JAVA Programming

AF647483

JAVA Programming

Dr. RAJIV CHOPRA
Ph.D. (Computer Science)
M.Tech. (IT), MIT
BE (Computer Science & Engineering) and CCEH Certified
Assistant Professor
Department of Computer Science/Information Technology
GTBIT, GGSIPU
Delhi

Publishing Globally

NEW AGE INTERNATIONAL (P) LIMITED, PUBLISHERS
New Delhi • Bangalore • Chennai • Cochin • Guwahati
Hyderabad • Kolkata • Lucknow • Mumbai
Visit us at **www.newagepublishers.com**

Copyright © 2015, New Age International (P) Ltd., Publishers
Published by New Age International (P) Ltd., Publishers
First Edition: 2015
Reprint: 2016

All rights reserved.
No part of this book may be reproduced in any form, by photostat, microfilm, xerography, or any other means, or incorporated into any information retrieval system, electronic or mechanical, without the written permission of the publisher.

BRANCHES

- **Bangalore** 37/10, 8th Cross (Near Hanuman Temple), Azad Nagar, Chamarajpet, Bangalore-560 018
  Tel.: (080) 26756823, Telefax: 26756820, **E-mail: bangalore@newagepublishers.com**
- **Chennai** 26, Damodaran Street, T. Nagar, Chennai-600 017
  Tel.: (044) 24353401, Telefax: 24351463, **E-mail: chennai@newagepublishers.com**
- **Cochin** CC-39/1016, Carrier Station Road, Ernakulam South, Cochin-682 016
  Tel.: (0484) 2377303, Telefax: 4051304, **E-mail: cochin@newagepublishers.com**
- **Guwahati** Hemsen Complex, Mohd. Shah Road, Paltan Bazar, Near Starline Hotel, Guwahati-781 008
  Tel.: (0361) 2513881, Telefax: 2543669, **E-mail: guwahati@newagepublishers.com**
- **Hyderabad** 105, 1st Floor, Madhiray Kaveri Tower, 3-2-19, Azam Jahi Road, Near Kumar Theater Nimboliadda, Kachiguda, Hyderabad-500 027, Tel.: (040) 24652456, Telefax: 24652457
  E-mail: hyderabad@newagepublishers.com
- **Kolkata** RDB Chambers (Formerly Lotus Cinema) 106A, 1st Floor, S.N. Banerjee Road, Kolkata-700 014
  Tel.: (033) 22273773, Telefax: 22275247, **E-mail: kolkata@newagepublishers.com**
- **Lucknow** 16-A, Jopling Road, Lucknow-226 001
  Tel.: (0522) 2209578, 4045297, Telefax: 2204098, **E-mail:lucknow@newagepublishers.com**
- **Mumbai** 142C, Victor House, Ground Floor, N.M. Joshi Marg, Lower Parel, Mumbai-400 013
  Tel.: (022) 24927869, Telefax: 24915415, **E-mail: mumbai@newagepublishers.com**
- **New Delhi** 22, Golden House, Daryaganj, New Delhi-110 002
  Tel.: (011) 23262368, 23262370, Telefax: 43551305, **E-mail: sales@newagepublishers.com**

ISBN: 978-81-224-3882-6

₹ 350.00

C-16-05-9417

Printed in India at Ajit Printing Press, Delhi.
Typeset at Aakriti Graphics, Delhi.

PUBLISHING GLOBALLY
NEW AGE INTERNATIONAL (P) LIMITED, PUBLISHERS
7/30 A, Daryaganj, New Delhi-110002
Visit us at **www.newagepublishers.com**

Preface

This book attempts to provide a unified overview of the broad field of JAVA2 programming and its practical implementation. This book is a survey of the state of art. It breaks this massive subject intc comprehensible parts piece by piece. The objective is to focus on basic principles of JAVA2 programming with some leading edge topics. This book addresses a full spectrum of JAVA2 programming. The emphasis is to solve lot many programming examples using step-by-step practical implementation of JAVA2. To facilitate easy understanding of JAVA2, this book has been written in such a simple style that a student thinks as if a teacher is sitting behind him and guiding him.

This book is written as per the new syllabus of Object-Oriented Programming (OOP) in JAVA2 of Guru Gobind Singh Indraprastha University (GGSIPU) Delhi and also covers the syllabus of many other technical universities of India. It also covers the syllabus of B. Tech. (CSE/IT) BCA, MCA of Delhi University, Delhi, GGSIPU, MDU, RGTU, Nagpur University, UTU and so on. The book is intended for both academic and professional audience.

It is said,."To err in human, to forgive divine." In this light, I wish that the short comings of the book will be forgiven. But suggestions for the further improvement of the book will be incorporated.

Dr. Rajiv Chopra

Ph. D. (Computer Science)

// Acknowledgements

It is indeed a great pleasure to acknowledge our gratitude to many persons involved, directly or indirectly, in the production of this book. First of all, we would like to thanks the almighty God who gave us the inspiration to start and complete this task. I also thank undergraduate and graduate teaching assistants for providing valuable inputs on this text. I also thank my students for providing me comments and feedbacks on the type of book desired for JAVA2 programming.

I am also grateful to M/s New Age International (P) Limited, Publishers and the staff of editorial department for their encouragement and support throughout this project.

Finally, I would like to thank my parents and family members—Dr. J. R. Chopra, Ms. Sushma Chopra and my sweet, twin babies Arjeesh (son) and Arshitha (daughter). I appreciate their support, patience and many other contributions more than I can express in any acknowledgements here.

Dr. Rajiv Chopra

Ph. D. (Computer Science)

Contents

Chapter 1

Introduction to Java

1.0 INTRODUCTION

Computers can perform different jobs as they are programmable. This important job of programming is done by the programmers. It is an art as well as a science. It is also a science because programs do not work properly the first time as they are written. It needs a lot of analyzing (its space and time complexity), experimenting (with dry runs), redesigning, if needed. The programs should be functional, efficient, powerful and easy to use. This adds to its ***quality***. The solution to any problem is written in form of a program now. *A program is a set of instructions written in a programming language*. A programming language provides a medium for conveying the instructions to the computer. A program transforms the inputs to the outputs. To solve a problem, either bottom-up approach or top-down approach is followed. **In bottom-up approach or working backward approach** the problem can be solved by starting from the Goal state to the Start state. **In top-down approach or the problem decomposition technique**, however, a problem is decomposed into smaller units over and over again until each smaller unit is manageable. **Please note that a complex problem is simplified and solved by decomposing it into many simple problems**. And then finding sub-solutions for all of these sub-problems and finally combining these sub-solutions to get the solution as a whole. This is known as **divide-and-conquer strategy**. This approach of program development is also known as *stepwise refinement* or *modular decomposition* or *structured approach* or *algorithmic approach*.

Ada Lovelace is considered to be the first computer programmer.

JAVA is a new object-oriented programming language that was developed by James Gosling and his team at Sun Microsystems in California. The language was based on C and C++. The language was first called as Oak, named after the oak tree outside of Gosling's office. But this name was already taken by someone so the team renamed it as JAVA. **Also note that JAVA is known as a web programming language because of its use in writing programs called as applets** (to be discussed later) that run within a web browser. Even complete applications in Java can be written as we write in other programming languages. Many other object-oriented programming languages also exist like Simula, SmallTalk etc.

1.1 JAVA HISTORY

Several versions of Java exist today ever since Sum Microsystems released the first version of Java i.e. JAVA 1.0. This was followed by an updated version, JAVA 1.1. When Sun released the next version, Java 1.2, they changed the name of the language to JAVA 2. *Please remember that 2 is part of the name and not the version number.* So that version of the language was known as Java 2 version 1.2. The next version was Java 2 version 1.3. The current version is Java 2 version 1.4.

Let us show the history of JAVA in a tabular form.

Table 1.1: History of Java

Year	Features and versions of JAVA
1990	Sun Microsystems started *Stealth project* supporting applications of computers in the consumer electronics market.
1991	Green project started with the members of *Stealth project* such as James Gosling, Patrick Naughton and Mike Sheridan. New programming language called as Oak was created by Gosling.
1992	An intelligent remote control called *StarSeven* was delivered. The Green project was incorporated under the name FirstPerson.
1993	*Mosaic web browser* was introduced in the field of Internet.
1994	*HotJava web browser* was introduced by Sun Microsystems.
1995	Oak was renamed as Java.
1996	Sun released the first version 1.0 of JAVA with core features like I/O, utilities, network programming, and user interfaces like AWT, Applets and multithreading introduced.
1997	Sun released JDK 1.1 with new features like inner classes, JavaBeans, JDBC (Java Database Connectivity) and RMI (Remote Method Invocation).
1998	JAVA 2 platform, Standard Edition (J2SE) 1.2, code named as *Playground*, was released. It replaced JDK and JVM was equipped with JIT (Just-in-Time) compiler.
2000	J2SE 1.3, code named as *Kestral*, was released with key features like JavaSound APIs like audio playback, recording etc.
2002	J2SE 1.4, code named as *Merlin*, was released with key features like integrated XML parser, image I/O etc.
2004	J2SE 5.0 , code named as *Tiger*, was released with new features like enhanced for-loop, autoboxing/unboxing, enums, etc.
2006	JAVA SE 6.0, code named as Mustang, was released with new features like swing, JDBC 4.0 support etc.
2008	Java SE 7.0, code named as *Dolphin*, with native support for XML with its role in Web services.

Unlike most other software systems that usually settle into a pattern of small, incremental improvements, JAVA continued to evolve at an explosive space. We shall be studying the latest version JAVA 2 Platform Standard Edition with JAVA DEVELOPMENT KIT 5.0 (JDK1.4.2_07) in this book.

1.2 HOW JAVA WORKS?

JAVA is an object-oriented programming language similar to C++. It has been, however, simplified to eliminate language features that cause common programming errors. The source code is developed in either a plain text editor like a Notepad or Wordpad or an Integrated development Environment (IDE) like Netbeans IDE 7.0, JAVA creator or Gel or jEdit. *Please note that a java source file has* .java *extension similar to a word file that has an extension of* .doc, a *Pascal file has an extension* of .pas and a text file *that has an extension of .txt.*

JAVA source codes (programs/files with .java extension) are compiled into a format called as **bytecode** (i.e. files with .class extension) using Java compiler (javac.exe). If there is any error then the java compiler announces it else its class file is created by the Java compiler. Finally, this class file can be executed by a JAVA VIRTUAL MACHINE (java.exe) also known as Java Interpreter. It is shown in Fig. 1.1.

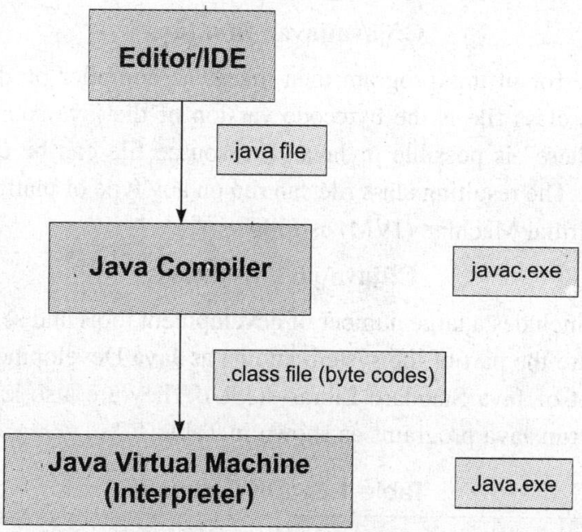

Fig. 1.1: JAVA's working

Compiled Java code can run on most computers because Java interpreters and runtime environments,(known as Java Virtual Machine (JVM)) exists for most operating systems (including UNIX and windows). Bytecodes can also be converted directly into machine language instruction by Just-in-Time (JIT) compiler. In nutshell, the process of compilation involves two steps:

Step 1: Source code is converted to bytecode i.e. the instructions for an imaginary machine called as the JAVA VIRTUAL MACHINE.

Step 2: This virtual machine is emulated by all Java interpreters. This allows us to execute a compiled Java program among different platform.

Notes:

1. Java is a general purpose programming language with a number of features that make the language well suited for its use on WWW.
2. Small Java applications are called as Java Applets. They run on the system by a Java-compatible web browser like Netscape Navigator or Microsoft Internet Explorer.

For example,

Create a java source file named as first.java as follows:

```
//Program1—first.java
class first
{
    public static void main (String args[ ] )
    {
        System.out.println("My First Java Program");
    }
}
```

We save this file, compile it and run it using Java compiler (javac). Say, this program file (first.java) is stored in a subdirectory—"c:\java". Now go to the command prompt then go to subdirectory Java and compile this source program as follows:

C:\java\javac first.java

Now if there is no error in this program then the javac compiler produces a file—first.class in the same directory. This class file is the bytecode version of the java source file. The concept of – "Write-once, Run anywhere" is possible in Java. The source file can be compiled on any platform that has a javac compiler. The resulting class file can run on any type of platform, using Java interpreter (java), that has a Java Virtual Machine (JVM) as follows:

C:\java\java first.class

JAVA environment includes a large number of development tools and several classes and methods. The development tools are the part of the system known as Java Development Kit (JDK). The classes and methods are the part of Java Standard Library (JSL). They are also known as Applications that are used to develop and run Java programs as shown in Table 1.2.

Table 1.2: JDK Contents

Tool	Usage
Appletviewer	Allows us to run Java applets without using any Java compatible browser.
Java	Java Interpreter, which runs applets and applications by reading and interpreting byte code files.
Javac	It is the Java compiler that translates Java source code to bytecode files that the interpreter can understand.
Javadoc	Creates HTML format documentation from Java source code files.
Javah	Produces header files for use with native methods.
Javap	Java disassembler, that enables you to convert bytecode files into a program description.
Jdb	Java debugger that helps you to find errors in your programs.

Please note that with most of the other programming languages, we either compile or interpret a program so that we can run it on our system. However, in Java, a program is both compiled as well as interpreted. *Also note that with the compiler, we first of all translate a program into an intermediate language called as Java Bytecodes* i.e. platform-independent codes interpreted by the interpreter on the Java platform. The interpreter parses and runs each Java bytecode instruction on the computer. Compilation is done just once but interpretation is done each time the program is executed. The entire concept is shown in Fig. 1.2.

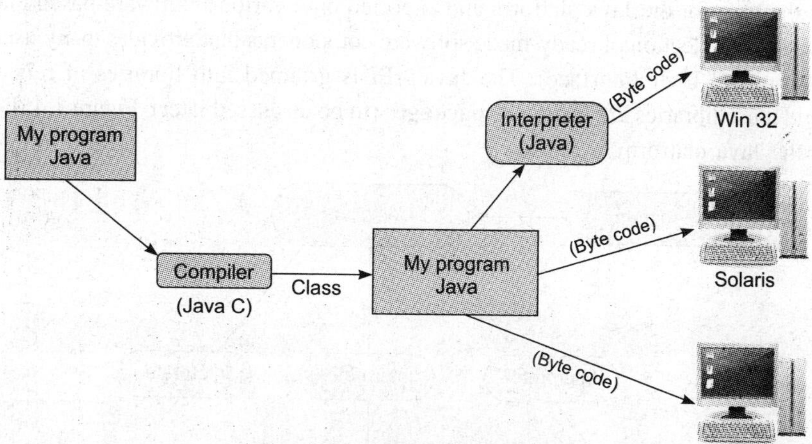

Fig. 1.2: Overall flowchart

Thus, we can think of Java bytecodes as the machine code instructions for the **Java Virtual Machine (JVM).** Every Java interpreter, whether it is a development tool or a web browser that can run applets, is an implementation of the JVM. **Also understand that these bytecodes make "write once, run anywhere" also possible.** This means that you can compile your program into bytecodes on any platform that has a Java compiler. Then the bytecodes can be run on any implementation of the JVM. This means that as long as a computer has a JVM, the same program written in Java Programming language can be run on WINDOWS 2K, a SOLARIS WORKSTATION or on an iMAC.

1.3 JAVA VIRTUAL MACHINE (JVM)

Java platform consists of a JAVA VIRTUAL MACHINE and a package of ready made software components. It is shown in Fig. 1.3. This package is known as Java Application Programming Interface (API).

As we know that all programming languages use compilers to convert source code into machine code for a specific computer. But Java is somewhat different because Java produces a bytecode of a source code and this bytecode is run by this JAVA VIRTUAL MACHINE (JVM). *Also understand that JVM is actually software* and *not a hardware unit.* Its job is to convert bytecode into machine code for a specific computer. Thus, we can say that JVM is an interpreter for a bytecode. Java

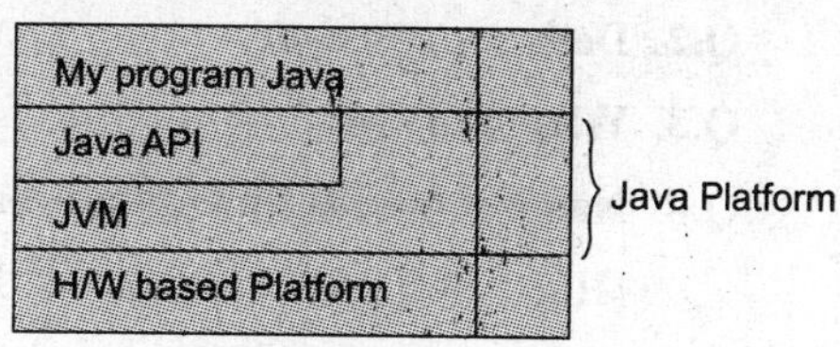

Fig. 1.3: JVM

bytecodes were made machine-independent so that they could be run on a variety of machines. That is why, you need only JVM for each platform. Also **note that these bytecodes are not machine specific**.

From Fig. 1.3, it is crystal clear that Java platform has two main components:

(*a*) JVM—JAVA VIRTUAL MACHINE.

(*b*) JAVA API—JAVA APPLICATION PROGRAMMING INTERFACE.

JVM is the base for the Java platform and is ported onto various hardware-based platforms. While Java API is a large collection of ready-made software components that provides many useful capabilities like GUI (Graphical User Interface). The Java API is grouped into libraries of related classes and interfaces and these libraries are known as **packages** (to be discussed later). Figure 1.4 shows a program running on the Java platform.

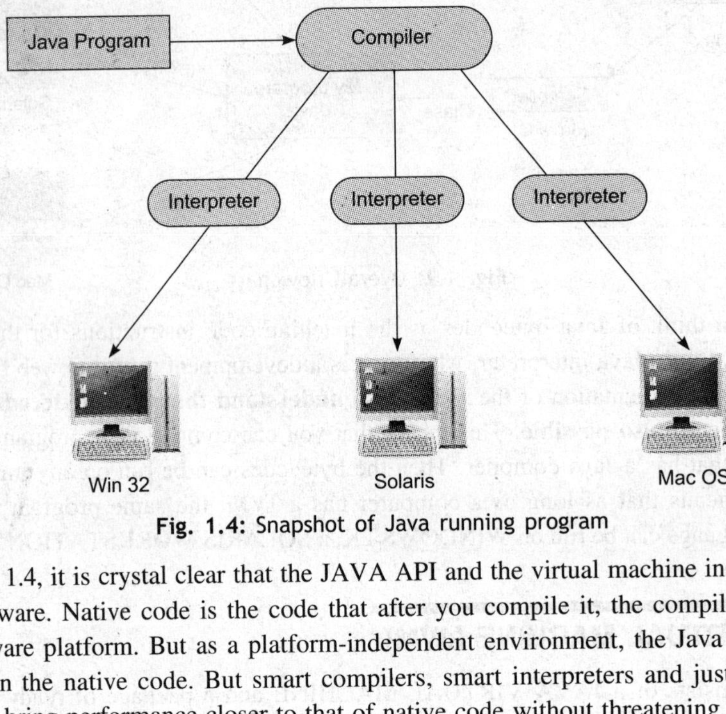

Fig. 1.4: Snapshot of Java running program

From Fig. 1.4, it is crystal clear that the JAVA API and the virtual machine insulate the program from the hardware. Native code is the code that after you compile it, the compiled code runs on a specific hardware platform. But as a platform-independent environment, the Java platform can be a bit slower than the native code. But smart compilers, smart interpreters and just-in-time bytecode compilers can bring performance closer to that of native code without threatening portability.

Before we discuss further, please answer the following questions:

Q.1. What is a compiler?

Q.2. Define a bytecode.

Q.3. What is JVM?

Q.4. Name some runtime data areas of JVM.

[**Hint:** Heap, Stack, Registers, Method area, Runtime constant Pool]

Q.5. What was the earlier name of Java? [*GGSIPU, B. Tech(CSE/IT)-5th sem, August 2009*]

Ans. Oak.

Q.6. What actually JVM is—Interpreter or Compiler?

[GGSIPU, B. Tech(CSE/IT)-5th sem, Sept. 2010]

Q.7. What is the difference between JDK and JRE? How Java is platform independent in case of JRE? *[GGSIPU, B. Tech(CSE/IT)-5th sem, Oct. 2010]*

Q.8. Briefly explain JVM, JDK and JRE? *[GGSIPU, B. Tech(CSE/IT)-5th sem, Dec. 2011]*

[**Hint:** JRE is important set of tools that are required in order to display Java applications on server. Such application can include software and games. JRE works as the communicator between OS in question and Java based programs.]

1.4 JUST IN TIME COMPILER (JIT)

Each web browser that supports Java has a JAVA VIRTUAL MACHINE (JVM) built right into it and it loads .class file. It is also evident that when a program is interpreted, it generally runs substantially slower than it would run if compiled to an executable code. But remember that the use of bytecode enables the Java run-time system to execute programs faster. Sun has introduced Just In Time Compiler (JIT) for bytecode. Just In Time Compiler (JIT compiler) is a part of JVM. Its job is to take the generic i.e. cross-platform bytecodes and compile them into more machine-specific instructions allowing the program to run faster. Even though it is referred to as a JIT compiler, it is the part of the virtual machine. When JIT is a part of JVM, it compiles bytecode into executable code in real-time, on demand basis. This is so because JVM performs various run-time checks that can be done only at the run-time. Instead, JIT compiles the code as it is needed during execution. JVM code is designed so that it is easy to translate it into machine instructions for real machines, so the second part of the translation to real machine instructions is done in the browser on the user's machine. **Please understand that the browser takes the applet JVM code that it gets from the server and translates from JVM code to the machine code the browser is using.** This compiler in the browser is often **called as a JIT compiler**. **Also understand that JIT means that the last part of the compilation is done before running the program**.

1.5 JAVA FEATURES

When JAVA was released publicly by Sun Microsystems in 1996 (USA) then its authors also wrote a white paper in US magazine that explains their design goals and some of them are discussed below.

1. **Simple:** JAVA is simple and easy to understand. Peter Naughton, one of the authors of Java quoted that—"We wanted to build a system that could be programmed easily without a lot of erotic training and which leveraged today's standard practice. So, even though we found that C++ was unsuitable, we designed Java as closely to C++ as possible in order to make the system more comprehensible. Java omits many rarely used, poorly understood confusing features of C++ that, in our experience, brings more grief than benefit" [1]. From these statements, we find that Java inherits the C/C++ syntax and many of the object-oriented features of C++. Java is simple as compared to C++ because:

   (*a*) Unstructured goto statement has been removed.

(*b*) Java has no preprocessor.

(*c*) No structures and unions.

(*d*) Pointers are not supported.

2. **Object-oriented:** The authors of Java quoted that "Object-oriented design is a technique for programming that focuses on the data (=objects) and on the interfaces to that object. To make an analogy with carpentry, an "object-oriented" carpenter would be mostly concerned with the chair he was building and secondarily with the tools used to make it. A non object-oriented carpenter would think primarily of the tools. The object-oriented facilities of Java are essentially those of C++" [1]. There are no global functions in Java rather all functions are invoked through an object. Thus, Java is a pure object-oriented programming language. Java believes that everything is an object. It provides features like abstraction, encapsulation, inheritance and polymorphism. **Please understand that anything in Java is embedded into a class.**
3. **Compiled and Interpreted:** Java source programs are translated into bytecode by Java compiler and this bytecode is interpreted by the JAVA interpreter. Thus, Java is both compiled and interpreted. When a Java source program is compiled, it lists all errors in that program. And when this program is error free, it is interpreted by the interpreter which executes it line by line. It takes some extra time for debugging a program. *Please understand that the Java interpreter can execute Java bytecode directly on any machine to which the interpreter has been posted. Also note that as linking is more incremented and lightweight process, the development process can be much more rapid and exploratory.*
4. **Portable:** Java is portable because the bytecode produced by a Java compiler can be run on any platform that has Java interpreter. This portability is because of Java wide library—the libraries that are a part of the system defined portable interfaces. For example, there is an abstract windows class and implementation of it for UNIX, Windows and the Macintosh. Java authors quoted that—"unlike C and C++, there is no implementation-dependent aspect of the specification. The sizes of the primitive's data types are specified, as is the behavior of arithmetic on them".
5. **Robust: Java is a strictly typed language.** It checks your code at compile time as well as at the run-time. Thus, Java programs are less error prone. Java provides an easy and wide exception handling package to make it more robust language. Authors of Java once quoted- "Java is intended for writing programs that must be reliable in a variety of ways. Java puts a lot of emphasis on early checking for possible problems, later dynamic checking and eliminating situations that are error-prone. The single bigger difference between Java and C++ is that Java has a pointer model that eliminates the possibility of overwriting memory and corrupting data."
6. **Multithreading:** Java supports multithreading programming environment that allows you to write programs that do many things simultaneously. **Please note that even the core of Java is multithreaded.**
7. **Secure:** Java does not allow a programmer to manipulate the memory of a system. Authors of Java once quoted—"Java is intended to be used in network distributed environments; towards

that end a lot of emphasis has been placed on security. Java enables that construction of virus-free, tamper-free systems."

8. **Distributed:** Java programs can access data across a network. So, it is distributed. Java is a complete language to build distributed application. The authors of Java once quoted—"Java has an extensive library of routines for coping with TCP/IP protocols like HTTP and FTP. Java application can open and access objects across the Net via URL with some ease when accessing a local file system." There is now a separate architecture, the Java 2 Enterprise Edition (J2EE) that supports very large scale of distributed applications.
9. **Architectural Neutral:** Java first converts source program into bytecode which can be run on a variety of computers having different operating systems. For example, if Java programs are written on WINDOWS-XP and we want to use it on LINUX or any other platform then without any modification, it can be run on LINUX platform; just needed is Linux compatible JVM. The authors of Java once quoted—"The compiler generates an architecture-neutral object file format—the compiled code is executable on many processors, given the presence of the Java runtime system. The Java compiler does this by generating bytecode instruction, which has nothing to do with particular computer architecture. Rather they are designed to be both easy to interpret on any machine and easily translated into native machine code on the fly."
10. **High Performance:** Java programs are faster as compared to programs written in other interpreter-based programming languages.
11. **Dynamic:** Java provides an efficient way for maintaining different versions of an application. In many ways, JAVA is more dynamic language than C++. It was designed to adapt to an evolving environment. Libraries can freely add new methods and instance variable without any effect on their clients.

1.6 JAVA TOOLS

JDK stands for JAVA DEVELOPMENT KIT. To write rapid Java applications or applets, we need a tool to write, test and debug our programs. All of these activities are the part of JDK only. Some vital Java tools are as follows:

1. **The javac Compiler:** Java programs are created in any text editor like Notepad. We just need to open the text editor, type our program and save this program with the extension .java. Every Java source file must have one public class definition. This source file is converted to bytecode by the Java compiler, javac. The javac compiler converts this .java file that you create to a .class file which contains byteccde.

   Syntax is:

   javac filename.java

   Please note here that filename.java is the name of the Java source file. After execution of this statement, we get a bytecode file—filename.class, which is interpreted by the Java interpreter, Java.

2. **The Java Interpreter:** The Java interpreter, java, is used to execute the java class file produced by the javac compiler.

   Syntax is:

   java filename.class

3. **The jdb Tool:** It is used to debug a Java program.

   Syntax is:

   jdb filename.class

4. **The javap Disassembler:** To get back the Java code from the bytecode, we can use Java disassembler called as javap.

   Syntax is:

   javap filename.class

   Please note that you can also get back the Java codes of more than one file using a Java disassembler as follows:

   javap file1.class file2.class file3.class

   Also note that the filenames must be separated by spaces.

5. **The javadoc Tool:** It is a document generator that creates HTML page documentation for the classes that you create. To use javadoc, you have to embed the statements between /** and */.

   Syntax is:

   javadoc filename.java

   Again if you specify more than one file then they must be separated by spaces.

6. **The javah Tool:** It creates header and stub files that let you extend your Java code with the C language.

   Syntax is:

   javap filename.class

7. **The Appletviewer:** Applets are small programs that are not executed on its own rather they are first embedded into web pages and then they are executed using a Java enabled web browser. We can also run these applets using the appletviewer. We can also test our applets using the appletviewer.

   Syntax is:

   Appletviewer filename.html

1.7 USING JAVA WITH OTHER STOOLS

Java can be made to work with internet and with WWW. Let us now discuss these two cases.

Case 1: Java and Internet.

Case 2: Java and WWW.

Case 1: Java and Internet

The first application written in Java was HotJava. It is a web browser to run applets on Internet. Java is strongly associated with Internet. Internet users can use Java to create applet programs and run them locally using a Java enabled web browser. We can even download an applet from a remote (far off) computer. We can, thus say that Java applets have made the Internet a true extension of the storage system of the local computer. Internet users can also create their own site containing Java applets that could be used by other users of the Internet. It is this ability that makes Java a unique programming language for the Internet. This is the reason as to why Java is known as Internet programming language.

Case 2: Java and WWW

WWW stands for WORLD WIDE WEB. It provides a consistent means to access any type of information in a much more simplified manner. *Please note that WWW is different from an Internet because WWW is just one of the many technologies that the Internet makes possible*. WWW contains web pages. A web browser is required to retrieve these web pages. The first web browser was Mosaic. Others are like Netscape Navigator, Microsoft's Internet Explorer, Chrome etc. These are graphical web browsers meaning that they can display graphics as well as text. A web page contains HTML tags that enable us to find, retrieve, manipulate and display document world wide.

Note: JAVA made the web more interactive and dynamic as it can be easily used in web page.

Please remember the following points now:

1. **Internet** is a massive network of networks, a networking infrastructure. It collects millions of computers together globally. Information that travels over the Internet does so via a variety of languages known as protocols.
2. **WWW or World Wide Web or simply a web** is a way of accessing information over the medium of the Internet. It is an information sharing model that is built on top of the Internet. Web uses HTTP protocol to transmit data. Web services, that use HTTP to allow applications to communicate in order to exchange business logic, use the web to share information. Web also uses browsers to access web documents called as web pages that are linked to each other via hyperlinks. Web documents also contain graphics, sounds, text and video.
3. Web is just one of the ways that information can be disseminated over the Internet.
4. The Internet (not the web), is also used for email, which relies on SMTP, Usenet news groups, instant messaging and FTP.
5. So, web is just a portion of Internet but the two terms are not same and should not be confused.

We are in a position to answer the following questions now.

Q.1. What do you mean by Internet, Intranet and Extranet?

[**Hint: Intranet** is a network that operates locally by some one or more Internet services like email, www etc. Thus, we can say local Internet is an Intranet.

Internet is the network of networks which operates globally and connect local network outside for everyone. It uses a common set of rules or protocols like TCP/IP suite.

Extranet is the combination of Internet and Intranet. When we connect our Intranet to Internet, on authentication for special users that is compulsory for company is called as Extranet. ***For example,*** VPN-Virtual Private Networks.]

Q.2. What do you mean by ISP?

[Hint: ISP or Internet Service Provider is a company that operates Internet facility globally or locally and makes money monthly or yearly for it.

For example, Reliance, BSNL, Primus and Bharti (Airtel).]

Q.3. The Java compiler generates ....

Q.4. JVM stands for ....

Q.5. What are bootstrap class loader and user-defined class loader?

[Hints: The main task of JVM is to load .class files and to execute the bytecode they contain. JVM contains a class loader which loads .class files, that are compiled versions of the user programs and JAVA APIs. Please understand that only the mandatory .class files from JAVA APIs are loaded into JVM. Java application can use 2 types of class loaders:

(a) Bootstrap loader or primordial or system or default class loader—that loads classes in default way from the local disk, usually.

(b) User-defined class loader—is not the part of JVM implementation. During execution, a Java application can install a user-defined class loader like other .class files.]

Q.6. Distinguish between structured programming and OOP.

[Hint: The differences are given in the tabular form below:

Structured programming	Object-oriented programming
1. Top-down approach is followed.	1. Bottom-up approach is followed.
2. The main focus is on algorithm and control flow.	2. The main focus is on objects and classes.
3. A program is divided into a number of sub-modules or functions or procedures.	3. A program is organized by having a number of classes and objects.
4. Functions are independent of each other	4. Each class is related in a hierarchical manner.
5. It views data and functions as two separate entities.	5. It views data and functions as a single entity.
6. Software reuse is not possible.	6. Software reuse is possible.
7. Functions call is used.	7. Message passing is used.
8. Function abstraction is used.	8. Data abstraction is used.
9. Data-driven technique is used.	9. It is driven by delegation of responsibilities.
10. Algorithm is given importance.	10. Data is given more importance.
11. No encapsulation—data and functions are separate.	11. Encapsulation is done here and it treats code and data as a single unit called as a class.
12. Costlier maintenance.	12. Cheaper maintenance.

Q.7. Distinguish between abstraction and encapsulation.

[Hint: The differences are given in the tabular form below:

Abstraction	Encapsulation
1. It separates Interface and Implementation.	1. It groups together related concepts into one item.
2. It provides access to a specific part of data.	2. It hides data and the user cannot access the same directly (data hiding).
3. It gives a coherent picture of what the user wants. The degree of relatedness of an encapsulated unit is defined as cohesion. High cohesion is achieved by means of good abstraction.	3. Coupling means dependency. Good systems have low coupling. Encapsulation results in lesser dependencies of one object on other objects in a system that has low coupling. Low coupling may be achieved by designing a good encapsulation.
4. Abstraction is defined as a data type called as a class which separates interface from implementation.	4. Encapsulation packages data and functionality and hides the implementation details (information hiding).
5. The ability to encapsulate and isolate design from execution information is known as abstraction.	5. Encapsulation is a concept embedded in abstraction.

Q.8. Distinguish between function call and message passing.

[Hint: The differences are given in the tabular form below:

Function call	Message passing
1. Function call may use zero or more arguments.	1. Message passing uses at least one argument that identifies the receiving agent.
2. It always identifies a single piece of executable code.	2. The function name is called as message selector. The same name may be associated with different receiving agents.
3. It is applied to data to carry out a task.	3. It is a way to access the data. Message may invoke a function defined for a specific purpose.
4. Consumer is responsible for choosing functions that operate properly on the data.	4. Supplier is responsible for choosing the appropriate message.
5. There is no designated receiver in the function call.	5. There is a designated receiving agent in message passing.

Q.9. Distinguish between interface and implementation.

[**Hint:** The differences are given in the tabular form below:

Interface	Implementation
1. It is a user's view point (what part).	1. It is the supplier's view point (How part).
2. It is used to interact with the outside world.	2. It describes how the delegated responsibility is carried out.
3. User is permitted to access the interfaces only.	3. Functions or methods are permitted to access the data. So, supplier is capable of accessing data and interfaces.
4. It encapsulates the knowledge about the object.	4. It provides the restriction of access to data by the user.

Q.10. What are the main concepts involved in Object-oriented programming? Write one line about each of these concepts. [*Delhi University, MCA-1st sem., 2008*]

Q.11. What are the main features of Java programming language? Give the advantages of Java over C++. [*GGSIPU, B. Tech. (CSE/IT)-5th sem., Dec. 2009*]

[**Hint:** Refer to section 1.5 for Java features. Advantages of Java over C++ are as follows:

C++	JAVA2
1. It is compatible with C source code, except for a few corner cases.	1. No backward compatibility with any previous language. But the syntax is highly influenced by C/C++.
2. Write once, compile anywhere (WOCA).	2. Write once, run anywhere/everywhere (WORA/WORE).
3. It allows procedural programming, functional programming, object-oriented programming and template meta-programming.	3. It strongly encourages an object-oriented programming paradigm.
4. It allows direct calls to native system libraries.	4. Call through the Java Native Interface and recently Java Native Access.
5. Exposes low-level system facilities.	5. Runs on a virtual machine. Does not always provide full access to the features and performance of the platform on which the software runs.
6. It only provides object types and type names.	6. It is reflective, allowing meta-programming and dynamic code generation at runtime.
7. Optional automated bounds checking.	7. Normally performs bound checking. HotSpot can remove bounds checking.
8. It supports native unsigned arithmetic.	8. No native support for unsigned arithmetic.

(Contd....)

9. Pointers, references and pass-by-value are supported.	9. Primitive and reference data types always pass by value. No pointers.
10. Explicit memory management.	10. Automatic garbage collection, no concept of destructor and usage of finalize() is not recommended.
11. It supports classes, structs and unions and can allocate them on heap or stack.	11. It supports classes only and allocates them on heap.
12. It allows explicit overriding types.	12. Rigid type safety except for widening conversions.

Q.12. Write short notes on email, internet and intranet services.

[GGSIPU, B. Tech. (CSE/IT)-5th sem., Dec. 2009]

Q.13. What is spaghetti code and how it is avoided in Java?

[Hint: It is a term used for the source code that has a complex and tangled control structure like the code that uses many GOTOs, exceptions, threads or other "unstructured" branching constructs. It is so called because the program flow tends to look like a bowl of spaghetti i.e twisted and tangled. This type of code may result because of less experienced programmers and complex software that underwent changes again and again. Thus, structured programming decreased the incidence of spaghetti code.]

Q.14. How can you force garbage collector in Java?

[GGSIPU, B. Tech. (CSE/IT)-5th sem., Sept. 2010]

[Hint: Garbage collection cannot be forced but only can be requested. Since JVM will not start the garbage collection immediately, JVM will invoke "system.gc" to request the garbage collection.]

Q.15. ***(a)*** **Describe the distributed and dynamic property of Java?**

(b) **What is the difference between JDK and JRE? How Java is platform independent in case of JRE?** *[GGSIPU, B. Tech. (CSE/IT)-5th sem., Sept. 2010]*

Q.16. Briefly explain the compilation process of Java program, by stating the role of class loader, byte code verifier and JSTL?

[GGSIPU, B. Tech. (CSE/IT)-5th sem., Dec. 2010]

[Hint: Class loader has already been discussed. Let us see a Java Bytecode Verifier now. It is a mini theorem prover that verifies that the language ground rules are respected.]

Q.17. Write short notes on:

(a) **JVM**

(b) **Byte code and Unicode.**

[Hint: We have already seen what JVM is and what is a bytecode. Let us now see what is Unicode? Characters set in Java are indices into 16-bit value that can be converted into integers and manipulated with the integer operators like +, –.]

[GGSIPU, B. Tech. (CSE/IT)-5th sem., Dec. 2011]

Q.18. Briefly explain JVM, JDK and JRE.

[*GGSIPU, B. Tech. (CSE/IT)-5th sem., Dec. 2011*]

Q.19. (*a*) What do you mean by bytecode? Explain its working.

(*b*) Why is Java more suitable as compared to other languages?

[*MDU, B.E. (CSE/IT)-8th sem., Dec. 2008*]

Q.20. What are class loaders? [*MDU, B.E. (CSE/IT)-8th sem., May 2009*]

Q.21. How does Java achieve portability?

[*GGSIPU, B. Tech. (CSE/IT)-5th sem. , Dec. 2013*]

Q.22. Why is Java considered as the best language for internet applications?

[*GGSIPU, B. Tech. (CSE/IT)-5th sem. , Dec. 2013*]

1.8 NATIVE CODES

The environment, in which you are using a subroutine written in other programming language such as C/C++, is called as a **native code**. Java provides the native keyword which is used to declare native code methods. Once declared, these methods can be called from inside your Java programs just as you call any other Java method. To declare a native method, precede the method with the native modifier as follows:

```
public native int sqr( );
```

Please note here that you do not need to define any body for the method. Also note that the native methods are linked to Java program dynamically at run -time by following a rather complex series of steps.

A native method is written in some other in some other language like C or C++ or assembly and compiled to the native machine code of a particular processor. Native methods are stored in dynamically linked libraries (DLL) or shared libraries. They are platform specific whereas Java methods are platform independent. *During execution of a Java program, a call to native methods loads the DLL containing the native method.*

Limitations/ drawbacks of Native codes

1. **Security Loss:** If you import a native method then there are chances of a virus invitation because native code is not confined to the Java execution environment.
2. **Portability Loss:** Since the native code is contained in a DLL, therefore a Java program that uses native methods will be able to run only on a machine for which a compatible DLL has been installed.

1.9 JAVA APPLICATION TYPES

Java applications are basically of four types:

1. **Applications: An application is a program that you execute from the MS DOS prompt or UNIX prompt.** Java provides both text-based and GUI-based applications. These are stand-alone programs. These do not require any web browser to execute. These are general-purpose programs (programs written in other languages like C/C++, Basic etc.) that run on any machine where the Java runtime environment is installed.
2. **Applets: The programs that reside on World Wide Web are known as applets.** The applets are downloaded by a browser to a client's system (that's your system) and are run by that browser. These applets are usually small in size to minimize download time. These applets are invoked by a HTML web page. Thus, applets are smaller Java programs that execute inside a web page. Applets need Java enabled web browser like Microsoft Internet explorer or hot Java, to run. *Please note that an applet is loaded and executed when it is embedded into a web page through a web server.* When users view the web page in which the applet is embedded, they interact with the applet. *Also note that applets have Graphical User Interface* (*GUIs*). An applet cannot access the resources of the local machine. Let us tabulate the differences between the two in a tabular form now.

Applications	Applets
1. Application programs use main ( ) method for initiating the execution of the code.	1. Applets do not use the main ( ) method for initiating the execution of the code. Applets, when loaded, automatically call certain methods of Applet class to start and execute the applet code.
2. These programs can run independently.	2. Applets cannot run independently. They run embedded into a web page on a web browser using HTML tag.
3. These can read from or write to the files on a local computer.	3. These cannot read from or write to the files on a local computer.
4. These can run some other program from the local computer.	4. These cannot run any program from the local computer.
5. Java language can use these libraries of other languages like C and C++ using native method.	5. Applets are restricted from using libraries from other languages.

3. **Servlets:** These programs extend the functionality of web services. Servlets do not have graphical interfaces. Java servlets are server-side components that can extend the functionality of a Java-enabled web server.
4. **Packages:** They are collections of classes that can be shared by other Java programs. Packages in Java are just like libraries in C/C++. Java provides packages like **java.lang, java.util, java.io etc.**

1.10 JAVA COMPARISONS WITH C AND C++

Let us compare the three—Java, C and C++ in a tabular form based on certain features.

Features	JAVA	C	C++
1. Goto, sizeof, typedef statement	No, not included	Yes, included.	Yes, included.
2. Struct, union, enum datatype	No, not included	Yes, included.	Yes, included.
3. Pointers	No, not included	Yes, included.	Yes, included.
4. Preprocessor directives like #include, #define)	No, not included	Yes, included.	Yes, included.
5. Break and continue	With label	Without label	Without label
6. Operator overloading	No, not included	No, not included	Yes, included.
7. Template classes	No, not included	No, not included	Yes, included.
8. Multiple Inheritance	Implemented using Interfaces	No, not included	Yes, included.
9. Global variables	No, not included	Yes, included.	Yes, included.
10. Header files	No, not included	Yes, included.	Yes, included.

We are in a position to answer the following questions now.

Q.1. What is the difference between applet and servlet?
[GGSIPU, B. Tech. (CSE/IT)-5th sem. Dec. 2009]

Q.2. Give the advantages of Java over C++. *[GGSIPU, B. Tech. (CSE/IT)-5th sem. Dec. 2009]*

Q.3. Is chaining there in Servlet? *[GGSIPU, B. Tech. (CSE/IT)-5th sem. Oct. 2010]*

[Hint: Yes, chaining exists in Servlet]

Q.4. Define what is a native code?

Q.5. Write main drawbacks of Applet? *[GGSIPU, B. Tech. (CSE/IT)-5th sem. Oct. 2010]*

Q.6. Write the differences between Servlet and JSP.
[GGSIPU, B. Tech. (CSE/IT)-5th sem. Oct. 2010]

Q.7. What are applets? Explain their usage. How are they different from Java programs.
[MDU, BE(CSE)-8th sem., May 2007]

Q.8. Why is Java more suitable as compared to other languages?
[MDU, BE(CSE)-8th sem., Dec. 2008]

Q.9. Discuss about the three major Java programming technologies as given by Sun.

[Hint: J2ME, J2SE and J2EE; J2SE (Java 2 Platform, Micro Edition) is the core Java language. It provides an environment for developing many different types of Java applications; it includes support for GUI programming, threads, input/output, networking, XML, CORBA, Applets, JavaBeans, RMI, security and database access.

J2ME is not a slimmed –down version of J2SE rather it establishes a procedure for defining what a particular JVM designed for an electronic device will provide. J2ME technology has 2 components:

(a) Configurations: That defines the type of JVM that is being targeted.

(b) Profiles: That describes specification details about the device that is being targeted. Each device has a profile listing standard Java APIs available for that device.

Please understand that configurations are composed of Java API and virtual machines designed to run on two different types of devices and are as follows:

(a) The 1st type of device is those with 128-512KB of memory. This configuration is called as the **Connected Limited Device Configuration (CLDC)** and the corresponding JVM is called as the **K Virtual Machine or KVM**.

(b) The 2nd configuration is for devices with more than 512KB of memory. This configuration is called as the Connected Device Configuration and uses the standard JVM, with all capabilities of a regular desktop computer.

Profiles are defined by the Java Community Process (JCP), which allows for input from any industry interested in a profile for a particular type of electronic device. **For example**, a profile would be created for cellular phones, with the profile defining the configuration to use for wireless phones and the Java APIs that will be available. Any company that had interest in wireless phones could join the JCP to help determine which configuration to choose and what Java API would look like for developing Java applications for cellular, wireless phones.

J2EE is a collection of Java technologies that create a platform for distributed applications. Both J2SE and J2EE allows for the most complex multi-tier software applications to be portable across multiple platforms. It consists of different technologies like EJB, JSP, XML etc.

Also understand that just as J2SE programs run in a JVM, J2EE applications run in a J2EE-complaint application server. The application server implements the J2EE specification, allowing developers to create applications that use any or all of the J2EE technologies but that are still platform independent. **For example**, some popular application servers are IBMs Web Sphere, BEA System's Web Logic and Macromedia's JRun.]

Q.10. Name some web browsers.

[Hint: Netscape, Firefox, Internet Explorer, Google Chrome etc.]

Q.11. Name some popular Java IDEs.

[Hint: Eclipse, Netbeans, JBuilder, MS Visual J#, AnyJ (free for Linux), BlueJ, JasmineIDE, TextPad, Ready, C_Forge, CodeGuide, CodeWarrior etc.]

Q.12. Is it possible to have more than one JDK version on a system?

[**Hint:** Yes]

Q.13. What is an IDE?

[**Hint:** Editor, compiler, debugger, trace facility etc. all are available in an IDE].

Q.14. What is a project?

[**Hint:** A collection of source and resources files]

Q.15. What is a compilation unit?

[**Hint:** Java source code file]

Q.16. Give the roles of bin and lib in JDK.

[**Hint:** bin directory contains all tools like javac, applet viewer, awt tool etc. so, executable files of the commands like javac, Java, AppletViewer are available in bin directory of JAVAHOME. While lib directory contains all packages and variables.]

□□□

Chapter 2

Java Fundamentals

2.0 INTRODUCTION

Java is a high-level programming language. It is developed to accommodate object-oriented concepts. It is a general purpose, concurrent, class-based and object-oriented programming language. It gives better performance for solving problems in distributed environment. Like any other programming language, Java has a vocabulary and a set of rules to use vocabulary. **Please understand that the vocabulary is a set of keywords and the grammar is the syntax of the language. Also understand that it is the Java compiler that provides keywords, syntax, data types and operators of Java.** The grammar of Java defines both lexical grammar and syntactic grammar. **The lexical grammar** defines the set of rules for forming input elements which are the starting point of the syntactic grammar. **The syntactic grammar** defines a set of rules that describe how sequences of input elements can form syntactically correct programs. A lexical element refers to a character or a grouping of characters that are considered valid in programs. Let us study these in this chapter.

2.1 MY FIRST JAVA PROGRAM—AN ANATOMY

Java is a **pure object-oriented programming language.** Therefore, whatever, you write in Java, it must be included in a class. Let us consider a simple Java program to understand this.

```
//This is my first Java program
//Program—first.java
class first
{
    public static void main(String args[]) //main method
    {
        System.out.println("Welcome to new world of Java");
    }
}
```

You are supposed to type and store this program in the following subdirectory:

C:\javaprog

And save it as first.java.

Line numbers 1 and 2 are comments that are simply ignored by the compiler as they do not generate any executable code. Actually, Java supports 2 types of comments:-

(a) **Single line comment:** It starts with a // and ends at the end of the line.

(b) **Multi-line comments:** That starts with /* and ends with */

Line no. 3 is class first. This statement declares a class by first using the keyword—class. The variable 'first' is an identifier that specifies the name of the class. This name is decided by the programmer. Programmer-defined names may be written in lowercase letters, uppercase letters or a mixture of both. This line is followed by an opening curly brace '{', (i.e line no. 4). **This curly brace indicates the start of the class body.** Now you can declare variables and methods. **Please note here that the member-functions (as they are called in C++) are known as methods in Java.** And finally the class body is terminated by a closing brace '}', (i.e. line no. 9).

Now, line no. 5 contains the statement as follows:

public static void main(String args[ ])

Also note the following points from this line no. 5:

1. Here, 'public' keyword is an access specifier which means that this method is also available to outside this class in which it is declared. This line is known as a **class header**. It marks the beginning of a class definition.
2. Next is the, 'static' keyword that declares that this main method can be called without any object of the class in which it is defined (here it is class first). Since it is a main( ) method so it is called by the Java interpreter implicitly. *Also note that since main( ) method does not return any value therefore its return type is declared as void.* Recall that as in C/C++, in Java too the program execution starts from the main( ) method only. *But please understand that the Java compiler will compile classes that do not contain a main( ) method but the Java interpreter will not run these classes.* And if you run a program that does not contain any main( ) method then it will report the following error message:

   Exception in thread "main" java.lang.NoSuchMethodError : main

   This error indicates that this program does not have a main( ) method. **Thus, in a Java program, one class must have a main( ) method.**
3. Any method receives information by variables specified within the set of parentheses that follow the name of the method. The **main( ) method receives an array of String arguments named args[ ]. Here, args receives any command line arguments.** This line is followed by an opening curly brace '{', (i.e. line no. 6). **This curly brace indicates the start of the method body.** Now you can declare variables, if you need.
4. Finally, the method is terminated by a closing brace '}', (i.e. line no. 8).
5. Line no. 7 in the main( ) method is:

   System.out.println("Welcome to new world of Java");

   This statement displays the message-'Welcome to the new world of Java' on to the screen. Here, 'system' is a predefined class that is defined in java.lang package. And 'out' is a predefined standard object of PrintStream class which is connected to the console. Then, the println( ) method is a member of the 'out' object and is used to display the information on to the screen. The println( ) statement is terminated by a semicolon.

6. All statements in Java are NOT terminated by semicolon. Like, comments do not have to end with a semicolon because they are ignored by the compiler, class headers and method headers do not end with a semicolon because they are terminated with a body of code inside braces. The braces '{'and '}' are not statements and hence we do not place any semicolon after them too.
7. While saving a Java program, the programmer must be very careful. This is so because a Java program may have one or more classes but one class must have a main( ) method and your program should match with this particular class name.
8. You should use .class extension when using the Java command.
9. A Java program must have at least one class definition.
10. You may create more than one class in a file but you may only have one public class per **Java file.**
11. When a Java file has a public class, the name of the public class must be the same as the name of the file without the .java extension. For instance, in the program given above, there is a public class named **first**, so it is stored in a file named as **first.java.**
12. Java is case-sensitive language. It means that it regards uppercase letters as being totally different characters from their lowercase counterparts.
13. The curly braces are also named as left and right braces or opening and closing braces or opening and closing flower braces.
14. Just remember that the total number of opening braces must be equal to the total number of closing braces in any program. Be it any programming language.
15. In the sample program, we have encountered the following special characters:

Table 2.1: Special Characters

Characters	Name	It's meaning
//	Double slash	Start of the comment
()	Opening and closing parentheses	Used in method header.
{ }	Opening and closing curly braces	Encloses a group of statements like contents of a class or a method
" "	Quotation marks	Encloses a string of characters like a message that is to be printed on to the screen.
;	Semicolon	Marks the end of a complete programming statement.

2.2 IDENTIFIERS, VARIABLES AND KEYWORDS

In Java program, every word is classified as either an identifier or a keyword. Identifiers are the names that we specify for the variables, types, classes, objects, methods and labels in the Java program. Declaring these in declaration section creates identifiers. An identifier is a programmer-defined name that represents some element of a program. **Variable names and class names are the examples of identifiers.**

Rules for Naming Identifiers

The following rules are used when naming identifiers:

1. An identifier is a combination of one or more letters a–z, A–Z, digits, underscores (_) or dollar sign characters in which the first letter must be a letter or an underscore or a dollar ($) sign.
2. An identifier can be of any length.
3. Uppercase and lowercase characters are distinct.
4. They cannot include spaces.
5. For example, area, radius, first_name are some identifiers.

Keywords: Are those special words whose meanings are prefixed by the Java compiler. **Please note that you cannot use keywords to name classes or variables. Also note that the keywords are also called as the reserved words**. Some examples of **Java's keywords** are as follows:

Abstract, char, double, for, int, private, super, try, Boolean, class, else, goto, interface, protected, switch, void, break, const, extends, if, long, public, synchronized, volatile, byte, continue, final, implements, native, return, this, while, case, default, finally, import, new, short, throw, catch, do, float, instanceof, package, static, transient.

But please remember the following points regarding identifiers:

1. Always choose names for variables that give an indication of what they are used for. This increases program's understandability.
2. Although $ is a legal identifier character, it is normally used for special purposes. So, don't use it in your variable names.
3. Combine two words into one to form a variable like "itemsordered". But we can follow **Hungarian notation** here i.e. we can capitalize the first word of the 2nd word and rewrite the variable name as "itemOrdered". This makes it self-documenting i.e. we can make out what this variable is storing.

Variable names: Are the type of identifiers only. Variables are temporary data holders. Variable names/ identifiers must begin with a letter, underscore or dollar sign, use ASCII or Unicode characters. They are case sensitive too. *But please remember that they cannot be the reserved words of JAVA.* Variables are declared with a data-type. *Also remember that Java is a strongly typed language as the variable can only take a value that matches its declared type.* This enforces good programming practice and reduces error also to a larger extent. When the variables are declared, they may or may not be assigned a value. Thus, variable is a memory location where data is stored during run-time. When we execute any program, by default it goes into memory and it takes some space in memory which is denoted by a variable name in a program. We cannot access data from memory directly until we know where data is stored in memory. *Please understand that by using variables we assure that which value will be stored in which memory location and that we can use that location data by a variable. Also understand that the variables names should be meaningful as it self-documents a program.* We shall be studying these in detail a bit later.

We are in a position to solve some examples now.

Example 1: Identify from the following, whether they are valid variable names or not. Give reasons.

Day of Month, 3dgraph, jan2014, mix#5, day of week.

[**Ans.** Let us tabulate these variables and discuss:

Variable name	Valid/ Invalid
Day of Month	Valid variable.
3dgraph	Invalid as identifiers cannot begin with a digit.
jan2014	Valid.
Mix#5	Invalid as identifiers may only use alphabetic letters, digits, underscores or dollars.
Day of week	Invalid as identifiers cannot contain spaces.

Example 2: Explain as to why the following variable identifiers are invalid:

```
int main;
int static;
int constant;
```

[**Hint:** All these variables are invalid as they all use the reserved keywords of Java. Java keyword can not be used as a variable name].

Example 3: Give three properties of a variable.

[**Hint:** A variable has 3 properties:- a memory location to store the value, the type of data stored in memory location and the name used to refer to the memory location].

Example 4: What are separators? Describe various separators in Java?

[GGSIPU, B. Tech(CSE/IT)-5th sem., Dec. 2011]

[**Hint:** Separators help us to define the programs structure like parentheses ( ), braces { }, period(.) and semicolon (;)].

Example 5: Define Shadowing.

2.3 DATA TYPES (IN JAVA)

As we know that a data type signifies the type of information is being stored in a variable. Data types are especially important in Java because it is a strongly typed language. This means that all operations are type-checked by the compiler for type compatibility. Illegal operations will not be compiled. Thus, strong type checking helps to prevent errors and enhance reliability (i.e. failure-free operation of the software).

Figure 2.1 shows the classification of different data types in Java.

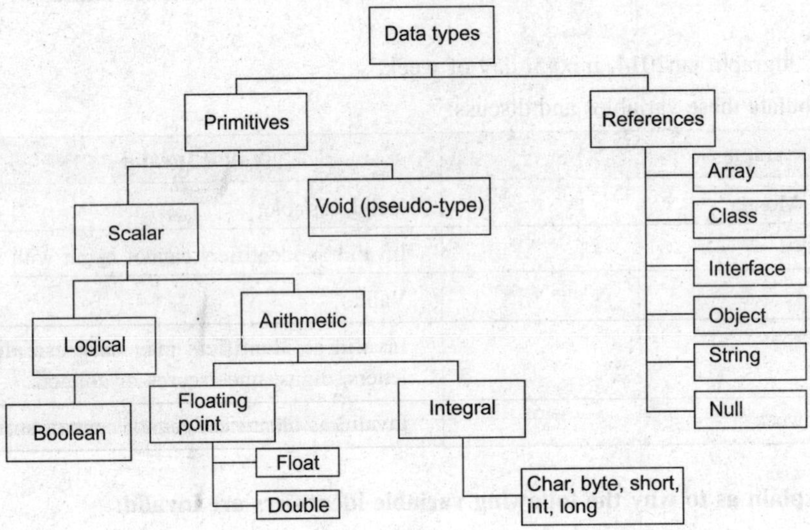

Fig. 2.1: Classification of Java data types

In general, Java supports two types of in-built data types as follows:

(a) Object-oriented.

(b) Non object-oriented.

Java supports two types of object-oriented or primitive data types:

(a) Primary data types.

(b) Secondary data types.

2.3.1 Primary Data Types

Primary data types are the data types that are built into the Java language. They are also called as **standard data types**. Java provides four types of primary data types, namely- Integers, Floating-point numbers, characters and Booleans.

Integers: They are whole-valued signed or unsigned numbers. It includes byte, short, int and long types of data. All of these are signed, positive and negative values. *Please note that Java does not support unsigned integer literals. Also note that if you have an expression involving bytes, shorts, ints, longs and literal numbers then the entire expression is promoted to long before the calculation is done.* The following table shows their sizes and ranges:

Table 2.2: Data Types and Their Sizes.

Data types	Size	Range
Integers		
Byte	8 bits	–128 to +127
short	16-bits	–32768 to +32767
int	32-bits	-2^{31} to $2^{31} - 1$
long	64-bits	-2^{63} to $2^{63} - 1$
Floating-point numbers		
float	32-bits (IEEE 754)	–3.4e38 to 3.4e38
double	64-bits (IEEE 754)	–1.7e308 to 1.7e308
Characters		
char	16-bits	0 to 65,536
Boolean		
boolean	1-bit	True/false
object	n/a	n/a

Primitives are not full-fledged objects in Java. They are treated as lightweight containers for storing and accessing a value. *Please note that since they are not the objects, they cannot be used where an object is required.* For example, storing primitive values in a java.util. Collection requires the primitive be wrapped in a special wrapper class such as java.lang.Integer or java.lang.Double. *Also note that each primitive in Java has a corresponding wrapper class.*

2.3.2 Secondary Data Types

The data types that are defined from the primary data types are called as **secondary data types. For example**, arrays, classes, strings etc.

Non object-oriented data types

Object references are variables that refer to Java objects. Instead of holding a primitive value, they hold the memory address of the object. The object may be a user-defined class or it may be one of the classes included in the Java APIs such as java.lang.String or java.util.List.

The following table lists the corresponding reference types of the primitive types provided with the language.

Table 2.3: Primitive Data Types

Data type in Java	Wrapper class	Size (bits)
byte	System.Byte	8
short	System.Short	16
int	System.Integer	32
long	System.Long	64
char	System.Character	16
boolean	System.Boolean	—
float	System.Float	32 (IEEE 754)
double	System.Double	64 (IEEE 754)

These data types are called as primitive **because they are not created from classes. They allow a variable to hold a single value.** Variables do not have attributes or methods.

Please remember the following points here:

1. All floating point numbers follow IEEE std. 754 specifications.
2. There are 3 floating point values—positive infinity, negative infinity and NaN (not a number). These values denote overflows and errors. Also note that the result of certain invalid operation like 0/0 or the square root of a negative number yields **NaN**. The result of dividing a positive number by 0 is **positive infinity**.
3. The type void is not a type in Java; it is only a pseudo type. The void type is used to represent the absence of information.
4. Scalar types are predefined and void is a pseudo type.
5. There is a special reference type in Java called as **null**. It is not possible to declare a variable of null type since it has no name.
6. It is not possible to cast to null type also.
7. The null reference can be cast to any reference type.
8. It is the only possible value of an expression of null type.
9. In Java, primitive types have corresponding reference types. **The act of converting a primitive type variable** (like int, float, double etc.) **to a reference to the corresponding type** (like Integer, Float, Double etc,) **is known as boxing. And the reverse process is known as unboxing**. During assignment or calling of constructor, the automatic transformation of wrapper types into their primitive equivalent is known as **unboxing**.

We are in a position to answer the following questions now.

Q.1. Define and WAP on the concept of Autoboxing and Unboxing principle?

[GGSIPU, B. Tech.(CSE/IT)-5th sem., Sept. 2010]

[Hint: //program to convert int into Integer

```
int inative =0;
inative = new Integer(5);   // auto-unboxing
Integer intObject = 5;   // autoboxing
//storing int a into vector vt
int a=10;
Vector <integer> vt = new Vector <integer> ();
vt.add(a);
int  n = vt.element.At(0);

//autoboxing also works with comparison
int a = 10;
Integer b = 10;
System.out.println (a==b);
```

OUTPUT: true

//another example of boxing/unboxing of character value

```
public class MainClass {
public static void main(String args[]) {
Boolean booleanObject = true;
if (booleanObject) {
System.out.println("b is true");
}
Character ch ='x';   // box a char
Char ch2 = ch;  //unbox a char
System.out.println("ch2 is" + ch2);
}
}
```

OUTPUT: b is true
Ch2 is x]

Q.2. What are wrapper classes? *[GGSIPU, B. Tech. (CSE/IT)-5th sem., Dec. 2012]*

2.4 LITERALS (CONSTANTS)

Literals or constants can be thought of as the read-only memory variables. Numerical literals are generally used in expressions.

Types of Literals

The following Fig. 2.2 shows the classification tree of literals:

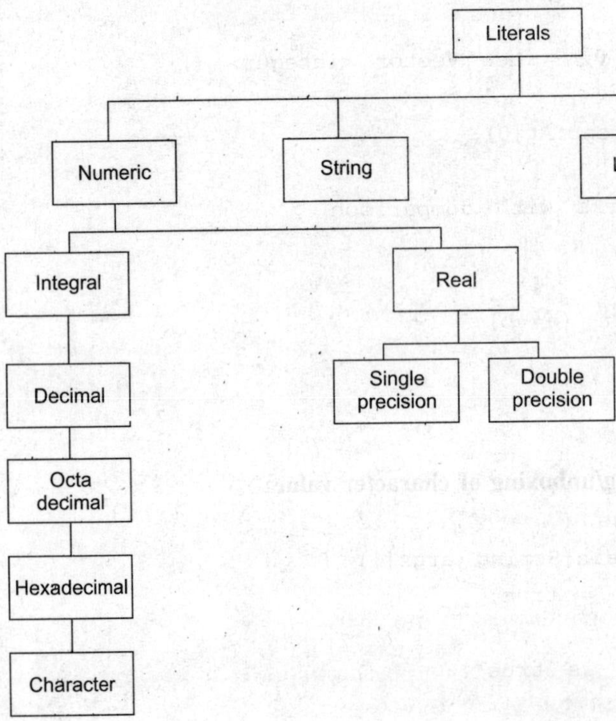

Fig. 2.2: Classification of literals

1. **Integer Literals:** Are numeric data. An integer literal can be a decimal integer literal, octal integer literal (i.e. the number with a zero prefix) and hexadecimal integer literal (i.e. the number with a 0x prefix).
2. **Floating-point Literals:** Are numeric data with a decimal point.
3. **Boolean Literals:** Are true or false.
4. **Character Literals:** Are enclosed in single quotes.
5. **String Literals:** Are enclosed in double quotes.

Examples of valid literals are:

189

–100

015

0x12ff

9.0

0.31412

2.47e40

1197e–10

'p'

"hello"

Examples of Invalid literals are:

+5 (no plus sign)

123,25 (no comma allowed)

0448 (cannot contain digit 8)

0x-25 (cannot contain a –ve sign after 0x)

123,45.55 (no comma allowed)

+12.85 (no plus sign)

'tc' (only 1 character within single quotes)

But please remember the following points regarding literals:

1. We can also have a long integer constant by appending a lowercase 'l' or an uppercase 'L' to the integer literal as follows: 78965L, – 15677889l etc.
2. By default, the floating-point literals are double precision. To make it a float literal, append an 'F' or 'f' to the constant as follows: 8.0f or 3.1417f.
3. In Java, strings are not like C/C++. Here, strings are object types. Thus, Java includes extensive string-handling capabilities that are both powerful and easy to use.
4. The literals **true** and **false** are the logical values that can be used in a program.
5. An object reference can be converted to Boolean. Any reference other than *null* is true.
6. Special characters except +, –, e, p, F, f, D, d and . are not allowed.
7. Floating literals must end with f or F.
8. Double literals must end with d or D.
9. The exponent of the floating literals written in exponential form must be an integer.
10. Either the integer part or the fractional part (not both) may be missing.

11. Either the decimal point or the exponent (not both) may be missing.
12. Both the integer and fractional parts consists of a sequence of digits only.
13. Java is a strongly-typed language which means that it only allows you to store values of compatible data types in variables. For instance, a double value is not compatible with a float variable because a double can be much larger or much smaller than the allowable range for a **float.** Thus, the following code will cause an error:-.

    float numb;

    numb = 88.9; //Error !!

    But the following is correct way of writing the above 2 instructions:

    float numb;

    numb = 88.9F; //will work !!

    That is, you can force a double literal to be treated as a float. However, by suffixing it with the letter f or F, this may be done.
14. In E notation the number 5.1718 * 10^8 will be written as 5.1718E8.
15. The scientific notation E can be uppercase or lowercase i.e. both E and e are correct.
16. The contents of a **boolean** variable may not be copied to a variable of any type other than **boolean.**
17. String literals cannot be assigned to char variables as string literals are enclosed in double quotation marks.

Let us now discuss about the Unicodes in Java.

Unicodes: As we know that characters are internally represented by numbers. Each character is assigned a unique number. When a character is stored in memory, it is actually the Unicode number that is stored. When the computer is instructed to print the value on the screen, it displays the character that corresponds with the numeric code. Unicode is an international encoding system that is extensive enough to represent all of the characters of this world. Java uses Unicode. Unicode is a set of numbers that are used as codes for representing characters. Each Unicode number requires two bytes of memory, so char variables also occupy 2 bytes. When a character is stored in memory, it is actually the numeric code that is stored. When the system is instructed to print the value, it displays the character that corresponds with the numeric code. In Unicode, letters are arranged in alphabetic order. Because 'A' comes before 'B', the numeric code for the character 'A' is less than the code for the character 'B'. The code for 'A is 65 and the code for 'B' is 66. The following program demonstrates this:

```
//program to show that when you work with characters, you are actually
working with numbers
public class charnumb
{
     public static void main(String args[])
```

```
    {
        char letter;
        letter = 65;
System.out.println(letter);
        letter = 66;
System.out.println(letter);
    }
}
```

OUTPUT: A

B

Conclusions: When we think of the characters A, B, and C being stored in memory, it is really the numbers 65, 66 and 67 that are stored. Recall that the number 65 is the code for A, 66 is the code for B and so on. So, A, B, C are being stored in memory as 65, 66, 67. This is so done because computers can only work on numbers directly and not characters. But to make them work on characters they are actually stored as integers only.

Before we discuss further, answer the following questions:

Q.1. Is the variable name salary the same as Salary? Why or why not?

Q.2. Which of the following is a character literal—'R' or "R"?

Q.3. What is wrong with the following statement- char alpha ="P";

Q.4. What are variables? List rules for naming variables in Java.

Q.5. Write short notes on UNICODE.

Q.6. How ASCII code is different from Unicode, convert 'A' into Unicode format?
[GGSIPU, B. Tech. (CSE/IT)- 5th sem., Oct. 2010]

Q.7. Write short notes on—
(a) UNICODE.
(b) Wrapper class. *[GGSIPU, B. Tech.(CSE/IT)-5the sem., Dec. 2011]*

Q.8. The 16-bit coding scheme employed in Java programming is called?
[GGSIPU, B. Tech.(CSE/IT)-5th sem., Dec. 2011]

2.5 ESCAPE SEQUENCES

An escape sequence basically consists of a backslash (\ ) followed by a letter or by a combination of digits. They are used to move the cursor from one position to the other or to specify certain actions like alerting. **They are so called because the backslash allows us to escape from the usual**

interpretation of the single-quote character. The following Table 2.4 shows different types of escape sequences:

Table 2.4: Escape Sequences

Escape sequence	Meaning
\n	New line-it advances the cursor to the next line for subsequent printing.
\t	Horizontal tab (cursor moves towards right columnwise)
\v	Vertical tab
\b	Backspace,
\r	Carriage return-causes the cursor to g to the beginning of the current line, not the next line.
\f	Form feed
\a	Alert (alarm)
\'	Single quotation mark
\"	Double quotation mark
\ddd	Octal character (ddd)
\uxxxx	Hexadecimal UNICODE character (xxxx)
//	Causes a backslash to be printed.

Please note that a single character is represented by an escape sequence formed by a backslash followed by one or more characters. Also note that in Java some of the non-graphic characters are known as white space characters. They are blank, new line, horizontal tab and form feed.

Although we have to type two characters to write an escape sequence, they are stored in memory as a single character. There is no space between the backslash and the control character following it.

2.6 VARIABLES

Are the type of identifiers only. Variables are temporary data holders. Variable names/identifiers must begin with a letter, underscore or dollar sign, use ASCII or Unicode characters. They are case sensitive too. But please remember that they cannot be the reserved words of JAVA. Variables are declared with a data-type. *Also remember that Java is a strongly types language as the variable can only take a value that matches its declared type.* This enforces good programming practice and reduces error also to a larger extent. When the variables are declared, they may or may not be assigned a value. Thus, variable is a memory location where data is stored during run-time. When we execute any program, by default it goes into memory and it takes some space in memory which is denoted by a variable name in a program. We cannot access data from memory directly until we know where data is stored in memory. *Please understand that by using variables we assure that which value will be stored in which memory location and that we can use that location data by a variable. Also understand that the variables names should be meaningful as it self-documents a program.*

There are three types of variables, mainly used in Java:

1. **Local Variables:** They are declared in a method, constructor or block. When a method is entered, an area is pushed onto the call stack. *Please note that this area contains slots for each local variable and parameter. When the method is called,* the parameter slots are initialized to the parameter values. When the method exits, this area is popped off the stack and the memory becomes available for the next called method. *Please note that parameters are essentially local variables which are initialized from the actual parameters. Also note that local variables are not visible outside the method.*
2. **Instance Variables:** They are declared in a class but outside a method. **They are also called as member or field variables.** When an object is allocated in the heap, there is a slot in it for each instance variable value. Therefore, an instance variable is created when an object is created and destroyed. Visible in all methods and constructors of the defining class, should generally be declared private but may be given greater visibility.
3. **Class/Static Variables:** They are declared with the static keyword in a class but outside a method. *Please note that there is only one copy per class, regardless of how many objects are created from it.* They are stored in static memory. It is rare to use static variables other than declared final and used as either public or private constants.

For example,

```
// a program1 showing all three of its types
Class myClass
      {
         // Instance variable
      public int n1;

      // Class variable
      public static int n2;
      void myfunction( )
      {
      //Local variable
        int n3;
            }
   }
```

Program-1

Variables Declaration

Variables are declared using this syntax:

<data type> <variable-name>;

Where data type will replace the type of value stored in variable and variable-name will replace the name of the variable. **For example,**

int numb1;

Here, data type = int and variable name = numb1. *Please understand that when we are create a variable, we are creating an instance of its types.* Thus, the capabilities of a variable are determined by its type. For example, a variable of type Boolean cannot be used to store floating-point value.

Variable Initialization

The general syntax of variable initialization is as follows:

type var = value;

Where, value is the value that is given to var when var is created. The value must be compatible with the specified type. **For example,**

```
int counter = 1;       //give counter an initial value of 1
char ch = 'r';         // initialize ch with the letter r
float f = 3.1417f      // f is initialized with 3.1417
```

But keywords and reserved words may not be used as variable names. For example,

```
int main;
int static;
int constant;
```

Furthermore, these variable names are case-sensitive too i.e. salary and Salary are two different variable names, as given by the user.

Variable Scope

Each of the three variable types in Java has a different scope. A variable's scope defines for how long a variable lives in the program memory and when it expires. *Please note that once a variable goes out of scope, its memory space is marked for garbage collection by the JVM and the variable may no longer be referenced. Also note from the above program-1, that both n1 and n2 are declared within myClass but outside of any of its methods, only one method exists in this example.* On the other hand, n3 is declared within myfunction. Local variables must be declared within methods. This includes being declared within code blocks nested inside of a method—within an if, while or for block etc. Please understand here that a variable is local to the code block within which it is declared. Being declared within a method body makes a variable local to that method. Being declared within an if- block makes a variable local to that if-block. Also understand that this means that a variable cannot be used outside of the curly braces within which it was declared. In fact, it can only be used from the line it is declared on until the code block ends. Local variables have the most limited scope. They are only valid from the line they are declared on until the closing curly brace of the method or the code block within which they are declared.

Instance variables are in scope as long as their enclosing object is in scope. An instance variable is a part of the object that contains it and cannot live in isolation, independently of it. Each instance of an object has its own version of instance variables. For example, if an Admission class declares that there is an admnDate instance variable then every Admission object will have its own value for admndate.

Class variables are in scope from the point the class is loaded into the JVM until the class is unloaded. Classes are loaded into the JVM the first time the class is referenced; often when the first object of that class is instantiated with the new operator. They are most long-lived kind of variable and come closest to being a global variable. A class variable's value is shared by all instances of that class. So, even if there are ten Admission mode objects that contain a class variable named currentDate, the value that currentDate contains is shared by all ten objects—there is only one currentDate.

We have already discussed about the variable types earlier.

Variable Visibility: The visibility or the access scope of instance and class variables defines what objects can read and modify that variable. There are four possible visibility modifiers: public, protected, private and no modifier. But if no visibility modifier is included with an instance or class variable then it is said to have default visibility. It is also called as **package-private and package-protected. Please remember that as a general rule you should make your instance and class variables private unless you have a reason to make them more visible to other classes. And keeping an object's data hidden is called as encapsulation.**

The following Table 2.5 lists the four access specifiers and their visibility:

Table 2.5: Access Specifiers/ Modifiers

Modifier	Can be accessed by
Public	Any class
Protected	Owning class, any subclass, any class in the same package.
No modifier	Owning class, any class in the same package.
Private	Owning class

But please remember the following points regarding variables:

1. A variable can hold only one value at a time.
2. When you assign a new value to a variable, the new value takes the place of the variable's previous contents.
3. The symbol = that is used for variable initialization is known as an **assignment operator**.
4. The assignment operator only changes the contents of its left operand. (operators perform operations on data. The data that operators work with are called as **operands.** The assignment operator has two operands.

5. When a variable is declared inside a method, it must have a value stored in it before it can be used.
6. The variables holding data of scalar data types are known as **scalar variables.**
7. The variable names are also known as **declarators.** The declarators are separated by a comma when more than one declarator is written in a declaration. The declaration ends with a semicolon.
8. A variable can be declared as final to store a constant value.
9. You cannot have two local variables with the same name in the same scope. This applies to the parameter variables also. A parameter variable is a local variable only. So, you cannot give a parameter variable and a local variable in the same method the same name.
10. But you can have a local variable or a parameter variable with the same name as a field. When you do so, the name of the local or parameter variable shadows the name of the field. This means that the field name is hidden by the name of the local or parameter variable. For example,

```
public void readLength (double len)
  {
     int length;    //local variable
   length = len;
  }
```

Herein, a local variable is given the same name as the field. So, the local variable's name shadows the field's name. When the statement length = len; is executed, the value of len is assigned to the local variable length, not to the field.

2.7 OPERATORS

The task of computation is known as **operation.** The data items that the operators act upon are called as **operands**. An **operator** is a symbol or a keyword that specifies an operation to be performed. If an operator uses a symbol like +, –, * etc. then it is called as a **symbolic operator**. If a particular keyword is used as an operator then it is called as a **named operator**. The operator that uses a single operand is called as a **unary operator** and that which uses two operands is known as a **binary operator**. A **ternary operator** uses three operands.

Each variable must be associated with a memory location for data storage. Each function must be associated with a part of a program which invokes it. Each program must be associated with the execution environment for performing the task specified by the program. *The association of a program to a suitable entity is called as binding. The time during which the choice of binding takes place is known as binding time.* Binding can occur during *compile time or execution time. The binding that takes place during compilation is known as compile time binding or early binding or static binding.* On the other hand, *the binding that takes place during program execution is called as execution time binding or late binding or dynamic binding. Please understand that late binding provides flexibility whereas early binding provides efficiency.*

Also understand that any valid combination of constants, variables and operators constitutes an expression and the result of the expression after its evaluation is known as the *value of an expression.* Like 5+5 =10, the evaluation of an expression always yields a value. *Please note that the operands in an expression may be of similar data types or of different data types*. When an operator uses operands of different data types then the operation is known as a *mixed mode operation. Also note that the evaluation of an expression takes place only if both the operands have a type that is compatible with the type required by the operand.* Else type conversions are done and this will be discussed a bit later.

Types of Operators

Operators can be classified on the following basis:

1. Based on number of operands—unary, binary and ternary.
2. Based on notations used—symbolic and named.

In Java operators are classified as follows (see Fig. 2.3):

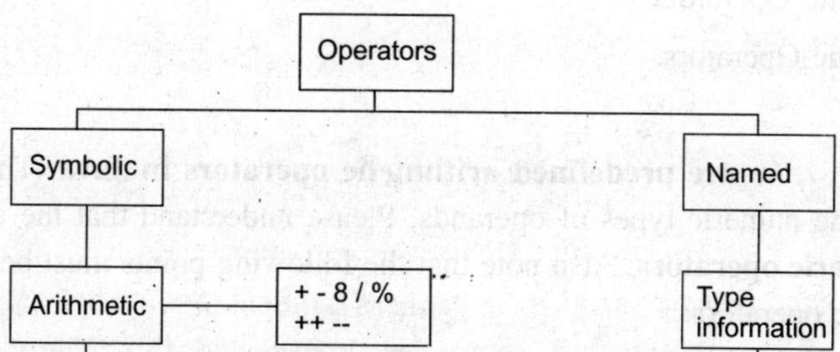

Fig. 2.3: Operator's classification in Java

We shall be studying these operators one by one now.

2.7.1 Arithmetic Operators

As we know that, arithmetic expressions are formed by using numeric values/variables and arithmetic operators. **They are also known as numeric expressions.** The simple binary arithmetic expression takes the form:-

Operand1 op operand2

Where

Operand1—represents the left side operand.

Operand2—represents the right side operand.

Op —— represents one of the arithmetic operators + - * / %.

Like, p +q, t-20, a % b, a*b a/b etc.

Arithmetic operators are of 2 types:

(a) Binary Arithmetic Operators.

(b) Unary Arithmetic Operators.

The operators +, –, *, /, % are predefined arithmetic operators in Java. The binary arithmetic operators allow only the numeric types of operands. Please understand that the arithmetic operators are also called as **numeric operators**. Also note that the following points must be kept in mind while using binary arithmetic operators:

1. The binary division (/) operator uses the left-hand operand as the **dividend** and the right-hand operand as the **divisor.**
2. The division operator gives floating quotient value for floating operands.
3. Integer division by 0 is an error whereas floating point division by 0 yields an infinity or NaN result.
4. If both the operands of / are integral types, the fractional part of the quotient is truncated and the result is integer type.
5. The modulus operator (%) can only be applied to integer as well as floating point operands.
6. x % y yields a result value such that (x / y) * y + (x % y) is always equal to x if x and y are integral types.
7. The operator % on floating point operation behaves similar to that of the integer remainder operator. This can be compared with the library function **fmod** in C. The remainder operation defined by IEEE 754 is not followed.
8. The following Table 2.6 shows both the operators:

Table 2.6: Arithmetic Operators

Binary arithmetic	
Operators	**Operation**
+	Addition
–	Subtraction
*	Multiplication
/	Division
%	Modulus
Unary arithmetic Operators	**Operation**
+	Unary plus; indicates positive value.
–	Unary minus; negates an expression
++	Increment a value by 1
––	Decrement a value by 1
!	Logical complement operator; inverts the value of a Boolean.

The following program tests these arithmetic operators:

```
Class ArithmeticOperator {
    public static void main (String[] args) {
        int result = 1+2;      // result is now 3
        System.out.println(result);

        result = result -1;   // result is now 2
        System.out.println(result);

        result = result * 2;        //result is now 4
        System.out.println(result);

        result = result/2;          //result is now 2
        System.out.println(result);

        result = result + 8;        //result is now 10
        result = result % 7; //result is now 3
        System.out.println(result);
        }
}
```

Also note that you can also combine the arithmetic operators with the simple assignment operators to create compound statements. For example, x+=1; and x=x+1; both increment the value of x by 1.

NOTE: The operator + can also be used for concatenating (joining) two strings together.

This is shown in the program below:

```
Class ConcatOperator {
    public static void main(String[] args) {
    String s1= "Rajiv";
    String s2 = "Chopra";
    String ConcatString = s1 + s2;
    System.out.println(ConcatString);
}
}
```

OUTPUT: Rajiv Chopra

Let us now test the working of unary operators.

```
Class UnaryOperator {
    public static void main (String[] args) {
        int result = +1;        // result is now 1
        System.out.println(result);

        result--; // result is now 0
        System.out.println(result);

        result++; // result is now 1
        System.out.println(result);

        result = -result;     //result is now -1
        System.out.println(result);

        boolean success = false;
        System.out.println(result);    //false
}
}
```

Please note that the increment/decrement operators can be applied before (prefix) or after (postfix) the operand. The statement result++ and ++result will both end in result being incremented by one. Also note that only difference is that the prefix version (++result) evaluates to in the incremented value whereas the postfix version (result ++) evaluates to the original value. If you are just performing a simple increment/decrement, it doesn't matter which version you choose. But if it is a larger expression then it makes a significant difference. The following program shows the use of unary operators:

```
Class PrePostOperator {
    public static void main(String[] args) {
    int i =3;
      i++;
    System.out.println(i);          // "4"
     ++i;
    System.out.println(i);          //"5"
    System.out.println(++i);        //"6"
    System.out.println(i++);        //"6"
    System.out.println(i);          //"7"
    }
  }
```

2.7.2 Relational and Equality Operators

The equality and relational operators determine if one operand is greater than, less than, equal to or not equal to another operand. The majority of these operators will probably look familiar to you as well. **But please remember that you must use "==" and not "=" when testing if two primitive values are equal.** Relational and equality operators require two operands. The relational operation performs comparison of two numeric values. An equality operation tests whether both the operands represent the same value. The operands may be any arithmetic types. These operators when applied on the operands produce logical values. Expressions that use relational and equality operators are called as **relational expressions.** They are listed in Table 3.7 below:

Table 3.7: Relational Operators

Operation	Symbol	Result
Greater than	>	True or false
Greater than or equal to	>=	True or false
Less than	<	True or false
Less than or Equal to	<=	True or false
Equal to	==	True or false
Not equal to	!=	True or false

The following program tests these operators:

```
Class ComparisonOperator
 {
   public static void main(String[] args)
    {
      int val1= 1;
      int val2 = 2;

      if(val1 == val2)
      System.out.println("value1 == value2");

      if(val1 != val2)
      System.out.println("value1 != value2");

      if(val1 > val2)
      System.out.println("value1 > value2");

      if(val1 < val2)
      System.out.println("value1 < value2");

      if(val1 <= val2)
      System.out.println("value1 <= value2");
     }
   }
```

OUTPUT:

```
value1 != value2
value1 < value2
value1 <= value2
```

2.7.3 Logical Operators

In Java, logical operators may be bitwise or conditional.

The binary bitwise logical operators are shift operators and & (bitwise AND), | (bitwise OR) and ^ (bitwise XOR) operators. **Bitwise complement operator is the unary bitwise logical operator.**

There are two binary conditional logical operators: && (logical AND), || (logical OR) and one unary conditional logical operator ! (negation operator logical NOT).

Please understand that bitwise operators are mainly used for operating on the single bits of an integral variable while conditional operators operated on Boolean expressions.

Let us now classify different types of logical operators. They are shown in Fig. 2.4.

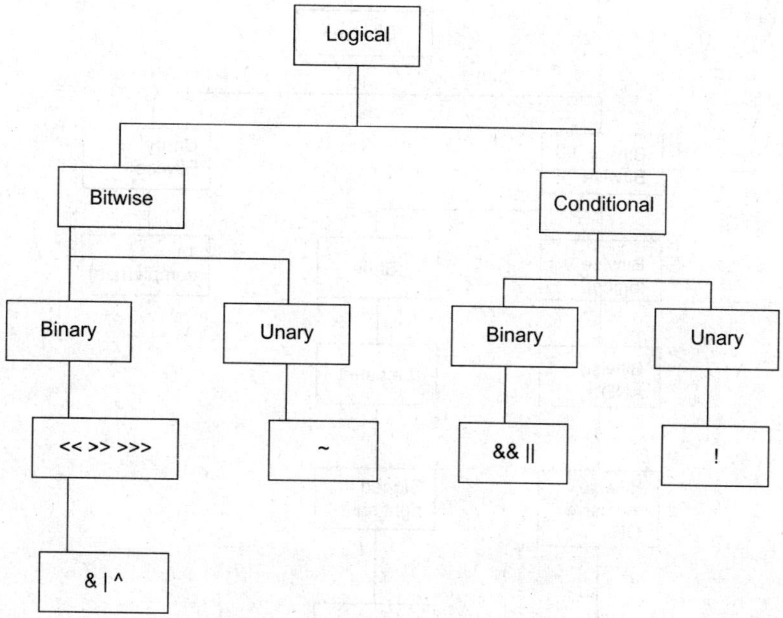

Fig. 2.4 Categories of logical operators

Bitwise Logical Operators

To manipulate individual bits of an integral type, Java supports 7 special operators known as **bitwise logical operators**. These operators are used for modifying bit patterns (binary representation). They are shown in Table 2.8 below.

Table 2.8: Bitwise Logical Operators

Operator	Meaning
&	Bitwise AND
|	Bitwise inclusive OR
^	Bitwise exclusive OR (XOR)
<<	Left shift
>>	Signed Right shift
>>>	Unsigned Right shift
~	One's Complement (unary)

The bitwise logical operators &, || and ^ are called as **logical bitwise AND, logical OR and logical bitwise EXCLUSIVE OR operators respectively.**

Let us now categorize logical operators also. It is shown in Fig. 2.5.

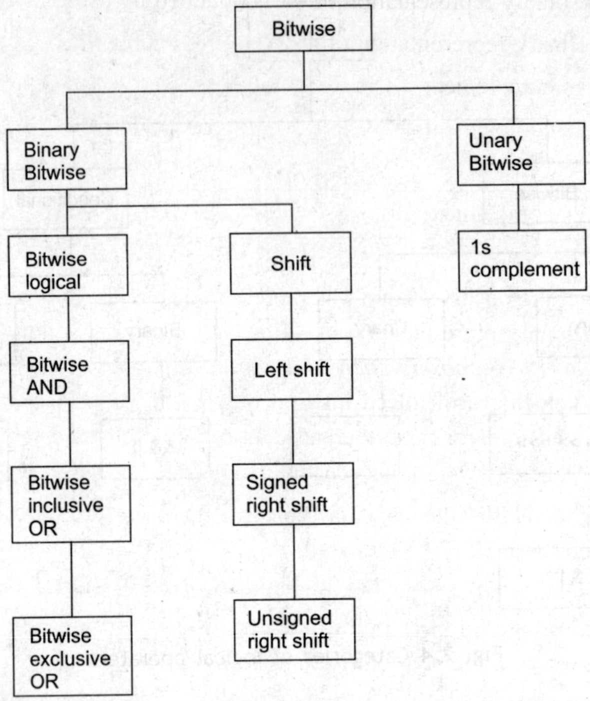

Fig. 2.5: Types of logical operators

The operator & performs a bitwise AND between two integral operands. The operator & compares each bit of the left operand with the corresponding bit of the right operand. For each bit the result is 1, if both the bits compared are 1; otherwise, the result is 0. This is shown in Table 2.9 below.

Table 2.9: The & Operations

Compared bits	Result
0 & 0	0
0 & 1	0
1 & 0	0
1 & 1	1

Please note that the positive values are internally represented in its binary form. The negative value is represented in 2s complement form. Also we know that the 2s complement is obtained by adding 1 to 1s complement of a number. 1s complement is obtained by inverting 0 to 1 and 1 to 0 of the binary representation of the magnitude of a number.

For example, the binary representation of –4 is obtained by using 2s complement as follows:

Binary representation of 4	= 00000100
1s complement	= 11111011
1s complement + 1	= 11111011 +
	00000001
2s complement	= 11111100

Just remember that the positive value 4 is represented as 00000100 whereas –4 is represented as 11111100. Given the binary representation of –4 as well as 4, the 2s complement of –4 is 4 and 2s complement of 4 is –4. *Please observe here that the negative value always has the most significant bit MSB) to be 1.* When the result of an integral bitwise operation has 1 as its MSB in its binary representation for signed integral type operands, its 2s complement is obtained to get the absolute value of the number. A negative sign precedes the magnitude to represent it as a negative value.

As already explained, that the int data type in Java uses 32 bits for its bit patttern. Similar operations are done on these 32 bits data too.

Bitwise AND is often used to mask off some bits. **Masking is defined as an operation by which the desired bits of a binary number or bit pattern are set to zero.** The operator & is very useful here. This can be shown with the help of an example too.

Say, given number = 58 (decimal)	= 00000000000000000000000000111010
Mask	= 11111111111111111111111111110000
Then the result = 48	= 00000000000000000000000000110000

Thus, in the result, the four LSBs are masked.

NOTE: To mask the alternate bits (starting from LSB) of an 8-bit binary number, the mask is selected as 10101010. Thus, the mask is selected in such a way that the bits to be masked off must be zero and the remaining bits are 1. This concept can be extended to any number of bits.

Bitwise Inclusive OR (|)

The | operator performs a bitwise OR between two operands. It compares each bit of the first operand with the corresponding bit of the second operand. *Please remember that for each bit, the result is 0, if the two bits compared are both 0; otherwise, the result is 1.* That is,

Table 2.10: The | Operation

Compared bits	Result
0 | 0	0
0 | 1	1
1 | 0	1
1 | 1	1

Even ¦ operator can be used to perform another type of masking in which the desired bits of a binary number can be set to 1. For this type of masking the second operand is selected in such a way that the bits to be set as 1 must be selected as 1 and the remaining bits are 0.

For example, to set the 4 LSBs of an integer value, the operation is performed as follows:

Say, given number is 187 = 00000000000000000000000010111011

Mask is = 00000000000000000000000000001111

Result is = 00000000000000000000000010111111

Bitwise Exclusive OR (^)

The operator ^ performs a bitwise exclusive OR between two operands. This operator compares each bit of the first operand with the corresponding bit of the second operand. For each bit the result is 0, if the two bits compared have the same value; otherwise, the result is 1. This is shown in table below:

Compared Bits	Result
0 ^ 0	0
0 ^ 1	1
1 ^ 0	1
1 ^ 1	0

The ^ operator can be used to perform another type of masking in which the desired bits of a binary number can be complemented. For this type of masking, the second operand is selected in such a way that the bits to be complemented are set as 1 and the remaining bits as 0.

For example, to complement the 5 LSBs of an integer value, the operation is performed as follows:

Say, given number is 214 (dec.) = 00000000000000000000000011010110

Mask is = 00000000000000000000000000011111

Result is = 00000000000000000000000011001001

In Java, there are 2 binary logical operators also. They are && (AND), || (OR) and one unary logical operator ! (NOT). Logical operators require operands as the logical values. The following Table 2.11 lists the logical operators in Java:

Table 2.11: Truth Table for Logical Operators

Operation	Symbol	Result
Logical AND	&&	True or false
Logical OR	||	True or false
Logical NOT	!	True or false

The result of && is true, if and only if both the operands are true, otherwise the result is false. The result of || is false if and only if both the operands are false else the result is true. **Please note that these operators are also known as short-circuiting logical operators.** The logical expression a && b is equivalent to a & b (assuming a and b are Boolean expressions) except that b is evaluated only if a is true. Also observe from the above table that if one of the logical values is false using &&, the result is false. Hence, if the 1st operand is or left operand is false, there is no meaning in evaluating the 2nd operand. *And this process in which the compiler omits the evaluation of the second operand if the first operand's value is false is known as short-circuiting.* Such short-circuiting operation is also known as **lazy evaluation of expression.** Similarly, the logical expression a || b is equivalent to a | b (assuming 'a' and 'b' are Boolean expressions) except that b is evaluated only if a is false. Using the 2nd operand in the subsequent expressions may not perform the intended operation because of short-circuiting operation. **Also one must take care while short-circuiting operators are used as the 2nd operand may not be evaluated at all.**

This is shown in Table 2.12 below:

Table 2.12: Truth Table for && and ||

Condition	Result of &&	Condition	Result of ||
True && True	True	True || True	True
True && False	False	True || False	True
False && True	False	False || True	True
False && False	False	False || False	False

The logical operator ! (logical negate or NOT) requires only one operand which represents a logical value true or false. The result of the operation is true if and only if the operand is false else the result is false. This is shown in Table 2.13 below:

Table 2.13: Truth Table for !

Condition	Result
! False	True
! True	False

Please note that the operand follows the operator !, while using this operator. Also note that there is a difference between the bitwise operators & and | from the logical operators && and ||. The & and | operators yield Boolean values when applied to Boolean values. They are similar to && and || operators but not *subjected to short-circuit* evaluation.

Note: A logical expression is any valid combination of logical values, variables and logical operators.

2.7.4 Shift Operators

These operators work with integer primitives only. They shift the left operand by the number of bits specified by the right operand. **Please note that with these operators the value of the new bit is shifted into the number.** For << (left shift), the new bit that appears in the low order position is always zero. SUN had to define two types of right shift because the high order bit in integer primitives indicates the sign. The >> right shift propagates the existing sign bit, which means a negative number will still be negative after being shifted. The >>> right shift inserts a zero as the MSB. (note: 0 means the number is +ve). **Also note that when doing bit manipulations on primitives shorter than 32 bits, the compiler promotes all operands to 32 bits before performing the operation.** But if the right operand is larger than 31 bits for operation on 32-bit integers, the compiler uses only the five lowest order bits i.e. values of 0 through 31. With a 64-bit integer as the right operand, only the six lowest order bits i.e. values of 0 through 63, are used. Therefore, in line 1 given below:

1. a = b << 1024;

b is shifted by only 1 bit. This also means that the sign bit is totally ignored.

In line 2, as follows:

2. a = c >> –1;

The right shift is not turned into a left shift by the minus sign.

Please note that the assignment operator (=) can also be combined with the shift and bitwise operators, just as with the arithmetic operators.

The following points may be remembered regarding shift operators:

1. The right shift operators >> and >>> and the left shift operator << move the bit patterns to the right or left respectively.
2. The general form of the shift expression is:

   leftop op n

   where leftop— is the left operand that can be of integral type.

   Op— is any one of the shift operators >>, >>> and <<.

   n— is the number of bit positions to be shifted. It must be of integer type only.
3. *In right shift*, the left operand is shifted to the right by n number of bit positions whereas *in the left shift*, the left operand is shifted to the left by n number of bit positions.
4. Usually the shift operators are used for computational purposes or to extract a single bit.
5. There is no arithmetic left shift operator. Left shift operation is performed as logical left shift only.
6. To divide an integer by 2, the variable or constant is shifted right by 1-bit position.
7. To divide by 4, it is shifted right by 2-bit positions and so on.
8. To multiply integers by powers of 2, the left shift can be used.

9. Signed numeric values are represented in memory by reserving the MSB as a sign bit. The sign bit is filled with 1 for a negative value and 0 for a positive value.
10. In a right shift operation, MSB will be shifted to the right and the sign bit is filled with 0.
11. It is mandatory to retain the sign bit of leftop having negative value to effect shift operation correctly. In such cases, the vacated bits will be filled with 1.
12. If the vacated bits are simply filled with zeros without considering this factor, it is called as **logical shifting.**
13. If the sign bit is filled with 1 for negative left operand in right shift expression, it is called as **arithmetic shifting.**
14. Java compilers implement a logical right shift in which zero is shifted to the leftmost bit position (vacated bit) if the leftop is of type unsigned.
15. If the leftop is signed, the bits shifted in from the left are the same as the bit value formerly occupying the left-most bit positions resulting in arithmetic right shift.
16. The logical shift right is represented by >>> operator and the arithmetic right shift is represented by >> operator.
17. Explicit type casting or coercion (to be studied a bit later) may result in the opposite operation to that inferred from the data type of leftop. **For example,** if a is an int variable, the expression-

    (int) ((uint) a >> 5);

    It performs a logical right shift instead of the default arithmetic right shift for int type.

2.7.5 1s Complement Operator

One's complement (1s) complement operator (~) needs one operand only. This operator converts all 1-bits to 0 and vice versa. The result is 1s complement of the operand. *Please note that ~ operator can operate on the entire bit pattern and not on the individual bits. Also note that it is clear that* ~(~6) *is* 6. In general, ~(~n) is n only. This operator can be used for encoding of the secret message too as it will then invert each and every message bit.

2.7.6 Assignment Operators

The equal to operator (=) is an assignment operator in any programming language. In Java also, there are 3 types of assignment operations:

(a) Simple assignment.

(b) Compound assignment.

(c) Assignment expression.

Syntax:

lvalue = expression

where,

lvalue — represents a memory location where a value may be stored(a variable name).

expression — may be a constant or a variable or a combination of constants, variables and operators.

= is an assignment operator.

For example, u=77, u=v, area = 3.1417 * r * r and so on.

General format of the compound assignment is:

lvalue operator = expression

where,

operators may be one of these: + – * ? % << >> & ^

lvalue and expression are same as given above.

NOTE: lvalue operator = expression is a shorthand notation for
lvalue = lvalue operator expression.

In Java, an assignment operation is treated as an expression because the operation has a result. The result of an assignment is the value that was assigned. It is useful in multiple assignments.

For example 1, u=v=0

It is equivalent to u = (v=0), resulting to a=0 and b=0.

Example 2, a=7 + (b=8 + (c =2)) – 4 will evaluate to-

a=13, b=10 and c=2.

Please note here that if a semicolon (;) is placed at the end of an assignment expression, the result is an assignment statement. For example, u=80 is an assignment expression whereas u=80; is an assignment statement. *Also note that if the two operands in an assignment operation are of different data types, the right side operand is automatically converted to the data type of the left side.* Depending on the type of the left operand, boxing, unboxing, narrowing or widening conversion will take place. We shall be studying these a bit later.

2.7.7 Conditional / Ternary Operator

The conditional assignment operator is the only Java operator that takes three operands. This is same as C/C++. **This is also referred to as compact if. Also it is called as a ternary operator as it takes three operands.**

Syntax:

Expression1 ? Expression2 : Expression3;

Here, Expression1, Expression2 and Expression3 are the three operands. Expression1 is a Boolean expression, which is tested. It is just like a Boolean expression in the parenthesis of an if-statement. If **Expression1** is true then **Expression2 is executed else Expression3 is executed.**

For example,

z = x > y? x : y;

Please note here that the operand to the left of the ? must evaluate as boolean and the other two operands must be of the same type or convertible to the same type, which will be the type of result. The result will be the operand to the left of the colon if the **boolean** is true, else it will be the right operand. It is also possible to write this statement as follows:-

(expr1) ? expr2 : expr3;

Here, if expr1 is evaluated as true then expr2 will be executed else expr3 will be executed. Thus, you can use this conditional operator to create short expressions that work like if-else statements (to be discussed shortly). This ternary operator is powerful and unique also.

But please remember the following points regarding conditional operators/ternary operators:

1. You can even add parentheses around the sub-expressions in a conditional expression like,

   number = (x > 10) ? 100 : 250;

   This simply means that if x > 10 then number (variable) is assigned a value of 100 else it is assigned a value of 250.
2. The conditional operator gives you the ability to pack decision-making power into a concise line of code.
3. The parentheses are placed around the conditional expression because the + operator has higher precedence than the ? : operator. Without parentheses, the + operator would work as a concatenation operator only.
4. You can never use a void method as an argument to the ? : operator.
5. The following class **condi-oper** implements the same:-

```
Class condi-oper
  {
     public static void main (String args [ ])
    {
      int a = 10;
      int b= 20;
      int c= 30;
    int large = a > b ? (a > c ? a: c) : (b > c ? b : c);
System.out.println("The greatest of the 3 numbers is" + large);
    }
}
```

This program prints the largest of three numbers.

2.7.8 New Operator

When you create an instance of a class, you need to allocate memory for it. To allocate memory you need to use new operator. Please understand that you can allocate memory for an object in two different ways:

(a) classname objectname;

objectname = new classname( );

(b) classname objectname = new classname ( );

For example 1, Car Maruti;

Maruti = new Car( );

Example 2, Car Maruti = new Car( );

Also note that you can use new operator to allocate memory for array elements. Also you can use new operator inside the methods only.

This new operator is used to create objects dynamically on the heap. By generating an object, the memory for its fields and methods are allocated. We shall be studying this operator again a bit later.

We are in a position to solve some questions now.

Q.1. Rewrite the following statements using combined assignment operators to perform the following operations:

(a) Add 5 to u.

(b) Subtract 8 from salary.

(c) Multiply v by 8.

(d) Divide total by 2.

(e) Store in temp the remainder of u divided by v.

Q.2. Give the output of the following code:

```
int u = 5;
int v = u++;
int v2 = ++x;
```

[Hint: v gets a value of 5, before incrementing u and v2 gets the value of 7, after incrementing].

Q.3. What will be the result of the following statements:

(a) double result;

result = 5 / 2;

(b) double result;

result = 5.0 / 2;

[Hint: (a) result = 2. It is not 2.5 because 5 and 2 are integers.

(b) result = 2.5. It is so because 5.0 is double type.

Thus, we can say that Java does division according to the operand types. If both the operands of an operator are integers, then the result will be integer. To get decimal results, at least one of the operand has to be either double or float].

Q.4. Is &&= a valid operator?

[Hint: No].

Q.5. What will be the values of x and y:

(a) x = 5; y = ++x;

(b) x=5; z=x++;

[Hint: (a) x =6; y =6

(b) x=6; z=5**].**

Q.6. Right shifting shifts bits right and that the bits shifted off the right end are lost. In which case the MSBs become LSBs and the bits are not lost?

[Hint: In rotations of bits, bits are not lost**].**

Q.7. Is minus sign a unary or a binary operator or both? Explain.

[Hint: both. As a unary operator, the minus sign causes the algebraic sign of the right operand to be changed. As a binary operator, the minus sign causes its right operand to be subtracted from its left operand**].**

Q.8. Operator & has the same effect as the operator &&. Why or why not?

[GGSIPU, B. Tech (CSE/IT)- 5th sem., Aug. 2009]

[Hint: No, as the operator & works on bits whereas && works on Boolean values—true or false].

Q.9. Find the error (s) if any in the following code. Also correct the errors and give the output:

(a)
```
class Scope
{
    {
        int x = 10;
        int y =20;
        System.out.println("x="+x);
        System.out.println("y="+y);
    }
        int x = 20;
      System.out.println("x="+x);
      System.out.println("y="+y);
}
```

(b)
```
int i=40;
char c1 = i, c2 = 40;
System.out.println("c1i="+c1i);
System.out.println("c2j="+c2j);
```

(c) short s = 100;

```
s = s * 2;
System.out.println("s="+s);
```

(d) boolean b;

```
int i =0;
b = i;
System.out.println("b="+b);
```

(e) double d =23.34; int i=30;

```
short s = 45;
char c = 70;
int sum = d + I + s + c;
System.out.println("sum="+sum);
```

[*DU, MCA 1st Sem., 2009-10*]

[Hint: (a) 10

20

20

20

This is so because first x and y variables are local to that block within braces. Similarly, 2nd x is local to that block. Once the scope of one local block finishes, then only the control comes to the next block.

(b) Error; as c1i and c2j are not defined.

(c) 200.

(d) b=0

(e) 168].

Q.10. Write the output of the following code segments:

(a) int a=9, b=1;

a >> b+2;

(b) int a=7, b=5, c=7;

a | 4+ c>>b&7.

(c) int a=10, b=5;

if (a! =10 & b++ <10)

a = b;

System.out.println("a="+a);

System.out.println("b="+b);

[*DU, MCA 1st Sem., 2009-10*].

Q.11. Explain right and left shift operators with examples.

[*GGSIPU, B. Tech (CSE/IT)- 5th sem., Dec. 2013*].

Q.12. What can go wrong if you replace && with & in the following code:

String a = null;

if (a!=null && a.length ( ) > 10)

}}

[GGSIPU, B. Tech (CSE/IT)- 5th sem., Aug. 2009].

[Hint: A single ampersand here would lead to NullPointerException].

Q.13. Write your comments for the below code:

```
Class Temp{
    public static void main(String s[ ]) {
      byte b =10;
      byte a = 20;
      byte c = a + b;
      System.out.println("C=" +c);
  } }
```

[GGSIPU, B. Tech (CSE/IT)- 5th sem., Oct. 2010]

[Hint: The above expression prints the value of c].

2.8 STRING CONCATENATION

Another interesting and important concept in Java is here. Java strings are sequences of Unicode characters. There is a pre-defined class called as String in Java library. In an expression, if one operand is of type String, the string conversion takes place on the other operand to produce a string at execution. The result is a reference to string object of the concatenated string. That is,

String3 = String1 + String2;

When the + operator is used with strings, it is known as the *string concatenation operator. Please understand that to concatenate means to append and thus the string concatenation operator appends one string to another.* For example,

System.out.println("This is a " + "Java book.");

This statement will display:

This is a Java book.

So, the + operator produces a string that is the combination of two strings used as its operands. We can also use this + operator to concatenate the contents of a variable to a string. **For example,**

numb= 100;

System.out.println("The value of numb is: " + numb);

This statement will display:

The value of numb is 100;

The second line here uses the + operator to concatenate the contents of the numb variable with the string "The value of numb is:" Also understand here that although numb is not a string, the +

operator converts its value to a string and then concatenates that value with the first string. Thus, the above output is seen.

There are other situations also where this + operator is useful like, in the following statement there is an error:

System.out.println("Enter a value that is less than 10000 and more than the salary of each employee.");

The error is because you have continued your message string on the next line. To remove this error, concatenation operator (+) is used as follows:

System.out.println("Enter a value that is less than 100000"

+ "and more than the salary"

+ "of each employee");

Please note here that we have broken up the argument into smaller string literals and then used the string concatenation operator to spread them out over more than one line.

Another situation occurs, when the contents of a variable are part of the concatenation:

sum = 1024;

System.out.println("Total sum is=" + sum);

Thus, 1024 will be printed as output along with the string (enclosed in the double codes). **Also note here that placing a quotation mark (s) around a variable name changes the program's result.** Say,

int numb;

numb = "10";

This will result in an error as we have declared numb as integer type but we are assigning a string constant to it. So, only integers can be stored in the variable numb. Just remember the following points here:

1. 10 and "10" are not the same.
2. Strings are intended for humans to read and numbers are used for computation purpose.
3. You cannot perform math on strings. Before numbers can be displayed on to the screen, they must first be converted to strings.
4. Both print and println handle this conversion automatically when you send numbers to them. (We will discuss this a bit later).

2.9 OPERATOR PRECEDENCE AND ASSOCIATIVITY

We can build mathematical expressions with several operators. Now, if the statement is as follows:

Sum = 80 + u + v + 100;

Then the value of sum can be printed without any problem, provided some values to u and v. But if the expression is as follows:

Average = 10 + 5 / 2;

What will be the final value in variable average? Here, the result could be 7 or 12 depending upon when division takes place. So, there must be some rule or priority or precedence to these operators. And certainly the need for operator precedence arises. The answer is 12 *because division operator has a higher precedence than addition operator*. Mathematical expressions are evaluated from left to right. *When two operators share an operand, then the operator with the highest precedence works first.* Multiplication and division have higher precedence than addition and subtraction. That is,

– (unary negation) (highest precedence)

* / % ↓

+ = (lowest precedence)

Please note here that the multiplication, division and modulus operators have the same precedence. Also note that if two operators sharing an operand have the same precedence, they work according to their associativity. Associativity is either left to right or right to left. That is,

– (unary negation) has right to left associativity.

* / % have left to right associativity.

+ – have left to right associativity.

Special Notes:

1. Parts of mathematical expression may be grouped with parentheses to force some operations to be performed before others. For instance,

   salary = (u+v+w) / 3.0;

   Here, (u +v + w) will be performed first as they are enclosed in parentheses and then the result is divided by 3.0. Otherwise, if you will not put braces then you will get a wrong result i.e. w would be divided by 3 first and then the result will be added to v and u and then assigned to the variable salary. This is incorrect. In nutshell, we can say that parentheses can be used to override/overcome some of the operators also that are on higher priority or we can say that have a higher precedence.

2. In Java, raising a number to a power requires the Math.pow method. This is a very useful method because (unlike other programming languages), Java does not have an exponent operator. For example,

   power_of_x_to_y = Math.pow (3.0, 2.0);

   Note that the method takes two double arguments. It raises the first argument to the power of the second argument and returns the result as a double. To display/ print this result also we can write like this:

   System.out.println(Math.pow(3.0, 2.0));

The following Table 2.14 lists the operators according to their precedence order:

Table 2.14: Showing Operator Precedence and Hierarchy

<table>
<tr><th>Precedence level</th><th>Operator</th><th>Operation</th><th>Associativity</th><th>Comments(if any)</th></tr>
<tr><td>1. Primary Expressions</td><td>f(parameter list)</td><td>Function call</td><td>left to right</td><td></td></tr>
<tr><td>2. Unary expressions</td><td>(exp)
a[exp]
p.q
!
~
+
–
x++ or ++x
y—or —y
new
(data type)</td><td>Parenthesized expression.
Array element access
Member access
Logical NOT
1s complement
Unary plus
Unary minus
Autoincrement
Autodecrement
Object creation
Cast operator</td><td>left to right
left to right
left to right
right to left
right to left
right to left
right to left
right to left
right to left
right to left
right to left</td><td></td></tr>
<tr><td>3</td><td>*
/
%</td><td>Multiplication
Modulus
Division</td><td>left to right
left to right
left to right</td><td></td></tr>
<tr><td>4</td><td>+
–</td><td>Addition
Subtraction</td><td>left to right
left to right</td><td></td></tr>
<tr><td>5</td><td><<
>>
>>></td><td>Left shift.
Signed right shift.
Unsigned right shift.</td><td>left to right
left to right
left to right</td><td></td></tr>
<tr><td>6</td><td><
<=
>
>=
Instanceof</td><td>Less than
Less than or equal to
Greater than
Greater than or equal to
Instance of a class</td><td>left to right
left to right
left to right
left to right
left to right</td><td></td></tr>
<tr><td>7</td><td>==
!=</td><td>Equal to
Not equal to</td><td>left to right
left to right</td><td></td></tr>
<tr><td>8</td><td>&</td><td>Bitwise AND</td><td>left to right</td><td></td></tr>
<tr><td>9</td><td>^</td><td>Bitwise XOR</td><td>left to right</td><td></td></tr>
<tr><td>10</td><td>|</td><td>Bitwise OR</td><td>left to right</td><td></td></tr>
<tr><td>11</td><td>&&</td><td>Logical AND</td><td>left to right</td><td></td></tr>
<tr><td>12</td><td>||</td><td>Logical OR</td><td>left to right</td><td></td></tr>
<tr><td>13</td><td>? :</td><td>Conditional/ternary</td><td>right to left</td><td></td></tr>
<tr><td>14</td><td>= += –= *=
/= %= >>=
>>>= <<=
&= ^= |=</td><td>Simple and compound assignment</td><td>right to left</td><td></td></tr>
</table>

Thus, when several operators appear in one expression, the evaluation takes place according to certain predefined rules called as **hierarchy rules**. These rules specify the order of evaluation called as **precedence level or priority of operators or hierarchy of operators**. The highest precedence level is 1 and the lowest level is 14. Operators shown on the same level have equal precedence. Associativity or grouping refers to the order in which Java evaluates the operations having the same precedence level. *Please note that such operations are evaluated either from right to left or from left to right according to the specific types of operator used. Also note that parentheses may be included in an expression to change the order of evaluation.* They force the enclosed operations to be performed first because parentheses have higher precedence. But if the parentheses are nested then the innermost parentheses are evaluated first and then the next innermost parentheses and so on. In nutshell, Java is rich in operators having different precedence levels, thus the programmers can make use of parentheses to ensure that an expression is evaluated as intended.

2.10 TYPE CASTING (OR COERCION) IN JAVA

Scalar data types can be explicitly converted into the desired data types. In certain programs, there may be many situations in which one data type may need to be converted to another data type. This is achieved by means of the process of **type conversions or coercion in Java.** This is accomplished by using a **cast operator.**

Syntax is:

(dataType) expression

where expression is converted to the target dataType that is enclosed within the parentheses. The expression may be a constant or a variable. **Please note that the data type must be any scalar type or void. If it is void, the operand must be other than the void type expression.** The name of the data type to which the conversion is to be made is enclosed in parentheses and placed directly to the left of the expression.

For Example 1, (float) 5 converts the integer constant 5 to the float value 5.0. so, (float) 1/5 will be evaluated as 1.0/5.0 yielding 0.22 whereas 1/5 yields 0. *Please note here that (float) is the cast operator.*

Example 2, (double) (1+2) converts the integer constant 3 to double. Here also the type within the parentheses is called as the **cast operator**.

Types of Coercion

There are basically two types of coercions or type castings in Java:

(a) Implicit Casting/ Implicit Coercion.

(b) Explicit Casting/ Explicit Coercion.

Let us discuss these one by one now.

I Implicit Casting/ Implicit Coercion

It means simply assigning one entity to another without any transformation guidance to the compiler. This type of casting is not permitted in all kinds of transformations and it may not work for all application scenarios.

For example,

```
int u = 800;
long v = u;   // Implicit casting
```

II Explicit Casting/ Explicit Coercion

It means very specifically informing the compiler about the transformation that is expected.

For example,

```
long u = 800.00;
v = (int) u;   //Explicit casting
```

Note: If you will do implicit casting for the cases where explicit casting is desired then the compiler will report an error by throwing an exception— *"Incompatible type for =. Explicit cast needed to convert long to int"*.

But sometimes it may be desired to cast across different parameter types like from int to long, long to int etc. Otherwise an error may be reported. The following example illustrates this.

In the following code, an error is reported:

```
1 int t =550;
2 long h =t;        //Implicit casting
3 int t = 250;
4 long h = t;       //Implicit casting
5 t = h;
```

Let us see why?

In statement no. 4, h gets 550.00. But in statement no. 5, we are assigning this value of h to the variable t and t happens to be of integer type. **Please remember that the rule is that you cannot put long to int because here in this example, size of t is less than the size of h.** This has naturally to do something with the storage space allocated for each of the fundamental data types in Java. For example, variables declared int are allocated 32 bits of memory whereas long is allocated 64 bits. Thus, while it is easy to allocate an int into a long (32 into 64)—without loss of data, the compiler finds it difficult to put a long into int (64 into 32). Thus, it forces the programmer to do an explicit casting as follows:

```
1. int t =550;
2. long h =t;        // Implicit casting
3. t = (int) h;      // Explicit casting
```

Please understand that here an explicit conversion allows us to overcome the above error. Also understand that the numeric data types that can be implicitly cast are as follows:

+byte (8 bits) to short, int, long, float, double

short (16 bits) to int, long, float, double

int (32 bits) to long, float, double

long (64 bits) to float, double

that is,

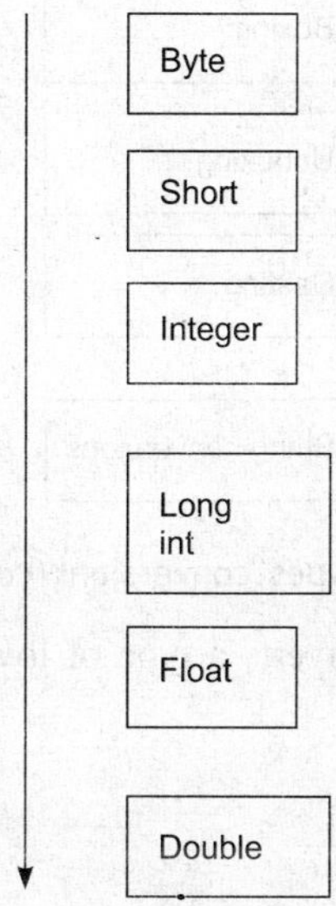

Advantages of coercion/ type casting:

1. It helps to avoid truncation in a division like ½.
2. It treats a data type as other data type when the cast operator is applied.

But the following conversions are **not** allowed:

1. any primitive type to any reference type.
2. the null value to any primitive type.
3. any primitive to Boolean.
4. a Boolean to any primitive.

The evaluation of expressions involves type conversions whenever the operands are not compatible. *It is this process of conversion of one data type into another data type within an expression that is called as type conversion.* Type conversions in Java are of different types as shown in Fig. 2.6.

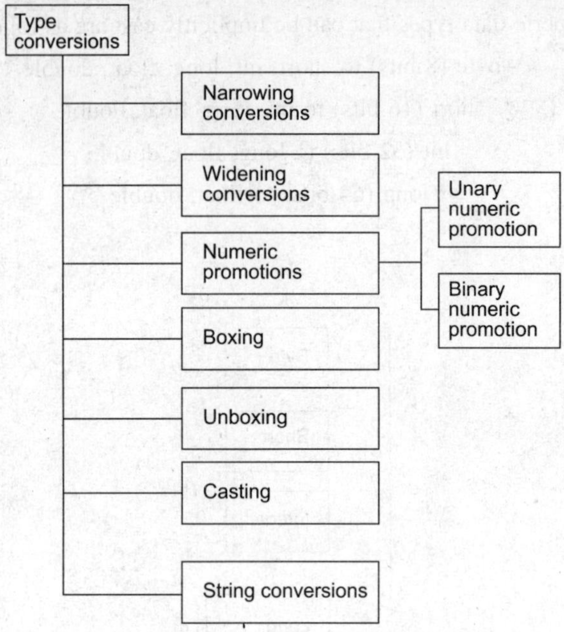

Fig. 2.6: Types conversions/coercion

The widening primitive conversion converts a type of lower rank to a type of higher rank. The ranking order (crescent) is given below:

1. byte
2. short, char
3. int
4. long
5. float
6. double.

The narrowing conversion converts a type of higher rank to a type of lower rank. Both of these operations are shown in table below:

WIDENING PRIMITIVE CONVERSION

Type from	Converted to
Byte	short, int, long, float or double
Short	int, long, float or double
Char	int, long, float or double
Int	long, float or double
Long	float or double
Float	Double

Similarly, the narrowing primitive conversion table is as follows:

NARROWING PRIMITIVE CONVERSION

Type from	Converted to
Short	byte or char
Char	byte or short
Int	byte, short or char
Long	byte, short, char or int
Float	byte, short, char, int or long
Double	byte, short, char, int, long or float

Please note that the conversion of byte to char combines both widening and narrowing conversion. Also note that the byte is converted to an int using widening conversion and then the resulting int is converted to a char by narrowing conversion.

Boxing conversions converts values of primitive type to corresponding values of reference type. **Unboxing conversions** convert values of reference type to corresponding values of primitive type. Both boxing and unboxing conversions are shown in Table 2.15 below:

Table 2.15: Boxing Conversion

Type from	Boxed to
Boolean	Boolean
Byte	Byte
Char	Character
Short	Short
Int	Integer
Long	Long
Float	Float
Double	Double

Similarly, unboxing conversions are as follows:

Type from	Unboxed to
Boolean	boolean
Byte	byte
Character	character
Short	short
Integer	integer
Long	long
Float	float
Double	double

This casting conversion is applied to the operand of a cast operator. The type of the operand expression must be converted to the type explicitly named by the cast operator. There is a String conversion to type String from every other type including null type when binary + operator is used. When one argument is String, the other one is converted to String.

Numeric promotion is applied to the operands of an arithmetic operator. It is used to convert the operands of a numeric operator to a common type so that an operation can be performed. There are two types of numeric promotion—

(a) Unary numeric promotion and

(b) Binary numeric promotion.

Unary numeric promotion is applied on operands of expressions using operators like unary plus, unary minus, bitwise complement and bitwise shift operators. It is also applied on index expression and dimension expression in arrays. The **rules** followed here are as follows:

1. If the operand is of compile-time type Byte, Short, Character or Integer, it is subjected to unboxing. The result is then promoted to a value of type int.
2. Otherwise, if the operand is of compile-time type Long, Float or Double, it is subjected to unboxing.
3. Otherwise, if the operand is of compile-time type byte, short or char, unary numeric promotion promotes it to a value of type int.
4. Otherwise, a unary numeric operand remains as is and is not converted.

On the other hand, binary numeric promotion is performed on the operands of arithmetic operators *, /, +,– ,numerical relational operators <, <=, >, >=, = = ,!=, integer bitwise operators &, ^, || and some cases of conditional operator. *Please understand that a data type is automatically converted into another type by the compiler by means of the rules described in Java.*

The following **rules** are applied when an operator applies binary numeric promotion to a pair of operands, each of which must denote a value that is convertible to a numeric type:

1. If one of the operands is a reference, unboxing conversion takes place.
2. If one of the operands is of type double, the other operand is converted to type double.
3. Else, if one of the operands is of type float, the other operand is converted to type float.
4. Else, if one of the operands is of type long, the other operand is converted to type long.
5. Else, both the operands are converted to type int.

In assignment statements, where values of lower-ranked data types are stored in variables of higher-ranked data types, Java automatically converts the lower- ranked value to the higher ranked type. **This process of automatic conversion of lower ranked value to the higher type is called as widening conversion.** For example,

```
double u;
int v =20;
u=v;   // performs a widening conversion
```

Please note that the widening conversions also take place automatically when an argument is passed to a method. If the argument's data type is ranked lower than the parameter variable's data type, the argument's value will be converted to match that of the parameter variable. On the other hand, *the process of conversion of a value to a lower-ranked type is called as a narrowing conversion. For example, converting a double to an int. Also note that because narrowing conversions can potentially cause loss of data, so Java does not automatically perform them.*

Please remember the following points regarding these conversions:

1. When a cast operator (unary) is applied to a variable, it does not change the contents of the variable. It only returns the value stored in the variable, converted to the specified data type.
2. If one of the operator's operand is a **double**, the value of the other operand will be converted to a double. The result of the expression will be a **double**. For example,

   temp = u + v;

   Assume u is double and v is an int. The value in v will be converted to a **double** prior to the addition. The result of the addition will be a double, so the variable *temp* must also be a **double.**
3. If one of the operator's operand is a **float**, the value of the other operand will be converted to a **float.** The result of the expression will be a **float**. For example,

   z = x * y;

   Assume that x is a **short** and y is a **float**. The value in x will be converted to a **float** prior to the multiplication. The result of the multiplication will be a **float**, so the variable z must also be either a double or a **float**.
4. If one of the operator's operand is a **long**, the value of the other operand will be converted to a **long**. The result of the expression will be a **long**. For example,

   d = a – b;

   Assume that the variable a is a **long** and b is **short.** The variable b will be converted to a **long** prior to the subtraction. The result of the subtraction will be a **long,** so the variable c must also be a **long, float or double.**
5. It is always safe to convert from a variable type that can hold less information to a type that can hold more information. So, the following conversions are safe to perform:-

   byte-> short -> int -> long -> float ->double
6. A conversion of a **byte to a char** loses information despite the fact that a **char** uses 16-bits (whereas a byte uses 8) because **char** is unsigned and does not allow negative values. Therefore, the compiler requires a specific cast to convert **byte to char.**
7. The first step in converting a float or double to an integer type is conversion to either a long, if the destination is long or int for all other integer type. The final step is dropping any excess bits. *Please note that you may get some surprising results here because all special floating-point values like NaN and POSITIVE_INFINITY, turn into integer values without any complaint from the compiler or an exception.*
8. The compiler is intelligent enough to realize that the values can be cast to byte without loss of information.

9. Java permits a short to be stored in an int but does not permit a double to be stored in an int. It is due to the reason that a double can store fractional numbers and can hold values much larger than an int can hold. If Java were to permit a double to be assigned to an int, a loss of data would be likely.

10. The primitive data types are ranked. One data type outranks another if it can hold a larger number. This is analogous to the ranking of officers in the military. For example, a float outranks an int and an int outranks a short. The following are the numeric data types in order of their rank:

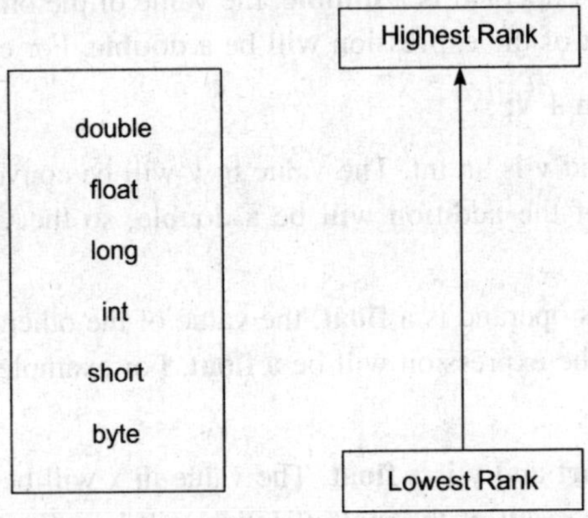

Please note that the higher a data type appears in the list, the higher is its rank.

11. If the evaluation of an expression yields a different value during the evaluation of the same expression again, such a state is known as **side effect**. The side effect makes changes in the state of the execution of the environment. For example,

    Assume an initial value of 10 to a variable x. Then the expression—

    a= x*5 + 10 always yields 60 for x=10. Even if it is evaluated again and again, the value of a will be 60 only, with x=10. Thus, this expression does not have any side effect. But if the expression is modified as follows:-

    x= ++x *5+10, it results in side effect. **In nutshell, we can say that some expressions may have side effects and some may not.** The expression ++x yields a value of 11 after evaluation. This is so because it is equivalent to x = x +1. The value of x is incremented by 1 and assigned to x. It increments the variable x and returns a newly incremented value. If the same expression is executed again, the value will be different. **Hence, the operator ++ has a side effect after evaluation.**

Before we discuss further, let us solve some questions now.

Q.1. Give the final results/outputs of the following statements in Java:

(a) u = (long) 5.8;

(b) int numb = (int) 15.555;

(c) val = (float)u;

(d) temp = (byte)number;

[Hint:

(a) The cast operator is applied to the expression 5.8. The operator returns the value of 5, which is assigned to the variable u.

(b) The cast operator is applied to the expression 15.555. The operator returns 15, which is then assigned to the variable numb.

(c) The cast operator returns the value in u, converted to a float. The converted value is assigned to the variable value.

(d) The cast operator returns the value in number, converted to a byte. The converted value is assigned to the variable temp].

Q.2. Define what is side effect?

Q.3. (a) Define and WAP on the concept of Autoboxing and Unboxing principle?

(b) Explain the effect of comparison operator "==" on the string with a short program.

[GGSIPU, B. Tech.(CSE/IT)-5th sem., Sept. 2010]

Q.4. (a) What is the difference between narrowing and widening conversion. Give an example of both type.

(b) What will be the result if you add a float, int and byte?

[GGSIPU, B. Tech.(CSE/IT)-5th sem., Dec. 2011]

Q.5. (a) Casting does not affect the original object or value. True or false.

(b) It is said that java is purely O. O. language, however, it has primitive data types such as int, char, short, long, byte, double, float, Boolean. What is the solution provided by Java for using primitive types as objects?

[DU, MCA 1st sem., 2001 Onwards]

Q.6. What will happen if you attempt to compile and run the following code? Explain your answer.

```
integer ten = new Integer (10);
long nine = new Long (9);
System.out.println (ten + nine);
int i =1;
System.out.println (i + ten);
```

(a) 19 followed by 20.

(b) 19 followed by 11.

(c) 10 fol' owed by 1.

(d) Error: cannot convert java lang Integer. *[DU, MCA 1st sem., 2001 Onwards]*

2.11 CONTROL FLOW STATEMENTS

Normally the program execution flows in a sequential manner. But it is not mandatory for all situations. To change the flow of execution in a program from one point to another, Java provides following types of control statements (see Fig. 2.7). Every programming language defines its own syntax for statements. A sentence is terminated by a period and a statement is terminated by a semicolon in a program. *For example*, by placing a semicolon at the end of an assignment expression, an assignment statement is obtained. *Please understand that an operation is represented by an expression and it becomes an instruction by a statement.* Hence, a program requires operations represented by statements. A set of statements may be represented as a group in a program. As we know that a program contains a sequence of declarations and action statements. Each statement is executed only once in the order it appears and then the execution flow is said to be from top to bottom. Practically speaking, it may be needed to modify the execution path and transfer the control from one part of the program to another. And this can be achieved with the help of control flow statements (or control structures or control constructs). Also understand that a block encloses a sequence of statements between braces. The opening brace specifies the beginning of a block and the closing brace marks the end of a block. Blocks define the scope of the variables that have been declared. They support nesting too. **Such set of statements that are enclosed within a block are called as embedded statements.**

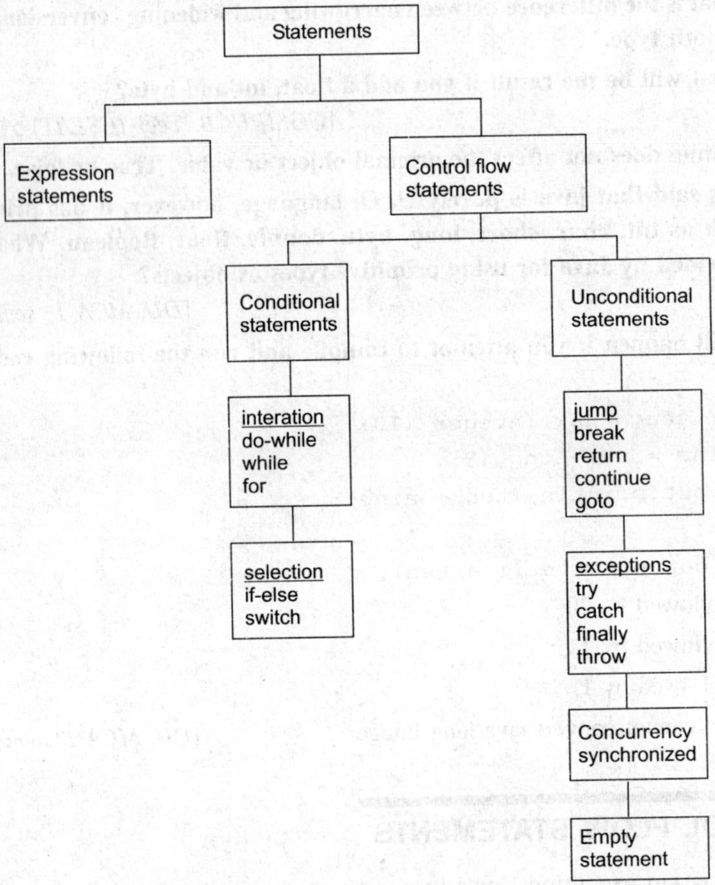

Fig. 2.7: Types of control flow statements

From Fig. 2.7, it is crystal clear that the statements are put under two categories basically:

(a) Expression statements.

(b) Control flow statements.

Please note that an empty statement has no action to be performed. It is simply represented by a semicolon. When an expression is terminated by a semicolon it is known as an **expression statement or a simple statement**. For example, u-v+w and count==0 when ending with semicolons result in mere evaluation of a value and there is no side effect. Hence, they are not allowed as statements in Java. **Also note that all expressions are not allowed as valid statements.** A valid expression statement is formed from the following expressions ending with a semicolon—assignment, increment/decrement expression, method invocation, object creation. An assignment statement is an assignment expression ending with a semicolon. A post increment or post decrement or pre increment or pre decrement expression ending with a semicolon is known as **increment/decrement statement.** A method (may be user-defined or predefined in inbuilt library) invocation ending with a semicolon is known as **invocation statement**. An object creation statement makes use of new operator in its statement. And an expression that has an emerging side effect after its evaluation is a valid expression statement.

Control flow statements actually modify the sequential execution path of a program. This execution flow can be altered by basing on a condition evaluated at runtime or directly. As shown in Fig. 2.7, they are also of two types namely:

(a) Conditional execution.

(b) Unconditional execution.

Let us discuss these one by one now.

I Conditional Execution

The flow of execution may be transferred from one part of a program to another based on the result of the conditional test carried out. This is known as a *conditional execution.* Conditional control flow statements make use of Boolean expressions for conditional tests and embedded statements as part of them. It is important to note that if there is a single statement in a conditional control flow statement, braces are optional but for multiple statements, braces are required; else you may get an error.

Let us discuss their types one by one now.

(i) Selection statements: In selective control constructs, the statement part is selected for execution based on result of the conditional test represented by a Boolean expression. Java supports the following types of selection statements:-

(a) if

(b) if-else

(c) if-else-if

(d) switch-case

We will be studying these in detail in next sub-sections.

(ii) Iteration statements: Sometimes the execution of certain statements needs to be repeated until a given condition is satisfied or it may have to be repeated for a known number of times. Such repetitions are carried out by using iterative control constructs or repetitive control constructs or loop constructs. Java supports the following types of loop constructs:

(a) while

(b) do-while

(c) for

(d) enhanced for

We will be studying these in detail in next sub-sections.

II Unconditional Execution

If the flow of execution is transferred from one part of a program to another part without carrying out any conditional test then it is known as an *unconditional execution*. Unconditional execution is achieved by means of *jump statements*. A jump statement transfers control to a target location. Such location may be in the same block or outside the block. This may result in complex execution paths also. Java supports the following types of unconditional control constructs:

(i) Jump statements like break statement, continue statement and return statement.

(ii) Exception and Error statement- Exceptions are defined as the errors that arose from unexpected conditions that make it impossible to continue the execution of an application without a specific handling. Whereas, errors are of more general category consisting of bugs, exceptions or general program errors. They include:

(a) throw statement.

(b) try-catch-finally statements.

(c) assert statement.

We will be studying these in detail in next sub-sections.

(iii) Concurrency/Synchronization statements: Synchronization statements help programmers in correctly designing multi-threaded and concurrent applications. They comprise of only one statement which provides the most low-level structure for synchronizing block of statements. They include:

(a) synchronized statement

We will be studying these in detail in next sub-sections.

2.11.1 Decision Making Statements

Let us study if-else control construct.

The if..else statement

The if statement is followed by a logical expression in which data is compared and a decision is made based on the result of comparison. Its syntax is:

Syntax:

```
if (testcondition)
    {
      Statement (s);
    }
else
    {
      Statement (s);
    }
```

Here, when the ***testcondition*** is true then the statements enclosed in the **if clause** is executed; otherwise statements enclosed in the **else clause** is executed.

The **if statement** is used to create a decision structure which allows a program to have more than one path of execution. It can be represented by a flowchart also:

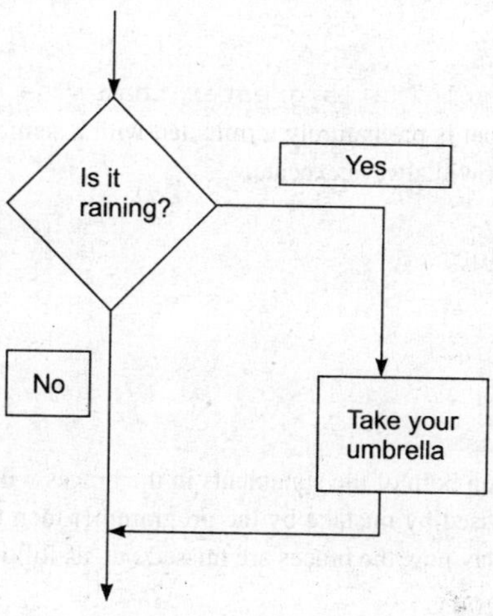

Fig. 2.8: if-else decision structure logic flowchart

Relational operators like >, <, >=, <=, = =, != may be used. **But please remember that when you use <= or >= operator then there is no space between them.**

Even though an **if statement** usually spans more than one line, it is really one long statement. **For example,** the following if statements are identical except for the style in which they are written:

```
if (salary > 100000)
        System.out.println("It is a good salary");

if (salary > 1000000) system.out.println("It is a good salary");
```

Also note that in both of these examples, the compiler considers the if statement and the conditionally executed statement as one unit, with a semicolon properly placed at the end. Indentions and spacing are for human readers of a program, not the compiler.

Rules for using if statements:

Rule 1: The conditionally executed statement should appear on the line after the *if statement.*

Rule 2: The conditionally executed statement should be indented one level from the *if statement.*

Recall that in most of the editors, when you press the tab key, you are indenting by one level. By indenting the conditionally executed statement, you are causing it to stand out visually. This is so you can tell at a glance what part of the program the *if statement* executes. This is the standard way of writing if statements.

NOTE:

1. Don't put semicolons after the if(testcondition) portion because the if statement is incomplete without its conditional part. But if you place a semicolon here, then the compiler assumes that you have terminated. No error will be displayed but the compiler will assume that you are placing a null statement there. Also note here that the null statement (that is an empty statement that does nothing), will become the conditionally executed statement. The statement that you intended to be conditionally executed will be disconnected from the if statement and will always execute. For example,

```
int u=5, v=10;
 if ( u>v);
   System.out.println("u is greater than v" + u);
```

   The if statement in this code snippet is prematurely terminated with a semicolon. Because the println statement is not connected to the if statement, it will always execute.

2. Now consider another example,

```
if( salary > 200000)
    {
    tax = .30 * basic;
    bonus = 800;
      }
```

   Herein, if the condition is true, then both of the statements in the braces will be executed in the order they appear. But if say the braces were left/missed by mistake by the programmer then the if statement conditionally executes only the very next statement i.e. say now the braces are missed out, as follows:

```
if( salary > 200000)
    tax = .30 * basic;
    bonus = 800;
```

   In this case, only the statement tax = .30 * basic will be executed conditionally and the other one (bonus=800;) will always be executed.

We are in a position to write a simple program now.

Program-1: To find the greater of two numbers that are read from the keyboard and then displaying the greater number.

Solution-1:

```
    // use of if-else
import java.io.*;
class large
```

```
{
    public static void main(String args[ ])
    {
      try
        {
     DataInputStream din = new DataInputStream(System.in);
     int u, v;
     System.out.println("Enter first number:");
     u = Integer.parseInt(din.readLine( ));
     System.out.println("Enter second number:");
     v = Integer.parseInt(din.readLine( ));
     if (u > v)
         System.out.printn("First number is greater than second
 number");
        else
         System.out.printn("Second number is greater than first
 number");
       }
     Catch(Exception e)
       {

        }
     }
}
```

OUTPUT (after running):

Enter first number: 800

Enter second number: 100

First number is greater than second number

Please note here that the reading of values from the keyboard is not as simple as you have seen in other higher programming languages like C/C++. Also note that since Java is a strongly typed language, therefore it first checks whether you have read the correct data value or not and then it stores that value in appropriate variable. We shall be studying about this in detail later.

Next let us see the working and the syntax of nested if-else.

When an if-else control appears as a statement in another if-else, it is known as a **nested if-else construct**. For example,

```
if (boolExpr1)
    if  (boolExpr2)
    if (boolExpr3)       {
        stml1;
```

```
        }
        else  {
              Stml2;
        }
       else  {
          Stml3;
    }
```

This code is very confusing!!! **Please note here that there is no else part for the first if construct.** The compiler associates the else part with the closest inner if construct which does not have an else part. Thus, each else part is associated with the respective if. To avoid this confusion, it is better to use braces appropriately for the association of **else** part with its **if.** By using the braces, any **else** part may be associated with a particular **if** construct. **Also note that since Java is a free-format language, the Stmt part following if (boolExpr) or else may be written on the same line for clarity.**

Let us now see the if-else-if control construct.

The else-if control construct follows the if control construct to have multiple decision making.

Syntax:

```
    if   (boolExpr1)
     {
         Stml1;
     }
     else
         if  (boolExpr2)
         {
             Stml2;
         }
         else
            if  (boolExpr3)
            {
             Stml3;
            }
             ..........
             else if (boolExprN-1)
             {
                 StmlN-1;
             }
             else  {
                 StmlN;
             }
```

Herein, if any **boolExpr** returns true value, the **Stmt** associated with that **if** is executed and then the next statement to the whole **else if** construct is executed. If no expression returns true value then the last **else** part is executed. If there is no instruction needed for the last **else** part, then it can be omitted or it can be used for displaying the error messages due to invalid conditions. **We are in a position to write a simple program now.**

Program-2: Write a Java program to check whether the given year is a leap year or not. A leap year is a year which is divisible by 4 and not divisible by 100 or divisible by 400.

Solution:

```
        //leap year program

    import java.util.Scanner;
    class LeapYear {
        public static void main (String [] args)  {
            Scanner sc = new Scanner(System.in);
            int y;
            System.out.printf("Enter the year in four digits: ");
            y = sc.nextInt ( );
            if (( y % 4 ==0 && y%100 != 0) || (y %400==0 ))
                System.out.printf ("%d is a leap year", y);
            else
                System.out.printf("%d is not a leap year", y);
                }
            }
```

OUTPUT:

Enter the year in four digits: 2000

2000 is a leap year

Explanation:

For making use of the methods to read data from the keyboard, the following statement must be written to create the necessary object for reading purpose. The keyboard is represented by the standard input stream System.in. The keyboard is linked with the scanner for user's ease. An object of type **Scanner** needs to be created to make use of methods in it for reading various types of keyboard inputs. Once a **Scanner** object is created, the same can be used for reading other inputs with the scope of the code. Thus, the first import statement is must.

The standard output stream System.out represents the selected output peripheral for the program. It is normally mapped to the screen of the computer. The method println ( ) of this standard output stream is used to display the output on the screen.

Before we discuss further, please answer the following questions:

Q.1. Write a Java code that reads a character from the keyboard and then uses the = = operator to compare it with the character 'A'.

[Hint:

```
char input;
System.out.print ("Enter a character: ");
input = Keyboard.readChar ();
if (input == 'A')
```

```
System.out.println("You entered the letter A."); ]
```

Q.2. Write an if statement that multiplies salary by 0.50 if designation is senior.

Q.3. Write an if-else statement that assigns 0 to the variable b and assigns 1 to the variable c if the variable a is less than 10. Otherwise, it should assign -99 to the variable b and assign 0 to the variable c.

Let us now discuss a cleaner way of programming using switch statement.

Switch statement

Java provides an extremely handy **switch-case construct** to facilitate selecting between multiple alternatives. Within the block of code controlled by a **switch statement,** the programmer can place **case statements** and (optionally) a **default statement. For example,**

```
switch (x) {
    case 0 : str = "none"; break;
    case 1 :
        str = "single" ; break;
    case 2 :
        str = "pair" ;
        break;
    default : str = "many" ;
}
```

Each case keyword is followed by an integer constant, followed by a colon. **Please note that the code block belonging to each *case* can immediately follow the colon on the same line or on separate lines.** If the value of x is not one of the values provided for in case statements, the **default statement** code is executed. **Also note that if there is no default statement and no exact match, execution resumes after the *switch* block of code.**

In the program example above, break statements are used that terminate the code for each *case* and cause execution to continue after the **switch code block. Please understand that if a break does not appear, execution falls-through to execute code in subsequent *cases*. For example,**

```
Switch(x)   {
    Case 0 : System.out.print("A,   ");
    Case 1: System.out.print("B, "); break;
    default: System.out.println("Java?");
}
```

Herein, a value of 0 for x would cause output of "A, B,".

Also understand that most of the errors that occur when we work with switch structures seem to be related to forgetting about fall-through. Therefore, we must always carefully check for the *break statements* whenever we write a program using *switch statement.* The block of code associated with *each case* can be as simple as a single statement or it can be hundreds of LOC. Also, this code block can have another switch statement. But for better readability for our ease we should convert any complex code into a separate method and simply call that method from the case statement.

The following points may be remembered regarding this switch statement:

1. The expression in a **switch statement** must evaluate to one of the 32-bit or smaller integer types: **byte, char, short or int.** The compiler checks that the legal range of the integer type covers all of the constants used in **case statements** in the **switch code block.**
2. The compiler throws an error if the legal range of the integer type in the switch statement does not cover all of the constants used in **case statements.**
3. Each **case statement** must have a literal constant or a value the compiler can evaluate as a constant of a 32-bit or smaller integer type.
4. It cannot have a **float constant, a long constant, a variable, an expression, a String or any other object.**
5. The compiler checks that the constant is in the range of the integer type in the switch statement.
6. If you are using a byte variable in the switch statement, the compiler objects it, if it finds case statement constants outside the -128 through 127 range that a byte primitive can have.
7. The code block associated with a case must be complete within the case. That is, we can't have an if-else or loop structure that spreads across multiple case statements.
8. Constants in case statements can be integer literals or they can be variables defined as **static and final.**
9. If *continue label* is used instead of break in switch statement then the next statement following it will not be executed rather it will resume the loop with the next value of iterator.
10. The switch statement is an alternative to if-else or if-else-if control construct.
11. The expressions and case labels are restricted to the following types: byte, short, char, int and enum.
12. The expression is evaluated first and its value is then matched against the ***case labels*** that must be constant values. When a match is found, the statement following that case will be executed. If there is no match with any of the case labels, the statement following the default (if present) will be executed.
13. Different case statements in a switch-case statement may be arranged in any order.
14. The *Case Expressions* of each *case* statement must be unique.

Switch versus if-else (a comparison)

The if-else statement can handle ranges for instance as follows:

```
if(marks > 80 && marks <=100)
        //statements
else if(marks > 70 && marks <=90)
        //statements
```

But unfortunately, the switch cannot handle these ranges. Each switch case label must be a single value and that value must be an integer or a character. You cannot even use a floating case label. As far as the ranges or floating point number are countered, you must use if-else construct. On the other hand, if the case labels are integer constants or character constant then the switch statement is more efficient, easier to write and understand.

We are in a position to write some programs using switch statement now.

Example 1: Write a Java program to check whether an alphabet is a vowel or not.

Solution:

```
import java.util.Scanner;
class SwitchSample {
        public static void main(String [ ]  args) {
            int ch;
            Scanner sc = new Scanner (System.in);
            System.out.println("Enter a letter:");
            ch = sc.next( ).charAt(0);
            System.out.printf("Entered char: %c\n", ch);
            Switch (ch)   {
             Case 'a':
             Case 'e':
             Case 'i':
             Case 'o':
             Case 'u':
                System.out.printf("%c is a vowel\n", ch);
                 break;
             default:
                        System.out.printf("%c is not a vowel", ch);
            }
        }
}
```

OUTPUT (after running):

Enter a letter;

u

Enter char: u

u is a vowel

Example 2: Write a Java program to suitable the operation of a numerical calculator with the functions +, –, / and *. *[GGSIPU, B. Tech.(CSE/IT)-5th sem., Dec. 2013]*

Or

Write a Java class Calculator for performing binary operations (only +, -, * and /) on integers. The program will be get input on the command line. *[DU, MCA- 1st sem., 2001 and onwards]*

Solution:

```
import java.io.*;
class Calculator{
```

```
public static void main(String args[ ]) throws IOException {
InputStreamReader is=new InputStreamReader(System.in);
BufferedReader br = new BufferedReader(is);
String s1, s2,s3;
int a,b,n;
int result=0;
System.out.println("Enter the value of a:");
s1= br.readLine( );
a=Integer.parseInt(s1);

System.out.println("Enter the value of b:");
s2= br.readLine( );
b=Integer.parseInt(s2);

System.out.println("\n\n");
System.out.println("1. SUM");
System.out.println("DIFF");
System.out.println("MULTI");
System.out.println("DIV");
System.out.println("Enter your choice");
s3= br.readLine( );
n = Integer.parseInt(s3);
switch(n) {
case 1:
      result = a+b;
      break;
case 2:
      result = a-b;
      break;
case 3:
      result = a/b;
      break;
case 4:
      result = a*b;
      break;
}
System.out.println("Result is" + result);
}
}
```

OUTPUT (after running):

Enter the value of a

10

Enter the value of b

5

1. SUM
2. DIFF
3. MULTI
4. DIV

Enter your choice

4

Result is 2

Before we discuss further, please answer the following questions:

Q.1. Give the output of the following code snippet:

```
char ch='q';
switch(ch)
   {
     default:
    System.out.println("Default Value");
   case 'a':
      System.out.println("character is a.");
      break;
   case 'b':
      System.out.println("character is b.");
      break;
   case 'c':
      System.out.println("character is c.");
      break;
   case 'd':
      System.out.println("character is d.");
   }
```

[*DU, MCA-1st sem., 2001 onwards*]

Q.2. Simulate a calculator using switch statement.

[*GGSIPU, B. Tech.(CSE/IT)-5th sem., Dec. 2009*]

Q.3. Which of the following is an invalid jump statement—return, break, continue or goto.

[**Hint:** goto].

Q.4. Give the output of the following code:

```
public class Main
 {
   public static void main(String [ ] args)
     {
      int i =0;
      while(i <=4 )
        {
           Switch(i)
            {
            Case 1:
               System.out.print(++i +  " ");
            Case 2:
               System.out.print(i + " ");
            Case 3:
               System.out.print(i-- +  " ");
      }
      i+=2;
      }
    }
  }
```

[**Hint:** OUTPUT: 2 2]

Q.5. Give the output of the following code:

```
public class Main
 {
   public static void main(String [ ] args)
    {
      int ch;
      ch = 3.0;
      switch(ch)
       {
        Case 3:
             System.out.print("DR.");
        Case 2:
             System.out.print("RAJIV");
        Case 1:
             System.out.print("CHOPRA");
         }
       }
  }
```

[**Hint**: Error is reported].

Q.6. Write a Java program to print the student's results as per the following scale:

Marks	**Class**
>=60	First class
>=50	Second class
>=35	Third class
<35	Failed

[**Hint:**

```
import java.util.*;
public class result {
   public static void main(String [ ] args) {
     Scanner keyboard=new Scanner(System.in);
     int N;
     System.out.print("enter the student marks:");
     N = keyboard.nextInt( );
     if (N<35)  {
        System.out.println("Failed");
     }
     else {
        switch(N/10)  {
             case 3:
           case 4: System.out.println("Third Class"); break;
           case 4: System.out.println("Second Class"); break;
           default: System.out.println("First Class"); break;
        }
        }
     }
   }
```

Q.7. Write a Java program to create a menu for a typical banking system.

[GGSIPU, B. Tech. (CSE/IT)-5th sem., Dec. 2013]

[**Hint:** Use switch statement]

2.12.2 Looping Statements

A loop is part of a program that repeats. **A loop is a control structure that causes a statement or group of statements to repeat.** Java has three types of looping structures, namely:

(a) while loop.

(b) do-while loop.

(c) for loop.

Let us discuss these one by one now.

While loop:

The while loop construct is used when a single statement or a group of statements is to be executed repeatedly as long as a given condition is satisfied. It consists of a ***Boolean expression (boolExpr)*** for modeling the condition and one or more statements ***(Stmt).*** Firstly, the ***boolExpr*** is evaluated. If it returns true, the ***Stmt*** in the while loop is executed. The loop is terminated when the ***boolExpr*** yields a false value. The ***boolExpr*** is an expression that yields a Boolean literal or simply a Boolean literal. The **syntax and the working of a while loop** is shown in Fig. 2.9.

Syntax:

```
while (boolExpr)
      {
        Stmt;
      }
```

Working:

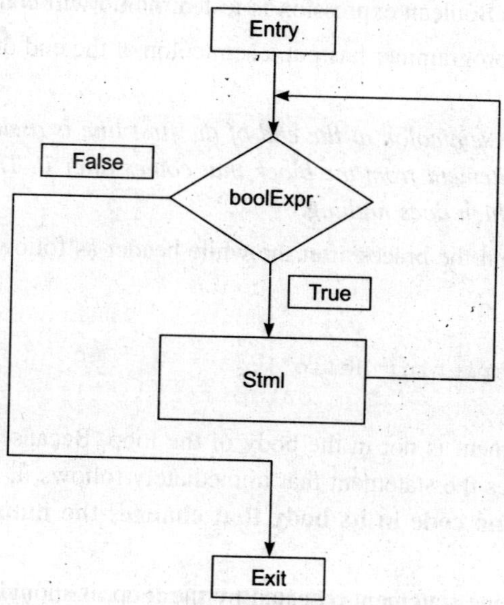

Fig. 2.9: Syntax and working of a do-while loop

Explanation: The first line shown in the syntax is also known as **a loop header.** The ***Stmt part*** is executed when the ***boolExpr*** returns true value. When it returns false value, the loop is terminated. It is possible to exit the while loop without executing the statement part in the loop if the ***boolExpr*** yields false value for the first time. **Thus, the minimum number of times the while loop is executed is zero. Please understand that since the condition is tested before entering the body of the loop, so it is also known as pre-tested loop or a top-tested loop. Also understand that when the *boolExpr* returns always true value, the loop becomes an infinite loop. For example,**

```
while (true) {
      Stmt;
   }
```

This is an **infinite loop.** Here, the Boolean literal true is used in place of boolExpr. It may also be written as follows also to form an infinite loop:

```
while (! false) {
        Stmt;
    }
```

Thus, if a loop does not have a way of stopping, it is called as an infinite loop. **An infinite loop continues to repeat until the program is interrupted. For example,**

```
int numb =1;
while(numb <=5)
   {
      System.out.println("Hello");
   }
```

This is an infinite loop because it does not contain a statement that changes the value of the numb variable. Each time the Boolean expression is tested, numb wiil contain the value 1.

Now say by mistake the programmer has put a semicolon at the end of the while loop as follows:

```
while(numb <=5);
```

Please note here that the semicolon at the end of the first line is assumed to be a null statement and disconnects the while statement from the block that comes after it. This while loop, will forever, execute the null statement, which does nothing.

Now say, you forget to put the braces after the while header as follows:

```
int numb =1;
while(numb <=5)
      System.out.println("Hello");
        numb++;
```

Here, the numb++ statement is not in the body of the loop. Because the braces are missing, the while statement only executes the statement that immediately follows it. **This loop will also execute infinitely because there is no code in its body that changes the numb variable. The rules that you must follow are:**

Rule 1: If there is only one statement repeated by the loop, it should appear on the line after the while statement and be indented one additional level.

Rule 2: If the loop repeats a block, each line inside the braces should be indented.

There is no semicolon at the end of the loop header. Also note that this while loop works just like as if statement that executes over and over again as long as the expression in the parentheses is true. Each repetition of a loop is known as **iteration**. But the important feature of this loop is that it will never iterate if the Boolean expression is false to start with.

Applications of while loop

1. It can be used to create input routines that repeat until acceptable data is entered.
2. This loop is useful for input validations also. We define input validation as the process of inspecting data given to a program by the user and finding out if it is valid.
3. The read operation that takes just before the loop starts is known as a **priming read.**

Before we discuss further, let us solve some examples based on while-loops.

Q.1. Give the general logic of performing input validation.

[Hint: The following steps are used for input validation

1. Read the first input value.
2. Check whether the value is valid or invalid.
3. If it is invalid, then display the error message and read another value.
4. Else continue with the rest of the program.]

Q.2. Give the output of the following code snippet:

```
int i =40;
while (i >=0) {
   if( i%2 ==0)
      System.out.print(i+ " ");
   i++;
  }
```

[Hint: It prints 40. Try to change i++ to i– – and find your result].

Q.3. Write a Java program to print the reverse of a number.

[Hint:

```
import java.util.Scanner;
class DigitOfNumbers {
   public static void main(String[ ] args)  {
     Scanner sc= new Scanner(System.in);
     System.out.println("Enter a number:");
     int n = sc.nextInt ( );
     System.out.printf("The reversed number is:");
     while (k !=0) {
      //extract the individual digits by repeated mod and division
            int m = n % 10;
            k=n/10;
            n=k;
            System.out.printf("%d",m);  //print the digit.
               }
            }
     }
```

OUTPUT (after running):

Enter a number: 321

The reversed number is: 123].

Q.4. Write a Java program to find the GCD (Greatest Common Divisor) of two positive numbers by different methods.

Method 1: The GCD of two positive numbers is defined as the largest common divisor of both the integers. Like, GCD of 24 and 36 would be:

Divisors of 24 are 1, 2, 3, 4, 6, 8, 12, 24

Divisors of 36 are 1, 2, 3, 4, 6, 9, 12, 18, 36

Then the largest/greatest common divisor is 12. So, the GCD of 24 and 36 is 12.

Or

Method 2: You can use **Euclid's algorithm** as follows to find the GCD of two numbers:

while m is greater than zero

do

if n is greater than m, swap m and n.

subtract n from m.

end

final n is the GCD.

Or

Method 3: Another algorithm may be followed-

1. Read 2 numbers a ,b.
2. Repeat through step-5 while a not equals to 0.
3. Set gcd =a
4. a = b % a
5. b = gcd
6. Print gcd
7. Exit

[Hint: Method 1:

```
import java.util.Scanner;
class Gcd
 {
  public static void main(String[ ]  args)
  {
   Scanner sc = new Scanner(System.in);
   System.out.println("Enter two numbers:");
  int n1 = sc.nextInt ( );
  int n2 = sc.nextInt ( );
  int greaterNumber = n2;
  int gcd =1;
```

```
//assign the greater value to the greaterNumber variable
if (n1 > n2)
    greaterNumber = n1;
//start finding GCD from the minimum gcd: 2
int index =2;

//keep checking unless the index is larger than the greater
value and the
//greater value is larger than 2
while (index <= greaterNumber && greaterNumber > 2)
 {
  if ((n1 % index ==0) && (n2 % index ==0))  {
     gcd = index;
 }
//check the next value
index++
}
//print the GCD
System.out.printf("Greatest Common Divisor (GCD) =%d", gcd);
}

      }
```

OUTPUT (after running):

Enter two numbers

6

9

Greatest Common Divisor (GCD) = 3

Method 2:

```
public class GCD {
   public static int gcd(int m1, int n1)  {
     int m = m1;
     int n = n1;
     int temp;
     while (m >0) {
       if(n > m) {temp =n; n=m; m=temp; }
        m = m - n }
     return n; }
   public static void main(String args[ ]) {
     System.out.println(gcd(24,18)); }
   }
```

OUTPUT: 6

Method 3:

```
import java.util.*;
public class GCD
  {
   public static void main(String args[ ])
    {
     int a ,b, gcd;
     a=b=gcd=0;
       Scanner s =new Scanner(System.in);
       System.out.println("Enter two numbers:");
       a =s.nextInt( );
     b= s.nextInt( );
     while(a!=0)
     {
     gcd =a;
     a= b% a;
     b=gcd;
   }
  System.out.println("GCD =" + gcd);
  }
        }          ].
```

Q.5. Enter a number from the keyboard and find out the Fibonacci series using while-loop.

[Hint:

```
import java.util.Scanner;
public class Fibonacci
  {
   public static void main(String args [ ])
        {
        int a=0, b=1, c=0, size;
        Scanner s=new Scanner(System.in);
        System.out.println("Enter a range");
        size = s.nextInt( );
        System.out.println("\n");
        System.out.printl(a+"\n" +b);
        while(c <= size)
          {
           c = a +b;
           if(c<=size)
           System.out.print(c+ "\n");
           a=b;
           b=c;
```

```
            }
        }
    }
```

OUTPUT (after running):

Enter a range

50

0

1

2

3

5

8

13

21

34].

Q.6. Write a Java program to read a number from the keyboard and find its factorial.

[Hint:

```
import java.util.Scanner;
public class Facto
  {
        public static void main(String args[ ])
         {
            int fact=1, b, c;
            Scanner s = new Scanner(System.in);
            System.out.println("Enter a number:");
            b = s.nextInt ( );
            c = b;
            while(c >0)
             {
                  fact = fact * c;
                  c--;
            }
            System.out.println("\nFactorial of b is:" +fact);
        }
  }
```

OUTPUT (after running):

Enter a number: 3

Factorial of 3 is 6

Q.7. Write a program to check whether a given number is a palindrome or Not.

[*GGSIPU, B. Tech.(CSE/IT)-5th sem., Dec. 2013*]

[Hint: The algorithm is given first:

1. Initialize s=0.
2. Read number, num.
3. Set b=num.
4. Repeat through step-7 until (num >0)
5. r=num % 10
6. s=(s*10) + r
7. num = num/10
8. If b equals to s then print "b is a palindrome" else print "b is not a palindrome"
9. Exit.

```
//palindrome program
   import  java.util.Scanner;
   public class Palindrome
      {
       public static void main(String args[ ])
       {
        int num, b, s=0, r;
        Scanner s1 = new Scanner(System.in);
        System.out.println("Enter a number:");
        num=s1.nextInt( );
        b=num;
       while (num > 0)
        {
        r = num % 10;
        s= (s * 10) + r;
        num = num/10;
      }
      if (b ==s)
            System.out.println(b+ " is a palindrome");
      else
            System.out.println(b+ " is not a palindrome");
      }
   }
```

OUTPUT (after running):

Enter a number

121

121 is a palindrome

Run2:

Enter a number

123

123 is not a palindrome

Q.8. Write an algorithm and hence a Java program to check whether a given number is an Armstrong number or not.

[Hint: The algorithm and hence the program is as follows:

1. Initialize s=0
2. Read number, num
3. Set b = num
4. Repeat through step-7 while num greater than 0
5. r=num%10
6. s=s+(r*r*r)
7. num=num/10
8. If b equals to s then print "it is an Armstrong number" else print "it is not an Armstrong number"
9. Exit.

The program follows now:

```
import java.util.Scanner;
public class Armstrong
  {
    public static void main(String args [ ])
     {
    Scanner s1 = new Scanner(System.in);
    int num, b, s=0, r;
    System.out.println("Enter a number:");
    num = s1.nextInt ( );
    b = num;
    while (num > 0)
        {
        r = num % 10;
        s=s+ (r *r*r);
        num = num/10;
         }
       if ( b ==s)
    System.out.println(b+ " is an Armstrong number");
     else
```

```
System.out.println(b+ "not an Armstrong number");
        }
    }
```

OUTPUT (after running):

Enter a number: 153

153 is an Armstrong number

Run2:

Enter a number: 15

15 is not an Armstrong number

Q.9. Write a Java program to check whether the given number is binary or not.

[Hint:

```
import java.util.Scanner;
public class BinaryTest
 {
     public static void main(String args[ ])
       {
       int r=0,c=0, num, b;
       Scanner s1=new Scanner(System.in);
       System.out.println(Enter a number:");
       num = s1.nextInt ( );
       b = num;
       while(num > 0)
         {
           if((num % 10 ==0) || (num%10==1))
           c++;
           r++;
           num=num/10;
           }
       if(c==r)
         System.out.println(b+ "is a binary number.");
       else
         System.out.println(b+ is not a binary number.");
       }
     }
```

OUTPUT (after running):

Enter a number:

12345

12345 is not a binary number.

Enter a number:

11001011

11001011 is a binary number.

Q.10. Write two Java programs to compute the gcd of two numbers using:

(a) Brute force method.

(b) Euclid's method.

And now compare their execution times. Discuss your results.

[Hint: The basic idea used here is:

1. Start the clock (stopwatch).
2. Run the method.
3. Stop the clock.
4. Report the elapsed time.

Please note that there is no clock or stopwatch standard class but we can time the execution by using the Date class from the java.util package. Before we call the method we want to time. We record the start time by creating a Date object. After the method is completed, we record the end time by creating a second Date object. Calling the getTime method of the date class returns the number of milliseconds (1ms = 1/1000s). so, by subtracting the start time from the end time, we can get the elapsed time in milliseconds. That is,

```
Date startTime = new date ( );
//the method call
Date endTime = new date ( );
long elapsedTimeInMilliseconds=endTime.gettime( )-startTime.getTime( );
```

And here goes the complete program:

```
import java.util.*;
import javax.swing.*;

class gcd_time {
     private static final int BRUTE_FORCE = 0;
     private static final int EUCLID =1;

     public static void main(String [ ] args) {
          gcd_time tester = new gcd_time( );
          tester.start ( );
          }

     public gcd_time( ) {
     }
```

```
    public void start( ) {
        long bruteForceTime, euclidtime;
        int m, n;
        while (isContinue ( )) {
            m = getPositiveInteger( );
            n = getpositiveInteger( );

        //time the brute-force method
        bruteForceTime = timemethod(m, n, BRUTE_FORCE);

        //time the Euclidean method
        euclidTime = timemethod(m, n, EUCLID);

        System.out.println("M:" + m);
        System.out.println("N:" + n);
        System.out.println("Brute-Force time is: "+ bruteForceTime);
        System.out.println("Euclidean Time is: "+ euclidtime + "\n");
        }
    }

    private long timeMethod(int m, int n, int type) {
        Date startTime, endTime;
        startTime = new Date( );
        if (type == BRUTE_FORCE) {
            gcd_bruteforce(m, n);
            }
    else {
            gcd(m, n);
    }

  private int getPositiveInteger( ) {
            int input;
            string inputStr;

            while ( true) {
                inputStr = JOptionpane.showInputdialog(null,
                                            "Enter positive integer:");
                input = Integer.parseInt(inputStr);
                if( input >= 0) break;
                JOptionPane.showMessageDialog(null, Input must
                                                    be 0 or more");
```

```
            return input;
        }

    private boolean isContinue( ) {
            int result;
            result = JOptionPane.showConfirmDialog(null, "Run test?",
                        "Confirmation", JOptionPane.YES_NO_OPTION);
            return (result == JOptionpane.YES_OPTION);
            }

    private int gcd_bruteforce(int m, int n) {
            //assume m, n >=1
            int last = Math.min(m, n);
            int gcd;
            int i=1;
            while (i <=last) {
                if(m % i ==0 && n % i ==0) {
                    gcd = i;
                }
                i++;
            }
            return gcd;
                }

    private int gcd(int m, int n) {
            //assume m, n>= 1
            int r = n % m;
            while(r !=0) {
                n = m;
                m = r;
                r = n % m;
            }
                return m;
        }
  }
```

OUTPUT (after running):

M: 4567820

N: 2147483640

Brute-force time: 240

Euclidean Time: 0

The following observations are made here:

1. The brute-force solution given here is quite inelegant.
2. The brute-force approach derives the solution by applying the definition of the greatest common divisor directly. Given two positive integers M and N, where M <=N, we find their greatest common divisor(GCD) by dividing M and N with values from 1 to M. The last integer that divided both M and N perfectly (i.e. there is no remainder), is the greatest common divisor. For example, say two numbers are 24 and 36. The numbers that divide 24 and 36 perfectly are 1, 2,3, 4,6 and 12. so, the GCD is 12.
3. The fraction 24/36 is reduced to its simplest form 2/3 by dividing 24 and 36 by 12. *Please note that we can see if a number j divides another number i perfectly by using the modulo arithmetic. Also note that if i %j ==0, then j divides i perfectly because the remainder of the division is 0.*
4. The second solution given here is Euclid's solution and is more elegant.
5. Say the two numbers are 44 and 16. **Please note that the gcd(44,16) =4. Let us see how Euclidean works.** First divide 44 by 16. The remainder is 12. We have the relation:

   $$44 = 2 * 16 + 12$$

   From this we can say that the GCD (G) that divides 44 and 16 must also divide 12. If it doesn't, then we get a contradiction. If a number G can divide 16 perfectly but cannot divide 12 perfectly, then

   44 % G = (2 *16 +12) %G will result in a non-zero value. This is a contradiction.

   So, now we can reduce the problem of finding gcd(44, 16) to gcd (16,12). We repeat the process as follows:

   $$16 = 1 * 12 + 4$$

   Now we reduce the problem to gcd(12,4). Since 12 = 3 * 4 + 0, shows no remainder, we finish the process and return the answer 4 as the GCD. In nutshell, the sequence of reduction is:

   gcd (44,16) = gcd (16,12) =gcd (12,4) = 4.
6. The working is very clear, that is,

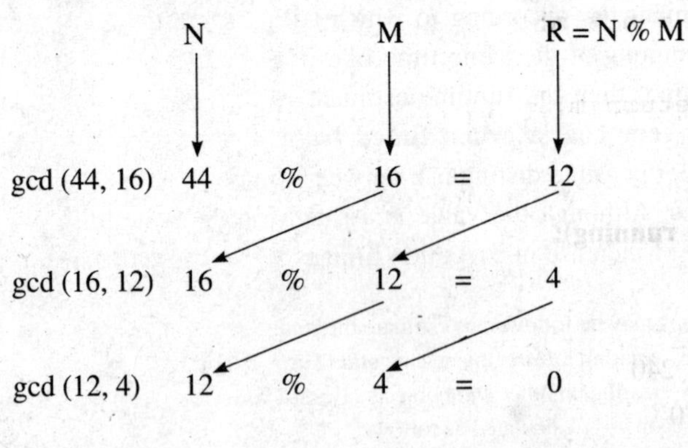

From this working, it is crystal clear that M at one stage becomes N in the next stage and the remainder R becomes M in the next stage. Also understand that we repeat this process until the remainder becomes 0. The value of M at the end of the repetition is the required GCD. The values of count, n, m and r for the second method are as follows:

Count	n	m	r
0	44	16	12
1	16	12	4
2	12	4	0

Please note that the first column shows the number of times the while loop is executed. So, the first row shows the values of n, m and r after zero repetitions i.e. before the while statement is executed. The 3rd row shows the values after the 2nd repetition is completed. Now at the point where the 3rd repetition is attempted, the value of r is 0, so the while loop is terminated and the value of m, which is 4, is now returned.

7. **Which method is better?** Both the versions produce correct results. But the brute-force method is easier to understand because **it reflects the definition of GCD clearly.** We always prefer a simpler and clearer method but only when its performance is relatively same as that of better version. Here, the Euclidean method of gcd outperforms the gcd_bruteforce method as it finds the solution much faster than the brute force method. **Please understand that the gap widens further when the values of M become large.**
8. **Comparisons of the time as obtained as outputs is as follows:**

   The value of 0 for Euclidean time does not imply that it took no time to compute the result. This means that the time it took was so small that we were not able to detect it by the method we used. Please note that for the brute-force approach, the difference for the Euclidean approach is not discernible. Also note that detailed analysis tells us that the running time for the brute-force approach is linearly proportional to the input size M, while the Euclidean approach is logarithmically proportional to the input size, M. So, for the second comparison in the sample run, there will be 1,457,689,098 divisions performed in gcd_bruteforce but only log 1,457,689,098 = 9 divisions. Practically speaking, it will be twice this number because we are executing m % i ==0 && n % i == 0. **But please keep in mind that the value we get for the elapsed time is rough estimate only.** For one thing, the values we get for the elapsed time differ dramatically according to which CPU we run the program on and whether other processes are running at the same time like if a garbage collection routine kicks in while a method is running, then the runtime estimate can be way off. **Also keep in mind that the granularity is very coarse when timed from a high-level language such as Java. For example,** it is not possible distinguish between the program that runs in 5ms and the program that runs in 6ms. Although the value is a rough estimate, it still gives us useful information such as the rate of increase in execution time as we increase the size of input values.

NOTES: The following steps may be followed to estimate the running time of a loop statement:-

1. Record the *start time* by creating a ***Date*** object, say, **startTime,** before the loop statement.
2. Record the *end time* by creating another ***Date*** object, say, **endTime,** after the loop statement.
3. Elapsed time (in milliseconds) is calculated as follows:
   elapsedTime = [endTime.getTime ( ) – startTime.getTime( );]

do-while loop:

The general syntax of do while loop is as follows:

```
do
  {
    Statement(s);
  } while (test-condition);
```

The do-while statement evaluates the test condition at the end of the loop. This loop guarantees that the loop will be executed at least once. *While loop is called as a pretest loop or entry-controlled loop whereas do-while loop is known as posttest loop or exit-controlled loop.* Also a loop may be used inside another loop also. Such loops are called as *nested loops*. Also you can use any type of loop inside one loop. The rules for nested loops are as follows:

Rule-1: An inner loop goes through all of its iterations for each iteration of an outer loop.

Rule-2: Inner loops complete their iterations before outer loops do.

Rule-3: To get the total number of iterations of a nested loop, multiply the number of iterations of all the loops.

Working of do-while loop:

It is similar to the while loop only but here the condition is evaluated after the statement is executed once. Its flowchart is as follows:

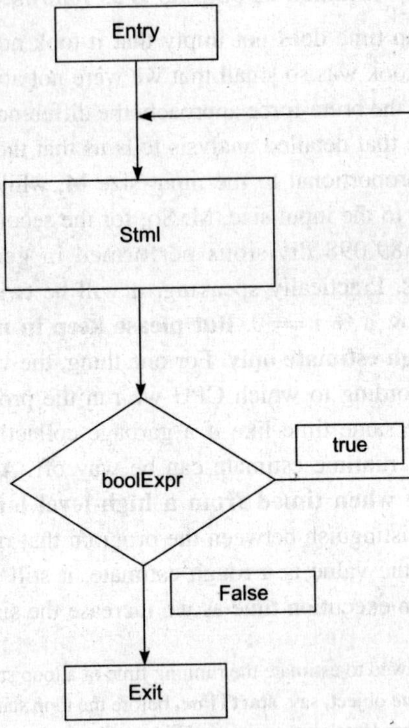

Please note that it is important to place a semicolon (;) after closing the Boolean expression in do-while loop construct. This loop construct executes the statement part in the loop before the boolExpr is evaluated. **Also note that it is because of this reason that the minimum number of times the do-while loop is executed is one. The loop is terminated when the boolExpr yields false value.** Because the condition is tested after execution of the body of the loop, so it is also known as **post-tested loop or bottom-tested loop.**

Notes:

1. The do-while loop is same as that of repeat-until control construct of PASCAL language except that the loop is terminated when the test condition returns false value.
2. The do-while loop is a posttest loop which means its Boolean expression is tested after each iteration.
3. The do-while loop must be terminated with a semicolon.

Before we discuss further about the for-loop, let us solve some questions now.

Q.1. Write an algorithm and hence a Java programs to develop a multi-table program.

[Hint: The algorithm is as follows:-

1. Initialize a=1.
2. Initialize b=1.
3. Print a*b
4. Increment b by 1 i.e. b = b+1
5. Repeat step 3 to 5 until (b <=3).
6. Increment a by 1 i.e. a=a+1.
7. Repeat step 2 to 7 until (a<=3).
8. Exit.

The Java program is as follows:

```
public class MultiTable
    {
        public static void main(String args[ ])
        {
            int a, b;
            a=1;
            do
                {
                b=1;
                do
                    {
            System.out.println("Value of a and b is" + (a *b));
                b++;
                } (while(b<=3);
                a++;
```

```
            }while(a<=3);
        }
    }
```

OUTPUT (after running):

Value of a and b is 1

Value of a and b is 2

Value of a and b is 3

Value of a and b is 3

Value of a and b is 4

Value of a and b is 6

Value of a and b is 3

Value of a and b is 6

Value of a and b is 9

Q.2. Distinguish between while and do-while loops.

[Hint:

While loop	Do-while loop
1. The test condition is evaluated first.	1. It enters into the loop first and then the test condition is evaluated.
2. The minimum number of times a while loop will be executed is zero.	2. This loop will be executed atleast once.
3. It is also known as a pre-test loop or entry-controlled loop.	3. It is also known as a post-test loop or exit-controlled loop.

4. It's syntax is:
while(test-condition)
{
Statement(s);
}
	4. It's syntax is:
	do{
	statement(s);
	while(test-condition);

5. No need of semicolon.	5. Semicolon is must after the while statement in this loop.

Let us discuss the most important for-loop now.

For loop:

The most common, frequently used and versatile loop used in many programs is the for-loop. It is used when the loop is repeated for a known number of times. In Java, it can be used to execute for a known number of times or execute the loop repeatedly based on specific conditions.

Syntax:

```
for ( expression-1; boolExpr; expr3)
{
    statement(s);
}
```

Flowchart:

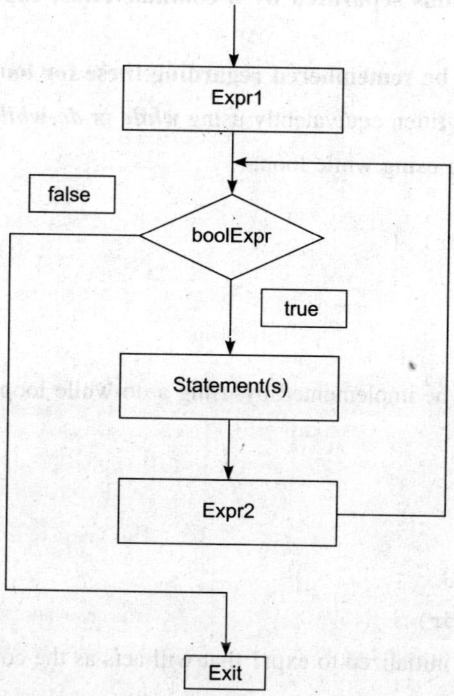

Working: The working of the for-loop is as follows:

1. First of all, expr1 is evaluated. It is usually used to initialize a counter.
2. Then, boolExpr is evaluated to check for the condition for execution. If it returns a true value, then
   (a) statement in the loop is executed.
   (b) Expr2 is evaluated.
   (c) The control is then transferred to step-2.
3. If boolExpr returns a false value then the loop is terminated.

Please note that this means that the working of the for-loop is as follows:

```
for (expr1; boolExpr; expr2)
{
    statement(s);
}
```

That is, firstly, ***expr1*** is evaluated. Then the condition is checked. If it is true then the loop enters into the body (after { braces) and executes the statements within it. After one iteration is over, the control goes back to ***expr2*** and then again the ***boolExpr*** condition is checked. This is how a for loop works. **Also note here that any one, two or all of the three expressions can be omitted in a for loop but the two semicolons (;) must be placed separating the expressions. Also expr1 and expr2 can be lists of expressions separated by a comma. Thus, expr1 or expr2 may become compound statements also.**

The following points may be remembered regarding these for loops:

1. A for loop can also be written equivalently using ***while*** or ***do-while loops*** as follows:

   For loop implementation using while loop:-

```
expr1;
while (boolExpr) {
   statements;
   expr2
}
```

   Similarly, for loop may be implemented by using a do-while loop also:-

```
expr1;
do {
   statements;
   expr2
   }
while (boolExpr);
```

2. Any valid value can be initialized to expr1 that will acts as the counter.
3. The minimum number of times a for-loop is executed is zero.
4. It is also possible to declare the counter variable in for-loop itself like,

```
for ( int count=1; count< 10; count++) {....}
```

5. We can also nest any of these three loops (discussed so far) into one another. Such loops are also called as **nested loops. Please note that the loops should not overlap each other. Also note that one type of loop construct can be nested in another type of loop construct also.** For instance, a for-loop may be nested within a while loop or do-while loop and vice versa. This depends on the program statement that you are solving.
6. We can also control the operation of a loop with break and continue statements, with and without labels. The break statement immediately terminates the loop code block whereas the continue statement skips any remaining code in the block and continues with the next loop iteration.
7. A variable/iterator/counter variable that is declared in a for- statement can be referred to only inside the loop.
8. The following is the bare minimum for-loop with missing parts-

```
for (;;){ }
```

9. These loops are *counter-controlled loops*. We can also write *user-controlled loops* i.e. the loops that allow the user to decide the number of iterations.
10. The first line of the for-loop is also known as a **loop header.**
11. Also note that there is no semicolon after expr3.
12. For-loop is also a *pretest loop* as it checks for the condition before it performs an iteration.
13. It is also possible to execute more than one statement in the initialization expression and the expr3 (increment/decrement). Just remember that when you use multiple statements in any of the parts of the for-loop header then simply separate the statements with commas. For instance,
```
for ( int i=1, j=2; i<10; i–) {...}
```
14. The following is the for-loop as an infinite loop:
```
for (;  ;)
```
15. A new feature of this for loop is that it is also able to iterate through collections without the explicit use of iterators. Please understand that iterators are the programming patterns used to provide a simple sequential access to a collection of objects without knowing a priori the type and the size of the specific collection accessed (to be discussed later).

Before we discuss further, please solve the following questions:

Q.1. Write a program to implement Fibonacci series using for loop control structure.

[GGSIPU, B. Tech.(CSE/IT)-5th sem., Dec. 2013]

[Hint: Fibonacci series is a series of numbers in which the first number is 0 and second is 1. The next number is obtained by adding the previous two numbers i.e

F1=0

F2=1

F3= F2 + F1

In general, Fn = F(n–1) + F(n–2) (where n is positive number). The program follows:
```
class Fibonacci
{
 public static void main(String args [ ])
 {
   int i, n, f1, f2, f3;
  n=12;          //first 12 fibonacci numbers are displayed
  if(n <=1)
     System.out.println(n);
  else
  {
     f1 =0;
     f2 =1;
     f3 = f1 + f2;
     System.out.println(f3);
```

```
for (i=2; i<=n; i++)
    {
        f3 = f1 + f2;
        f1 = f2;
        f2 = f3;
        System.out.print("\t" + f3);
    }
  }
 }
}
```

OUTPUTS (after running):

0 1 1 2 3 5 8 13 21 34 55 89 144

Dry run:

f0	f1	f3 = f1 + f2
0	1	1
		1
1	1	2
1	2	3

Let us now rewrite this program using for-loop:-

```
class fibonacci
{
   public static void main(String args [ ] )
   {
        int i, f0=0,f1=1,f2;
        System.out.println(f0+ " "+f1);
        for(i=3;i<=10;i++)
        {
            f2= f1 + f0;
            System.out.print(" "+f2);
            f0 = f1;
            f1 = f2;
        }
   }
}
```

OUTPUT (after running):

0 1 1 2 3 5 8 13 21 34

Q.2. Write a Java program using for loops to check whether the given number is Armstrong or not. An Armstrong number is a 3 digit number which is equal to the sum of the cubic values of the individual digits in it. For example, 153= 1 **3 + 5 **3 + 3 **3 and thus is an Armstrong number. Also modify your program to generate these types of numbers from 100 to 999.

[Hint: The program follows:

```
class Armstrong
 {
  public static void main(String args [ ]) throws IOException{
  InputStreamreader is=new InputStreamReader(System.in);
  BufferedReader br = new BufferedReader(is);
  String s1;
  int num, n, d;
  int sum =0;
  System.out.println("Enter any three digit number:");
  s1 = br.readLine();
  num = Integer.parseInt(s1);
  n = num;
  while(num!=0)
   {
       d= num % 10;
       num = num/10;
       sum = sum + d*d*d;
  }
  if (sum==n)
       System.out.println("Number is Armstrong!!!");
  else
       System.out.println(Number is not Armstrong!!!");
   }
  }
```

OUTPUT (after running):

Enter any three digit number

123

Number is not Armstrong!!!

OR

//the modified program to find **Armstrong numbers** between 100 to 999.

```
import java.util.Scanner;
class ArmstrongNumber {
  public static void main(String [ ] args) {
       int n, a, b, c;
       for(int i=100;i<1000;i++) {
          a = i%10;
          b = i%100/10;
          c = i/100;
          n = a * a * a + b * b * b + c*c*c;
          if (i==n)
                System.out.printf("%d"\t",i);
          }
       }
    }
```

OUTPUT (after running):

153 370 371 407

Q.3. Write a Java program to compute the factorial of an integer.

[Hint:

```
import java.util.Scanner;
class Fact {
    public static void main(String [ ]  args) {
        int n;
        Scanner sc = new Scanner (System. in);
        System.out.println ("Enter your number:");
        n = sc.nextInt ( );
        long f =1;
        for (int i =1; i<=n; i++)
            f  *= i;
        System.out.printf("Factorial is %d", f);
      }
  }
```

OUTPUT (after running):

Enter your number:

4

Factorial is 24

Q.4. A very popular series in mathematics is the sine series. Now write a Java program to find the value of sin(x) from the series as follows:

Sin(x) = x –x3 / 3! + x5 / 5! –x7 / 7! + ...

[Hint:

```
import java.util.* ;
class SineSeries {
  public static void main(String [ ]  args) {
        int deg, n;
        Scanner sc = new Scanner(System.in);
        System.out.println ("Enter the number of terms: ");
        n = sc.nextInt ( );
        System.out.println ("Enter the angle in degrees:"):
        deg = sc.nextInt ( );
        float x, s = 0.0f, t;
        x = (float) Math.PI *deg/180;
        s = x;
        t = x;
        for(int i=1; i<=n;i++) {
            t = (-t*x*x) / ( (2 * i) * (2*i+1) );
            s = s+t;
        }
        System.out.printf("Sin(%d) = %f ", deg, s);
    }
}
```

OUTPUTS (after running):

Enter the number of terms:

20

Enter the angle in degrees:

90

Sin (90) = 1.000000].

Q.5. Write a Java program to generate perfect numbers. We define a perfect number as a positive integer that equals the sum of its positive integer divisors, including unity but excluding the number itself. Like, 6 is a perfect number as 6 = 1 + 2 + 3.

[Hint:

```
import java.util.Scanner;
class PerfectNum {
  public static void main(String [ ] args)  {
      int n;
```

```
Scanner sc = new Scanner(System.in);
//read n-number of prefect numbers you want.
System.out.println("Enter your n:");
n = sc.nextInt ( );
int sum, count =0;
for(int i=4;; i++) {
    sum =0;
    for (int j=1; j<=i/2; j++)  {
        if (i % j ==0)
            sum+=j;
    }
    if (sum ==i) {
        System.out.printf("%d\t", sum);
        ++count;
        }
      if (count ==n)
    break;
  }
 }
}
```

OUTPUTS (after running):

Enter your n:

4

6   28   496   8128

Q.6. If a loop has a counter variable, would it be normally written as a while statement or a for statement? In a for-loop, which of the –initialization, test and update parts are optional? Which of the initialization, test and update parts allow the use of commas? Give examples(s) to explain this. [*DU, MCA 1st Sem., 2001 onwards*]

Q.7. Write a Java program to draw the following triangle:

```
*
*   *
*   *   *
*   *   *   *
*   *   *   *   *
*   *   *   *   *   *?
```

[**Hint:** Let us write its algorithm first:

1. Read *row* variable i.e. the number of rows.
2. Initialize i=0.
3. Repeat through step-9 while i less than row.

4. Initialize j=0.
5. Repeat through step-7 while j less than or equals to i.
6. Print "*"
7. j = j+1
8. Move to new line.
9. i = i + 1
10. Stop and exit.

And here is the program:

```
import java.util.Scanner;
public class Triangle1
  {
    public static void main(String args [ ] )
    {
        Scanner s1 = new Scanner(System.in);
        int row, i, j;
        System.out.println("Enter the number of rows:");
        row = s1.nextInt ( );
        System.out.print("\n");
        for(i=0; i<row; i++)
        {
            for(j=0; j<=i; j++)
              {
                   System.out.print (" * ");
              }
            System.out.print("\n");
        }
      }
    }
```

OUTPUT (after running):

```
Enter the number of rows:
6
*
*    *
*    *    *
*    *    *    *
*    *    *    *    *
*    *    *    *    *    *
```

Q.8. Write a Java program to draw the following triangle:

1

01

101

0101

10101

010101

1010101 ?

[Hint: Let us write its algorithm first of all:

1. Read number of rows, *row.*
2. Initialize i=1.
3. Repeat through step-8 while i less than or equals to *row.*
4. Initialize j=0.
5. Repeat through step-7 while j less than i.
6. Print (i-j) % 2
7. j=j+1
8. Move to the next line.
9. Stop and exit.

And here is the program:

```
import java.util.Scanner;
public class Triangle2
  {
  public static void main(String args [ ] )
    {
      Scanner s1 = new Scanner(System.in);
      int row, i, j;
      System.out.println("Enter the number of rows:");
      row = s1.nextInt ( );
      System.out.print("\n");
      for(i=1; i<row; i++)
      {
          for(j=0; j<i; j++)
            {
                System.out.print( (i-j) % 2);
            }
          System.out.print("\n");
      }
    }
  }
```

Q.9. Write a Java program to print the following triangle now:

```
*   *   *   *   *   *   *
*   *   *   *   *   *
*   *   *   *   *
*   *   *   *
*   *   *
*   *
* ?
```

[Hint: Let us develop its algorithm first:

1. Read the number of rows, *row*.
2. Initialize i = row.
3. Repeat through step-9 until i is greater than 0.
4. Initialize j=0
5. Repeat through step-7 until j less than i.
6. Print "*".
7. j=j+1
8. Move to newline.
9. i=i-1
10. Stop and Exit.

And here goes the program:

```
import java.util.Scanner;
   public class Tria
     {
     public static void main(String args [ ] )
       {
       int row, i, j;
       Scanner s1 = new Scanner(System.in);
       System.out.println("Enter the number of rows:");
       row = s1.nextInt ( );
       for(i=row; i>0;i- - )
           {
             for(j=0;j<i;j++)
             {
                    System.out.print(" * ");
              }
           System.out.print("\n");
           }
         }
     }
```

OUTPUT (after running):

Enter the number of rows

7

```
*   *   *   *   *   *   *
*   *   *   *   *   *
*   *   *   *   *
*   *   *   *
*   *   *
*   *
*                         ].
```

Q.10. Write a Java program to print the following triangle:

1

12

123

1234

12345

123456

1234567 ?

[**Hint:** Let us develop its algorithm first:

1. Read the number of rows, *row*.
2. Initialize i = 1.
3. Repeat through step-9 until i is less than or equals to *row*.
4. Initialize j=1.
5. Repeat through step-7 until j less than or equals to i.
6. Print j.
7. j=j+1
8. Move to new line.
9. i=i+1
10. Stop and Exit.

And here is the program:

```
import java.util.Scanner;
   public class Tria
     {
     public static void main(String args [ ] )
       {
```

```
        int row, i, j;
        Scanner s1 = new Scanner(System.in);
        System.out.println("Enter the number of rows:");
        row = s1.nextInt ( );
        for(i=; i<=row; i++)
            {
            for(j=1; j<=i; j++)
                {
                    System.out.print(j);
            }
        System.out.print("\n");
        }
    }
}
```

OUTPUT (after running):

Enter the number of rows

7

1

12

123

1234

12345

123456

1234567

Q.11. Now write a Java program to print the following triangle:

7777777

666666

55555

4444

333

22

1 ?

[**Hint:** Let us develop its algorithm first:

1. Read the number of rows, *row*.
2. Initialize i = row.
3. Repeat through step-9 until i greater than 0.

4. Initialize j=0.
5. Repeat through step-7 until j less than i.
6. Print i.
7. j=j+1
8. Move to new line.
9. i=i-1
10. Stop and Exit.

And here is the program:

```
import java.util.Scanner;
   public class Triang
     {
        public static void main(String args [ ] )

        {
            int row, i, j;
            Scanner s1 = new Scanner(System.in);
            System.out.println("Enter the number of rows:");
            row = s1.nextInt ( );
            for(i=row; i>0; i- - )
               {
                   for(j=0; j<i; j++)
                     {
                         System.out.print(i);
                       }
                   System.out.print("\n");
               }
        }
     }
```

OUTPUT (after running):

Enter the number of rows

7

7777777

666666

55555

4444

333

22

1

Q.12. Write an algorithm and hence a Java program to print the following pattern:

```
          *
         ***
        *****
       *******
      *********
     *********** ?
```

[**Hint:** Let us develop its algorithm first:

1. Read the number of rows, *row*.
2. Initialize i = 0.
3. Repeat through step-17 until I less than or equals to row.
4. Initialize j=1.
5. Repeat through step-7 until j less than or equals to row-i.
6. Print " ".
7. j=j+1
8. Initialize j=1.
9. Repeat through step-11 until j less than or equals to i.
10. Print "*".
11. j=j+1
12. Initialize j=1.
13. Repeat through step-15 until j less than i.
14. Print "*".
15. j=j+1
16. Move to new line.
17. i=i+1
18. Stop and Exit.

And here is the program:

```
import java.util.Scanner;
   public class Tri
   {
      public static void main(String args [ ] )
         {
            int row, i, j;
            Scanner s1 = new Scanner(System.in);
            System.out.println("Enter the number of rows:");
            row = s1.nextInt ( );
            for(i=0;i<=row;i++)
```

```
            {
        for(j=1;j<=row-i;j++)
                System.out.print(" ");
        for(j=1;j<=i;j++)
                System.out.print("*");
        for(j=1;j<=i;j++)
                System.out.print("*");
        System.out.print("\n");
        }
      }
    }
```

OUTPUT (after running):

Enter the number of rows

6

```
          *
         ***
        *****
       *******
      *********
     ***********
```

Q.13. Write a Java program to draw a PASCAL TRIANGLE **as follows:**

```
        1
      1   1
    1   2   1
  1   3   3   1
1   4   6   4   1
```

[Hint: Let us develop its algorithm first:

1. Set a=1, q=0.
2. Read the number of rows, *row*.
3. Repeat through step-15 until q is less than *row*.
4. Initialize p=30-3*q
5. Repeat through step-7 until p is greater than *row*.
6. Print " "
7. p=p-1
8. Initialize b=0.
9. Repeat through step-13 until b is less than or equal to q.
10. If b equals to 0 or q equals to 0 then set a=1 else set a=(a*(q-b+1)/b).

11. Print (" ");
12. Print a
13. b=b+1
14. Move to the next line.
15. q=q+1
16. Stop and exit.

And here goes the program:

```
import java.util.Scanner;
   public class PascalTri
     {
     public static void main(String args [ ] )
       {
            int a=1,p,q=0,row, b;
            Scanner s1 = new Scanner(System.in);
            System.out.println("Enter the number of rows:");
            row = s1.nextInt ( );
            System.out.println("\nPascal Triangle\n");
            while(q<row)
                {
                  for(p=30-3*q; p>0;p–)
                      System.out.print("   ");
                   for(b=0;b<=q;b++)
                      {
                      if(b==0 || q==0)
                         a=1;
                      else
                         a=(a*(q-b+1)/b;
                      System.out.print(" "+a);
                      }
            System.out.print("\n");
            q++;
            }
          }
       }
```

OUTPUT (after running):

Enter the number of rows

5

```
        1
      1   1
    1   2   1
  1   3   3   1
1   4   6   4   1 ].
```

Q.14. Write a Java program to display the Floyd triangle.

[**Hint:** Let us write its algorithm first:

1. Initialize a=1.
2. Read the number of rows, *row*.
3. Initialize i=0.
4. Repeat through step-12 until i less than row.
5. Initialize j=0.
6. Repeat through step-10 until j less than or equals to i.
7. Print a
8. If a less than 10 then print " " else print " ".
9. a = a+1
10. j=j+1
11. Move to the next line.
12. i=i+1
13. Stop and exit.

And here goes the program:

```
import java.util.Scanner;
   public class Floyd
     {
     public static void main(String args [ ] )
       {
          int a=1,i, j, row;
          Scanner s1 = new Scanner(System.in);
          System.out.println("Enter the number of rows:");
          row = s1.nextInt ( );
          System.out.println("\n");
          for(i=0;i<row;i++)
           {
              for(j=0;j<=i;j++)
                {
                  if(a<10)
                  System.out.print(a+ "  ");
```

```
                    else
                    System.out.print(a+ "  ");
                    a++;
                }
            System.out.print("\n");
            }
        }
    }
```

OUTPUT (after running):

Enter the number of rows

4

1

2 3

4 5 6

7 8 9 10].

Q.15. Write a Java program to generate a sequence of numbers using for loop construct and print them in specified format:

1

2 3

4 5 6

7 8 9 10

11 12 13 14 15 ?

[Hint:

```
import java.util.Scanner;
Class Sequence {
  public static void main(String [ ]  args) {
      int k=1;
      System.out.printf("%d\n",k);
      for(int i=1;i<5;i++) {
          System.out.printf("%d\t",++k);
          for(int j=0; j<i; j++) {
                k+=1;
                System.out.printf("%d\t",k);
          }
          System.out.printf("\n");
          }
      }
  }
```

OUTPUT (after running):

1

2 3

4 5 6

7 8 9 10

11 12 13 14 15].

2.11.3 Other Statements

The break Statement

When a break statement is executed inside a loop, it skips the remaining statements of that loop and the control is immediately transferred outside the loop.

Syntax:

break;

For example,

```
Class BreakDemo
  {
     public static void main(String args [ ])
       {
          int i, j;
          for(i=1; i<=3;i++)
            {
               for(j=1;j<=3;j++)
                 {
                       if(i= =j)
                            break;
                       else
                            System.out.println(i+ "\t"+j);
                 }
            }
       }
  }
```

OUTPUT (after running):

2 1

3 1

3 2

Please note that when a break statement appears inside a loop or in a switch statement, it terminates the execution at that point and transfers execution control to the statement immediately following the loop or switch statement. So, it does an early exit from any loop or switch statement. *Also note that when multiple statements are nested within each other, a break transfers control to its immediate outer level.*

However, the break statement should be avoided in a loop (whenever possible) because it bypasses the loop's logic and makes the code difficult to understand and debug.

Another variant of break statement:

The **syntax** is:

break label_name;

For example,

```
.
.
.
{
    Statement;
    break kk;
}
.
kk:
.
.
.
```

Where label_name is an identifier and not a number. There is no need of declaring these labels as they are just user-defined labels. When compiler encounters the label (like kk in this example), the control jumps to the statement labeled as kk and executes the statements following that label. *Please understand that if these statements appear before a break statement, the flow is in backward direction. If the statements appear after a break statement, the flow is in forward direction.*

The continue Statement

Syntax:

continue;

A *continue* statement is used within the loops to end the execution of the current iteration and proceed to the next iteration. Thus, it provides a method of skipping the remaining statements in that iteration after the continue statement. *Please note that a continue statement should be used only in loop constructs and not in selective control constructs. Also note that using a continue statement in selective control constructs results in compilation error.*

While loop and continue together

With respect to the while loop, it means that the program jumps to the *Boolean expression* at the top of the loop. If the expression is still true, the next iteration begins.

do-while loop and continue together

In a do-while loop, the program jumps to the *boolean expression* at the bottom of the loop, which determines whether the next iteration will begin.

For loop and continue together

In a for loop, *continue* causes the *update expression (i.e increment/decrement part of the for loop)* to be executed and then the test expression is evaluated.

However, even the continue statement should also be avoided because like the break statement, it also bypasses the loop's logic and makes the code difficult to understand and debug.

Selection of loops—while, do-while or a for loop

Most of the repetitive algorithms can be written with any of the three loops discussed above. But each loop works best in different situations. Let us see how?

1. **The while loop:** As we have studied that a *while loop* is a pretest loop. *Please understand that this loop is ideal to be used when you do not want the loop to iterate if the condition is false from the beginning.* It is also ideal if you want to use a sentinel value to terminate the loop. A sentinel value is a special value that cannot be mistaken as a member of the list and it signals that there are no more values to be entered. When the user enters the sentinel value, the loop terminates.
2. **The do while loop:** As we have already studied that *do while loop* is a sort of posttest loop. *Please understand that this loop is ideal to be used in situations where you always want the loop to iterate at least once.*
3. **The for loop:** As studied earlier, the *for loop* is a pretest loop that has in built expressions for initializing, testing and updating. These expressions make it very convenient to use a loop control variable as a counter. *Please understand that the for loop is ideal in situations where the exact number of iterations is known.*

The return Statement

A return statement is used only in methods (functions in C and member-functions in C++ are known as methods in Java). It terminates method's execution by transferring the control to the calling method. Thus, if a method has to return a value then you may write:-

return ***expression;***

On the other hand, **for a void type of method that does not return any value,** the following **syntax** is used:

return;

Please understand that a return statement unconditionally transfers control to the calling method from the called method. This means that all statements between the return statement and the end of the method are skipped. That is why, such a statement is normally placed at the end of a method but it is possible to use it when specific conditions apply and an early termination is required. **Also understand that the use of return statement at the end of the method is essential in case of methods that return a type different from *void.***

Note: For methods having a void return type, this statement can be omitted and will be implicitly added by the compiler.

Block Statements

A group of statements enclosed within the flower/curly braces comprises a block. Thus, a block contains a statement list—a sequence of statements. **A statement in a block is called as an embedded statement and it can be a labeled, a declaration or a simple statement. Please note that a block is also called as a compound statement.** It is also valid to have no statements or an empty statement in a block. A block is syntactically similar to a single statement. **Also note that no semicolon is placed after the closing brace that ends a block.** When there is no statement in a block, it is called as an **empty block. A block having empty statement is not an empty block since it contains a valid statement.** That is,

```
{ }     //is empty block
{ ; }   //non-empty block
```

Empty statement: A statement that does nothing is known as an empty statement. It is written as a single semicolon as follows:

```
;          //empty statement
```

Please remember that an empty statement is also known as a null statement. This statement helps a programmer to introduce some delays in the program execution. Actually, they do nothing and just bypass certain machine cycles, thereby, producing delays. **For example,**

```
for( int i=0; i<100; i++)
    {
        ;        // null statement
    }
```

Similarly, we can use it in while and do-while loops also.

We are in a position to solve some examples now.

Q.1. Define what is a sentinel value and why is it used?

Q.2. Write a Java program to that reads numbers 1 to 10 through the keyboard and displays their squares in a tabular format.

[Hint:

```
public class sqr
{
    public static void main(String[ ] args)
    {
            int number, maxValue;    // number is loop control variable
            System.out.println("Displaying the table of numbers and their
                    squares:");

            //get the maximum value to display
            System.out.print("Till what number you want the squares?");
```

```
            maxValue = Keyboard.readInt ( );

            //display your table now
            System.out.println("Number        Number Squares");
            System.out.println("--------------------------------------");
            for( number=1; number <=maxValue; number++)
            {
                System.out.println(number + "\t\t" + number * number);
            }
        }
    }
```

Q.3. Give the outputs of the following program snippets:

(a) int x, y;

```
for (x=1, y=1; x <=5; x++)
{
  System.out.println(x + "plus" + y + "equals" + (x + y));
}
```

[**Hint: Both** x and y are initialized to 1. Thus, we get the following output-

1 plus 1 equals 2

2 plus 1 equals 3

3 plus 1 equals 4

4 plus 1 equals 5

5 plus 1 equals 6].

(b) int x, y;

```
for(x=1;y=1; x<=5;x++,y++)
{
System.out.println(x + "plus" + y + "equals" + (x + y));
}
```

[**Hint:** The loop update expression is x++, y++. Thus, we get the following output:

1 plus 1 equals 2

2 plus 2 equals 4

3 plus 3 equals 6

4 plus 4 equals 8

5 plus 5 equals 10].

Q.4. Give an example to show the use of a sentinel value.

[Hint:

```
while (result != -1)
 {
     result = result + 20;
 }
```

Here, the value –1 was chosen for the sentinel because it is not possible to have a negative result. Thus, this makes it possible for the loop to terminate immediately if the user gets –1 as the result].

Q.5. Try to simulate a clock using nested for-loops. What inferences you draw from your program regarding for-loops.

[Hint:

```
 //simulation of a clock

import java.text.DecimalFormat;
public class Clock
  {
   public static void main(String[ ] args)
   {
     DecimalFormat fmt = new DecimalFormat("00");
     for (int hours = 1; hours <=12; hours++)
      {
       for (int minutes = 0; minutes <=59; minutes++)
        {
          for (int second = 0; seconds <=59; seconds++)
           {
             System.out.print(fmt.format (hours)  + ":");
             System.out.print(fmt.format (minutes)  + ":");
             System.out.print(fmt.format (seconds));
           }
         }
       }
     }

   }
```

OUTPUT (after running):

01:00:00

01:00:01

01:00:03

(The loop continues to count…)

12:59:57

..

12:59:58

12:59:59

The following conclusions are drawn from this program:

1. An inner loop goes through all of its iterations, for each iteration of an outer loop.
2. Inner loops complete their iterations before outer loops do.
3. To get the total number of iterations of a nested loop, multiply the number of iterations of all the loops].

Q.6. Write a Java program that reads for the number of students and the number of test scores per student. Then it displays the average score for the student.

[Hint:

```
public class Aver_test
{
    public static void main(String [ ] args)
    {
        int n,              //number of students
          numTests,         //number of tests per student
          score,            //test score
          total;            //test scores in total
        double average;    //average test score
        System.out.println("TEST AVERAGING PROGRAM");

        // read number of students
        System.out.print("Enter number of students:");
        numTests = Keyboard.readInt ( );

        //get number of test scores per student
        System.out.print("How many test scores per student?);
        numTests = Keyboard.readInt ( );


        // Calculate for each student
        for (int student =1; student <=numStudents; student++)
        {
            total = 0;      //set total to 0
            //get the test scores for a student
            for (int test = 1; test <=numTests; test++)
            {
               System.out.print("Enter score " + test + "for
                      student" + student + ": ");
                score = Keyboard.readInt ( );
                total += score;    // add score to total
```

```
                        }

                    //calculate and display the average
                    average = total / numTests;
                    System.out.println("The average score for student"
                        + student + "is" + average);
                        System.out.println ( );
                    }
                }
            }
```

OUTPUT (after running):

TEST AVERAGING PROGRAM

Enter number of students: 2

How many test scores per student? 3

Enter score 1 for student 1: 80

Enter score 2 for student 1: 85

Enter score 3 for student 1: 90

The average score for student 1 is 85.0

Enter score 1 for student 2: 60

Enter score 2 for student 2: 80

Enter score 3 for student 2: 80

The average score for student 1 is 73.3].

Q.7. Write a nested loop that displays 5 rows of '#' characters. There should be 10 '#' characters in each row.

Q.8. Do as directed:

(a) Convert while loop to a do-while loop in the code below:-

```
int x=1;
while (x >0)
 {
     System.out.print("Enter a number: );
     x = Keyboard.readInt ( );
}
```

(b) Convert for-loop to a while loop in the code below:-

```
for( int i = 10 ; i > 0; i–)
{
     System.out.println(1 + "seconds to go");
}
```

(c) Write an input validation loop that asks a user to enter a number in the range of 1 through 100.

(d) Write a Java program that displays a table of centigrade temperatures 0 to 50 and their Fahrenheit equivalents. The formula used is:

$$C = 5/9\ (F-32)$$

where C and F have their usual meanings. Try to use a loop to display your table.

Q.9. Develop a program to find the roots of a given quadratic equation. Use switch statements and loops to display your roots.

Q.10. The distance a body travels in free fall is given by the formula:-

$S= -gt^2$ **where** s is the distance traveled in feets,

T is the time in seconds to travel the distance s,

G is a constant and is equal to 32.2 feet per second^2.

[Hint:

```
for (i=1; i<=100; i++)
{
    float s = 0.5 * 32.2 * i *i;
    System.out.println("i" + "\t" + s);
}
```

].

Q.11. Write a Java program to read a number from the keyboard and to add each of its digit.

[Hint:

```
import java.util.Scanner;
public class SumDigit
 {
   public static void main(String args [ ] )
   {
     int r, sum=0, num;
     Scanner s1 = new scanner(System.in);
     System.out.println("Enter a number:");
     num = s1.nextInt ( );
     while(num > 0)
      {
        r = num % 10;
        sum = sum + r;
        num = num /10;
      }
   System.out.println("The sum of digits is= \t" +sum);
   }
}
```

OUTPUT (after running):

Enter a number

123

The sum of digits is=6].

Q.12. Give and discuss the output of the following code:

```
int price;
for (int width =11; width <=20; width++) {
   for(int length =5; length <=25; length +=5) {
      price = width * length * 19;
      System.out.print("   " + price);
      }
      //finished one row; now move on to the next row
      System.out.println(" ");
   }
```

[**Hint:** The outer for statement is set to range from the first row (width =11) to the last row (width=20). For each repetition of the outer for, the inner for statement is executed, which ranges from the first column (length = 5) to the fifth column (length = 25). The loop body of the inner for computes the price of a single item and prints out this price. So, the complete execution of the inner for-loop, which causes its loop body to be executed 5 times, completes the output of one row. The following shows the sequence of values for the two control variables:

width	length
11	
	5
	10
	15
	20
	25 (this completes the printing of the first row)
12	
	5
	10
	15
	20
	25 (this completes the printing of the first row)
13	
	5
	10
:	
:	

].

Q.13. What will be the value of sum after the following nested for–loops are executed:

(a)
```
int sum =0;
for (int i = 0; i < 5; i++)  {
   sum = sum + i;
   for (int j = 0; j < 5; j++)  {
       sum = sum + j;
   }
}
```

(b)
```
int sum =0;
for( int i = 0; i < 5; i++) {
   sum  =  sum + i;
   for(int j = i; j < 5; j++)  {
     sum  =  sum +j;
   }
}
```

Q.14. What is wrong with the following nested for loop?

```
int sum = 0;
for (int i = 0; i < 5;  i++)  {
   sum =  sum + i;
   for (int i  = 5; i > 0; i- -)  {
      sum = sum + j;
   }
}
```

2.12 ARRAYS

Say, we wish to store the marks of 3000 students of our college, if I use variables then more than 3000 variables are required. This is very tedious and cumbersome. So, to solve this type of problem, we use array that uses a common name with a subscript representing the index of each element. Thus, **an array is an ordered sequence of finite data items of the same data type that shares a common name.** The common name **is the array name and** each individual data item **is known as an element of the array.**

An array is defined as a set of similar type of elements that are stored contiguously in memory. This means that the elements of an array are stored in the subsequent memory locations starting from the first memory location of the block of memory created for the array. Each element of an array can be referred to by an array name and a subscript or an index. **Please**

note that all elements of an array should be of similar type. In Java, arrays are slightly different than C/C++. Arrays can have one of more dimensions—one dimensional or multidimensional. One dimensional array uses a single index and a two dimensional array uses two indexes and so on. Also note that a 1D array can be used to represent a list of data items and it is also known as a vector or a list. Similarly, a 2D array can be used to represent a table of data items consisting of rows and columns. It is also known as a matrix. A 3D array can be used to represent a collection of tables. This concept can go on to more than 3-dimensions also.

The dimension of the array is known as the **rank of the array**. Like, a 1D array has rank 1, a 2D array has a rank of 2 and so on. Also understand that the number of subscripts is determined by the rank of an array. The size or length of each dimension is represented by an integral value greater than or equal to 0. The total number of elements in an array is the product of the sizes of each dimension in an array. If any one or more of the dimensions of an array have size 0 then the array is known as an *empty array*. Arrays are reference data types in Java. An array may be regular or ragged. A ragged/jagged array is a 1D array which contains *arrays as elements*. A regular array is a multidimensional array where each dimension contains the same number of elements, while this is not generally true for jagged arrays.

NOTE: 2D regular arrays are also known as rectangular arrays.

Also note that the size of an array is not the part of the array data type.
The overall classification of arrays in Java is shown in Fig. 2.10.

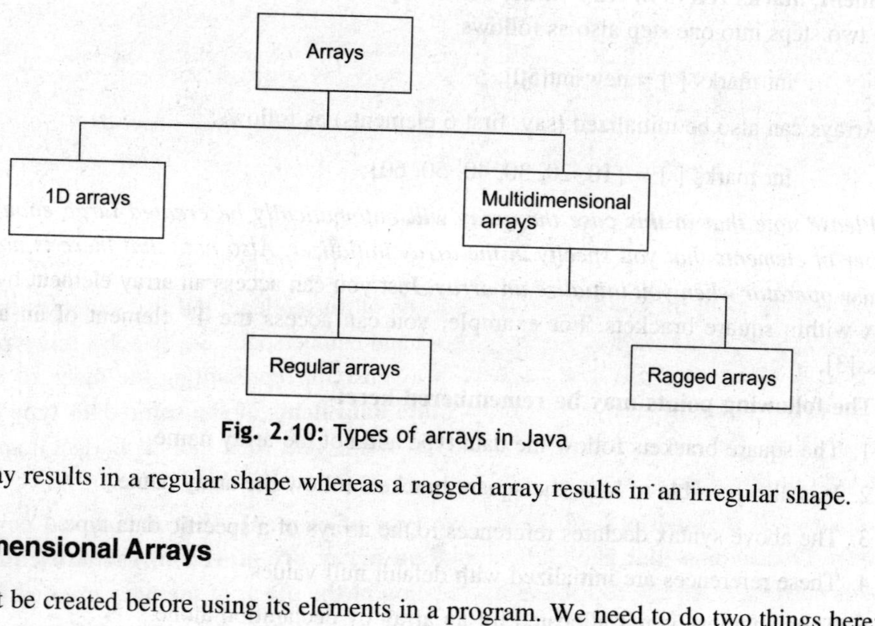

Fig. 2.10: Types of arrays in Java

A regular array results in a regular shape whereas a ragged array results in an irregular shape.

2.12.1 1-Dimensional Arrays

An array must be created before using its elements in a program. We need to do two things here:

(a) Declare the array.

(b) Instantiate an array.

Please understand that the syntax for declaration of an array depends on its number of dimensions and shape. Also understand that only the declared arrays can be instantiated. It is worth mentioning here that it is also possible to combine declaration and instantiation in a single statement itself.

In Java, one dimensional array is declared as follows:

datatype arrayname[ ];

Java provides another way of declaring an array as follows:

datatype [ ] arrayname;

Here, *datatype* specifies the type of the elements in array *arrayname.*

For example, the following statements declare an array of integers:-

```
int marks[ ];
int [ ] marks;
```

Please note that this statement just declares that 'marks' is an array variable, no array actually exists. So, to create an actual array, you must use **new operator** as follows:

```
arrayname = new datatype[size];
```

Thus, to create an array, *marks*, of 50 integer numbers, we can write:-

```
marks = new int[50];
```

After this statement, *marks* will refer to an array of 50 integers. **Also note that prior to this statement, marks refers to Null value, which represents an array with no value.** You can achieve these two steps into one step also as follows:

```
int marks [ ] = new int[50];
```

Arrays can also be initialized (say, first 6 elements) as follows:

```
int marks [ ] = {10, 20, 30, 40, 50, 60};
```

Please note that in this case the array will automatically be created large enough to hold the number of elements that you specify in the array initializer. Also note that there is no need of using the new operator when you initialize an array. Just you can access an array element by specifying its index within square brackets. For example, you can access the 4th element of an array marks as marks[3].

The following points may be remembered here:

1. The square brackets follow the data type and not the array name.
2. It is also possible to have the square brackets follow the array name.
3. The above syntax declares references to the arrays of a specific data type.
4. These references are initialized with default null values.
5. Thus, memory is not allocated for an array by declaration alone.
6. The data type of elements and the rank of the array are identified from the declaration.
7. The size of an array representing the length of dimension is not part of array's type. That is why, the size of the array is not mentioned it its declaration.

8. The declaration also does not enclose any integer value in-between the opening and closing square brackets.
9. Note here that like C/C++, in Java array indexing starts from 0 and that they are integer expressions.
10. An array having size equal to 0 is known as an **empty array.**
11. In the following declaration,

    float [ ] x;
    x = new float[5]; //array x has 5 elements
    This means that,

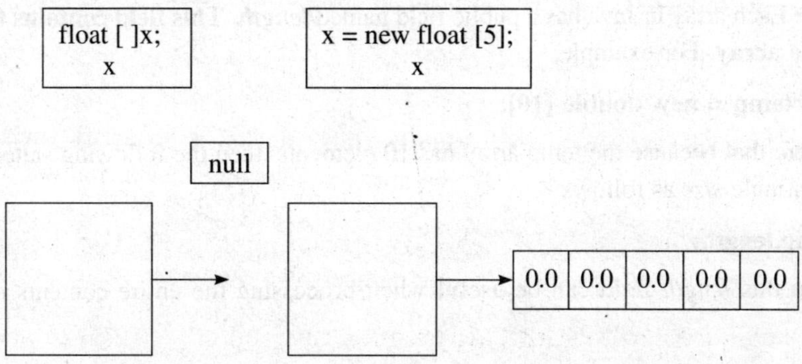

Fig. 2.11: Memory allocations of array

12. The following statement:

    double [ ] d = new double[15];

    creates an array that can hold **a maximum of 15 double values.**
13. Once an array is created, its size cannot be changed.
14. The subscript of the last element in an array is one less than the total number of elements in the array.

    For example,

```
class array_demo
{
   public static void main(String args[ ])
   {
      int a[ ] = {2,4,6,8,10};
      int i;
      for ( i = 0; i < 5; i ++)
         System.out.print(a[i] + "\t");
   }
}
```

OUTPUT (after running):
2 4 6 8 10

Please note here that Java strictly checks to make sure that you do not try to store or reference values outside of the range of the array. It is Java's runtime system that does all this work. If you try to go outside the array boundary then also Java reports it as an error as follows:-

Exception in thread "main" java.lang.ArrayIndexOutOfBoundsException....

So, we have to be careful while using arrays in Java too.

As already explained earlier, regular arrays may be 1D or multidimensional. More than 3D arrays are rarely used. Regular array is the simplest form of 1D-array. It is also created using the 2 steps mentioned above.

Array length: Each array in Java has a public field named ***length.*** **This field contains the number of elements in the array.** For example,

double [ ] temp = new double [10];

Please note here that because the temp array has 10 elements, then the following statement would assign 10 to the variable *size* as follows:

size = temp.length;

Also note that this *length* field can be useful when processing the entire contents of an array. That is,

```
for (int i=0; i<temp.length; i++)
    System.out.println(temp[i]);
```

This loop steps through an array and displays the contents of each element. The array's length field is used in the test expression as the upper limit for the loop control variable.

NOTE: 1. You cannot change the value of an array's *length* field.
2. *length* is not a method here rather it is a property available in Java.

How to read array from the keyboard?

Consider the following code snippet:

```
int n;          //n = size of array
int [ ] numbers;
System.out.print(" Enter total number of elements in array:");
n = Keyboard.readInt ( );
numbers = new int[size];
```

Thus, Java allows you to use an integer to specify an arrays size declarator. This makes it possible for the user to specify the array size.

It is also possible to reassign an array reference variable to a different array as follows:

```
//create an array referenced by the numbers variable
int [ ] numbers = new int [10];
//reassign numbers to a new array
numbers = new int[5];
```

Here, the 1st statement creates a 10-element integer array and assigns its address to the numbers variable i.e. the numbers variable holds the address of an int array. The 2nd statement then allocates a 5-element integer array and assigns its address to the numbers variable. **Please note that the address of the 5-element array takes the place of the address of the 10-element array.** After this statement executes, the numbers variable references the 5-element array instead of the 10 element array. **Also note that since the 10-element array is no longer referenced so it becomes a candidate for garbage collection and that the next time the garbage collector runs, the array will be destroyed.**

The issue of copying arrays:

Array is an object. There is a difference between an array and the variable that references it. Thus, the array and the reference variable are two separate entities. This difference becomes essential when you wish to copy the contents of one array to another. The following is the **wrong way** of copying an array:-

```
int [ ]  a1 = {1, 3, 5, 7};
int [ ] a2 = a1;        //error, no copying will be done.
```

These two statements will not copy the contents of a1 to a2. Instead it makes a copy of the address that is stored in a1 and stores it in a2. Thus, after this statement executes, both the a1 and a2 variables will reference the same array. Recall that this is also known as **shadow copying.**

Correct way:

We observed from the above example that we **cannot copy** an array by merely assigning one array reference variable to another. *Please remember that to copy an array you need to copy the individual elements of one array to another as follows:*

```
int [ ] firstArray = { 1, 2, 3, 4, 5, 6, 7, 8, 9};
int [ ] secondArray = new int [5];
for( int i=0; i < firstArray.length; i++)
    secondArray[i] = firstArray[i];
```

The loop in this code copies each element of *firstArray* to the corresponding element of *secondArray.*

Alternative solution:

Using System class's *arraycopy ( ) method,* we can efficiently copy data from one array into another. This method requires five arguments as follows:

public static void arraycopy (Object source, int srcIndex, Object dest, int destIndex, int length)

Where, the two Object arguments indicate the array to copy from and the array to copy to.

The three integer arguments indicate the starting location in each of the source and the destination array and the number of elements to copy. This is shown in Fig. 2.12.

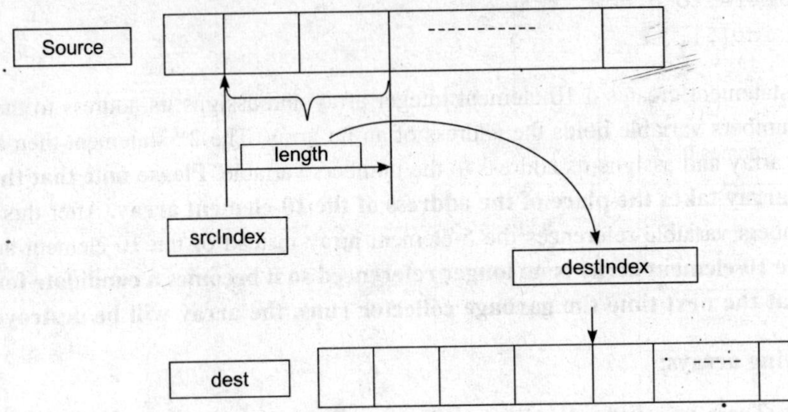

Fig. 2.12: Showing how arrayCopy( ) method works

Class Objects for Arrays

Every array has an associated Class object, shared with all other arrays with the same component type. The direct superclasss of an array type is Object. Every array type implements the interfaces Cloneable and java.io.Serializable.

Array of Characters is Not a String

In Java, unlike C, an array of char is not a string and neither a String nor an array of char is terminated by NULL character. ***Please note that a String object is immutable*** i.e., its contents never change while an array of char has mutable elements. The method tocharArray in class String returns an array of characters containing the same character sequence as a String. The class **StringBuffer** implements useful methods on **mutable arrays** of characters.

If an array variable v has type A[ ], where A is a reference type, then v can hold a reference to an instance of any array type B[ ], provided B can be assigned to A. Else we will get an exception.

String Arrays in Java

An array of *String objects* may be created. But if the array is un-initialized then each String in the array must be created individually. **For example,**

String [ ] names = { "Rajiv", "Ajay", "Amit"};

Please note that in memory, an array of *String objects* is arranged differently than an array of primitive data type. Also note that in order to use a String object, you must have a reference to the *String object.* So, we can say that an array of String objects is really an array of references to String objects. The *names variable* will reference an array of references to ***String objects.*** This is shown diagrammatically also.

The ***names*** variable holds the address of a ***String*** array. A ***String*** array is an array of references to ***String*** objects.

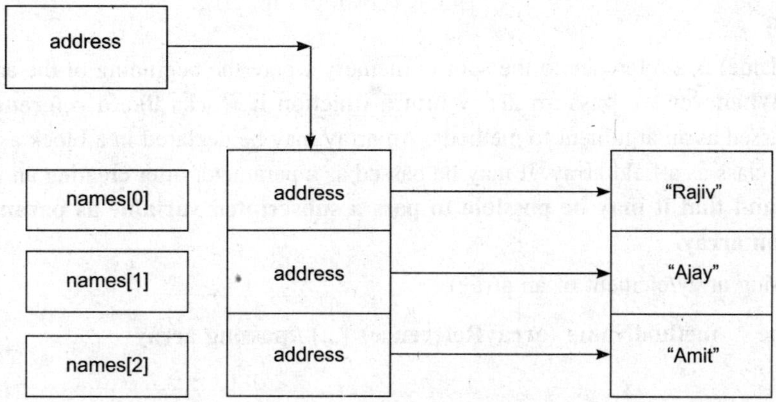

Please note here that each element in the *names* array is a reference to a *String* object. The names [0] element references a String object containing "Rajiv", the names [1] element references a String object containing "Ajay" and so on.

As we do with the primitive data types, here also an initialization list automatically causes an ***array of String objects*** to be created in memory. **And that if you do not provide an initialization list, you must use the new keyword to create the array. That is,**

String [ ] names = new String[2];

This statement creates an array of 2 references to ***String objects***. Also **note that the array is an array of 2 un-initialized String references and that as they do not reference any objects, they are set to *null*.** That is, an uninitialized ***String*** array is as follows:

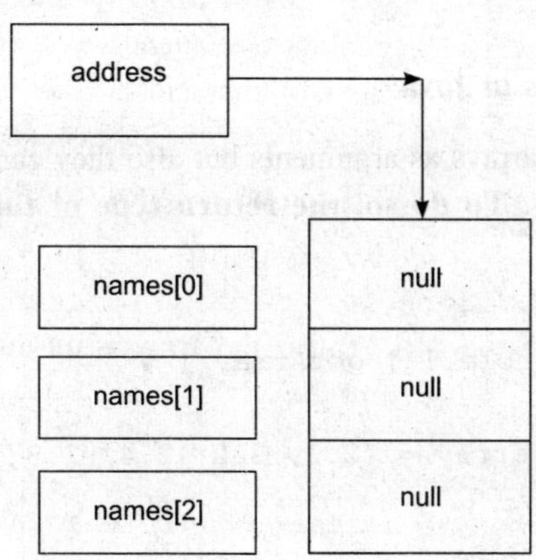

Passing an Array as a parameter to methods in Java

Practically speaking, an array is a reference. For example,

int [ ] a;

Here, a (array name) is a reference to the spot in memory where the beginning of the array is stored. **The rule is:-"Whenever we pass an array into a function it works like a reference variable."** Array can be passed as an argument to methods. An array may be declared in a block as a local array or declared in a class as a field array. It may be passed as a parameter after creating an instance of it. **Please understand that it may be possible to pass a subscripted variable as parameter to pass an element of an array.**

Syntax (of passing array/element of an array):

dataType methodName (arrayReference) {...} //passing array

Syntax2:

dataType methodName (subscriptedVariable) {...} //passing an element of an array.

Example 2. The following is a method prototype with an array as a *formal parameter-*

```
public static void print(int[ ] a);
```

This means that the method print ( ) can change the values in the array (the actual parameter) that is passed to it.

Example 3. The following program initializes or assigns the given value to all elements of the array, a.

```
public static void initialize(int [ ] a, int value) {
    for (int i = 0; i< a.length; i++)
            a[i] = value;
    }
```

Returning Arrays from Methods in Java

Not only can the methods accept arrays as arguments but also they can return arrays. **A method can return a reference to an array. To do so, the return type of the method must be declared properly.**

For example,

```
public static double [ ] getArray ( )
{
    double [ ]  array = {2.1, 2,2, 2.4, 2.8 };
    return array;
}
```

Here, the getArray method is a public static method that returns an array of ***doubles.*** **Also note that the return type listed in the method header is double [ ].** Inside the method an array of

double is created, initialized with some values and referenced by the array variable. The return statement then returns the ***array*** variable. *Please note that by returning the array variable, the method is returning a reference to the array. Also note that this method's return value may be then stored in any compatible reference variable.*

Before we discuss about the multidimensional arrays, let us summarize the arrays as follows:

1. Do not index into an array with an invalid index.
2. Not initializing all of the values of an array results in errors.
3. Saying a=10; will not assign 10 to each element of the array,a. This is not syntactically correct **because the LHS is not an integer variable while the RHS is an integer expression.**
4. You must differentiate between an array index and the values stored in an array at a particular index.
5. All array accesses are checked **at run time.** An attempt to use an index that is less than 0 or greater than or equal to the length of the array causes an ***ArrayIndexOutOfBoundsException*** to be thrown.
6. An array may hold at most the number of elements specified by its size. **It may hold no data if the size is zero.**
7. An array name followed by a subscript enclosed within the square brackets refers to the individual elements in it.
8. The subscript can be *byte, short, char or int.* it cannot be ***long type.***
9. The elements are stored in **consecutive/succesive memory locations.**
10. Subscripted array variables are treated as ordinary variables.
11. Subscripted array variable uses the subscript enclosed within square brackets whereas ordinary variable does not have any subscript.
12. By incrementing the value of the subscript by one, the data stored in the subsequent memory location is obtained. **Please note here that ordinary variables do not have such facility.**
13. Accessing an array element is easier irrespective of the size of the array. **The value of the subscript gives the position of the element in the array.**
14. Arrays may be **1D or multi dimensional.**
15. Arrays may be **regular or ragged.**
16. 2D regular arrays have all rows having same number of columns.
17. 1D ragged array may have rows with equal or different column size.
18. An array instance created is always an array type.
19. When an instance of an array is created, the rank and size of each dimension are specified and remain constant throughout the lifetime of the instance. It is not possible to change the rank and size of the dimensions of an existing array.
20. During array initializations, the **new** keyword followed by the array type name and brackets may be omitted. Only the initializers are enclosed within appropriate braces. **The sizes must be constant values.**

21. An array is a reference data type.
22. String is not an array of characters. String is different from array of characters.
23. The data type of elements, the shape of an array and the number of dimensions are part of the type of array. Thus, an array contains only these details in its declaration.
24. Array's size is not the part of array's type. So, the declaration of an array does not contain its size.
25. An array declaration does not reserve any memory.
26. An instance of the array is created dynamically using **new operator.**
27. **It is only in the place of array creation using *new operator*,** the values within square brackets mention the size. In other places, they refer to the indices or subscripts only. **The subscript must be an integral constant.**
28. **The size of the array must be an integer greater than or equal to 0.** After creation of arrays, the values of the subscripted variables assume default values, if there are no initializers.
29. **The array subscripts must always start at zero.**
30. **The last array variable's subscript is always [size –1] i.e., one less than the size of the array.**
31. You cannot index an array backwards like a[–1], a[–2] etc. **Also note that it is illegal to refer to the elements that are out of array bounds. For example,**

    For an array of size 8, the array bound is from a [0] to a [7] only. **Java compiler checks on the array bounds and report errors, if any, at compile time.**
32. While executing a program, a value of an array type can be null or a reference to an instance of that array type.
33. Initialization of an array may be combined with instantiation by using initializers.
34. **Array elements are initialized to their default values,** if they are not explicitly initialized by using initializers, when an instance is created.
35. **Arrays have a field named *length* and String objects have a method named *length*.** So, when you work with String arrays, do not get confused. In the following example, both field length and the method length ( ) are used:

    ```
    for (int i = 0; i < names.length; i++)
            System.out.println(names[i]. length ());
    ```

    Note here that a method will always have a braces of ( ) type.
36. Even the arrays of class objects may be created. **For example,**

    ```
    Item[ ] inventory = new Item[2];
    ```

This declares an array of three objects. The variable that references the array is named ***Item.*** As with String arrays, each element in this array is a reference variable i.e.,

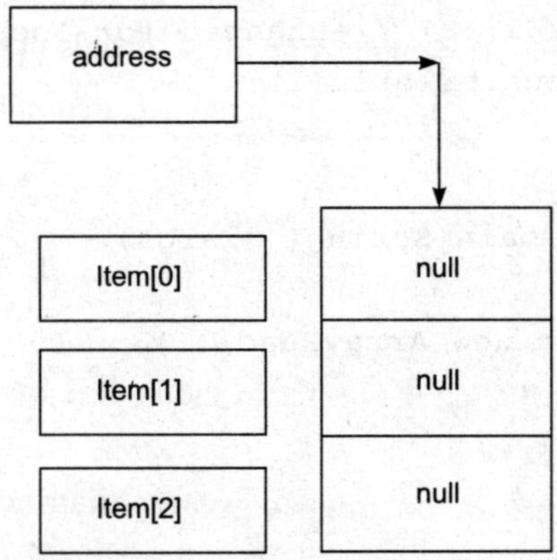

Please note from the figure that each element of the array is initialized with the ***null*** *value. Also note that this shows that the array elements do not yet reference objects. You must create the objects that each element will reference. For instance, the following loop creates objects for each element:*

for (int i = 0; i < Item.length; i++)

Item[i] = new Item( );

We shall be studying this a bit later in detail.

We are in a position to solve some questions based on 1D arrays now.

Q.1. Write a Java program to read an array, a, and to display array elements.

[Hint:

```
    //To read an array and to display its elements
import java.util.Scanner;
class ArrayRead {
    int [ ] a;
    void ReadArray( )
      {
            a = new int [5];
            Scanner sc = new Scanner(System.in);
            System.out.println("Enter the array elements:");
            for(int i=0; i<5; i++)
                a[i] = sc.nextInt ( );
      }
```

```
    void PrintArray ( )
     {
            System.out.println("Array elements are: ");
            for (int i :a) //enhanced for-loop
            System.out.println(i);
        }


public static void main(String[ ] args)
    {
    ArrayRead  obj = new ArrayRead ( );
    obj.ReadArray ( );
    obj.PrintArray ( );
    }
}
```

OUTPUTS (after running):

Enter the array elements:

1

2

3

4

5

Array elements are:

1

2

3

4

5

Please note here that within the loop, the variable i is initialized as 0 to start the subscript at zero. Also note that after reading the array elements, these elements can be accessed in any order and can be used in the same way as scalar variables].

Q.2. Write a Java program to initialize an array with the following values: 10, 20 30, 40, 50. Also display your entire array.

[Hint:

```
    //Array initializations
import java.util.Scanner;

class Array {
```

```
    int [ ] a;

    Array ( )
    {
      a = new int [ ]  {10, 20, 30, 40, 50};
    }

 void printArray ( )
    {
      System.out.println("Array elements are: ");
      for (int i = 0;  i < a. length;  i++)
           System.out.println(a[i]);
    }

 public static void main(String [ ] args)
  {
    Array obj = new Array ( );
    Obj.printArray ( );
  }
 }
```

OUTPUT (after running):

Array elements are:

10

20

30

40

50

Q.3. Write a simple Java program that reads and displays an array of strings.

[Hint:

```
import java.util.Scanner;
class StringArray {
     String [ ] s;

     void readString( )
         {
         s= new String[3];
         Scanner sc = new Scanner(System.in);
         System.out.println("Enter your strings:");
         for (int i =0; i<5; i++)
```

```
            s[i] = sc.next ( );
        }

    void printArray ( )
    {
        System.out.printl("Given strings are:");
        for (String i : s)
            System.out.print(i+ ", ");
    }

public static void main(String [ ]  args)
{
    StringArray obj = new StringArray ( );
    obj.readString ( );
    obj.printArray ( );
}
}
```

Output (after running):

Enter your strings:

Dr.

Rajiv

Chopra

Given strings are:

Dr., Rajiv, Chopra].

Q.4. Can you use == operator to compare two arrays. If no, why and then what is done?

[**Hint:** // wrong way

```
Say, the firstArray is:
    int [ ] firstArray ={2, 4, 6, 8, 10};

And the secondArray is:
    int [ ] secondArray = {2, 4, 6, 8, 10};
Now if we write,
    if (firstArray == secondArray)            //this is an error
        System.out.println("Arrays are same");
  else
        System.out.println("Arrays are not the same");
```

This is so because when you use == *operator* with reference variables, the operator compares the memory addresses that the variables contain and not the contents of the objects referenced by the variables. *Please note that because the two array variables in this code reference different objects in memory, they will contain different addresses.* Thus, the result of the Boolean expression *firstArray == secondArray* is false and the code reports that the arrays are not the same.

Let us write the correct code now.

```
int [ ] firstArray = { 2, 4, 6, 8, 10};
int [ ] secondArray = {2, 4, 6, 8, 10};
Boolean arraysEqual = true; //flag variable
int i =0;
//find out whether arrays are the same size.
if (firstArray.length != secondArray.length)
    arraysEqual = false;
//check whether the elements contain the same data
while (arraysEqual  && i < firstArray.length)
{
    if (firstArray [i] != secondArray [i])
        arraysEqual = false;
    i++;
}
if (arraysEqual)
    System.out.println("The arrays are equal.");
else
    System.out.println("The arrays are NOT equal."); ].
```

Q.5. Write Java codes to do the following:

(a) To sum the values in an integer array.

(b) To average the values in a numeric array.

(c) To find the highest and lowest values in an integer array.

[Hint:

(a) To sum the values in an array, we must keep a loop counter with some accumulator variable. It is this loop that adds the value in each array element to this accumulator. That is,

```
int [ ]  a = new int[100];
//loop to add
int total =0; //initialize accumulator
for (int i = 0; i <  a.length;  i++)
     total += a[i];
```

(b) To compute the average we need to sum the values in the array, first of all. Then divide it by the number of elements in the array. That is,

```
Double [ ] marks = new double[10];
//computing average
```

```
double total =0;      //initialize accumulator
double average;       //will hold the average
for (int i =0; i < marks.length; i++)
     total += marks[i];
average = total/ marks.length;
```

Please note here that the last statement, which divides total by marks, length, is not inside the loop. This statement will execute only once, after the loop has finished its iterations.

(c) //for finding the highest value in an array

```
int [ ] numbers = new int[25];
int highest = numbers[0];
for (int i =1; i < numbers.length; i++)
{
     if (numbers[i] > highest)
          highest = numbers[i];
}
```

Similarly, for finding the lowest number, the code is as follows:-

```
int [ ] numbers = new int[25];
int lowest = numbers[0];
for (int i =1; i < numbers.length; i++)
{
     if (numbers[i] < lowest)
          lowest = numbers[i];
}
```

Also note that when the loop has finished, *lowest* variable will contain the *lowest/smallest* value in the array.

Q.6. To sort means to arrange the elements of an array in either ascending or descending order. By default, it is in ascending order. Can you suggest any in-built method in Java that does this? If so, write a Java program for the same.

[Hint:

//Java API provides a class, ***Arrays***, which has a static method named ***sort.*** The sort method accepts an array as its argument and sorts its elements inascending order. If an array is sorted in ascending order, it means that the values are from lowest to highest. So, to use the Arrays.sort method, we simply pass the array that is to be sorted as an argument. That is, the following statement calls the Arrays.sort method, passing numbers array as an argument:

Arrays.sort(numbers);

This sorts the array mentioned as parameter. But to use this method you must write the following header:

import java.util.Arrays;

Also note that the Arrays class is the part of the java.util package. Without this statement, the Java compiler cannot access the class. Here is the complete program:

```
//sorting arrays
public class Sort
{
    public static void main(String [ ] args)
    {
        int [ ]  numbers = { 10, 5, 11, 15, 2, 1, 6};
        //display the unsorted array elements
        for (int i=0; i < numbers.length; i ++)
            System.out.print(numbers[i] + " ");
        System.out.println( );

        //sort the array
        Arrays.sort(numbers);

        //display the sorted array elements
        for (int i=0; i < numbers.length; i++)
            System.out.print(numbers[i] + " ");
        System.out.println( );
    }
}           ].
```

Q.7. Write a Java program to show how a reference to an array can be returned from a method. Explain your program.

[Hint:

```
public class ReturnArray
{
    public static void main(String[ ] args)
    {
        double [ ] values;
        values = getArray( );
        for(int i = 0; i < values.length; i++)
            System.out.println(values[i]);
    }
//the getArray method returns a reference to an array of doubles
public static double[ ] getArray( )
  {
        double [ ] array = {2, 4, 6, 8, 10};
        return array;
  }
}
```

OUTPUT (after running):

2

4

6

8

10

Working: Consider the following statement in the main method :-

values = getArray ( );

It assigns the array created in getArray to the array variable ***values.*** Then the *for- loop* displays the value of each element of the values array].

Q.8. Can you modify the above program in question number 7 to create an array of a specified size and fill it with the values entered by the user.

[Hint:

```
public static double [ ]  getArray (int size)
{
    double [ ] array = new double[size];
    System.out.println("Enter a series of"+array.length+"numbers.");
    for (int i = 0; i < array.length; i++)
      {
      System.out.print("Number " + (i+1) + ":");
      array [i ] = Keyboard.readInt ( );
      }
      return array;
}          ].
```

Q.9. How can you call String methods from an array element?

[Hint: The ***String objects*** have several **methods. For example,** the *toUpperCase* method returns the uppercase equivalent of a String object. **Please understand that as each element of a String array is a *String object*, you can use an element to call a *String method.* For example,** we can call the toUpperCase method from element 0 of the *names* array as follows:

```
System.out.println(names [ 0 ] . toUpperCase ( ));
```

Thus, for each element of this array, we must use a loop as follows:

```
public class StringArrayMethods
 {
   public static void main(String [ ] args)
   {
      String [ ] names = { "Rajiv" , "Mayur", Ajay" };
```

```
      //display each string in the names array in uppercase now
        for ( int i=0; i < names.length; i++)
            System.out.println (names [i] .toUpperCase ( ));
      }
   }
```

OUTPUT (after running):

RAJIV

MAYUR

AJAY].

Q.10. Write two separate Java programs to:

(a) Search for an element in an 1D array. If the value is found in array, the element's subscript is returned else –1 is returned.

(b) Using the searchArray classes sequentialSearch method.

[Hint:

(a) public static int sequen_search (int [ ] array, int value)

```
{
    int i, element;     // i is loop controller
    Boolean found;      // flag variable showing search results
    // element 0 is the starting point of the search
    i =0;
    // store the default values—element and found.
    element = -1;
    found= false;
    // search the array now.
    while (!found && i < array.length)
    {
        if (array[ i] == value)
        {
            found = true;
            element = i;
        }
        i++;
    }
        return element;
    }
}
```

Please note here that –1 is returned when the search value is not found in the array. This is so because –1 is not a valid subscript.

(b) Now, let us use the searchArray class and here is the program:

```
public class TestSearch
{
 public static void main(String [ ] args)
  {
     int [ ] tests = {80, 85, 100, 93, 75 };
     int results;

     results = SearchArray.sequentialSearch(tests, 100);
     if (results == -1)
     {
        System.out.println("Could not score 100" + "on any test");
     }
     else
     {
        System.out.println("You scored 100 on" + "test" + (results
                                                          + 1));
     }
  }
}
```

OUTPUT (after running):

You scored 100 on test 3].

Q.11. What are parallel arrays? What is their use?

[**Hint:** Parallel arrays are two or more arrays that hold related data and the related elements of each array are accessed with a common subscript. For example,

```
for ( int i = 0; i < names.length;  i++)
{
    System.out.println("Name:" + names[ i ] );
    System.out.println("Address:" + address[ i ] );
}
```

Please note that here the two arrays used are of same type (char type) but is is also possible to have two arrays of different types.

Uses: Parallel arrays are particularly useful when the related data is of different types].

Q.12. Write a Java program to store the names of 10 countries and their corresponding currency.

[**Hint:** (a) Define two arrays that may be used in parallel to store the names of the countries and their currencies.

(b) Write a loop now that uses these arrays to print each country's name and its currency].

Q.13. Write a Java program to calculate different statistics from monthly rainfall averages. Try to compute the following:

(a) Average annual rainfall.

(b) Average for odd months.

(c) Average for even months.

(d) Quarter averages.

[Hint:

```
import jacax.swing.*;
class rainfall_stat {
    public static void main (String [ ] args) {
        String [ ] monthName = { "January" , "February", "March",
                                 "April", "May", "June", "July",
                                 "August", "September", "October",
                                 "November", "December" };
        double [ ] rainfall = new double[12];
        double [ ] quarterAverage = new double[4];
        double annualAverage, sum, difference;
        double oddMonthSum, oddMonthAverage, evenMonthSum,
               evenMonthAverage;

        // for average annual rainfall
        sum = 0.0;
        for( int i =0; i < rainfall.length; i++)  {
        // reading rainfall  for month
            rainfall [ i ] = Double.parseDouble (
            JOptionPane.showInputDialog(null, "Rainfall for"
                     + monthName[i]));
            sum += rainfall[i];
        }
        annualAverage = sum / 12.0;
        System.out.format( "Annual Average Rainfall:%5.2f\n\n",
                    annualAverage);

        // for odd and even month averages

    //for odd months average calculation
    for( int i =0; i < rainfall.length; i+=2)
    {
```

```
        oddMonthSum += rainfall[i];
    }

    oddMonthAverage = oddMonthSum / 6.0;

    //for even months average calculation
    for( int i =0; i < rainfall.length; i+=2)
    {
        evenMonthSum += rainfall[i];
    }

    evenMonthAverage = evenMonthSum / 6.0;
    System.out.format" "Odd  Month Rainfall Average: %4.2f\n",
                        oddMonthAverage);
    System.out.format" "Even Month Rainfall Average: %4.2f\n",
                        evenMonthAverage);

    //for quarter averages now.
    for (int i =0; i< 4; i++) {
        sum = 0;
        for( int j =0; j<3; j++) { //compute the sum of one quarter
            sum += rainfall[3*i + j];
        }
    quarterAverage[i] = sum / 3.0;        //average for quarter i+1
    System.out.format( Rainfall Average Qtr %2d:%5.1f\n", i+1,
                                              quarterAverage[i]);
    }
  }
}
```

The following points may be noted regarding this program:

1. We do not specify the size of the array (as above) if the array elements are initialized at the time of declaration.
2. The size of the array is determined by the number of values in the list.
3. We assume here that the *rainfall array* is declared and all 12 values are read in.
4. We compute in the above program the average rainfall for the odd months (i.e. January, March,….) and for the even months (February, April,….)
5. In the quarter average calculation, the inner for-loop is used to compute the sum of one quarter.
6. The values of i, j and 3i+j are as follows:-

i	j	3 * i + j
0	0	0
	1	1
	2	2
1	0	3
	1	4
	2	5
2	0	6
	1	7
	2	8
3	0	9
	1	10
	2	11

Q.14. Write a Java program to show working of the bubble sort program. Also search for an element, x, in this array. If found, then also display its position.

[Hint: //to implement bubble sort

```
class arr_sort {
    public static void main (String [ ] args) {
        int i, j, temp =0;
        int arr[ ] = {20, 10, 40, 30, 80 };
        int n = arr.length;
        int brr[ ] = new int[n];
        System.out.println("The given array (unsorted) is: ");
        for( i = 0; i < n; i++)  {
            System.out.print("  " + arr[i]);
        }
        System.out.print("\n");
        for (i =0; i <n-1; i++) {
            for (j=0; j< n-1-i; j++){
                if (arr[j] < arr[j+1]) {
                    temp = arr[j+1];
                    arr[j+1] = arr[j];
                    arr[j] = temp;
                    }
                }
            }

    System.out.println("The sorted array is: ");
    for(i =0; i < n; i++)  {
```

```
        System.out.println("  " + arr[i]);
     }
     System.out.println("\n");
     }

     System.out.println("\nEnter the value to be searched");
        x = s1.nextInt( );
     for(i=0; i < n; i++)
      {
        if(x ==a[i])
        System.out.println(x+ "is located at locationà"+(i +1));
       }
     }
```

OUTPUT (after running):

The given array (unsorted) is: 20

10

40

30

80

The sorted array is:

10

20

30

40

80].

Q.15. Write a Java program that returns the location (index) of the element with the largest value in an integer array.

[Hint:

```
public class SortArray {
   //method maxPos, returns an int and takes in an int array and the
   //current index to begin finding the max value.
  public static int maxPos (int arr[ ] , int index)          {
     int max = index;
     for(int i = index+1; i < arr.length; i++)
        if (arr[i] > arr[max])
           max = i;
           return max; ].
```

Q.16. Write a Java program to evaluate a polynomial using Horner's method.

[Hint:

```
import java.util. *;
public class Horners {
  public static double eval(int n, double x, double c[ ] )
  {
    //nth order polynomial has n+1 coefficients stored in c[0]
    //through c[n]
    // y= c[0] + x* (c[1] + x*(c[2] + x *(c[3] + ...x*(c[n-1] +c[n]*x))))
    double y = c[n] * x;
    if(n<=0) return c[0];
    for(int i =n-1; i > 0; i- -)
            y = (c[i] + y) * x;
    return y + c[0];
  }
 public static void main (String[ ] args)
  {
    double [ ] coeff;
    Scanner keyboard = new Scanner(System.in);
    System.out.println ("Enter the order of the polynomial");
    int ord = keyboard.nextInt ( );
    coeff = new double[ord + 1]
   System.out.println ("Enter coefficients of the polynomial");
   for (int i =0; i<=ord; i++)
   coeff[i] = keyboard.nextDouble( );
   System.out.println("x value where we want to calculate
          polynomial value");
   double xval = keyboard.nextdouble ( );
   System.out.println("Polynomial value=" + eval(ord, xval, coeff));
 }
}
```

OUTPUTS (after running):

Enter the order of the polynomial

3

Enter coefficients of the polynomial

2

–3

–1

4

X value where we want to calculate polynomial value

2

Polynomial value= 24.0].

Q.17. Write a Java program to count the frequency of each alphabetic character in a string that is read from the keyboard.

[Hint:

```
import java.util.*;
public class freq {
    public static void main(String[ ] args) {
    int index;
    char c;
    int [ ] freq = new int[26];
    Scanner stdin = new Scanner (System.in);
    //initializing frequency array to 0s
    for(index = 0; index < 26; index++)
    freq[index] = 0;
    System.out.println("Enter your line of text:\n");
    String inp = stdin.nextLine( );
   for (index = 0; index < inp.length ( ); index++) {
        c = inp.charAt(index);
        if( c >= 'A' && c<='Z')
            freq[c - 'A'] ++;
        if( c >= 'a' && c<='z')
            freq[c - 'a'] ++;
   }
   System.out.println("Letter\tfrequenct\n");
   for (index = 0; index < 26; index++)
   System.out.println((char) ('A + index) + "\t" + freq[index]);
   }
}
```

The students are advised to run this program.].

Q.18. Write a Java program to read a decimal number from the keyboard and convert it into its binary form.

[Hint: Let us write its algorithm first of all:

1. Initialize i=0.
2. Read the decimal number, say, *num.*
3. Create two integers a[ ] and b[ ].
4. Repeat through step-7 while *num* greater than 0.

5. a[i] = num % 2.
6. i = i+1
7. num = num/2
8. Set k = i -1
9. Initialize j=0
10. Repeat through step-14 while j less than i.
11. b[j] = a[k]
12. Print b[j]
13. k = k -1
14. j = j + 1
15. Exit.

And here goes the program now:

```
import java.util.Scanner;
public class Conversion
   {
     public static void main(String args[ ] )
     {
         int num, i=0, j, k;
         Scanner s1 = new Scanner(System.in);
         System.out.println("Enter your decimal number:");
         num = s1.nextInt( );
         int a[ ] = new int[20];
         int b[ ] = new int[20];
         while (num > 0)
              {
                     a[i] = num % 2;
                     i++;
                     num = num/2;
              }
         k = i - 1;
         System.out.print("\n\n");
         for (j = 0; j < i; j++)
             {
                     b[j] = a[k];
                     System.out.print(b[j]);
                     k- - ;
              }
         }
     }
```

OUTPUT (after running):

Enter a number

7

111].

Q.19. Write a Java program to print the elements of an array after deleting the duplicate elements from it.

[Hint:

```
import java. util. Scanner;
public class Duplicate
  {
      public static void main(String args[ ])
          {
              int c, t, x, y;
              Scanner s= new Scanner (System.in);
              System.out.println("Enter your array size:");
              y = s.nextInt( );
              int a[ ] =new int[y];
              int b[ ] = new int[y];
          System.out.println("Enter your array elements:");
          for (c=0; c<a.length; c++)
              {
                a[c] = s.nextInt( );
              }
  System.out.println("\n DISPLAYING THE ARRAY ELEMENTS\n");
    for (c =0; c < a.length; c++)
        {
          System.out.print(a[c] + " ");
        }
    System.out.print("\n");
    for (t=0; t <a.length; t++)
        {
          for(x=t+1; x <a.length; x++)
              {
                if (a[t] == a[x])
              a[x] =0;
              }
          }
          y=0;
          for( c= 0; c <a.length; c++)
          {
```

```
                if (a[c] != 0)
                {
                        b[y] = a[c];
                        y ++;
                }
        }
        System.out.println("\nAfter deleting duplicate elements\n");
        for (x=0; x <y; x++)
            {
            System.out.print(b[x] + " ");
            }
            }
    }
```

OUTPUTS (after running):

Enter the array size

5

Enter your array elements

10

20

30

20

50

The array elements are
10 20 30 20 50

After deleting duplicate elements

10 20 30 50].

Q.20. It is desired to write a Java program that generates random numbers, count even and odd numbers in them and display their counts.

[Hint:

```
    import java.util. *;
    public class ArraySplit {
        public static void main (String args[ ] ) {
            Random rand = new Random ( );
        int anArray[ ] = new int[Math.abs(rand.nextInt ( ) ) % 100];
      //creating memory for an integer array of random size
      //now creating random elements and storing in the array
      for(int i=0; i< anArray.length; i++)
      anArray[i] = Math.abs(rand.nextInt ( ) ) % 100;
```

```
int oddCnt = 0;          //counts the odd numbers in the array
int evenCnt = 0;         //counts the even numbers in the array
//go through each element in the array and determine if odd or
//even and increase oddCnt or evenCnt as appropriate.
for (int i = 0; i <anArray.length; i++)
{
  if ( anArray[i] % 2 == 0)    //number is even
  evenCnt++;
else            //number of odd
  oddCnt++;
}
System.out.println("The number of odd numbers in the array
                    is:" + oddCnt);
System.out.println("The number of even numbers in the array
                    is:" + evenCnt);
  }
}
```

2.12.2 Multi-Dimensional Arrays

In Java, multi-dimensional arrays are actually arrays of arrays. Each dimension has its own set of square of brackets. A 2D array is declared as follows:-

datatype arrayname [ ] [ ];

Here, ***datatype*** specifies the type of the array elements. It can also be declared as follows:-

datatype [ ] [ ] arrayname;

Please understand that after declaring a 2D array, it must be created using *new operator*. For example,

int a[ ] [ ];

a = new int [5] [10]; //create an array of size (5 * 10)

This can be written as one statement also:

int a[ ] [ ] = new int [5] [10];

Also note that when you allocate memory for a multidimensional array, you need only to specify the memory for the first (leftmost) dimension. For example,

int a[ ] [ ] = new int [5] [10]; is equivalent to the following statements:

```
int a[ ] [ ] = new int [5] [ ];
    a[0] = new int[10];
    a[1] = new int[10];
    a[2] = new int[10];
```

This type of allocation is required when you do not need to allocate same number of elements for each dimension. So, the length of each dimension is under the programmer's control.

Syntax for regular 2D array:

```
dataType [ ] [ ] arrayName = new dataType[M] [N] {
                        {val11, val12, ...., val1N},
                        {val21, val22,....., val2N},
                        ..............
                       {valM1, valM2,.....valMN}
                   };
```

Where,

dataType: is any valid data type.

arrayName: is the name of the array.

M: is the row size of the array.

N: is the column size of the array.

val11,......,valMN: are initializers/ values of array elements.

The following points are worth mentioning here:

1. The expression [M] [N] is evaluated from left to right.
2. Each array index must start from 0 (zero).
3. The array size may be omitted in its initialization.
4. The number of rows and the number of elements in each row are counted from the initializers to fix the row size and column size respectively.
5. 2D arrays follow the same rule as 1D arrays do.
6. Here also the problems like array index out of bound, confusion of array elements and its subscripts may occur.
7. Arrays can contain arrays.

We are in a position to answer some questions now.

Example 1: Write a Java program that reads the elements of a 2D array and then echoes them.
Solution:

```
import java.util.*;
public class two-d-Array {
    public static void main(String [ ] aa)  {
      int i, j, m, n, a[ ] [ ];
    Scanner keyboard=new Scanner(System.in);
    System.out.printf("Enter number of rows
                               and columns:\n");
    m = keyboard.nextInt( );
```

```
            n = keyboard.nextInt( );
            a = new int[m] [n];   //allocating memory
            //reading the 2D array
            for(i = 0; i < m; i++)  {
                for(j =0; j < n; j++)  {
                    System.out.printf("Enter the next
                                        element\n");
                    a[i][ j] = keyboard.nextInt( );
                    }
                  }
            // echoing the array now

            for(i = 0; i < m; i++)   {
                for(j =0; j < n; j++)   {
                    System.out.printf("array
                        elements " + a[i][j]);
                        }
                    }
        }
```

Simulations: Let us see how a (2 * 3) i.e., m=2 and n=3 matrix is read into a 2d array. That is, the given data is stored in the given array as follows:

2	2	2
3	3	3

Let us simulate the working of the program now.

m	n	i	j	a[i][j]	Comments
2	3				
		0	0	2	Say, user enters 2 that is stored in a[0][0].
			1	2	Say, user enters 2 that is stored in a[0][1].
			2	2	Say, user enters 2 that is stored in a[0][2].
			3		Comes out of the inner for loop. Thus, till this point, 1st row is read.
		1	0	3	Say, user enters 3 that is stored in a[1][0].
			1	3	Say, user enters 2 that is stored in a[1][1].
			2	3	Say, user enters 3 that is stored in a[1][2].
			3		Comes out of the inner for loop. Thus, till this point 2nd row is read.
		2			Comes out of the outer for loop. By now all elements of matrix of size m *n are read.

Please understand that we can print and manipulate the data of any 2d-array by traversing row-by-row and in each row column-by-column fashion. Also understand here that we can also do the opposite traversals of this array.

Example 2: Write a JAVA program which reads n student marks in 5 tests into a 2d array such that one row contains one student marks in 5 tests. Also calculate the mean of each test and covariance matrix for the student data. It is given that, if the data matrix, a, is (n * d) then the mean vector is calculated as follows:

Mean[j] = 1/n Σ a[i][j], I =0 to n, j = 0, ...d–1

And the covariance matrix is d * d matrix with diagonal matrix as variances and off-diagonal elements as co-variances. The diagonal elements are positive values as they are variances,

COV[i][j] = 1/n Σ a[k][i] – Mean[i])*(a[k][j] – Mean[j], i, j= 0,....d-1; k =0 to n.

Solution:

```
import java.util. *;
public class meancovariance {
    public static void main(String [ ] aa) {
        int i, j, k, l, n, a[ ] [ ];
        Scanner keyboard = new Scanner (System.in);
        System.out.printf("Enter number of students\n");
        n = keyboard.nextInt ( );
        a=new int[n] [5];     //allocate memory
        //read 2d array first
        System.out.printf("Enter student marks\n");
        for (i =0; i < n; i++) {
          for (j=0; j < 5; j++) {
              a[i] [j] = keyboard.nextInt( );
              }
          }
    //allocate memory for mean and covariance matrices
        float [ ] MEAN= new float[5];
        float [ ] [ ] COV=new float [5][5];
        System.out.printf("Mean vector\n");
        for (i =0; i <5; i++) {
           MEAN[i] = 0;
           for (j=0; j<n; j++)
              MEAN[i] += a[j][i];
              MEAN[i] /=n;
           System.out.printf ("\nCovariance Matrix\n");
           for (i = 0; i < 5; i++) {
              for (j = 0; j < 5; j++)  {
                  COV[i][j] =0;
                  for (k = 0; k < n; k++)
```

```
                    COV[i][j] += (a[k][i] -
                MEAN[i]) * (a[k][j] - MEAN[j]);
                COV[i][j] /=n;
                System.out.printf("%f\t", COV[i][j]);
                }
            }
        }
```

OUTPUTS (after running):

Please run yourself!!

Example 3: Write a JAVA program that prints out all powers of 2 to the 30th power. Store your results in an array. The nth element of the array should store 2^n.

Solution:

```
public class power_of_two {
     public static int[ ] powers ( ) {
          int [ ] P = new int[31];
          int ax=1;   //accumulator
          int i = 0;
          int j =0;
          while (i <P . length)  {
               P[i] = ax;
               System.out.println(ax);
               ax <<=1; //bitwise left shifting by 1
                           //doubles the value.
               i++;
               }
               return P;
          }
     public static void main(String[ ] a) {
          int [ ] val = powers ( );
          }
     }
```

Students must run this program and check the results.

Example 4: Write a Java main program that generates random numbers and stores them in a 2D array.

Solution:

```
import java.util.*;
public class random_numbers {
    public static void main(String args[ ] ) {
        Random rand = new Random ( );
      int arr[ ] = new int[Math.abs(rand.nextInt ()) % 100];
      for(int i=0; i < arr.length; i++)
```

```
                arr[i] = Math.abs(rand.nextInt ( )) % 100;
            }
        }
```

Example 5: Write a JAVA program to sum the rows of a 2D array.

[Hints:

```
int [ ] [ ] numb = { {1,  2,   3,   4   },
                     {5,  6,   7,   8   },
                     {9,  10,  11,  12  } } ;
int total;
for( int row = 0; row < numb.length; row++)
 {
    //set accumulator to 0.
    total = 0;

    //sum a row
    for(int col = 0; col < numb[row].length; col++)
        total += numb[row][col];

    //displaying rows total
            System.out.println("Total of row" + row + "is" + total);
 }
```

Please note here that the *total* variable is being used as an accumulator that is initialized to 0 just before the inner loop executes. This is so because the inner loop sums the elements of a row and stores the sum in *total*. So, this *total* variable must be set to zero, before each iteration of the inner loop.

Now, try this for summing the columns of a 2d array].

Example 6: How do you pass 2d arrays to methods? Give an example to explain.

Solution: When a 2d array is passed to a method, the parameter must be declared as a reference to a 2d array. Any 2d int array can be passed as an argument to the method. For example,

```
public class param_pass
 {
    public static void main (String[ ] args)
     {
        int [ ] [ ] numb = { { 1, 2, 3, 4 },
                             { 5, 6, 7, 8 },
                             {9, 10, 11, 12 } };
    System.out.println("The elements of the array are :");
        showArray(numb);
    System.out.println("Sum of the value is:"
             + arraySum(numbers));
}
```

```
    private static void showArray(int [ ] [ ] array)
    {
        for ( int row = 0; row < array.length; row++)
        {
            for(int col = 0; col < array[row].length; col++)
                System.out.print(array[row] [col] + " ");
            System.out.println ( );
        }
    }

    private static int arraySum(int [ ] [ ] array)
    {
        int total = 0;
        for(int row =0; row < array.length; row++)
        {
            for (int col=0; col < array[row].length; col++)
                total += array[row][col];
        }
        return total;
    }
}
```

Example 7: Discuss some of the Random class's methods.

Solution: JAVA API has a Random class that is used to generate random numbers. This class uses an algorithm to generate a sequence of random numbers that are very useful when we write programs for game simulations. The following are some of the Random's class methods:

Method	Meaning
nextDouble ( )	Returns the next random number as a double. Number will be in the range of 0.0 and 1.0.
nextFloat ( )	Returns the next random number as a float. Number will be in the range of 0.0 and 1.0.
nextInt ( )	Returns the next random number as an int. Number will be in the range of an int.
nextInt(int n)	This method accepts an integer argument as n. it returns a random number as an int. Number will be within the range of 0 and n.
nextLong ( )	Returns the next random number as an long. Number will be in the range of an int.

Also note that this class is part of the java.util package. Thus, in a program that uses this class, we must include the following statement:

```
import java.util.Random;
```

Example 8: Is there any limit on the dimensions array?

Solution: There is no limit to the number of dimensions an array can have. We can also declare 3d, 4d and higher dimensional arrays. But it would be better to instead use an array of objects with each object containing an array.

Example 9: Write a JAVA program to find the transpose of a given matrix.

Solution:

```
import java.util.Scanner;
class transpose
    {
        public static void main(String args[ ] )
         {
            int i, j, t, r, c;
            Scanner s1 = new Scanner(System.in);
          System.out.println("Enter number of rows:");
            r = s1.nextInt( );
          System.out.println("Enter number of cols::");
            c = s1.nextInt( );
            //put elements into the array
          System.out.println("\nEnter array elements:");
            int a[ ] [ ] =new int[r][c];
            int b[ ] [ ] =new int[c][r];
            for(i=0; i<r; i++)
              for(j=0;j<c;j++)
                  a[i][j] =s1.nextInt( );
          System.out.println("Elements of array are:\n");
            for(i=0; i<r; i++)
              {
                  System.out.print("\n");
                      for(j=0; j<c; j++)
                        {
                  System.out.print(a[i][j]+"\t");
            }
        }
   for (i=0; i<r; i++)
    {
       for (j=0; j<c; j++)
       {
          b[i][j] = a[i][j];
       }
   System.out.println("\nAfter transposing:");
   for (i = 0; i < c; i++)
       {
```

```
System.out.print("\n");
for(j=0; j<r; j++)
  {
  System.out.print(b[i][j] + "\t");
  }
 }
}
}
```

OUTPUT (after running):

Enter number of rows:

3

Enter number of columns:

3

Enter array elements:

1

2

3

4

5

6

7

8

9

Elements of array are:

1 2 3

4 5 8

7 8 9

After transposing:

1 4 7

2 5 8

3 6 9

Example 10: Write a JAVA program to multiply two matrices using the concept of anonymous array. *[GGSIPU, B. Tech(CSE/IT)-5th semester, 2nd term., Oct. 2010]*

Solution:

```
Class Matrix_Multiply {
    public static void main(String [ ] args) {
    int array [ ] [ ] = {{5,6,7}, {4,8,9}};
    int array1[ ] [ ] = {{6,4},{5,7}, {1,1}};
    int array2[ ] [ ] = new int[3][3];
    int x=array.length;
    System.out.println("Matrix 1:");
    for(int i = 0; i < x; i++) {
    for(int j=0; j<=x; j++) {
    System.out.print(" " + array[i][j]);
    }
    System.out.println( );
    }
    int y=array1.length;
    System.out.println("Matrix 2:");
    for(int i = 0; i < y; i++) {
    for(int j=0; j< y-1; j++) {
    System.out.print(" " + array[i][j]);
    }
    System.out.println ( );
    }
    for(int i = 0; i < x; i++) {
    for(int j=0; j<y-1; j++) {
    for(int k=0; k<y; k++) {.
    array2[i][j] += array[i][k] * array1[k][j];
      }
     }
    }
    System.out.println("Multiplication of matrices:");
    for(int i=0; i <x; i++) {
    for( int j=0; j<y-1; j++) {
       System.out.print(" " +array2[i][j]);
    }
    System.out.println ( );
    }
     }
}
```

There is no limit to the number of dimensions an array can have. We can also declare 3d, 4d and higher dimensional arrays. But it would be better to instead use an array of objects with each object containing an array.

2.13 STRINGS

A string is commonly considered as a sequence of characters stored in memory. String literals are specified using double quotes as follows:

"Rajiv is a prolific author"

"God is Great!!!"

Java implements strings using the String class and StringBuffer class. *Please remember that both of these two string classes are declared as final and defined in the java.lang package.*

The String class supports strings that are immutable. That is, we can use the String class when you are working with strings that cannot change. On the other hand, StringBuffer is used when you want to manipulate the contents of the string. *Also understand that when you add two String objects together, a third object is created.* For example,

```
String msg = "Rajiv";

msg += " is an author.";
```

Here, the original String "Rajiv" is not changed. Instead, a new String is created with the value "Rajiv is an author." And is assigned to the variable msg.

String objects can be created by using the **new** keyword or by using a literal. For example,

```
String str = new String("Rajiv");
```

Or

```
String str = "Rajiv";
```

Please note that if you construct two Strings using the same String literal without the new keyword then only one String object is created. For example,

```
String str1 = "Rajiv";

String str2 = "Chopra";
```

Also note here that both str1 and str2 point to the same String object in memory. As explained earlier also, String objects are immutable. Thus, if we attempt to modify str1, a new modified String is created. However, the original String referred to by str2 remains unchanged.

Note:

1. The StringBuffer object allows strings to be concatenated without creating a new object.
2. StringBuffer objects are mutable which means their contents can be changed. For example,

```
StringBuffer str1 = new StringBuffer("12345");
str1.append("6789");   //now str1 contains "123456789"
```

Just observe that how this differs from the String object:

```
String str2 = new String("12345");
str2.concat("6789");    //now str2 contains "12345"
```

Let us now discuss the String Class methods. They are as follows:

Table 3.17: String Class Methods

Methods	Meanings
str1.length ( );	Returns the number of characters contained in String str1.
str1.CharAt(n);	Returns nth character of string str1
str1.indexOf('x');	Returns position of first occurrence of 'x' in the string str1.
str1.indexOf('x', n);	Returns the position of 'x' after nth position in the string str1.
str2 = str1.toLowerCase ( );	Converts the String str1 to all lowercase.
str2 = str1.toUpperCase ( );	Converts the String str1 to all uppercase.
str2 = str1.replace('x', 'y');	Replaces all occurrences of 'x' with 'y' in String str1.
str2 = str1.trim ( );	Removes the leading and trailing blank spaces in String str1.
str1.equals(str2);	Returns true if str1 is equal to str2
str1.equalsIgnoreCase(str2);	Returns true if str1 is equal to str2, ignores the case of characters.
str1.concat(str2);	Returns concatenated string of str1 and str2.
str1.substring(n);	Returns the substring starting from the nth character.
str1.substring(n, m);	Returns the substring starting from nth character upto mth character (not included mth character).
str1.compareTo(str2);	Returns negative if str1<str2, positive if str1>str2 and zero if str1=str2.
String.valueOf(p);	Returns a String object of the parameter p (simple type or object).
String.valueOf(var);	Returns a String object of the variable 'var.
p.toString( );	Returns a string representation of the object 'p'.

Let us put it in a nutshell now:

1. In Java, strings are sequences of Unicode characters.
2. A predefined class called as ***String*** is provided in the standard Java library.
3. Java implements strings as objects of type ***String.***
4. Each string constant is also treated as an instance of String class.
5. A ***String*** variable reference can also be made to refer to some other ***String*** object.
6. As studied that strings are constants. So, their values (contents) cannot be modified after they are created.
7. Please understand that the technique of using fixed (non-mutable) strings enables the implementation of JVM to be more efficient (in terms of memory requirements).
8. Both the string and Stringbuffer classes are defined in java.lang package. They are available to all programs automatically.

9. Both are declared ***final.*** This means that none of these classes can be inherited now.
10. Java supports 3 classes for string manipulations, namely:
    (a) **String** class: It generates immutable strings.
    (b) **StringBuffer** class: It creates flexible strings.
    (c) **StringTokenizer:** It is used for extracting tokens i.e., atomic units, from the strings.

We are in a position to solve some questions now.

Example 1: Write a Java program to show the usage of the String functions.

Solution:

```
class Str_func
 {
  public static void main(String args[ ] )
     {
       String str1 = "God is great";
  System.out.println("Length of string=" + str1.length ( ));
  System.out.println("Equivalent Uppercase is=" +
                                        str1.toUppercase( ));
  System.out.println("Equivalent Lowercase is=" +
                                        str1.toLowerCase ( ));
  System.out.println("Character at 5th position="
                                        +str1.charAt(4));
  System.out.println("Index of element 'g'
                                        is="+str1.charAt(4));

  System.out.println("Substring from 4 to 5 ="
                                   +str1.substring(4,8));
      String str2 = "rajiv";
      String str3 = "RAJIV";
    if (str2.equals(str3))
      System.out.println("Both strings are equal");
    else
      System.out.println("Both strings are not equal");
    if (str2.equalsIgnoreCase(str3))
      System.out.println("Both strings are equal");
   else
      System.out.println("Both strings are not equal");
      }
    }
```

OUTPUTS (after running):

Length of string = 12

Equivalent Uppercase = GOD IS GREAT

Equivalent Lowercase = god is great

Character at 5th position = i

Index of element 'g' is = 8

Substring from 4 to 8 = is

Both strings are not equal

Both strings are equal.

From this program it is clear that String type is a class the results that are returned by these functions are stored in a variable, displayed or may be used in computations also the String class allows you to create objects for holding strings. It has various methods that allow a programmer to work with strings.

Example 2: What is the general form of the method call (of any class inbuilt in Java)?

Solution: The general form of any method call is:

variable.method(arguments...)

where ***variable*** is the name of a variable that references an object, ***method*** is the name of the method and arguments is 0 or more arguments that are passed to the method. **Please remember that if no arguments are passed to the method then a set of empty parentheses must follow the name of the method.**

Example 3: Can we convert strings to numbers also?

Solution: Yes, we can do so by using some methods as follows:

Method	Purpose	Examples
Byte.parseByte	Converts a string to a byte.	byte num;num = Byte.parseByte(str);
Double.parseDouble	Converts a string to a double.	double num;num = Double.parseDouble(str);
Float.parseFloat	Converts a string to a float	float num;num = Float.parseFloat(str);
Integer.parseInt	Converts a string to an int.	int num;num = Long.parseLong(str);
Short.parseShort	Converts a string to a short.	short num;num= Short.parseShort(str);

These methods are the part of Java's wrapper class.

Example 4: Write java programs to do the following on strings:-

(a) To Concatenate two strings.

(b) To show usage of equals () method and == operator.

(c) To check if the given string is a palindrome or not.

(d) To convert string to a character array.

Solution:

(a) It is possible to merge two or more strings to create a single long string. **This process of**

appending more than one string is known as concatenation of strings. This is done by using the + operator. **Please note that it is also possible to do this same operation by using the concat( ) method.** The following program solves part-a:

```
class Concat {
      public static void main(String args[ ] )  {
            String fname = "Rajiv ";
            String lname = "Chopra: an author of 21 books." ;
            System.out.println("Name:" + fname + lname);
            System.out.println( fname.concat(lname) );
            }
      }
```

OUTPUTS (after running):

Name: Rajiv Chopra: an author of 20 books.

Rajiv Chopra: an author of 20 books.

(b) Please understand that the equals ( ) method and the == operator perform two different operations. The equals ( ) method compares the character contents of the ***String*** object. **The = = operator compares two object references.** Let us write its program now:

```
Class Equals {
      public static void main(String args[ ] ) {
            String book1 = "OOP";
            String book2 = new String(" Using Java");
            String book3 = book2.intern ( );
System.out.println("book1 = = book2 " + (book1 = = book2));
System.out.println("book1 = = book3 " + (book1 = = book3));
System.out.println("book1.equals(book2) " + (book1.equals(book2));
System.out.println("book1.equals(book3) " + (book1.equals(book3));
            }
      }
```

OUTPUTS (after running):

book1 = = book2	false
book1 = = book3	true
book1.equals(book2)	true
book1.equals(book3)	true

(c)
```
class  Palindrome_check  {
      public static void main(String args[ ] ) {
         String actual  =  "TOOT" ;
         String reverse = new StringBuffer(actual) .reverse ( ).toString ( );
            if (reverse.equals(actual))
```

```
                System.out.println("Actual string:" + actual + "is a
                                                           palindrome");
            else
                System.out.println("Actual string:" + actual+ "is NOT a
                                                           palindrome");
            }
    }
```

OUTPUTS (after running):

Actual string : TOOT is a palindrome.

(d)
```
public class Convert_String_To_Array {
    public static void main(String [ ] args) {
        String lang = " Java";
        Char[ ] oop= lang.toCharArray ( );
        System.out.printf("The given string is %s\n", lang);
        System.out.printf("The converted array of characters:\n");
        for(int i=0; i < oop.length; i++) {
          system.out.print(oop[i]);
          }
        }
    }
```

OUTPUT (after running):

The given string is Java

The converted array of characters:

Java

Let us now discuss the StringBuffer class.

StringBuffer class

It implements a flexible set of character sequence i.e. at any particular instant of time, it contains some particular sequence of characters. But the advantages here is that the length and the content of the sequences can be changed through the methods. *Please understand that it implies that the StringBuffer objects are mutable* i.e., the length of storage buffer can be changed after its creation. On the other hand, the standard *String* objects are immutable (that cannot be changed). *Also note that this means that methods are synchronized whenever each of the individual threads are involved.*

NOTE: The existing implementation of the + (concatenation operator) is based on the Stringbuffer class only.

There are two important operations provided here:

1. append ( ) method: This method always adds the specified characters at the end of the string buffer.
2. insert ( ) method: It adds the given characters at a specified position.

The append ( ) method returns a reference to the StringBuffer instance that actually contains the string added. **Please note that since a reference to the updated StringBuffer instance is returned it is possible to concatenate multiple strings by chaining the calls. That is,**

obj = obj.append("R").append("A").append("J").append("I").append("V");

this will return RAJIV as the output.

Some more methods as supported by this StringBuffer class are as follows:

Method	Its usage (purpose)
public int length ( );	Returns the length of the buffer.
public synchronized void setChatAt(int index, char ch)	Replaces the character at the specified position.
S1.setLength(int n);	Truncates or extends the buffer.
public StringBuffer append(String str);	Appends the string to this string buffer.
public StringBuffer append(int i);	Appends the string representation of the int argument to this string buffer.

NOTE: Similarly, the append of other data items (like float, char etc.) is also supported by this class.

Not only this, this particular class also supports three constructors (a function with the same name as that of a class) as follows:-

1. **Stringbuffer ( )** — It creates an empty string buffer and reserves memory for 16 characters.
2. **Stringbuffer(int length);** — It creates an empty string buffer with an initial capacity of the length given as argument.
3. **StringBuffer(String str)** — It creates a string buffer with 16 plus the length of the argument string.

We will study constructors in details a bit later.

Before we discuss further, let us solve some questions on strings now.

Example 1: Write a simple Java program to sort an array of strings using bubble sort technique.

Solution:

```
public class bubble_sort_strings {
      static String name[ ] ={"RAJIV", "AJAY", "GEETIKA", "AMAN" };
      public static void main(String [ ] args)   {
            int n=name.length;    //length member of any array
```

```
                //object returns number of elements of it.
                for(int i=0; i <n; i++) {
                  for(int j=i+1; j<n; j++) {
                     if(name[j].compareTo(name[i] < 0) {
                          String temp = name[i];
                          name[i] = name[j];
                          name[j]=temp;
                          }
                     }
                for(int i=0; i<n; i++) {
                   system.out.println(name[i]);
                }
           }
```

OUTPUTS (after running):

AJAY

AMAN

GEETIKA

RAJIV

Example 2: What are vectors? How are they created?

Solution: Vectors are better data structures than arrays as they expand automatically when new data is added to them. They can hold only Objects and not primitive types like int. To put it in a vector, we put it inside an object (like to save an integer value use the Integer class) or you can define your own class. **Please understand that we have to convert simple data types to objects.** This can be done using the wrapped classes.

How to create them? We must first of all import either java.util.vector; or import java.util.*; Also understand that vectors are implemented with an array and that when that array is full then to add an additional element, a new array must be allocated. This takes time. To save this time, we can also create a vector with a size that it will commonly be, when full. This is how it is done:

Vector v = new Vector ( ); //creates a vector with default initial size

Vector v = new Vector(100); //creates a vector with an initial size 100.

Example 3: Write a Java program to read a string from the keyboard and to determine whether it is a palindrome or not? *[GGSIPU, B. Tech.(CSE/IT)-5th sem. Dec. 2011]*

Solution: Let us write its algorithm first:

Step-1: Read string, *str.*

Step-2: Set *size* = str.length ( );

Step-3: Create a byte array reference b[ ].

Step-4: b [ ] = *str*.getbytes ( );

Step-5: Create a byte array b1[ ] of size, *size.*

Step-6: Initialize i=size -1;

Step-7: Repeat through step-10 while (i>=0).

Step-8: set x= size- (i+1);

Step-9: b1[x] = b[i];

Step-10: i=i-1;

Step-11: set count=0

Step-12: reset i=0

Step-13: Repeat through step-15 while (i < size).

Step-14: if(b1[i] == b[i]) then count = count +1.

Step-15: i=i+1;

Step-16: if count==size then print "String given is a palindrome".
else print "string is not a palindrome".

Step-17: Stop and exit.

And here goes the program:-

```
import java.util.Scanner;
public class palin
    {
        public static int count=0;
        public static void main(String args[ ] )
            {
                Scanner s= new Scanner(System.in);
                System.out.println("Enter the string");
                String str= s.nextLine( );
                int size=str.length( );
                byte b[ ] =str.getBytes( );
                byte b1[ ] = new byte[size];
               for(int i=size – 1; i >=0; i- - )
                 {
                    int x=size-(i +1);
                      b1[x] = b[i];
                 }
               for(int i=0; i<size; i+ +)
                 {
                   if (b1[i] = = b[i])
                      {
```

```
                    count ++;
                }
            }
        if (count = = size)
         {
            System.out.println(str+ " is a palindrome.");
        }
        else {
            System.out.println(str+" is not a palindrome.");
            }
        }
    }
```

Example 4: Write a Java program to read a string from the keyboard and to check how many vowels and consonants are present in that string.

Solution:

```
import java.util.*;
public class vowels
    {
        String input;
        Char ch;
        void stringout ( )
         {
            System.out.println("Enter a string of characters:");
            Scanner s=new Scanner(System.in);
            input=s.nextLine( );
            int vowel=0, consonant=0;
            int length = input.length ( );
            char [ ] chinput=input.toCharArray( );
            for (int i=0; i < length; i++)
              {
                if (chinput[i] = = 'a') || (chinput[i]= = 'e') ||
(chinput[i]= = 'i') || (chinput[i]= = 'o') || (chinput[i]= = 'u') ||
(chinput[i]= = 'A') || (chinput[i]= = 'E') || (chinput[i]= = 'I') ||
(chinput[i]= = 'O') || (chinput[i]= = 'U')) {
                vowel + +;
            }
            else {
                consonant++;
                }
            }
```

```
        System.out.println(input.length( ));
        System.out.println("vowels:" + vowel);
        System.out.println("Consonants:" + consonant);
        }
        public static void main(String a[ ] )
          {
              vowels ss= new vowels ( );
                    ss.stringout( );
          }
        }
```

Example 5: Write a Java program to reverse a string.

[GGSIPU, B. Tech.(CSE/IT)-5th sem. Oct. 2010]

Solution:

```
public class reverse {
        static void reverse( )
         {
             String a =" Rajiv Chopra";
             System.out.println("\nOriginal string: " +a);
             StringBuffer b = new StringBuffer(a).reverse ( );
             System.out.println("Reverse character string is: " +b);
             System.out.println("\n");
        }

public static void main(String[ ] args)
   {
       reverse ( );
   }
}
```

Example 6: In "PigLatin", a word such as KING is replaced by INGKAY and TROUBLE is replaced by OUBLETRAY and so on. The first vowel of the original word becomes the start of the translation, any proceeding letters being shifted towards the end and followed by AY words that begin with vowels are left unchanged. Write a Java program to translate the word in piglatin.

Solution:

```
import java.io.*;
public class PigLatin
{
       public static void main(String [ ] args) throws IOException
          {
              System.out.println("Enter a name:");
BufferedReader br = new Bufferedreader(new InputStreamreader(System.in));
String input = br.readLine( );
```

```
System.out.println(input);
char[ ] chinput = input.toCharArray( );
for (int i= 0; i <chinput.length; i++)
    {
if (chinput[i] = = 'a') || (chinput[i]= = 'e') || (chinput[i]= = 'i') ||
                                (chinput[i]= = 'o') || (chinput[i]= = 'u')
      {
          String ss = input.substring(i).toUpperCase( ) + input.substring(0,
                                                     i).toUpperCase( ) + "AY";
          System.out.println(ss);
          break;
        }
      }
   }
}
```

OUTPUT (after running):

Enter a name

sai

sai

AISAY

Example 7: Write a Java program to read a string from the keyboard and to do the following operations:

(a) Extract the middle character of the string.

(b) Check whether the string entered from keyboard is a palindrome or NOT.

(c) Counting the number of vowels in the string.

(d) Counting the total number of characters in this string?

Solution:

```
import java.io.*;
public class string
 {
     public static void main(String args[ ]) throws IOException
        {
          BufferedReader br= new BufferedReader(new
                                  InputStreamReader(System.in));
          System.out.print("\nEnter your string:");
          String s = br.readLine( );
          int l=s.length( );
System.out.println("\n extracting middle character from this string....");
     if (l % 2 ==0)
      {
          int m1=l/2-1
```

```
        int m2=m1 +1;
        System.out.println("\nThe mid characters are....."
                              +s.charAt(m1)+ "and "+s.charAt(m2));););
    }
    else
     {
        int m = l/2;
      System.out.println("\nthe mid character is: " +s.charAt(m));
    }
    int t=0,i,j=1;
    for(i=0; i< l; i++)
     {
        if(s.charAt(i) = = s.charAt(j -1))
         {
             j - - ;
         }
         else
          {
             t=1;
         }
     }
System.out.println("\n\t\t******");
System.out.println("\nChecking whether the enètered string is a palindrome
                                                              or NOT?");

    if( t= = 0)
     {
        System.out.println("\nIt is a palindrome");
    }
    else
     {
        System.out.println("\n It is NOT a Palindrome");
   }
    int c=0;
    for(i =0; i <1; i++)
      {
        if(s.charAt(i) = = 'A' || s.charAt(i) = = 'a' || s.charAt(i) =='E'
|| s.charAt(i) = = 'e' || s.charAt(i) = ='I' || s.charAt(i) = = 'i' ||
s.charAt(i) = = 'O' || s.charAt(i) = = 'o' || s.charAt(i) = = 'U' ||
s.charAt(i) = = 'u' )
     {
         c++;
     }
   }
 System.out.println(\n\t\t********");
```

```
System.out.println("Counting the number of vowels in the string….");
System.out.println(\nNumber of vowels in the given string is:" + c);
        c= 0;
        int k, z;
System.out.println("\n\t\t******");
System.out.println("\nTotal number of characters in the given string
are…");
    for (j= 0; j < l; j++)
      {
        z=0;
        if (j > 0)
          {
            for (k=j-1; k>=0; k–)
              {
                if (s.chatAt(j) = = s.charAt(k))
                  {
                    z =1;
                  }
          }
    }
if (z = =1)
  {
    continue;
  }
for (i =0; i < l; i++)
  {
    if(s.chatAt(j) = = s.charAt(i))
      {
        c++;
      }
  }
System.out.prinln(" " +s.charAt(j) +" is repeated" +c + "times");
    c=0;
    }
      }
  }
```

NOTE: The students re advised to run this program on their own.

The basic idea is very simple:

```
    for each character ch in the string {
        if (ch is a vowel) {
            increment the counter
        }
    }
```

Example 8: Write a Java program to count the number of words in a given string.

Solution:

```
import javax.swing.*;
class word_count {
    private static final char BLANK =' ';
    public static void main(String [ ] args) {
        int index, wordCount, no_of_characters;
String sentence = JOptionPane.showInputDialog(null, "Enter a sentence:");

    no_of_characters = sentence.length( );
    index =0;
    wordCount = 0;
while (index < no_of_characters ) {
    //ignore blank spaces
    while( index < no_of_characters && sentence.charAt(index) = =
                 BLANK) {
                 index++;
        }
    //locating the end of the word now
    while (index < no_of_characters && sentence.charAt(index)
                                         !=BLANK) {
            index ++;
        }
        //another word is found so increment the counter
        wordCount++;
        }
    //displaying the results now
System.out.println(Input sentence:" + sentence);
System.out.println("\n");
System.out.println("Word count: " + wordCount + "words");
    }
}
```

2.14 COMMAND-LINE ARGUMENTS

Command line arguments are used to receive information into a program when you run it. They are received to main ( ) method. A command line argument is the information that directly follows the programs name on the command line when it is executed. They are stored as strings in the String array passed to main( ). Inside the parentheses of the method header is the declaration of a parameter named ***args.*** This parameter is an array name. As its declaration indicates, it is used to reference an array of ***Strings.*** *Please note that the array being passed into the args parameter comes from the O.S. command-line.*

For example,

```
class command_line
 {
     public static void main(String args[ ] )
      {
          int i, length;
          length = args.length;
          for (int i=0; i< length; i ++)
           {
               System.out.println("Argument [" + (i+1) + "]"- "
                                              + args[i]);
           }
      }
 }
```

OUTPUTS (after running):

C:\javaprog\javac CommandLineDemo.java

C:\javaprog\javac CommandLineDemo Rajiv is a prolific author

Argument[1] = Rajiv

Argument[2] = is

Argument[3] = a

Argument[4] = prolific

Argument[5] = author

Also note that if you want to pass numeric values as command-line arguments to main ( ) then they are collected as strings first and then we have to convert them into numerical values.

From the program it is observed that any item types on the command-line that must be separated by spaces/blanks, after the class name are passed into the ***main method.*** Here, in this example five arguments are being passed into args[ ] array as shown in the output above. The for-loop in this program, just displays each argument.

In nutshell, arguments may be passed from the OS command-line into the main method of a Java program.

We can also display the length of arguments i.e. total number of arguments passed as follows:

System.out.println("Length of command-line arguments is=" + args.length);
for(String s : args)
System.out.println(s);

If these statements are also added to the above code then we get the following output:

Length of command-line argument is= 5

Rajiv is a prolific author

Thus, now the program iterates on the args array and displays it.

Summary

This chapter lays a complete foundation of how can you start to write good Java programs. It discusses about the program's anatomy—variables, literals, constants, strings and so on. Operator precedence and associativity form the part of this chapter. Also dealt in this chapter are the concepts of concatenation, coercion, arrays, and command-line arguments. Several programming examples have been solved for the student's convenience.

❑❑❑

Chapter 3

Java Classes

3.0 INTRODUCTION

The central core concept of any object-oriented programming language is the reusability of the code. It may be any object-oriented programming language but the need to encapsulate the data and the functions to be performed under one roof. A class is one such data structure that encapsulates both data members (data) and functions (called methods in Java) into a single unit. And this single unit is called as a **class.** Thus, class is used to define new data types. That is why classes are called as **user-defined data types**. We can even restrict the data access. We can build hierarchies of classes. *Please understand that classes help you to reuse data and code. Also understand that when you instantiate a class you create an object.* In nutshell, we can say that a class is a template for an object and an object is an instance of a class.

The class is at the **core** of Java. It is a logical construct upon which all Java language is built because it defines the shape and the nature of an object. Class is a template for an object and an object is an instance of the class. As an object is an instance of the class only so we can use the terms object and instance interchangeably. A class is the blueprint for an object and objects use methods to communicate between them. It specifies the attributes and methods that a particular type of object has. Almost all non-trivial programs will have many objects of the same type. We write instructions to create objects. A class, however, must be defined before you create an instance (object) of the class.

In languages like C, we have structures. Both are different. Let us see the differences between the two now.

Table 3.1: Structure v/s Class

Structure	Class
1. It is defined by using the keyword **struct**.	1. It is defined by using the keyword **class**.
2. It is available in C only.	2. It is available in all of the object-oriented programming languages like C++, JAVA2, C# etc.
3. By default, the data is public.	3. By default, the members (data and functions) are private.
4. The **variable** is used to access its members.	4. An **object** is used to access its members.

We shall be studying all these concepts and many more in this chapter.

3.1 OBJECTS AND CLASSES

The need is to map the real world entities to object-oriented programming languages. The concept is very simple.

Real world → has entities.

Abstraction → implemented by the properties of these entities and the operations to perform.

Properties are the data itself and operations are the functions in the programming language. Thus, there is a mapping of abstraction to a program.

The software structure that supports data abstraction is known as a class. A class is a data type capturing the essence of an abstraction. It is characterized by a number of features. A class is a prototype or a blueprint or a model that defines different features. A feature may be a data or an operation. Data are represented by instance variables or data variables in a class. *Please understand that the operations are also known as behaviors or methods (in Java) or member functions (in C++).*

For example, car represents a class and there are a number of instances of car. Each instance of car is an object. Also note that the class car does not physically mean a car. An object is also known as class variable because it is created by the class data type.

NOTE: Each object in an object-oriented system corresponds to a real world thing that may be a person, a product or an entity.

Let us now tabulate the differences between the two.

Table 3.2: Comparisons between a Class and on Object

Class	Object
1. Class is a data type.	1. Object is an instance of class data type.
2. It generates object.	2. It gives life to a class.
3. It is a prototype or model.	3. It is a container for stroing its features.
4. It does not occupy memory location.	4. It occupies memory location.
5. It cannot be manipulated because it is not available in the memory.	5. It can be manipulated.
6. It is the collection of similar types of object that has same attributes and methods.	6. It is the working instance of a class.
7. It is a logical entity that does not consume memory.	7. Being a processes entity it consumes some memory depending upon the data members.
8. **Example:** Student will be a class having enroll_no, sname, sage as its attributes or properties and marks( ), fees ( ) may be its methods.	8. **Example:** Student, car, bike may be its objects.

Please remember the following points here:

1. Instantiation of an object is defined as the process of creating an object of a particular class.
2. An object has—**states (or properties), operations and identity.**
3. **Properties** maintain the internal state of an object.
4. **Operations** provide an appropriate functionality to the object.
5. **Identity** distinguishes one object from the other.
6. **Object name** is used to identify the object.
7. **Object name** is itself an identity.
8. **The functions** control the properties of an object. They act and react to messages.
9. **The behavior** of an object depends on the properties.
10. **For example,** in a student marksheet, the result ( ) behavior depends on the data called marks. The property of resultStatus may be modified based on the marks.
11. A class is a way to bind the data describing an entity and its associated functions together in a single unit.
12. Space in memory is set up only when objects are defined in the main ( ) program and not during the class specification.
13. A class facilitates program's modifiability.
14. Assign values to the data members of an object and not to the class.

3.1.1 Declaring a Class

A class is declared by using the keyword—**class.** A class definition consists of two parts:-

(a) class header.

(b) class body.

The class header consists of the keyword **class** followed by the identifier, *classname.* The data members and methods are defined in the class body. In Java, curly or flower braces i.e { and } mark the beginning and the end of a class or a method. The syntax in general is as follows:-

Syntax:

```
class classname     → class header
{
     //data members
     ......                  → class body
     ......
     //methods ( )
}
```

Here, the *classname* is the name of the class and it is mandatory. The *classname* is used to refer to the class and to create the instances of the class. The class body consists of the class data members, class methods and the access specifiers of these class members (to be discussed a bit later). Please note that each class definition introduces a new data type. For example,

```
class Stud
  {
     //data members
     ….
     ….
     //methods
  }
```

Here, the ***Stud*** is a user-defined data type.

Rules and Conventions for naming Classes:

1. A class name must not be a keyword in Java.
2. A class name must begin with a letter, an underscore (_) or '$' symbol.
3. It must not contain embedded spaces or periods (.).
4. A class name can also contain characters from various alphabets like Greek, Japanese etc.
5. Begin class names with an uppercase letter.
6. The class body consists of fields, methods and constructors (to be studied later).

Fields or member data are the member variables of a class. They can be of any valid data type. They are declared as variables in the class body. *Please understand that the values of the fields can be read using a predefined method or the values may be initialized in the declaration itself.* The syntax is:

Syntax:

accessModifier dataType field1, field2,….,fieldN;

where, **dataType** is any valid data type (primitive or reference),

field1, field2,….,fieldN represent field variables names.

accessModifier [optional] (to be studied a bit later).

Field variable names atart with a lowercase letter. *Also understand that Camel-casing is done if the name has more than word.* Camel is a programming language. Camel casing is done when we have multiword names. In this method, *each word except the first one capitalizes its first letter.*

A method performs an operation required by the class. It is the actual interface to start the objects action. It may be used to read, manipulate or display the fields. The syntax is as follows:

Syntax:

```
accessModifier returnType methodName (dataType1 arg1, …,  dataTypeN argN) {
local variable declarations;   //optional
action statements;
}
```

Where, **returnType** is the data type of the value returned by the method.

methodName represents the name of the method.

(dataType1 arg1,..,dataTypeN argN) are the arguments separated by Commas,

accessModifier [optiona] (to be studied later)

A method declaration tells about what a method does, how its actions are performed and how it is used? It consists of a method header and its body. *Please note here that the method header should not end with a semicolon if the method body follows it.* The body of the method declaration is also called as a block. While the methodName and the argument list forms its signature. *Also note that this does not include thereturnType.*

A good programmer of Java should also use meaningful names for a methodName which reflects the actions performed by the method. For example, readData( ) may be used to read values of the fields. **A methodName is an identifier.**

NOTE: The naming convention is the same as that of the naming convention of a field.

Also note the following points from these concepts:

1. Arguments in the method declaration declare formal parameters.
2. 0, 1 or more parameters may be used.
3. Each parameter must be preceded by its data type.
4. More than one parameter declaration must be separated by commas.
5. Each parameter name has to be accompanied by the desired data type.
6. This may not be true for fields and local variables.
7. A ***returnType*** may be any valid data type or void.
8. If a method does not return a value, ***void*** is specified as the ***returnType*** in the method header.
9. It is optional to include an empty ***return*** statement in a method having void as its ***returnType.***
10. It is not possible to include a ***return*** statement to return a value from a method using **void** as its ***returnType***
11. When a class is defined, no data is stored or memory is allocated. Only when objects of a class are created (declared), memory is allocated.

3.1.2 Class Members

The class consists of two types of members as follows:-

I. MEMBER DATA.

II. METHODS.

Let us study them one by one now.

Member Data

The data or variables defined inside a class are called as **data members or instance variables**. Data members of a class are declared in the same way as we declare variables in C/C++. For declaraing a data member, the syntax is as follows:-

Syntax:

datatype varname;

Here, *varname* is the variable name of ***datatype***. The datatype can be any valid Java data type, either in-built or user-defined.

For example,

```
class Distance
  {
      int meter;
      float cms;
  }
```

Proper indentation is must here. But as Java is a free-from of language, so we can also define the above class as follows:

class Distance {int meter; float cms: }

Methods

The functions of a class are called as methods in Java. They are defined inside a class. They have been discussed earlier.

3.1.3 Method Overloading

Method overloading is used when we want to create several methods that perform closely related tasks.

For example, the following class Sample has a method that returns the absolute value of an integer, another method returns the absolute value of a float and a third that returns the absolute value of a double. These three methods perform the same essential operations and thus it is appropriate to use the same name for them. Java supports method overloading in which we create three methods with the same name. This is shown below:

```
class Sample
 {
     public int abs(int a)
      {
          if ( a < 0)
              a= -a;
          return a;
```

```
        }

        public float abs(float b)
         {
              if ( b < 0)
                   b= -b;
              return b;
        }

        public double abs(double c)
         {
              if ( c < 0)
                   c= -c;
              return c;
        }

    }
```

We have used three abs ( ) methods in this example. Now how will the compiler find out which one to execute out of these three similar named functions/methods. *Please understand here that the compiler at the time of compilation, resolves this problem depending upon the parameters passed. Also remember that overloading of methods is not done on the return type of the method.* That is, the following is illegal:

```
int add(int m, int n)
  {
     //......
   }

long add(int x, int y)   //incorrect
  {
     //....
   }
```

This shows that two functions differing only in their **return types cannot be overloaded. Either they should have different number of parameters or different data types.**

NOTE: Two or more methods in a class may have the same name as long as their parameter lists are different.

Before we discuss further, let us write some programs now.

Example 1: Write a Java program to compute the square of a number that may be an integer or a double. Read your number from the keyboard and display your results.

Solution:

```
// uses the concept of method overloading
public class MyMath
```

```
{
    public static int square(int number)
    {
        return number * number;
    }

    public static double square(double number)
    {
        return number * number;
    }
}

public class Overloading
{
    public static void main(String [ ] args)
    {
        int i;
        double d;

        System.out.println("\n\tEnter your integer number:");
        i = Keyboard.readInt( );
        System.out.println("The square of the number is:" +
                                        MyMath.square(i));

        System.out.println("\n\tEnter your double number:");
        d = Keyboard.readDouble( );
        System.out.println("The square of the number is:" +
                                        MyMath.square(d));

    }
}
```

OUTPUTS (after running):

Enter your integer number: 2

The square of the number is: 4

Enter your double number: 1.2

The square of the number is: 1.44

Explanation: Both of these methods accept an argument and return its square. **The process of matching a method call with the correct method is known as binding.** When an overloaded method is being called, Java uses the method's name and parameter list to determine which method to bind the call to. Here, when an int argument is passed to square, then the version of the method that has an int parameter is called. Same thing happens with double.

Example 2: Can we overload main ( ) method in Java? Give example.

[GGSIPU, B. Tech(CSE/IT), 5th sem., Oct. 2009]

Solution: Yes, we can overload main method in a Java class. But in order to run a class the JVM will look for **public static void main(String[ ] args) {..}** only. Else it will show an error i.e. the execution will start only in this method. **For example,**

```
public classMainExample {
    public static void main(String[ ] args) {
        MainExample me=new MainExample( );
        System.out.println("Test");
        main (4);
        System.out.println(me.main("Main method example)):
    }

public static void main(int k) {
System.out.println("test 3");
}

String main(String s) {
    return s;
}
}
```

OUTPUT:

Test

Test 3

Main method example

3.1.4 Creating an Object

An object is an instance of a class. An object is declared in the same way as we declare variables of basic data types such as int or float.

Syntax:

classname objectname;

Here, ***classname*** is the name of the class and ***objectname*** is the name of the object. *Please note that in Java an object does not reserve memory space when it is declared.* The declaration of an object simply tells the compiler that this variable can refer to an object of type *classname. Also note that memory is allocated to an object using new operator as follows:*

1st way: classname objectname;
objectname = new classname( );

2nd way: classname objectname= new classname( );

The new operator dynamically allocates memory to an object and returns a reference to it.

For example,

Line No. 1: Distance dobj; //declare reference to an object

Line No. 2: Dobj = new Distance ( ); //allocate memory to a Distance object

Line No. 1, will simply declare a reference ***dobj*** to an object of type Distance. **Also understand that at this stage, the value of *dobj*** is null. The null value indicates that it does not yet point to an actual object. The ***dobj*** points to an actual object of type Distance just after the following statement:

dobj = new Distance( );

Line no. 1 and line no. 2 means the following:

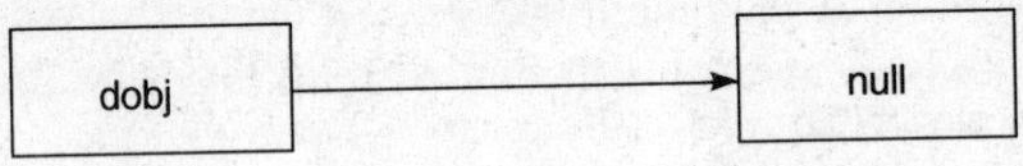

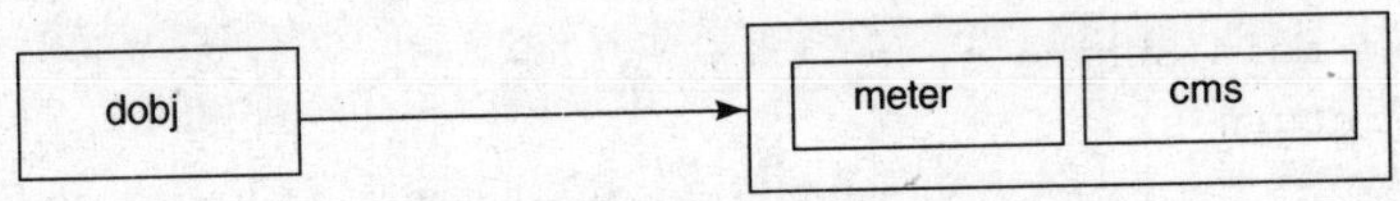

Please remember the following points regarding objects:

1. Objects are the physical instantiations of classes.
2. Objects are the variables of type class.
3. Many objects of different classes can be created, used and destroyed in the course of program's execution.
4. Declaring an object does not create an object.
5. You can declare an object with the same name.
6. Garbage collection is the heap of JVM. It is used to store all of the objects created by an executing Java program. Java's new operator creates objects. Memory for new objects is allocated on the *heap* at run time. Thus, *garbage collection is the process of automatically freeing objects that are no longer referenced by the program.* This frees up the programmer from the task of keeping track of when to free allocated memory. To see how garbage collection works let us see an example. Consider three (3) statements as follows:

   Line no. 1: Rectangle rectangle1;

   Line no. 2: rectangle1 = new Rectangle( );

   Line no. 3: rectangle1 = new Rectangle( );

For line no. 1, the picture of the memory is:

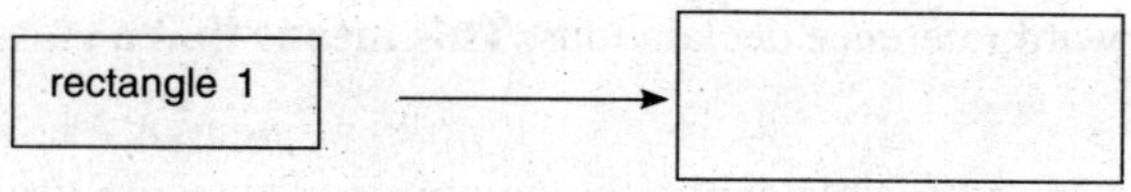

For line no. 2, the picture of memory is:

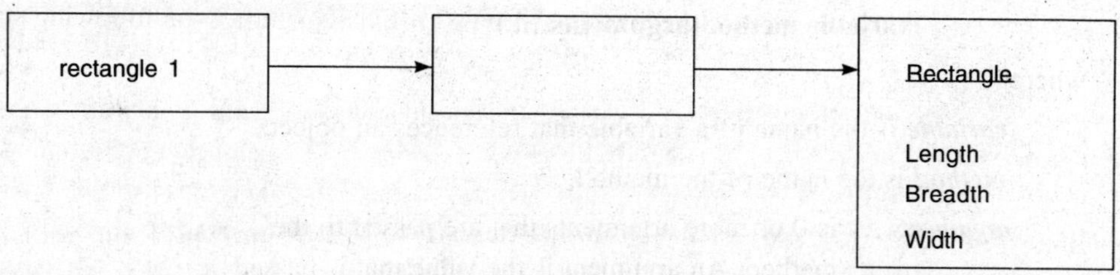

For line no. 3, the picture of memory is:

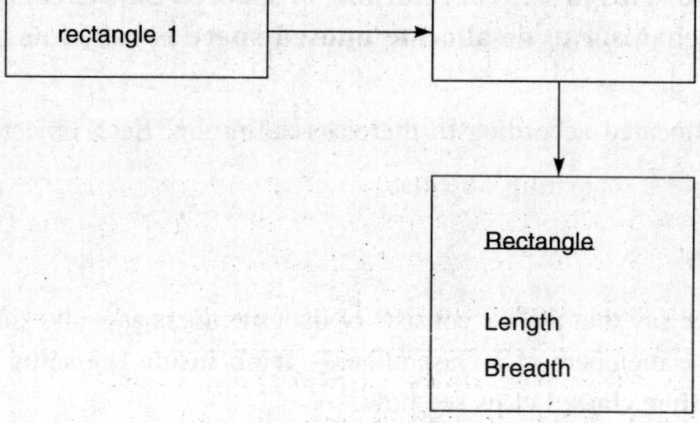

Now the garbage collected is:

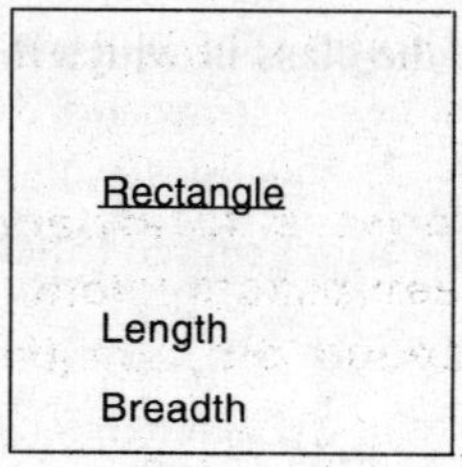

Please note here that the identifier rectangle1 is a reference to the object. When an object no longer has a reference it can no longer be accessed. Also understand that Java actually searches for such objects and destroys them. This process is known as garbage collection in Java.

7. Java does not allow forward reference declarations. **This means that a class must be declared before its use.**
8. The fields and methods are accessible explicitly via objects if they are declared as public else they are accessible only within their own classes (if they are declared as private).
9. The general form of a method call is as follows:

   variable.method(arguments.....)

   where,

   variable is the name of a variable that references an object,

   method is the name of the method,

   arguments... is 0 or more arguments that are passed to the method. An argument is the value that is passed into a method.

   This is called as the **sending of messages**.
10. Please remember that when an object is created, some amount of memory space is allocated for storing this object. If this allocated but unused space is not returned to the system for other uses, the space gets wasted. **This process of returning of space to the system is known as de-allocation and the mechanism to de-allocate unused space is called as garbage collection.**
11. For each object, memory is allocated according to the class definition. Each object gets its own set of variables.

3.1.5 Accessing Class Members

From the basic definition of a class, we say that a class consists of data members as well as methods. The principle is that we can access the members of a class either— **from inside the same class in which they are defined or from another class.** Let us see how?

Case 1: Accessing Data Members.

Case 2: Accessing Methods.

Case 1: Accessing Data Members

A data member can be accessed inside the class in which they are defined. **For example,**

```
class Distance
  {
      int meter;
      float cm;

      void setdata (int mm, float cc)
```

```
        //This method sets data members to 'mm' and 'cc' respectively.
        {
              meter = mm;
                cm = cc;
        }
   }
```

Please understand that a data member can be used in a different class by creating an object of that class and then referring to that data member using the dot '.' Operator. For example,

```
class Sample
 {
      Distance d;    // declaring an object of the Distance class

      void putdata( )
       {
             d = new Distnace( ); //allocating memory to an object.
             d.meter = 80;   //accessing data members of 'd'
             d.cm = 35.8f;
       }
 }
```

Case 2: Accessing Methods

A method can be accessed inside the class in which they are defined by using parentheses and a semicolon. *Also understand that one method of a class can invoke another method of the same class using the name of the method.* For example,

```
class Distance
 {
      int meter;
      float cm;

      void setdata(int mm, float cc)
       {
             meter = mm;
             cm = cc;
             increment( );    //calling increment( ) method from the
//same class.
       }

      void increment ( )
      {
            meter++;
            cm++;
      }
 }
```

Please note that a method can also be accessed from a different class by creating an object of that class and then invoking that method using the dot '.' Operator. For example,

```
class Sample
 {
    Distance d; // declaring an object of the Distance class

    void putdata( )
     {
        d=new Distance( ); //allocating memory to an object
        d=setdata(55, 45.7f);
     }
 }
```

Here, we have called **method setdata( )** of the class Distance from the class **Sample.**

But keep in mind that the fields and methods are accessible explicitly using objects only if they are declared as public else they are accessible only within their own classes, if they are declared private.

Also remember that in case of large Java programs, try to store your program of each class in a separate program file. Like it is a good programming practice to declare a separate class that contains the main( ) method.

Whenever we call a method of some object, we use dot notation. Just as we can call a method of another object, it is possible to call a method from a method of the same object. For example,

Class A

```
{
public void myMethod( ) {
    BClass obj =
        new BClass( );

    obj.doWork ( );
}
```

Class B

```
public void doWork( ) {
    .....
}
public void myMethod( ) {
    doWork( );
}
```

Please note here that dot notation is necessary when you are calling a method of another object. On the other hand, dot notation is optional when you are calling a method of the same object. **Also note that no dot notation is necessary when you call a method from another method of the same class.**

Any class can include the main method. For a program to be executable, the designated main class must include the main method. Other classes in the program may or may not include the main method. It is NOT relevant to the execution of the program. Methods may be user-defined methods or pre-defined methods. User-defined methods are defined by the coder who codes. The pre-defined methods are the inbuilt functions that almost all programming languages provide. They are also known as **dynamic link libraries** (DLLs). Another category is that methods may return a value or may not. Methods that return values are actually called as functions. For example, a method to find the factorial of a number must return the result, so it will be a function. While a method to clear the screen will not return any value from the method. Furthermore, a method may be recursive or non-recursive.

Recursion is the process in which a method calls itself again and again (to be studied a bit later). The methods discussed so far are instance methods except main ( ). They can be invoked only by instances of classes or objects. The instance methods are also known as **non-static methods**. The main ( ) method is an example of a static method. All pre-defined methods are static methods. Recursion is possible only with non-static methods. It is not possible with static methods as recursions in static method results in stack overflow.

Before we discuss further, let us write a simple program now.

Example 1: Write a Java program that creates a class as Student and stores his enrollment number as well as his name.

Solution:

```
class Student {
        int id_no;    // this class has 2 data members
        String name;

        //there are 3 methods in this class

        public void setEnroll_no (int my_id)
            {
            id_no = my_id;
            }

        public void setName (String my_name)
            {
              name = my_name;
            }

        public void disp_data( )
            {
            System.out.println("ID No.: " + id_no);
            System.out.println("Name:" + name);
            }
        //and hence the main program now

        public static void main(String [ ]  args)
            {
            Student s1;
            s1= new Student ( );
            Student s2 = new Student( );
            s1.id_no = 1;
            s1.name = "Rajiv";
            s1.disp_data( );
            s2.setID_no(2);
```

```
            s2.setName("Ajay");
            s2.disp_data( );
            }
      }
```

OUTPUTS (after running):

ID No: 1

Name: Rajiv

ID No.: 2

Name: Ajay

Explanation: There are some rules that are clear from this example, as follows:

1. A method can also invoke other methods defined in the same class directly or via objects of its own class.
2. Static methods cannot invoke non-static methods from its class directly. For example, *main* ( ) method cannot directly access methods such as *disp_data*( ) but it can access it by using references to objects like *s1.disp_data*( ).
3. The compiler does not allow the static methods to access member fields as they do not exist unless the object is created and to call other member methods, which can potentially access member data.

3.1.6 The main( ) Method

In Java program, there may be many classes and each class may have one or more methods. But *please remember that the method that the compiler executes first is the main( ) method*. The syntax is as follows:

Syntax:

```
public static void main(String args[ ])
 {
      //.....
}
```

Also note the following from the above syntax:

1. The main ( ) method is declared as public so that Java interpreter can access it.
2. The method does not return any value and hence it is declared as void.
3. The static modifier is used so that an instance of the class cannot be created to call the main ( ) method.
4. The primary name of the file in which the code is written and the name of the class that has the main ( ) method should be same. For example,

```
Class Demo_Class
      {
```

```
    public static void main(String args[ ] )
      {
      //....
    }

  }
```

Thus, the **name of this file must be** Demo_Class.java.

5. The order of the modifiers and access specifiers may be interchanged but the return type, void, must be specified immediately before the method name.
6. For example,

```
//stored in Demo_Class.java

class Distance
 {
    int meter;
    float cm;

    void set_data(int mm, float cc)
    {
      meter = mm;
      cm = cc;
    }

    void display( )
    {
      System.out.println(meter+ "  " + cm);
    }
 }

Class Demo_Class
 {
   public static void main(String args[ ] )
   {
      Distance d;
      d = new Distance(0);
      d.set_data(85, 95.5f);
      d.display( );
   }
}
```

OUTPUT (after running):

85   95.5

7. The class contains main( ) method to start the execution of the program. The main( ) method is mandatory for every Java program that you write.
8. A Java program may contain more than one class but only one class can contain main( ) method in a single program.
9. A single class may contain more than one method also.
10. The controlling class of every Java application must contain a main( ) method having one of the following signatures:

    public static void main(String [ ] args)

    or

    public static void main(String args[ ])
11. The main( ) method is declared as static because it must be called by the operating system when our program begins. Thus, it is called before any objects have been instantiated. We shall be studying this in detail a bit later.

3.1.7 Passing Arguments to a Method

Like other programming languages, Java programs can also pass arguments and do many other tasks. In the previous example program, we invoke set_data( ) method that receives two arguments—one int type and the other float type, of the class Distance from the class Class_Demo. **Please note that the method which calls a method is called as calling method and the method which is being called is called as a called method.** When we call a method, the calling method passes arguments to the called method. In Java, arguments are passed to a method in two ways:

(a) Call by Value.

(b) Call by Reference.

Let us discuss these one by one now.

I. CALL BY VALUE

In Java, all arguments of primitive data types are passed by value. It means that the value of the actual arguments cannot be altered by the called method. The called method receives the value of the actual arguments in the duplicate copies. The called method only manipulates the duplicate copies and *thus any changes made in the duplicate copies are not reflected back in the calling program* i.e., main method.

For example,

```
class ValuePass
{
    static void swap(int aa, int bb)  //called method
    {
        int t;                   //receives duplicate values
        t = aa;
        aa=bb;
```

```
            bb=t;
        }

public static void main(String args[ ] )    //calling method
  {
     int a, b;
     a= 60;
     b= 80;
     System.out.println("Before calling swap( ) method");
     System.out.println("A= " + a + "B=" +b);
         swap(a, b);
     System.out.println("After calling swap( ) method");
     System.out.println("A= " + a + "B=" +b);
  }
}
```

OUTPUT (after running):

Before calling swap( ) method

A=60 B=80

After calling swap( ) method

A=60 B=80

Explanation: Here, we have declared the method swap( ) as **static.** We shall study this static word a bit later. The above output shows that the value of actual arguments remains same even when the function swap( ) is called. That is, *the change is not reflected back in the main program.*

Actually, local variables are used for temporary purposes like storing intermediate results of a computation. The member data of a class are accessible from all instance methods of the class, local variables and parameters are accessible only from the method in which they are declared and they are available only while the method is being executed. *But please remember that because separate memory space is allocated for each parameter during the execution of the method, the parameter is local to the method and thus changes made to the parameter will not affect the value of the corresponding argument.*

II. CALL BE REFERENCE (only objects)

In Java, arguments are the **objects** that are passed by reference to the called method. In this method of parameter passing, any change made to the object by the called method is **reflected back in the calling method** i.e., the main ( ) method. When we are passing objects to a method then the changes made to the object itself are reflected back to the caller **because the calling side still has the same reference to the object**.

For example,

```
class Obj
 {
    int a, b;

    void set_data(int aa, int bb)
        {
            a=aa;
            b=bb;
        }
        static void swap(Obj t)
         {
            int temp;
            temp = t.a;
            t.a = t.b;
            t.b = temp;
        }
        void display( )
         {
            System.out.println("A=" + a + "B=" +b);
          }
    }

Class Reference_passing
  {
    public static void main(String args[ ] )
     {
    Obj p = new Obj( ); //allocate memory to obj
    p.set_data(60, 90);
  System.out.println("Before calling swap( ) method");
  p.display( );
  Obj.swap(p);  //object 'p' being passed to swap
                //method of Obj class
  System.out.println("After calling swap( ) method");
  p.display( );
 }
}
```

OUTPUT (after running):

Before calling swap( ) method

A=60 B=90

After calling swap( ) method

A=90 B=60

Explanation: Here, we have declared the display( ) method static. We shall be studying the static keyword a bit later. The output of the above program clearly shows that the changes made to the passed object inside the method do affect the actual object. That is,

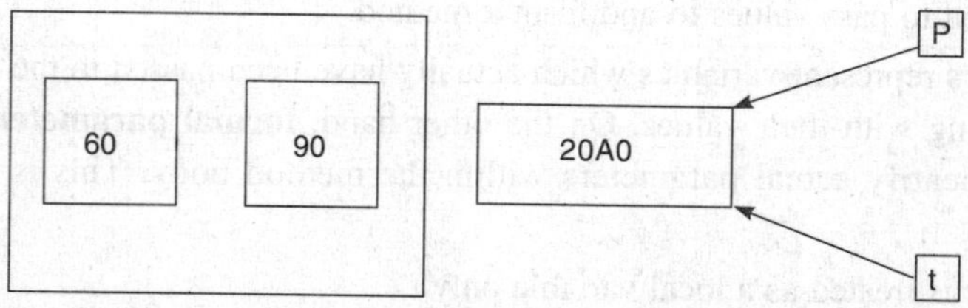

Please remember the following points regarding parameter passing in Java:

1. When passing an argument to a method, the parameters data type must be compatible with the parameter variable's type. Else an error occurs.
2. Even if no arguments are passed to any method, you must still put the parentheses following the method name.
3. Even the following statement is valid:-
   System.out.println("My name is" + oo.get_name( ));
   This statement calls the oo.get_name( ) method.
4. A method that gets a value from a class's field but does not change is known as an *accessor method.*
5. A method that stores a value in a field/ member data or in some other way changes the value of a field is known as a *mutator method.*
6. *Avoid stale data*—when the value of an item is dependent on other data and that item is not updated when the other data is changed, it is said that the item has become stale. So, provide a method that returns the result of the calculation rather than storing it in a field as this value may become incorrect as soon as the fields get changed.
7. A method may have multiple parameter variables allowing you to pass multiple arguments to the method. When an argument is passed to a method, it is passed by value. This means that the parameter variable holds a copy of the value passed to it. Changes made to the parameter variable do not affect the argument.
8. The order is important here. **Please remember that the arguments are passed to the parameter variables in the order that they appear in the method call** i.e. the first argument is passed into the first parameter, second argument is passed into the second parameter and so on.
9. Each instance of a class has its own set of fields which are known as *instance fields.* You can create several instances of a class and store different values in each instance's fields. The methods that operate on an instance of a class are known as *instance methods.*
10. Whenever a method does not have any parameter it is known as a *parameter-less method or a method without parameters.*

11. The parameters or arguments in a method invocation are called as actual parameters or actual arguments.
12. Parameters in a method declaration are known as **formal parameters** or **formal arguments**. As a general rule, **just remember that a function header is always formal**.
13. Parameters are used to pass values to and from a method.
14. **Actual parameters** represent variables which actually have been passed to the method during the invocation along with their values. On the other hand, **formal parameters** are only the placeholders to identify actual parameters within the method body. This is the difference between the two.
15. A value parameter is treated as a local variable only.
16. The expressions or variable references of an argument are evaluated from left to right during execution. The data type of an argument must be assignment compatible with the data type of the matching parameter.
17. The resulting value of each parameter becomes the initial value of each parameter during the method invocation.
18. Also note that the data type of each argument does not precede the actual arguments name.
19. If there is more than one argument then they are separated by commas.
20. Actual arguments may be in form of variables or constants or expressions of appropriate data types.
21. It is not required for the actual parameters to be exactly of the same type of formal parameters. **Please understand that the compiler will try to find an applicable type conversion from the actual parameter types to formal parameter types. If not found, it will issue an error.**
22. We can also send class type of objects to functions. **But please remember that whenever we pass an object to a method, we are actually passing the address or reference, of an object to the method.**
23. Thus, when we pass an object to a method, we are not sending a copy of an object but rather a reference to the object.
24. Local variables and parameters are erased when the execution of a method is completed.
25. Parameters, declarations and statements in a method are optional in a method declaration. When all these are omitted, the method is known as a *dummy method or an empty method. A dummy method has no action to perform.*
26. Control of flow of execution of the statements is transferred to the calling method after reaching the ***return statement.*** Else the control is transferred to the calling method after reaching the closing brace of the method body of the called method.
27. *Java passes method arguments by value and not by reference.* That is, the local copies are made whether the argument and the parameter share the same name or not.
28. We cannot invoke an instance method with the object only.
29. Instance methods of a class have to be invoked only with the object of that class.
30. The object cannot point to NULL. This gives a 'NullPointerException' error.

31. Class methods cannot call instance methods of the same class.
32. Instance methods can call all other methods of the same class.
33. The number of arguments in the method call must match the number of parameters in the method definition.
34. Local copies (different from arguments) are created even if the parameters and arguments share the same name.
35. Parameters are input to a method and they are local to the method. Changes made to the parameters will not affect the value of the corresponding arguments.

Before we discuss further, let us solve some problems now.

Example 1: Write a Java program to find the square of a number, x.

Solutions:

```
class Square_finder {
        double x;
        double square ( )
        {
            return x * x;
        }

public static void main(String args[ ] ) {
    double y;
    Square_finder s= new Square_finder( );
    s.x = 50;
    y= s.square( ) * 10;    //method call
    System.out.println(y); //gives 25000.0 output
y= Math.pow(s.x, 2) * 10; // pow( ) is inbuilt method
System.out.println(y);
```

OUTPUT (after running):

25000.0

25000.0

Explanation: When the method call is executed, the method is invoked and in the place of the method invocation s.square ( ), the returned value is substituted. The in-built method pow (a, b) in Math class may be used to find a raised to b (a^b).

Example 2: As we know that speed = distance/ time. Now write a Java program that calculates the distance traveled by reading speed and time from the keyboard.

Solution:

```
import java.util.Scanner;
class Distance {
        float speed;
```

```
        float speed ( ) {
            Scanner sc = new Scanner(System.in);
            System.out.println("Enter your speed:");
            speed = sc.nextFloat( );
            return speed;
        }
    float calculate (float h) {
        return speed * h;
        }
    public static void main(String args[ ] ) {
        Distance d= new Distance ( );
        d.read( );
        float hour = 20.2f;
    System.out.println("Speed=" + d.speed + "and Hour=" +hour);
    System.out.println("Distance traveled= + d.calculate(hour));
    }
}
```

OUTPUTS (after running):

Enter your speed: 80

Speed=80.0 and Hour= 20.2

Distance traveled= 1616.0

Example 3: Write a Java program that shows the technique of returning values from methods.

Solution:

```
class fact
  {
    int num=4;
    int i;

    int factorial( )
     {
        int f=1;
        for(i=1; i<num; i++)
          {
            f=f * i;
          }
            return f;
     }
  }

class facto_demo
  {
    public static void main(String args[ ] )
```

```
        {
            fact obj=new obj( );
            int fac=obj.factorial( );    //store result in fac
            System.out.println("factorial of the number is=" +fac);
        }
    }
```

Example 4: Write a Java program to read the dimensions of a box, say its length and its width and thus to compute its area. Try to pass multiple arguments to a method.

Solution:

```
    public class box
    {
        public void set(double len, double w)
    {
        length = len;
        width = w;
    }
public static void main(String args[ ] )
        {
            Rectangle box = new Rectangle( );
            double blength, bwidth;

            //read length and width dimensions
        System.out.println("Enter your box's length: ");
            blength = Keyboard.readDouble( );
        System.out.println("Enter your box's width: ");
            bwidth = Keyboard.readDouble( );

        //now pass blength and bwidth to the set method
            box.set(blength, bwidth);

            //display the results
        System.out.println("The box length is=" +box.getLength( ));
        System.out.println("The box width is=" +box.getWidth( ));
        System.out.println("The box area is=" +box.getArea( ));
        }
    }
```

OUTPUTS (after running):

Enter your box's length: 55

Enter your box's width: 100

The box length=55.0

The box width=100.0

The box area=5500.0

Explanation: When the statement,

box.set(blength, bwidth);

is executed, the value stored in the Blength variable is passed into the len parameter and the value stored in the bwidth variable is passed into the w parameter.

3.1.8 Instance Variables, Methods and Classes

Each instance of a class has its own set of fields, which are known as instance fields. *Please understand that we can create several instances of a class and store different values in each instance's fields.* The methods that operate on an instance of a class are known as *instance methods. All methods given before are instance methods except the main*( ). They can be invoked only by the instances of classes or objects. The instance methods are also known as non-static methods. The keyword static is used here. We shall be studying about this a bit later.

3.2 INHERITANCE

Inheritance is the process of creating new classes (called as derived classes) **from the existing class** (called as base class). **The base classes are also known as super classes or the parent classes or an ancestor and the derived classes are known as subclasses or the child classes or descendents.** The subclass inherits all of the capabilities of the super class but can add new features and refinement of its own. **For example**, a child inherits the properties from both of its parents. Practically speaking, the superclass represents the generalized properties and the subclass represents specialization in which the behavior of the super class is modified. Inheritance is not limited to one level only. A subclass can be a superclass of other classes also. This forms an **inheritance hierarchy.** For example,

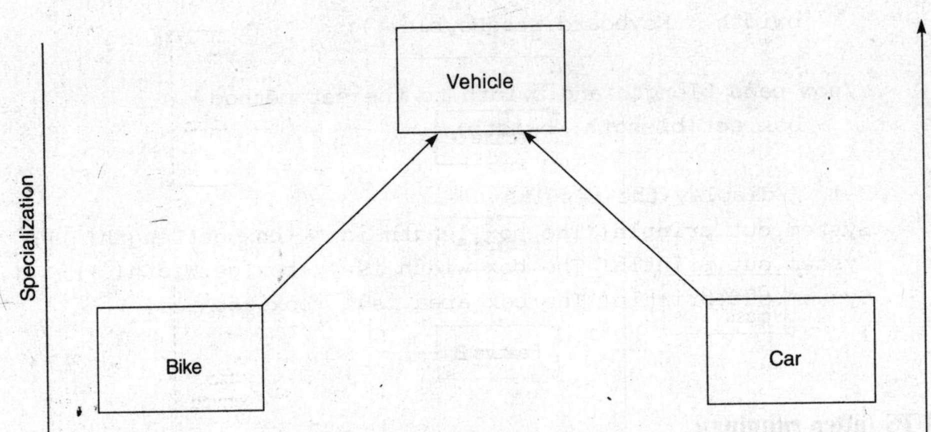

Fig. 3.1: Inheritance concept

Please note here that vehicle is a superclass or the base class or the parent class while Bike and Car are the subclasses or derived classes or child classes. These subclasses are derived from the base class—Vehicle. Also note that we draw the arrows from each subclass to its superclass because a subclass can refer to the items defined in its superclass but not vice versa. Also observe that there are two arrows on the left and the right side. The arrow on the left i.e. from top to bottom shows the concept of **specialization** while the other arrow on the right hand side shows the concept of **generalization**. That is to say that the vehicle class is specialized to the two subclasses (Bike and Car) while the two subclasses are generalized to one class as Vehicle. This can go to any level till the system has been completely delineated. When an object is a specialized version of another object then we say that there is a "is a" (ISA) relationship between them. For example, Joe is a father.

The arrow in Fig. 3.1 shows the concept of ***derivation.*** Actually, the derived class inherits all of the capabilities of the base class and can add some refinements and extensions of its own. **The base class remains unchanged.** Java provides support for single inheritance only i.e. each class is allowed to have one direct base class and each base class can have unlimited number of derived classes. There is no limit on these derivations. This results in a sort of **class hierarchy.** This is shown in Fig. 3.2. From the Fig. 3.2, it is crystal clear that the derived class inherits all features of the base class (A, B and C) and adds its own features (D).

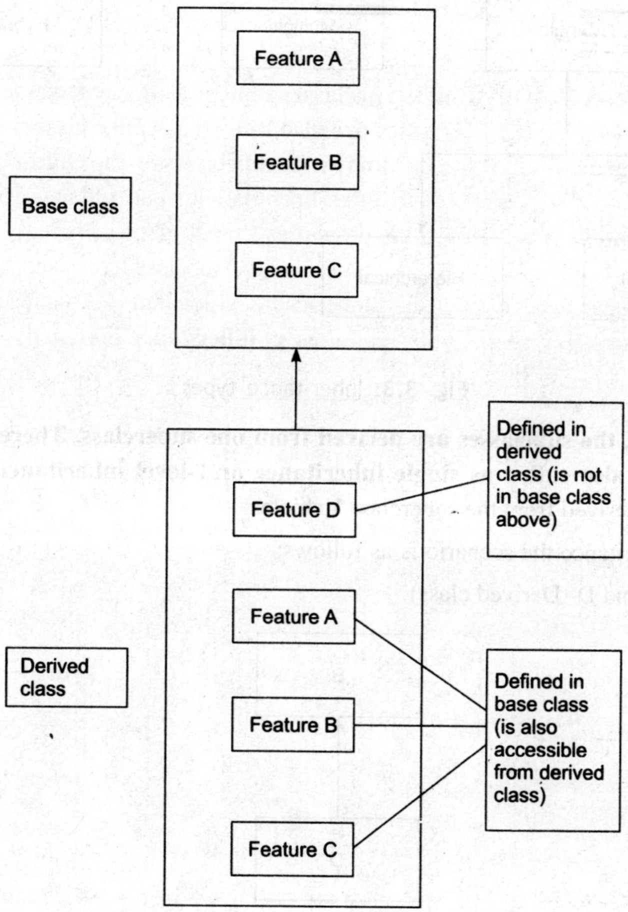

Fig. 3.2: Inheritance concept

3.2.1 Types of Inheritance

There are three main types of inheritance in Java. They are as follows:

(a) Single Inheritance.

(b) Multiple Inheritance.

(c) Hybrid inheritance.

The overall chart of inheritance types is as follows:

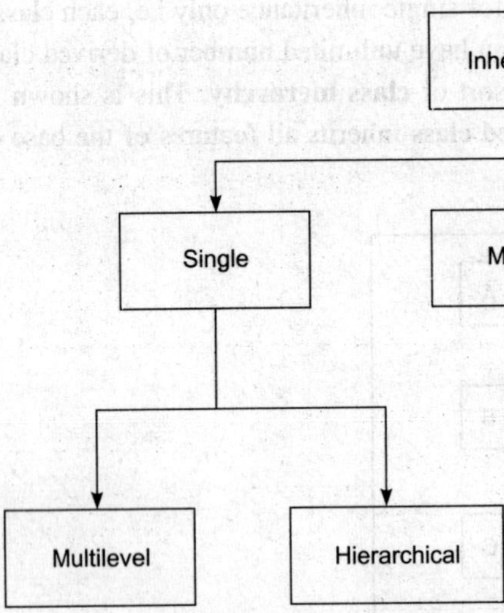

Fig. 3.3: Inheritance types

In single inheritance, the subclasses are derived from one superclass. There is only a sub class and its parent. It is also called as single inheritance or 1-level inheritance. For example, the subclass Bike can be derived from the superclass Vehicles.

That is, in single inheritance the scenario is as follows:

(where B-Base class and D- Derived class)

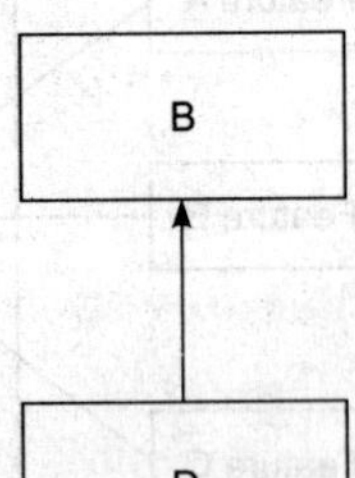

Fig.3.4: Single inheritance

On the other hand, in multiple inheritance subclasses are derived from more than one superclass. When a subclass is derived from a derived class then it is known as **multilevel inheritance**. The derived class inherits the data members and methods of all of its superclasses. It can go till any number of levels. For example,

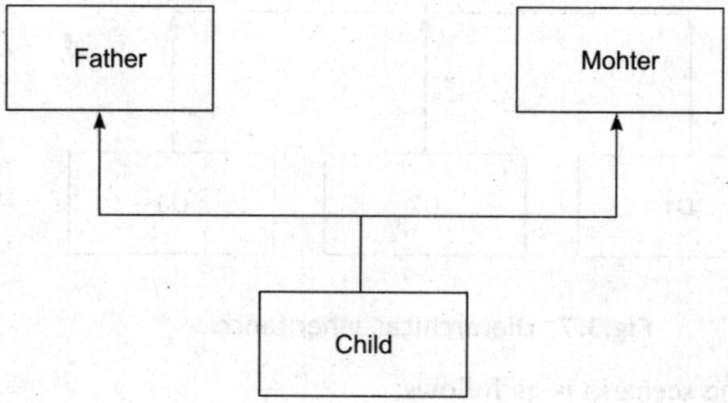

Fig. 3.5: Multiple inheritance

In general, we can say that here in multiple inheritance, the scenario is as follows:

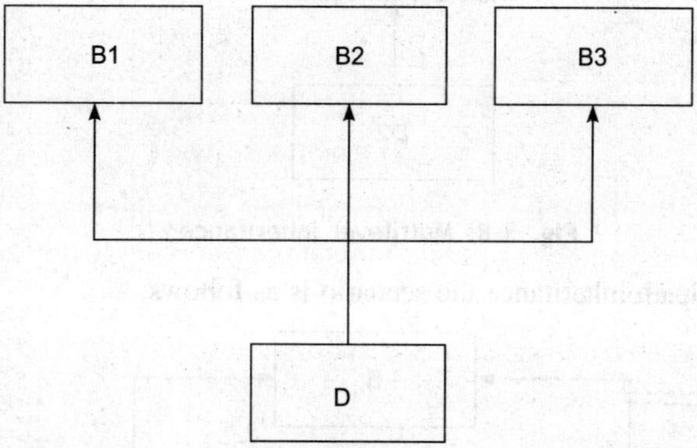

Fig. 3.6: Multiple inheritance

It is also possible to have **hybrid inheritance** by combining single and multiple inheritances.

Thus, the mechanism of inheriting the features of more than one base class into a single class is known as **multiple inheritance.** But please remember that Java does not support multiple inheritance but multiple inheritances in Java can be achieved by using *interfaces* (to be discussed shortly).

In hierarchical inheritance, the scenario is as follows:

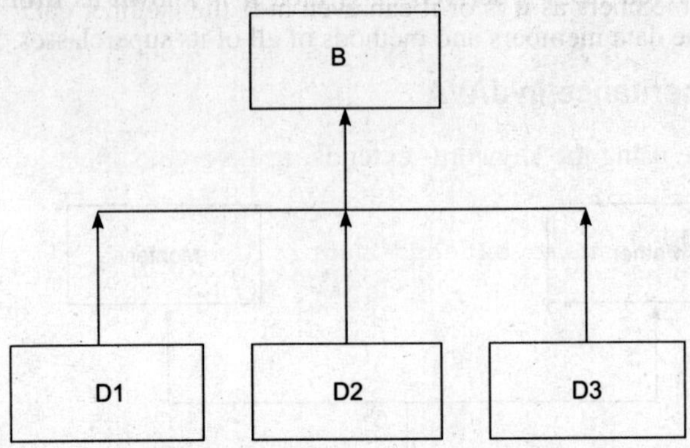

Fig.3.7: Hierarchical inheritance

In multilevel inheritance, the scenario is as follows:

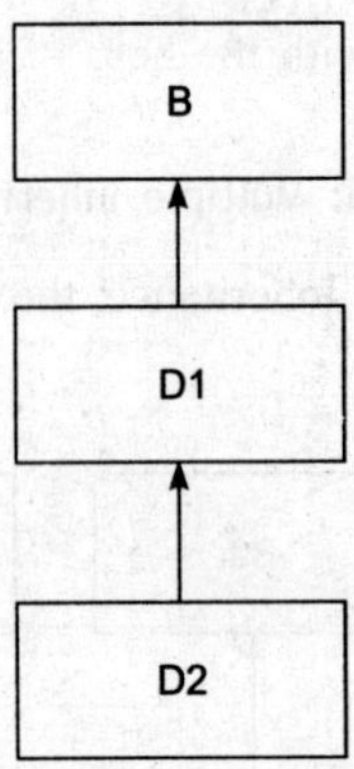

Fig. 3.8: Multilevel inheritance

However, in hybrid/ multipath inheritance the scenario is as follows:

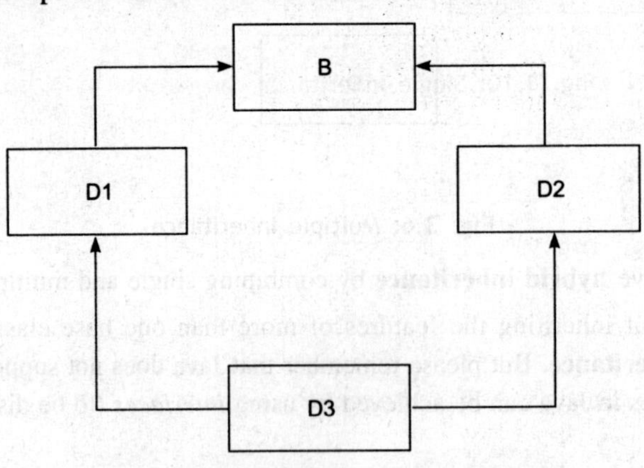

Fig.3.9: Hybrid/Multipath inheritance

During inheritance, a subclass inherits variables and methods from its superclass and all of its ancestors. The subclass can use these members as it is or it can even hide the member data/variables.

3.2.2 Implementing Inheritance in JAVA

Java implements inheritance using the keyword- **extends, to derive a subclass from the superclass.**

Syntax:

```
public class subclassname extends superclassname
 {
      //.......
      //.......
 }
```

Here, the *subclassname* is the name of the subclass or derived class and *superclassname* is the name of the superclass or base class. **Recall that, in inheritance the basic properties of the superclass are extended to the subclass.** The subclass inherits data members and methods from the superclass; it may add its own data members as well as methods.

Let us show the concept of single inheritance with the help of an exampie program. It's diagram is as follows:

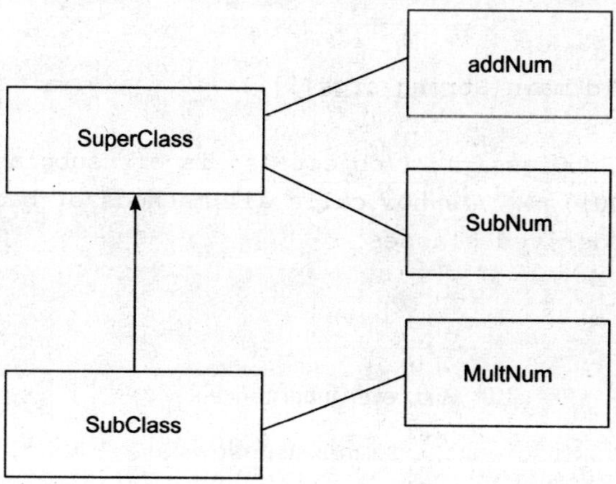

Fig. 3.10: Single inheritance concept

```
// Single Inheritance Example
class SuperClass
  {
    void addNum(int x, int y)
      {
        int z;
        z= x+ y;
        System.out.println("Addition of numbers=" +z);
      }
```

```
    void subNum(int x, int y)
      {
          int z;
          z= x-y;
System.out.println("Difference of numbers=" +z);
      }
    }

class SubClass extends SuperClass
 {
    void multNum(int x, int y)
      {
          int z;
          z=x * y;
  System.out.println("Multiplication of numbers=" + z);
    }
}

class inherit_Demo
 {
    public static void main(String args[ ] )
      {
    SubClass s= new SubClass( ); //object 's' is of  subclass
    s.addNum(100, 200);      //s now calls all methods of base and
s.subNum(100,50);  //derived classes
s.multNum(5,6);
   }
  }
```

OUTPUT (after running):

Addition of numbers = 300

Difference of numbers = 50

Multiplication of numbers = 30

But please remember that the SubClass can be the Superclass for another SubSubClass. In such cases, a class inherits not only from its immediate superclass but also from any superclass upwards.

Also keep the following points in mind when implementing inheritance:

1. A derived class can be declared if its base class is already declared.
2. Once a base class is declared, one or more derived classes can be inherited from it.
3. The derived and base classes may be used in another class.

4. Three-steps are very common here—declare a base class, inherit a derived class from it and then declare a new class to make use of both the above classes.
5. When a class is derived from another class, the public members of the base class become public members of the derived class.
6. The private members of the base class cannot be accessed by the derived class.
7. **Please note that inheritance does not work in reverse.** This means that the derived class inherits members from the base class and not the vice versa. Also this implies that it is possible for a base class to call a derived class's method.
8. Members of a class that are declared private are not inherited by subclasses of that class.
9. Only members of a class that are declared protected or public are inherited by subclasses declared in a package other than the one in which the class is declared.
10. Subclasses don't inherit a superclass's member if the subclass declares a member with the same name. **In case of member variables,** the member variable in the subclass hides the one. On the other hand, **in case of methods, the method in the subclass overrides the one in the superclass.**

3.2.3 Method Overriding

In general, when a method is called using an object then the Java looks for the method definition in the object's class. If it cannot find in the subclass then it checks one level up in the hierarchy of classes. But if the same method name appears in both the subclass and superclass with the same signature (same number of arguments with the same type) then the method is said to be **overridden.** Thus, we can say that method overridden is a concept where the same method name is used in both the subclass and superclass with the same signature. In such a case when a method is called by an object of the subclass then it is the subclass's method which would be called i.e. subclass method overrides superclass method. *Please understand that this means that the method defined in the superclass is overridden or hidden from the objects of subclass.*

Rule:" Subclass has a higher priority here."

Let us consider an example program to understand this.

For example,

```
class First
{
        int a;

        void set_data(int aa)
         {
                a = aa;
        }

        void display( )
```

```
        {
            System.out.println("A= " +a);
        }
    }

class Second extends First
{
    int b, c;

    void set_data(int bb, int cc)
        {
            b= bb;
            c = cc;
        }

    void display( )
        {
            System.out.printl("B=" + b);
            System.out.printl("C=" + c);
        }
    }

class Overload_Demo
    {
        public static void main(String args[ ] )
        {
            First f = new First( ); //object of first class
            Sec s= new Second( );   //object of second class
            f.set_data (-1);
            s.set_data(100, 90);
            f.display ( );
            s.display ( );
        }
    }
```

OUTPUTS (after running):

A= -1

B= 100

C= 90

Also understand that this does not mean that you can't call the base class method in the derived class. You can call the base class method in the derived class method using the 'super' keyword along with the name of the method. So, the methods set_data( ) and display ( ) in the example above can be rewritten as follows:

void set_data(int aa, int bb, int cc)

```
{
    super.setdata(aa);
    b = bb;
    c= cc;
}

void display( )
{
    super.display( ); //calling display( ) method of superclass
    System.out.println("B= " +b);
    System.out.println("C= " +c);
}
```

OUTPUTS (after re-running):

A= -1

A=100

B= 100

C= 90

Also note that a superclass method (now hidden for objects of subclass) *is overridden by the subclass method only when they have identical names and identical arguments*. If there is any mismatch then the two methods are simple treated as overloaded methods (to be discussed shortly). The return types of the overridden methods must be identical. So, overriding occurs when two or more functions/ methods have *same names, same signatures and same return types*.

Let us put it in a nutshell now:

1. Method overriding is needed as we know that the derived class is more specialized than the base class. So it becomes mandatory for the derived class to replace inadequate base class methods with more suitable ones.
2. In order for a derived class method to override a base class method, it must have the same signature.
3. When an object of the derived class invokes the method, it invokes the derived class's version of the method and not the base class's.
4. A derived class may call an overridden base class method by prefixing its name with the super keyword and a dot (.) operator.
5. Method overriding and method overloading discussed earlier are two different concepts.

Let us tabulate the differences between the two now.

Table 3.3: Differences between method overloading and method overriding.

Method overloading	Method overriding
1. The process of defining functions having the same name with different parameter list is called as **overloading method**.	1. When methods of the subclass having same name as that of superclass, overrides the methods of the superclass then it is called as **overriding methods**.
2. It is a relationship between methods in the same class.	2. It is a relationship between subclass method and a superclass method.
3. It is static binding –at the compile time.	3. It is dynamic binding—at the runtime.
4. It is the concept of **compile time polymorphism or early binding.**	4. It is the concept of **run-time polymorphism or late binding.**
5. It may or may not be observed during inheritance.	5. It is observed during inheritance.
6. Return types do not affect overloading.	6. Return types, method names and signatures, of both overridden methods must be identical.

Explanations: When a method overrides another method, they both have same signatures. Overloaded methods can appear within the same class. On the other hand, overriding can only take place in an inheritance relationship.

If two methods have the same name but different signatures, they are overloaded. This is true where the methods are in the same class or where one method is in the base class and the other method is in the derived class. If a method in a derived class has the same signature as a method in the base class, the derived class method overrides the base class method. *Please understand that the difference between overloading and overriding is very important as it can affect the accessibility of the base class methods in a derived class. When a derived class overloads a base class method, both methods may be called with a derived class object. Also understand that when a derived class overrides a base class method, only the derived class's version of the method can be called with a derived class object.*

3.3 ENCAPSULATION AND POLYMORPHISM

The process of wrapping up of the data and methods into a single unit is called as encapsulation. In Java, the basis of encapsulation is a class. It is also known as *information hiding* since it involves hiding of many of the important details of an object from the user. User cannot directly access data that resides in an object. It can be accesses by the methods of an object. And this insulation of data from direct access by the program is called as *data hiding*.

Polymorphism means the ability of having more than one form. Poly means "many" *and morphs* means "forms" and thus polymorphism **here means many forms of a function**. It is the facility that helps different objects to react differently to the same operation. Java supports **run-time polymorphism** with the help of overridden method. As discussed earlier, when an objects method is called, Java looks for the method definition in the objects class. If it cannot find then it checks one level up in the hierarchy of classes. But remember that *if the same method name is used in both the subclass and superclass with the same signature then when the method is called by an object of the subclass then the method defined in the superclass is overridden.* Thus, polymorphism is directly or indirectly related to method overriding.

Polymorphism is a process in which a class to an overridden method is resolved at run-time rather than at the compile time. **This process is also called as late binding or dynamic binding**. Also understand that when you use inheritance, the objects of subclasses can be assigned to super class reference. It means that the superclass reference can refer to an object of any of its subclass.

Let us understand this with the help of an example.

Consider the following class hierarchy:

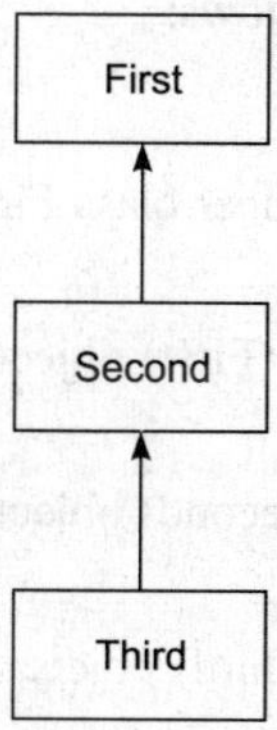

Now we define classes as follows:

```
class First
  {
     //.....
     void display( )
        {
          //....
        }
  }
class Second extends First
 {
     //....
     void display ( )    //Method Overridden
        {
          //......
        }
}
class Third extends Second
 {
```

```
  //….
  void display( )      //method overridden
   {
      //….
   }
}
```

Say now three objects are created as follows:

First f= new First( );

Second s= new Second( );

Third t= new Third( );

These three statements create three objects of classes—First, Second and Third respectively. Let us now create a reference of a superclass First as follows:

First fref;

This superclass reference can refer to object of super class First as well as its subclasses-Second and Third as:-

fref = f;   //valid—refer to super class (First) object

…

fref = s;   //valid—refer to subclass (Second) object

…

fref = t;   //valid—refer to subclass (Third) object

Now when we call a method display( ) using fref then the compiler invokes that particular version of display( ) that is being referred by the type of the object rather than type of the reference variable. *So, please note here that when an overridden method is called through a super class reference then it is the type of the object being referred to that determines which version of an overridden method will be executed.* For example,

```
class First
 {
    void display( )
     {
        System.out.println("First");
     }
}

class Second extends First
{
    void display( )
    {
        System.out.println("Second");
     }
```

```
}


Class Third extends Second
{
    void display( )
    {
        System.out.println("Third");
    }
}

Class RefSuperDemo
{
    public static void main(String args[ ] )
    {
     First f = new First( );
     Second  s = new Second( );

     Third f = new Third( );

     First fref; //super class reference
     fref = f; //refer to super class (First) object
     fref.display( );

     fref = s; //refer to sub class (Second) object
     fref.display( );

     fref = t; //refer to sub class (Third) object
     fref.display( );
     }
  }
```

OUTPUT (after running):

First

Second

Third

Note: You can also assign an object of a subclass type to an object of superclass type. Thus, the following assignment is also completely valid:

```
First f = new First( );
Second s= new Second( );
f=s;
```

In nutshell, we can just say that:

1. A reference variable can reference objects of classes that are derived from the variable's class.
2. In Java, a reference variable is polymorphic because it can reference objects of types different from its own as long as those types are related to its type through inheritance.
3. *The process of matching a method class with the correct method definition is known as binding.*
4. Java performs *dynamic binding or late binding* when a variable contains a polymorphic reference. This means that the JVM (discussed earlier) determines at runtime which method to call, depending on the type of object that the variable references. Thus, it is the *object's type* that determines which method is called not the *variable's type.*
5. You can also use parameters to polymorphically accept arguments to methods.
6. ISA relationship as discussed earlier, does not work in reverse.
7. The encapsulation mechanism allows easier modification of program code.
8. Polymorphism makes possible smooth and easy extension and modification of a program.

3.4 CONSTRUCTORS, FINALIZERS AND DESTRUCTORS

Like C++, Java provides a special member function for initializing the data members of a class called as **constructors**. It is executed automatically when an object of the class is created. Constructors are of two types:

1. Constructors with no arguments.
2. Constructors with arguments.

The constructors have exactly the same name as the class of which they are the members. **For example,**

```
Class dist
 {
        int meter;
        float cms;

        dist( )    //no arguments constructor
         {
              meter = 5;
              cms= 55.0f
           }
        ......
      }
```

Thus, a constructor is a special method with the same name as that of a class. In the above example, whenever an object, say d1, of the dist class is created as

dist d1 = new distance( );

The constructor is executed and it initializes the member variables to the specified values 5 and 55.0f respectively.

The following are some of the rules:

1. The constructor has the **same name as that of the class** in which it is defined. This is so because when an object is created then the Java compiler must know which functions should be called implicitly.
2. A constructor has **no return type** because it is called implicitly and returning a value would not make sense.
3. **Parameterized Constructors:** Java also provides constructors that receive arguments. Such constructors are called as **parameterized constructors**. For example,

```
class Distance
 {
        int meter;
        float cm;

  Distance (int mm, float cc)
  //parameterized constructors
   {
     meter = mm;
     cm = cc;
   }
  ....
 }
```

Note that here the constructor has two arguments in its arguments list. This argument list is used to initialize the data members of an object when it is created. Now, whenever an object, say d2, of the Distance class is created as:

Distance d2= new Distance(30,55.5f);

The parameterized constructor is executed and it initializes the data members to the specified values 30 and 55.5f respectively. Similarly, you can create other objects as follows:-

Distance d3= new Distance(40,65.5f);

Distance d2= new Distance(50,75.5f);

Now let us write a complete program showing all these concepts of constructors:-

```
class Distance
 {
    int meter;
    float cm;

    Distance( )             //no argument constructor
     {
       meter = 25;
       cm = 25.5f;
     }
```

```
    Distance(int mm, float cc)    //parameterized constructor
      {
         meter = mm;
         cm = cc;
      }

void display( )
{
    System.out.println(meter + " " + cm);
 }
}

class Constructor_demo
 {
     public static void main(String args[ ] )
      {
     Distance d1, d2;
 d1 = new Distance( );   //calling no argument constructor implicitly
 d2= new Distance(30, 55.0f); //calling no argument constructor
 //implicitly
 d1.display( );
 d2.display( );
  }
}
```

OUTPUT (after running):

```
25    25.5
30    55.0
```

Also note that in this program we have used more than one constructor in the same class. This is called as **overloaded constructor**. Overloaded constructors are distinguished by the list of the arguments they have. Each constructor has a unique list of parameters with respect to the number and the types of the argument.

Please understand here that if our program has only one constructor, as follows:

```
Distance (int mm, float cc)
  {
     meter = 5;
     cm = 15.5f;
  }
```

Then the compiler would not let you create a Distance object any other way. It means that all declarations of Distance object must have two arguments of type *int and float* respectively. If you try to create an object of Distance class some other way, say,

Distance d1 = new Distance ( );

Or

Distance d2 = new Distance (55);

Then you will encounter the following error message:

No constructor matching Distance( ) found in class Distance

No constructor matching Distance(int) found in class Distance

Also note that if you don't specify any type of constructor and you create an object of Distance as follows:

Distance d1 = new Distance ( );

Then, the compiler calls **the default constructor** even though it was not defined explicitly. This process is done automatically.

Conclusion: If you write a constructor then the compiler say— "You have written a constructor, so you know what you are doing and therefore you should write all type of constructors". If you do not write any type of constructor then the compiler says— "you are bound to need some constructor, so let me make one for you".

A Copy Constructor

A copy constructor is a constructor that *replicates or duplicates an existing object.* That is why it is called as a *copy constructor*. A copy constructor is called *whenever you initialize an instance*, using *values of another instance of the same class type.* For example,

```
Distance (Distance d)   //copy constructor
{
    meter = d.meter;
    cm = d.cm;
}
```

Let us now study—**what is the order of invocation (calling) of constructors in Java?**

We have already studied that when an object is created, it calls the default constructor. **When we create an object of the subclass, it automatically calls the super class constructor prior to the subclass constructor. For example,**

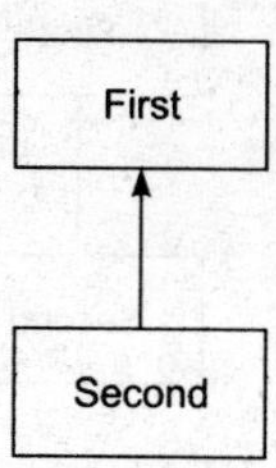

```
class First
  {
     First ( )
      {
          System.out.println("My first constructor.");
      }
}

class Second extends First
 {
     Second( )
      {
          System.out.println("My second constructor.");
      }
}
```

Now we create an object of Second class as follows:

Second s= new Second( );

It will invoke the constructor of the class First and then the constructor of the class Second and displays the following result:

My first Constructor.

My second constructor.

Please note that this is absolutely true for the default constructor only (or zero-argument constructor). But if you have constructors with arguments then you need to explicitly call the super class constructors. And the super class constructors are called by using a keyword—super, as follows:

super (list_of_arguments);

Here, the list of arguments consists of one or more arguments needed by the constructor in the super class. There are two rules to be followed here:

Rule 1: The super( ) class must appear as the first statement in the subclass constructor.

Rule 2: super( ) always refer to the superclass immediately above the calling class.

The following program shows this.

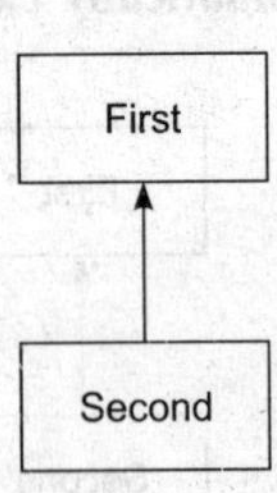

```
class First
 {
    int a;
   First(int aa)
    {
         a=aa;
    }
}


class Second extends First
{
     int b, c;
     Second (int aa, int bb, int cc)
       {
          super(aa);    //calling superclass one-argument
//constructor…this is must here else you will
//get an error.
          b= bb;
          c= cc;
      }

int sum( )
 {
    return (a + b + c);
  }
}

Class CallConstructor_demo
 {
    public static void main(String args[ ] )
     {
         Second s= new Second(250, 300, 500);
         int d= s.sum( );
         System.out.println("Addition= " +d);
      }
    }
```

OUTPUT(after running):

Addition = 1050

Also note that it is necessary to call superclass constructor in the subclass constructor else the compiler will report an error message. When you invoke the super call with some arguments then it must match the order and the type of the instance variable declared in the superclass.

You can also invoke the superclass constructor with an object of subclass as an argument. For example,

```
class First
 {
    int a;

    First( ) //zero argument or default constructor
      {
        a = -1;
        b = -1;
      }

    First(int aa) //parameterized constructor
     {
        a= aa;
      }

First (First obj)  //object constructor
  {
    a = obj.a;
  }

void display ( )
  {
    System.out.println("A=" +d);
  }
 }

class Second extends First
 {
    int b, c;
    Second( )
      {
      super( );    //calling superclass zero arg. Constructor
    b = -1; //Rule: super( ) must appear as first statement in
//all subclass constructors else error.
    c = -1;
    }

    Second(int aa, int bb, int cc)
```

```
      {
Super(aa);    //calling superclass one-argument constructor
b= bb;
c= cc;
}

//in subclass we call-
// a. superclass's zero arg. Constructor
// b. superclass's 1 arg. Constructor
// c. superclass's 1 obj Constructor. All use super( )

Second(Second obj)
 {
     super(obj);     //calling superclass one object constructor
      b = obj.b;
      c = obj.c;
}

     void display( )
{
super.display( ); //calling display( ) method of superclass
//i.e., we have 3 calls-
//1) super( );
//2) super(aa);
//3) super(obj);
      System.out.println("B=" +b);
      System.out.println("C=" +c);
        }
 }
class RefSuper_demo
 {
     public static void main(String args[ ] )
      {
           Second s1= new Second( );
           Second s2 = new Second(100, 200,300);
           Second s3 = Second(s2);
           First f;

           f = s1;
           f.display( );

           f = s2;
           f.display( );
```

```
        f = s3;
        f.display( );

    }
}
```

Please observe the following constructor in this program:-

```
Second(Second obj)
 {
    super(obj);     //calling superclass one object constructor
    b = obj.b;
    c = obj.c;
}
```

Here, we have called super( ) with an object, obj, of subclass Second. This is completely valid because reference variable of superclass can refer to an object of any subclass derived from that superclass.

But please remember the following points regarding constructors:

1. The name of the constructor is the class name itself.
2. A constructor does not return any value and hence does not have a return type.
3. The arguments may be omitted if no value is to be passed to a constructor.
4. The argument list defines the **signature of the constructor.**
5. A constructor is called when an object is created and it is required by JVM:
6. Their declaration is not necessary.
7. The compiler implicitly provides a parameter-less constructor if and only if no constructor is defined.
8. Space is allocated in memory for the object and its fields are initialized by executing the body of the constructor.
9. A class may have more than one constructor.
10. Java compiler differentiates constructors based on the number of arguments and their types.
11. When there is no constructor declared in the class, the compiler provides a no argument default constructor, which will invoke the no-argument constructor of the base class.
12. A constructor may be static or non-static. Non-static constructors are also called as **instance constructors** because they are called to initialize new instances. While **static constructors** are known as **class constructors** because if defined, they are called before the first object of that specific class is created in a program.

13. Class constructors provide a useful way to initialize static members while this is not possible during their declaration.
14. Since class constructors are automatically called by the JVM, they are subject to some restrictions like there can be only at most one class constructor defined per class and another one that the class constructor must be parameter-less.
15. A public parameter-less instance constructor called as default constructor is implicitly declared for any value type, if no constructor is defined. This default constructor returns a default value for the value type. The default value is a zero-initialized instance.
16. All of these declarations initialize the float variable f to 0.0f only-

    float f = new float( ); is same as float f = 0.0f; or float f;
17. Actually, when a constructor is invoked, the following sequence of operations is performed:
    1. All **data fields** are initialized to their **default value.**
    2. All field initializers and initialization blocks are executed, in the order in which they appear in the class declaration.
    3. If the first line of constructor calls a second constructor, then the second constructor is executed.
    4. The body of the constructor is executed.
18. super keyword in Java is used for two purposes as follows:
    (a) Accessing the variables and calling methods of the super class.
    (b) Calling the constructors of the super class.
19. The term **default constructor** in Java can mean two things:
    (a) **The constructor that Java provides is known as a default constructor.** It sets all of the class's numeric fields to 0, Boolean fields to false and char fields to the Unicode value 0. If the class has any fields that are reference variables, the default constructor sets them to the special null value which means that they do not reference anything.
    (b) This term is also applied to any constructor that does not accept arguments. Such a constructor is also called as a **default constructor.**
20. They can also be private or public type.
21. Constructors are of three types—default constructor, argument constructor and copy constructor.
22. **Constructor Chaining:** It occurs when a derived class constructor invokes the constructors of its base class, implicitly or explicitly. In such a scenario, there will be a whole chain of constructors that will be called, all the way back to the original/ultimate base class. This is observed when the inheritance tree is very deep.

Before we discuss further, let us solve some examples based on constructors and its types.

Example 1: Compare and contrast constructors and methods in Java.

Solution:

Feature	Constructors	Methods
Purpose	1. To create an instance of a class.	1. To group Java statements.
Modifiers	2. Cannot be abstract, final, native, static or synchronized.	2. Can be abstract, final, native, static or synchronized.
Return type	3. No return type, not even void.	3. void or valid return type.
Name	4. Same name as that of a class.	4. Any name except the class.
This	5. Refers to another constructor in the same class. If used, it must be the first line of the constructor.	5. Refers to an instance of the owing class. Cannot be used by static methods.
Super	6. Calls the constructor of the parent class. If used, must be the first line of the constructor.	6. Calls an overridden method in the parent class.
Inheritance	7. They are not inherited.	7. Methods are inherited.
Compiler supplies	8. If a class has no constructor, a no-argument constructor is automatically supplied (default constructor).	8. Does not apply here.
Compiler automatically gives a default call to the super class constructor	9. If the constructor makes no zero or more argument calls to super, a no-argument call to super is made.	9. Does not apply.

Example 2: Write a Java program to implement the Student class using constructors.

Solution:

```
Class Student {
    int id_no;
    String name;

    //Student class has 2 constructors
    Student ( ) {  //no argument constructor
        id_no = 0;
        name= " ";
        }

    Student (int my_id, String my_name)
    {    //2 argument constructor
        id_no = my_id;
```

```
    name = my_name;
}
        // student class has 3 methods
        public void setID_no(int my_id)
    {
      id_no = my_id;
}

public void setName(String my_name)
  {
    name = my_name;
  }

public void displayData ( ) {
  System.out.println("ID No.: " + id_no);
  System.out.println("Name: " + name);
 }
}

    //class with main method now

    class MyStudent {
        public static void main (String [ ] args) {
        Student student1 = new Student ( );    //no-arg.
//Constructor is called here
Student student2 = new Student(2, "Rajiv"); //2 arg.
//Constructor is called now
        student1.displayData( );
        student1.setID_no(1);
        student1.setname("Arjeesh" );
        student1.displayData( );
        student2.displayData( );
         }
        }
```

OUPUT (after running):

ID No.: 0

Name:

ID No.: 1

Name: Rajiv

ID No.: 2

Name: Arjeesh

Example 3: Write a Java program to add and subtract two complex numbers.

Solution:

```
class ComplexNumber {

//two instance variables to represent real and imag. parts of a
//complex number
private double myRealPart;
private double myImagPart;
//default constructor
public ComplexNumber ( ) {
    myRealPart = 0.0;
    myImagPart = 0.0;
 }

    //constructor to create a complex number with only the real part
    public ComplexNumber( double realPart) {
        myRealPart = realPart;
        myImagPart = 0.0;
    }

 //constructor to create a complex number with both real & imag. //part
    public ComplexNumber( double realPart, double imagPart) {
        myRealPart = realPart;
        myImagPart = imagPart;
    }

//constructor to copy one complex number to another
public ComplexNumber( ComplexNumber copy) {
    myRealPart = copy.getRealPart( );
    myImagPart = copy.getImagPart( );
  }

 public double getRealPart ( ) {
    return myRealPart;
  }

public double getImagPart ( ) {
  return myImagPart;
}

//method to add 2 complex numbers
public ComplexNumber add (ComplexNumber nbr) {
  //calculate real and imag. parts of new complex number
```

```
double r = getRealPart( ) + nbr.getRealPart( );
double i = getImagPart( ) + nbr.getImagPart( );

//create new complex number object using new values
ComplexNumber newNumber = new ComplexNumber(r, i);
return newNumber;
}

//method to subtract 2 complex numbers
public ComplexNumber subtract (ComplexNumber nbr) {
  //calculate real and imag. parts of new complex number
double r = getRealPart( ) - nbr.getRealPart( );
double i = getImagPart( ) - nbr.getImagPart( );

//create new complex number object using new values
ComplexNumber newNumber = new ComplexNumber(r, i);
return newNumber;
}

//method to return string representation of complex number
public String toString( ) {
    return myRealPart + " + " + myImagPart + "i";
   }
} //end class ComplexNumber

//class to test this ComplexNumber class
public class ComplexNumberTest {
     public static void main(String args [ ] ) {
          // the number 0
     ComplexNumber zero = new ComplexNumber( );
          // the real number 42
     ComplexNumber one = new ComplexNumber(42.0);
          //the imag number 2i
     ComplexNumber two = new ComplexNumber(0.0, 2.0);
          //the complex number 2+3i
     ComplexNumber twoPlusThreeI = new ComplexNumber(2.0, 3.0);
          ComplexNumber a = one.add(twoPlusThreeI);
          ComplexNumber b = one.subtract(twoPlusThreeI);
          System.out.println("Zero=" + zero);
          System.out.println("one=" + one);
          System.out.println("two=" + two);
          System.out.println("twoplusThreeI=" +
```

```
twoPlusThreeI);
        System.out.println("one + twoPlusThreeI= "+a);
        System.out.println("one- twoPlusThreeI= " +b);
        }
    }
```

OUTPUTS (after running):

Zero = 0.0 + 0.0i

one = 42.0 + 0.0i

two = 0.0 + 2.0i

twoPlusThreeI = 2.0 + 3.0i

one + twoPlusThreeI = 44.0 + 3.0i

one - twoPlusThreeI = 40.0 - 3.0i

Example 4: Modify the above program to multiply and divide two complex numbers. Just write the two methods *mult* and *div* for the same.

Solution:

```
    public ComplexNumber mult (ComplexNumber nbr)
      {
        //calculate real and imag parts of new complex number
        double r= myRealPart * nbr.myRealPart - myImagPart*
nbr.myImagPart;
        double i= myImagPart * nbr.myRealPart + myImagPart*
nbr.myImagPart;
    //create a new complex number object using the new values
    ComplexNumber newNumber = new ComplexNumber(r, i);
        return new Number;
      }
    public ComplexNumber div (ComplexNumber nbr)
      {
        //compute real and imag part of new complex number
        float p = nbr.myRealPart*nbr.myRealPart + nbr.myImagPart *
nbr.myImagPart;
        double r = (myRealPart * nbr.myRealPart - myImagPart*
nbr.myImagPart) / p;
        double i = (myImagPart * nbr.myRealPart -myRealPart
* nbr.myImagPart)/p;
          //create a new complex number using the new values
     ComplexNumber newNumber = new ComplexNumber(r, i);
        return newNumber;
        }
```

Example 5: Write a Java program that implements a stack of characters. A stack is a data structure that works on LIFO principle i.e., Last-In-First-Out.

Solution:

```
public class stack {
      char a[ ] ;
      int top;
      int sz;
      public stack(int sz) {
        a = new char[this.sz = sz];
       top = -1;
        }

      public boolean isempty ( ) {
            if (top < 0) return true;
            else
            return false;
            }

      public boolean isfull( ) {
            if (top = = (sz-1)) return true;
            else
            return false;
            }

      public void push(char v) {
            if(isfull( )) {
            System.out.println("Stack is full\n");
            System.exit(-1);
            }
            a[++top] = v;
            }

      public char pop( ) {
            if(isempty( )) {
                  System.out.println("Stack is empty\n");
                  System.exit(-1);
              }
            return (a[top--]);
            }

      public char peek ( ) {
            if(isempty( )) {
```

```
            System.out.printf("Stack is empty\n");
            System.exit(-1);
            }
            return (a [top]);
            }

      public String toString( ) {
            String P=" ";
            for(int i=0; i<=top; i++) P += a[i];
            return P;
      }

   public static void main(String args[ ] ) throws Exception{
        stack A= new stack(10);
        String x=" raj";
        int i;
        for(i=0; i<x.length( ); i++)
             A.push(x.charAt(i));
        while(!A.isempty( ) )
             System.out.println("%c", A.pop( ));
             System.out.println ( );
        }
   }
```

OUTPUT (after running):

Jar

Finalizers in Java

Some times an object will need to perform some action when it is destroyed. **For example,** an object needs to close the open files or to ensure that the related tasks are completed before the object is forgotten. To handle such scenarios, Java provides special functions, known as **finalizers.** They are special functions that are called just before an object is garbage collected. **This process is also known as finalization.**

How to create a finalizer?

Simply, define the finalize( ) method as follows:

```
protected void finalize ( )
 {
     //...
 }
```

Please understand that the Java runtime calls this finalize( ) method just before a class is garbage collected. Here, the keyword protected is a specifier that prevents access to finalize ( ) by code defined outside the class. Also remember that this method is only called just prior to garbage collection rather than when an object goes out of scope. Therefore, you cannot predict when. Even if finalize ( ) will be executed it will be done within microseconds. In nutshell, one must not rely on finalize( ) method for normal program execution and provides some other means of releasing of system resources, used by the object.

So, if a class has a method named finalize, it is called automatically just before an instance of the class is destroyed by the garbage collector. If you wish to execute code just before an object is destroyed, you can create a finalize method in the class and place the code there. The finalize( ) method accepts no arguments and has no *void* return type. The garbage collector runs periodically and you cannot predict exactly when an object's *finalize* method will execute.

Destructors

There is no need of destructors in Java as Java has a garbage collection mechanism that will be discussed next.

3.5 GARBAGE COLLECTION

In Java, objects are dynamically created by using ***new operator.*** But it is very interesting to note and to argue that when happens when an object goes out of scope or you can say when an object is no longer needed by the system? To answer this question, let us consider the following situation:

```
d1= new Dist(10, 20.5);
d1= new Dist(100, 200.55);
```

That is,

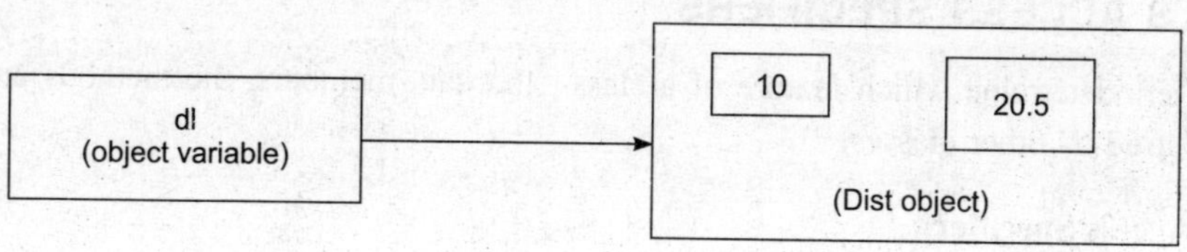

The object d1 initially references the object representing meter= 10 and cm = 20.5

When the second statement (above) is executed, the situation is as follows:

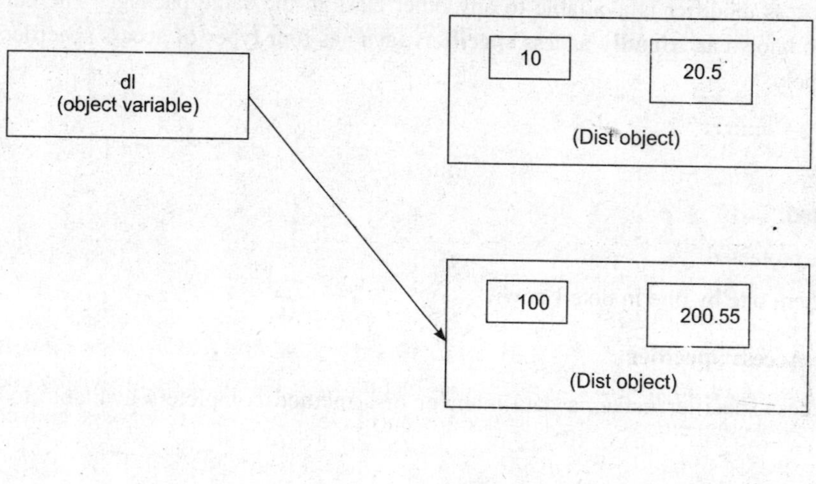

The object d1 now references to a new object representing the object, meter= 100 and cm = 200.55. **Please note that since there is no reference to the first object, it will be automatically discarded by the garbage collector.** Here, two objects are created in this code but only one object variable is there. After the first statement, the distance object d1 points to the object representing meter=10 and cm=20.5. After the 2nd statement, d1 points to the object representing meter=100 and cm= 200.55 and nothing points to the first object (the address of object is removed).

In C++, we use delete operator to free memory. But in Java, this deallocation is done dynamically. Java automatically reclaims memory used by an object when no object variables refer to that object. **This process is known as garbage collection.** Thus, there is no explicit need to destroy objects in Java (as done in C++)

NOTE: An object's finalize( ) method may only be invoked once by the garbage collector.

Also note that when an object is created, a certain amount of memory space is allocated for storing this object. If this allocated but unused space is not returned to the system for other uses, the space gets wasted. **This process of returning of space is called as deallocation and the mechanism to deallocate unused space is called as garbage collection.** This process of destroying of all such objects is done automatically when an object no longer has any references. It is the JVM that periodically runs a process known as *garbage collector*, which removes unreferenced objects from memory.

3.6 JAVA'S ACCESS SPECIFIERS

Access specifiers determine which feature of a class—the data members, the methods and the class itself, may be used by other classes.

The default Access Specifier

Classes written so far have default access. By default access, we mean that a class is available to any other class in the same package (a package is a collection of classes). Similarly, a variable or a method without any access modifier is available to any other class in the same package. The default access specifier is also known as **friendly access specifier.** Java has four types of access specifiers or access modifiers, namely:

1. public.
2. private.
3. protected.
4. private protected.

Let us study them one by one in detail now.

1. The public Access Specifier

The public access specifier makes a data member or a method completely available to all classes.

Also note that when a class is defined as public, it can be accessed by any other class. For example,

```
public class Sample
 {
      public int count;
      public void increment( )
      {
            //....
      }
 }
```

2. The private Access specifier (within a package)

The private access specifier hides a data member or a method from all classes. A private data member can be used by *methods defined in it's own class but not by the objects of any other class.* For example,

```
class Sample
  {
      private int count;
      private void increment( )
      {
            //....
       }
  }
```

Also note here that classes cannot be declared as private *because the classes are to be available to other classes in the same package.*

3. The protected Access Specifier (package-to-package)

The protected access specifier applies to data members as well as the methods of a class. The protected data members and methods *will be available to all classes in the same package.* They will also be *available to subclasses in other packages subjected to certain conditions.*

For example,

```
class Sample
 {
      protected int count;
      protected void increment( )
      {
            //.....
      }
 }
```

4. The private protected Access specifier

A member can be declared with two keywords—private and protected together also, as follows:-

Private protected int number;

The private protected access specifier makes a member visible in all subclasses regardless of what package they are in. Such members are not accessible by other classes in the same package.

For example,

Consider that we have two packages 'A' and 'B' as follows:

- Package 'A' has one super class- 'X' and one subclass 'XX' of 'X'. The class 'X' has a protected method-'M'.
- Package 'B' has a class 'Y' , derived from the class 'X' and a subclass 'YY' of 'Y'.

The scenario is as follows:

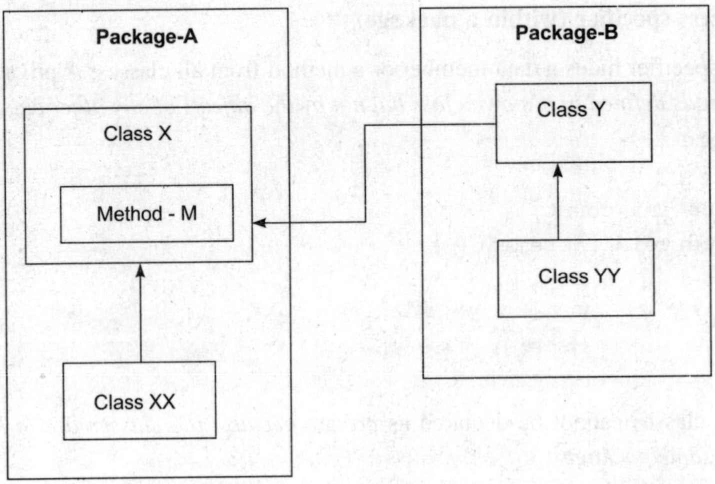

Fig. 3.11: Showing the relationship between access specifiers

Please note here from the figure that the method 'M' can be invoked by the classes 'X' and 'XX' in the same package- 'A' as well as by the class 'Y' in package- 'B'. Also note that if class Y is not inherited from class X then, class Y cannot use method-M.

The following Table 3.4 explains this.

Table 3.4: Compares Different Access Specifiers

Access	Public	Protected	Default (friendly)	Private	Private protected
From the same class	Yes	Yes	Yes	Yes	Yes
From any class in the same package	Yes	Yes	Yes	No	No
From any class outside the package	Yes	No	No	No	No
From a subclass in the same package	Yes	Yes	Yes	No	Yes
From a subclass outside the package	Yes	Yes	No	No	Yes

Let us now compare these access specifier's usage (where and when used):

Table 3.5: Access Specifiers

Modifier/ specifier	Used with	Description
public	Classes, Interfaces, Constructors, Inner classes, Methods	Field variables, a class or interface may be accessed from outside its package. Constructors, inner classes, methods and field variables may be accessed from wherever their class is accessed.
protected	Constructors, Inner classes, Methods	Field variables may be accessed by other classes in the same package or from any subclasses of the class in which they are declared.
private	Constructors, Inner methods	Field variables may be accessed from within the class in which they are declared.
No modifier	Classes, Interfaces, Constructors, Inner classes, Methods	Field variables may be accessed from within the package in which they are declared.

From these discussions we find that access modifier can be applied either to class declarations or to class member declarations. Hence, the actual access to the class member is controlled by the combination of the two access modifiers: 1st the access modifier of the class is evaluated and then the access specifier of the member.

The following Fig. 3.12 shows all these concepts:

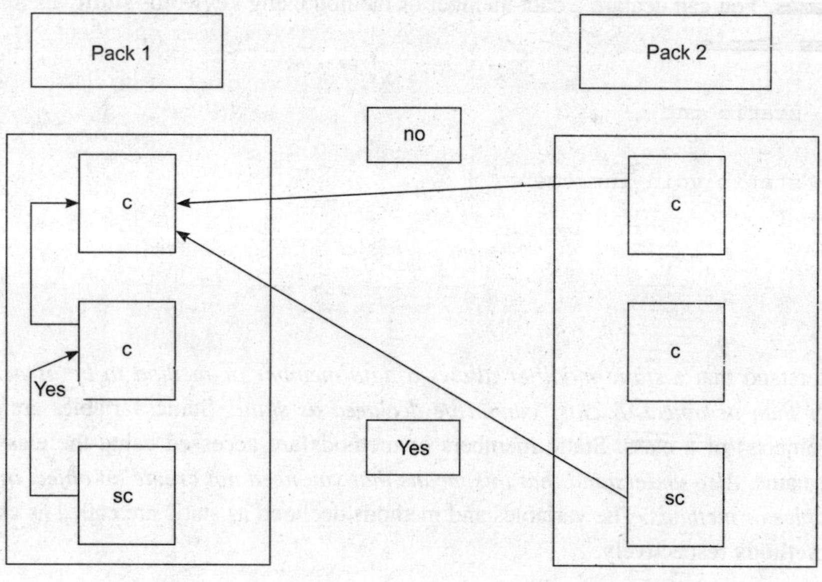

Fig. 3.12: Role of packages

For example,

```
class X {                          yes  public:
    private int i;                              ....
    public:                             //all other are no, even
        method( )   yes                 //protected is no
        {
            i;
            protected j;
class Y {
        i=20;           no
        .....
        .....
    }
```

3.7 JAVA'S MODIFIERS—STATIC AND FINAL

Java provides two types of modifiers—static and final. We shall study these now.

3.7.1 The Static Modifiers

Java provides static modifier that determines how the data members of a class and methods are used in other classes. You can declare a data member or method using keyword **'static'** as follows:-

```
class Sample
 {
    static int n;
    //...
    static void increment( )
     {
        //...
     }
 }
```

Please understand that a *static modifier allows a data member or method to be associated with its class rather than its object. A class cannot be declared as static.* Static variables are shared by all instances (objects) of a class. Static members or methods are accessed using the class name rather than object name. *Also understand that this means that you need not create an object in order to call static variables or methods.* The variables and methods declared as static are called as **class variables** and **class methods** respectively.

For example 1,

```
main( ) method in Java is static.
```

Example 2,

```
class Example
{
      public static void main(String args[ ] )
       {
            int number;
            //...
            number = Sample.n;          //accessing static member using
                                        //class name itself i.e., Sample
            Sample.increment( );        //accessing static method
      }
}
```

Also note that you cannot access non-static data members from a static method because non-static data members are instance variable that is, non-static data members are accessed using an object.

Java supports definition of global methods and variables that can be accessed without creating objects of a class. **Such members are called as static members.** They are common to a class. A method or a field may be of static type. The ***static members of a class*** are defined with the keyword ***static.*** There are two things here:

1. A field/member data's dataType is preceded by the static keyword in its declaration.
2. In a ***static method*** definition, the keyword static precedes the ***returnType*** in the method header.

NOTE: The members defined without the static keyword are known as non-static members. The non-static members are instance members. A static member is a member that is only one per class. But a non-static member is a member that is one per object for each object of that class type.

So, what are static fields/member data?

Sometimes it is desired to share an instance of a field by all objects of a class. Such fields are common to a class and are called as *static fields or class fields. Please understand that when a static field in a class is declared, all objects created from that class share a single copy of that field. Also understand that a static field takes one storage location.* For static fields, there is exactly one variable even when no object is created or any number of objects are created. It can be used even if the class is never instantiated.

So, what are static methods then?

Just as we have static data members/fields, similarly we have *static methods*. Class methods are specific to the class itself but not on a specific object of that class. They usually perform operations on static fields. When a static method is invoked, there is no specific instance of the class for the method to operate on. That is why, instance fields cannot be referenced in a static method. Also note that it will be a error if you refer to *this* (to be discussed shortly) in a static method. The instance fields may be passed as parameters to static methods. This indirect method helps us to make use of the instance fields also. *Please note that static methods perform class-related tasks and non-static methods do object-related operations. Also note that telling a static method to operate on non-static fields is analogous to telling someone that you go on a vehicle, without showing any instance of a vehicle like which vehicle-car, bike or bus.*

NOTE: Static methods are generally used to group related library functions that do not depend on data members of its class like Math library functions.

Please remember the following points regarding 'static':

1. A static class member belongs to the class and not the objects instantiated from the class.
2. Both instance fields and instance methods are associated with a specific instance of a class and they cannot be used until an instance of the class is created.
3. It is possible to create a field/data member and even a method that does not belong to any instance of a class. **Such members are known as static fields and static methods.**
4. When a value is stored in a static field, it is not stored in an instance of the class. An instance of the class need not even exist in order for the values to be stored in the class's static fields.
5. Static methods do not operate on the fields that belong to any instance of the class.
6. Instead they can operate only on static fields.
7. You can think of static fields and static methods as belonging to the class instead of an instance of the class.
8. When a field is declared as ***static,*** there will be only one copy of the field in memory, regardless of the number of instances of the class that might exist. **For example,**

    ```
    private static int count = 0;
    ```

    Please note here that this initialization of count to 0 will takes place only once irrespective of the number of instances of the class that are created. Also note that Java automatically stores 0 in all of the un–initialized static member variables.
9. When a class contains a static method then it is not mandatory for an instance of the class to be created in order to execute the method.
10. If a method is declared as static and they belong to a class, so it may be called without any instances of the class being in existence.
11. Static methods are useful as they can be called directly from the class as needed.
12. They are mostly used to create utility classes that perform operations on data but have no need to collect and store data.
13. The only restriction with static methods is that they cannot refer to non-static members of the class. *Please understand that this means that any method called from a static method must also be static.* It also means that if the method uses any of the class's field, they also must be static.

14. A static member is accessed using the notation as follows:-

    ClassName.staticMemberName

15. The method body of a static method of a class cannot reference a non-static variable of that class. It can access only the static fields and static methods of that class.
16. A static member can be accessed in the static body directly in the same manner as an instance member in an instance method.
17. A non-static variable can be passed as a parameter to a static method. So, it is possible to use the value of an instance variable in a static method by passing it as a parameter to it.
18. By passing an explicit object reference as a parameter to the static method, non-static members may be accessed in it.
19. A static constructor is used to initialize static variables. It is invoked only once no matter how many objects are created.
20. A static method cannot refer to this or super at all.

We are in a position to solve some problems now.

Example 1: Write any Java program to show the usage of static methods.

Solution:

```
class comparison {
        public static int max(int a, int b)
          {
              if (a > b)
                return a;
              else
                 return b;
        }

        public static String_max(String a, String b)
        {
        if (a.compareTo (b) > 0)
        return a;
        else
        return b;
        }
}

Class MyClass
  {
     public static void main(String args[ ] )
       {
```

```
        String s1= "Rajiv";
        String s2 = "Chopra";
        String s3 = "author";
        int a = 85;
        int b = 95;

System.out.println(Comparison.max(a, b); //check number
System.out.println(Comparison.max(s1, s2); //check names
System.out.println(Comparison.max(s1, s3); //check names
    }
}
```

OUTPUTS (after running):

95

Chopra

Rajiv

Example 2: What is a static initializer?

Solution: If we need to perform more than a simple assignment to initialize a class variable then we define a static initializer. A static initializer is a code that gets executed when a class is loaded into the Java system. It is defined as follows:

```
    class XYZ {
        ...
        static {
            //code to initialize class variables and perform other tasks
            }
            ...
        }
```

Example 3: What is static import? What are its types?

Solution:

The purpose of the import statement is to include the classes in the program. It is like using #include directive in C/C++. We can also have a static import. They are of two types:

(a) **Single static import:** It is used to import a particular static member of a class.

(b) **Static import on demand:** It is used to import all static members of a class.

3.7.2 The Final Modifier

It will be discussed a bit later.

3.8 THE FINAL KEYWORD

The *final* keyword can be used in a variable declaration to make the variable a named constant. Named constants are initialized with a value and that value cannot change during the execution of the program. An initialization value must be given when declaring a variable with the final modifier. Otherwise, you will get an error. **Note that you cannot write any statement that changes the value of a final variable. For example,**

final double PI = 3.14;

Similarly, during inheritance, a final class cannot be inherited. Hence, it cannot have any derived class. The ***final*** keyword is used in a class to make that class as a final class. Only a **concrete class** with all its members and methods can be declared as final. We cannot declare an abstract class (without any body) as final class. **Please note that as a final class is known to never have any derived classes, it is possible to transform the invocations of virtual functions on final class objects into non-virtual invocations.** For example,

```
final class sample
        {
          ......
        }
```

When an instance method declaration includes a final modifier in its header, the method is called as a **final method**. A final method overrides an inherited virtual method with the same signature. The final modifier can only be used in combination with the override modifier. A final method cannot be overridden in the derived classes.

Note: Final classes and final method are opposite to abstract classes and abstract methods. Final classes are useful to prevent unauthorized access to a class by 3rd party who has not signed any agreement. Final methods are useful to avoid problems caused by overriding the existing functionality. On the other hand, abstract methods and classes foster the extension, final methods and classes limit it.

Applications: As we know that there are several inbuilt functions/methods in Java that are very useful for the programmer. Now, if the source code for these methods is accidentally changed by the user or the programmer then we loose its use. We can prevent such happenings by declaring these methods as final methods only.

The final keyword is used for security reasons also. But it has different usages depending on the context in which it is being used:-

1. *final* Data Member

   Whenever we declare a member data as final then it means that its **value could not be changed** at any cost. A final data member is declared as follows:

   final float PI = 3.14f;

   final char sex = 'M';

2. *final* Method

Whenever we declare a method as final then it means that this method **cannot be overridden** in its subclasses. *Please note that the function of a final method is just reverse of an abstract method.* A final method is declared as follows:

```
final void decrement( )
{
    //....
}
```

Also note that a final method behaves like inline functions in C++.

3. *final* Class

A final class **cannot be inherited** at any cost. The function of a final class is just the reverse of an abstract class. The final class is declared as follows:-

```
final class classname
{
    //....
}
```

Also understand that such classes are preferred where we do not want to make any changes in them.

4. *final* Object

The final object is a constant object and it must be initialized to an object at the point of declaration. The final object **can never be changed to point to another object**.

In nutshell, we can conclude that:

1. **A *final* member** data **cannot be changed** after its initialization.
2. **A *final* method cannot be overridden** by a subclass.
3. **A *final* class cannot be inherited.**
4. **A *final* object must be initialized to an object** at the point of declaration and it can never be changed to point to another object.

3.9 ABSTRACT CLASS

An abstract class is not instantiated but other classes are derived from it. An abstract method has no body and must be overridden in a derived class. *An abstract method is a method that appears in a base class but expects to be overridden in a derived class.* An abstract method has a header only and *no body*. The **syntax of** an abstract method is as follows:

AccessSpecifier abstract ReturnType MethodName(ParameterList);

Please note here that the keyword abstract appears in the header. Header ends with a semicolon.

There is no body for the method. *Also note that when an abstract method appears in a class, the method must be overridden in a derived class.* If the derived class fails to override the method, an error will result. Abstract methods are used to ensure that a derived class implements the method. When a class contains an abstract method, you cannot create an instance of the class. Abstract methods are commonly used in abstract classes. An abstract class is not instantiated itself but serves as a base class for other classes. *Please remember that an abstract class represents the generic or abstract form of all classes that are derived from it.* A class becomes abstract when you place the abstract keyword in the class definition. The general *syntax* is:

public abstract class ClassName

We cannot define a shape. But we can define a square, triangle, rectangle, circle or a square. This is because a square can be described by its sides, a circle by its radius and so on. But unfortunately a shape has no dimensions. In other words, we can say that shape is abstract. Thus, we can say that a shape is an abstract class. Similarly, we can say vehicles, mammals etc will be the examples of abstract classes. An abstract class defines the common properties and behavior of other classes. **It is used as a base class to derive specific classes of the same kind.** It defines properties common to all of its derived classes.

NOTE: You cannot create an object of an abstract class. Abstract methods have public scope. An abstract method has no body rather it has just a declaration.

Please understand that *an abstract class may contain an abstract method as well as a concrete method* (i.e. with body). For example,

```
abstract class Sample
 {
     //….
     void display ( )          //concrete method
      {
          System.out.println("Calling concrete method…");
      }

     public abstract void putdata( );  //abstract method
 }
```

Also understand that it is not mandatory to override a concrete method in its subclasses but if you declare an abstract method in a class then this abstract method should necessarily be overridden by all its subclasses. Thus, a subclass must override an abstract method defined in its super class. For example,

```
    abstract class Shape
     {
         //….
     }
public class Reactangle extends Shape
```

```
{
    float length, breadth;
    ......
    public float area( )
        {
            return (length * breadth);
        }
```

Observe that here the area( ) method of the abstract super class—shape, has been overridden in the rectangle class. If the Rectangle class does not override the method, the class will inherit the abstract method from the parent class. **If a class has at least one abstract method then it is necessary to declare that class as an abstract class.**

Let us see a complete program now.

The class diagram is as follows:

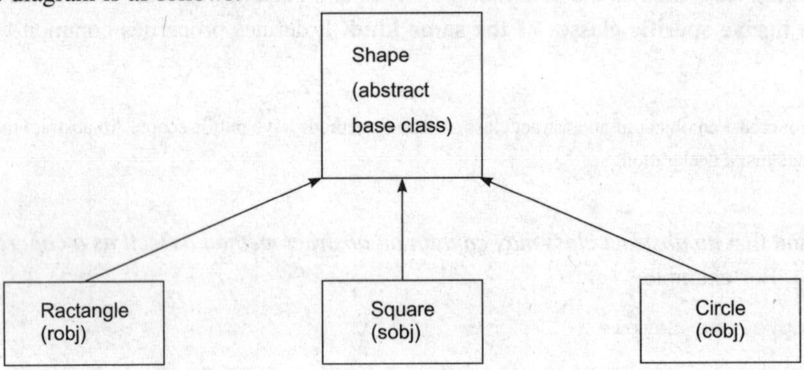

Its implementation is as follows:

```
abstract class Shape
  {
     abstract void setdata( );
     abstract float area( );
}

class Rectangle extends Shape
 {
     float length, breadth;

     void setdata( )
      {
          length = 10.0f;
          breadth = 25.0f;
      }
```

```
      float area( )
       {
           return (length * breadth);
       }
   }

class Circle extends Shape
 {
      float radius;

      void setdata( )
       {
           radius = 15.0f;
       }

      float area( )
       {
           return (radius * radius * 3.14f);
       }
       }

class Square extends Shape
  {
      float length;
      void setdata( )
       {
           length = 20.0f;
       }

      float area ( )
       {
           return (length * length);
       }
      }

class Abstract emo
 {
      public static void main(String args[ ] )
       {
           Shape ssref;  //is valid reference of abstract base class but
shape
//ssref = new Shape ( ) gives an error.
           float a;
```

```
        Rectangle robj = new Rectangle( );   //you can create object of
//derived class as they are not abstract.
        robj.setdata( );

        ssref = robj;
        a= ssref.area( );  //calls area( ) of rectangle class as reference
//has been set to robj of rectangle subclass.
        System.out.println("Area of rectangle= " + a);

        Circle cobj = new Circle( );
        cobj.setdata( );

        ssref = cobj;
a= ssref.area( );
        System.out.println("Area of circle= " + a);

        Square sobj = new Square( );
        sobj.setdata( );

        ssref = sobj;
        a= ssref.area( );
        System.out.println("Area of square= " + a);
        }
       }
```

OUTPUT (after running):

Area of a rectangle = 250.0

Area of a circle = 707.1428

Area of a square = 400.0

All abstract classes are public by default and also cannot be instantiated. **Also note that constructors and static methods cannot be declared as abstract.**

Please keep the following points in mind before you write programs:

1. Abstract class is designed to be inherited only. It cannot be instantiated.
2. A class containing one or more abstract methods implies that the class itself should be abstract.
3. Any non-abstract class that is derived from the abstract class must override the abstract method.
4. An abstract class may or may not include abstract methods.
5. It may also include concrete methods and fields/data members.
6. A non-abstract class does not allow abstract methods.

7. The main reason behind the designing of an abstract class is to provide a base root type and define an interface of operations which cannot be specified further along with a common behavior. Derived class will be in charge of specifying these operations.

We are in a position to write some programs on abstract classes now.

Example 1: Write a Java program to declare an abstract class Solid and implements Cylinder, Cone and Sphere by inheriting from Solid abstract class. Try to compute the surface area and its volume.

Solution:

```
import java.util.Scanner;

abstract class Solid
  {
     double radius;

     public abstract void  surfaceArea( );
     public abstract void  volume( );
     public abstract void  readRadius( );

     public double baseArea(double r)
      {
         double p;
         p= Math.PI * r * r;
         return (p);
      }
  }


class Cylinder extends Solid
  {
     double height;
     public Cylinder (double h)   //constructor
     height = h;
  }

public void readRadius( )
  {
     Scanner sc = new Scanner (System.in);
     System.out.println("Enter the radius of cylinder:");
     radius = sc.nextDouble( );
  }
```

```
        public void surfaceArea( )
          {
              double bArea;
              double totalArea;
              bArea = baseArea(radius);
              totalArea = 2 * Math.PI * radius * height + 2 * bArea;
        System.out.println("\nSurface area of cylinder is:", total Area);
          }

        public void volume( )
          {
    System.out.println("\nVoulme of the cylinder is:" + height
* (baseArea(radius)) * 1/3);
          }
    }

class Cone extends Soild
  {
    double height;

    public Cone(double h)   //constructor
      {
        height = h;
      }

    public void readRadius( )
      {
        Scanner sc = new Scanner(System.in);
        System.out.println("\nEnter the radius of cone:");
        radius = sc.nextDouble( );
      }

    public void surfaceArea( )
      {
        double area;
        double slantHeight;

        slantHeight = Math.sqrt(radius * radius + height * height);
        area = Math.PI * radius * slantHeight;
        System.out.println("\nSurface area of cone is:" + area);
      }
```

```
    public void volume ( )
     {
         double volume;

         volume = (1.0/3) * (baseArea(radius)) * height;
    System.out.println("Volume of cone is: " + volume);
    }
  }

class Sphere extends Solid
    {
         public void readRadius( )
           {
              Scanner sc = new Scanner(System.in);
         System.out.println("\nEnter the radius of sphere:");
         radius = sc.nextDouble( );
    }

    public void surfaceArea( )
      {
         System.out.printf("\nSurface area of sphere is:", 4 *
baseArea(radius));
      }

    public void volume( )
     {
         double volume;
         volume = (4.0/3) * (baseArea(radius)) * radius;
    System.out.printf("\nVolume of sphere is:", volume);
    }
    }

class MySolid
 {
    public static void main(String args[ ] )
      {
         Solid s = new Cylinder(7);

         s.readRadius( );
         s.surfaceArea( );
         s.volume( );
```

```
        s= new Cone(7);
        s.readRadius( );
        s.surfaceArea( );
        s.volume( );
        s = new Sphere( );
        s.readRadius( );
        s.surfaceArea( );
        s.volume( );
    }
}
```

OUTPUTS (after running):

Enter the radius of cylinder:

10

Surface Area of Cylinder: 1068.14

Volume of cylinder is 2199.11

Enter the radius of cone:

10

Surface Area of Cone is 383.48

Volume of cone is 733.04

Enter the radius of sphere:

10

Surface area of sphere is 1256.64

Volume of sphere is 4188.79

Explanation: The volume( ) and the area( ) methods identify property of every solid but it depends on the type of solid that is considered. That is why, a generic base class Solid exposing these methods is defined but their actual implementation is given in the derived classes. So, Solid class must be an abstract class.

Example 2: Consider a college system in which a student may be an undergraduate or graduate student or none of these. Such students who are neither undergrads nor grads are named as non-regular students. Write two separate programs (with and without abstract classes) to implement such a college system. Which approach is better? Comment.

Solution:

Two cases arise here:

Case 1: Student must be an Undergraduate or Graduate.

Case 2: Student is neither an Undergraduate or Graduate rather a non-regular student.

Case 1:

```
abstract class Student
  {
     protected final static int num_of_tests = 2;
     protected String name;
     protected int[ ] test;
     protected String courseGrade;

     public Student ( )
       {
          this("No Name");
       }

     public Student(String studentName)
       {
          name = studentName;
          test = new int[num_of_tests];
          courseGrade = "*****";
        }

     abstract public void computeCourseGrade( ); // abstract method
    //with no body, just a semicolon.

     public String getCourseGrade( )
       {
          return courseGrade;
       }

     public String getName( )
       {
          return name;
        }

     public int getTestScore(int testNumber)
       {
          return test[testNumber -1];
       }

     public void setName(String newName)
     {
        name = newName;
     }
```

```
    public void setTestScore(int testNumber, int testScore)
     {
         test[testNumber -1] = testScore;
     }
   }
```

Explanation: Observe that the abstract class Student has an incomplete definition because the class includes the abstract method *computeCourseGrade* that does not have a method body. The objective is that its implementation is to be left with the sub-classes. *Also understand that if its subclass does not provide its implementation then that means that it is also abstract and thus no instances of its subclass can also be created.* This means that an abstract class can only make sense when it is a superclass, we frequently use the term **abstract superclass.** The intent of an abstract class is to define code common to all its subclasses and leave some portions i.e. abstract methods, to be completed by the individual subclasses.

NOTE: Math class is not an abstract class.

Case 2:

There are two ways of handling this situation. One is to make the Student base class non-abstract that is now it can be instantiated (objects can be created now). The 2nd method is to add another, 3rd subclass, say another_student. This is shown with the help of a class diagram also.

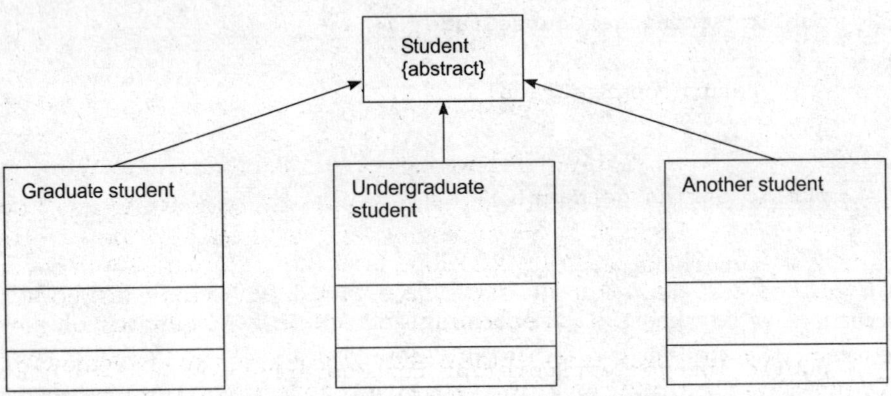

This 2nd approach is implemented below:

```
class another_student extends Student
 {
   public void computeCourseGrade( )
     {
        int total =0;
        for(int i=0; i< num_of_tests; i++)
```

```
            {
               total +. = test[i];
            }
         if (total / num_of_tests > = 50)
            {
               courseGrade = "Pass";
            }
               else {
                     courseGrade = "Not passed";
                    }
                 }
         }
```

Which method is better? It all depends on the given scenario that one wishes to implement. If modifications are easier by 1st method then use 1st method or else use the 2nd method.

3.10 THIS REFERENCE

Let us understand this with the help of an example.

<pre>Class Marks
 {
     int mark, rank;
     Sample(int mark, int rank)
     {
          mark = mark;
          rank = rank;
     }
     .....
 }</pre>
	<pre>Class Marks
	{
	     int mark, rank;
	     Sample(int mark, int rank)
	     {
	          mark = mark;
	          mark = rank;
	     }
	     .....
	}</pre>

In this scenario, how do body statements distinguish between method parameters and fields having the same name? Here, this reference is needed. *Please remember that every method of a class has access to the keyword this. Also remember that the reference this holds the address of the current object on which the method was invoked.* The *this reference* is passed to every method as a hidden argument. So, the constructor has an implicit *this argument.* It is not shown in the signature of the method or constructors because the compiler automatically passes it to the method during invocation. Whenever, a method accesses the fields in its class, it implies that it is accessing fields in the object referred to by ***this parameter.*** The same is also true when a method invokes another method in the same class. When a constructor is invoked, a reference to the newly allocated object or instance is automatically passed to the constructor. The object can be accessed from within the constructor as ***this.***

Whenever there is a fight between local variables and member fields, local variables win and is given a higher priority. Formal parameters are treated as local variables. Local variables cannot be named as formal parameters. For example,

In the following programming statement,

this.age = age;

this.age refers to a field variable which is a class member and variable 'age' on the right side of the assignment, refers to the parameter passed to the constructor. The keyword ***this*** is used as a reference, an object name, of a current class. The mechanism of accessing the current object is thus obtained now. The ***this reference*** is allowed in the block of a constructor or non-static method.

In the left hand side code, ***this*** is not explicitly used. The compiler cannot explicitly associate this with mark and rank variables because both names are used as parameters in the constructors. The parameters are treated as local variables inside the constructor or a method. So, the instance fields are hidden by these parameters. In such scenarios, ***this*** is used to mark the current object reference. It is necessary to use *this reference* to an instance field to distinguish it from the parameters. Also note that *this reference* is used to pass a reference pointing to the current object as a parameter to other methods.

So, please remember the following points regarding *this* reference:

1. ***this*** keyword is the name of a reference variable that is available to all non-static methods.
2. An object can use the ***this*** variable to refer to itself.
3. The ***this*** variable contains the address of the calling object.
4. The ***this*** reference variable is available to a class's non-static methods.
5. If a method's parameter has the same name as a field in the same class then the parameter name shadows the field name.
6. Many Java programmers give parameters the same names as the fields to which they correspond and then they use the ***this*** keyword to refer to the field names.
7. ***this*** keyword is also used to call one constructor from another constructor in the same class.
8. ***this*** is also called as a **self-referencing pointer because it is used to refer to the receiving object of a message from within this object's method.**
9. Inherited methods are called from the method of a subclass without using dot notation or by using dot notation with the reserved word ***this.***

Before we discuss further, let us solve some problems now.

Example 1: How this reference can be used to pass reference to the current object?

Solution:

Consider the following code snippet:

a = t.add(this);

It passes ***this*** as a reference to the current object by invoking ***add method*** of object ***t.***

Example 2: Consider the following code snippet. Do you need this reference here? Why or why not?

```
class Car {
    String numberPlate = " ";
    double speed = 0.0;
    double maxSpeed = 80.0;
  void floor( )
    {
    speed = maxSpeed;
    }
  }
```

Solution: Inside the Car class, you don't need to prefix the field names with ***this*** like this.numberPlate or this.speed or this.maxSpeed. **Please note that here just numberPlate , speed and maxSpeed are sufficient.** The *this* may be implied here. That is because the floor ( ) method must be called by a specific instance of the Car class and this instance knows what its data is. Thus, we can also say that every object has its own floor( ) method.

Tip: Use this, as a new programmer in your codes, explicitly.

Example 3: Explain how you can call a constructor from another constructor by using *this*?

Solution:

The syntax for calling a constructor from another constructor of the same class is as follows:-

this(<parameter-list>);

Rule "The constructor that matches the parameter list will be called." We can add more statements after the *this* statement in a constructor but not before it. That is, the call to this in a constructor must be the first statement of the constructor.

3.11 WRAPPER CLASSES

Let me ask a simple question? Is array a data type or a data structure? The following points will answer this intelligent question:

1. Array is **a data type** supported by Java and the **array data structure** is created using the array type.
2. **Array** is a data type and with respect to the structuring of data, **array is a data structure.**
3. So far we have used only primitive data structures in all Java programs.
4. All primitive data structures are created using primitive type declarations. **For example,**
   int x;
   creates an integer data structure (primitive) capable of holding integer values in it.
5. But we cannot easily create data structure of any type like stack, queue, linked list, tree, set, hash table etc. as Java does not provide in-built types.

6. But Java provides several interfaces and classes by means of the Java Collection Framework (JCF). This collection framework is similar to C++ STL (Standard Template Library) only. The architecture of JCF enables representation and manipulation of collections.
7. **Collection** is the root interface of the collection framework hierarchy. It is an interface representing a group of objects. Each object is known as its **element.**
8. Collections are also called as **containers** because they are in general, data structures designed to hold generic (any) type of objects. Thus, containers or collections are used to store the objects only. They allow you to store, organize and access objects in an efficient manner.
9. Collections are basically defined through a set of interfaces to facilitate the programmer to have flexible implementations based on their requirements.
10. JCF provides many APIs (Application Programming Interfaces) for the manipulation of data structures like maps, sets, trees, arrays and hash tables.
11. Advantages of collections/ containers are:-
    (a) It creates data structures containing heterogeneous types.
    (b) Size of container is resizable.
    (c) It reduces the burden of designers, programmers and users.
    (d) Increased productivity of programming resulting in RAD (Rapid Application Development)
    (e) Interoperability among unrelated APIs is possible.
    (f) It enables software reuse also.
12. Disadvantages of collections/ containers are:-
    (a) Proper care is needed during casting/coercion operations.
    (b) Compile-time type checking is not possible.
13. JCF consists of interfaces, implementations and algorithms.
14. **Interfaces** represent a promised behavior of methods that will be implemented later on.
15. **Implementation** refers to the actual implementation of these interfaces using concrete data structure that can be easily reused also.
16. **Methods** refer to functions performing tasks like searching and sorting on objects.
17. All these components are included in the Java APIs for dealing with the common data structures used to solve problems.
18. To access these objects in a container we use either enhanced for –loop or an Iterator.
19. An iterator is an object that has methods to traverse the collection classes. **This process of traversing of the elements of a collection using an Iterator object is called as an iterating process.** Please understand that when the iterator ( ) method of the Collection interface is invoked, it returns an Iterator object. It is this Iterator object that is used to traverse through the container to access each element in it. In nutshell, we can say that iterators are used to access the elements of the data structures created from the collection classes.

20. Also understand that using an iterator to traverse the collection is the only safe way to modify a collection during iteration.
21. It is not mandatory to place the iterator methods in the try-catch block (to be discussed later). This type of behavior of an iterator is also known as **fail-fast** meaning that the iterator fails quickly and cleanly rather than behaving erractically.
22. The following table shows the Collection interfaces, the method they use and the operations they perform. These help us to write better Java programs:

Collection interfaces	Classes implemented for interfaces given in column-1	Basic operations	Group operations	Query operations	Array operations	Iterator method
Set	HashSet, TreeSet	Add ( ) Remove ( )	addAll ( ) remove All ( ) retainAll ( )	Size ( ) Contains ( ) isEmply ( )	toArray ( ) toArray (Object []a)	hasNext ( ) next ( ) remove ( )
List	LinkedHashset, ArayList, LinkedList					
Deque	ArrayDeque, LinkedList					
Map	HashMap, TreeMap, LinkedhashMap					

23. There are some legacy(old) collection classes also that exist in Java like Vector, Stack, Dictionary, HashTable, Properties, Enumeration.

    Now, just understand that collections cannot handle basic, primitive data types like int, floor and char. They are converted into object types by using the Wrapper classes that are supported by the java.lang package. Wrapper classes as supported by Java are as follows:

Basic/ primitive data type	Wrapper class
int	Integer
char	Character
long	Long
float	Float
double	Double
boolean	Boolean

NOTE: These conversions are preformed by the compiler only.

24. Java's collection classes have been extended and implemented with generic type also. Generic types are the types which include in their definition other types as parameters. It abstracts a specific set of functionalities, behaviors and algorithms. This is done by using type placeholders for the instances they work on. These can be member data, formal method parameters and local method variables.
25. That is why, **generic types are also called as parametric types.**
26. Generic data types allow programmers to define classes and encapsulate into them algorithms which operate on generic parameters.
27. Thus, it is possible to define a generic behavior that applies to different data types.
28. List is an ordered collection of elements that allows duplicate elements. Also it allows easy access of the elements using some index.
29. Java provides two implementations of the List interface — **ArrayList and LinkedList.**
30. There are two versions of the ListInterface also but the new one supports the generic programming model as explained earlier.
31. The new List interface definition is as follows:

    public interface List <E> extends Collection <E>

    Because the List interface extends the Collection interface, it has all the methods available in the Collection interface like add/remove elements, searching for an element inside the collection, clear off all the elements, get the iterator of the collection, and get the size of the collection. Please understand that all of these methods have a control over the specific position of the List.
32. Both **ArrayList and LinkedList** implementation may be used but there is no hard and fast rule for the selection out of the two. **ArrayList** provides additional methods to control over its size while **LinkedList** provides methods to add/remove elements from its head and tail.
33. Wrapper classes are immutable i.e., once you create an object, you cannot change the object's value.
34. The Character class is a wrapper class for the char data type. It provides numerous methods for testing and converting character data.
35. The wrapper classes allow us to use the many Java utility classes that manipulate objects for manipulating primitive values. **For example,** if we are creating a calculator application, we can store the intermediate numeric results as Double **objects** on a **Stack.**

How to convert Strings to Primitives using Wrapper classes?

There are six parser methods in Java—parseInt, parseDouble, parseFloat, parseLong, parseByte and parseShort. They take a String as an argument and convert it to the corresponding primitive. They throw a **NumberFormatException** if the string is not properly formed. **For example,**

```
String str1 = "220";
int n = Integer.parseInt(str1);
```

String str2 = “220.20”;

double d = Double.parseDouble(str2);

How to convert Primitives to Strings using Wrapper classes?

You can also convert primitives to strings **using toString( ) method** of wrapper classes. **For example,**

int n = 220;

String str1 = Integer.toString(n);

Double d= 22.20;

String str2 = Double.toString(d);

The ***Character wrapper class*** provides some static methods for converting the case of the character. Each method accepts a ***char argument*** and returns a ***char*** value. The methods for case conversions are as follows:

Method-I

Char toLowerCase(char ch);

This method returns the ***lowercase*** equivalent of the argument passed to ***ch.***

Method-II

Char toUpperCase(char ch);

This method returns the ***uppercase*** equivalent of the argument passed to ***ch.***

Also note that if the toLowerCase method’s argument is an uppercase character, the method returns the lowercase equivalent.

We are in a position to solve some problems now.

Example 1: What are wrapper classes? [GGSIPU, B. Tech. (CSE/IT)-5th sem., Dec. 2012].

Solution: A wrapper class is a class that contains data or an object of a specific type and has the ability of performing special operations on the data or object. Wrapper classes correspond to the primitive data types in the Java language.

Example 2: Write a Java program to compute the area of a circle and to do this till the user enters “Y” from the keyboard.

Solution:

```
import java.io.*;

public class CircleArea
 {
     public static void main(String[ ] args)
      {
```

```
            DecimalFormat formatter = new DecimalFormat("0.00");
            double radius, area;
            char choice;
            do {
                //read circle's radius
                System.out.println("Enter the radius of circle:");
                radius = Keyboard.readDouble( );
                //calculate and display area
                area= Math.PI * radius * radius;
            System.out.println("The area is: " + formatter.format(area));
            System.out.print("Do you wish to continue? (Y or N)");
            choice = Keyboard.readChar( );
            } while (Character.toUpperCase(choice) = = 'Y');
        }
    }
```

OUTPUTS (after running):

Enter the radius of circle: 10

The area is: 314.16

Do you wish to continue? (Y or N) **y**

Enter the radius of circle: 15

The area is: 706.86

Do you wish to continue? (Y or N) **n**

Example 3: Write a Java program to show the basic operations of the list containing ArrayList implementation. Will your program change if the same operations are to be performed with LinkedList implementation? Explain.

Solution:

```
    //ArrayList implementation
package com.javabook.collection;  // we will study package a bit later
import java.util.ArrayList;
import java.util.List;

public class ArrayList_demo {
    public static void main(String args[ ] args) {
        List<String> arrayList = new ArrayList<String> ( );
    //add 5 items
    for (int i = 0; i < 5; i ++)
      {
     arrayList.add ("Item" + i);
```

```
      }

      // print first 4 elements/items
      for (int i = 0; i < 4; i ++)
         {
            System.out.println(arrayList.get (i) );
         }

         System.out.println("Length of current list is: " + arrayList.size( ));

//change the last item now
arrayList.set(4, "Item 3");

//remove the last one item now
System.out.println(arrayList.remove(4));
System.out.println("Length of current list is: " + arrayList.size( ));
  }
}
```

OUTPUTS(after running):

Item 0

Item 1

Item 2

Length of current list is: 3

Item 2

Length of current list is 2

Explanation: This program adds three items into a String list, prints the elements, resets the value of the 3rd element, then removes the 3rd element from the list. Also note that there exist same item two at both index three and index four.

By simply replacing the ArrayList to the LinkedList, the same result will be shown and nothing else needs to be changed.

Example 4: Write a Java program to read a set of integers along the command line and to find their average. Use wrapper classes.

Solution:

```
public class avg {
     public static void main(String args[ ] ) {
          int s = 0;
```

```
    //loop to traverse command line one by one

    for ( int i =0; i <a.length; i++)
     s+= Integer.parseInt((a[i]));

    //each number is stored as String. Use parseInt method of
//Integer class to convert string to integer and add it to s.

double avg = s/ (double) a.length; //typecasting result to double
system.out.println("Average=" + avg);
 }
}
```

Summary

In this chapter, we have studied what a class is? What are its objects? Why should a class be created and how should it be created? Also studied are the various access specifiers that make a class unique. We have also studied the concept of final, static and instant variables and class members. Also studied finalizers, wrapper classes. Several programming examples have also been solved.

❑❑❑

Chapter 4

Interfaces and Packages

4.0 INTRODUCTION

As we have studied in C++ that deriving of a single new class from two or more base classes is known as multiple inheritance. Also we have studied that this type of inheritance results in ambiguity when two or more base classes have the methods with the same name. Fortunately, **Java does not support multiple inheritance.** But at the same time it cannot overlook the benefit of multiple inheritance also. Thus, to enjoy the benefits of multiple inheritance, **Java provides interfaces. An interface forces the classes to implement certain methods with certain signatures.** An interface takes the abstract concept one step ahead.

4.1 INTERFACES

Interfaces are used to define a promised behavior of a class. So, using interface you can specify **what** a class must do, but not **how** it does? *Please understand that once an interface is defined, you can implement any number of classes from this interface. Also understand that one class can implement any number of interfaces.* That is,

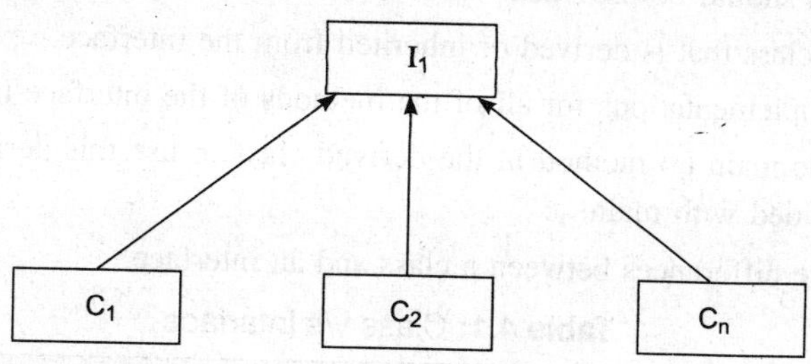

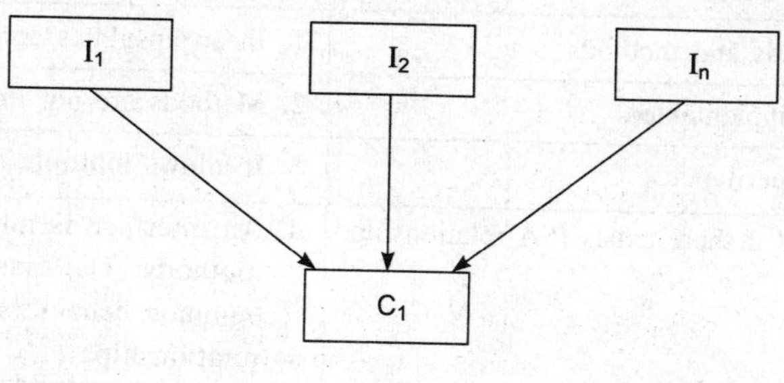

Syntax:

An interface is defined like a class but uses a keyword **interface** rather than **class** as follows:

```
public interface InterfaceName
  {
     //.......
  }
```

Here, the access specifier is used either public or not used. An interface contains constant values (final variables) and methods declarations. *Please note that the difference between an interface and a class is that the methods in an interface are only declared and not implemented* i.e., the methods do not have a body. In other words, there can be no default implementation of any method specified within an interface.

Notes:

1. Methods of abstract class need to be overridden in subclasses (as done earlier).
2. Methods of interface need to be overridden by the classes that implement them.
3. An interface cannot be instantiated.
4. A class is declared to inherit the interface and all methods of the interface are implemented in it.
5. This derived class may have main ( ) method or another class with main ( ) may be written to make use of the interface.
6. Inheriting an interface is mandatory for programs using interfaces.
7. It is a good programming practice to cast the object reference to the interface type.

To implement an interface, the following steps are followed:

1. We declare the interface with methods showing their promised behaviors and no implementation should be provided.
2. (a) Declare a class that is derived or inherited from the interface.
   (b) Provide implementations for all of the methods of the interface in this derived class.
   (c) Provide the main ( ) method in the derived class or use this derived class in some other class provided with main( ).

Let us now tabulate the differences between a class and an interface.

Table 4.1: Class v/s Interface

Class	Interface
1. It encapsulates fields and methods.	**1.** In encapsulates contracts.
2. The methods are implemented.	**2.** Methods are not implemented.
3. It allows single inheritance.	**3.** It allows multiple inheritance.
4. A class is inherited if there exists ISA relationship.	**4.** An interface is inherited to implement the methods. The class is derived to execute common behaviors even if there is no ISA relationship.

Another important distinction at this point of juncture is between an abstract class and an interface.

Table 4.2: Abstract Class v/s Interface

Abstract class	Interface
1. An abstract class is declared with the keyword **abstract**.	1. An interface uses the keyword **interface**.
2. It can contain both abstract methods and non-abstract/concrete methods.	2. All methods in an interface are treated as abstract methods even though there is no abstract keyword in the methods.
3. Abstract classes define a common base type whose instances can only be obtained through specialization of the type i.e. by implementing non-abstract derived classes.	3. Interfaces define only a set of related operations that are expected to be implemented by some instances.
4. When the design requires the presence of a common base class, an abstract class must be defined.	4. When the design requires the ability of a set of operations, an interface must be defined.
5. Abstract class may contain non-final and final variables.	5. Interface contains variables that must be static and final.
6. Abstract class may contain non-public members.	6. Members in an interface are public by default.
7. Abstract class is used to "extend".	7. Interface is used to **"implements"**.
8. Abstract class can be used as a single inheritance.	8. Interface can be used to achieve multiple inheritance.
9. Abstract class can **"extend"** another class and **"implements"** multiple interfaces.	9. Interface can extend another interface.
10. Abstract class can be invoked if main( ) exists.	10. Interface is absolutely abstract.
11. Abstract class is less flexible.	11. Interface is more flexible than abstract class because one class can only "extend" one superclass but "implements" multiple interfaces.

Interfaces are similar to classes but they lack instance variables and their methods are declared without any-body. *Please note that the variables declared inside interfaces are implicitly final and static meaning that they cannot be changed by implementing class and all methods that declare inside interfaces are implicitly abstract methods meaning that there are no default implementations of any method specified within an interface.*

Interfaces are reference data types supporting multiple implementations i.e. a class can implement more than one interface, interaction between two event handling code in GUI based programming, inheritance from diverse concepts where ISA relationship does not hold good, supports functional decomposition and a pure design concept. *Please note that it is also possible to implement each interface by a separate class resulting in hierarchical inheritance. Also note that a class is a mix of design and implementation whereas an interface is an expression of a pure design.*

For example,

```
public interface BankEmployee
 {
     static final int count =25;
          void set_data( );
          void disp_data( );
 }
```

It may be observed here that as the methods of an interface have to be overridden by the classes that implement it, so they cannot be declared final. The data members may be public, static or final. Here, **public** ensures that it can be accessed in unrelated classes; **static** ensures that you cannot create an object of the interface and **final** ensures that the value is not changed in the classes that implement the interface.

Thus, we can say that interfaces cannot contain constants, private data members, constructors and destructors, non-public members and static members. All members of an interface are public by definition. You will get an error if any other access specifier is used. The interfaces follow the naming convention starting with the uppercase letter 'I'.

Interfaces are the part of Java language. Java compiler ensures that when a class is initiated from an interface to implement the methods of the interface, the class will do it.

Applications: Interfaces are useful in developing rapid GUI applications where components like buttons, menus, textboxes etc are involved. When an end user initiates an action by operating the visual component, the client's code communicates with the application program. Such codes are known as **event handlers** (to be discussed a bit later).

4.1.1 Implementing Interfaces

Once an interface has been defined, one or more classes can implement that interface. The keyword **implements** is used to implement an interface by a class. It's syntax is:-

Syntax:

```
class ClassName implements InterfaceName
 {
     //.....
 }
```

Please note that each class that includes an interface must implement all of the methods.

For example,

```
class Manager implements BankEmployee
     {
         //....
```

```
        void set_data( )
         {
             //.....
         }

        void display( )
         {
             //...
         }
    }
```

Diagrammatically,

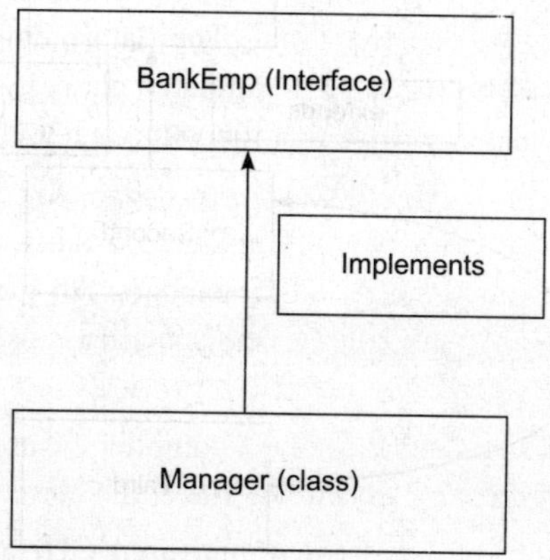

We are in a position to solve some problems now.

Example 1: Which interface must an object implement before it can be written to a stream as an object? *[GGSIPU, B. Tech. (CSE/IT)-5th sem., Sept. 2010]*

Solution: An object must implement Serialization or Externalizable interface.

Example 2: What is externalizable interface used for?

[GGSIPU, B. Tech. (CSE/IT)-5th sem., Oct. 2010]

Solution: It is used for Serialization.

4.1.2 Extending Interfaces

Like classes, interfaces can also be extended. *Please understand that it means that an interface can be sub-interfaced from other interfaces. The new sub-interface will inherit all of the members of the super interface. A new interface is inherited from the old interface using the keyword:- "extends".*

Syntax:

```
Interface SubInterfaceName extends SuperInterfaceName
 {
     //...
 }
```

Just keep the following points in mind regarding interfaces:

1. The keyword "implements" is used to implement an interface by a class while a new interface is inherited from the old interface using the keyword "extends".
2. When a class implements that inherits another interface, it must provide implementation for all of the methods defined within the *interface chain.*

We are in a position to solve an example now.

Example 1: Consider the following class diagram and implement it using interfaces.

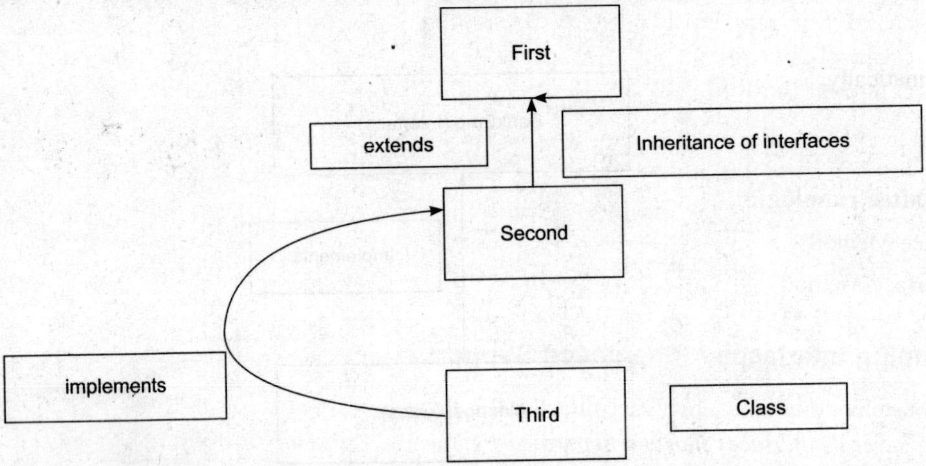

Solution:

```
    // program for extended interface demo

interface first
  {
    void show1( );
  }

interface second extends first
  {
    void show2( );
  }

class third implements second
 {
   public void show1( ) // implementing first interface method declaration
    {
    System.out.println("First Interface Method");
    }

   public void show2( ) // implementing second interface method declaration
    {
```

```
    System.out.println("Second Interface Method");
    }
  }


Class Extend_Interface_Demo
 {
    public static void main(String args[ ] )
     {
        third t = new third( );  //class obj t
        t.show1( );
        t.show2( );
     }
 }
```

OUTPUT (after running):

First Interface Method

Second Interface Method

4.1.3 Grouping Interfaces / Inheritance Support in Java

Java does not support multiple inheritance directly. But Java enjoys the *benefits of multiple inheritance by grouping several interfaces that are separated by commas, into one interface*. The **syntax** is as follows:

```
interface InterfaceName1
  {
     //...
  }

interface InterfaceName2
 {
     //...
 }

interface InterfaceName3 extends InterfaceName1, InterfaceName2
 {
     //...
 }
```

Note that an interface can extend an interface but a class will implement the interface. Also note that the sub-interfaces are too interfaces so you cannot define the methods declared in super interfaces. When we implement a class from a sub-interface then it is the duty of this class to define all of the methods of super-interfaces as well as sub-interfaces.

Before we discuss further, let us solve a program example now.

Example 1: Implement the following class-interface hierarchy:

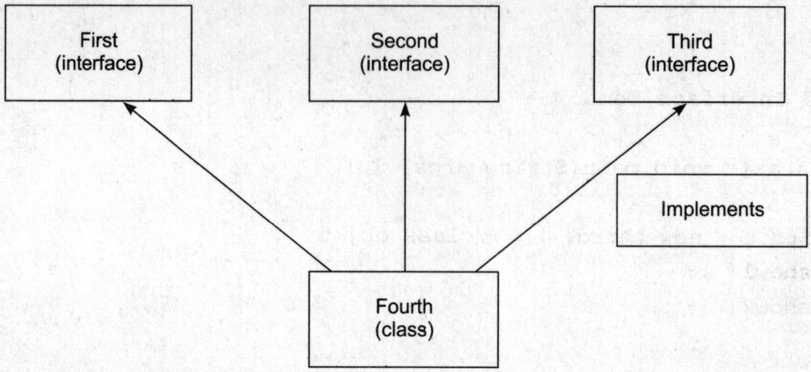

Solution: Here, is the program:

```
interface first
  {
     void show1( );
   }

interface second
  {
     void show2( );
   }


interface third
  {
     void show3( );
   }

class fourth implements first, second, third
  {
    public void show1( )    //implementing 1st interface method
    {
       System.out.println("First Interface Method");
     }

    public void show2( )   //implementing 2nd interface method
    {
       System.out.println("Second Interface Method");
     }
```

```
    public void show3( )     //implementing 3rd interface method
     {
        System.out.println("Third Interface Method");
     }
  }

class Group_Interface_Demo
  {
    public static void main(String args[ ])
     {
        fourth f = new fourth( );
        f.show1( );
        f.show2( );
        f.show3( );
     }
  }
```

OUTPUTS (after running):

First Interface Method

Second Interface Method

Third Interface Method

Please note that polymorphism is also possible in interfaces because inheritance is involved in the implementation of an interface. Also understand that it is possible to have two or more classes that implement the same interface with different implementations. It is through the instances of the class that the polymorphic behaviors are achieved for the given interface. Interfaces support:

- Hierarchical inheritance.
- Multilevel inheritance.
- Multiple inheritances.

Let us now consider one example of each.

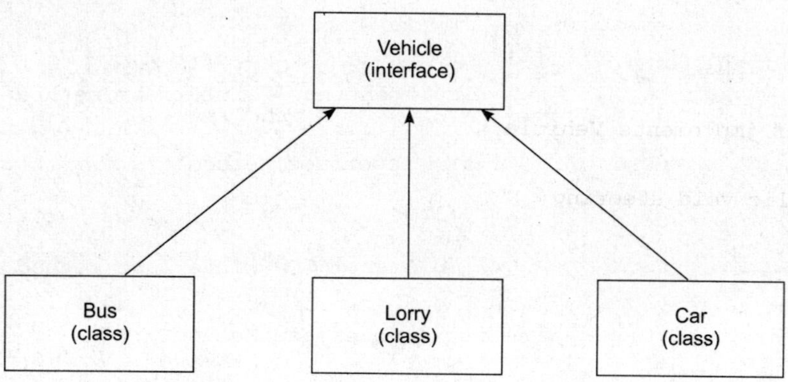

```
//hierarchical inheritance example demo—implementing class
//diagram above.

interface Vehicle
{
   void steering( );
   void brake( );
 }

class Bus implements Vehicle
 {
     public void steering( )
       {
          System.out.println("Steering is round.");
     }

      public void brake( )
      {
    System.out.println("Always use brakes to stop the bus.");
     }
}

class Lorry implements Vehicle
 {
     public void steering( )
      {
          System.out.println("Steering is round.");
     }

      public void brake( )
      {
    System.out.println("Always use brakes to stop the Lorry.");
      }
 }

 class Car implements Vehicle
  {
     public void steering( )
       {
```

```
        System.out.println("Steering is round.");
    }

      public void brake( )
      {
    System.out.println("Always use brakes to stop the car.");
    }
}

class My_Vehicle
 {
    public static void main(String args [ ] )
     {
          Vehicle b = new Bus( );
           b.steering( );
              b.brake( );

          Vehicle v= new Lorry( );
          v.steering( );
          v.brake( );

          Vehicle c= new Car( );
          c.steering( );
          c.brake( );
       }
   }
```

OUTPUTS (after running):

Steering is round.

Always use brakes to stop the bus.

Steering is round.

Always use brakes to stop the Lorry.

Steering is round.

Always use brakes to stop the car.

Let us now see an example of **multilevel inheritance.**

Consider the following class hierarchy:

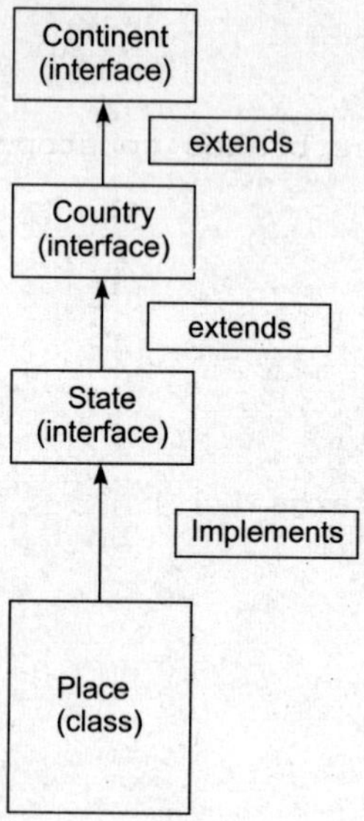

And here is the program.

```
interface I_Continent
 {
    void count_Display( );
 }

interface  I_Country  extends I_Continent
 {
    void show_Country( );
 }

interface I_State  extends I_country
 {
    void display_State( );
}

//now a class is created that implements all these interfaces

class Place implements I_State
{
    public void cont_Display( )
```

```
  {
       System.out.println("Continent is Asia");
  }

 public void show_Country( )
  {
       System.out.println("Country is India");
  }

 public void display_State( )
  {
       System.out.println("State is Delhi");
  }

 void location( )
  {
       System.out.println("Place is GTB Nagar");
   }

 public static void main(String args[ ] )
  {
       Place p = new Place ( );
       IContinent cont = p;
       cont.contDisplay( );
       ICountry country = p;
       country.showCountry( );
       Istate state = p;
       state.displayState( );
       p.location( );
 }
   }
```

OUTPUT (after running):

Continent is Asia

Country is India

State is Delhi

Place is GTB Nagar

Please note here that the class Place implements the base interface IState. Istate is inherited from the interface ICountry which is inherited from the interface IContinent. The class **Place** will implement these two interfaces also i.e. ICountry and IContinent.

Let us consider an example of multiple inheritances now.

Consider the following class hierarchy:

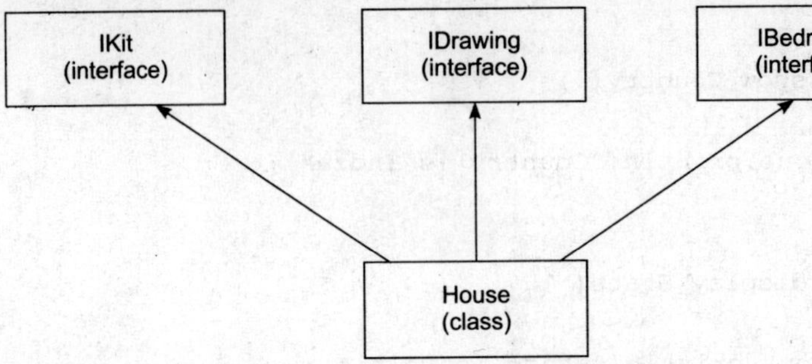

And here goes the program.

```
interface I_Kit
  {
     void store( );
  }

interface I_Drawing
 {
     void showcase( );
 }

interface I_Bedroom
  {
     void ac( );
  }

class House implements I_Kit, I_Drawing, I_Bedroom
  {
     public void store( )
      {
          System.out.println("Please put your groceries inside the shelf.");
      }

     public void show( )
      {
        System.out.println("Keep the prizes and medals in showcase");
       }

     public void ac( )
      {
          System.out.println("AC is must in the room.");
```

```
    }

    public static void main(String args[ ] )
    {
        House h = new House( );
        h.store( );
        h.show( );
        h.ac( );

        IKit k = new House( );
        k.store( );

        I_Drawing d = h;
        d.show( 0;
        IBedRoom b = h;
        b.ac( );
    }
}
```

OUTPUTS (after running):

Please put your items inside the shelf.

Keep the prizes and medals in showcase.

AC is must in the room.

We are in a position to differentiate between an interface and an abstract class.

Table 4.3: Interface v/s Abstract Class

Interface	Abstract class
1. An interface can have only method signatures as their implementation are left for the classes.	1. An abstract class can have method definition i.e. non-abstract methods.
2. A class can implement any number of interfaces i.e. interfaces provide a mechanism to implement multiple inheritance.	2. A class can only extend a single class (abstract/non-abstract) i.e. multiple inheritance using classes.
3. An interface is just a specialization or prescription f· : the promised behavior.	3. An abstract class is an "incomplete class" that requires further specialization.
4. An interface is used when you want to call the methods with their signatures in your classes.	4. An abstract class is generally used when you want to initiate a hierarchy of core specialized classes.
5. Interfaces can be used to support callbacks (just as pointers to function in C/C++).	5. An abstract class just defines the properties that are common to all of its derived classes e.g. shape class.

Note: A class can implement several interfaces at once whereas a class can extend only one parent class.

4.2 PACKAGES

As we know that a class library is a collection of classes that supports the development of programs. A compiler is provided with a class library. Each class in a class library provides a different functionality. Java Programmers always use methods in a class library to develop their programs. They are not in the Java language definition. Like, String is a class. It is not an inherent part of Java language. It is the part of Java Standard class Library that is available in any JDE (Java development Environment). The class libraries are organized as **packages. We define a package as a container for classes. This is done to avoid name collisions.**

However, *please note that two classes with the same name can coexist without any conflict, if each class is declared in a separate package. Also note that a package is not a type.* They are used to organize the different types to avoid name clashes. They have no access restrictions also. They are always public.

Purpose of packages:

1. They are used to avoid class name collisions.
2. They enable class reusability.
3. Software distribution is also easier now.
4. They protect classes from the access by the external classes.

Thus, we can say that a package is a collection of classes and interfaces of similar nature. Two packages may have classes of the same name. But within a package, each class has unique name. They are stored on the disk in their own directories/folders and sub-directories or subfolders.

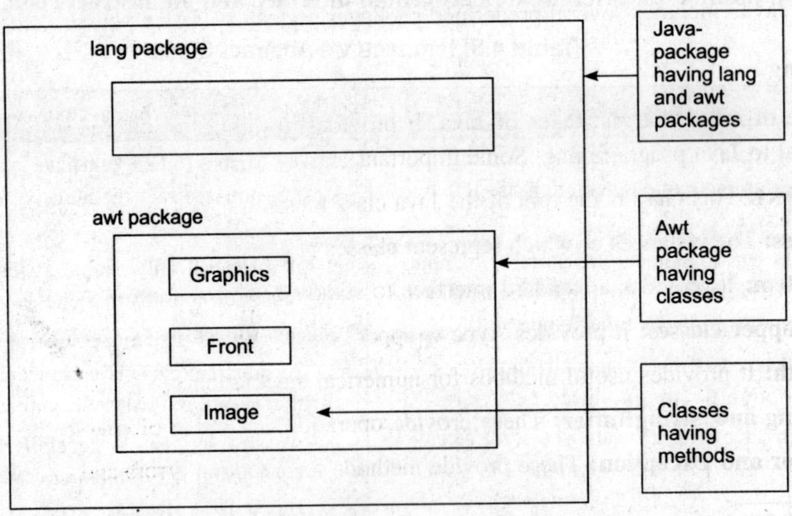

Fig. 4.1: Hierarchical structure of packages in Java

The compiler is informed where the package is located. Packages are organized in a hierarchical structure type. For instance, a package named as "Java" contains the package "awt" which in turn contains many classes required for implementing GUIs. *Also understand that it is possible to nest packages within each other.* This is analogous to that O.S. a folder containing another folder. Thus, Java package contains "lang", "awt" packages, awt package contains classes and classes contain methods. Java package can be used in a Java program by using the **import statement.**

Its **syntax** is as follows:

```
import PackageName.*; // imports an entire package-PackageName
import PackageName.ClassName; //imports a class-ClassName from
                                             //package Packagename
```

For example,

```
import java.awt.*;
```

Note here that a dot (.) separates an element. *Please note that this shows that a hierarchy has been followed while creating these in-built packages.* The first import statement above, imports all classes or interfaces of the awt package (to be discussed later). After importing the packages, we can create an object of the classes within that package.

Packages are of two types and are discussed next.

4.2.1 In-built Packages

Java also as some standard set of supportive classes that are grouped in packages. **Classes with related functionality are bundled together in the same package whether they share code, data or neither.** Every class contained in the package has a unique name that cannot conflict with class names defined elsewhere. Java2 includes several predefined packages and some of them are as follows:

1. Java.lang

This is one of most vital packages of Java. It provides a number of classes and interfaces that are fundamental to Java programming. Some important classes of this package are as follows:-

- **Object:** This class is the root of the Java class hierarchy.
- **Class:** The instances of which represent classes at run-time
- **System:** It provides a standard interface to standard input, output or error.
- **Wrapper classes:** It provides "type wrapper" classes for every Java primitive data type.
- **Math:** It provides useful methods for numerical calculations.
- **String and StringBuffer:** These provide operations on string of characters.
- **Error and Exception:** These provide methods for handling errors and exceptions

NOTE: Of all the packages, package java.lang is exceptional because it is automatically imported.

2. Java.util

This package contains classes and interfaces that support Collection API, date/ calendar operations, internationalization, parsing and basic event processing. Some important classes of this package are as follows:

- **Date and Calender classes:** These classes work with dates and calendars. The date and time are encapsulated in **Date** class.
- **StringTokenizer class:** This class provides methods to parse a string.

3. Java.io

This package provides input/output related classes. Input and output in Java is in the form of streams i.e. a sequence of bytes that flow from source to destination. Classes in this package are put under two categories:

(a) ByteInputStream and Byteoutputstream classes.

(b) CharacterReader and CharacterWriter classes.

4. Java.awt

This package provides all graphical classes that are required for creating a standard GUI programs. It is the largest package of the entire class hierarchy. This package has classes for creating push buttons, labels, check boxes, textboxes, list boxes, menus and many other components.

5. Java.net

This class consists of classes that support network programming. The classes included are as follows:

- **Socket**
- **ServerSocket**
- **DatagramSocket**
- **MultioutSocket**

6. Java.applet

This is one of the smallest packages in Java. This class provides the basic functionality for the creation of applets.

Please understand that applets are the small programs that run inside the web page. It has an Applet class that provides methods to display images, play songs etc.

4.2.2 User Defined Packages

It is possible in Java to create our own packages in order to organize related classes. **Such packages are known as user-defined packages.**

The syntax is:

```
package PackageName;
```

Here, **package** is the reserved keyword of Java and **PackageName** is the name of user-defined package. **Please understand that you can make only one package declaration in a source Java program.** After the package declaration all classes declared within that file will belong to the specified package.

For example,

```
package mypackage;
public class First_Class
 {
       //......
 }
```

We need to save this source file as **First_Class.java.** When you compile this file (First_class.java), its class file, FirstClass.class is stored in the same directory with the name of the package. *Also understand that if now you want to use the classes of this package then go to one level higher and then you can import a class or all of the classes of this package, mypackage.*

For example,

Say, this package mypackage, has the following path:

C:\>j2sdk1.4.2\mypackage

And that the two files—FirstClass.java and FirstClass.class files are stored in C:\>jdk\mypackage\ then before using the classes of mypackage, you must go one level higher, say,

C:\> j2sdk1.4.2

And then import the classes of mypackage in a file, say, "FirstDemo.java" as follows:

```
import mypackage.*;
public class FirstDemo
 {
       public static void main(String args[ ] )
        {
             FirstClass f= new FirstClass( );
        }
 }
```

Save this file as Firstdemo.java in C:\j2sdk1.4.2\ directory and then compile and execute this file. **Please note that if you do not go up one level higher and try to import the classes of mypackage** like you store the file FirstDemo.java in directory C:\>j2sdk1.4.2\mypackage\ then you will get the error message: "can't find class FirstClass". **Also note that if you want to use classes of mypackage from anywhere then you will have to set CLASSPATH variable.**

Let us now see what is this CLASSPATH variable?

The CLASSPATH specifies the specific location that the Java compiler will consider as the root of any packages hierarchy. Say, you create a class FirstClass.java in a package called **javatemp.** You must first compile the file FirstClass.java. This results in FirstClass.class being stored in the **javatemp directory.** Say now you want to use this FirstClass.class in the file FirstDemo.java, which is stored in your directory c:\j2sdk1.4.2 then you will have to explicitly set the CLASSPATH variable as follows:

Set CLASSPATH = %CLASSPATH% ; c:\javatemp

Summary: There are two methods to use a class defined in a package:

1. Change to one directory up one level and then use the class defined in a package.
2. Set the CLASSPATH variable appropriately and use the class defined in a package from anywhere.

The complete program follows now:

```
//program—FirstClass.java
package mypackage;
public class FirstClass
 {
    public FirstClass( )
     {
        System.out.println("First Constructor");
     }
}
```

Save this file as "FirstClass.java" in a directory c:\j2sdk1.4.2\mypackage and compile it.

```
//program—SecondClass.java
package mypackage;
public class SecondClass
 {
    public SecondClass( )
     {
        System.out.println("Second Constructor");
     }
}
```

Save this file as "SecondClass.java" in a directory c:\j2sdk1.4.2\mypackage and compile it.

```
//program—FirstDemo.java
import mypackage.*;
public class FirstDemo
 {
    public static void main(String args[ ])
     {
     FirstClass f = new FirstClass( );
     SecondClass s = new SecondClass( );
     }
   }
```

Save this file as "FirstDemo.java" in a directory c:\j2sdk1.4.2\mypackage and compile it. Finally, execute the file – **"FirstDemo.class"** and check your results.

However, please note that classes defined in the same package are automatically visible without need to specify any import statement.

4.3 JAVA API PACKAGES

It is good to make a group of related classes and interfaces into packages as it makes the usage of classes easier and also its location. So, we can say that package is a collection of related classes and interfaces providing access protection and namespace management.

4.3.1 What is API?

API stands for **Application Programming Interface.** An API is the definition of how a programmer can access the functionality contained within a code library. **An API is an interface which is used for accessing an application or a service from a program.** An API makes it possible makes it possible to use programs from within programs. That is why; it is the foundation for modular systems with clearly defined interfaces between separate components. Java comes with many code libraries that provide **pre-written functionality** for programmers.

For example, Swing is a user interface code library,

```
import javax.swing.*;
```

Swing's API provides the access to the graphical components in Swing.

So, API can be regarded as the local equivalent of a protocol because it is used for the same purposes and defines the same thing. But please remember that traditionally APIs are used for interfaces on one computer while protocols are used for distributed scenarios. An API can be contrasted with a graphical use interface or a command interface or a program. Both are direct user interfaces only.

4.3.2 Java API

In general, Java contains three components as follows:

(a) The Java language.

(b) The Java Virtual Machine (JVM).

(c) The Java API.

The Java language defines the syntax and semantics of the Java programming language. It defines basic vocabulary like primitive types, if/else blocks, the syntax of class declaration, exception syntax, variable scoping rules and every thing else necessary for any programming language to work.

The JVM executes Java bytecode. In conventional way, we produce Java bytecode by compiling code that conforms to the Java language. **Please note that you can compile the code written in other languages into Java bytecode.**

The Java API is the set of classes included with the Java Development Environment. These classes are written using the Java language and run on the JVM. The Java API includes everything from collection classes to GUI classes.

4.3.3 Types of Java APIs

There are three types of Java Programming Language Application Programming Interfaces (API):

(a) Official Core Java API.

(b) Optional official APIs.

(c) Unofficial APIs.

I. Official Core Java API

These APIs are contained in the JDK or JRE, of one of the editions of the Java Platform. The three editions of the Java Platform are Java ME (Micro Edition), Java SE (Standard Edition) and Java EE (Enterprise Edition).

Table 4.4: Packages

Name	Packages that contain API	History
Abstract Window Toolkit (AWT)	java.awt	First released version 1.0
Swing	javax.swing	Included in J2SE 1.2 and later
Accessibility	javax.accessibility	
Drag and Drop	java.awt.datatransfer and java.awt.dnd	
Image I/O	javax.imageio	
Sound	javax.sound.midi	
Java Database Connectivity (JDBC)	java.sql javax.sql	
Java Cryptography Extension (JCE)	javax.crypto javax.crypto.interfaces javax.crypto.spec	Included as part of J2SE 1.4 and later. Available as an optional package to versions 1.2 and 1.3.
Java Authentication and Authorization Service (AAS)	javax.security.auth	Included in J2SE 1.4 and released as an optional package with version 1.3.
Java Secure Socket Extension (JSSE)	javax.net javax.net.ssl java.security.cert	A set of packages the enable secure Internet communications. Included as part of J2SE 1.4 and later.
Java Native Interface (JNI)		Allows Java code running in JVM to call and be called by native applications and libraries written in other languages like C, C++ and assembly.
Java Management Extensions (JMX)	javax.management javax.management.loading javax.management.modelmbean javax.management.monotor javax.management.openmbean javax.management.relation javax.management.remote javax.management.remote.rmi javax.management.timer	A technology that supplies tools for managing and monitoring applications, system objecys, devices like printers and service-oriented networks. Included as part of J2SE 1.5 and later was an optional package prior to this.

II. Optional Official APIs

These APIs can be downloaded separately from the Sun Microsystems official site. The specification of these APIs is defined according to a Java Specification Request (JSR). Sometimes some of these APIs are later included in the core APIs of the platform. **For example,** Swing.

These APIs are as follows:

Table 4.5: APIs

Name	History
Java Advanced Imaging (JAI)	An API that provides a set of interfaces that support a high-level programming model allowing to manipulate images easily.
Java Communications API	JCA
Java Data Objects (JDO)	A specification of Java objects persistence.
JavaHelp	A full-featured extensible help system that enables you to incorporate online help in applets, components, applications, OS and devices.
Java Media Framework (JMF)	An API that enables audio, video and other time-based media to be added to Java applications and applets.
Java Naming and Directory Interface (JNDI)	An API for directory services.
Java Speech API (JSAPI)	This API allows for speech synthesis.
Java 3D (J3D)	A scene graph-based 3D API.
Java Open GL (JOGL)	A wrapper library for OpenGL.

III. Unofficial APIs

These APIs are developed by third parties but not related to any JSRs. For example,

(a) Eclipse.

(b) JScience—Numerical Analysis

(c) Javolution—real-time libraries.

(d) Rendering libraries— Cobra HTML parser and Renderer library.

(e) Windowing Libraries— Standard Widget Toolkit (SWT).

NOTE: The print and println methods are part of the API and provide ways for output to be displayed on the standard output device. For example, in the following statement of Java-

```
System.out.println("Java is easy….");
```

System is a class that is the part of Java API. The System class contains **objects** and methods that perform system-level operations. One of the objects contained in the System class is named **out.** The **out object** has **methods** like print and println for performing output on the system console or standard output device.

4.3.4 Java API Overview

The following are the JAVA APIs as given by the Sun Microsystems:-

1. **JDK 1.0.2 API:** It is the API that ships with version 1.0.2 of the JDK (i.e. Java Development Kit). It includes eight (8) basic packages— *java.lang, java.io, java.util, java.net, java.awt, java.awt.image, java.awt.peer and java.applet.*
2. **JDK 1.1 API:** It is the current release of JDK. It is a superset of JDK 1.0.2 that brings improvements in functionality, performance and quality to Java.
3. **JAVA Enterprise API:** It supports connectivity to enterprise databases and legacy/old applications. With these APIs, corporate developers are building distributed client/server applets and applications in Java that run on any OS or hardware platform in the enterprise. This API presently covers 4 areas—JDBC, Java IDL, Java RMI and JNDI. Let us define these one by one now.

   JDBC is Java Database Connectivity, a standard SQL database access interface, providing uniform access to a wide range of relational databases. Microsoft has provided this open database connectivity.

   Java IDL is developed to the OMG Interface Definition Language specification as a language-neutral way to specify an interface between an object and its client on a different platform.

   Java RMI is remote (far) method invocationbetween peers or between client and server, when applications at both ends of the invocation are written in Java.

   JNDI is Java Naming and Directory Interface. It is a new addition to JavaSoft platform APIs. It provides Java applications a unified interface to multiple naming and directory services in the enterprise. As part of the Java Enterprise API set, JNDI enables seamless connectivity to heterogeneous enterprise naming and directory services. Java developers can now build powerful and portable **directory-enabled applications** using this industry-standard interface.
4. **JavaBeans API: The JavaBeans API define a portable, platform-neutral set of APIs for software components.** JavaBean components are able to plug into existing component architectures like MS OLE/COM/Active-X architecture, OpenDoc and Netscape's LiveConnect. End users are able to compose together JavaBeans components using application builders. **For example,** a button component could trigger a bar chart to be drawn in another component or a live data feed component could be represented as a chart in another component. JavaBeans is available in JDK. Beans developers will also need to download the Beans Development Kit from the JavaBeans web pages.
5. **Java Security API:** They are the framework for developers to easily and securely include security functionality in their applets and applications. This functionality includes cryptography

with digital signatures, encryption and authentication. An intermediate subset of the Security API is included in JDK 1.1. This subset is known as **"Security and Signed Applets."**

6. **Java Server API:** Java server API is an extensible framework that enables and eases the development of a whole spectrum of Java-powered Internet and Intranet servers. The APIs provide uniform and consistent access to the server and the administrative system resources required for developers to quickly develop their own Java Servlets i.e., executable programs that users upload to run on networks or servers.

7. **Java Commerce API:** This API brings secure purchasing and financial management to the web. **JavaWallet** is the initial component that defines and implements a client-side framework for credit card, debit card and e-cash transactions.

8. **Java Media API:** It allows developers and users to easily and flexibly take advantage of a wide range of rich, interactive media on the web. The Media APIs encompass these areas: Java 2D, Java Media Framework, Java Collaboration, Java Telephony, Java Speech, Java Animation and Java 3D. **Java 2D** provides an abstract imaging model that extends the 1.0.2 AWT package including line art, images, color, transforms and compositing. **JMF or Java Media Framework** specifies a unified architecture, messaging protocol and programming interface for media players, capture and conferencing. JMF will be published as three APIs—the Java Media player will be published first, Java Media Capture and Java Media Conference APIs will be published subsequently. JMP is an API for synchronization, control, processing and presentation of compressed streaming and stored timed media including video and audio. **Java collaboration allows for interactive two-way, multi-party communications** over a variety of networks. **Java Telephony** integrates telephones with computers. It provides basic functionality for first-party and third-party call control. **Java Speech** provides Java-based speech recognition and speech synthesis (text-to-speech). **Java animation provides for motion and transformations of 2D objects.** It makes use of **Java Media** Framework for synchronization, composition and timing. **Java 3D** provides an abstract, interactive imaging model for behavior and control of 3D objects.

9. **Java Management API:** It provides a rich set of extensible Java objects and methods for building applets that can manage an enterprise network over Internets. It has been developed in collaboration with SunSoft and a broad range of industry leaders like Bay Networks, Cisco Systems, Computer Associates, Compuware, LandMark Technologies, Novell etc.

10. **Java Embedded API:** These APIs specify how the Java API may be subsetted for embedded devices that are incapable of supporting the full Java Core API. **Please remember that it includes a minimal embedded API based on java.lang, java.util and parts of java.io**. It defines a series of extensions for particular areas like networking and GUIs.

4.3.5 Some Java API Packages

The following table shows the API specification for version 6 of the Java Platform, Standard Edition:

Table 4.6: Java API Packages

API packages	Purpose
java.applet	It provides the classes necessary to create applet.
java.awt	It contains all classes for creating user interfaces and for painting graphics and images
java.awt.color	It provides classes for color spaces.
java.awt.datatransfer	It provides interfaces and classes for transferring data between and within applications.
java.awt.dnd	Drag and Drop is a direct manipulation gesture found in many Graphical User Interface systems that provides a mechanism to transfer information between two entities logically associated with presentation elements in the GUI.
java.awt.event	It provides interfaces and classes for dealing with different types of events fired by AWT components.
java.awt.font	It provides classes and interfaces related to fonts.
java.awt.image	It provides classes and interfaces for creating and modifying images.
java.awt.print	It provides classes and interfaces for a general printing API.
java.beans	It contains classes related to developing beans (components based on the Java Beans architecture).
java.io	It provides for system input and output through data streams, serialization and the file system.
java.lang	It provides classes that are fundamental to the design of Java programming language.
java.math	It provides classes for performing precise integer and decimal arithmetic.
java.net	It provides classes for implementing networking applications.
java.rmi	It provides the RMI package.
java.security	It provides classes and interfaces for the security framework.
java.sql	It provides the API for accessing and processing data stored in a data store like a file or an RDBMS, using Java programming language.
java.text	It provides classes and interfaces for handling text, dates, numbers and messages (free from natural languages).
java.util	It contains the collections framework, legacy collection classes, event model, date and time facilities, internationalization and different utility classes like a string tokenizer, a random number generator, a bit array etc.

We are in a position to solve some questions now.

Q.1. Write down the order in which the APIs are released.

[**Hint:** As per Sun Microsystems Inc., the API are released in the following order:

- JDK 1.0.2 API
- JDK 1.1 API
- Java Enterprise API—JDBC, Java RMI, Java IDL and JNDI.
- JavaBeansTM API.
- Java Security API.
- Java Server API.
- Java Commerce API/ Java Wallet.
- Java Media API—Java 2D, JMF, Java Collaboration, Java Telephony, Java Speech, Java Animation and Java 3D.
- Java Management API.
- Java Embedded API.]

Q.2. What is a Collection API? [*GGSIPU, B. Tech. (CSE/IT)-5TH sem., Dec. 2011*]

[**Hint:** It is a set of classes and interfaces that support operation on collections of objects. These classes and interfaces are more flexible, more powerful and more regular than vectors, arrays and hashtables.

Example of classes are HashSet, HashsetMap, ArrayList, Linkedlist, TreeSet, TreeMap.

Example of interfaces are Collections, set, List and Map.]

Q.3. Is Iterator a Class or Interface?

[**Hint:** It is an interface that is used to step through the elements of a Collection].

Q.4. Are the imports checked for validity at the compile time?

[**Hint:** Yes, the imports are checked for the semantic validity at the compile time.]

Q.5. What is an Externalizable interface?

[**Hint:** It is an interface that contains two methods—***readExternal*** and ***writeExternal***. These methods give you a control over the serialization mechanism. Thus, if your class implements this interface, you can customize the serialization process by implementing these methods.]

Q.6. Write a program to show inheritance concept in interface.

[*GGSIPU, B. Tech. (CSE/IT)-5TH sem., Dec. 2009*]

[Hint:

```
interface face
 {
  int add;
  void sum(int a, int b);
    { }
}
class demo implements face
  {
  void sum (int a, int b)
   {
    x=a;
    y= b;
    add = x + y;
    System.out.println("Addition =" + add);
  }
}

class my_demo
 {
  public static void main(String args[ ] )
    {
    demo d = new demo ( );
    d.sum(33, 22);
   }
}
```

Q.7. What are the similarities/differences between an abstract class and and an interface?

[GGSIPU, B. Tech. (CSE/IT)-5TH sem., Dec. 2011 and Dec. 2012]

Solution:

Abstract class	Interface
1. An abstract class is declared with the keyword **abstract.**	1. An interface uses the keyword **interface.**
2. It can contain both abstract methods and non-abstract/concrete methods.	2. All methods in an interface are treated as abstract methods even though there is no abstract keyword in the methods.
3. Abstract classes define a common base type whose instances can only be obtained through specialization of the type i.e. by implementing non-abstract derived classes.	3. Interfaces define only a set of related operations that are expected to be implemented by some instances.
4. When the design requires the presence of a common base class, an abstract class must be defined.	4. When the design requires the ability of a set of operations, an interface must be defined.
5. Abstract class may contain non-final and final variables.	5. Interface contains variables that must be static and final.
6. Abstract class may contain non-public members.	6. Members in an interface are public by default.
7. Abstract class is used to "extend".	7. Interface is used to **"implements"**.
8. Abstract class can be used as a single inheritance.	8. Interface can be used to achieve multiple inheritance.
9. Abstract class can **"extend"** another class and **"implements"** multiple interfaces.	9. Interface can extend another interface.
10. Abstract class can be invoked if main( ) exists.	10. Interface is absolutely abstract.
11. Abstract class is less flexible.	11. Interface is more flexible than abstract class because one class can only "extend" one superclass but "implements" multiple interfaces.

Q.8. (a) Why multiple inheritances of classes is not there in Java?

(b) What is a package? Explain the packages with an example and how to import packages. Explain the compilation of a newly designed package.

[GGSIPU, B. Tech. (CSE/IT)-5TH sem., Dec. 2012]

Q.9. Explain with an example how to create a package.

[GGSIPU, B. Tech. (CSE/IT)-5TH sem., Dec. 2013]

Q.10. What statement must appear at the beginning of each class source file that is the part of a package?

Summary

In this chapter, we have studied and compared interfaces as well as classes. We have also seen that what a package is? Package organizes the related classes into groups just as you have books in a library. A Java programmer can create his own package of classes using package statement. A Java package is used by using an import statement in a program.

Chapter 5

Exception Handling

5.0 INTRODUCTION

Large monolithic programs may become very complex. This results in more errors. To make a program error free in the first instance is a tedious job. This is so because the programmer has not anticipated all possible situations that might occur while you run a program. These errors may be due to syntax mistakes, incorrect input, corrupt files or other physical device problems. **An exception is an abnormal condition that arises in a code-sequence at run-time and disrupts the normal flow of a program.** That is why; error handling becomes mandatory when you develop applications that need to take care of unexpected situations. Java provides exceptions to provide error-handling capabilities for its programs. *Please understand that when an exception occurs in any program, it creates an exception object and hands it off to the runtime system.* The exception object contains necessary information like its type and the state of the program when the error occurred, about the exception. The run-time system is then responsible for finding the code to handle this error. *Also understand that in Java terms, creating an object and handing it to the run-time system is called as throwing an exception.* An exception is an object that is generated in memory as a result of an error or an unexpected event. When an exception is generated, it is said to be **thrown.** An application must detect this exception as otherwise it will halt the application. To solve this problem Java allows us to create exception handlers. An exception handler is a part of the code that responds to the exceptions when they are thrown. And this process of intercepting and responding to exceptions is called as exception handling. *Please note that if your code does not handle an exception when it is thrown, the default exception handler deals with it. Also note that it is this default exception handler that prints an error message.*

There is a class ***Exception*** to solve these problems in Java.

Let us now see what is this Exception class?

Exceptions in Java are actual objects. The class at the top of the hierarchy is called **Throwable.** Two classes are derived from the **Throwable** class—**Error and Exception.**

Instances of Error **are internal errors like *VirtualMachineError,*** in Java Run Time Environment. The ***Exception class*** is used for exceptional conditions that have to be trapped in a program. The Exception class has been sub-classed into two categories—***IOException*** and ***RunTimeException.*** Run-time exceptions are those exceptions which occur within the Java runtime system **like** ArrayIndexOutOfBoundsException, ArithmeticException or NullPointerException. *Please note that run-time exceptions can occur anywhere in a program.*

Let us see the complete hierarchy now (see Fig. 5.1).

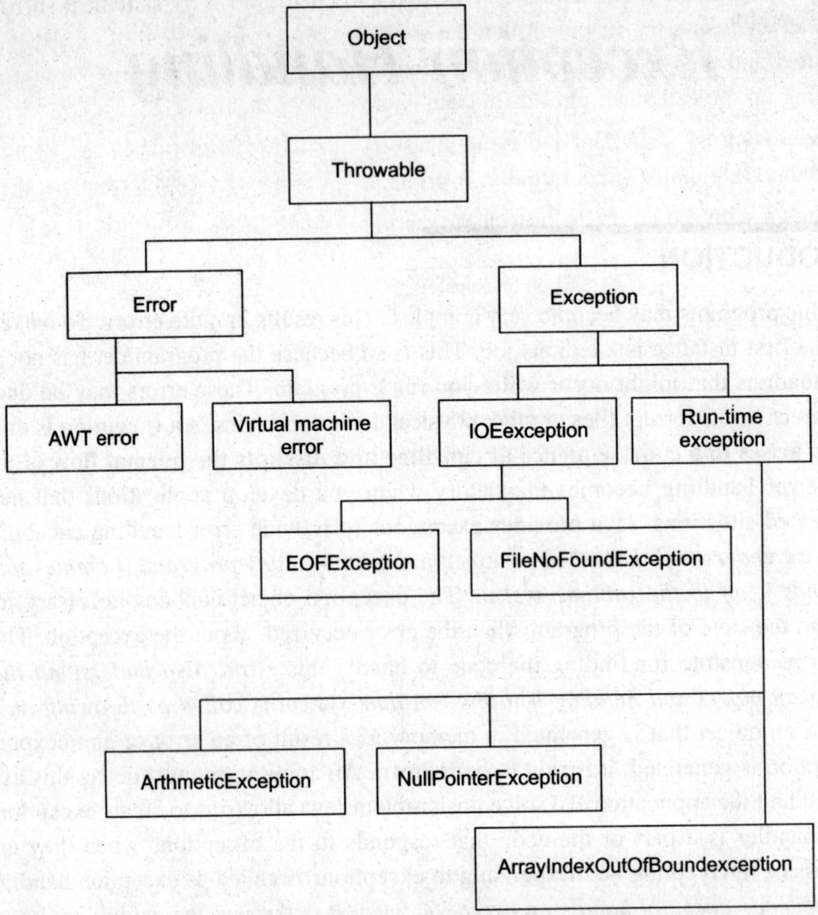

Fig. 5.1: Classification of errors and exceptions in Java

An exception is an abnormal condition in Java Program that occurs at run –time and cause Java program to stop. Please understand that when Java program stops or interrupts, Java throws an exception. Then, Java throws *this exception* to a part of the program that will *catch* it.

NOTE: You should not try to catch most exceptions but you should catch all exceptions that are caused by events on which you have no control like I/O problems.

Sequences of events that occur when exception occurs in Java are as follows:

Step-1: It looks the code that caused the exception inside a try statement that can handle the exception. (we shall study try a bit later). If the try statement has a catch clause that can handle this type of exception then it goes to that code. After catch clause is executed, execution resumes after the end of the entire try statement. It is not possible to return to the point at which the exception was thrown.

Step-2: If there is no try statement around the code that threw the exception, ***Java goes up the stack call*** and looks at the statement that called this method and checks for a try statement surrounding the call. If it finds an enclosing try statement that has a catch clause for this kind of exception, the catch clause is executed and then execution continues after that try statement. Please understand that Java continues moving up the call stack until it finds an enclosing try statement.

Step-3: If no enclosing try statement and catch clause is found, the exception is caught by the initial Java system method that called main initially. It prints an error message and terminates the program.

This may be shown with the help of a flowchart (see Fig. 5.2)

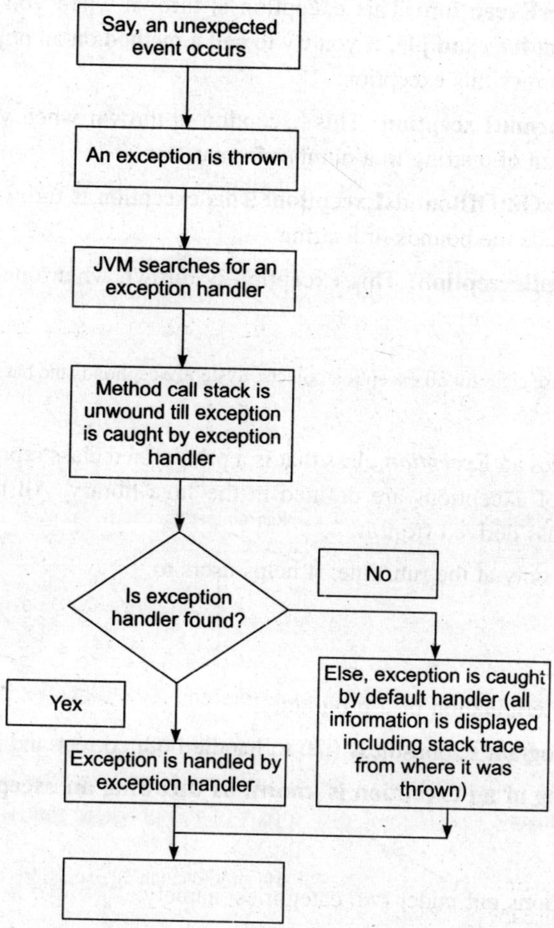

Fig. 5.2: Flowchart for exception handling

NOTES:

1. Say, a user creates a file on disk and later someone deletes it. Then when later the application attempts to open the file to read from it then an error occurs because it does not exist. So, exception is thrown.
2. JAVA API documentation lists all of the exceptions that can be thrown from each method.

5.1 JAVA'S COMMON EXCEPTIONS

Java has several predefined exceptions inside the standard package **java.lang.** Some of the common exceptions are as follows:

1. **The ArithmeticException:** This exception is thrown when an exceptional arithmetic condition **like divide-by-zero** is encountered in a program.
2. **The ArrayIndexOutOfBoundsException:** This exception is thrown when an attempt is made to access an array element beyond the array index.
3. **The NullPointerException:** This exception is thrown when you try to use null where an object is required. **for example,** if you try to call a method on an object which is just declared, not created, it throws this exception.
4. **The NumberFormatException:** This exception is thrown when you attempt to perform an invalid conversion of a string to a number format.
5. **The StringindexOutOfBoundsException:** This exception is thrown when you try to attempt to an index outside the bounds of a string.
6. **The InterruptedException:** This exception is thrown when one thread interrupts another thread.

NOTE: Exception is the base class for all exception objects; SystemException is the base class for all run-time error.

The Java library provides an ***Exception*** class that is a pre-defined class representing ***System.Exception*** data type. A number of exceptions are defined in the Java library. All these exceptions are either Exception type or a class derived from it.

An exception is raised only at the run-time. It helps users to:

(a) notify the error,

(b) save all work,

(c) allow graceful termination of a program,

(d) improve the program's robustness (i.e. to handle both correct and incorrect data).

This process of raising of an exception is known as throwing an exception.

Types of Exceptions

Actually, Java **Exceptions** put under two categories, namely:

1. **Unchecked Exceptions:** Server problems that normally are treated as fatal or situations that probably reflect program bugs are unchecked exceptions. Fatal situations are represented by the Error class. Probable bugs are represented by the ***RunTimeException class.*** These exceptions are usually something that should have been prevented by more careful programming.

   For example, you should never get ***NullPointerException or ArrayindexOutOfbounds*** exception. If you get so, then it means that there is something wrong in your program and you must fix it. *Please remember that you don't catch unchecked exceptions.* Instead, you fix your program so that it can't produce one of these. But ***NumberFormatException*** is one of exceptions of this type that is usually caught.

2. **Checked Exceptions:** Conditions that can readily occur in a correct Java program are called as checked exceptions. These are represented by the ***Exception class.*** These are usually error in the input data. The programmer has no control over the input the user gives you like filenames. If the user gives you a bad value, it may cause an exception when you use it. *Please understand that you need to check for bad input using a try statement.*

5.2 METHODS OF EXCEPTION HANDLING

We have seen that when an unexpected error occurs in a method, Java creates an object of the type Exception. After creating the Exception object, Java sends it to the program. **This is called as throwing an exception.** The exception object contains information about the type of error and the state of your program when the exception occurred. Now it is our responsibility to handle this using an exception handler.

5.2.1 The Try Block

The try block contains the code that might throw an exception.

Syntax:

```
try
{
    //statements that may cause  an exception
}
```

If an exception occurs then the remaining statements, in the statements enclosed in a try block, is skipped and the exception handler code within the catch block is executed.

5.2.2 The Catch Block

A try block must have at least one catch block that follows it immediately. We must associate an exception handler with the try block by providing one or more catch handlers immediately after the try block. Its syntax is as follows:

Syntax:

```
try
    {
        //statements that may cause  an exception
    }

catch(Exception e)
{
    //exception handler statement
}
```

Also note that there may be more than one catch block, each of them catching a specific type of exception:

```
try
   {
      //statements that may cause  an exception
   }

catch(Exception1 e1)
 {
     //exception handler statement
 }
catch(Exception2 e2)
 {
     //exception handler statement
 }


catch(Exception3 e3)
 {
     //exception handler statement
 }
```

We are in a position to solve some examples now.

Example 1: Write a Java program to implement try-catch when trying to divide by zero.
Solution:

```
    // program to demonstrate try-catch working

 class try_catch_demo
 {
    public static void main(String args[ ])
    {
        try
        {
            int a=100, b=100,c;
            c= a/ (a-b);
            System.out.println("\nDivide by zero successful.");
        }

catch (ArithmeticException ae)
 {
 System.out.println("Catching an arithmetic exception.");
```

```
 System.out.println("Divide by zero unsuccessful.");
}

System.out.println("This is nice.....");

try
 {
     int p[ ] = new int[5];
     p[1] = 6;
     p[2] = 5;
     p[3] = 1974;
     p[4] = 19;
     p[5] = 67;
 System.out.println("Violating array boundary condition successful.");
        }

        catch (ArrayIndexOutOfBoundsException aoe)
         {
System.out.println("Catching an array index out of
bounds exception.");
System.out.println("Violating array boundary condition
   unsuccessful.");
            }
          }
        }
```

OUTPUTS (after running):

Catching an arithmetic exception.

Divide by zero unsuccessful.

This is nice......

Catching an array index out of bounds exception.

Violating array boundary condition unsuccessful.

Example 2: Write Java programs to do the following tasks:-

(a) use of StringIndexOutOfBoundException.

(b) NullPointerException.

Solution:

(a)
```
import java.io.*;
class testing_your_string
{
    public static void main(String args[ ] )
    {
```

```
        try
        {
            String s = "Rajiv Chopra";
            Char ch = s.charAt(5);
        }

        catch (Exception ae)
        {
            System.out.println(ae);
        }
    }
}
```

(b)

```
class null_exception
{
    public static void main(String args[ ] )
    {
        int a[ ] = null;
        int b;
        try {
            b= a [1]; //null pointer
        }
    catch (ArithmeticException ae)
    {
        System.out.println(e.Message( ));
    }
    catch (NullPointerException e1)
    {
        System.out.println("Null Pointer Exception" + e1);
    }
    catch (Exception e)
    {
        System.out.println("Error");
    }
    }
}
```

5.2.3 The Throw Statement—within the Method

The throw statement is used to throw an exception **within the method**. In order to throw an exception, we find an appropriate exception class, create an object of that class (using new operator) and use the throw statement. Its syntax is as follows:

Syntax:

throw objName;

Please understand that here the compiler gives an error if the object objName does not belong to a valid Exception class. Also understand that the throw statement is commonly used in programmer-defined exception.

5.2.4 The Throw Statement—by the Method

The throw statement is used to specify the list of exceptions that are thrown by the method. The throw keyword is used after the signature of the method and followed by the name of one or more exceptions.

For example,

```
void show( ) throws Exception1, Exception2, Exception3
  {
      //....
  }
```

Here, the show( ) method can throw an exception of either Exception1 type or Exception2 type or Exception3 type. *Please understand that adding the throws keyword does not mean that the exceptions occur rather it provides additional information with the method definition about the possible exceptions that might occur.*

Before we discuss further, let us solve some programs now.

Example 1: Write a Java program to show the working of the throws statement by the method.

Solution:

```
class try_catch_demonstration
 {
      public static void main(String args[ ] )
        {
            try
              {
                  sample ( );
              }

             catch(NullPointerException ne)
              {
                System.out.println("Catching an exception" + ne);
              }
        }

static void sample( ) throws NullPointerException
  {
      System.out.println("Throwing a null pointer exception..");
      throw new NullPointerException( );
  }
}
```

OUTPUTS (after running):

Throwing a null pointer exception.

Catching an exception—java.lang.NullPointerException

Example 2: What is the difference between throw and throws?

[GGSIPU, B. Tech. (CSE/IT)-5th sem., Dec. 2011]

Solution: Throw is a statement and is used to throw an Exception explicitly. On the other hand, **throws** is a clause that is generally used for checked exception or for user-defined exception. (Please refer to the sections above).

Example 3: What are checked and unchecked exceptions?

[GGSIPU, B. Tech. (CSE/IT)-5th sem., Dec. 2011]

Solution: Please refer to the sections above.

5.2.5 The Finally Block

When an exception occurs, the remaining statements in the try block are ignored. Sometimes it is vital to process certain statements, no matter whether an exception is raised or not. The **finally block** is used for this purpose.

For example,

```
try
 {
     OpenFile( );  // a method that opens a file
     OutputToFile( );   //method that writes to a file
 }

catch(Exception1 e1)
 {
     //exception handler statement
  }

finally( )
  {
     CloseFile( ); // a method to close a file
  }
```

The file which was opened in OpenFile ( ) method has to be closed irrespective of whether an exception is raised or not. **Please understand that the code in the finally block is executed regardless of whether an exception is thrown or not. The finally block follows the catch blocks.**

For example,

```
class try_catch_finally_demo
  {
    public static void main(String args[ ] )
     {
```

```
//put in try, the portion of code where you doubt an error can occur
        try
         {
              int a=100, b=100,c;
              c= a / (a-b);
        System.out.println("Division by zero successful");
          }

        catch (ArithmeticException ae)    //try must have a catch
          {
               System.out.println("Divide by zero unsuccessful.");
          }
         finally( )   //control has to come here at any cost
          {
              System.out.println("Avoid dividing by zero.");
          }
        }
      }
```

OUTPUTS (after running):

Divide by zero unsuccessful.

Avoid dividing by zero.

5.2.6 Catching all Exception Handler

It may be the scenario that it is not possible for a **Java programmer to provide a specific catch handler for every possible exception.** Java provides the facility to **create a catch handler** that catches every possible exception as follows:-

```
catch (Exception e)
  {
     //......
   }
```

This will catch any exception, so if you use it then write it at the end of all catch handlers. *Please note that this is just like a default in switch statement as studied earlier.*

```
try
 {
     //statements;
 }

catch(ArithmeticException ae)
 {
```

```
        //......
    }
catch(ArrayIndexOutOfBoundsException aoe)
    {
        //......
    }
catch(Exception e)
    {
        //......
    }
```

Also note here that since the last catch handler can catch any exception, so we write it at the end as otherwise you will get an error message. This also means that the order as given above should not be changed else you will get an error as 'Catch not reached".

Before we discuss further, let us solve some examples now.

Example 1: Write a Java program using exceptions to compute the roots of a given quadratic equation. Throw an exception if discriminant becomes less than 0.

Solution:

```
import java.util.*;
public class quad_equ {
        public double[ ] roots(double a, double b, double c) throws
    NoRootsException {
      if (a < 0) throw new NoRootsException( );
      double  [ ] r= new double[2];
      double t= b * b - 4 * a * c;
      if (t < 0) throw new NoRootsException( );
        t=Math.sqrt(t);
      r[0] = (-b+t) / (2.0 * a);
      r[1] = (-b-t) / (2.0 * a);
      return ( r );
      }

public static void main(String args[ ] )
   {
      Quad_equ Q= new Quad_equ( );
      Scanner kbd= new Scanner(System.in);
 System.out.println("Enter the coefficients of quad equation");
      double a = kbd.nextDouble( );
      double b = kbd.nextDouble( );
      double c = kbd.nextDouble( );
      try {
            double  [ ] root = Q.roots(a, b, c);
```

```
        System.out.println("roots are\t" + root[0] + "\t" + root[1]);
            }
        catch(NoRootsexception s) {
          System.out.println(s);
         }
        }
        class NoRootsException extends Exception {
              public String toString( ) {
                return "Roots cannot be computed";
              }
             }
```

Example 2: What is the difference between *throw* and *throws*?

Solution: Exceptions that are thrown by Java runtime systems can be handled by try and catch blocks. With throw exception we can handle the exceptions thrown by the program itself. If a method is capable of causing an exception that it does not handle, it must specify this behavior. So the callers of the method can guard against that exception.

Example 3: Differentiate between Exception and Error in Java.

Solution: Exception and error are the subclasses of the throwable class. **Exception class** is useful exceptional conditions that user program should catch. With exception class we can subclass to create our own custom exception.

Error defines exceptions that are not expected to be caught by your program. **For example, Stack Overflow.**

Example 4: Define what is a Resource Leak?

Solution: The process of freeing up other resources that might have been allocated at the beginning of a method is known as Resource Leak.

Example 5: Can we have a catch block without try block?

Solution: No, because try-catch and try-finally form a unit.

Example 6: Show three different ways of using catch.

Solution:

1. catch(Exception e) : It throws general Exception object that can be caught by any object.
2. catch(Error err): It throws Error type object. Any object which is derived from Error type will be caught here.
3. catch(Throwable t): It throws Throwable type object.

Example 7: What happens to the Exception object after exception handling?

Solution: It will go for Garbage Collector and frees the memory.

Example 8: How many exceptions can we define in throws clause?

Solution: We can define multiple exceptions in throws clause.

5.3 CREATING YOUR OWN EXCEPTION CLASSES

It is also possible to create your own exceptions by just using already existing exceptions in the system. To create your own exceptions, extend the **Exception class.** The extended class contains constructors, data members and methods like any other class. The **throw** and **throws** keywords are used while implementing **user-defined exceptions.** The following program explains this. The class hierarchy is as follows:

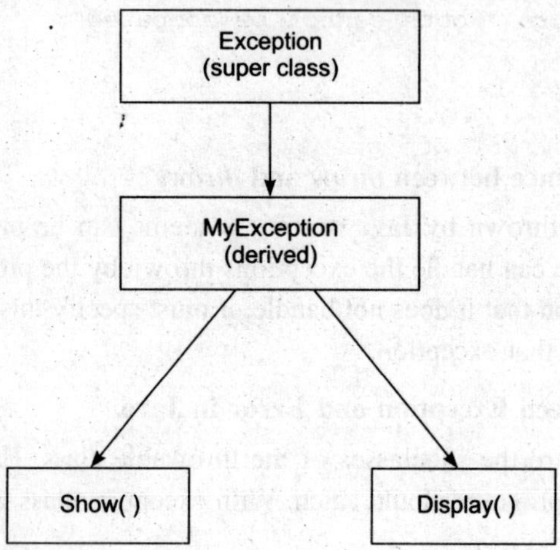


```
//user-defined exceptions
class MyException extends Exception
 {
     MyException( )
       {
        }

MyException(String str)
      {
          Super(str);   //rule
      }
 }

Class UserException
 {
     public static void main(String args[ ] )
       {
          try
           {
               show( );
           }
```

```
catch(MyException e)
        {
            System.out.println(e.getMessage( ));
        }

        try
         {
            display( );
         }
        catch(MyException e)
         {
            System.out.println(e.getMessage( ));
         }
      }

    static void show( ) throws MyException//method-1
     {
        System.out.println("Throwing my own exception from show( )");
        throw new MyException( ); //throwing an exception without args.
     }

static void display( ) throws MyException  //specifying an exception
                                             //(method-2)
  {
    System.out.println("Throwing my own exception");
    throw new MyException("Originated in display( )"); //throwing an
                                             //argument with 1 argument
  }
}
```

OUTPUTS (after running):

Throwing my own exception from show( )

Null

Throwing my own exception

Originated in display( )

Explanations: Herein, a class called **MyException** is extended from the **Exception class.** The user class has two methods—**show( )** that throws a user-defined exception—**MyException (without arguments)** and **display( ) that throws a user-defined exception-MyException (with arguments).** The **throws** keyword tells about the exception thrown by the method.

We are in a position to solve some examples now.

Example 1: Write a Java program that reads the voters age and if it is less than 18 years then error is displayed else the program continues in a normal fashion.

Solution:

```
class User_Defined_Exception extends Exception
{
        int age;
    User_Defined_Exception(int x)
    {
        age = x;
    }

    String toString( )
     {
        'return("Age below requirement(" + age +") ");
     }
    }
    class ExecutionClass
     {
        public void vote(int x) throws User_Defined_Exception
         {
            System.out.println("Voting Condition");
            if (x < 18)
                throw new User_Defined_Exception(x);
              System.out.printn("You are eligible to vote");
         }
     }
    class Main_Class
     {
        public static void main(String args[ ] )
         {
            ExecutionClass obj = new ExecutionClass( );
         try
           {
            obj.vote(22);
            obj.vote(12);
            catch(User_Defined_Exception e)
             {
                System.out.println("Error occurred" + e);
             }
            }

     }
```

Explanation: herein, toString( ) method has been used. ToString( ) and getMessage( ) are the methods of every exception class.

Example 2: Write a Java program to define your own exception and to ensure that the radius of a circle is not zero or negative.

Solution: There are three steps involved in order to solve this problem.

Step-1: Defining your own exception:

```
import java.lang.Exception;
class InvalidRadiusException extends Exception
 {
    private double r;

    public InvalidRadiusException(double radius)
     {
        r= radius;
     }

    public void printError( )
     {
        System.out.println("Radius + r+ is not valid");
     }
    }
```

Step-2: Throw the exception:

```
class circle
  {
   double x, y, r;
    public Circle(double centreX, double centreY, double radius)
      throws InvalidRadiusException {
   if(r < 0)
     {
       throw new InvalidRadiusException(radius);
     }
   else {
      x= centreX;
      y= centreY;
      r= radius;
      }
     }
   }
```

Step-3: Catch the exception now:

```
Class Circle_test
{
    public static void main(String args[ ] )
    {
        try {
            Circle c1 = new Circle(10, 10,-1);
            System.out.println("Circle is created");
            }
        catch(InvalidRadiusException e) {
            e.printError( );
              }
            }
        }
```

Example 3: Distinguish between a general catch clause and a specific catch clause.

Solution: A catch followed by a block without the parenthesized information is known as a general catch clause. Its syntax is as follows:

Syntax:

```
catch {.....}
```

This is equivalent to:

```
catch (System.Exception) {.....}
```

That is why, a *catch* statement with System.Exception cannot be included in a *try* statement whenever a general catch clause is also available in the same *try* statement. *Please note that a catch statement will be executed only if an exception occurs in try statement. Also understand that the ordering of catch statements is very important in Java2.* If there is no match of exceptions in all specific catch statements for a thrown exception, general catch statement is executed. A catch block may contain a throw statement with no expression to re-throw its current exception. Also note that the try statement may be nested and the inner try may have a finally block and the outer try may have another one.

NOTE: The finally block is optional. If a finally block is present it will be executed both if an exception occurs and is an exception does not occur.

Example 4: Write a Java program to check whether the amount is sufficient in the bank account and to raise an exception if it is not so.

Solution:

```
//insufficient funds example-file insufficient_funds.java
import java.io.*;
public class Insufficient_Funds_Exception extends Exception
  {
    private double amount;
    public Insufficient_Funds_Exception(double amount)
      {
```

```
        this.amount = amount;
      }

   public double getAmount( )
    {
        return amount;
   }
    }

   //checking account example—file checking_account.java
   import java.io.*;
   public class CheckingAccount
    {
        private double balance;
        private int number;
        public CheckingAccount(int number)
         {
            this.number = number;
         }

        public void deposit(double amount)
         {
            balance += amount;
         }

        public void withdraw(double amount) throws
                        Insufficient_Funds_Exception
         {
            if (amount < = balance)
             {
                balance -= amount;
             }
             else
              {
                 double needs = amount - balance;
            throw new InsufficientFundsException(needs);
              }
          }

        public double getBalance( )
         {
            return balance;
          }
```

```
        public int getNumber( )
        {
            return number;
        }
    }

//main program now

public class Bank_Demo
{
    public static void main(String args[ ] )
    {
        CheckingAccount c = new CheckingAccount(285);
        System.out.println("Depositing Rs. 1000…");
        c.deposit(1000.00);
        try {
            System.out.println("\nWithdrawing Rs. 400..");
            c.withdraw(400.00);
                System.out.println("\nWithdrawing Rs. 800..");
            c.withdraw(800.00);

            } catch(Insufficient_Funds_Exception e)
            {
    System.out.println("Oops! Cannot withdraw" + e.getAmount( ));
            e.printStackTrace( );
            }
        }
    }
```

Students are advised to run this program on their own.

Summary

Exceptions in Java are no more the exceptions from any Java program. This is so because if there is no exception handling then certain unpredictable situations in a program cannot be dealt with. Exception handling also helps in the testing of the code as it provides a sort of validation only. Java provides classes that are defined in java.lang package for handling exceptions. They are handled by using the keywords try, catch, throw, throws and finally. Actually, the statement that might cause an error is embedded in a try block. The catch block is used to process the exception occurred. There can be more than one catch block for a try block. *The throw keyword is used to throw an exception. The throws keyword is, however, used with methods that throw an exception.* The code in finally block is executed irrespective of whether an exception is raised or not. Also you can create an exception classes by extending the class exception.

Chapter 6

Managing I/O Streams and Stream Files

6.0 INTRODUCTION

We are all aware of the IPO cycle of Java. That is, every Java program accepts Input (I) from user (like from a disk, from memory or another program) and output (O) can be produced on any destination (like a file or monitor or a program) after processing (P). **This is known as a IPO cycle.**

Please understand that Java manages its input and output systems using streams where a stream is a general term given to the **flow of data from a source to a destination over a communication channel. A stream is a path along which data flows.** It is analogous to a river or a pipe along which water flows. However, a file is different. A file stores data on a hard disk while a stream does not store information but opens channels to read/write information to a given source like a file. Our Internet also uses streams in between client and servers.

6.1 JAVA STREAMS

Java2 provides two basic streams—**an input stream** and **an output stream.**

The rule is that—"You can only read from the input stream and only write to an output stream." Figure 6.1 shows both of these streams.

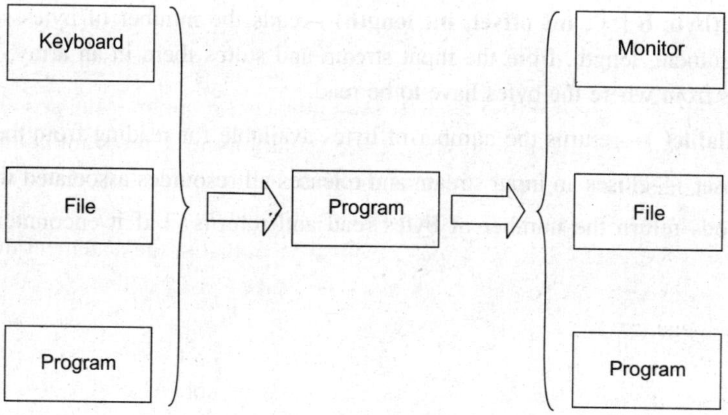

Fig. 6.1: Roles of input and output streams

Also understand that Java2 implements streams within a class hierarchy defined in the *java.io* package. These classes are divided into two major categories:

(a) Byte Streams.

(b) Character Streams.

NOTE: Older versions of Java (i.e. Java 1.0) provided only the byte stream classes. So, all I/O were byte-oriented only. Then Java 1.1 introduced character streams. At the lowest level, all I/O are still byte-oriented.

Let us study these in detail now.

6.2 BYTE STREAM CLASSES

Java byte stream classes are derived from two main abstract classes as follows:

(a) InputStream.

(b) OutputStream.

These abstract classes are sub-classed to provide a variety of Input-Output capabilities. The *InputStream class* lays the foundation for the input class hierarchy whereas the *OutputStream class* lays the foundation for the output class hierarchy.

Let us study these two classes now.

I. InputStream Class: The **InputStream class** provides a constructor as shown below:

InputStream ( );

This constructor creates an instance of the class. The InputStream class defines several methods, that its subclasses must implement:

(a) **int read( )**—reads a byte of data from the input stream.

(b) **int read(byte b[ ])**—reads bytes of data from the input stream and stores them in the array.

(c) **int read(byte b [ ] , int offset, int length)**—reads the number of bytes specified from the third argument, length, from the input stream and stores them in an array. The 2nd argument specifies from where the bytes have to be read.

(d) **int available( )**—returns the number of bytes available for reading from the input stream.

(e) **void close( )**—closes an input stream and releases all resources associated with it.

The read methods return the number of bytes read and returns -1 if it encounters END-OF-FILE (EOF).

The InputStream class hierarchy is shown in Fig. 6.2.

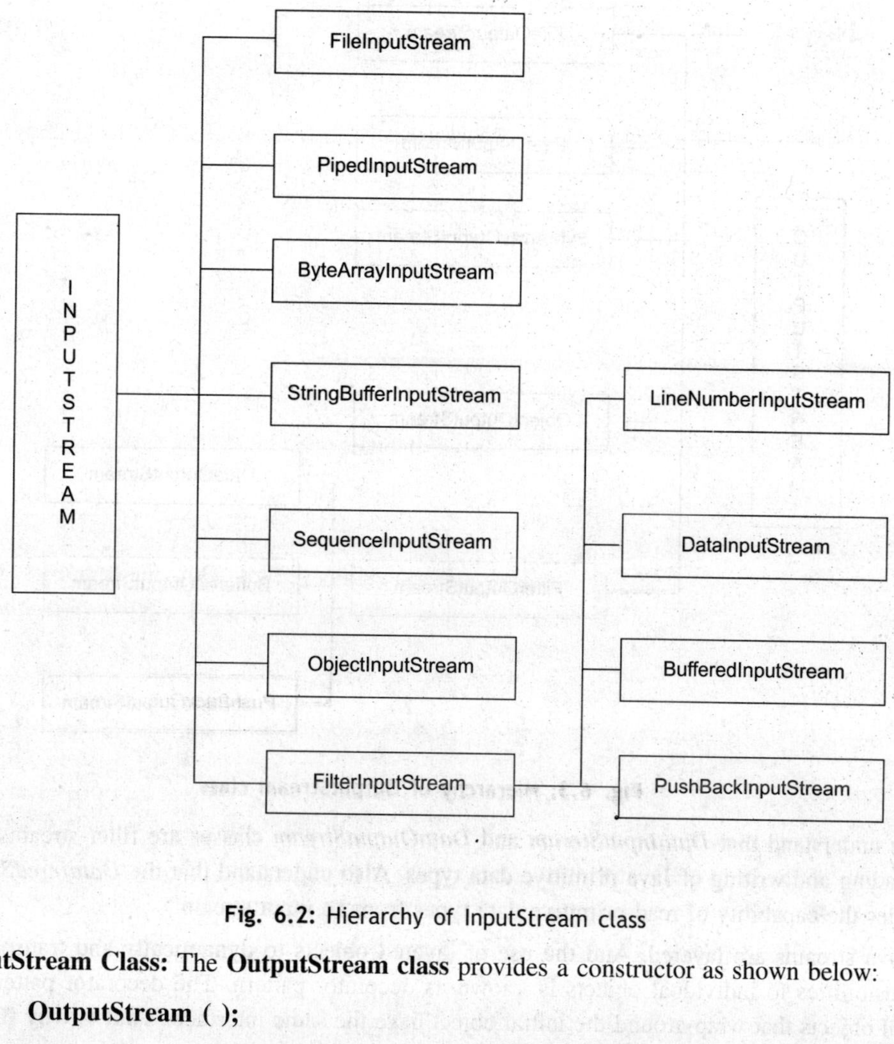

Fig. 6.2: Hierarchy of InputStream class

II. OutputStream Class: The **OutputStream class** provides a constructor as shown below:

OutputStream ( );

This constructor creates an instance of the class. The **OutputStream class** defines several methods that its subclasses must implement:

(a) **int write(int n)**—writes a specified byte of data to the output stream.

(b) **int write(byte b[ ])**—writes an array of bytes of data to the output stream.

(c) **int write(byte b[ ] , int offset, int length)**—writes a subpart of array to the output stream.

(d) **void flush( )**—flushes any byte that the stream has buffered.

(e) **void close( )**—closes an output stream.

The OutputStream class hierarchy is shown in Fig. 6.3.

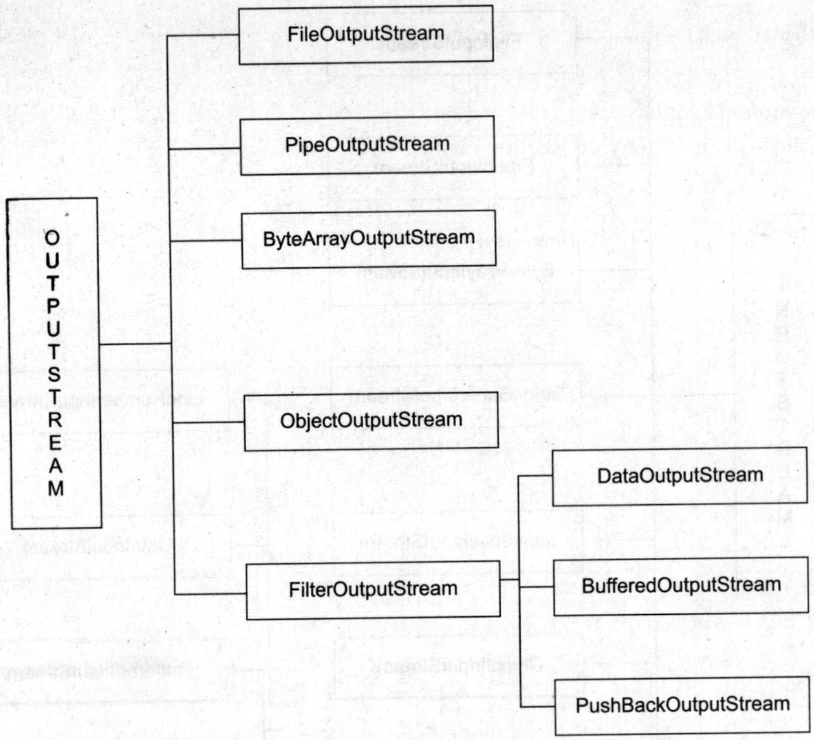

Fig. 6.3: Hierarchy of OutputStream class

Please understand that *DataInputStream* and *DataOutputStream* classes are filter streams that allow the reading and writing of Java primitive data types. Also understand that the *DataInputStream* class provides the capability of read primitive data types from an input stream.

Java streams are layered. And the use of layered objects to dynamically and transparently add responsibilities to individual objects is known as decorator pattern. The decorator pattern specifies that all objects that wrap around the initial object have the same interface. **That is why filter classes exist in the Java IO library.** The abstract **filter class is the base class** for all the decorators. **Please note that a decorator must have the same interface as the object it decorates.** It can further extend the interface to support extra functionalities.

6.3 CHARACTER STREAM CLASSES

Character streams are used to work with any text that is represented by ASCII character set or Unicode. Java 1.1 introduced two abstract classes, namely, **Reader and Writer** classes for Unicode I/O. *Please note here that Unicode is used to represent data such that each character is represented by 16 bits. Also note that byte-streams, however, work on 8-bits of data.*

The Reader Class—The character-oriented abstract class Reader has two constructors:

(a) **Reader( )**—that creates an instance of the class.

(b) **Reader(Object lock)**—that creates an instance of the class, critical section will synchronize of the lock.

The **Reader class** supports InputStream class methods like **read( ), available( ), close( )** and so on. Figure 6.4 shows the class hierarchy of **Reader class.**

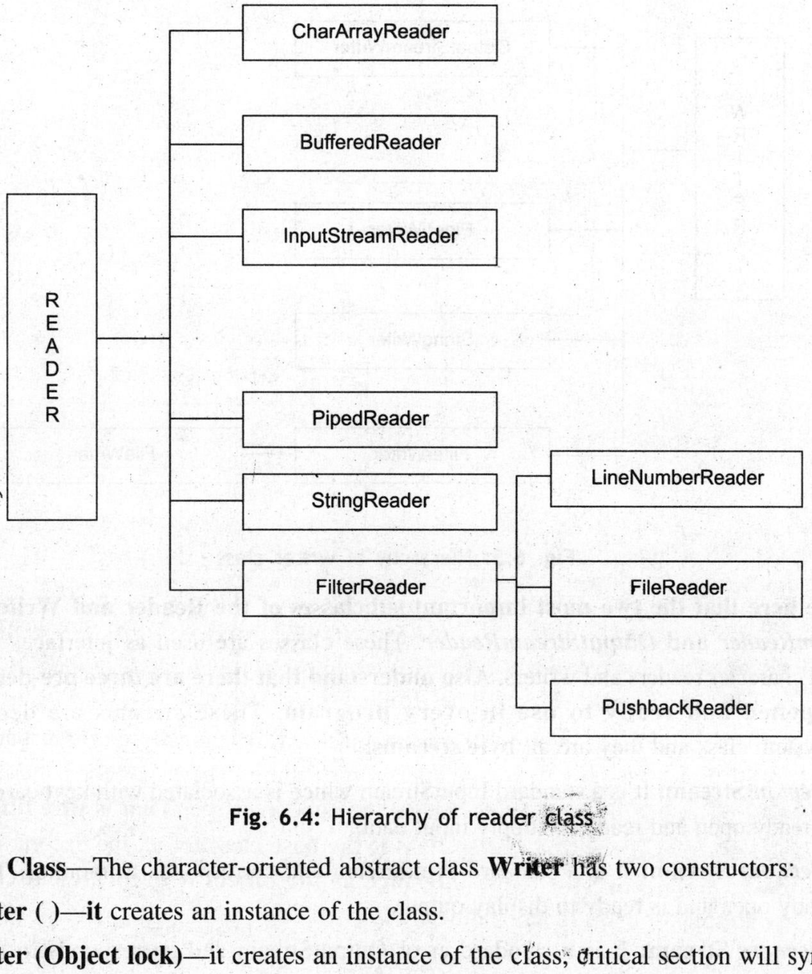

Fig. 6.4: Hierarchy of reader class

The Writer Class—The character-oriented abstract class **Writer** has two constructors:

(a) **Writer ( )—it** creates an instance of the class.

(b) **Writer (Object lock)**—it creates an instance of the class, critical section will synchronize on lock.

Similarly, the **Writer class supports OutputStream class methods like write( ), flush( ) and close( ).**

Fig. 6.5 shows the class hierarchy of **Writer class:**

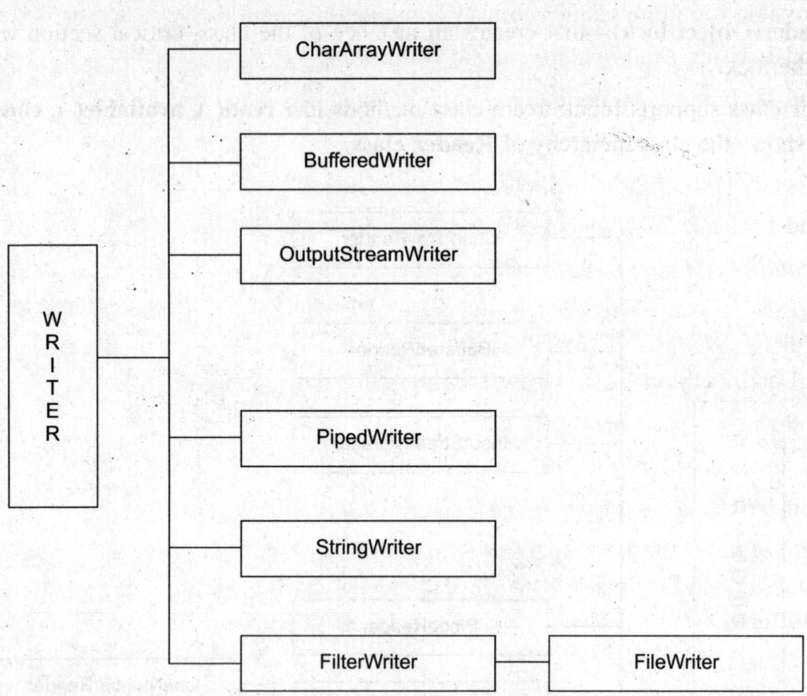

Fig. 6.5: Hierarchy of writer class

Please note here that the two most important subclasses of the Reader and Writer classes are *InputStreamReader* and *OutputStreamReader*. These classes are used as interfaces between byte streams and character readers and writers. **Also understand that there are three pre-defined streams already opened and ready to use in every program.** These streams are declared in the java.lang.System class and they are all **byte streams:**

(a) ***System.in* Stream:** It is a standard InputStream which is associated with keyboard. This stream is already open and ready to supply input data.

(b) ***System.out* Stream:** It is a standard PrintStream and corresponds to monitor. This stream is already open and is ready to display output.

(c) ***System.err* Stream:** It is a standard error OutputStream and corresponds to monitor. This stream is already open and is ready to accept output data.

These different filter streams may be used in many possible ways. The manner in which you deal with those streams depends only on the top level of the stream. Just remember that the underlying complexity has been hidden by the internal implementations.

6.4 READING FROM KEYBOARD

It is possible for a programmer to read primitive data from the keyboard by two methods:

Method-I: Using *DataInputStream* and *DataOutputStream* Classes.

Method-II: Using *InputStreamReader* and *OutputStreamReader* Classes.

Let us study both of these methods one by one now.

Method-I: Using *DataInputStream* and *DataOutputStream* classes.

The ***DataInputStream* and *DataOutputStream* Classes** are also used to read and write Java primitives data types. To read from console, we create an object of the ***DataInputStream class and call the*** *readLine ( ) method.* For example,

DataInputStream dis = new DataInputStream(System.in);

String str = dis.readLine( );

Method-II: Using *InputStreamReader* and *OutputStreamReader* Classes.

The *InputStreamReader* and *OutputStreamReader* Classes are used to convert data between the byte and Unicode character streams. Buffered character I/O is supported by the **BufferedReader and BufferedWriter classes.** The readLine( ) method of the BufferedReader class is used to read line of text from the keyboard, the file or other input streams. For example,

InputStreamReader isr = new InputStreamreader(System.in);

BufferedReader br = new BufferedReader(isr);

String str = br.readLine( );

The readLine( ) method receives input from the keyboard in form of string. Now, this string is converted into corresponding primitive data type using **Wrapper classes.** For example,

If you receive "92" from the keyboard using ***readLine( ) then use the parseInt( ) method*** of Integer wrapper class as follows:

int n = Integer.parseInt(str);

Similarly, if you want to read a float then use the Float wrapper class as follows:

float val = Float.parseFloat(str);

Please recall that Java provides support for input and output through the classes of java.io package. Therefore, while using these classes we must import java.io package in our programs.

We are in a position to solve some programming examples now.

Example 1: Write a Java program that reads the temperature in Fahrenheit from the keyboard and then displays its equivalent temperature in Celsius.

Solution:

```
// program temperature convertor
import java.io.*;
```

```
class TempConvert
  {
     public static void main(String args[ ])
      {
         try
          {
         DataInputStream dis = new DataInputStream(System.in);
        try
         {
     System.out.println(\nEnter temperature in Faherenheit: ");
     String str = dis.readLine( );
     float farh = Float.parseFloat(str);
     float cel = (farh -32)/ 1.8f;
     System.out.println("Temperature equivalent in Celsius :" +cel);
        }
     catch(NumberFoematException e)
      {
         System.out.println("Incorrect input..");
      }
     }
     catch (Exception e)
      {
        }
     }
   }
```

OUTPUT (after running):

Enter temperature in Faherenheit: 100

Temperature equivalent in Celsius: 37.77778

Example 2: Write a Java program to implement Unix CAT utility in Java.

[*GGSIPU, B. Tech.(CSE/IT)-5th sem., Dec. 2009*]

Solution:

```
import java.io.*;
class Cat {
        public static void main(String args[ ])
          {
            String thisLine;

            //loop across the arguments
            for(int i = 0; i <args.length; i++) {
              //open file for reading
            try {
            BufferedReader br = new BufferedReader(new
```

```
                                           FileReader(args[i]));
                while((thisLine = br.readLine( )) != null) {
                  {
                    System.out.println(thisLine);
                   }  //while ends
                } //try ends

                catch(IOException e) {
                  System.out.println("Error: " + e);
                }
             }  //end for-loop
             }  //end of main
             }
```

6.5 FILE STREAM CLASSES

In Java, there are four types of File Stream classes and are as follows:

(a) FileInputStream class—for byte input.

(b) FileOutputStream class—for byte output.

(c) FileReader class—for character input.

(d) FileWriter class—for character output.

6.5.1 The FileInputStream and FileOutputStream Classes

The **FileInputStream Class** allows you to read input from a file. The **FileOutputStream Class** allows to write output to a file stream.

For example,

FileInputStream infile = new FileInputStream("Student.dat");

FileOutputStream outfile = new FileOutputStream("fee.dat");

After creating a file input stream you can read bytes from the stream using **read** ( ) methods. Similarly, after a file output stream you can write bytes to the stream using **write( ) methods.** The **FileInputStream** throws a **FileNotFoundException** if the given file is not present. But in case of **FileOutputStream,** if the given file is not present then it will create a new file with this name. If there is already a file with this name then it will delete its previous contents and places new contents on it. However, if you do not want to delete its previous contents then you will create a **FileOutputStream** as follows:

FileOutputStream outfile = new FileOutputStream ("fees.dat", true);

Please note here that the 2nd argument is a *Boolean argument.* If it is set *true* then the new contents are appended after the previous contents.

The following program demonstrates this.

```
import java.io.*;
class FileDemo1
{
  public static void main(String args[ ] )
  {
    try
     {
     int a[ ] = {10,20,30,40,50};
   FileOutputStream fos = new FileoutputStream("MyFile1.txt");
   System.out.println("Writing data to file—\"Myfile1.txt\"");
   for(int i = 0; i < a . length; i + +)
       fos.write(a[i]);
   fos.close( );
   }

  catch(IOException e)
   {
       System.out.println("\nFile I/O error");
   }

   try
    {
      int n;
   FileInputStream fis = new FileInputStream("Myfile1.txt");
   boolean eof = false;
   System.out.println("Reading data to file—\"MyFile1.txt\"");
   while (!eof)
     {
       n = fis.read( );
       if(n == -1)
         eof = true;
       else
           System.out.println(n);
     }
       fis.close( );
   }

   catch(IOException e)
       {
           System.out.println("\nFile I/O error");
  }
 }
}
```

OUTPUT (after running):

Writing data to file—"MyFile1.txt"

Reading data to file—"MyFile1.txt"

10

20

30

40

50

6.5.2 The FileReader and FileWriter Classes

The **FileReader** class is the main class used when reading character stream from a file. The **FileWriter** class allows to write output to a file stream. **For example,**

FileInputStream infile = new FileInputStream ("Student.dat");

FileOutputStream outfile = new FileOutputStream ("fees.dat");

After creating a file input stream you can read bytes from the stream using ***read( ) methods.*** Similarly, after a file output stream you can write bytes to the stream using ***write( ) methods.*** The **FileInputStream** throws a **FileNotFoundException** if the given file is not present. But in the case of **FileOutputStream** if the given file is not present then it will create a new file with this name. If there is already a file with this name then it will delete its previous contents and places new contents on it. However, if you do not want to delete its previous contents then you will create a **FileOutputStream** as follows:

FileOutputStream outfile = new FileOutputStream ("fees.dat", true);

Please note here that the 2nd argument is a Boolean argument. If it is set true then the new contents are appended after the previous contents. The following program demonstrates this.

```
import java.io.*;
import java.lang.*;
public class FileDemo1
 {

     public static void main (String args[ ])
      {
          try
            {
                 int a[ ] = {1,2,3,4,5};
          FileWriter fw = new FileWriter("Myfile2.txt");
          System.out.println("Writing data to file—\"Myfile2.txt\"");
          for (int i = 0; i < a.length; i++)
               fw.write(a[i]);
```

```
        fw.close( );
        }
       .catch(IOException e)
          {
            System.out.println("\nFile I/O error");
          }

        try
          {
            int n;
        FileReader fr = new FileReader("MyFile2.txt");
        boolean eof = false;
        System.out.println("Reading data to file - \"Myfile2.txt\"");
        while (!eof)
          {
            n = fr.read( );
            if (n = = -1)
                eof = true;
            else
                System.out.println(n);
          }
            fr.close( );
          }
          catch(IOException e)
            {
                System.out.println("\nFile I/O error");
            }
          }
```

OUTPUT (after running):

Writing data to file- "Myfile2.txt"

Reading data to file- "Myfile2.txt"

1

2

3

4

5

We are in a position to answer some questions now.

Example 1: What is a stream?

Solution: A stream is simply a sequence of data items, usually eight bytes.

Example 2: Write a Java program to do the following operations:

(a) to create an empty file and delete it.

(b) To find all files and subdirectories in a directory.

Solution:

(a) import java.io.*;

```
public class BasicTest{
    public static void main(String args) throws Exception
    {
        File file = new File("newFile.dat");
        System.out.println("File exists? " +file.exists( ));
        if(!file.exists( ))
    {
System.out.println("File created? " + file.createNewFile( ));
    }
    else
    {
        System.out.println("File deleted?" + file.delete( ));
    }
    }
    }
```

(b) import java.io.*;

```
public class FileFinder{
    public static void main(String args [ ]) throws Exception
    {
        //if no argument is there, start with current directory
        String dirName = ".";
        if (args.length = =1) {
            dirname = args [0];
        }
        File dir = new File(dirName);
        if (!dir.isDirectory( )) {
          System.out.println(dirName + "is not a dir");
          System.exit(1); //quit if it is a file
        }
        String [ ] files = dir.list( );
        for(int i =0; i <files.length; i++)
        {
            File file = new File(files[i]);
            System.out.println(file.getAbsolutePath( ));
            if (file.isDirectory( )) {
```

```
            //recursive call to next level
            main (new String [ ] { file.getPath( ) } );
            }
        }
      }
    }
```

Example 3: Write a program to read from console and write these data into file, again read that file and print the content onto console? ***[GGSIPU, B. Tech.(CSE/IT)-5th sem., Dec. 2010]***

Solution:

```
import java.io.*;
class EX13A
 {
    void printInputStream(InputStream s)
     {
        try
          {
             System.out.print(" [ ");
             while (s.available( ) > 0)
               {
                  System.out.print(s.read( ));
               }
             System.out.println(" ]");
             s.reset( );
             }
          catch (Exception e)
             {
    System.err.println("Error displaying array: " + e);
             }
         }
    public static void main(String args [ ])
       {
          byte buf1 [ ] = {1,2,3,4,5};
    //create an input stream based on buf1
  InputStream is1 = new ByteArrayInputStream (buf1);

  EX13A example = new EX13A( );
  example.printInputStream(is1); //print the stream as is.

  buf1[0] = 0; //modify the array outside of the stream.
  example.printInputStream(is1); //print it again.
  byte buf2[ ] = {6, 7, 8, 9}; //create another array
  buf1 = buf2;   //and assign it to buff1
```

```
        example.printInputStream(is1);   //print it one last time
        //create another input stream based on buf2 that works
        //with the last two bytes of the array only.

    InputStream is2 = new ByteArrayInputStream(buf2, 2, buf2.length - 2);
        example.printInputStream(is2);   //finally print is2
      }
    }
```

OUTPUT (after running):

[12345]

[02345]

[02345]

[89]

Summary

In this chapter, we have studied that the classes of the java.io.package provide support for input and output operations in Java2. **A stream is a flow of bytes traveling from the source to the destination over a communication path.** Java byte stream classes are derived from two main abstract classes—***InputStream and OutputStream.*** Java 1.1 introduced 2 abstract classes—**Reader and Writer classes for Unicode I/O.** We can read primitives data from the keyboard using the **DataInputStream and DataOutputStream classes.** The ***InputStreamReader and OutputStreamReader classes*** are used to convert data between the byte and Unicode character streams. Buffered character I/O is supported by the ***BufferedReader and BufferedWriter classes.*** The ***readLine( ) method*** is used to read a line of text from the console, the file or other input streams. Java has four types of FileStream classes—***FileInputStream, FileOutputStream, FileReader and FileWriter.***

Chapter 7

Threading and Multithreading

7.0 INTRODUCTION

Java meets the real world requirements of creating interactive, networked programs for the programmers. To achieve this objective, Java provides the facility of multi-threaded programming in which you write programs that do several things simultaneously. Java provides a built-in support for multithreaded programming. A multithreaded program contains two or more parts that can run concurrently. **Each part of such a program is called as a thread.** Each thread defines a separate path of execution. **Multithreading is a specialized form of Multitasking.** Actually, multitasking is put under two categories as follows:

(a) **Process-based:** In process-based multitasking, two or more programs run concurrently. **For example**, you can run MS WORD and MS EXCEL at the same time. Two applications are available in memory and the processor (by means of OS) switches to the application you are actively working on.

(b) **Thread-based:** In time-based multitasking, a single program is divided into two or more parts and they perform two or more tasks simultaneously. **For example,** MS WORD can do spell-check while formatting is being done.

Please understand that multithreading helps you to write efficient programs that make efficient use of CPU i.e. the idle time can be kept to minimum. Also understand that this is especially significant for the interactive networked application because the idle time is common.

NOTE: In traditional single threaded environment, your program has to wait for each of the tasks to finish before it can proceed to the next one. This will result in more idle time. But multithreading lets you gain access to this idle time and allows you to use it.

Many a times in a Java program we encounter a statement like,

```
System.exit (0);
```

Now this statement causes the program to end. **It is always required whenever you use the JOptionPane class to display dialog boxes.** Unlike the console programs that you write, a program that uses this JOptionPane class to display dialog boxes does NOT automatically stop executing when the end of the main method is reached. This is because the JOptionPane class causes an additional process to run in the computer. If the system.exit method is not called then this process known as thread, will continue to execute, even after the end of main method has been reached. This example shows the utility of threads.

NOTE: The System.exit method requires an integer argument. This argument is an exit code which is passed back to the OS.

The operating system supports two types of multitasking-*cooperative multitasking* and *preemptive multitasking*. In *cooperative multitasking* each application is responsible for relinquishing (freeing) control to the processor to enable it to execute other application. Older versions of OSs followed this method of multitasking. On the other hand, in *preemptive multitasking*, the processor is responsible for executing each application in a certain amount of time called as *time slice*. The processor then switches to the other applications, giving each its time slice. Please note that now the programmer is free from the burden of relinquishing control from one application to another as the OS is taking care of this job. Modern OSs like WIN 95, WIN 98, WIN NT and WIN 2000 use this method of multitasking.

7.1 CREATING AND RUNNING A THREAD

Java extends the concept of switching between different programs to that of switching between several different functions (i.e. threads), executing simultaneously within a single program. This capability is known as *multithreading*. A process that is made up of only one thread is said to be **single-threaded**. A single threaded application can perform only one task at a time. When one task completes, another one starts. A process that is made up of more than one thread is a **multithreaded process.** A multithreaded program divides up its time slices among several independent threads of control in it. *Please understand that multiple threads in a process run at the same time, perform different task and interact with each other.*

NOTE: Java includes multithreading primitives as a part of the language itself in the classes Thread, ThreadGroup and threaddeath of the *java.lang package.*

Let us differentiate between a process and a thread.

Table 7.1: Differences between a Process and a Thread

Process	Thread
1. Processes **cannot** share the same memory.	1. Threads **share** memory and files.
2. Process creation is **time consuming**.	2. Thread creation is **not time consuming**.
3. Process execution is **very slow**.	3. Thread execution is **very fast**.
4. It takes **more time** to terminate a process.	4. It takes **less time** to terminate threads.
5. Process is **loosely coupled** i.e. lesser resource sharing.	5. Threads are **tightly coupled** i.e. more resource sharing.
6. It is a **heavy weight** process as it requires more resources.	6. It is a **light weight** process as it requires fewer resources.

Now, there are two ways of creating a new thread in Java as follows:

Method-I: Create a new class, say *MyThread,* as a subclass of the

Thread class and override the method *run( ).*

Method-II: Declare a class implementing the *Runnable interface*

Method-I: Using a subclass of a Thread class:

We create a subclass of the ***Thread class.*** **This new subclass must define its own run( ) method to override the run( ) of the Thread class. Its syntax is as follows:**

```
public class  MyThread extends Thread
 {
    public void run( )
     {
        //.....
     }
 }
```

Please understand that it is necessary to override the run( ) method of the Thread class because it is the run( ) method that performs the task.

Let us write a program to understand this.

```
//thread example demo
Class MyThread extends Thread
{
public void run( )
{
   for(int i=1; i<5; i++)
     System.out.println("child thread name is" + getName( ) + " I = " + i);
  System.out.println("Exit from Child thread" + getName( ));
}

Class ThreadDemo
  {
     public static void main(String args[ ])
      {
         MyThread t1 = new MyThread( );
         MyThread t2 = new MyThread( );
         MyThread t3 = new MyThread( );
         t1.setName("First");
         t2.setName("Second");
         t3.setName("Third");
         t1.start( );
         t2.start( );
         t3.start( );
         System.out.println("Exit from Main thread");
      }
  }
```

Also understand that in this program we have used two methods—getName( ) and setName( ). The **getName( ) method** is used to receive the name of the specific thread and **the setName( ) method** is used to set the name of the specified thread. **The start method starts the execution of the thread.**

OUTPUT(after running):

Exit from Main thread

Child thread name is First I = 1

Child thread name is First I = 2

Child thread name is Second I = 1

Child thread name is Third I = 1

Child thread name is Second I = 3

Child thread name is Third I = 2

Child thread name is First I = 4

Child thread name is Second I = 3

Child thread name is Third I = 3

Child thread name is First I = 5

Child thread name is Second I = 4

Child thread name is Third I = 4

Exit from Child thread: First

Child thread name is Second I = 5

Child thread name is Third I = 5

Exit from Child thread: Second

Exit from Child thread: First

Method-II: Implementing the Runnable Interface:

We can create a new thread by implementing the Runnable interface. The class Thread itself is an implementation of Runnable. The Runnable interface requires the run( ) method to be implemented.

Syntax is:

```
public class MyThread implements Runnable
 {
     public void run( )
       {
          //......
       }
  }
```

```
Let us write a program to understand this.
// thread demo using runnable
class MyThread implements Runnable
 {
    Thread t1, t2, t3;
    MyThread( )
     {
        t1 = new Thread(this, "First");
        t2 = new Thread(this, "Second");
        t3 = new Thread(this, "Third");

        t1.start( );
        t2.start( );
        t3.start( );
     }

    public void run( )
     {
        String str = new String( );
        for(int i=1; i<=5; i++)
         {
            str = Thread.currentThread( ).getName( );
        System.out.println("Child thread name is" +str + "I = " +i);
         }
        System.out.println("Exit from child thread: " + str);
        }
      }

 class ThreadDemo
  {
    public static void main(String args [ ])
     {
        MyThread t  = new MyThread( );
        System.out.println("Exit from Main thread");
     }
  }
```

OUTPUT (after running):

Exit from Main thread

Child thread name is First I = 1

Child thread name is First I = 2

Child thread name is Second I = 1

Child thread name is Third I = 1

Child thread name is Second I = 3

Child thread name is Third I= 2

Child thread name is First I = 4

Child thread name is Second I = 3

Child thread name is Third I= 3

Child thread name is First I = 5

Child thread name is Second I = 4

Child thread name is Third I = 4

Exit from Child thread: First

Child thread name is Second I = 5

Child thread name is Third I = 5

Exit from Child thread: Second

Exit from Child thread: First

Please note that you cannot call *getName( )* inside *run( )* method directly because there is no Thread like object *'this'* in runnable whereas there is in Thread. Therefore, first call the thread class static method *currentThread( )* which returns the *thread object* and then call the *getName( ) method* to get the name of the Thread currently running.

7.2 THE THREAD CONTROL METHODS

Java provides many methods, defined in the java.lang.Thread class that control the execution of a thread. Some important methods are as follows:

1. void start( ) throws IllegalThreadStateException

A thread execution starts by calling ***start( ) method*** which, in turn, calls the ***run( ) method*** automatically. This method throws an exception ***IllegalThreadState Exception,*** if the code is trying to start a thread that has already been started.

2. void stop( )

The ***stop( ) method*** stops the execution of a thread no matter what the thread is doing. When the code executes this ***stop( ) method,*** it immediately kills the thread and the resource allocated to this thread are reclaimed.

3. void suspend( )

The ***suspend( ) method*** temporarily stops the execution of a thread. When the code executes ***suspend( ) method,*** it saves all of the states and resources of the thread.

4. void resume( )

The ***resume( ) method*** resumes the execution of a suspended thread. After execution of this method, if the suspended thread has a higher priority than the running thread, the running thread will be preempted otherwise this resumed thread will wait in queue for its turn. Both ***suspend( ) and resume( ) methods*** can lead to deadlock and therefore they should be avoided.

5. static void sleep(long sleepTimeInMilliseconds) throws InterruptedException

This ***sleep( ) method*** causes the called thread to sleep for a minimum of the specified time period. This method throws an ***InterruptedException*** while a thread is sleeping or any time you interrupt it.

6. void join( ) throws Interrupted Exception

The thread who call this method waits for itself to die, **for example**, by coming to the end of the ***run( ) method.***

7. static void yield( )

This ***yield( ) method*** temporarily stops the execution of the caller's thread and places the caller's thread at the end of the queue to wait for another turn. This method actually provides chances to execute other threads of either the same priority or the lower priority.
Some other useful methods of the ***Thread class*** are **getname( ), setName( ), isAlive( ), toString( )** etc.

To understand these methods, let us write a small program now.

```
//Thread methods demo
class MyThread extends Thread
  {
     public void run( )
      {
         try
           {
              for(int i=1; i<=5; i++)
              {
    System.out.println("Child thread name is " + getname( )+ "I =" + i);
              Thread.sleep(1000);
              }
           }

    catch(InterruptedException e)
      {
      }
       System.out.println("Exit from child thread"+ getName( ));
     }
   }
```

```
class ThreadMethodDemo
  {
     public static void main(String args[ ])
      {
        MyThread t1= new MyThread( );
        MyThread t2= new MyThread( );

        t1.setName("First");
        t2.setName("Second");

        t1.start( );
        t2.start( );

        System.out.println("First thread is alive: " + t1.isAlive( ));
        System.out.println("Second thread is alive: " + t2.isAlive( ));

        try
          {
            System.out.println("Waiting for first thread to finish...");
            t1.join( );
            System.out.println("Waiting for second thread to finish...");
            t2.join( );
          }

        catch(InterruptedException e)
          {
          }
        System.out.println("First thread is alive:" + t1.isAlive( ));
        System.out.println("Second thread is alive:" + t2.isAlive( ));
          }
        }
```

OUTPUT (after running):

First thread is alive: true

Second thread is alive: true

Waiting for first thread to finish...

Child thread name is First I = 1

Child thread name is Second I = 1

Child thread name is First I = 2

Child thread name is Second I = 2

Child thread name is First I = 3

Child thread name is Second I = 3

Child thread name is First I = 4

Child thread name is Second I = 4

Child thread name is First I = 5

Child thread name is Second I = 5

Exit from Child thread First

Exit from Child thread Second

First thread is alive: false

Second thread is alive: false

7.3 THE THREAD LIFE CYCLE

Just as a process goes through different states, so does these threads. This is shown in Fig. 7.1.

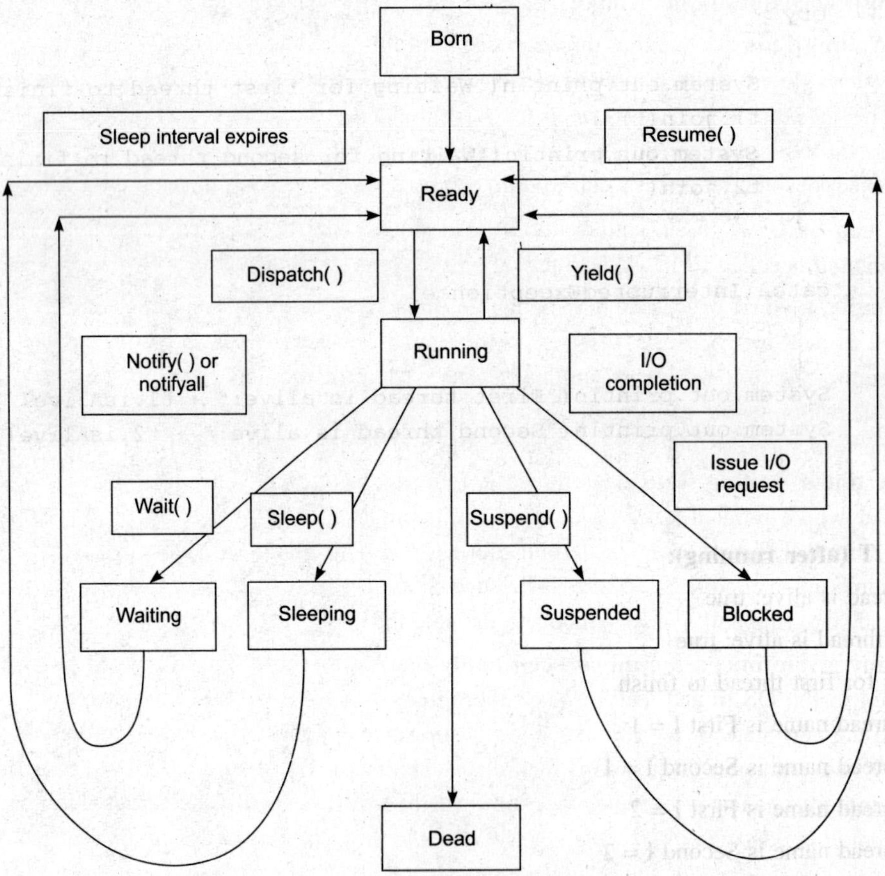

Fig. 7.1: UML diagram showing various thread states

Let us discuss these stages now.

1. **Born State:** The thread when created will be in born state.
2. **Ready State:** The thread remains in this state until the thread's ***start method*** is called. This causes the thread to enter the **ready state.**
3. **Running State:** The highest priority thread enters the running state when the system assigns a processor to the thread i.e. the thread starts executing.
4. **Blocked State:** A thread comes into a blocked state when it issues an input/output request. And once this input/output request accomplishes, the blocked thread comes into ready state. A blocked thread cannot use a processor even if one is available.
5. **Sleep State:** A running thread comes into sleep state when it calls the sleep method. A sleeping thread becomes ready when its resume method is called by another method. A sleeping thread can not use a processor even if one is available.
6. **Suspended State:** A running thread comes into a suspended state when it calls suspend method. A suspended thread becomes ready when its resume method is called by another thread. A suspended thread cannot use a processor even if one is available.
7. **Waiting State:** A running thread comes into this waiting state when it calls wait method. A waiting thread waits in a queue associated with the particular object on which wait was called. The first thread in a wait queue for a particular object becomes ready on a call to ***notify( )*** issued by another thread associated with that object. However, all waiting threads for a given object become ready on a call to ***notifyall*** by another thread associated with that object.
8. **Dead State:** A thread enters into a dead state when its run method completes or the ***stop method*** is called for it. A dead thread will eventually be disposed of by the system.

For example, a word processor may contain a thread that periodically writes a copy of the current document to disk for recovery purposes. If the thread did not sleep between successive backups, it would require a loop in which it continually tests whether it should write a copy of the document to the disk. This loop would consume processor time without performing productive work, thus reducing system performance. In this case, it is more efficient for the thread to specify a sleep interval and enter **the timed waiting state.** This thread is returned to the runnable state when its sleep interval expires, at which point it writes a copy of the document to disk and reenters the **timed waiting state.** A **runnable thread** enters the terminated state when it completes its tasks or otherwise terminates due to some error condition. In the UML state diagram, the **terminated state** is followed by the UML final state (the bull's –eye symbol) to indicate the end of the state transitions.

At any given time, a thread can be in only one state. These states are JVM states as they are not linked to the OS thread states. When the object of a user **Thread class** is created, the thread moves to the new state. After the invocation of the start( ) method, the thread shifts from the new to the ready state (runnable) state and is then dispatched to running state by the JVM thread scheduler. After gaining a chance to execute, the run( ) method will be invoked. *Please note that when the run( ) method is invoked directly, the code in it is executed by the current thread and not by the new thread as the thread object is not assigned to the virtual machine scheduler.* Depending on the program operations or invocation of methods like wait( ), sleep( ) and suspend( ) or an I/O operation, the thread moves to the waiting, sleeping and blocked states respectively. **Also note here that the thread is still alive.** After the completion of the operation that blocked it (I/O or sleep) or receiving an external signal that wakes it up, the thread moves to the ready state. Then the JVM thread scheduler moves it to the running state in order to continue the execution of remaining operations. When the thread completes its execution, it will be moved to terminate state. A dead thread can never enter any other state, not even if the start( ) method is invoked on it.

Before we discuss further, we shall solve some examples now.

Q.1. Show the execution of the following mathematical equation using multiple threads.

$$p = \sin(x) + \cos(y) + \tan(z)?$$

Solution: From the given equation we find that all these trigonometric operations sin, cos and tan are independent operations i.e. there are no interdependencies between them. So, they can be executed in parallel (concurrently) also. And then finally there results can be combined to produce the final result as shown in Fig. 7.2 below:

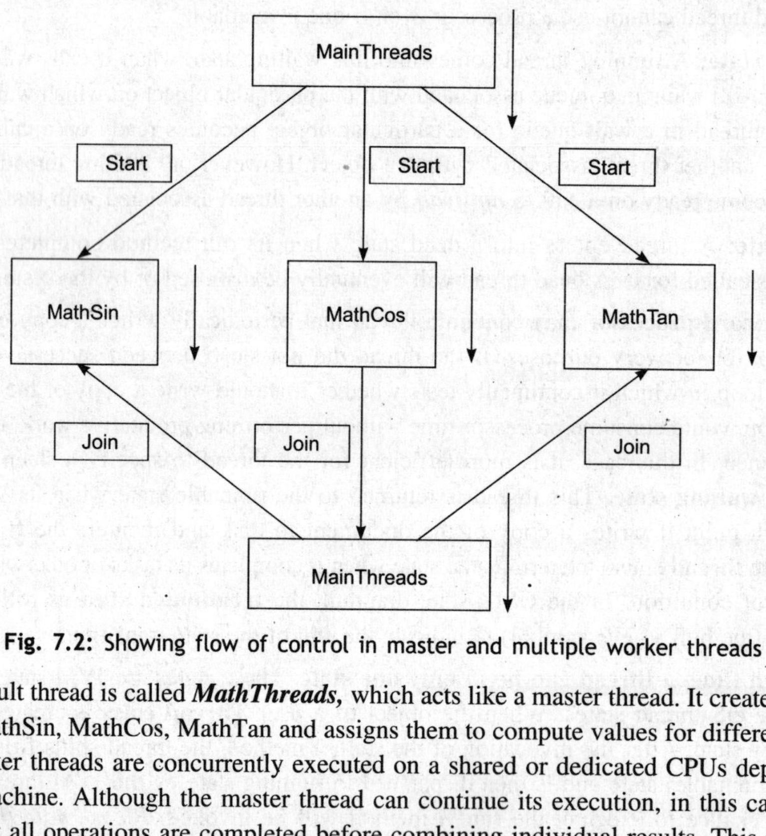

Fig. 7.2: Showing flow of control in master and multiple worker threads

The main/default thread is called ***MathThreads,*** which acts like a master thread. It creates three worker threads i.e. MathSin, MathCos, MathTan and assigns them to compute values for different data inputs. All three worker threads are concurrently executed on a shared or dedicated CPUs depending on the type of the machine. Although the master thread can continue its execution, in this case, it needs to make sure that all operations are completed before combining individual results. This is achieved by waiting for each thread to complete by invoking ***join( ) method*** associated with each worker thread. *Please understand that the execution or completion of threads does not need to be in the order of* *their start i.e. invocation of start( ) method. Also understand that because of the different operations being performed within JVM, threads and different applications running at different times, it is hard to predict the precise time at which the context-switching occurs.* It is possible to enforce the order of execution to some extent by setting different priorities for threads.

Q.2. Write a program to show multithreading concept?

[GGSIPU, B. Tech. (CSE/IT)- 5th sem. Dec. 2009]

Solution: Please refer to sections 7.1 and 7.2 of this chapter.

Q.3. What are the basic differences between extending the Thread class and implementing the runnable interface, in order to create a thread? Which one of these will you prefer to create a thread? *[GGSIPU, B. Tech. (CSE/IT)- 5th sem. Oct. 2010]*

Solution: Please refer to sections 7.1 and 7.2 of this chapter.

Q.4. Name the interface that is necessary to implement while converting a class into thread. Create three thread child classes and explain how these child thread start executing?

[GGSIPU, B. Tech. (CSE/IT)- 5th sem. Dec. 2011]

Solution: Please refer to sections 7.1 and 7.2 of this chapter.

Q.5. Why do we need start( ) and run( ) method both. Can we achieve it only with run method?

[GGSIPU, B. Tech. (CSE/IT)- 5th sem. Dec. 2011]

Solution: Please refer to sections 7.1, 7.2, 7.3 and 7.4 of this chapter.

Q.6. What is synchronization with respect to multi-threading?

[GGSIPU, B. Tech. (CSE/IT)- 5th sem. Dec. 2010]

Solution: Please refer to sections 7.1 and 7.2 of this chapter.

Q.7. (a) Why should the sleep( ) method of thread class be enclosed in a try catch block?

(b) Explain Inter Threads Communication and suspending, resuming and stopping threads.

[GGSIPU, B. Tech. (CSE/IT)- 5th sem. Dec. 2012]

Solution: Please refer to sections 7.1, 7.2, 7.3 and 7.4 of this chapter.

Q.8. (a) Explain wait( ) methods related to thread.

(b) What is multithreaded programming? Show how threads can be created in Java ?

[GGSIPU, B. Tech. (CSE/IT)- 5th sem. Dec. 2013]

Solution: Please refer to sections 7.1 and 7.2 of this chapter.

7.4 THREAD PRIORITIES

The Java Runtime Environment (JRE) executes threads based on their priority. Each thread has its own priority. **Please note here that the threads with higher priority executes before the threads with low priority.** When a thread is being executed and a new thread with higher priority becomes ready then the running process is preempted and the new ready thread, with the higher priority, schedules for execution. **Also note that you can set the priority of a thread by an integer in the**

range of 1 to 10. You can change the priority of a thread using ***setPriority( ) method of the Thread class.*** **Its syntax is as follows:**

t.setPriority(n);

Here, 't' is a Thread object and 'n' is an integer in the range of 1 to 10, the argument 'n' can also take any of the following constants:

MIN_PRIORITY represents integer number 1.

MAX_PRIORITY represents integer number 10.

NORM_PRIORITY represents integer number 5.

These constants are declared in ***Thread class.*** By default, when a thread is created it has NORM_PRIORITY.

Similarly, the ***getPriority( ) method*** is used to get the priority of a thread. **Its syntax is as follows:-**

n =t.getPriority( );

Here, 't' is a Thread object.

Let us write a program to show its demo now.

```
// program thread priority
class MyThread extends Thread
 {
    public void run( )
     {
     for(int i=1; i<=3;i++)
       System.out.println("Child thread name is" + getName( ) +" I=" +i);
       System.out.println("Exit from Child thread" + getName( ));
     }
 }

class ThreadPriorityDemo
 {
   public static void main(String args[ ] )
    {
      MyThread t1 = new MyThread( );
      MyThread t2 = new MyThread( );
      MyThread t3 = new MyThread( );

    System.out.println("First thread priority- " +t1.getPriority( ));
    System.out.println("Second thread priority- " +t2.getPriority( ));
    System.out.println("Third thread priority- " +t3.getPriority( ));

    t1.setPriority(1);
    t2.setPriority(10);
```

```
    t3.setPriority(5);

    System.out.println("First thread priority- " +t1.getPriority( ));
    System.out.println("Second thread priority- " +t2.getPriority( ));
    System.out.println("Third thread priority- " +t3.getPriority( ));

    t1.setName("First Thread");
    t2.setName("Second Thread");
    t3.setName(Third Thread");

    t1.start( );
    t2.start( );
    t3.start( );
    System.out.println("Exit from Main thread");
  }
}
```

OUTPUT (after running):

First thread priority-5

Second thread priority-5

Third thread priority-5

First thread priority-1

Second thread priority-10

Third thread priority-5

Child thread name is Second Thread I = 1

Child thread name is Second Thread I = 2

Child thread name is Second Thread I = 3

Exit from Child thread Second Thread

Exit from Main Thread

Child thread name is Third Thread I = 1

Child thread name is Third Thread I = 2

Child thread name is Third Thread I = 3

Exit from Child Thread Third Thread

Child thread name is First Thread I = 1

Child thread name is First Thread I = 2

Child thread name is First Thread I = 3

Exit from Child Thread First Thread

In java, all thread instances the developer created have the same priority, which the process will schedule fairly without worrying about the order. Please understand that it is vital for different threads to have different priorities. Also understand that important threads should have higher priorities than the less important ones. For example, the garbage collector thread just needs the lowest priority to execute. It means that it will not be executed before all other threads are scheduled to run. It is possible to control the priority of the threads by using the Java APIs. The ***Thread.setPriority( ) method*** will do this job.

7.5 THREAD SYNCHRONIZATION

When two or more threads need to share a resource (i.e. a variable, or a statement or a set of statements), it must ensure that the resources will be used by only one thread at a time. This can be achieved by making a resource—-**synchronized and this process is known as synchronization.** Java provides the coordination between different threads by using **synchronized methods or synchronized statement.** Java provides synchronization by using the keyword—**synchronized.**

Let us study these two methods one by one now.

I. Synchronized Methods.

II. Synchronized Statements.

Synchronized Methods: As studied earlier also, that normally the data members of a class are declared private and the methods of the class are public. You can achieve the synchronization by making a method synchronized. **Please note that you can invoke only one synchronized method for an object at any given point in time.** Therefore, only one thread can call a synchronized method at a time.

Each object contains a single lock that is also named as a **monitor.** This monitor is automatically the part of an object. **Also note that when you call a synchronized method that object is locked and no other synchronized method of that object can be called until the first one finishes and releases the lock.** It means that if a thread is executing a synchronized method then all other threads those try to call it one, the same instance have to wait it.

To understand this method further, let us write its program now.

```
//demo of thread synchronization
class Synch
 {
   synchronized public static void show(String name) //synchronized method
   {
     System.out.print("[" + name);
     try
     {
          Thread.sleep(1000);
     }

catch(InterruptedException e)
```

```
    {
      System.out.println("Interrupted");
     }
      System.out.printl("]");
     }
   }

class MyThread extends Thread
 {
   String msg = new String( );
   public MyThread(String str)
   {
     msg = str;
   }

  public void run( )
   {
      Synch.show(msg);
   }
 }

class Thread_Synch_Demo1
 {
    public static void main(String args[ ])
     {
        MyThread t1 = new MyThread("First");
        MyThread t2 = new MyThread("Second");
        MyThread t3 = new MyThread("Third");
        MyThread t4 = new MyThread("Fourth");

        t1.start( );
        t2.start( );
        t3.start( );
        t4.start( );
     }
 }
```

OUTPUT (after running):

[First]

[Second]

[Third]

[Fourth]

But very surprisingly, if I remove the word "synchronized" from the show( ) method of Synch class as follows:

```
public static void show(String name) //synchronized method
   {
     System.out.print("[" + name);
     try
      {
          Thread.sleep(1000);
      }

catch(InterruptedException e)
    {
     System.out.println("Interrupted");
     }
     System.out.printl("]");
    }
```

```
Then the output will be as follows:-
[First[Second[Third[Fourth]
]
]
]
```

NOTE: You should not make all methods *synchronized* because it will make all threads wait for locks released and only one thread will access any object at any point in time.

Synchronized Statements: Sometimes you wish to use a method of third party's class and you do not access the source code of that particular class. In such a case, you cannot add ***'synchronized'*** to the appropriate method within the class. For this you can simply out calls to the methods defined by this class inside a synchronized block as follows:

```
synchronized (obj)
  {
      //.....
  }
```

Here, ***obj*** is a reference to the object being synchronized. If you want to synchronize only one statement then the curly braces are operational.

Let us write a program to understand this now.

```
class Synch
 {
    public void show(String name)
     {
```

```
      System.out.print("[" + name);
      try
        {
            Thread.sleep(1000);


        }


catch(InterruptedException e)
     {
            System.out.println("Interrupted");
     }
            System.out.printl("]");
     }
  }


class MyThread extends Thread
  {
    String msg = new String( );
     Synch s;
    public MyThread(Synch sy, String str)
    {
      s = sy;
      msg = str;
    }


   public void run( )
    {
      synchronized(s)
       {
          s.show(msg);
       }
     }
     }


class Thread_Synch_Demo2
  {
      public static void main(String args[ ])
        {
            Synch sref = new Synch( );
            MyThread t1 = new MyThread("First");
            MyThread t2 = new MyThread("Second");
            MyThread t3 = new MyThread("Third");
            MyThread t4 = new MyThread("Fourth");
```

```
        t1.start( );
        t2.start( );
        t3.start( );
        t4.start( );
       }
   }
```

OUTPUT (after running):

[First]

[Second]

[Third]

[Fourth]

That is, this program also produces the same output as the previous one.

We are in a position to solve some examples now.

Q.1. What is the difference between notify( ) and notifyAll( )?

Solution: A ***notify( )*** is used to unblock one waiting thread. While ***notifyAll( )*** is used to unblock all of them. Using ***notify( )*** is preferable (for efficiency) when only one blocked thread can benefit from the change, for example, when freeing a buffer back into a pool. ***notifyAll( )*** is necessary (for correctness) if multiple threads should resume, for example, when releasing a "writer" lock on a file might permit all "readers" to resume.

Q.2. Name three ways by which a thread can enter the waiting state.

Solution: A thread can enter the waiting state by invoking its sleep( ) method, by locking on I/O, by unsuccessfully attempting to acquire an object's lock or by invoking an object's wait( ) method. It can also enter the waiting state by invoking its suspend( ) method.

Q.3. Consider the very popular—Producer and Consumer problem. Now write two separate programs—with and without synchronization. Show how synchronization is achieved?

Solution: There are two parts of this question. Let us write the code one by one.

Case 1: Producer/Consumer Relationship without Thread Synchronization.

Case 2: Producer/Consumer Relationship with Thread Synchronization.

```
//code for case-1
public class NoSync {
    public static void main(String   args[ ])
  {
    SharedHolder h = new SharedHolder( );
    Producer p = new Producer(h);
    Consumer c = new Consumer(h);
    p.start( );    //start threads
```

```
      c.start( );
    }
  }

class Producer extends Thread {   //single level inheritance
  {
     private SharedHolder pHold;
     public Producer(SharedHolder h) {
      pHold = h;
     }

      public void run( ) { //user-defined run( )
       for(int count=0; count< 5; count++) {
            pHold.setData(count);
            System.out.println("Producer set shared data to" +count);
            try {
                  sleep(int)(Math.random( ) * 3000));
                }
            catch(InterruptedException e) {
                 System.err.println("Exception" + e.toString( ));
                }
              }
            }
          }

class Consumer extends Thread {        //single level inheritance
  {
     private SharedHolder cHold;
     public Producer(SharedHolder h) {
      cHold = h;
     }

public void run( ) {    //user-defined run( ) to override run( ) of
                        //inbuilt Thread class.
   int val;
 val = cHold.getData( );
System.out.println("Consumer retrieved: " + val);
while(val !=4) {
   try{
         sleep(int) (Math.random( ) * 3000));
       }
     catch(InterruptedException e) {
         System.err.println("Exception" +e.toString( ));
     }
```

```
  val = cHold.getData( 0;
  System.out.println("Consumer retrieved: " +val);
   }
  }
}
    class SharedHolder {
          private int sharedData;
          public void setData(int val) { sharedData = val;} //sets data
          public int getData( ) { return sharedData; }
          }
```

OUTPUT(after running):

Consumer retrieved: 0

Producer set shared data to 0

Producer set shared data to 1

Consumer retrieved: 1

Producer set shared data to 2

Producer set shared data to 3

Producer set shared data to 4

Consumer retrieved: 4

This output shows that the slow consumer cannot cope with the fast producer and looses some data.

```
//code for case-2 (with sync)
class SharedHolder {
    private int sharedData;
    private Boolean writable = true;
    public synchronized void setData(int val) {
          while (!writable) {
                try { wait( ); }    //wait producer
                catch(InterruptedException e) {
                      System.err.println("Exception" +e.toString());
                      }
                }
                sharedData = val;
                writable = false;
                notify( );    //activate consumer now
                }

    public synchronized int getData( ) {
        while(writable) {
          try { wait( );}
```

```
        catch(InterruptedException e) {
            System.err.println("Exception" + e.toString( ));
            }
        }
        writable = true;
        notify( );
        return sharedData;
    }
}
```

OUTPUT(after running):

Producer set shared data to 0

Consumer retrieved: 0

Producer set shared data to 1

Consumer retrieved: 1

Producer set shared data to 2

Consumer retrieved: 2

Producer set shared data to 3

Consumer retrieved: 3

Producer set shared data to 4

Consumer retrieved: 4

From the output of thread synchronization we see that there is a perfect coordination between the threads i.e. the producer places a data and waits till the consumer consumes it and similarly consumer waits till the producer places a new data.

Summary

In this chapter, we have studied what is a thread and how is it different from a process. **A thread is a sequence of flow of control in a program.** A multithreaded program contains two or more threads and each thread defines a separate path of execution. Java creates thread by two methods—by implementing the ***Runnable interface*** and by extending the ***Thread class.*** A thread can have these main states—Born, Ready, Running, Blocked and Dead. The threads are scheduled on the basis of their priorities. The setPriority and getPriority( ) methods are used to change and get the priority of a thread. **Coordination between different threads is known as thread synchronization. The *synchronized* keyword** is used to ensure that no two threads access the same object simultaneously. Also a very popular producer-consumer problem is also implemented in Java in this chapter by using both the methods—without and with synchronization.

Chapter 8

Applets and Event Handling

8.0 INTRODUCTION

Actually there are two types of programs in Java, the applications and the applets. So far we have studied only Java applications and nothing about applet programming has been studied. An applet is a small Java program that runs on Java enabled Internet web browser like Internet Explorer, Firefox, Opera etc. An applet is not run from the command line like an application rather an applet is a small pre-compiled Java program that can be run using an in-built Java tool appletviewer or a Java enabled web browser. Java programs are written to run on World Wide Web (WWW) using applets.

8.1 JAVA APPLETS VERSUS JAVA APPLICATIONS

The programs that reside on WWW servers are known as **applets.** The applets are downloaded by a browser to a clients system and are run by that browser. **Please note that these applets are usually small in size to minimize the download time.** These applets are invoked by a HTML web page.

Applications are, however, stand-alone programs. These do not require any web browser to execute. These are the general-purpose programs (programs written in other languages like C, C++ and BASIC etc) that run on any machine where the Java runtime environment is installed. They are run by a Java compiler and Java interpreter. **Also note that the main difference between an applet and an application program is that an applet can dynamically change its output according to the user input whereas an application produces the same output over and over.** There are many other differences, let us tabulate them now.

Table 8.1: Application v/s Applets

Applications	Applets
1. Application programs use main ( ) method method for initiating the execution of the code.	1. Applets do not use the main ( ) method for initiating the execution of the code. Applets, when loaded, automatically call certain methods of Applet class to start and execute the applet code.
2. These programs can run independently.	2. Applets cannot run independently. They run embedded into a web page on a web browser using HTML tag.
3. These can read from or write to the files on a local computer.	3. These cannot read from or write to the files on a local computer.
4. These can run some other program from the local computer.	4. These cannot run any program from the local computer.
5. Java language can use these libraries of other languages like C and C++ using native method.	5. Applets are restricted from using libraries from other languages.

Let us now list the features of an applet.

Features of applets:

1. An applet does not contain a main( ) method whereas an application must contain a main( ) method.
2. Applets cannot load or run any program stored on the user's system whereas applications can run.
3. Applets are first embedded into a web page and then this page is loaded into memory using Java-enabled web browser. There is no such step to run application programs.
4. Applets cannot read or write files on the users system whereas application programs can.
5. Applets cannot communicate with other servers on the network.

8.2 CREATING APPLETS

An applet is a Java program that can be embedded in a web page. Applets are run on any Java-enabled web browser or appletviewer tool included in JDK.

8.2.1 The Applet Class

The java.applet package is the smallest package in the Java API. It has only one Applet class. All applets are subclasses of this Applet class. **For example,**

```
import java.applet.*;
public class Applet1 extends Applet
{
    //....
}
```

The Applet class has over 20 methods that are used to display images, play audio files and respond when you interact with it. **Please note that Applets do not have main( ) method.** All applets must be declared public. Use javac to compile applets and appletviewer or Java-enabled web browser to execute them.

The Graphics Class: The ***Graphics class*** is an abstract class that represents the display area of the applet on the web page. It is a part of **java.awt** package. It is used for drawing on the display area of the applet. The graphics class provides a **drawString method** to display text on the applet. It also requires position to be specified.

An applet displays the information on the screen by using **paint( ) method** defined in **java.awt.Graphics** class and it takes an instance of the Graphics class as parameter.

For example,

```
import java.applet.*;
import java.awt.*;
public class Applet1 extends Applet
```

```
{
    public void paint(Graphics g)
    {
     g.drawString("Welcome to my first applet",20,20);
    }
}
```

The **Graphics class** also provides methods to draw various graphics and manage fonts and colors. Some of these methods are as follows:

1. **drawLine(x1, y1, x2, y2)**—draw line from points (x1,y1) to (x2,y2).
2. **drawRec(x1, y1, width, height)**—draw a rectangle from point (x1,y1) as the top corner with width and height specified.
3. **fillRect(x1, y1, width, height)**—draw a filled rectangle.
4. **drawOval(x1, y1,width, height)**—draw an oval.
5. **fillOval(x1, y1,width, height)**—fill an oval.
6. **setColour(c)**—sets the text foreground color specified by the argument 'c'. Here, 'c' is an object of the class Colour.
7. **setBackColour(c)**—sets the text background color specified by the argument 'c'.
8. **setFont(f)**—sets the font. Here, 'f' is an object of the class Font.

8.2.2 HTML for JAVA Applets

As we have seen the Java source files, similarly HTML files are also text files with special character sequences. These special character sequences characterize your document. **These special characters are called as tags.** Each tag consists of symbols placed between left and right angled bracket. Most HTML tags use <tag> and </tag> sequence to set or unset the relevant characteristics. A slash (/) in a tag signifies the end of that tag section. The entire block of a HTML file must be in the HTML block. The HTML block is marked by an opening HTML tag <HTML> and a closing tag </HTML>. The HTML section consists of Comment block, HEAD block and BODY block. The Comment section begins with a character sequence <! and ends with a character >. Comments can be included anywhere in a webpage. **Web browser ignores all such comments.**

The HEAD block defines the title for the page and other attributes for heading. The HEAD block begins with a <HEAD> tag and ends with a </HEAD> tag. The text enclosed in the tags <TEXT> and </TEXT> will appear in the title bar of the Java-enabled web browser when it displays the web page. Like comments, the HEAD block is optional.

The BODY block includes all of the text matter about the web page, along with images in the IMG block and applets in the Applet block. The BODY block starts with a <BODY> tag and ends with a </BODY> tag. The IMG block is used to include a image in a HTML file. Actually, web browser can display image files in GIF (Graphics Interchange Group) and JPEG (Joint Photographic Expert Group). Any bold and italic text must be enclosed in the B and I block respectively.

For example,

```
<HTML>
     <HEAD>
          <TITLE>
               This is the beginning of first applet
          </TITLE>
     </HEAD>
     <BODY>
          <H1> WELCOME
          <I>  TO
          <B>  JAVA Applet World </B> </I> </H1>
     </BODY>
</HTML>
```

Let us save this file as "sample.html". now open this file in web browser—Internet Explorer. After opening, it produces output as follows:

Welcome to Java Applet World

8.2.3 Adding JAVA Applets to an HTML Document (The Applet Tag)

A Java applet is added to a HTML document using <APPLET> tag. This tag specifies the location of the class file (bytecode version of a Java source file) and the display area allocated to the applet. Say, we have a java source file—Applet1.java as follows:

```
//Applet1.java
import java.applet.*;
import java.awt.*;
public class Applet1 extends Applet
 {
     public void paint(Graphics g)
      {
          g.drawString("Welcome to my first applet", 20,20);
      }
 }
```

Please understand that when you compile this file, it produces "Applet1.class" file.

8.2.4 Viewing an Applet in JAVA-enabled Web Browser

Now that you have to include this .class file in APPLET tag an HTML document—"first.html" as follows:

```
<HTML>
     <HEAD>
          <TITLE>
               First Applet
          </TITLE>
```

```
    </HEAD>
    <BODY>
        <H2>
        <APPLET>
            CODE = "Applet1.class"        <! Calling java .class file
            WIDTH = 450
            HEIGHT = 200>
        </APPLET>
        </H2>
    </BODY>
</HTML>
```

Save this file as "first.html". This code uses the <APPLET> tag. It has three attributes:

- **CODE**—specifies the name of the applet's main class file.
- **WIDTH**—specifies the width of the applet window on the web page.
- **HEIGHT**—specifies the height of the applet window on the web page.

Some other important attributes are as follows:

- **ALIGN**—specifies the alignment of the applet with respect to the rest of the web page, this could be set to LEFT, RIGHT, MIDDLE, TOP.
- **HSPACE**—specifies the space in pixels on each side (left and right) of the applet.
- **VSPACE**—specifies the space in pixels on each side (top and bottom) of the applet.
- **CODEBASE**—indicates an alternative folder or alternative website for the browser to locate the applet's class file.
- **ALT**—specifies a short text message that should be displayed if the browser understands the applet tag but cannot run current Java applet.
- **NAME**—makes it possible for the applets to communicate with each other.
- **PARAM NAME and VALUE**—parameters that are used to retrieve the information that the applet can retrieve. The PARAM tag must be written between <APPLET> AND </APPLET> tag.

Now, you get the applet started and the following is displayed:
WELCOME TO MY FIRST APPLET.

8.2.5 Viewing an Applet in Appletviewer

It is also possible to run an applet using appletviewer at the command prompt as follows:

```
C:\appletviewer first.html
```

The appletviewer produces the window with the following string:

```
Applet
    Welcome to my first applet



Applet started.
```

Let us now summarize the entire process of development of an applet in an HTML document:

1. Write a Java source file and compile it into a class file (.class)
2. Write the HTML document that contains an <APPLET> and </APPLET> tag.
3. Use Java-enabled web browser, such as Internet Explorer or an appletviewer to run this applet.

8.2.6 Passing Values to Applets

The APPLET tag can consist of other tags. One of the tags written between <APPLET> and </APPLET> is the PARAM tag. The PARAM tag is used to pass values to your applet. The PARAM tag has two arguments—NAME and VALUE. The NAME argument specifies the name of the parameter and VALUE defines its value.

Syntax:

<PARAM NAME = "paramname" VALUE = "information"

For example,

<PARAM NAME = "aname" VALUE = "RAJIV CHOPRA"

Please note that you can retrieve the value from the PARAM tag of the HTML file using getParameter( ) method of the APPLET class.

Syntax:

String paramvalue = getparameter("paramname");

We are in a position to solve an example now.

```
import java.applet.*;
import java.awt.*;
public class Applet2 extends Applet
 {
   public void paint(Graphics g)
   {
         String str = getParameter("aname");
```

```
        g.drawString(str, 30,30);
    }
}
```

Compile this file and embed "Applet2.class" file in an HTML document as follows:-

```
<HTML>
    <BODY>
        <APPLET
            CODE = "Applet2.class"
            WIDTH = 150
            HEIGHT = 50>
        <PARAM NAME= "aname" VALUE="RAJIV CHOPRA">
        </APPLET>
    </BODY>
</HTML>
```

Save this file. The following output is produced by appletviewer tool:

Applet

RAJIV CHOPRA

Applet started.

However, remember that some OS require uppercase letters while some permit lowercase letters also. But to avoid confusion we have used uppercase letters only.

Before we discuss further, let us solve some examples now.

Example 1: Write a method to display an applet in the browser, so that the contents are contained in a rectangle around the phrase "Exercise Applet". Have the applet be one pixel less than the size specified on the web page and the phrase starting at the coordinates 5, 15.

Solution:

```
public void paint(Graphics g) {
//draw a rectangle around the applet's display area
g.drawRect(0,0, getWidth( ) -1, getHeight( ) -1);
//draw the current string inside the rectangle
g.drawString("Exercise Applet", 5, 15);
}
```

Example 2: Can applets communicate with each other?

Solution: At this point of time, applets may communicate with other applets running in the same virtual machine. *Please remember that if the applets are of same class then they can communicate via shared static variables. Also remember that if the applets are of different classes then each will need a reference to the same class with static variables.* In any case, the basic idea is to pass the information back and forth through a static variable.

An applet can also get references to all other applets on the same page using the getApplets( ) method of java.applet.AppletContext. Once you get the reference to an applet, you can communicate with it using its public members.

It is conceivable to have applets in different virtual machines that talk to a server somewhere on the net and store any data that needs to be serialized there. Then when another applet needs this data, it could connect to this same server. Implementing this is non-trivial.

Example 3: My application/applet loads images, but they aren't drawn on the screen. What's going on?

Solution: When you load an image (using java.awt.Toolkit.getImage), the function returns immediately and the image is loaded asynchronously. This means that sometimes an image isn't ready to be drawn because it hasn't yet loaded. Depending on when the image is loaded and when it is drawn, the problem can be intermittent and hard to track down. If your application or applet must display the image, you can have it wait until the image is fully loaded. For example, an animation applet may not have any useful work to do until the images are loaded. To wait for images, you need to use the java.awt.MediaTracker class. Mediatracker allows you to register an image with the tracker and have your application or applet wait until the image is ready. Please note that this isn't limited just to applets loading images over a network—from my own experience it can happen loading a small (< 100 bytes) image from a local file system.

To register an image, you assign it an image number and call the ***addImage*** method. Then you can call the ***waitFor(int) or waitForAll( ) methods.***

```
//Pass media tracker any component (like a canvas or an applet)
MediaTracker tracker = new MediaTracker(this);

//add images
tracker.addImage (myImage1, 0);
tracker.addImage (myImage1, 1);

//wait for images
try {
        tracker.waitForAll( );
    } catch (InterruptedException ie) { }
```

Once you start the wait, your application will block until the image has loaded. Then, you can call ***java.awt.Graphics.drawImage*** to display the image to your applet or application.

Example 4: Write an applet in Java to calculate principal interest on given amount.

Solution:

```
import java.awt.*;
import javax.swing.JOptionPane;
import java.applet.Applet;
/*<applet code ="Interest" width = 200 height = 100>
    <param name = rate value=monthly>
</applet>*/

public class Interest extends Applet
{
    String rate;
    public void start( )
    {
String s= JOptionPane.showInputDialog("Enter your principal amount:");
int p= Integer.parseInt(s);
s= JOptionPane.showInputDialog("Enter your rate:");
int r= Integer.parseInt(s);
s= JOptionPane.showInputDialog("Enter your time:");
int t= Integer.parseInt(s);
rate= getParameter("rate");
if(rate.equals("monthly"))
{
    double amount = (p * t * r) / (100 * 12);
    JOptionPane.showMessageDialog(null, "simple interest=" + amount,
"simple interest", JOptionPane.INFORMATION_MESSAGE);
}
else
{
    double amount = (p * t * r)/ 100;
    JOptionPane.showMessageDialog(null, "simple interest=" + amount,
"simple interest", JOptionPane.INFORMATION_MESSAGE);
}
}
}
```

8.3 LIFE CYCLE OF AN APPLET

There are four important phases in the life cycle of an applet:

1. **Initialization occurs** when the applet is loaded. This is implemented by the init( ) method. To implement a specific initialization process such as setting up an initial state, loading images or fonts, init( ) method is overridden.

2. **An applet is started** after it is initialized. Starting can also occur if it is in a stopped state. The method start( ) can be overridden to implement start operation. An applet is stopped when the user goes to a different web page and comes back to the page containing applet. Initialization occurs only once whereas starting occurs any number of times.
3. **Stopping occurs** when the user leaves the page containing the applet or when an applet stops itself by calling **stop( ) method**.
4. **Destruction** is done using the **destroy ( ) method.** This method performs cleanup process when the browser exits.

Please note that in simple applications these methods are not overridden. Thus, in nutshell we can summarize the lifecycle of an applet as follows:

Init ( ) → Start ( ) → Stop ( ) → Destroy ( )

[i.e ISSD]

Its pictorial representation is as follows:

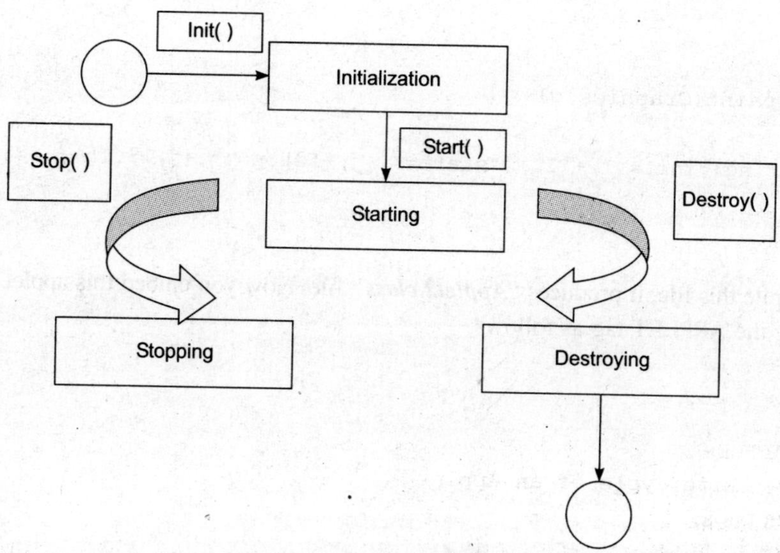

Fig. 8.1: Life cycle of an applet

To understand this further let us write a small applet program now.

```
//applet.java
import java.applet.*;
import java.awt.*;
public class Applet2 extends Applet
 {
String str;
int i=0;
int j=0;
```

```
int k=0;

public void init( )
 {
    i++;
 }

public void start( )
 {
    j++;
 }

public void stop( )
 {
    k++;
 }

public void paint(Graphics g)
 {
    g.drawString("init= " + I + "start=" +j +"stop= " +j,15,15);
 }
}
```

When you compile this file, it produces ***"Applet2.class"*** file. Now you embed this applet in an HTML document using the APPLET tag as follows:

```
<HTML>
    <HEAD>
        <TITLE>
            Life Cycle of an Applet
        </TITLE>
    </HEAD>
    <BODY>
        <H2>
        <APPLET
            CODE = "Applet2.class"
            WIDTH = 250
            HEIGHT = 150
            ALIGN = BOTTOM >
        </APPLET>
        </H2>
    </BODY>
</HTML>
```

Save this HTML file as "life.html". This produces the output as shown below as it is run using the appletviewer tool:

```
Applet
        Init = 1 Start = 1 Stop = 1

Applet started.
```

Also note that when you minimize this and maximize again then appletviewer shows the output as follows:

```
Applet
        Init = 1 Start = 2 Stop = 2

Applet started.
```

This output clearly shows that the variable 'j and 'k' gets updated.

Let us study the update( ) and repaint( ) methods now.

The ***update( ) method*** takes a Graphics class object as a parameter. It clears the screen and calls the ***paint( ) method.***

The ***repaint( ) method*** is used to redraw the applet area. **Please note here that the repaint( ) method calls the update( ) method to signal that the applet has to be updated. Also note that**

the default action of the update( ) method is used to clear the applet area and call the paint( ) method.

To show the use of these two methods, let us write a simple program now.

```
//Applet.java
import java.applet.*;
import java.awt.*;
public class Applet3 extends Applet
 {
int a=0;
int b=0;
int c=0;
int d=0;

public void init( )
 {
    a++;
    repaint( );
 }

public void start( )
  {
    b++;
    repaint( );
  }

public void stop( )
 {
    c++;
    repaint( );
  }

public void destroy( )
 {
   a++;
    repaint( );
  }

public void paint( )
 {
 System.out.println("A= " +a + "B=" +b + "C=" + c + "D=" +d);
 }
}
```

When you compile this file, it produces ***"Applet3.class"*** file. Now you embed this applet in an HTML document using the APPLET tag as follows:

```
<HTML>
    <HEAD>
        <TITLE>
            Life Cycle of an Applet
        </TITLE>
    </HEAD>
    <BODY>
        <H2>
        <APPLET
            CODE = "Applet3.class"
            WIDTH = 250
            HEIGHT = 150
            ALIGN = BOTTOM>
        </APPLET>
        </H2>
    </BODY>
</HTML>
```

Save this HTML file as "life.html" and run this HTML document to check the output.

8.4 JAVA EVENT HANDLING

User's clicking of a button, entering a text, clicking of mouse or any other interface related action in an applet results in the occurring of an **event. Almost all GUI application programs have events.** The GUI application waits for a user to perform some action. The user controls the sequence of operations that the application executes through a GUI. **This approach is known as event-driven programming.**

8.4.1 Components of an Event

An event consists of three components as follows:

1. Event object.
2. Event source.
3. Event handler.

Event object: An event is normally generated in an application when user presses a key or clicks a mouse. The OS senses this event and data associated with it.

For example, the time at which the event occurred, type of event etc. This information (data) is then passed onto the application to which event belongs.

Event source: An event source is an object that generates an event. The major user interface components that generate the events are Button, Checkbox, Choice, List, Menu item, Scrollbar, Text component and Window. **For example,** the Button component generates action events when it is pressed or text component generates text events when the user types a character. When we click on a button, an ***ActionEvent*** object is generated. This object of the ***ActionEvent class*** contains the information about the event.

Event-handler: An event handler is a method that understands the event and processes it. The event-handler method takes an **Event object** as a parameter.

Class Object is the root of the class hierarchy. Every class has Object as a superclass. All objects, including arrays, implement the methods of this class.

java.util.EventObject: The java.util.EventObject is the root class from which all event state objects shall be derived. It belongs to ***java.util package***. Most other event classes are present in the ***java.awt.event package.***

Some important events are listed below:

1. **ActionEvent:** An **ActionEvent** object is generated when a component is activated.
2. **AdjustmentEvent:** An **AdjustmentEvent** object is generated when scroll bars and other adjustable elements are used.
3. **ContainerEvent:** A **ContainerEvent** object is generated when components are added or removed from a container.
4. **FocusEvent: A FocusEvent** object is generated when a component receives focus for the input.
5. **ItemEvent: An ItemEvent** object is generated when an item from a list, a choice or a checkbox is selected.
6. **KeyEvent:** A **KeyEvent** object is generated when a key is pressed from a keyboard.
7. **WindowEvent:** A **WindowEvent object** is generated when a window activity like minimizing or closing occurs.
8. **MouseEvent: A MouseEvent object** is generated when the mouse is pressed.
9. **PaintEvent: A PaintEvent object** is generated when a component is painted.
10. **TextEvent: A TextEvent object** is generated when the text of a text component is modified.

Please remember that the *getSource( )* method of the *EventObject* class returns the object that initiated the event. The *getID( ) method* returns the event ID that represents the nature of the event. For example, if a mouse event occurs, you can find whether the event was a click, a drag, a move, a press or a release from the event objects.

8.4.2 Event Listener Interface

Event handling is achieved with the use of listener interfaces that are defined in java.awt.event package. *Please understand that when an event occurs, an event object of the suitable type is created.* This object is passed to the listener interface. In Java, there are a number of in-built interface listeners for different types of event handling. In nutshell, we can say that:

$$\text{Events} \xrightarrow{\text{handled by}} \text{Interface} \xrightarrow{\text{has}} \text{methods}$$

(Now we create classes that inherit these methods of interface. This class's object is to be registered with the event source).

The following Table 8.2 shows the listener interfaces and the event sources which uses them:

Table 8.2: Listener Interface and Event Objects

Interface	Events generated by
ActionListener	Button, List, MenuItem, TextField.
AdjustmentListener	Scrollbar
ItemListener	Checkbox, CheckboxMenuItem, Choice, List
TextListener	TextComponent
ComponentListener	Component
ContainerListener	Container
FocusListener	Component
KeyListener	Component
MouseListener	Component
MouseMotionListener	Component
WindowListener	Window

Please observe here that these interfaces declare one or more methods each of which handle a specific event. For example, *ActionListener* has a method ***actionPerformed( ), Windowlistener*** interface has methods—windowClosing( ), windowClosed( ), windowIconified( ) etc. **Also observe that the classes which inherit these interfaces must implement these interfaces in order to respond to certain types of events.**

Syntax (for implementing a Listener interface):

```
    class classname implements xxxListener
      {
         //implements all methods declared in the xxxListener interface
      }
```

```
Please note here that 'xxx' represents Action, Item, Mouse, Key or Window
etc.
For example,
    class MyListener implements ActionListener//class (user's
//defined) is implementing interface
```

```
    {
        public void actionPerformed(ActionEvent ae)
                   {
                          //code to handle the event
                   }
    }
```

In order to receive the events, the MyListener's object (user defined class's object) has to be registered with the event source by invoking its addxxxListener(listener object).

For example,

```
//....
Button b1 = new Button("Hello");
b1.addActionListener(new MyListener( ));
add(b1);
//....
```

Herein, a button 'b' is registered with ***addActionlistener( ) method.***

Please note that it is the combination of event and event-handler that provides a framework for event-driven programs. The following is the sequence of events for a single event connected to an event handler:

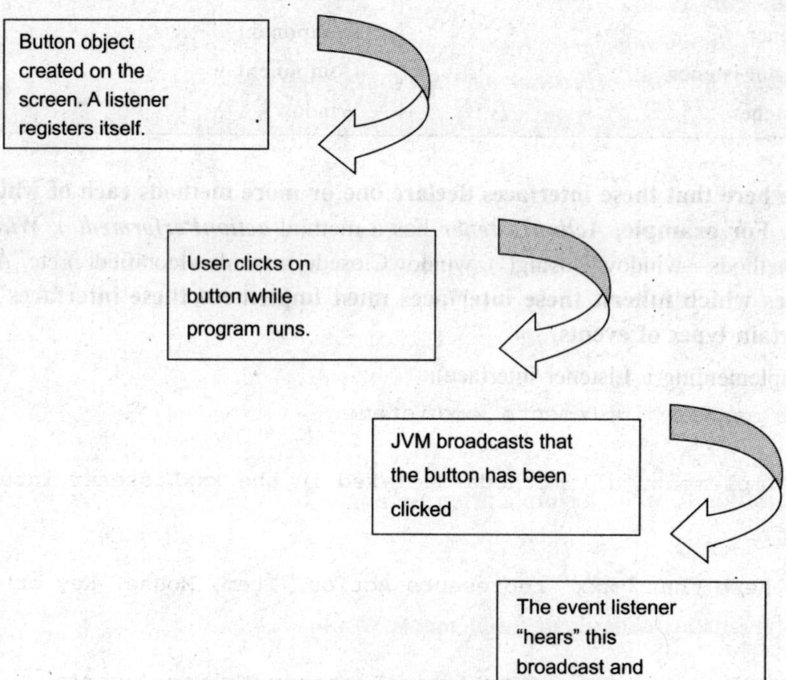

Fig. 8.2: Sequence of events

Please note that you need two things to respond to events properly:

1. You must create an event handler.
2. You must register the events you wish to handle with that event handler.

Also note that you need to do two things to create an event handler:

1. Implement a Listener for the type of event you wish to process.
2. You must provide a public method that will receive notifications when the events occur.

For example, to handle a button click, you must implement the ***java.awt.event.ActionListener*** class and provide a public ***actionPerformed*** method. **The *actionPerformed method*** takes one parameter—a ***java.awt.event.ActionEvent object*** that contains information about the event like a source item that generated it.

8.5 WINDOW EVENT

A low-level event that indicate that a window has changed its status is called as a **window event**. This low-level event is generated by a Window object when it is opened, closed, activated, deactivated, iconified or deiconified or when the focus is transferred into or out of the Window.

In order to handle window events, you have to implement the ***WindowListener interface***. Then this object has to be registered with the window by invoking its ***addWindowListener( ) method by passing a listener object.***

The ***WindowListener interface*** has seven methods in it. So, the implementing class has to override all these methods. The ***WindowListener*** interface looks as below:

```
interface WindowListener extends EventListener
  {  //promises
     public void WindowClosing(WindowEvent e);
     public void WindowClosed(WindowEvent e);
     public void WindowOpened(WindowEvent e);
     public void WindowIconified(WindowEvent e);
     public void WindowDeIconified(WindowEvent e);
     public void WindowActivated(WindowEvent e);
     public void WindowDeactivated(WindowEvent e);
  }
```

We are in a position to write a simple program now:

import java.awt.*;

import java.awt.event*;

public class MyFrame **extends** Frame **implements** WindowListener

{

......

```
   Myframe( ) {
```

```
        super("My Frame");
        setSize(300,200);
        setVisible(true);
        addWindowListener(this);
        }

 public void WindowClosing(WindowEvent e)
   {
    System.out.println("Window is closing");
    dispose( );
    System.exit(0);
   }

    public void WindowClosed(WindowEvent e)
    {
        System.out.println("Window closed");
    }
public void WindowOpened(WindowEvent e)
    {
        System.out.println("Window opened");
    }

public void WindowIconified(WindowEvent e)
    {
        System.out.println("Window iconified");
    }

public void WindowDeiconified(WindowEvent e)
    {
        System.out.println("Window deiconified");
    }

public void WindowActivated(WindowEvent e)
    {
        System.out.println("Window activated");
    }

public void WindowDeactivated(WindowEvent e)
    {
        System.out.println("Window deactivated");
    }
```

```
    public static void main(String args[ ]) {
        myFrame mf = new MyFrame( );
    }
}
```

Adapter classes:

Java provides adapter classes that implement the corresponding listener interface containing more than one method. The methods in these classes are empty. The listener class that you define can extend the Adapter class and override the methods that you need. The Adapter class used for the WindowListener interface is the WindowAdapter class.

In the previous program, we found that even though we were interested only in the ***windowClosing*** event still we had to supply null bodies for all the methods in the ***WindowListener*** interface. To make things a little more convienent, a concept called adapter classes can be used.

In Java AWT event-handling, for some of the Listener interfaces (like the *WindowListener)* you might want to implement only one or two functions to handle the one or two events of interest but the *XXXListener* interface may specify half a dozen methods. The language rules are such that you must implement all of the methods in an interface even if just give them empty bodies, as in the W*indowListener* above. The package java.awt.event provides adapters that implement all of the methods with null bodies, thus, allowing you to override as few methods as you like. They are as follows:

- ComponentAdapter
- MouseMotionAdapter
- WindowAdapter
- ContainerAdapter
- MouseAdapter
- FocusAdapter
- KeyAdapter

Please note that these adapters are the classes that provide empty bodies for all the methods in the corresponding XXXListener interface. For example, the *WindowAdapter* class looks like this:

public abstract class WindowAdapter implements WindowListener

```
{
    public void WindowClosing(WindowEvent e) { }
    public void WindowClosed(WindowEvent e) { }
    public void WindowOpened(WindowEvent e) { }
    public void WindowIconified(WindowEvent e) { }
    public void WindowDeIconified(WindowEvent e) { }
    public void WindowActivated(WindowEvent e) { }
    public void WindowDeactivated(WindowEvent e) { }
}
```

If you declare your event handler as a subclass of one of these adapters, you can provide only one or two methods you want, instead of implementing all of the methods in the interface. Let the inheritance do the work.

Since Java classes have only one parent, you can't use this technique if you already inherit from some other class. In the previous example, the *MyFrame* class already extends *Frame* and hence you can't again inherit from **WindowAdapter** class. Here is an example showing how the *WindowAdapter* class is used when you are interested in is the W*indowClosing* event only:

```
import java.awt.*;
import java.awt.event.*;
public class MyFrame extends WindowAdapter {
   Frame f;
   MyFrame( ) {
        f = new Frame("My Frame");
        f.setSize(300,200);
        f.setvisible(true);
        f.addWindowListener(this);
        }

        public void windowClosing(WindowEvent e)
        {
             System.exit(0);
        }

        public static void main(String args[ ])
         {
             MyFrame m = new MyFrame( );
         }
        }
```

Please note that we can reduce the code size further by using inner classes. They allow you to put the event handling class and method right next to the place where you declare the control or register the callback listener. Anonymous classes are a refinement of inner classes allowing you to combine the definition of the class with the instance allocation. The above code is rewritten below using anonymous class:

```
import java.awt.*;
import java.awt.event.*;
public class MyFrame extends Frame {
     MyFrame( ) {
          super("My Frame");
          setSize(300,200);
          setVisible(true);
```

```
        addWindowListener(new WindowAdapter( )
        {
            public void windowClosing(WindowEvent e)
            {
                System.exit(0);
            }
        }

        }

        public static void main(String args [ ])
        {
            MyFrame m = new MyFrame( );
        }
        }
```

How to handle action events as generated by componets like Buttons, MenuItems, Lists etc.? These events can be handled just as we did for window events, by implementing the corresponding listener (ActionListener) and registering this with the event source. The *ActionListener* interface has only one method in it and the class that implements this should override this method. **For example,**

```
import,java.awt.*;
import java.awt.event.*;
import java.applet.*;
class MyClass extends Applet implements ActionListener {
Button b1, b2;
public void init( ) {
    b1 = new Button("First");
    b2 = new Button("Second");
    add(b1);
    add(b2);
    b1.addActionListener(this);
    b2.addActionListener(this);
    }
public void actionPerformed(ActionEvent e) {
  if(e.getActionCommand( ).equals("First")) {
    //handle this event here
    }
else if(e.getSource( ) = = b2) {
    //handle this event here.
    }
  }
}
```

8.6 KEYBOARD AND EVENTS

An event that indicates that a keystroke occurred in a component is called as a **keyboard event**. This low-level event is generated by a component object like a text field, when a key is pressed, released or typed. The event is passed to every *KeyListener or KeyAdapter* object which is registered to receive such events using the component's ***addKeyListener*** method.

Note: *KeyAdapter* object implements *KeyListener* interface

Each such listener object gets this *KeyEvent* when the event occurs. *Please understand that the "key-typed" events are higher-level and generally do not depend on the platform or keyboard layout.* They are generated when a Unicode character is entered and are the preferred way to find out about the character input. In the simplest case, a key typed event is produced by a single key press e.g. 'a'. *Also understand that the "key pressed" and "key released" events are lower level and depend on the platform and keyboard layout.* They are generated whenever a key is pressed or released and are the only way to find out about keys that don't generate character input e.g. action keys, modifier keys etc. The key being pressed or released is indicated by the getKeyCode method which returns a virtual key code. Virtual key codes are used to report which keyboard key has been pressed rather than a character generated by the combination of one or more keystrokes like "A" which comes from shift and "a".

A mouse event is an event that indicates that a mouse action occurred in a component. A mouse action is considered to occur in a particular component if and only if the mouse cursor is over the unobscured part of the component's bounds when the action happens. Components bounds can be obscured by the visible component's children or by a menu or by a top-level window. This event is used both for mouse events (click, enter, exit) and mouse action events (moves and drags). This low-level event is generated by a component object for:

Mouse Events

- A mouse button is pressed.
- A mouse button is released.
- A mouse button is clicked (pressed + released)
- The mouse cursor enters the unobscured part of component's geometry.
- The mouse cursor exits the unobscured part of component's geometry.

Mouse Motion Events

- The mouse is moved.
- The mouse is dragged.

A *MouseEvent* object is passed to every *MouseListener or MouseAdapter* object which is registered to receive the interesting mouse events using the component's addMouseListener method. **Please**

remember that *MouseAdapter* object implements the *MouseListener* interface. Each such listener object gets a MouseEvent containing the mouse event.

Also remember that a *MouseEvent* object is also passed to every *MouseMotionListener or MouseMotionAdapter* object which is registered to receive mouse motion events using the component's *addMouseMotionListener* method. *MouseMotionAdapter* object implements the *MouseMotionListener* interface. Each such listener object gets a MouseEvent containing the mouse motion event.

When a mouse button is clicked, events are generated and sent to the registered MouseListeners. The state of modal keys can be retrieved using ***InputEvent.getModifiers( ) and InputEvent.getModifiersEx( ).*** The button mask returned by ***InputEvent.getModifiers( )*** *reflects only the button that changed state, not the current state os all buttons. To get the state of all buttons and modifier keys, use* ***InputEvent.getModifiersEx( ).*** The button which has changed state is returned by getButton( ). For example, if the first mouse button is pressed, events are sent in the following order:

Id modifiers		Button
MOUSE_PRESSED	:	BUTTON1_MASK BUTTON1
MOUSE_RELEASED	:	BUTTON1_MASK BUTTON1
MOUSE_CLICKED	:	BUTTON1_MASK BUTTON1

Please note that when multiple mouse buttons are pressed, each press, release and click results in a separate event. MOUSE_DRAGGED events are delivered to the Component in which the mouse button was pressed until the mouse button is released regardless of whether the mouse position is within the bounds of the Component. Please note that due to platform-dependent Drag and Drop implementations, MOUSE_DRAGGED events may not be delivered during a native Drag and Drop operation. *Also note that in a multi-screen environment, mouse drag events are delivered to the Component even if the mouse position is outside the bounds of the Graphics Configuration associated with that Component.* However, the reported position for mouse drag events in this case may differ from the actual mouse position:

I. **In a multi-screen environment without a virtual device:** The reported coordinates for mouse drag events are clipped to fit within *the bounds of the Graphics Configuration* associated with the Component.

II. **In a multi-screen environment with a virtual device:** The reported coordinates for mouse drag events are clipped to fit ***within the bounds of the virtual device*** associated with the Component.

8.7 USING AWT IN APPLICATIONS—CONTAINERS

The Abstract Windowing Toolkit (AWT) **refers to a set of classes, enabling the user to create a user friendly, Graphical User Interface (GUI).** It will also facilitate receiving user input from the mouse and the keyboard. The AWT classes are part of the java.awt package. The user interface consists of the following:

- **Components**—anything that can be put on the user interface. This includes buttons, check boxes, pop-up menus, text fields.
- **Containers**—this is a component that can contain other components. The examples include the Applet window, panels, dialog boxes.
- **Layout Managers**—these define how the components will be arranged in a container.

Please note that the statement import java.awt.*; imports all of the components, containers and layout managers necessary for designing the user interface.

Also note that the AWT components are heavy weight components (unlike swing components). The following are these components:

- Labels (java.awt.Label)
- Buttons (java.awt.Button)
- Checkboxes (java.awt.Checkbox)
- Single-line text fields (java.awt.TextField)
- Larger text display and editing areas (java.awt.TextArea)
- Pop-up lists of choices (java.awt.Choice)
- Lists (java.awt.List)
- Sliders and scrollbars (java.awt.Scrollbar)
- Drawing areas (java.awt.Canvas)
- Menus (java.awt.menu, java.awt.MenuItem, java.awt.CheckboxMenuitem)
- Containers (java.awt.Panel, java.awt.Window and its subclasses)

8.8 AWT COMPONENTS—LABELS, BUTTONS, CHECKBOXES CHECKBOX GROUP / RADIO BUTTONS, THE TEXT FIELD AND TEXT AREAS, THE CHOICE LISTS, THE LIST CONTROL, MENUS, LAYOUT MANAGER

Because all applets are containers, so components can be added directly to the applet windows. The following steps are required to add a component:

1. Create the component by creating an object of that class.
2. Call the Container's add method to add the component.

Labels

Labels display non-editable text. To create a label use one of the following methods:

- **Label ( )**—creates an empty label.

- **Label (string)**—creates a label with the given string.
- **Label(string, int)**—creates a label with the given string and right, left or center alignment.

Buttons

Clickable buttons can be created from the Button class. You can create a button by using either of the following methods of this Button class:

- **Button ( )**—creates a button without any label. Use setLabel(string) to display a text on the button.
- **Button(string)**—creates a button with the given string as the label.

Checkboxes

They are labelled or unlabelled boxes that can either be checked off or empty. They are used for selecting some option. Use one of the following methods to create them:

- **Checkbox ( )**—creates a checkbox without any label.
- **Checkbox (string)**—creates a labeled checkbox.

When many checkboxes are there, any number of them can be checked or unchecked. Checkboxes can be organized into groups so that only one of them can be checked at a time. The following statement creates a checkbox group:

Checkbox Group mygroup = new CheckboxGroup( );

To create a checkbox, belonging to this group, we use the following statement:

Checkbox c1 = new Checkbox("Delhi", myGroup, true);

We are in a position to write a small program now to create label, checkbox and buttons.

```
//to create label, checkboxes and buttons
import java.awt.*;
import java.applet.Applet;
    public class AddUserInterface extends Applet {
        Label l1 = new Label("Choose One", Label.CENTER);
        Checkbox c1= new Checkbox("Delhi");
        Checkbox c2= new Checkbox("GTB NAGAR");
        Button b1= new Button("Submit");
        Button b2= new Button("Cancel");
        public void init( ) {
            add (l1);
            add (c1);
            add (c2);
            add (b1);
            add (b2);
        }
```

The applet is viewed as shown below. In this "Choose One" is a label. **Please note in this code that there is no paint method.**

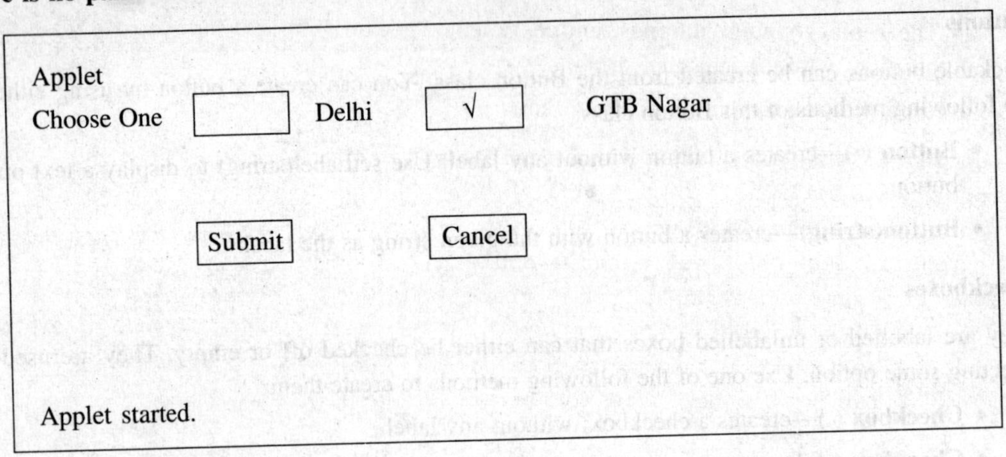

Text Fields

Text field is an editable component. Text field can be created by using one of the following methods of TextField class:

- **TextField ( )**—creates an empty text field.
- **TextField (string)**—creates a text field with specified string.
- **TextField (string, int)**—creates a text field with the specified string and specified width.

The TextField class has several useful methods:

1. **the getText( ) method**—returns the text in the field.
2. **the setText(string) method**—fills the field with the string.
3. **the setEditable(Boolean) method**—decides whether the field should be editable or not depending upon the Boolean value.
4. **the isEditable( ) method**—returns a boolean value indicating whether the field is editable or not.

Text Areas

These are editable text fields having **more than one line of input.** Use one of the following to create a text area:

- **TextArea ( )**—creates an empty text area.
- **TextArea (rows, characters)**—creates a text area of rows specified and width to accommodate the character specified.
- **TextArea(string)**
- **TextArea(string, rows, characters)**

The methods available in case of text field can also be used here. In addition to that, the following methods could be used:

- The **insert(string, charindex)** method inserts the indicated string at the position indicated by the second argument.
- The **replace(string, startpos, endpos)** method replaces the text between the given integer positions with the indicated string.

We are in a position to write a program now.

```
//applet to show the use of text field and text area
import java.awt.*;
import java.applet.Applet;
    public class UseText extends Applet {
Label l1 = new Label("Enter name", Label.CENTER); // draw
        //this label
        TextField t1 = new TextField("10"); //draw its textbox
        Label l2 = new Label("Enter message", Label.CENTER);
        TextArea t2 = new TextArea(5,10);
        Button b1 = new Button("Submit"); //draw buttons now
        Button b2 = new Button("Cancel");
        public void init( ) {
            add(l1); //add all of them now
            add(t1);
            add(l2);
            add(t2);
            add(b1);
            add(b2);
            }
        }
```

The applet is viewed as shown below:

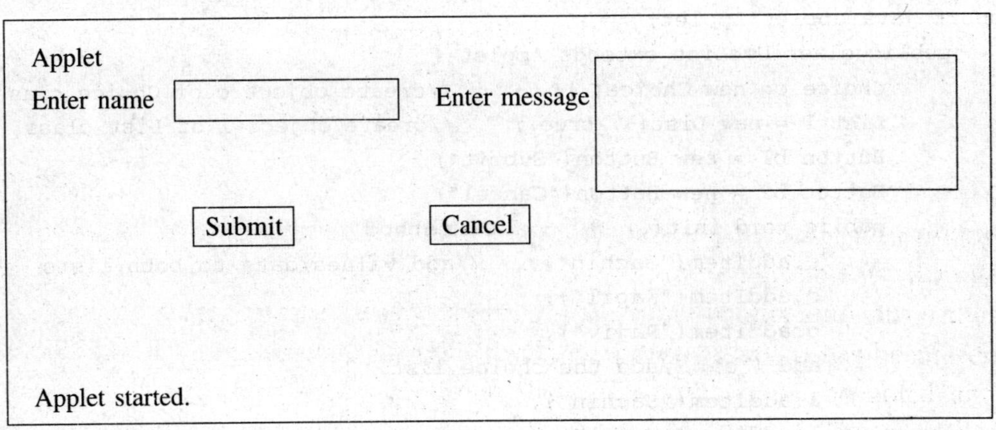

Choice lists

They are also called as **pop-up lists.** They enable a single item to be chosen from a list of items. Choice list is created and used as follows:

- Create an object of the class Choice.
- Add items to the list by using the method addItem (item) in the Choice class.
- Add the list as you do with any other component using the add (component) method.

The choice class has the following methods available:

- **getItem(index)**—returns text of the list item at the index position specified in the argument.
- **getItemCount( )**—returns the number of items in the list.
- **getSelectedIndex( )**—returns the index position of the currently selected item.
- **select(pos)**—selects the item at the indicated index position.
- **select(text)**—selects the first item in the list with the given text.

Scrolling lists

These are created from the **List class.** These are similar to choice lists. But here you can choose more than one item at a time. Scrolling lists do not pop-up. Multiple items are displayed at the same time. The list is created by choosing one of the following:

- **List ( )**—creates an empty scrolling list enabling only one item to be selected at a time.
- **List (item, boolean)**—creates a scrolling list with number of items equal to the first argument. The Boolean argument allows multiple selection is set to true.
- **addItem( )** method—is used to add items to the list.

We are in a position to write a simple program now to show the use of choice lists and scrolling lists.

```
//to show the use of choice lists and scrolling lists
import java.awt.*;
import java.applet.Applet;
    public class UseList extends Applet {
        Choice c= new Choice( );          //create object c of Choice class
        List l = new List(3, true);      //create object l of List class
        Button b1 = new Button("Submit");
        Button b2 = new Button("Cancel");
        public void init( ) {               //method
            c.addItem("Sachin");    //add values/data to both lists
            c.addItem("Kapil");
            c.additem("Rajiv");
            add ( c); //add the choice list
            l.addItem("Sachin");
            l.addItem("Kapil");
```

```
        l.addItem("Rajiv");
        add(l);
        add(b1);
        add(b2); //add buttons and scrolling lists now.
        }
    }
```

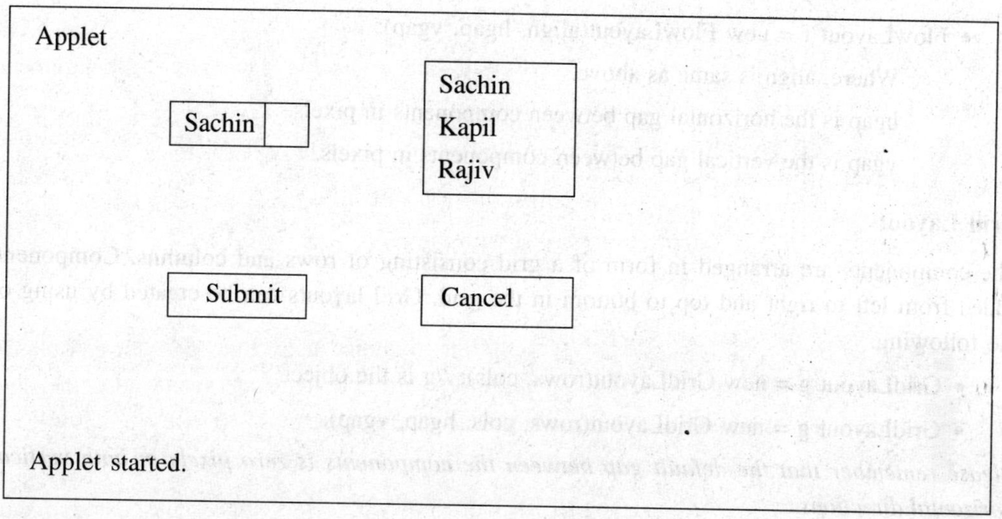

Now let us see how can we arrange the components on user interface?

Till this point we have studied how components can be added. **The components were added to the applet window by a *default layout mechanism.*** That is, the programmer could not control the way components were added to the window. ***By using layout managers, programmers can gain more control over the layout of an interface.***

The AWT contains five basic layout managers:

(a) FlowLayout

(b) GridLayout

(c) BorderLayout

(d) CardLayout

(e) GridBagLayout.

Technique used: To set a particular layout manager, an object of that type is created first and then the setLayout method is used.

Let us study these layouts now.

Flow Layout

This is the **default layout manager.** Components are added to the container from left to right. When there is no more space in row, components get added in the next row from left to right and so on.

Be default, the components on each row are centered. You can use any of the following to create the Flow Layout manager:

- FlowLayout f = new FlowLayout( ); //f is the object
- FlowLayout f = new FlowLayout(align);

  The align could be any one of the FlowLayout.LEFT, FlowLayout.RIGHT or FlowLayout.CENTER.
- FlowLayout f = new FlowLayout(align, hgap, vgap);

  Where, align is same as above,

  hgap is the horizontal gap between components in pixels.

  vgap is the vertical gap between components in pixels.

Grid Layout

The components are arranged in form of a grid consisting of rows and columns. Components are added from left to right and top to bottom in the grid. Grid layouts can be created by using one of the following:

- GridLayout g = new GridLayout(rows, cols); //g is the object
- GridLayout g = new GridLayout(rows, cols, hgap, vgap).

Please remember that the default gap between the components is zero pixels in both vertical and horizontal directions.

Border Layout

Here, the container is divided into five sections: north, south, east, west and center. Also remember that in *general, the central component is the largest and other components surrounding it will be smaller.* A border layout is created either by using a zero argument constructor or the one which takes hgap and vgap as arguments. Once the layout manager is set, the components are added by using the following statement:

add (place, component);

The argument, *place*, specifies the region in the container and the second argument specifies the *component* to be added.

In a single applet window, we can have multiple containers, each of one having it's own layout manager set to a particular type. The smaller containers are created from the panel class. The panels are filled with components before they are put into larger container. Panels are created and used as follows:

```
Panel p = new Panel( );
GridLayout g = new GridLayout(3, 3);
p.setLayout(g);
p.add(c1);
p.add(c2);
```

where c1 and c2 are the components added to the panel, p.

We are in a position to show the use of the above three layout managers.

```
//2 panels are used
import java.awt.*;
import java.applet.Applet;
public class UsePanel extends Applet {
    //create panels
    Panel p1 = new Panel( );
    Panel p2 = new Panel( );
    //create Layout managers
    GridLayout g = new GridLayout(2,2,2,2);
    BorderLayout b = new BorderLayout(2,2);
    //create buttons
    Button b11 = new Button("11");
    Button b12 = new Button("12");
    Button b21 = new Button("21");
    Button b22 = new Button("22");
    Button b1 = new Button("1");
    Button b2 = new Button("2");
    Button b3 = new Button("3");
    Button b4 = new Button("4");
    public void init( ) {
        //set the layouts
        p1.setLayout(g);   //1st panel gets grid layout.
        p2.setLayout(b);   //2nd panel gets border layout
        //add buttons to panel p1
        p1.add (b11);
        p1.add (b12);
        p1.add (b21);
        p1.add (b22);
        p1.setBackground(color.red);
 // add panel p1 to p2
 p2.add("North", p1);
 //add buttons to panel p2
 p2.add("West", b1);
 p2.add("East", b2);
 p2.add("South", b3);
 p2.add("Center", b4);
 p2.setBackground(Color.green);
 add(p2);
 }
 }
```

The above applet is viewed as follows:

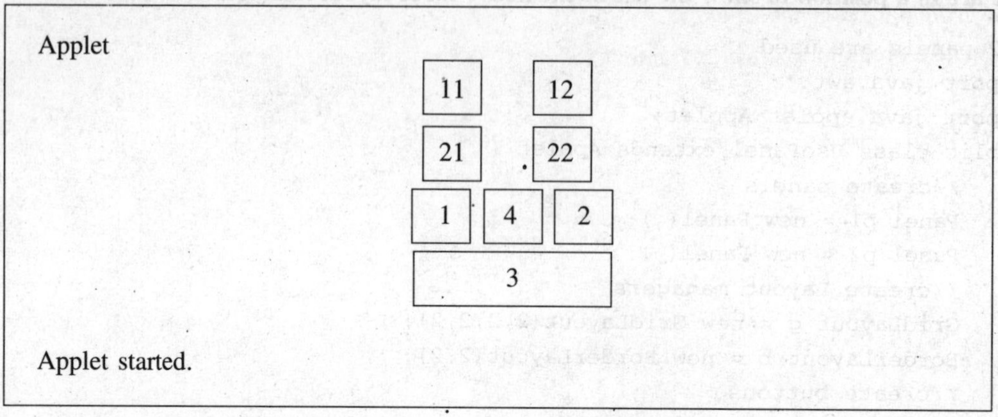

Please note that here the buttons labelled 11, 12, 21 and 22 are placed in the North region of Panel, p2. The North region is arranged as Grid Layout. The buttons labelled 1, 2, 3, 4 occupy the West, East, South and Center region of the Panel 2.

Grid Layout

This is a group of containers or components that are displayed one at a time. **Each container in the group is called as card.** You can use a panel to each card and each panel can have any number of components. A card layout is created similar to any other layout.

CardLayout c= new CardLayout( );

The **setLayout( ) method** is used to assign this layout manager for the container. The method **add(string, container)** is used to add a specific container or component to the card. After the card has been added to the main container such as an applet window, the card can be displayed by using the **show( )** method. **Only one card can be viewed at a time.**

Grid Bag Layout

This is an extension of the grid layout manager. A grid bag layout differs from grid layout as follows:

1. A component can occupy more than one cell in the grid.
2. The proportions between different rows and columns do not have to be equal.
3. Components inside grid cells can be arranged in different ways.

The class GridBagLayout is used to create an object for the layout manager. The class GridBagConstraints defines the properties of each component to be placed into the cell. The overall layout is defined by the relationships between the grid bag, the constraints and each component.

Let us now discuss about frames also.

Frames

These are subclasses of a class called **Window.** The Frame class provides a window with a title bar, close boxes and other window features. *Please note that dialog boxes are similar to frames but they* *do not have a title*. Frames are containers similar to panels. The default layout for frames is Border Layout. *Also note that you have to use the resize( ) method to provide a size for the window and the show( ) method to show the window.*

Let us write a program to create a frame.

```
import java.awt.*;
import java.applet.Applet;

public class ShowWindow extends Applet {
        Frame win;
        Button b1 = new Button("Open");
        Button b2 = new Button("Close");
        GridLayout g = new GridLayout(1,1);
        public void init( ) {
            win = new Frame("My Window");
            win.setLayout(g);
            win.add(b1);
            win.add(b2);
            win.resize(100,150);
            win.show( );
        }
    }
```

When this applet is viewed, a new window comes as shown below:

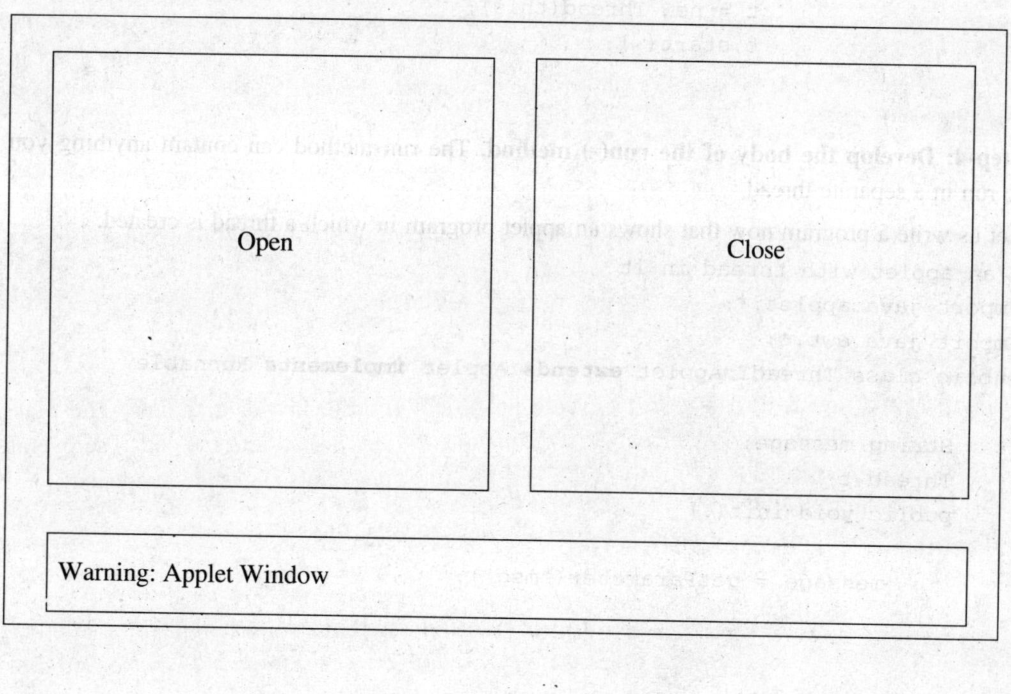

We are in a position to solve some examples now.

Example 1: What do you understand by threads in Applet? Explain the steps and with an example.

Solution: The only way to create threads in applet is by implementing the Runnable interface. The following steps may be followed:

Step-1: Declare your applet class as follows:

```
public class Sample extends Applet implements Runnable
  {
    .......
    ......
  }
```

Here, Sample is the name of the applet class.

Step-2: Add an instance variable to hold the applet's thread class as follows:

Thread t;

Here, 't' is the instance variable.

Step-3: Override the applet's start( ) method. In the new start( ) method, create a new thread and start it running as follows:

```
public void start( )
  {
      if (t == null)
       {
          t = new Thread(this);
          t.start( );
       }
  }
```

Step-4: Develop the body of the run( ) method. The run method can contain anything you want to run in a separate thread.

Let us write a program now that shows an applet program in which a thread is created.

```
//an applet with thread in it
import java.applet.*;
import java.awt.*;
public class ThreadInApplet extends Applet implements Runnable
  {
    String message;
    Thread t;
    public void init( )
      {
        message = getParameter("msg");
      }
```

```
    public void start( )
     {
         if (t == null)
           {
               t = new Thread(this);
               t.start( );
           }

public void run( )
  {
      Graphics g = getGraphics( );
      int i =0;
      while (true)
           {
          g.setColor(Color.black);
          g.drawString(message, 5 * i, 100);
          try {
               t.sleep(100);
               }
          Catch(InterruptedException e) { }
          g.setColor(Color.white);
          g.drawString(message, 5 * i, 100);
          i++;
          if (i > 79)
           i=0;
          }
       }
     }
```

HTML CODE FOR ABOVE APPLET IS:

```
<html>
<applet code=ThreadInApplet width=400 height=400>
<param name="msg" value="HelloWorld">
</applet>
</html>
```

When you run this program, it shows a text string Hello World moving from the left side of the applet window and disappearing at the right side. It then reenters the window from the starting left side, moves towards the right and disappears again. This process will be repeated. **Please note that you must not resize or maximize the applet window.** However, you can modify the program to get the same effect, irrespective of the window size.

Example 2: How will you display an image in an applet?

Solution:

```
//java code for displaying of an image in an applet
import java.applet.*;
import java.awt.*;

public class DisplayImage extends java.applet.Applet
 {
     String s;
     Image I;

public void init( )
       {
           s= getParameter("msg");
           i = getImage(getDocumentbase( ), s);
       }

public void paint(Graphics g)
  {
     d.drawImage(1, 100, 40, this);
  }
}
```

HTML CODE FOR ABOVE APPLET IS:

```
<html>
<applet code=DisplayImage width=400 height=400>
<param name="Img" value="Image1.gif">
</applet>
</html>
```

Example 3: Write a Java code to play an audio file.

Solution:

```
//java code for playing an audio file in an applet
import java.applet.*;
import java.awt.event.*;
import java.awt.*;

public class PlaySound extends Applet implements MouseListener
 {
     //to refer to the sounds
     AudioClip soundFile1;
     AudioClip soundFile2;
     public void init( )
```

```
{
//this loads the sounds from the server in the same way as an image.
soundFile1 = getAudioClip(getDocumentBase( ), "dataS.au");
soundFile2 = getAudioClip(getDocumentBase( ), "ShootS.au");

//when the applet gets here the sounds are loaded
//add the mouse lietsner
addMouseListener(this);
setBackground(Color.yellow);

//play the first sound to let the user know the applet is loaded
soundFile1.play( );
}

public void paint(Graphics g)
{
    g.drawString("Click to hear a sound", 20,20);
}

//play the second sound on a click
public void mouseClicked(MouseEvent evt)
{
    soundFile2.play( );    //play your sound file
}

//the mandatory methods
public void mousePressed(MouseEvent evt) { }
public void mouseReleased(MouseEvent evt) { }
public void mouseEntered(MouseEvent evt) { }
public void mouseExited(MouseEvent evt) { }
}
```

HTML CODE FOR THIS APPLET IS:

```
<html>
<applet code=PlaySound width=400 height=400>
</applet>
</html>
```

Example 4: Write an applet code to draw a line.

Solution:

```
import java.applet.*;
import java.awt.*;
```

```
public class DrawingLines extends Applet
 {
     int width, height;
     public void init( ) {
     width = getSize( ).width;
     height = getSize( ).height;
     setbackground(Color.black);
 }
public void paint(Graphics g) {
g.setColor(Color.green);
for( int i=0; i <10; ++i) {
g.drawLine(width, height, i * width / 10.0);
}
}
}
```

Summary

In this chapter, we have senn that an applet is a small program that can be executed using the ***appletviewer or Java-enabled web browser.*** The Applet class is the only class of the **java.applet** package. The APPLET tag is used to embed an applet in a web page. The **paint( ) method** draws the graphics of the applet in the drawing area. An application does not need a browser to run rather it needs javac and Java interpreter. An application starts with the main method only. Also we have seen that the init( ) method is the first method that is called when an applet is loaded into memory. The start( ) method is called immediately after the init( ) method and every time the applet gets the focus. The stop( ) method is called every time the user moves on to another web page or we can say when another applet gets the focus. The destroy( ) method is called just before the web browser is closed. The update( ) method clears the screen and calls the paint( ) method. The repaint( ) method calls the update( ) method to signal that the applet has to be updated.

Almost all GUI application programs have events like user moving the mouse or clicking a button. An event comprises of the three components—Event object, Event source and Event handler.

Also learnt in this chapter is that **layout management is the process that determines the size and position of components in a container.** Layout manager is used to organize the components into manageable groups. There are five commonly used layout managers but by default ***FlowLayout*** manager is the default manager for an applet.

Chapter 9

Animation and Images

9.0 INTRODUCTION

In Java, all drawing, including images and animations, takes place via a ***Graphics object.*** This is an instance of java.awt.Graphics class.

9.1 JAVA BASIC DRAWING TOOLS—THE GRAPHICS CLASS

Applets are very useful for drawing various objects. Most of them are available online and also within the Applet directory. As explained earlier, in Java all drawing is done by creating and object of Graphics class.

The Graphics class is an abstract class that represents the display area of the applet on the web page. It is a part of ***java.awt package.*** It is used for drawing on the display area of the applet. In the previous chapter, we have studied that the Graphics class provides a **drawstring method to display text on the applet.** It also requires the position to be specified. An applet displays the information on the screen by using the **paint( ) method** defined in ***java.awt.Graphics*** class, and it takes an instance of the Graphics class as a parameter. **For example,**

```
import java.applet.*;
import java.awt.*;
public class Applet1 extends Applet
 {
      public void paint(Graphics g)
      {
           g.drawString("Welcome to my first applet", 10, 10);
      }
}
```

The Graphics class also provides methods to draw various graphics and manage fonts and colors. Some of these methods with their prototypes are as follows:

1. **drawLine(int x1, int y1, int x2, int y2)**—It draws a line using the current color, between the points (x1, y1) and (x2, y2) in this graphics contexts coordinate system.
2. **drawArc(int x, int y, int width, int height, int startAngle, int arcAngle)**—It draws the outline of a circular arc or elliptical arc covering the specified rectangle.
3. **drawOval(int x, int y, int width, int height)**—It draws the outline of an oval.

4. **drawPolygon(Polygon p)**—It draws the outline of a polygon defined by the specified Polygon object.
5. **drawPolyline(int [ ] xPoints, int [ ] yPoints, int nPoints)**—It draws a sequence of connected lines defined by arrays of x and y coordinates.
6. **drawRoundRect(int x, int y, int width, int height, int arcWidth, int arcHeight)**—It draws an outlined round-cornered rectangle using this graphics context's current color.
7. **fillArc(int x, int y, int width, int height, int startAngle, int arcAngle)**—Fills a circular or elliptical arc covering the specified rectangle.
8. **fillOval(int x, int y, int width, int height)**—It fills an oval bounded by the specified rectangle with the current color.
9. **fillPolygon(int [ ] xPoints, int [ ] yPoints, int nPoints)**—Fills a closed Polygon defined by arrays of x and y coordinates.
10. **fillPolygon(Polygon p)**—It fills the polygon defined by the specified Polygon object with the graphics context's current color.
11. **fillRect(int x, int y, int width, int height)**—It fills the specified rectangle.
12. **fillRoundRect(int x, int y, int width, int height, int arcWidth, int arcHeight)**—It fills the specified rounded corner rectangle with the current color.
13. **getColor( )**—It gets this graphics context's current color.
14. **getFont( )**—It gets the current font.
15. **setColor(Color c)**—It sets this graphics context's current color to the specified color.
16. **setFont(Font font)**—It sets this graphics context's font to the specified font.

9.2 DRAWING LINES

In Java, a line is drawn by using **drawLine ( ) method with Graphics object,** say g, as follows:

g.drawLine(x1, y1, x2, y2);

This method draws a line using the current color between the points (x1, y1) and (x2, y2) in this graphics context's coordinate system. The parameter as follows:

x1 – the first point's x-coordinate.

y1 – the first point's y-coordinate.

x2 – the second point's x-coordinate.

y2 – the second point's y-coordinate.

We are in a position to solve an example now.

```
//Java program to draw four lines in four different colors (lines.java)
import java.applet.*;
import java.awt.*;
public class lines extends Applet
```

```
{
    public void paint(Graphics g)
     {
        g.setColor(Color.green);
        g.drawLine(10, 10,200, 200);

        g.setColor(Color.red);
        g.drawLine(50, 10,250, 200);

        g.setColor(Color.blue);
        g.drawLine(100, 10,300, 200);

        g.setColor(Color.black);
        g.drawLine(150, 10,350, 200);
 }
 }
```

And here is the program that shows a HTML file that displays the output:

```
<HTML>
     <BODY>
     <APPLET>
          CODE = "lines.class"
          WIDTH = 300
          HEIGHT = 300
        </APPLET>
        </BODY>
</HTML>
```

OUTPUT (after running):

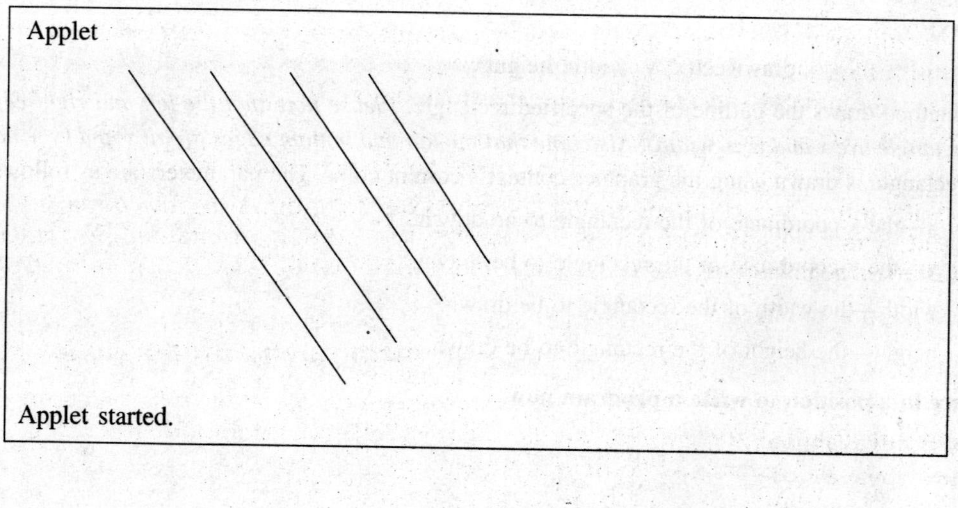

Please note that in the program- "lines.java", we have used the setColor( ) method. The setColor( ) method sets this graphics context's current color to the specified color.

setColor(Color c);

Also note that all of the subsequent graphics operations using this graphics context use this specified color. Here, the parameter 'c' is the new rendering color. It may have one of the following value at any time:

- black or BLACK – for black color.
- white or WHITE – for white color.
- red or RED—for red color.
- yellow or YELLOW—for yellow color.
- cyan or CYAN—for cyan color.
- blue or BLUE – for blue color.
- gray or GRAY – for gray color.
- darkGray or DARK_GRAY – for dark gray color.
- lightGray or LIGHT_GRAY –for light gray color.
- Magenta or MAGENTA – for magenta color
- Orange or ORANGE – for orange color.
- pink or PINK – for pink color.

We shall be studying these a bit later.

9.3 DRAWING RECTANGLES

The drawRect( ) method is used to draw to draw the outline of the specified rectangle. Its syntax is as follows:

Syntax:

drawRect(x, y, width, height);

This method draws the outline of the specified rectangle. *Please note that the left and right edges of the rectangle are x and (x + width). Also note that the top and bottom edges are at y and (y + height).* The rectangle is drawn using the graphics context's current color. The parameters are as follows:

x—the x-coordinate of the rectangle to be drawn.

y—the y-coordinate of the rectangle to be drawn.

width—the width of the rectangle to be drawn.

height—the height of the rectangle to be drawn.

We are in a position to write a program now.

```
import java.applet.*;
import java.awt.*;
```

```
public class rect extends Applet
 {
      public void paint(Graphics g)
       {
           g.drawRect(12, 12, 350, 350);
       }
 }
```

And the program that shows a HTML file that displays the output is:

```
<HTML>
     <BODY>
     <APPLET
          CODE = "rect.class"
          WIDTH = 450
          HEIGHT = 450>
     </APPLET>
     </BODY>
</HTML>
```

OUTPUT (after running):

Let us now discuss about the **fillRect( ) method.**

The **fillRect( ) method** fills the specified rectangle.

Syntax:

fillRect(x, y, width, height);

The fillRect method fills the specified rectangle. *Please note here that the left and right edges of the* rectangle are x and (x + width –1). *Also note that the top and bottom edges are at* y and (y + height–1). The resulting rectangle covers an area width pixel wide by height pixels tall. The rectangle is filled by the graphics context's current color. The parameters are as follows:

x—the x-coordinate of the rectangle to be filled.

y—the y-coordinate of the rectangle to be filled.

width—the width of the rectangle to be filled.

height—the height of the rectangle to be filled.

We are in a position to write a program now.

```
import java.applet.*;
import java.awt.*;
public class frect extends Applet
 {
     public void paint(Graphics g)
      {
          g.drawRect(12, 12, 350, 350);
      }
 }
```

And the program that shows a HTML file that displays the output is:

```
<HTML>
     <BODY>
     <APPLET
          CODE = "frect.class"
          WIDTH = 450
          HEIGHT = 450>
     </APPLET>
     </BODY>
</HTML>
```

OUTPUT (after running):

Say, now we want to draw a rounded rectangle (rounded from its corners). Then, in Java, we use the following method:

drawRoundRect(x, y, width, height, arcWidth, arcHeight);

This method draws an outlined round-cornered rectangle using this graphics context's current color.

Please note that the left and right edges of the rectangle are x and (x + width) respectively. Also note that the top and bottom edges are at y and (y + height). The parameters are as follows:

x—the x-coordinate of the rectangle to be drawn.

y—the y-coordinate of the rectangle to be drawn.

width—the width of the rectangle to be drawn.

height—the height of the rectangle to be drawn.

arcWidth—the horizontal diameter of the arc at the four corners.

arcHeight—the vertical diameter of the arc at the four corners.

We are in a position to write a program now.

```
import java.applet.*;
import java.awt.*;
public class rrect extends Applet
 {
     public void paint(Graphics g)
      {
           g.drawRoundRect(12, 12, 350, 350, 60, 60);
      }
 }
```

And the program that shows a HTML file that displays the output is:

```
<HTML>
     <BODY>
     <APPLET
          CODE = "rrect.class"
          WIDTH = 450
          HEIGHT = 450>
     </APPLET>
     </BODY>
</HTML>
```

OUTPUT (after running):

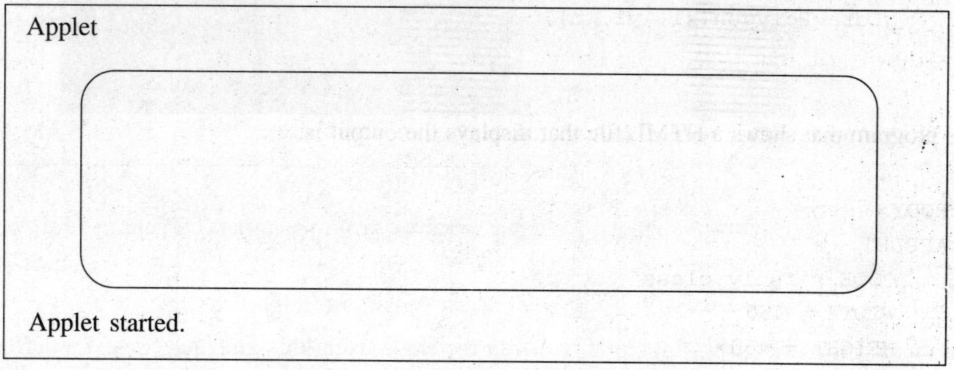

Just remember that as you have fillRect( ) method, you can use fillRoundMethod( ) in order to fill the specified rounded corner rectangle with the current color. The left and right edges of the rectangle are x and (x + width – 1), respectively. The top and bottom edges of the rectangle are y and (y + height – 1).

9.4 DRAWING POLYGONS

Again, the ***drawPolygon( ) method*** is used to draw a polygon. Its **syntax** is as follows:

drawPolygon(xPoints, yPoints, nPoints);

This method draws a closed polygon defined by arrays of x and y coordinates. Each pair of (x, y) coordinates defines a point. This method draws the polygon defined by nPoint line segments, where the first (nPoint – 1) line segments are line segments from (xPoints[i-1], yPoints[i-1] to (xPoints[i], yPoints[i]).

The figure is automatically closed by drawing a line connecting the final point to the first point, if those points are different. The parameters are as follows:

xPoints—an array of x-coordinates.

yPoints—an array of y-coordinates.

nPoints—the total number of points.

We are in a position to write a program now.

```
import java.applet.*;
import java.awt.*;
public class poly extends Applet
 {
     int x1 [ ] = {250, 20, 250, 300, 100};
     int y1 [ ] = {20, 150, 250, 100, 20};
     int n = 5;

     public void paint(Graphics g)
      {
          g.drawPolygon(x1, y1, n);
      }
 }
```

And the program that shows a HTML file that displays the output is:

```
<HTML>
     <BODY>
     <APPLET
          CODE = "poly.class"
          WIDTH = 450
          HEIGHT = 450>
```

```
    </APPLET>
    </BODY>
</HTML>
```

OUTPUT (after running):

9.5 DRAWING OVALS

The drawOval( ) method is used to draw an oval; Its syntax is as follows:

Syntax:

drawOval(x, y, width, height);

This method draws the outline of the specified oval. The result is a circle or ellipse that fits within the rectangle specified by the x, y, width and height arguments. *Please note that the oval covers an area that is* (*width* + 1) *pixels wide and* (*height* + 1) *pixels tall.* The parameters are as follows:

x—the x-coordinate of the upper left corner of the oval to be drawn.

y—the y-coordinate of the upper left corner of the oval to be drawn.

width—the width of the oval to be drawn.

height—the height of the oval to be drawn.

We are in a position to write a program now.

```
import java.applet.*;
import java.awt.*;
public class oval extends Applet
 {
     public void paint(Graphics g)
      {
          g.drawOval(12, 12, 350, 350);
      }
 }
```

And the program that shows a HTML file that displays the output is:

```
<HTML>
    <BODY>
    <APPLET
        CODE = "oval.class"
        WIDTH = 450
        HEIGHT = 450>
    </APPLET>
    </BODY>
</HTML>
```

OUTPUT (after running):

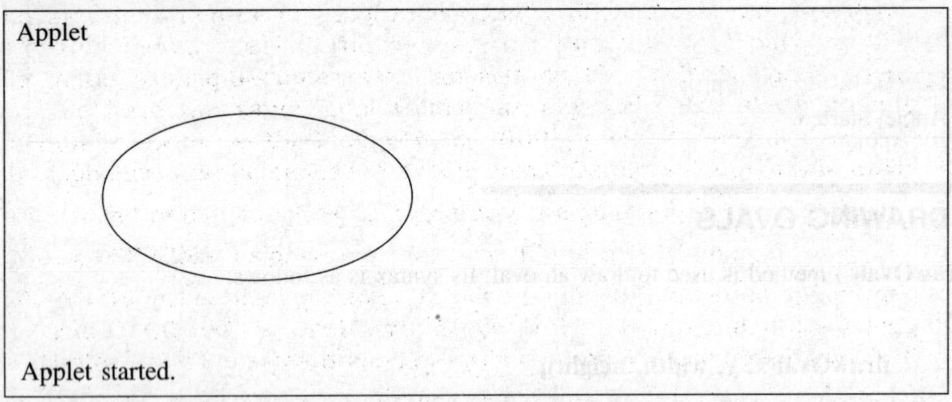

But if you want to draw an oval with the current color then use the following method:

fillOval(x, y, width, height);

This method fills an oval bounded by the specified rectangle with the current color. Here the parameters are as follows:

x—the x-coordinate of the upper left corner of the oval to be filled.

y—the y-coordinate of the upper left corner of the oval to be filled.

width—the width of the oval to be filled.

height—the height of the oval to be filled.

We are in a position to write a program now.

```
import java.applet.*;
import java.awt.*;
public class oval extends Applet
 {
    public void paint(Graphics g)
     {
        g.drawOval(12, 12, 350, 350);
```

```
        g.fillOval(12, 150, 250, 150);
    }
 }
```

And the program that shows a HTML file that displays the output is:

```
<HTML>
    <BODY>
    <APPLET
        CODE = "oval.class"
        WIDTH = 450
        HEIGHT = 450>
    </APPLET>
    </BODY>
</HTML>
```

OUTPUT (after running):

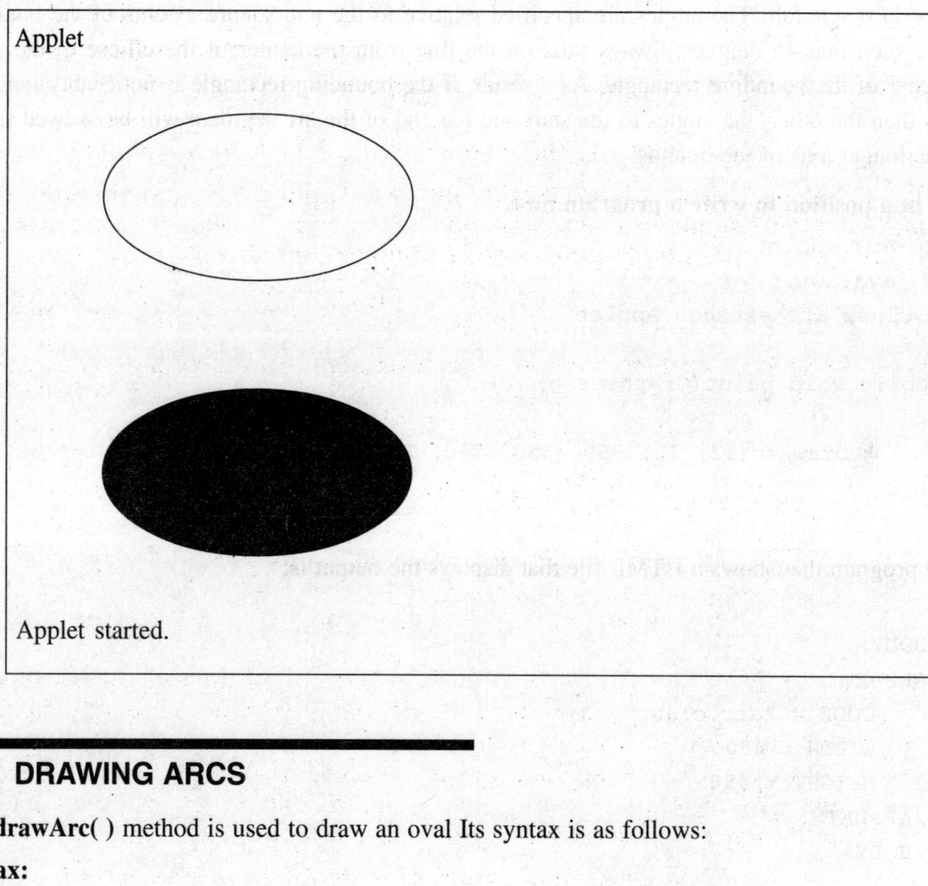

9.6 DRAWING ARCS

The drawArc( ) method is used to draw an oval Its syntax is as follows:

Syntax:

drawArc(x, y, width, height, startAngle, arcAngle);

This method draws the outline of a circular or elliptical arc covering the specified rectangle. The resulting arc begins at startAngle and extends for arcAngle degrees, using the current color. **Please note that the angles are interpreted such that 0 degrees is at the 3 o'clock position. Also note that a positive value indicates a counter-clockwise rotation while a negative value indicates a clockwise rotation.** The parameters are as follows:

x—the x-coordinate of the upper left corner of the arc to be drawn.

y—the y-coordinate of the upper left corner of the arc to be drawn.

width—the width of the arc to be drawn.

height—the height of the arc to be drawn.

startAngle—the beginning angle.

arcAngle—the angular extent of the arc, relative to the start angle.

The center of the arc is the center of the rectangle whose origin is (x, y) and whose size is specified by the width and height arguments. The resulting arc covers an area (width + 1) pixels wide by (height + 1) pixels tall. The angles are specified relative to the non-square extents of the bounding rectangle such that 45 degrees always falls on the line from the center of the ellipse to the upper right corner of the bounding rectangle. As a result, if the bounding rectangle is noticeably longer in one axis than the other, the angles to the start and the end of the arc segment will be skewed farther along the longer axis of the bounds.

We are in a position to write a program now.

```
import java.applet.*;
import java.awt.*;
public class arc extends Applet
{
     public void paint(Graphics g)
      {
          g.drawArc(12, 12, 350, 350, 250, 200);
      }
 }
```

And the program that shows a HTML file that displays the output is:

```
<HTML>
     <BODY>
     <APPLET
          CODE = "arc.class"
          WIDTH = 450
          HEIGHT = 450>
     </APPLET>
     </BODY>
</HTML>
```

OUTPUT (after running):

But if you want to draw a filled arc then use the following method:

fillArc(x, y, width, height, startAngle, arcAngle);

This method fills an arc.

We are in a position to write a program now.

```
import java.applet.*;
import java.awt.*;
public class farc extends Applet
 {
    public void paint(Graphics g)
     {
        g.fillArc(12, 12, 350, 350, 250, 150);
     }
 }
```

And the program that shows a HTML file that displays the output is:

```
<HTML>
    <BODY>
    <APPLET
        CODE = "farc.class"
        WIDTH = 450
        HEIGHT = 450>
    </APPLET>
    </BODY>
</HTML>
```

OUTPUT (after running):

9.7 COLOR MODELS

Java supports color in a portable, **device independent way**. The AWT color system allows us to specify any color we want. The ***color class*** is used to create a color combination. The color class has three constructors as follows:

Color(int r, int g, int b);

Color(int rgb);

Color(float r, float g, float b);

Please note here the following:

1. The 1st constructor takes three arguments; each argument takes a value between 0 and 255.
2. The 2nd constructor takes a single integer argument that is a mix of red, green and blue.
3. The final constructor takes three float values between 0.0 and 1.0, that specify the relative mix of red, green and blue.

The setForeground( ) and setBackground( ) methods are used to set the fore ground and back ground colors respectively. **But please remember that by default, the graphics objects are drawn in the fore ground color.** However, it can be changed by calling Graphics method setColor(c). Here, 'c' specifies the new drawing color. The getColor( ) method used to obtain the current color. Other important methods are getRed( ), getBlue( ) and getGreen( ). These 3 methods i.e. getRed( ), getBlue( ) and getGreen( ) are used to obtain the red, blue and green component of a color respectively.

We are in a position to write a small Java program now.

```
import java.applet.*;

import java.awt.*;
```

```
public class color_Demo extends Applet
 {
     public void paint(Graphics g)
       {
          Color c1 = new Color(255, 125, 125);
          Color c2 = new Color(155, 255, 185);
          Color c3 = new Color(125, 125, 255);
          g.setColor(c1);
          g.drawRect(20,20,50,50);
          g.setColor(Color.red);
          g.fillRect(60,20,100,50);
          g.setColor(Color.black);
          g.fillOval(20,220,100,50);
          g.setColor(c2);
          g.fillOval(160,120,100,50);
          g.setColor(Color.black);
          g.drawArc(60,200,100,250,120);
          g.setColor(c3);
          g.fillArc(160,200,100,50,150, 100);
         }
   }
```

And the program that shows a HTML file that displays the output is:

```
<HTML>
     <BODY>
     <APPLET
          CODE = "colordemo.class"
          WIDTH = 450
          HEIGHT = 450>
     </APPLET>
     </BODY>
</HTML>
```

OUTPUT (after running):

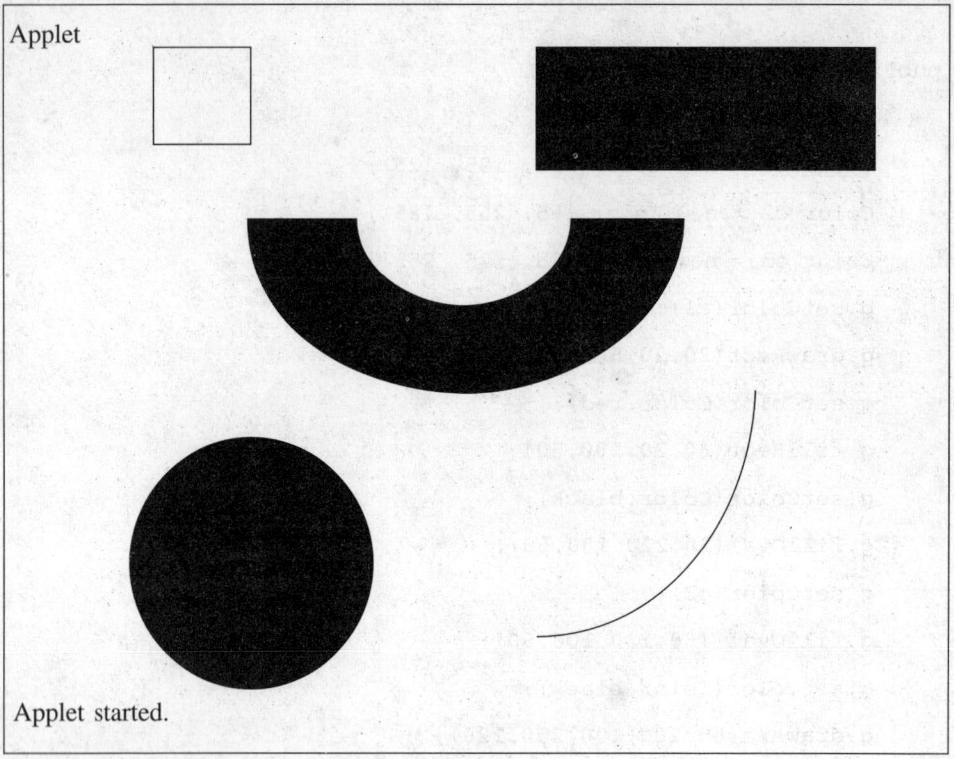

9.8 RENDERING TEXT

In order to render a text string, we call Graphics2D.drawString, passing in the string that we want to render. Java provides a number of fonts for management of text output in applets using the Font class. A font object can be created as follows:

Syntax:

Font f = new Font(name, style, size);

Here, '**name**' is the name of the font style of the Font, like Font BOLD and size is the size of the font.

Example:

Font f = new ("Arial", Font.BOLD, 12);

This Font class offers a wide variety of fonts like Times New Roman, Courier, Arial, Futura etc. Font names are strings representing the family of the font. Some of the font styles available are BOLD, PLAIN, ITALIC etc. **Please note that these are the integer constants and they can be added as follows:**

Font.BOLD + Font.ITALIC

Also remember that the Font class provides the following methods:

Table 9.1: Font Class Methods

Methods	Purpose
setFont(Font f)	Sets the graphics context's font to the specified font.
getFont( )	Returns the graphics context's font to the current font.
setForeground(Color c)	Sets the foreground color of an applet text.
setBackground(Color c)	Sets the background color of an applet text.
getStyle( )	Returns an integer value that indicates the current font style.
isPlain( )	Returns true if the font is plain.
isBold( )	Returns true if the font is bold.
isItalic( )	Returns true if the font is italic.
getSize( )	Returns an integer value that indicates the current font size.

Let us write a demo program now.

```
import java.applet.*;
import java.awt.*;
public class font_demo extemds Applet
 {
      Font f1, f2, f3;
      public void init( )
       {
            f1 = new Font(“Arial”, Font.BOLD, 14);
f2 = new Font(“Times New Roman”, Font.ITALIC, 16);
f3 = new Font(“Bookman Old Style”,
Font.BOLD+Font.ITALIC, 18);
      }

      public void paint(Graphics g)
      {
            g.se Font(f1);
            g.drawString(“My name is Dr. Rajiv Chopra”, 30, 40);
            g.setFont(f2);
            g.drawString(“My name is Dr. Rajiv Chopra”, 30, 100);
            g.setFont(f3);
            g.drawString(“My name is Dr. Rajiv Chopra”, 30, 160);
      }
}
```

And here is the program that shows a HTML file that displays the output:

```
<HTML>
    <BODY>
    <APPLET
        CODE = "font_demo.class"
        WIDTH = 450
        HEIGHT = 450>
    </APPLET>
    </BODY>
</HTML>
```

OUTPUT (after running):

```
Applet

    My name is Dr. Rajiv Chopra

    My name is Dr. Rajiv Chopra

    My name is Dr. Rajiv Chopra

Applet started.
```

Let us now discuss about the *fontMetrics* class.

Please note that it is true that the size of each font may differ and that fonts may be changed while your program is executing. There must be some way to determine the dimensions and various other attributes of the currently selected font. **For example,** to write one line of text after another implies that you have some way of knowing how tall the font is and how many pixels are needed between lines. And this is done with the help of fontMetrics class. **Also note that the Font Metrics class defines a font metrics object which encapsulates information about the rendering of a particular font on a particular screen.** This *fontMetrics class* defines several methods that help us to manage text output. The following table shows some of the used methods:

Table 9.2: FontMetrics Class Methods

Method	Meaning
bytesWidth(byte[ ] data, int off, int len);	Returns the total advance width for showing the specified array of bytes in the Font.
charsWidth(char[ ] data, int off, int len);	Returns the total advance width for showing the specified array of characters in the Font.
charWidth(char ch);	Returns the advance width of the specified character in this font.
charWidth(int ch);	Returns the advance width of the specified character in this font.
getAscent( );	Returns the **ascent** of the font.
getDescent( );	Returns the **descent** of the font.
getFont( );	Returns the font.
getHeight( );	Gets the standard height of a line of text in this font.
getLeading( );	Returns the space between lines of the text.
getMaxAdvance( );	Returns the width of the widest character. –1 is returned if this value is not available.
getMaxAscent( );	Returns the maximum **ascent** of the font.
getMaxDecent( );	Returns the maximum **decent** of the font.
getWidths( );	Returns the width of the first 256 characters.
stringWidth(String str);	Returns the width of the specified String str.

Let us now see, how can we display the multiple lines of text?

To display the multiple lines of text, we must manually keep track of the **current output position.** Each time a new line is desired, the Y-coordinate is updated to the beginning of the next line. The ***getLeading ( )*** method is used to determine the spacing between lines. Each time you like to display on the next line, we use ***getHeight( )*** method. This method returns the standard height of a line of text in this font. To start the output at the end of previous string, on the same line, use the ***stringWidth( )*** method that returns the width of the specified string.

Let us write a simple program now that displays multiple lines of text.

```
import java.applet.*;
import java.awt.*;
public class lines_demo extends Applet
 {
```

```
Font f1;
int x, y;

public void init( )
 {
    f1 = new Font("Arial", Font.BOLD, 14);
    setFont(f1);
 }

public void paint(Graphics g)
 {
    nextLine("My name is Dr. Rajiv Chopra", g);

    nextLine("My fathers name is Dr. J. R. Chopra", g);

    nextLine("My mothers name is Sushma Chopra", g);

    nextLine("I have 2 twin babies:-", g);

    sameLine("Arjeesh Chopra and", g);

    sameLine("Arshitha Chopra and", g);

    nextLine("Thanks to GOD!!!", g);
 }

 void nextLine(String s, Graphics g)
  {
    FontMetrics fm = g.getFontMterics( );
    y = y + fm.getHeight( );
    x=0;
    g.drawString(s, x, y);
    x = fm.stringWidth(s);
  }

 void sameLine(String s, Graphics g)
  {
    FontMetrics fm = g.getFontMterics( );
    g.drawString(s, x, y);
    x = x + fm.getWidth(s);
  }
 }
```

And here goes the HTML file that displays the output as follows:

```
<HTML>
    <BODY>
    <APPLET
        CODE = "lines_demo.class"
        WIDTH = 450
        HEIGHT = 450>
    </APPLET>
    </BODY>
</HTML>
```

OUTPUT (after running):

Applet

My name is Dr. Rajiv Chopra
My fathers name is Dr. J. R. Chopra
My mother name is Sushma Chopra
I have 2 twin babies: Arjeesh Chopra and Arshita Chopra
Thanks to GOD!!!

Applet started.

Let us now see how to center the text, left to right, top to bottom in a window even when the window is resized?

This program obtains ascent, descent and width of the string and computes the position at which it must be displayed to be centered.

```
//program to center the text
import java.applet.*;
import java.awt.*;
public class lines_demo2 extends Applet
 {
    Font f1;
    int x, y;

    public void init( )
     {
        f1 = new Font("Arial", Font.BOLD, 14);
     }

    public void paint(Graphics g)
     {
Dimension d = this.getSize( );
g.setColor(Color.red);
g.setFont(f1);
drawCenterString(Welcome to my zone", d.width, d.height, g);
    }

    void drawCenterString(String s, int w, int h, Graphics g)
     {
        FontMetrics fm = g.getFontMetrics( );
        x = (w-fm.stringWidth(s))/2;
    y = (fm.getAscent( ) + (h-(fm.getAscent( ) + fm.getDescent()))/2);
        g.drawString(s, x, y);
      }
    }
```

And here goes the HTML file that displays the output as follows:

```
<HTML>
    <BODY>
    <APPLET
        CODE = "lines_demo2.class"
        WIDTH = 450
        HEIGHT = 450>
```

```
        </APPLET>
    </BODY>
</HTML>
```

OUTPUT (after running):

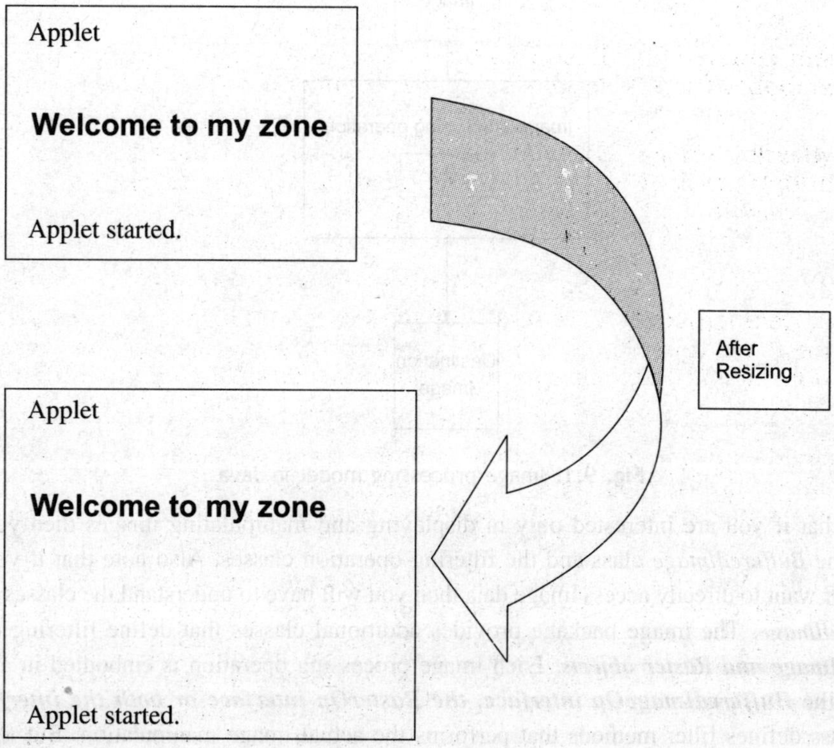

9.9 JAVA IMAGES

Different types of image formats exist. Java supports GIP (Graphic Interchange Format) or JPEG (Joint Photographic Experts Group) files that can contain pictures of just about anything. *Please remember that you can use any of the programs to create them as long as that program can save in GIF or JPEG format.* The abstract class *Image* is the superclass of all classes that represent graphical images. The image must be obtained in a platform-specific manner.

9.10 IMAGE PROCESSING

Image processing is defined as a type of signal processing in which the input is an image like frames of video and the outputs can be either an image or a set of characteristics or parameters related to the image.

Basic Model of JAVA 2D Image Processing

Fig. 9.1 shows the image processing model of Java.

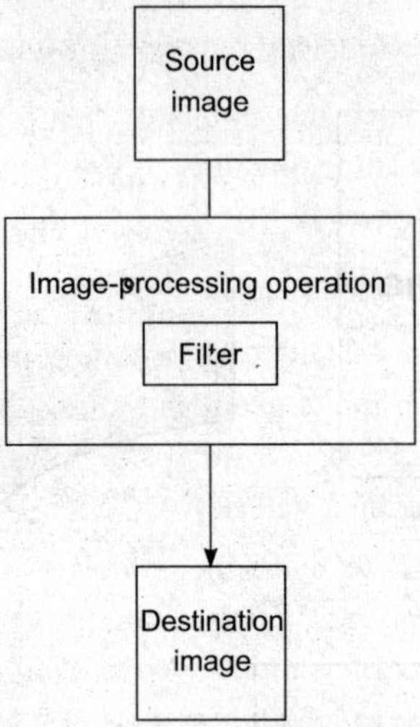

Fig. 9.1: Image processing model in Java

Please note that if you are interested only in displaying and manipulating images then you need to understand the *BufferedImage* class and the filtering operation classes. Also note that if you want to write filters or want to directly access image data then you will have to understand the classes associated with *BufferedImage.* The image package provides additional classes that define filtering operations on ***BufferedImage and Raster objects.*** Each image processing operation is embodied in a class that implements the ***BufferedImageOp interface, the RasterOp interface or both the interfaces.*** The operation class defines filter methods that performs the actual image manipulation. But we must be sure of where the images are placed whenever we try to use an image in Java. If this is known then only the image is accessed inside an applet using ***getImage( )*** method. And finally an image can be displayed by with ***drawImage( )*** method.

Images displayed by Java applet are retrieved either from the hard disk or from the web via a URL that points to the image file. Please note that usually you put images in the same directory as either the applet or the HTML file. Put the image with the applet .class file if different instances of the applet will use different images. Another way is to put all images in a common location and use PARAM tags in the HTML file to tell where the images are.

Let us now see how to load images?

If you know the exact URL for the image you wish to load, you can load it as follows:

URL imageURL = new URL("http://www.suncity.com/logo.gif");

Image img = getImage(imageURL);

This can be rewritten in one line also as follows:

Image img = getImage(new URL("http://www.suncity.com/logo.gif));

Also note here that the *getImage( )* method is used to access the image inside the applet. But if you do not know the exact path of the image but you know that it is in the same directory as the applet then you can use the ***getCodeBase( )*** method inside the ***getImage( )*** method as follows:

Image img = getImage(getCodeBase( ), "sun.gif");

The ***getCodeBase( )*** method returns a URL that points to the directory where the applet comes from. Finally, if the image file is stored in the same directory as the HTML file, use the getDocumentBase( ) method inside getImage( ) method as follows:

Image img = getImage(getDocumentBase( ), "sun.gif");

The ***getDocumentbase( )*** method returns a URL that points to the directory where the HTML file is stored. Load all of the images that your applet needs in the init( ) method. Actually, you do not want to load them in paint( ) method because if you do so then they will be reloaded every time your applet repaints itself and applet performance will be very poor.

An image can be displayed on an applet to make the applet aesthetically attractive. The Image class provides support for images in Java. Image objects are created using the methods of other classes. The getImage( ) method of the applet class is an easy way of retrieving an image from the disk. The ***ImageObserver interface*** present in the ***java.awt.image*** also provides a rich set of constants and methods that support the creation and loading of images. The drawImage( ) method can be used to display the image in the applet area. The set of graphics primitives in the Graphics class is really quite small. There are lines, rectangle, ovals, polygons etc. Remember that the Graphics class also provides the facility of loading bitmapped image in an applet by using an drawImage( ) method. The syntax is:

Syntax:

drawImage(img, x, y, bgcolor, observer);

This draw method draws as much of the specified image as is currently available. *The image is drawn with its top-left corner at (x, y) in this graphics context's coordinate space. Transparent pixels are drawn in the specified background color.* This operation is similar to that of the filling of a rectangle with the width and height of the specified image with the given color and then drawing the image on top of it but possibly more efficient. If the image has not yet been completely loaded then the ***drawImage( )*** returns false. It is important to note that as more of the image becomes available, the process that draws the image notifies the specified image observer. Its parameters are as follows:

img—the specified image to be drawn.

x- the x -coordinate.

y- the y-coordinate.

bgcolor—the background color to paint under the non-opaque portions of the image.

observer—object to be notified as more of the image is converted.

The ***drawImage( ) method*** draws as much of the specified image as is currently available.

Let us write a simple program now.

```
import java.awt.image.*;
import java.applet.*;
```

```
import java.awt.*;
public class Image1 extends Applet
 {
    private Image picture;
    public void init( )
    {
        picture = getImage(getDocumentBase( ), "cloud.gif");
    }

    public void paint(Graphics g)
    {
        g.drawImage(picture, 20, 20, this);
     }
  }
```

And here goes the HTML code that displays the output:

```
<HTML>
    <BODY>
    <APPLET>
        CODE = "Image1.class"
        WIDTH = 300
        HEIGHT = 300
       </APPLET>
       </BODY>
</HTML>
```

OUTPUT (after running):

However, if you want to stretch or compress the image to fit inside the specified rectangle, irrespective of the original size, then use the following drawImage( ) method as :

drawImage(img, x, y, width, height, bgcolor, observer);

This method returns true if the current output representation is complete and false otherwise. This method draws as much of the specified image as it has already been scaled to fit inside the specified rectangle. Here, the additional parameters are as follows:-

width—the width of the rectangle.

height—the height of the rectangle.

Please understand that a scaled version of an image will not necessarily be available immediately just because an unscaled version of the image has been constructed for this output device. Each size of the image may be cached separately and generated from the original data in a separate image production sequence.

We are in a position to write a simple program of displaying an image now.

```
import java.applet.*;
import java.awt.*;
public class img extends Applet
 {
 Image ima;
    public void init( )
     {
         ima = getImage(getCodeBase( ), "cloud.gif");
     }

    public void paint(Graphics g)
     {
         g.drawImage(ima, 20, 20, 200, 200, this);
      }
   }
```

Also note here that we have used the method—getImage( ). The getImage( ) method loads an image. Its syntax is as follows:

Syntax:

getImage(URL url, String name);

The getImage( ) returns an Image object that can then be painted on the screen. The url argument specifies the location from which the image is to be loaded. The name argument is usually the name os the image file, relative to the url argument. **Observe that in the above program, the statement:**

getImage(getCodeBase( ), "cloud.gif");

loads the file "cloud.gif" from the directory where the .class file is located. Actually, storing the image file with the .class file or .html file is purely a matter of personal choice. The getImage( )

loads an image from the file named as "cloud.gif" and stores it in the instance variable, ima. Then the paint( ) method displays the image in the rectangle specifying the coordinates (20, 20) to (200, 200). The parameter, ***this,*** (the applet itself) passed in the drawImage( ) call acts as the ImageObserver which monitors the drawing of the image. **The getCodeBase( ) method returns the URL of the .class file.**

And here is the program that shows a HTML file that displays the output:

```
<HTML>

    <BODY>

    <APPLET>

        CODE = "img.class"

        WIDTH = 300

        HEIGHT = 300

      </APPLET>

    </BODY>

</HTML>
```

OUTPUT (after running):

Herein, you also set the background color of the image using an additional parameter as follows:

drawImage(img, x, y, bgcolor, observer);

The additional parameter ***bgcolor*** specifies the background color to paint under the non-opaque portions of the image.

9.11 IMAGE FILTERING

In Java, the chunks of code that transforms an image in a predictable fashion are also supported. These are known as **image filters.**

For example, an image filter might remove the green and blue component of an image, leaving only the red. Or a filter might sharpen the lines or blur an image.

Now how to write simple filters?

In Java, an image filter requires a subclass of ***java.awt.image.ImageFilter*** and a subclass of ***java.awt.FilteredImageSource.*** The ***FilteredImageSource*** implements the ***java.awt.ImageProducer*** interface. It starts with an existing image but passes it through the ***ImageFilter*** before sending the pixels to an ***ImageObserver*** or ***ImageConsumer.***

The RGBImageFilter

The ***java.awt.image.RGBImageFilter*** class is an abstract subclass of ***java.awt.image.ImageFilter.*** It allows you to modify a single pixel at a time. It is used only when a pixel is independent of other pixels, to use this, you have to override in this class is – ***filterRGB( ).*** For the performance reasons, you may also wish to override ***filterRGBPixels( )*** and set the ***canFilterIndexColorModel*** field to true. This field determines whether or not the filter depends on the position of the pixel. If the ***canFilterIndexColorModel*** field is set to true the instead of filtering every pixel in the image, the limited number of entries in the image's color map are filtered instead. By default, it is assumed that the filter does depend on the position and the value of the field is ***false.***

We are in a position to write a small program that extracts only the blue parts of an image.

```
import java.awt.image.*;
public class BlueFilter extends RGBImageFilter
 {
     public void BlueFilter( )
      {
          canFilterColorModel = true;
      }

     public int filterRGB(int x, int y, int rgb)
      {
          return rgb & 0Xff0000ff;
      }
 }
```

Please note here that canFilterColorModel is set to true because the filtering is independent of the position. Also note that the bitwise & operator is used to select only the first 8-bits of the rgb value. The blue component is stored in the last 8-bits. FF is 11111111, so all blue component and transparency bits are retained. The remaining bits vanish.

An example, of a blue image filter:

To use blue image filter, you create a ***FilteredImage source object*** as follows:

Image src = getImage(getDocumentBase( ), filename); picture = createImage(new FilteredImageSource(src.getSource( ), new BlueFilter( )));

The ***getSource( ) method*** returns a reference to the ***ImageProducer*** which produced this image. Here is a simple applet that loads an image specified in a PARAM tag and uses the blue filter on it.

```
import java.awt.image.*;
import java.applet.*;
import java.awt.*;
public class BlueImage extends Applet
 {
     private Image picture;
     public void init( )
      {
          String filename = this.getParameter("blue.jpg");
          if (filename != null)
           {
          Image src = this.getImage(getDocumentBase( ), filename);
          this.picture = this.createImage(new FilteredImageSource
 (src.getSource( ), new BlueFilter( )));
            }
      }
     public void paint(Graphics g)
      {
          if (this.picture !=null)
               g.drawImage(this.picture, 0, 0, this);
          else
               g.drawString("Missing picture, 20, 20);
          }
}
```

Just as we have defined the blue filter, we can define the greyscale filter also which is used to convert an image to greyscale.

```
import java.awt.image.*;
public class GreyFilter extends RGBImageFilter
 {
     protected boolean canFilterIndexColorModel = true;
     public int filterRGB(int x, int y, int rgb)
      {
          int red = rgb & 0x00FF0000;
```

```
        red >>>= 16;

        int green = rgb & 0x0000FF00;
        green >>>= 8;

        int blue = rgb & 0x000000FF0000;
        int grey = (red + green + blue) / 3;
        return (0x000000FF << 24) | (grey <<16) | (grey << 8) | grey;
    }
  }
```

Please note that before averaging we have to shift the red and green components to the right 16 and 8 bits respectively. This forces them into range 0 to 255.

Let us write a program now.

```
import java.awt.image.*;
import java.applet.*;
import java.awt.*;
public class GreyImage extends Applet
 {
     private Image picture;
     public void init( )
      {
         String filename = this.getParameter("cloud.jpg");
         if (filename != null)
          {
         Image src = this.getImage(getDocumentBase( ), filename);
         this.picture = this.createImage(new FilteredImageSource
(src.getSource( ), new GreyFilter( )));
           }
      }

     public void paint(Graphics g)
      {
         if (this.picture !=null)
             g.drawImage(this.picture, 0, 0, this);
         else
             g.drawString("Missing picture, 10, 10);
         }
}
```

Before we close this chapter, let us solve some questions now.

Q.1. Create an applet to accept a flower name as a parameter and display it along with a message "is a beautiful flower", background color should be light gray. Text should be in Times Roman and size 40. [*GGSIPU, B. Tech.(CSE/IT)- 5th sem., Oct. 2010*]

Solution:

```
import java.awt.*;
import java.applet.*;
/* </applet code ="Sample" width=300 height=50>
</applet>
*/
public class Sample extends Applet {
String Flowername;
public void init( )
 {
     setBackground(Color.cyan);
     setForeground(Color.red);
     Flowername = "is a beautiful flower"
}

public void paint(Graphics g)
 {
     g.drawString(Flowername, 10, 30);
  }
}
```

Q.2. WAP to create a moving ball with human face in an applet.
[*GGSIPU, B. Tech.(CSE/IT)- 5th sem., Oct. 2010*]

Solution:

```
import java.awt.*;
import java.applet.*;
public class HumanFace extends Applet{
 private int mouseX, mouseY;
private boolean mouseclicked = false;
public void init( ) {
 }
public void paint(Graphics g) {
g.drawOval(40, 40, 120, 150);
g.drawOval(57, 75, 30, 30);
g.drawOval(110, 75, 30, 30);
g.fillOval(68, 81, 10, 10);
g.fillOval(121, 81, 10, 10);
g.drawLine(100, 100, 100, 117);
g.fillRect(60, 139, 80, 10);
```

```
    if (mouseclicked) {
        g.clearRect(60, 139, 80, 10);
        g.drawArc(70, 100, 60, 60, 0, -180);
        mouseclieck ed = false;
    }
}

public boolean mouseDown(Event e, int x, int y) {
    mouseX = x;
    mouseY = y;
    mouseclieck ed = true;
    repaint( );
    return true;
    }
}
```

Q.3. Explain how to implement an applet into a web page using applet tag?

[GGSIPU, B. Tech.(CSE/IT)- 5th sem., Dec. 2011]

Solution: To view an applet in the browser, the following steps are followed:

Compile the applet that you have written … the .java file so as to get the .class file. Then include the following code in your .html file:

<APPLET CODE = "XYZ.class" WIDTH = 100 HEIGHT=100>

</APPLET>

And then open the file using a java enabled browser.

Q.4. What is an image sprite? How is it applied using CSS? What is the benefit?

[GGSIPU, B. Tech.(CSE/IT)- 5th sem., Dec. 2011]

Solution: An image sprite is a collection of images put into a single image. A web page with many images can take a long time to load and generate multiple server requests. Using image sprites will reduce the number of server requests and save the bandwidth.

There is a single class that contains a reference to the CSS sprite image and several other classes that simply move the background into different positions.

Summary

When we used the ***System.out.println*** command in previous chapters, the resulting display was the standard white characters on a black background. But in Java, the ***Color class*** defines a color in terms of its red, green and blue components. There are three ways of doing this.

(a) Using the constructor as follows:

public Color(int r, int g, int b);

Each of these integers must be in the range 0 to 255. The integer ***r*** is the red component, ***g*** is the green component and ***b*** is the blue component. **For example,** a light blue would be defined as:

public Color(84, 84, 255);

Please note that this technique is capable of defining 16,777,216 shades of color. Normally, the human eye cannot perceive this many shades of color. So, a picture whose colors are digitally defined by this method does not suffer any degradation. When the Java interpreter transfers color data to your particular component, the number of colors actually displayed may be a lot different.

(b) Using the constructor as follows:

public Color(int rgb);

In this method, the integer ***rgb*** contains all three color components. As studied earlier, that Java integer is 32-bits long. The red component (in the range 0 to 255) is in bits 16 to 23 of the ***rgb integer***, the green component in bits 8 to 15 and the blue component in bits 0 to 7.

For example, the light blue color defined above, when written in binary, would be 010101000101010011111111, which in ordinary integer form is 2,774,271.

(c) Using the constructor as follows:

public Color(float r, float g, float b);

In this method, each of the color components is in the range 0.0 to 1.0. Also note that when we insert a decimal number into a statement it is taken as being of type double. To make it compatible with this version of Color, we need to follow it by an F.

Also we have studied that if you are creating a Java image then you must build an array in which each pixel is represented by an integer that expresses its color and then the entire array is transformed into an ***Integer object.***

Chapter 10

JDBC-ODBC

10.0 INTRODUCTION

It has been estimated that half of all software development involves client/server operations. A great promise of Java has been the ability to build platform-independent client/server data base applications. In Java 1.1, this has come to fruition with Java Database Connectivity (JDBC). JDBC is an API i.e. Application Programming Interface which consists of a set of Java classes, interfaces and exceptions and a specification to which both JDBC driver vendors and JDBC developers adhere when developing applications.

Most of the web applications today need to interact with the databases. A great promise of Java has been the ability to build platform independent client-server database applications.

10.1 DBMS

A database is a collection of tables where each separate table in a database contains related information. It is a repository of data in a tabular form. On the other hand, DBMS is a software that provides you with the mechanism to store, retrieve and modify data to the database.

The database may be either a flat-file database or relational database. **Please note that the relational databases are known as relational because they are set up to relate the data in multiple tables together using certain fields like primary keys and foreign keys.** The **primary key** in a table is used to access a certain record. The **foreign key** usually represents the primary key in another table that gives you an access to that table in an organized way.

For example, MS-ACCESS, MS-SQL SERVER, ORACLE, SYBASE, FOXPRO, PARADOX, PROGRESS, INGRESS etc. are some DBMS softwares. Each of these RDBMS stores data in its own format like MS-ACCESS stores in .MDB format whereas MS-SQL SERVER stores in .DAT file format.

Usually, what happens is that there are two-tiers. One is the front end GUI and the other tier is a backend like a DBMS. The front-end tier includes the forms designing and other things while the backend is a data store like DBMS. The most common example of this is our INTERNET that works on the client-server technology. The client works using some browser like chrome or Internet Explorer while the server is a huge database that actually responds to the users request.

10.2 ODBC

Microsoft established a common standard for communicating with different types of databases called as ***Open Data Base Connectivity.*** Unlike ODBC, most database clients were server specific. ODBC drivers abstract away vendor-specific protocols, providing a common Application Programming Interface (API) to database clients.

ODBC API is a set of library routines that enable your program to access a variety of databases. For this, you must first install a DBMS-specific ODBC driver and write your programs to interact with the specific ODBC driver. This is shown in Fig. 10.1.

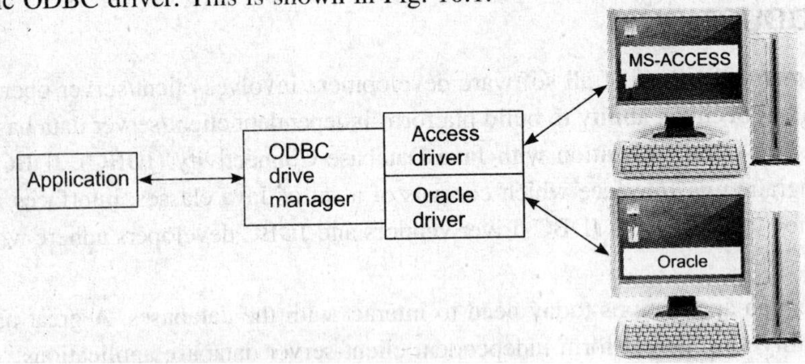

Fig. 10.1: Role of ODBC

10.3 JDBC

One of the major problems with databases has been the feature war between the database companies. There is a standard database language, Structured Query Language (SQL) but usually you must know which database vendor you are working with despite the standard. *Please note that JDBC (JAVA DATA BASE CONNECTIVITY) is designed to be platform-independent.* So, you do not need to worry about the database you are using while you are programming. But it is still possible to make vendor-specific calls from JDBC so you are not restricted from doing what you must. JDBC, like many of the APIs in Java, is designed for simplicity. The method class you make correspond to the logical operations you would think of doing when gathering data from a database: Connect to the database, create a statement and execute the query and look at the resultset. *Also note that to provide this platform independence, JDBC provides a driver manager that dynamically maintains all the driver objects that your database queries will need.* So, if you have three different kinds of vendor databases to connect to, you will need three different driver objects. The driver objects register themselves with the driver manager at the time of loading and can force the loading using the method Class.forName( ). That is,

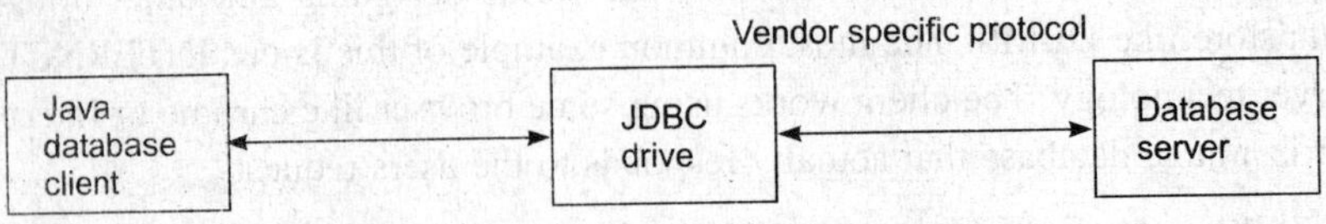

NOTE: JDBC Driver should be equipped with the corresponding vendor database driver in order for the Java programs to communicate with the underlying database.

Another way for the Java programs to communicate with different database engines is through JDBC-ODBC bridge. Microsoft established a common standard for communicating with databases, called as **Open Database Connectivity** (ODBC). Until ODBC, most database clients were server specific. ODBC drivers abstract away vendor-specific protocols, providing a common application programming interface to database clients. Please understand that by writing your database clients to the ODBC API, you enable your programs to access more database servers. So, your program interaction with different databases through jdbc-odbc bridge might look as shown in Fig. 10.2.

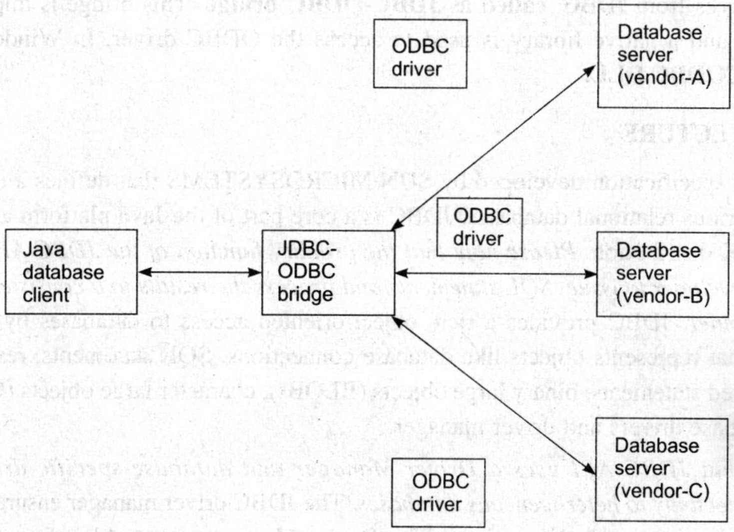

Fig. 10.2: JDBC-ODBC bridge allows Java database clients talk to databases via ODBC drivers

JDBC provides a database programming API for Java applications, since ODBC API is written in C language using pointers and other constructs that Java does not support, a Java program cannot directly communicate with an ODBC driver.

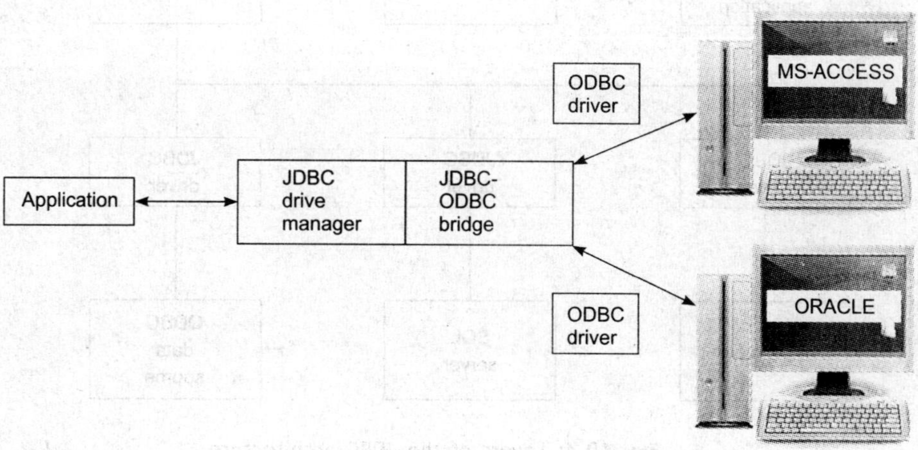

Fig. 10.3: Role of JDBC-ODBC

JavaSoft created JDBC-ODBC bridge driver **that translates the JDBC API to the ODBC API.** Your application interaction with different databases through JDBC-ODBC bridge might look something as shown in Fig. 10.3. It is clear from the figure that JDBC-ODBC bridge might look something as shown in this Fig. 10.3.

The JDBC Driver Manager: It is the backbone of the JDBC architecture. Its function is to connect a Java application to the appropriate driver specified in your Java program.

The JDBC-ODBC Bridge: As a part of JDBC, Sun Microsystems provides a driver to access ODBC data sources from JDBC, **called as JDBC-ODBC bridge.** This bridge is implemented as the ***JdbcOdbc.class*** and a native library is used to access the ODBC driver. In Windows, **this native library is JDBCODBC.DLL.**

JDBC ARCHITECTURE

JDBC is an API specification developed by SUN MICROSYSTEMS that defines a uniform interface for accessing various relational databases. JDBC is a core part of the Java platform and is included in the standard JDK distribution. *Please note that the primary function of the JDBC API is to provide a means for the developer to issue SQL statements and process the results in a consistent and database-independent manner.* JDBC provides a rich, object-oriented access to databases by defining classes and interfaces that represents objects like database connections, SQL statements, resultsets, database metadata, prepared statements, binary large objects (BLOBs), character large objects (CLOBs), callable statements, database drivers and driver manager.

Also note that JDBC API uses a Driver Manager and database-specific drivers to provide transparent connectivity to heterogeneous databases. The JDBC driver manager ensures that the correct driver is used to access each data source. The Driver Manager is capable of supporting multiple concurrent drivers connected to multiple heterogeneous databases. The location of the driver manager with respect to the JDBC drivers and the servlet is shown in Fig. 10.4.

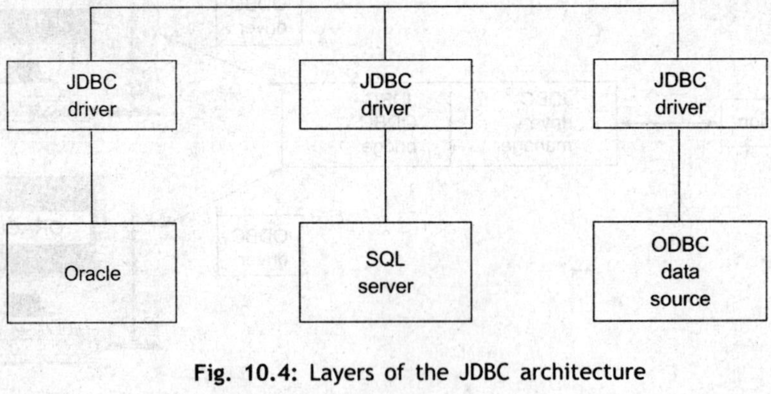

Fig. 10.4: Layers of the JDBC architecture

Please understand that the JDBC driver translates standard JDBC calls into a network or database protocol or into a database library API call that facilitates communication with the database. This translation layer provides JDBC applications with database independence. If the back-end database changes, only the JDBC driver needs to be replaced with few code modifications required.

There are four different types of JDBC drivers and are discussed below one by one.

Type 1: JDBC-ODBC Bridge

Type 1 drivers act as a **bridge between JDBC and another database connectivity mechanism such as ODBC.** The JDBC-ODBC bridge provides JDBC access using the most standard ODBC drivers. This driver is included in the Java 2 SDK within the **sun.jdbc.odbc package.** And finally the query is executed by the database. This driver has serious limitation for many applications. It is shown in Fig. 10.5.

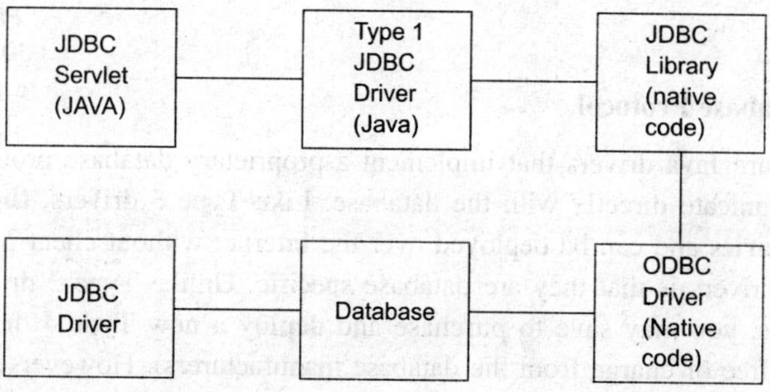

Fig. 10.5: Type 1 JDBC architecture

Type 2: Java to Native API

Type 2 drivers use the **JAVA NATIVE INTERFACE (JNI)** to make calls to a local database library API. This driver converts the JDBC calls into a database specific call for databases such as SQL, ORACLE etc. **Please note that this driver communicates directly with the database server.** It requires some native code to connect to the databse. Type 2 drivers are usually faster than type 1 drivers. **Also note that like type 1 drivers, these type 2 drivers also require native database client libraries to be installed and configured on the client machine.** This is shown in Fig. 10.6.

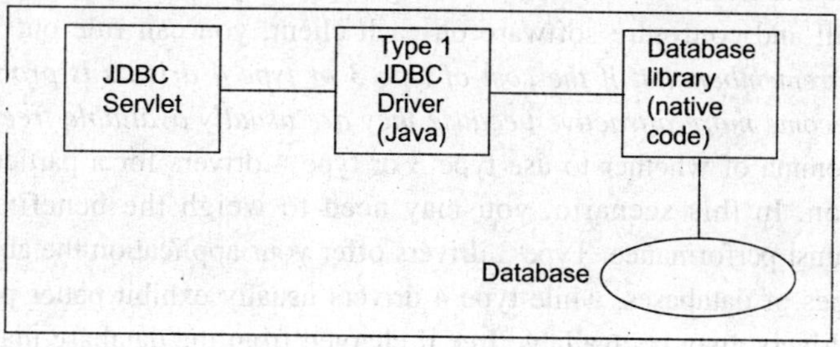

Fig. 10.6: Type 2 JDBC architecture

Type 3: Java to Network Protocol or ALL-Java Driver

Type 3 drivers are pure Java drivers that use a proprietary network protocol to communicate with JDBC middleware on the server. The middleware then translates the network protocol to database-specific function calls. **Please remember that type 3 drivers are the most flexible JDBC solution because they do not require native database libraries on the client and can connect to many different databases on the back end.** Type 3 drivers can be deployed over the Internet without any client installation. That is,

Java → JDBC Statements → SQL Statements → databases

This is shown in Fig. 10.7.

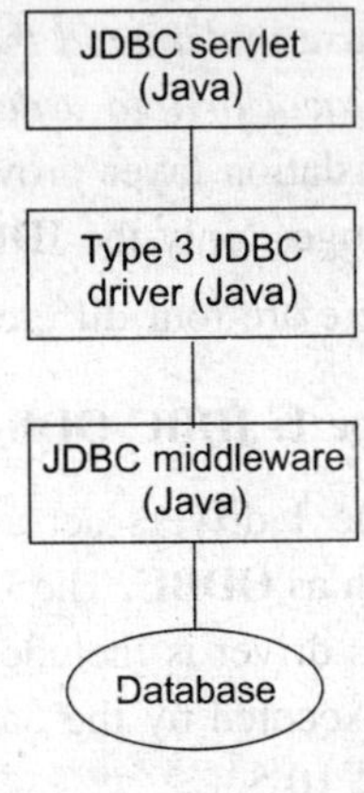

Fig. 10.7: Type 3 JDBC architecture

Type 4: Java to Database Protocol

Type 4 drivers are pure Java drivers that implement a proprietary database protocol (like Oracle's SQL *Net) to communicate directly with the database. Like Type 3 drivers, **they do not require native database libraries** and can be deployed over the Internet without client installation. But one drawback of type 4 drivers is that they are database specific. Unlike Type 3 drivers, if your back-end database changes, you may save to purchase and deploy a new Type 4 driver (some Type 4 drivers are available free of charge from the database manufacturers). However, *please note that as these Types 4 drivers communicate directly with the database engine rather than through middleware or a native library, they are usually the fastest JDBC drivers available.* This driver directly converts the Java statements to SQL statements. This is shown in Fig. 10.8.

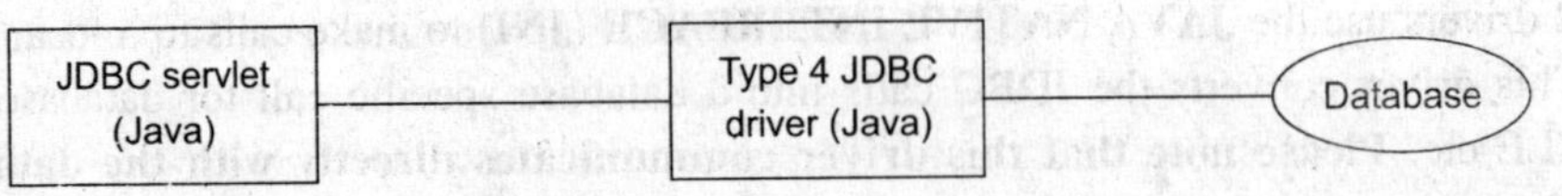

Fig. 10.8: Type 4 JDBC architecture

Now the question is, which one out of these four is the best driver for your application? It depends on the requirements of your particular project. If you do not have the opportunity or inclination to install and configure software on each client, you can rule out Type 1 and Type 2 drivers. *But please remember that if the cost of type 3 or type 4 drivers is prohibitive, then Type 1 and Type 2 may become more attractive because they are usually available free of charge.* Keeping price aside, the dilemma of whether to use type 3 or type 4 drivers for a particular application will continue to rage on. In this scenario, you may need to weigh the benefits of flexibility and interoperability against performance. Type 3 drivers offer your application the ability to transparently access different types of databases, while type 4 drivers usually exhibit better performance and like type 1 and type 2 drivers, may be available free if charged from the database manufacturer.

We are in a position to answer some questions now.

Example 1. What is the name of package that contains Java database related classes?

Solution: The java.sql package contains classes that help in connecting to a database, sending embedded SQL statements to the database and processing query results.

Example 2. How JDBC used with Java is advantageous?

[GGSIPU, B. Tech(CSE/IT)-5th sem., Dec. 2013]

Solution: Please refer to section 10.3 of this chapter.

Example 3: What are the two major components of JDBC?

Solution: One is the implementation interface for **database manufacturers** and the other is implementation interface for **application and applet writers.**

Example 4: JDBC has four components. Name them and explain them.

Solution: JDBC has four components as follows:

(a) The JDBC API.

(b) The JDBC Driver Manager.

(c) The JDBC Test Suite.

(d) The JDBC-ODBC Bridge.

The JDBC API: The JDBC application programming interface provides the facility for accessing the relational database from the Java programming language. The API technology provides the industrial standard for independently connecting Java programming language and a wide range of databases. Please understand that the user can not only execute the SQL statements, retrieve results and update the data but can also access it anywhere within a network because of it's "Write Once, Run Anywhere" (WORA) capabilities. Also understand that due to JDBS API technology, user can also access other tabular data sources like spreadsheets or flat files even in the heterogeneous environment. JDBC API is a part of the Java platform that have included ***Java Standard Edition(Java SE) and the Java Enterprise Edition (Java EE)*** in itself. The JDBC API has four main interfaces. The latest version of JDBC 4.0 API is divided into two packages: ***java.sql and javax.sql. Java SE and Java EE*** platforms are included in both the packages.

The JDBC Driver Manager: It is a very vital class that defines objects which connect Java applications to a JDBC driver. Usually, **Driver Manager is the backbone of the JDBC architecture.** It is very simple and small that is used to provide a means of managing different types of JDBC database drivers running on an application. **Please understand that the main job of JDBC database driver is to load all drivers found in the system properly as well as to select the most suitable driver from opening a connection to the database.** The Driver Manager also helps to select the most suitable driver from the previously loaded drivers when a new open database is connected.

The JDBC Test Suite: The function of JDBC driver test suite is to make ensure that the JDBC drivers will run user's program or not. The test suite of JDBC application program interface is very useful for testing a driver based on JDBC technology during the testing period. It ensures the requirement of Java Platform Enterprise Edition (JPEE).

The JDBC-ODBC Bridge: This bridge is also called as **JDBC type 1 driver.** It utilizes the ODBC driver to connect the database. **This driver translates JDBC method calls into ODBC function calls.** The bridge implements JDBC for any database for which an ODBC driver is available. **The bridge is always implemented as the sun.jdbc.odbc Java package and it contains a native library use to access ODBC.**

In nutshell, we can say that *the first two components of JDBC, the JDBC API and the JDBC Driver Manager manages to connect to the database and then build a Java program that utilizes SQL commands to communicate with any RDBMS. On the other hand, the last two components are used to communicate with ODBC or to test web application in the specialized environment.*

10.4 ODBC DRIVER

An application will work with the backend-database if and only if it is properly configured. Let us now study the steps involved in installing ODBC driver for your database:

Step-1: Select **Start | Control Panel**.

Step-2: Click **Administrative tools.**

Step-3: In **Administrative tools**, click **Data Sources** (ODBC).

Step-4: It will open **ODBC Data Source Administrator**. This dialog box contains a number of tables like "User DSN", "System DSN", "File DSN" etc. in which DSN stands for Data Source Name. It turns that for JDBC-ODBC bridge.

Step-5: Select **System DSN.** A dialog box opens.

Step-6: Click the ADD button.

Step-7: Select MS ACCESS Driver (*.mdb) in our case and click on **Finish** Button.

Step-8: A dialog thus pops up.

Step-9: Click Select in **ODBC Microsoft Access Setup** dialog box in order to select the database.

Step-10: Type the data source name and click Ok.

10.5 CONNECTIVITY OF JAVA WITH DATABASE USING JDBC: ODBC BRIDGE

With JDBC, understanding of the code is relatively simple. The confusing part is making it work on your particular system. **The reason for why this is confusing is that it requires you to figure out how to get your JDBC driver to load properly and how to set up a database using your database administrating software.** Of course, this process can vary radically from machine to machine but the process I have used to make it work under 32-bit windows might give you clues to help you attack your situation. Because most of your (programmers) have access to windows-95, I will be using MS ACCESS as my database server. After you learn how to connect to your database, the type of server that you are using won't matter as **JDBC provides a server-independent approach to database access.** This is one of its benefits.

Step 1: Find the JDBC Driver

As mentioned earlier, in order to query the underlying database the corresponding driver should be loaded and registered with the driver manager. As we are using MS ACCESS, we can make use of ***JdbcOdbcDriver*. Please note that this is the only one that comes with JDK 1.1.** This bridge allows you to access databases via Microsoft's Open Database ConnectivityAPI. **However, the JDBC-ODBC bridge is a temporary solution to database connectivity and has significant drawbacks also like requiring the bridge to be installed on your database users computers.** But for academic purposes this would suffice. **To force the loading of the driver use the statement:**

Class.forName("sun.jdbc.odbc.JdbcOdbcDriver);

This however does not imply a directory structure. You can load other JDBC driver such as pure Java driver, which does no depend on ODBC bridge.

Step 2: Configure the Database

Again this is specific to 32-bit windows. You might need to do some research to figure out for your own platform. First, open the control panel. When you open the "32bit ODBC" icon, you will see a tabbed dialog with a number of tabs, including "User DSN", "System DSN", "File DSN" etc. in which "DSN" MEANS "Data Source Name". It turns out that for the JDBC-ODBC bridge.

The only place where it is important to set up your database is "System DSN" but you will also want to test your configuration and create queries and for that you will also need to set up your database in "File DSN". Right now we will need to use only "System DSN".

Click on the "Add" button and add a new DSN. A dialog pops out and you should select the Microsoft Access Driver (in our case) and click on the "finish" button.

Another dialog box pops up asking for a DSN name. By this time, you should have created a database in the MS ACCESS. I have created a database called db1 in my MyDocuments folder. The DSN should be mapped on to the corresponding database by clicking on the select database button. Once these have been filed, the dialogs can be closed by clicking on the OK buttons. The DSN has been named as 'studentStats'. This name has to be remembered for future references to database in programs.

Step 3: Connecting to the Database with JDBC Bridge

To open a database, you must create a database URL that specifies:

(a) that you are **using JDBC with "jdbc"**.

(b) The **"subprotocol":** the name of the driver or the name of a database connectivity mechanism. Since the design of JDBC was inspired by ODBC, the first sub-protocol available is the **"jdbc-odbc bridge"**, specified by **"odbc"** and the one used in the subsequent examples.

(c) The database identifier. This varies with the database driver used but it generally provides a logical name that is mapped by the database administration software to a physical directory where the database tables are located. For your database identifier to have any meaning, you must register the name using your database administration software. The process of registration varies from platform to platform.

Please remember that all of this information is combined into one string, 'the database URL'. For example, to connect through the ODBC sub-protocol to a database identified as "studentStats", the database URL could be:

String dbUrl = "jdbc:odbc:studentsStats";

If you are connecting across a network, the database URL will also contain the information identifying the remote machine. When you are ready to connect to the database, you can call the static method DriverManager.getConnection( ), passing it the database URL. You get back a connection object that you can then use to query and manipulate the database:

Connection connl = DriverManager.getConnection("jdbc:odbc:studentStats");

Step 4: Create a Statement

Once you have established a connection to the database, you need to create a Statement object from which to execute your query. This is done as follows:

Statement stmtl = connl.createStatement( );

Also note that to create a Statement object, you must use the Connection.createStatement( ) method. As with nearly all class objects in the JDBC, statements cannot be instantiated using the new keyword. *Please note that the Statement created here is only one of the three types of statement objects.* The other two types of statement classes, PreparedStatement and CallableStatement, are sub classes of the Statement class. We shall be studying these three statements also a bit later.

Step 5: Execute the Statement

Finally, after all the preparations, we are ready to actually execute an SQL statement. The method used to execute a simple query is **Statement.executeQuery( ).** For example,

ResultSet rs = stmtl.executeQuery("Select * from student");

The code for a simple SQL query is simple. The ***executeQuery( )*** method takes an SQL query string as an argument and returns the results of the query as a **ResultSet object.** The ResultSet object contains both the data returned by the query and the methods for retrieving the data. There are several variations on execution methods. The ***executeUpdate( ) method*** is used to update the (write to) results and the execute( ) method is used for SQL statements that return multiple results.

Step 6: Retrieve the Results

After you have executed your SQL statement, your next task is to retrieve the results. **Please note that the results are stored in a ResultSet object.** Unlike the rest of the seven steps, retrieval of the data takes more than one line of code.

Also note that to retrieve the data out of the ResultSet and into a Java variable, you need to use one of the ResultSet "get" methods. The **"get"** methods retrieves the data from the ResultSet and converts it to a Java type. Each **"get" method** is used to retrieve a different Java type. **For example,** getInt( ) method can be used to retrieve an integer value from a particular column, **getString( )** is used to retrieve a string value. In all there are 17 "get" methods that can be used to retrieve SQL data into usable Java types. The "get" methods all take the column index as an argument and returns the value found in the current row of that column. By placing the "get" method in a loop and incrementing the row pointer using the **ResultSet.next( )** each time, you can step through the entire result set. For example,

```
while (rs. next( ) )
  {
      System.out.println(rs.getInt("student_id"));
      System.out.println(rs.getString("student_name"));
  }
```

Step 7: Close the Connection and Statement

The final steps in any database application should be to close the connection and any open statements. **Please note that the open connections can often cause trouble for databases and can also cause security problems.** While it is not absolutely necessary that you close every connection and its statement object, it is highly recommended. We simply add the lines as given below in our code:

```
stmtl.close( );
connl.close( );
```

Since nearly all of the methods in sql package have the potential to throw SQLException, we must either catch them or allow them to propagate up to the next level. Let us write a program now to implement all these concepts.

```
import java.sql.*;
/* The database student consists of several records of students. The fields
of the database are: id and Name.
```

Id	Name
101	Rajat
102	Amit
103	Manish
104	Ajay

```
              (studentStats.mdb)        */

class TryingJdbc {
    public static void main(String args[ ] ) {
      try{
         Class.forName("sun.jdbc.odbc.JdbcOdbcDriver");
         String dbUrl = "jdbc:odbc:studentStats";
    Connection connl = DriverManager.getConnection(dbUrl);
    Statement stmtl = connl.createStatement( );
    ResultSet rs = stmtl.executeQuery(Select * from student");
    while( rs.next( )) {
         System.out.println(rs.getInt("id"));
System.out.println(rs.getString("Name"));
```

```
        }
    }

    catch(Exception e) {
        e.getMessage( );
    }

    stmtl.close( );
    connl.close( );
     }
   }
```

A connection object represents a connection with a database. When we connect to a database by using the connection method, we can create a Connection object, which represents the connection to the database. An application may have one or more than one connections with a single database or many connections with the different databases also. **But please remember the following points regarding Connection object:**

1. It creates the Statement, *PreparedStatement and CallableStatement* objects for executing the SQL statements.
2. It helps us to *Commit or Rollback* a jdbc transaction.
3. If you want to know about the database or data source to which you are connected then the *Connection object* gathers information about the database or data source by the use of *DatabaseMetaData.*
4. It helps us to close the data source. The *Connection.isClosed( )* method returns true only if the *Connection.close( )* has been called. This method is used to close all the connections.

Also understand that firstly we need to establish the connection with the database. This is done by using the method —

DriverManager.getConnection( ). This method takes a string containing a URL. **The DriverManager class**, attempts to locate a driver that can connect to the database represented by the string URL. Whenever the ***getConnection( )*** method is called the **DriverManager class** checks the list of all registered Driver classes that can connect to the database specified in the URL.

Syntax:

```
String url = "jdbc:odbc:makeConnection";
Connection con = DriverManager.getConnection(url, "userID", "password");
```

10.6 java.sql PACKAGE

You are now in a position of being aware of some of the classes that are responsible for Java Database programming. The classes we have seen so far are: ***DriverManager, Connection, Statement and ResultSet.*** And please note that all these classes are grouped under the package java.sql.

Let us discuss about the Connection Interface now.

The Connection Interface

When a database connection is established using the ***getConnection( )*** method of **DriverManager**, it returns an object of the class that implements the Connection interface. This interface defines methods for interacting with the database via the established connection. It also defines several constants that describe the manner in which the database supports the committing of database transactions. The methods of Connection interface are used to manage a database connection, obtain information about a connection, roll back or commit database transactions and prepare SQL statements for execution. A number of methods are defined by the Connection interface. Particular methods of interest include the following:

- **close( )**—closes a database connection.
- **getMetaData( )**—returns an object of the **DatabaseMetaData interface** that can be used to obtain detailed information about the structure and capabilities of a database.
- **createStatement( )**—creates an SQL statement object.
- **prepareStatement( )**—creates an SQL **PreparedStatement object** using an SQL string. **PreparedStatement objects** are precompiled SQL that are more efficiently used.
- **prepareCall( )**—creates an SQL **CallableStatement object** using an SQL string. **CallableStatement objects** are SQL-stored procedure call statements. This interface also initiates objects that are used to execute SQL statements. The interfaces responsible for execution of SQL statements are **Statement, PreparedStatement and CallableStatement.**

Let us now discuss about the Statement Interface.

The Statement object is the most common type of object used. It is used to execute static SQL statements. **Please remember that static SQL statements are those that do not contain any IN or OUT parameters.** Static SQL statements can be updates, insert queries and even DDL SQL statements. As long as no parameters are to be passed to or from the database, **a Statement object** can be used. An object of the Statement interface is created by invoking the **createStatement( ) method** of the Connection interface. Statement objects cannot be created using the new keyword. Each statement object is associated with a single Connection object. Although you are free to have as many Statement objects per Connection as you want, a single Statement object cannot belong to more than one Connection. **Also note that when creating a Statement object, you do not specify the SQL statements and is not statically associated with any particular type of SQL operation.** The statement interface defines methods that are used to interact with databases via the execution of SQL statements. These methods also support the processing of query results returned via **ResultSet objects** and provide control over the mechanics of query processing. ***The execute( ), executeQuery( ) and executeUpdate( ) methods are the primary methods of interest in the statement interface.***

(a) The executeQuery( ) method executes an SQL statement (like the SELECT statements that queries the database and returns a ResultSet object).

(b) The executeUpdate( ) method executes an SQL statement like INSERT, UPDATE OR DELETE statement, that updates the database and returns the integer value of the row count associated with the SQL statement or 0 if the statement did not return a result.

(c) The *execute( ) method* executes an SQL statement that is written as a String object. It returns a Boolean value indicating whether a *ResultSet object* was produced as the result of the statement's execution. The *getResultSet( ) and getMoreResults( ) methods* are used to retrieve the ResultSet object. If the statement's execution returns an update count, *execute( ) returns false*. The update count can be retrieved using the *getUpdateCount( ) method.*

We are in a position to write a program now.

```
import java.sql.*;
class InsertDB {
    public static void main(String args[ ] ) {
     try {
        Class.forName("sun.jdbc.odbc.JdbcOdbcDriver");
        String dbUrl = "jdbc:odbc:studentStats";
        Connection c = DriverManager.getConnection(dbUrl);
        Statement s = c.createStatement( );
            /* Static SQL */
        String sql = "INSERT INTO student VALUES(1, 'Rajiv');
        int result = s.executeUpdate(sql);
            System.out.println(result + "records affected");
          }
    catch (Exception e) {
        e.getMessage( );
        }
    s.close( );
    c.close( );
    }
  }
```

The PreparedStatement Interface

The PreparedStatement is basically used for the execution of dynamic SQL statements and is created using the preparedStatement( ) method. Practically speaking, it is used when the SQL statement to be executed contains IN parameters. *Please note that the PreparedStatement is very unique as they are pre-parsed and pre-compiled by the database.* These results in quicker response times and lower work loads for the database server. For very large statements or statements that are repeated many times, **PreparedStatements** can provide significant improvements.

To understand this let us now see how SQL statements are executed by a typical database:

Step-1: The user enters an SQL statement and issues an execute request.

Step-2: The database parses the statement.

Step-3: The database uses the parsing to determine if the syntax is correct.

Step-4: The database compiles the statement.

Step-5: The database executes the statement.

As it is clear from these steps that each one of these steps takes time and more computer resources. If your application uses the same SQL statement over and over again, it must go through the same five steps each time. However, **if you use a prepared statement,** the database only has to do the first four steps one time that will further cut your work to 1/5 the of the original. The prepareStatement( ) method is used to create a PreparedStatement. Also note that unlike the Statement object, the PreparedStatement takes the SQL statement to be executed as an argument. Since the PreparedStatement is pre-compiled by the database at the time of its creation, the SQL statement must be known.

For dynamic SQL statements (i.e., those that contain IN parameters), **a placeholder is used to tell the database that it can expect a variable in that position.** Each variable in the statement is represented by a "?" which holds its place during compilation. When compiled, the placeholder is part of the statement and **therefore appears static to the compiler.** As a result, no matter what value is later assigned to the variable, the database does not need to recompile or parse the statement. At run time, you can assign values to the variables by using one of the **"set"** methods in the **PreparedStatement object.**

We are in a position to write a program now.

```
import java.sql.*;
class Jdbc {
    public static void main(String args[ ] ) {
     try {
        Class.forName("sun.jdbc.odbc.JdbcOdbcDriver");
        String dbUrl = "jdbc:odbc:studentStats";
        Connection c = DriverManager.getConnection(dbUrl);
                /* Dynamic SQL */
        String sql = "SELECT Name FROM student WHERE "+" Marks>?";
        PreparedStatement ps = c.prepareStatement(sql);
        ResultSet rs;
        System.out.println("List of the students with "+" marks > 70);
        ps.setInt(1, 70);
        rs = ps.executeQuery( );
        while(rs.next( ) ) {
            System.out.println(rs.getString("Name"));
         }
            }
    catch (Exception e) {
        e.getMessage( );
        }
    s.close( );
    c.close( );
    }
}
```

Let us put all of these concepts in one program now.

We try to develop a small DBMS only that can insert a new record, update record, delete records and display/list all of the records in a JAVA program now.

For database connectivity, we need to follow the seven steps as listed and explained earlier.

```
//DBMS IN JAVA
import java.sql.*;
import java.io.*;
import java.lang.*;
class dbms_java
 {
    static String dburl;
    static Connection con;
    public static void main(String args[ ] )
     {
        try
         {
            Class.forName("sun.jdbc.odbc.JdbcOdbcDriver");
            dburl = "jdbc:odbc:empStats";
            con = DriverManager.getConnection(dburl);
            int choice =1;
            while (choice !=0)
             {
                System.out.println( );
                System.out.println("1. Insert a new record");
                System.out.println("2. Update records");
                System.out.println("3. Delete records");
                System.out.println("4. Display records");
                System.out.println("0. Exit");
                System.out.println("Enter you choice:" );
            DataInputStream dis = new DataInputStream(System.in);
                try {
                    String str = dis.readLine( );
                    choice = Integer.parseInt(str);
                    switch (choice)
                     {
                        case 1:
                                addRecord( );
                                break;
                        case 2:
                                updateRecord( );
                                break( );
                        case 3:
```

```
                                        delRecord( );
                                        break( );
                              case 4:
                                        listRecord( );
                                        break( );
                         }
                       }
                       catch (Exception e)
                         {
                         }
                  }
               }
               catch (Exception e)
                 {
                 }
             }
             public static  void updateRecord( )
              {
                  try
                    {
      String sql = "Update empdata set name = 'Rajiv Chopra' where age=40";
                  Statement s = con.createStatement( );
                  s.executeUpdate(sql);
          System.out.println("Updated successfully");
                    }
             catch (Exception e)
               {
               }
          }
      public static void listRecord( )
       {
          try
           {
             Statement s = con.createStatement( );
             ResultSet rs = s.executeQuery("Select * from empdata");
             while (rs.next( ))
              {
                 System.out.println( );
                 System.out.print(rs.getString("name"));
System.out.print("\t" + rs.getInt("age"));
System.out.print("\t" + rs.getFloat("salary"));
              }
           }
catch (Exception e)
  {
```

```
}
    }
  public static void addRecord( )
   {
     try {
       String sql = "Insert into empdata values('Amit', 20,15000.50)";
       Statement s = con.createStatement( );
       s.executeUpdate(sql);
       System.out.println("Added successfully");
       }
       catch (Exception e)
        {
        }
    }
  public static void delRecord( )
   {
      try {
            String sql = "Delete from empdata where name='Amit'";
            Statement s = con.createStatement( );
            s.executeUpdate(sql);
            System.out.println("Deleted successfully...");
            }

      catch (Exception e)
       {
        }
      }
    }
```

The students are advised to compile and run this program and check the results.

Summary

As long as the application does not have any backend it is a **static application.** The moment some backend comes into play, it becomes a **dynamic application.** There are two things (called as **2-tiers**) involved here—one is the **front end GUI design** (like in Visual Basic GUI may be designed) and the other is the **back-end that is usually a data store like any RDBMS.** Now the **challenge is to connect the front end GUI design with a backend RDBMS.** And in this chapter we have studied how this can be done. Java uses ODBC as provided by Microsoft. The bridge that is formed between these 2 tiers is known as odbc:jdbc bridge that helps in this connectivity of front-end with the back-end. It uses *jdbc-odbc bridge* driver for translating the JDBC API to ODBC API. Furthermore, the java.sql package contains classes that help in connecting to a database, sending **embedded SQL statements** to the database and processing query results.

Multiple Choice Questions [MCQs]

(with Answers)

Choose the correct option(s)

1. Originally Java was named as

(a) Oak (b) Floak
(c) Cock (d) None of the above

2. The first graphical web browser for Internet is

(a) Mosaic (b) Chrome
(c) IE (d) None of the above

3. Java was developed by

(a) IBM (b) SUN
(c) Microsoft (d) Infosys

4. Which of the following web browser is used for running Java applets?

(a) NewJava (b) ColdJava
(c) HotJava (d) None of the above

5. The extension of the source code file in Java is

(a) .Java (b) .jva
(c) .jav (d) .class

6. The extension of the bytecode file is

(a) .byte (b) .bit
(c) .java (d) .class

7. JVM stands for

(a) Java Virtual Memory (b) Java Virtual Mechanic
(c) Java Virtual Machine (d) None of the above

8. JIT stands for

(a) Just-in-Time (b) Joy-in-Time
(c) Jam-in-Time (d) None of the above

9. API stands for

(a) Application Programming Interchange
(b) Advanced Programming Interchange

(c) Advanced Programming Interface
(d) Application Programming Interface

10. Java bytecodes are
(a) machine dependent (b) machine independent
(c) both 'a' and 'b' (d) none of the above

11. Which of the following is a Java compiler?
(a) javap (b) java
(c) javar (d) javac

12. Which of the following is a Java interpreter?
(a) javai (b) java
(c) javar (d) jdb

13. The tool used to debug all types of error
(a) jdb (b) java
(d) javar (d) javac

14. The tool used to get back the source file from a bytecode file is
(a) jdb (b) java
(c) javap (d) javac

15. The tool used as document generator in Java is
(a) javad (b) javadoc
(c) javac (d) javap

16. The tool used to create header and stub files in Java
(a) javap (b) javah
(c) javar (d) javac

17. The tool used to view applets
(a) Viewerapplet (b) Viewapple
(c) Appletview (d) AppletViewer

18. Which one of the following is not supported in Java?
(a) break (b) continue
(c) goto (d) all of the above

19. The collection of classes in Java is known as
(a) Interfaces (b) Packages
(c) API (d) None of the above

20. Which of the following is supported in Java?
(a) Single Inheritance (b) Multilevel Inheritance
(c) Multiple Inheritance (d) None of the above

21. The environment in which a subroutine written in other programming language, such as C/C++, is used, is called as

(a) Native code (b) HTML code

(c) Object code (d) None of the above

22. With javadoc, which of the following denotes a javadoc comment?

(a) /** (b) //#

(c) /* (d) //**

23. Java is a pure

(a) procedural programming language

(b) visual programming language

(c) object-oriented programming language

(d) none of the above

24. Which of the following is an essential method in every Java program?

(a) Main (b) String

(c) Strlen (d) None of the above

25. For displaying outputs in Java which command is used?

(a) Systemin (b) System.out

(c) System.log (d) None of the above

26. The ***out*** object is a predefined standard object of this class

(a) PrintStream (b) DisplayStream

(c) WriteStream (d) None of the above

27. Java is

(a) not a case sensitive language (b) a case sensitive language

(c) machine language (d) none of the above

28. Which of the following is a reserved word in Java?

(a) Catch (b) Caught

(c) Classic (d) None of the above

29. The primitive Java data type is

(a) string (b) bit

(c) byte (d) None of the above

30. What will be the result of the expression a % b; when a and b are of type int and their values are a = -17 and b= -6?

(a) 23 (b) 11

(c) 5 (d) -5

31. What will be the result of the expression a / b; when a and b are of type int and their values are a = -17 and b= 6?

(a) -2 (b) 5

(c) 2 (d) -5

32. What will be the output of the following statement?

System.out.println("The answer is" + 17 + 3);

(a) The answer is: 20 (b) The answer is: 173

(c) The answer is: 17 + 3 (d) None of the above

33. Which one of the following is a valid character constant?

(a) 'X' (b) '\t'

(c) "X" (d) Both 'a' and 'b'

34. What is the output of the following int?

x, y, z;

y = 1;

z = 5;

x = 0 – (++y) + z++;

System.out.println(x + "\t" + y + "\t" + z);

(a) 3 2 6 (b) -7 1 5

(c) 5 2 6 (d) None of the above

35. What is the output of the following?

int a = 23, b= 34;

a = ((a < (b) ? (b + a) : (b – (a);

(a) 11 (b) 57

(c) 23 (d) 34

36. In Java, this facility is used to derive new data types:

(a) Struct (b) Class

(c) Union (d) All of the above

37. .The functions in Java that are defined within a class are known as

(a) methods (b) inline functions

(c) inbuilt functions (d) none of the above

38. When 2 or more methods are defined in the same class, such methods are known as

(a) Doubling methods (b) Powering methods

(c) Full methods (d) Overloaded methods

39. .... term is used where a method is defined in the derived class with the same name and same signature as defined in base class

(a) doubling methods (b) powering methods

(c) overriding methods (d) overloaded methods

40. Which operator is used to create an object in Java?

(a) New (b) Create

(c) Make (d) None of the above

41. Which operator is used to access the data members of a class using object of the class?

(a) & (b) .

(c) - > (d) None of the above

42. In Java, all arguments of primitive data types are passed by

(a) address (b) reference

(c) value (d) none of the above

43. In Java, all arguments of object types are passed by

(a) address (b) value

(c) both 'a' and 'b' (d) reference

44. The command line arguments are received in

(a) main( ) (b) string( )

(c) equals( ) (d) none of the above

45. The main method is defined as

(a) static (b) final

(c) private (d) none of the above

46. The keyword that is used to implement the concept of inheritance is

(a) inherits (b) extends

(c) implements (d) none of the above

47. The keyword that is used to implement the concept of interfaces is

(a) inherits (b) extends

(c) implements (d) none of the above

48. The ability of the data to be processed in more than one form is known as

(a) polymorphism (b) inheritance

(c) data Hiding (d) interfaces

49. The special method that is called automatically when an object of a class is created is:

(a) Finalizers (b) Constructors

(c) Destructors (d) None of the above

50. The special method that is called automatically just before an object is garbage collected:

(a) Finalizers (b) Constructors

(c) Destructors (d) None of the above

51. The constructors that receive arguments also are known as:

(a) Argumentized (b) Parameterized

(c) Destructors (d) None of the above

52. What is called when you initialize an instance using values of another instance of the same class type?

(a) Extra Constructors (b) Simple Constructors

(c) Duplicate Constructors (d) Copy Constructors

53. The constructor of a base class is called in a derived class using keyword:
(a) Super (b) Base
(c) Old (d) None of the above

54. The specifier that hides a data member or a method from all classes is:
(a) Public (b) Private
(c) Protected (d) Private Protected

55. The specifier that makes a data member or a method completely available for all classes is:
(a) Private protected (b) Private
(c) Protected (d) Public

56. The specifier that makes a data member or a method available to the class in which they are defined as well as all classes in the same package is:
(a) Private protected (b) Private
(c) Protected (d) Public

57. The specifier that makes a data member or a method available to the class in which they are defined as well as all of its derived classes in any package is:
(a) Private protected (b) Private
(c) Protected (d) Public

58. Which keyword can protect a class in a package from accessibility by the classes outside the package?
(a) Private (b) Protected
(c) Final (d) Default

59. We would like to make a member of a class visible in all sub-classes regardless of what package they are in. Which one of the following keywords would achieve this?
(a) Private (b) Protected
(c) Private or Protected (d) Public

60. The use of protected keyword to a member in a class will restrict its visibility as follows:
(a) Visible only in the class and its subclass in the same package
(b) Visible in all classes in the same package and subclasses in other packages
(c) Visible only inside the package
(d) Visible only in the class where it is declared

61. A method is
(a) an entity that receives inputs and outputs
(b) a way of storing data
(c) a sequence of characters enclosed by quotes
(d) a type of system

62. The modifier allows a data member or method to be associated with its class rather than its objects

(a) Static (b) Friend
(c) Final (d) All of the above

63. If we declare a variable using reserved word 'final' in a class then

(a) its value can be changed (b) its value cannot be changed
(c) it can be changed in derived class (d) none of the above

64. A method defined as final in a class:

(a) Can be overridden in its subclass
(b) Can be rewritten in its subclasses
(c) Cannot be overridden in its subclasses
(d) None of the above

65. Select the true option.

(a) A final class can be extended by interfaces
(b) A final class can be extended by packages
(c) A final class can be inherited
(d) A final class cannot be inherited at any cost

66. Select the true option.

(a) A final object must be initialized to an object at the point of declaration
(b) A final object initializes its data members as 0
(c) A final object cannot be initialized to another object
(d) None of the above

67. All wrapper classes (except Character) defines this method to return the wrapper objects corresponding to the primitive data type?

(a) typeOf( ) (b) stringOf( )
(c) valueOf( ) (d) none of the above

68. The method used to convert String to integer primitive data types

(a) parseInteger( ) (b) parseInt( )
(c) Integer( ) (d) none of the above

69. The method used to convert String to short primitive data types

(a) parseShort( ) (b) parseSht( )
(c) Short( ) (d) none of the above

70. The method used to convert primitive data types to strings

(a) String( ) (b) StringTo( )
(c) StringChange( ) (d) toString( )

71. .... is used to enjoy the benefits of multiple inheritance in Java

(a) classes (b) interfaces
(c) editing tools (d) classes and interfaces

72. An interface contains

(a) only final variables (b) only final methods

(c) final variables and final methods (d) none of the above

73. When an interface is inherited by another interface, it uses this keyword

(a) extends (b) implements

(c) package (d) none of the above

74. When an interface is implemented by a class, it uses this keyword

(a) extends (b) implements

(c) package (d) none of the above

75. It we wish to create an object of a class which is defined elsewhere then we use

(a) export statement (b) passport statement

(c) import statement (d) none of the above

76. Wrapper classes are defined in this package

(a) java.lang (b) java.io

(c) java.net (d) none of the above

77. The package that provides all graphical classes that is required for creating a standard GUI programs

(a) java.lang (b) java.awt

(c) java.net (d) java.applet

78. The smallest package of Java language is

(a) java.lang (b) java.awt

(c) java.net (d) java.applet

79. A package can be created by this keyword

(a) package (b) interface

(c) userpackage (d) none of the above

80. This class is the root class of the Java class hierarchy

(a) class (b) object

(c) method (d) none of the above

81. The package that provides Date and Calender classes is

(a) java.lang (b) java.awt

(c) java.util (d) none of the above

82. The package that is automatically imported in a Java program when it is executed or compiled is

(a) java.lang (b) java.awt

(c) java.util (d) none of the above

83. The package that is imported in a Java program when we deal with stream classes in Java

(a) java.lang (b) java.io

(c) java.util (d) none of the above

84. The socket class is defined in this package

(a) java.lang (b) java.io
(c) java.util (d) java.net

85. The super class of all Exception and Error classes

(a) SuperErrors (b) SuperException
(c) Throwable (d) Both 'a' and 'b'

86. The subclass(es) of the Exception class is/are

(a) IOException (b) RunTimeException
(c) AWTError (d) Both 'a' and 'b'

87. When an attempt is made to access an element of an array beyond the array index, the exception thrown is

(a) ArrayOutOfBoundsException
(b) ArrayIndexBoundsException
(c) ArrayIndexOutOfBoundsException
(d) None of the above

88. In which package Java stream classes are provided

(a) java.io (b) java.awt
(c) java.net (d) None of the above

89. DataInput is

(a) an abstract class defined in java.io
(b) an interface that defines methods to read primitive data types
(c) a class we can use to read primitive data types
(d) an interface that defines methods to open files

90. Which exception is thrown by the read( ) method of InputStream class?

(a) Exception (b) FileNotFoundException
(c) IOException (d) None of these

91. Which of the following are pre-defined streams?

(a) System.in (b) System.out
(c) System.err (d) All of the above

92. Which of the following is byte input class for file handling?

(a) FileReader (b) DataInputReader
(c) FileInputStream (d) None of the above

93. Which of the following is character input class for file handling?

(a) FileReader (b) DataInputReader
(c) FileInputStream (d) None of the above

94. Which of the following is character output class for file handling?

(a) FileOutputStream (b) FileWriter
(c) DataOutputReader (d) None of the above

95. Which of the following is byte output class for file handling?

(a) FileOutputStream (b) FileWriter
(c) DataOutputReader (d) None of the above

96. Which of the following is character-oriented class for receiving input from keyboard?

(a) IOReader (b) InputStreamReader
(c) DataInputStream (d) None of the above

97. Which of the following is character-oriented class for displaying output on the screen?

(a) FileOutputStream (b) DataOutputStream
(c) OutputStreamWriter (d) None of the above

98. Which of the following is byte-oriented class for receiving input from keyboard?

(a) IOReader (b) InputStreamReader
(c) DataInputStream (d) None of the above

99. Which of the following is byte-oriented class for displaying output on the screen?

(a) FileOutputStream (b) DataOutputStream
(c) OutputStreamWriter (d) None of the above

100. While reading primitive data types from the keyboard, an object of the BufferedReader class takes the object of this class as its argument

(a) IOReader (b) IOWriter
(c) DataInputStream (d) InputStreamReader

101. The class used in multithreading programming, such as Thread, ThreadGroup and ThreadDeath, are defined in the package

(a) java.io (b) java.awt
(c) java.lang (d) None of the above

102. Which class must be extended in order to use multithreading?

(a) Thread (b) Runnable
(c) Threading (d) None of the above

103. Which interface must be implemented in order to use multithreading?

(a) Runnable (b) Thread
(c) Threading (d) None of the above

104. When we implement the Runnable interface, we must define the method

(a) resume( ) (b) init( )
(c) run( ) (d) start( )

105. How do you know the name of a thread?

(a) getName( ) (b) readName( )
(c) Name( ) (d) None of the above

106. How will you change the name of the thread?

(a) putName( ) (b) setName( )
(c) changeName( ) (d) None of the above

107. The method that starts the execution of a thread is

(a) resume( ) (b) init( )
(c) execute( ) (d) run( )

108. The method that temporarily stops the execution of a thread

(a) resume( ) (b) suspend( )
(c) execute( ) (d) run( )

109. The methods wait( ) and notify( ) are defined in

(a) java.lang.Runnable (b) java.lang.ThreadGroup
(c) java.lang.Thread (d) java.lang.Object

110. The following is a pre-defined constant in Java

(a) MIN_PRIORITY (b) MAX_PRIORITY
(c) NORM_PRIORITY (d) All of the above

111. What is the integer value of the pre-defined constant NORM_PRIORITY?

(a) 1 (b) 3
(c) 5 (d) 7

112. What is the integer value of the pre-defined constant MIN_PRIORITY?

(a) 1 (b) 3
(c) 5 (d) 7

113. What is the integer value of the pre-defined constant MAX_PRIORITY?

(a) 1 (b) 5
(c) 9 (d) None of the above

114. Java provides the coordination between threads by using the keyword

(a) Synchronization (b) Synchronized
(c) sync (d) None of the above

115. The method that is used to know the priority of a thread is

(a) setPriority( ) (b) getPriority( )
(c) Priority( ) (d) None of the above

116. These programs run when they are embedded into web pages

(a) Application programs (b) Applets
(c) Threads (d) None of the above

117. The smallest package available in JDK is

(a) java.applet (b) java.io
(c) java.net (d) java.lang

118. The method that is used to draw text on the applet area is

(a) drawText( ) (b) drawValue( )
(c) drawstring( ) (d) None of the above

119. This tool is used to view an applet

(a) ViewApplet (b) AppletView
(c) ViewerApplet (d) AppletViewer

120. When we invoke repaint( ) for a java.awt.Component object, the AWT invokes the method

(a) draw( ) (b) update( )
(c) show( ) (d) paint( )

121. The life cycle of an applet is

(a) init( ), start( ), paint( ), stop( )and destroy( )
(b) start( ), init( ), paint( ), stop( )and destroy( )
(c) init( ), start( ), paint( ), destroy( )and stop( )
(d) start( ), init( ), paint( ), destroy( )and stop( )

122. The method that can be used to remove a java.awt.Component object from the display is

(a) hide( ) (b) delete( )
(c) remove( ) (d) disappear( )

123. The setBackground( ) method is part of the following class in java.awt package

(a) Graphics (b) Applet
(c) Container (d) Component

124. This is not a data type

(a) Button (b) Protected
(c) int (d) void

125. The root class from which all events state objects shall be derived is

(a) java.EventObject (b) java.util
(c) java.util.Object (d) java.util.EventObject

126. Which of the following is a container control?

(a) Panel (b) Frame
(c) Dialog (d) All of the above

127. AWT stands for

(a) ALL WINDOW TOOLKIT
(b) ABSTRACT WINDOW TECHNIQUE
(c) ABSTRACT WINDOW TOOLKIT
(d) None of the above

128. Which of the following is not a control?

(a) Pictures (b) Labels
(c) Buttons (d) CheckBox

129. Which of the following is a control?

(a) TextArea (b) TextField

(c) List (d) All of the above

130. The following class is needed for implementing menus

(a) MenuBar (b) Menu

(c) MenuItem (d) All of the above

131. The method used to get the text of a label control

(a) getText( ) (b) getLabel( )

(c) getString( ) (d) None of the above

132. Checkboxes are added to the container using the method

(a) insert( ) (b) put( )

(c) add( ) (d) None of the above

133. A dialog box can be made resizable and movable by calling this method

(a) setResizable( ) (b) Resizable( )

(c) setSizable( ) (d) None of the above

134. The default layout manager is

(a) Grid Layout (b) Flow Layout

(b) Border Layout (d) Card Layout

135. Components are added from left to right and top to bottom in this layout

(a) Grid Layout (b) Flow Layout

(c) Border Layout (d) Card Layout

136. There are 5 sections –North, East, West and South, in this layout

(a) Grid Layout (b) Flow Layout

(c) Border Layout (d) Card Layout

137. In Java language, all drawing, including images and animations, take place through

(a) Graphics object (b) Animation object

(c) Applet object (d) None of the above

138. An applet displays the information on the screen by using

(a) init( ) (b) start( )

(c) paint( ) (d) None of the above

139. The method that sets the graphics contexts current color to the specified color is

(a) paintColor( ) (b) setColor( )

(c) putColor( ) (d) None of the above

140. The method that is used to obtain the current color is

(a) putColor( ) (b) setColor( )

(c) getColor( ) (d) None of the above

141. Java provides a number of fonts for text output in applets using
(a) Font class (b) FontMetrics class
(c) Both 'a' and 'b' (d) None of the above

142. The method that returns the space between the lines of the text is
(a) getFont( ) (b) getHeight( )
(c) getWidth( ) (d) getLeading( )

143. This abstract class is the superclass of all classes that represent graphical images
(a) Animation (b) Image
(c) Picture (d) None of the above

144. Images displayed by Java applet are retrieved from
(a) Hard disk
(b) Web via a URL that points to the image file
(c) Applet
(d) Both 'a' and 'b'

145. This method is used to access the image inside the applet
(a) getImage( ) (b) setImage( )
(c) putImage( ) (d) None of the above

146. JDBC stands for
(a) Java Document Base Connectivity (b) Java Data Base Connectivity
(c) Java Document Bridge Connectivity (d) None of the above

147. ODBC stands for
(a) Open Document Base Connectivity (b) Open Data Base Connectivity
(c) Open Document Bridge Connectivity (d) None of the above

148. Which of the following is NOT a database?
(a) MS ACCESS (b) ORACLE
(c) VISUAL BASIC (d) Dbase

149. A database is registered using this method of the class
(a) forClass( ) (b) forRegister( )
(c) forName( ) (d) None of the above

150. SQL statement is executed using
(a) executeQuery( ) method (b) executeStatement( ) method
(c) exQuery( ) (d) None of the above

151. The object that allows you to execute parameterized queries is
(a) PreparedObject (b) PreparedStatement
(c) PreparedClass (d) None of the above

152. To execute a simple Insert statement, this method is used
(a) executeInsert( ) (b) executeChange( )
(c) executeUpdate( ) (d) None of the above

153. To execute a simple Delete statement, this method is used

(a) executeDelete( )
(b) executeChange( )
(c) executeSet( )
(d) executeUpdate( )

154. The executeQuery( ) method takes an SQL statement as an argument and returns the result of the query as

(a) ResultSet object
(b) Result object
(c) RecordSet object
(d) None of the above

155. The modules that extend request/response oriented servers are known as

(a) Servlets
(b) Wavelets
(c) Leaflets
(d) None of the above

156. Which of the following is correct in order to successfully compile a source code file containing the public class 'test'

(a) It must import java.lang
(b) It must declare a public class named 'test'
(c) It must be named test.java
(d) It must have a package statement

157. Give the output

```
public class Main
{
    pubic static void main(String [ ] args)
    {
        char z= 'A' +55;
        System.out.print(z);
    }
}
```

(a) W
(b) x
(c) y
(d) z

158. What will be the values of the variables x, a and b after execution of the following code

```
int x, a = 6, b =7;
x = a++ + b++;
```

(a) x = 15, a =7, b =8
(b) x = 15, a =6, b =7
(c) x = 13, a =7, b =8
(d) x = 13, a =6, b =7

159. How many jump statements does Java supports?

(a) 1
(b) 2
(c) 3
(d) 4

160. If we have to do lot of random accesses then we must use

(a) Arrays
(b) ArrayList
(c) LinkedList
(d) None of the above

ANSWERS TO MCQS

1. a	2. a	3. b	4. c	5. a	6. d	7. c	8. a	9. d	10. b
11. d	12. b	13. a	14. c	15. a	16. b	17. d	18. c	19. b	20. c
21. a	22. d	23. c	24. a	25. b	26. a	27. b	28. a	29. c	30. d
31. a	32. c	33. d	34. a	35. b	36. b	37. a	38. d	39. c	40. a
41. b	42. c	43. d	44. a	45. a	46. c	47. c	48. a	49. b	50. a
51. b	52. d	53. a	54. b	55. d	56. c	57. a	58. d	59. c	60. b
61. a	62. a	63. b	64. c	65. d	66. a	67. c	68. b	69. a	70. d
71. b	72. c	73. b	74. a	75. c	76. a	77. b	78. d	79. a	80. b
81. c	82. a	83. b	84. d	85. c	86. d	87. c	88. a	89. b	90. c
91. d	92. c	93. a	94. b	95. a	96. b	97. c	98. c	99. b	100. d
101. c	102. a	103. b	104. d	105. a	106. b	107. d	108. b	109. d	110. d
111. c	112. a	113. d	114. b	115. b	116. b	117. a	118. c	119. d	120. b
121. a	122. a	123. d	124. b	125. d	126. d	127. c	128. a	129. d	130. d
131. a	132. c	133. a	134. b	135. a	136. c	137. a	138. b	139. b	140. c
141. c	142. d	143. b	144. d	145. a	146. b	147. b	148. c	149. c	150. a
151. b	152. c	153. d	154. a	155. a	156. b	157. b	158. c	159. d	160. b

Viva Voce Questions

(for JAVA PROGRAMMING LAB. Set-1 & Set-II)

Q.1. What is the difference between private, protected, and public?

Ans. These keywords are for allowing privileges to components such as java methods and variables.

Public: accessible to all classes.

Private: accessible only to the class to which they belong.

Protected: accessible to the class to which they belong and any subclasses.

Access specifiers are keywords that determines the type of access to the member of a class. These are:

* Public
* Protected
* Private
* Defaults

Q.2. What is the difference between an interface and an abstract class? Also discuss the similarities.

Ans. Abstract class is a class which contains one or more abstract methods, which has to be implemented by sub classes. Interface is a Java object containing method declaration and doesn't contain implementation. The classes which have implementing interfaces must provide the method definition for all the methods.

Abstract class is a class prefix with an abstract keyword followed by class definition. Interface is an interface which starts with interface keyword.

Abstract class contains one or more abstract methods where as Interface contains all abstract methods and final declarations.

Abstract classes are useful in a situation that some general methods should be implemented and specialization behavior should be implemented by child classes. Interfaces are useful in a situation that all properties should be implemented.

Differences are as follows:

* Interfaces provide a form of multiple inheritance. A class can extend only one other class.
* Interfaces are limited to public methods and constants with no implementation. Abstract classes can have a partial implementation, protected parts, static methods, etc.
* A Class may implement several interfaces. But in case of abstract class, a class may extend only one abstract class.

* Interfaces are slow as it requires extra indirection to find corresponding method in the actual class. Abstract classes are fast.

Similarities:

* Neither Abstract classes nor Interface can be instantiated.

How to define an Abstract class?

A class containing abstract method is called Abstract class. An Abstract class can't be instantiated.

Example of Abstract class:

```
abstract class testAbstractClass {
protected String myString;
public String getMyString() {
return myString;
}
public abstract string anyAbstractFunction();
}
```

How to define an Interface?

In Java, Interface defines the methods but does not implement them. Interface can include constants. A class that implements the interfaces is bound to implement all the methods defined in Interface.

Example of Interface:

```
public interface samplelnterface {
public void functionOne();
public long CONSTANT ONE = 100;
}
```

Q.3. How you can force the garbage collection?

Ans. Garbage collection is an automatic process and can't be forced. You could request it by calling System.gc( ). JVM does not guarantee that GC will be started immediately.

Garbage collection is one of the most important feature of Java. Garbage collection is also called automatic memory management as JVM automatically removes the unused variables/objects (value is null) from the memory. User program can't directly free the object from memory, instead it is the job of the garbage collector to automatically free the objects that are no longer referenced by a program. Every class inherits finalize( ) method from java.lang.Object, the finalize() method is called by garbage collector when it determines no more references to the object exists. In Java, it is good idea to explicitly assign null into a variable when no more in use. Java on calling System.gc( ) and Runtime.gc( ), JVM tries to recycle the unused objects, but there is no guarantee when all the objects will garbage collected.

Q.4. What's the difference between constructors and normal methods?

Ans. Constructors must have the same name as the class and can not return a value. They are only called once while regular methods could be called many times and it can return a value or can be void.

Q.5. Can you call one constructor from another if a class has multiple constructors.

Ans. Yes. Use this( ) to call a constructor from an other constructor.

Q.6. Explain the usage of Java packages.

Ans. This is a way to organize files when a project consists of multiple modules. It also helps resolve naming conflicts when different packages have classes with the same names. Packages access level also allows you to protect data from being used by the non-authorized classes.

Q.7. Explain in your own words the "bottom line" benefits of the use of an interface.

Ans. The interface makes it possible for a method in one class to invoke methods on objects of other classes, without the requirement to know the true class of those objects, provided that those objects are all instantiated from classes that implement one or more specified interfaces. In other words, objects of classes that implement specified interfaces can be passed into methods of other objects as the generic type object, and the methods of the other objects can invoke methods on the incoming objects by first casting them as the interface type.

Q.8. What are some advantages and disadvantages of Java Sockets?

Ans. Some advantages of Java Sockets: Sockets are flexible and sufficient. Efficient socket based programming can be easily implemented for general communications. Sockets cause low network traffic. Unlike HTML forms and CGI scripts that generate and transfer whole web pages for each new request, Java applets can send only necessary updated information.

Some disadvantages of Java Sockets: Security restrictions are sometimes overbearing because a Java applet running in a Web browser is only able to establish connections to the machine where it came from, and to nowhere else on the network. Despite all of the useful and helpful Java features, Socket based communications allows only to send packets of raw data between applications. Both the client-side and server-side have to provide mechanisms to make the data useful in any way.

Q.9. Explain the usage of the keyword transient?

Ans. Transient keyword indicates that the value of this member variable does not have to be serialized with the object. When the class will be de-serialized, this variable will be initialized with a default value of its data type (i.e. zero for integers).

Q.10. What's the difference between the methods sleep( ) and wait( )?

Ans. The code sleep (1000); puts thread aside for exactly one second. The code wait(1000), causes a wait of up to one second. A thread could stop waiting earlier if it receives the notify() or notifyAll ( ) call. The method wait( ) is defined in the class Object and the method sleep() is defined in the class Thread.

Q.11. What would you use to compare two String variables—the operator == or the method equals( )?

Ans. I will use the method equals( ) to compare the values of the Strings and the == to check if two variables point at the same instance of a String object.

Q.12. Why would you use a synchronized block vs. synchronized method?

Ans. Synchronized blocks place locks for shorter periods than synchronized methods.

Q.13. What access level do you need to specify in the class declaration to ensure that only classes from the same directory can access it?

Ans. You do not need to specify any access level, and Java will use a default package access level.

Q.14. Can an inner class declared inside of a method access local variables of this method?

Ans. It's possible if these variables are final.

Q.15. What can go wrong if you replace && with & in the following code:

Ans. String a=null; if(a!=null && a.length( ) > 10) {...}

A single ampersand here would lead to a NullPointerException.

Q.16. What's the main difference between a Vector and an ArrayList?

Ans. Java Vector class is internally synchronized and ArrayList is not synchronized.

Q.17. Describe the wrapper classes in Java.

Ans. Wrapper class is wrapper around a primitive data type. An instance of a wrapper class contains, or wraps, a primitive value of the corresponding type.

Following table lists the primitive types and the corresponding wrapper classes:

Primitive Wrapper

boolean - java.lang.Boolean

byte - java.lang.Byte

char - java.lang.Character

double - java.lang.Double

float - java.lang.Float

int - java.lang.Integer

long - java.lang.Long

short - java.lang.Short

void - java.lang.Void

Q.18. How could Java classes direct program messages to the system console, but error messages, say to a file?

Ans. The class System has a variable out that represents the standard output, and the variable err that represent the standard error device. By default, they both point at the system console. This how the standard output could be re-directed:

Stream st = new Stream (new FileOutputStream("output.txt")); System.setErr(st); System.setOut(st) ;

Q.19. How do you know if an explicit object casting is needed?

Ans. If you assign a superclass object to a variable of a subclass's data type, you need to do explicit casting. For example:

Object a; Customer b; b= (Customer) a;

Q.20. When you assign a subclass to a variable having a superclass type, the casting is performed automatically. Can you write a Java class that could be used both as an applet as well as an application?

Ans. Yes. Add a main( ) method to the applet.

Q.21. If a class is located in a package, what do you need to change in the OS environment to be able to use it?

Ans. You need to add a directory or a jar file that contains the package directories to the CLASSPATH environment variable. Let's say a class Employee belongs to a package com.xyz.hr; and is located in the file c:\dev\com\xyz\hr\Employee.javln this case, you'd need to add c:\dev to the variable **CLASSPATH**. If this class contains the method mainQ, you could test it from a command prompt window as follows:

c:\>java corn .xyz.hr.Employee

Q.22. What's the difference between J2SDK 1.5 and J2SDK 5.0?

Ans. There's no difference, Sun Microsystems just re-branded this version.

Q.23. Does it matter in what order catch statements for FileNotFound Exception and lOExceptipon are written?

Ans. Yes, it does. The FileNotFoundException is inherited from the IOException. Exception's subclasses have to be caught first.

Q.24. Name the containers which uses Border Layout as their default layout?

Ans. Containers which uses Border Layout as their default are: window, Frame and Dialog classes.

Q.25. You are planning to do an indexed search in a list of objects. Which of the two Java collections should you use: ArrayList or LinkedList?

Ans. ArrayList

Q.26. When should the method invokeLater( )be used?

Ans. This method is used to ensure that Swing components are updated through the event-dispatching thread.

Q.27. How can a subclass call a method or a constructor defined in a superclass?

Ans. Use the following syntax: super.myMethod to call a constructor of the superclass just write superQ; in the first line of the subclasss constructor.

Q.28. What do you understand by Synchronization?

Ans. Synchronization is a process of controlling the access of shared resources by the multiple threads in such a manner that only one thred can access one resource at a time. In non synchronized multithreaded application, it is possible for one thread to modify a shared object while another thread is in the process of using or updating the object's value. Synchronization prevents such type of data corruption.

E.g. Synchronizing a function

```
public synchronized void Method 1 ( )     {
      //Appropriate method-related code.
```

E.g. Synchronizing a block of code inside a function:

```
      public myFunction () {
      synchronized (this) {
      // Synchronized code here.
      }
}
```

Q.29. What's the difference between a queue and a stack?

Ans. Sacks works by last-in-first-out rule (LIFO), while queues use the FIFO rule.

Q.30. You can create an abstract class that contains only abstract methods. On the other hand, you can create an interface that declares the same methods. So can QU use abstract classes instead of interface?

Ans. Sometimes. But your class may be a descendent of another class and in this case the interface is your only option.

Q.31. If you're overriding the method equals() of an object, which other method you might also consider?

Ans. hashCode( )

Q.32. What is Collection API?

Ans. The Collection API is a set of classes and interfaces that support operation on collections of objects.

These classes and interfaces are more flexible, more powerful, and more regular than the vectors, arrays. and hashtables if effectively replaces.

Example of classes: HashSet, HashMap, ArrayList, LinkedList, TreeSet and TreeMap. Example of interfaces: Collection, Set, List and Map.

Q.33. How would you make a copy of an entire Java object with its state?

Ans. Have this class implement Cloneable interface and call its method clone ( ).

Q.34. How can you minimize the need of garbage collection and make the memory use more effective?

Ans. Use object pooling and weak object references.

Q.35. There are two classes: A and B. The class B need to inform a class A when some important event has happened. What Java technique would you use to implement it?

Ans. If these classes are threads I'd consider notify( ) or notifyAll( ). For regular classes you can use the Observer interface.

Q.36. Explain the Encapsulation principle.

Ans. Encapsulation is a process of binding or wrapping the data and the codes that operates on the data into a single entity. This keeps the data safe from outside interface and misuse. One way to think about encapsulation is as a protective wrapper that prevents code and data from being arbitrarily accessed by other code defined outside the wrapper.

Q.37. Explain the Inheritance principle.

Ans. Inheritance is the process by which one object acquires the properties of another object.

Q.38. Explain the Polymorphism principle.

Ans. The meaning of Polymorphism is something like one name many forms. Polymorphism enables one entity to be used as a general category for different types of actions. The specific action is determined by the exact nature of the situation. The concept of polymorphism can be explained as "one interface, multiple methods".

From a practical programming viewpoint, polymorphism exists in three distinct forms in Java:

* Method overloading
* Method overriding through inheritance
* Method overriding through the Java interface

Q.39. Is Iterator a Class or Interface? What is its use?

Ans. Iterator is an interface which is used to step through the elements of a collection.

Q.40. Explain the user defined Exceptions?

Ans. User defined Exceptions are the separate Exception classes defined by the user for specific purposed. An user defined can created by simply sub-classing it to the Exception class. This allows custom exceptions to be generated (using throw) and caught in the same way as normal exceptions.

Example:

```
class myCustom Exception extends Exception {
/ The class simply has to exist to be an exception
}
```

Q.41. What is OOP?

Ans. OOP is the common abbreviation for Object-Oriented Programming. There are three main principles of oops which are called Polymorphism, Inheritance and Encapsulation.

Q.42. Read the following program:

Ans.
```
public class test {
public static void main(String []args) {
int x = 3;
int y = 1;
if (x = y)
System.out.println("Not equal");
else
System .out.println("Equal");
}
}
```

What is the result?

A. The output is "Equal"

B. The output in "Not Equal"

C. An error at" if(x = y)" causes compilation to fall.

D. The program executes but no output is show on console.

Answer: C

Transient variable can't be serialize. For example if a variable is declared as transient in a serializable class and the class is written to an ObjectStream, the value of the variable can't be written to the stream instead when the class is retrieved from the ObjectStream the value of the variable becomes null.

Q.43. What is the difference between an Interface and an Abstract class?

Ans. An abstract class can have instance methods that implement a default behaviour. An Interface can only declare constants and instance methods, but cannot implement default behaviour and all methods are implicitly abstract. An interface has all public members and no implementation. An abstract class is a class which may have the usual flavours of class members (private, protected, etc.), but has some abstract methods.

Q.44. What is the purpose of garbage collection in Java, and when is it used?

Ans. The purpose of garbage collection is to identify and discard objects that are no longer needed by a program so that their resources can be reclaimed and reused. A Java object is subject to garbage collection when it becomes unreachable to the program in which it is used.

Q.45. Describe synchronization in respect to multithreading.

Ans. With respect to multithreading, synchronization is the capability to control the access of multiple threads to shared resources. Without synchonization, it is possible for one thread to modify a shared variable while another thread is in the process of using or updating same shared variable. This usually leads to significant errors.

Q.46. Explain different way of using thread?

Ans. The thread could be implemented by using runnable interface or by inheriting from the thread class. The former is more advantageous, because when you are going for multiple inheritance, the only interface can help.

Q.47. What are pass by reference and pass by value?

Ans. Pass by reference means the passing the address itself rather than passing the value. Pass by value means passing a copy of the value to be passed.

Q.48. What is HashMap and Map?

Ans. Map is Interface and Hashmap is class that implements this map.

Q.49. Difference between HashMap and HashTable?

Ans. The HashMap class is roughly equivalent to Hashtable, except that it is unsynchronized and permits nulls. (HashMap allows null values as key and value whereas Hashtable doesn't allow). HashMap does not guarantee that the order of the map will remain constant over time. HashMap is unsynchronized and Hashtable is synchronized.

Q.50. Difference between Vector and ArrayList?

Ans. Vector is synchronized whereas ArrayList is not.

Q.51 Difference between Swing and AWT?

Ans. AWT are heavyweight components. Swings are light-weight components. Hence Swing works faster than AWT.

Q.52. What is the difference between a constructor and a method?

Ans. A constructor is a member function of a class that is used to create objects of that class. It has the same name as the class itself, has no return type, and is invoked using the this operator. A method is an ordinary member function of a class. It has its own name, a return type (which may be void), and is invoked using the dot operator.

Q.53. What is an Iterator?

Ans. Some of the collection classes provide traversal of their contents via a java.utll.Iterator interface.

This interface allows you to walk through a collection of objects, operating on each object in turn. Remember when using Iterators that they contain a snapshot of the collection at the time the Iterator was obtained; generally it is not advisable to modify the collection itself while traversing an Iterator.

Q.54. State the significance of public, private, protected, default modifiers both singly and in combination and state the effect of package relationships on declared items qualified by these modifiers.

Ans. Public: Public class is visible in other packages, field is visible everywhere (class must be public too).

Private: Private variables or methods may be used only by an instance of the same class that declares the variable or method, A private feature may only be accessed by the class that owns the feature.

Protected: Is available to all classes in the same package and also available to all subclasses of the class that owns the protected feature. This access is provided even to subclasses that reside in a different package from the class that owns the protected feature.

Default: What you get by default ie, without any access modifier (i.e., public private or protected).It means that it is visible to all within a particular package.

Q.55. What is an abstract class?

Ans. Abstract class must be extended subclassed (to be useful). It serves as a template. A class that is abstract may not be instantiated (i.e., you may not call its constructor), abstract class may contain static data. Any class with an abstract method is automatically abstract itself, and must be declared as such.

A class may be declared abstract even if it has no abstract methods. This prevents it from being instantiated.

Q.56. What is static in Java?

Ans. Static means one per class, not one for each object no matter how many instance of a class might exist. This means that you can use them without creating an instance of a class. Static methods are implicitly final, because overriding is done based on the type of the object, and static methods are attached to a class, not an object. A static method in a superclass can be shadowed by another static method in a subclass, as long as the original method was not declared final. However, you can't overridden a static method with a nonstatic method. In other words, you can't change a static method into an instance method in a subclass.

Q.57. What is final?

Ans. A final class can't be extended i.e., final class may not be subclassed. A final method can't be overridden when its class is inherited. You can't change value of a final variable (is a constant).

Q.58. What if the main method is declared as private?

Ans. The program compiles properly but at runtime it will give "Main method not public"Message.

Q.59. What if the static modifier is removed from the signature of the main method?

Ans. Program compiles. But at runtime throws an error "NoSuchMethodError".

Q.60. What if I write static public void instead of public static void?

Ans. Program compiles and runs properly.

Q.61. What if I do not provide the String array as the argument to the method?

Ans. Program compiles but throws a runtime error "NoSuchMethodError".

Q.62. How can one prove that the array is not null but empty using one line of code?

Ans. Use Print args. length. It will print 0. That means it is empty. But if it would have been null then it would have thrown a NullPointe-Exception on attempting to print args. length.

Q.63. What environment variables do I need to set on my machine in order to be able to run Java programs?

Ans. CLASSPATH and PATH are the two variables.

Q.64. Can an application have multiple classes having main method?

Ans. Yes it is possible. While starting the application we mention the class name to be run. The JVM will look for the Main method only in the class whose name you have mentioned. Hence there is not conflict amongst the multiple classes having main method.

Q.65. Can I have multiple main methods in the same class?

Ans. No the program fails to compile. The compiler says that the main method is already defined in the class.

Q.66. Do I need to import java.lang package any time? Why?

Ans. No. It is by default loaded internally by the JVM.

Q.67. Can I import same package/class twice? Will the JVM load the package twice at runtime?

Ans. One can import the same package or same class multiple times. Neither compiler nor JVM complains about it. And the JVM will internally load the class only once no matter how many times you import the same class.

Q.68. What are Checked and UnChecked Exception?

Ans. A checked exception is some subclass of Exception (or Exception itself), excluding class RuntimeException and its subclasses. Making an exception checked forces client programmers to deal with the possibility that the exception will be thrown e.g., IOException thrown by java.io.FileInputStream's read() method. Unchecked exceptions are RuntimeException and any of its subclasses. Class error and its subclasses also are unchecked. With an unchecked exception, however, the compiler doesn't force client programmers either to catch the exception or declare it in a throws clause. In fact, client programmers may not even know that the exception could be thrown. e.g., StringIndexOhtOfBoundsException thrown by String's charAt() method and Checked exceptions must be caught at compile time. Runtime exceptions do not need to be. Errors often cannot be.

Q.69. What is Overriding?

Ans. When a class defines a method using the same name, return type, and arguments as a method in its superclass, the method in the class overrides the method in the superclass.

When the method is invoked for an object of the class, it is the new definition of the method that is called, and not the method definition from superclass. Methods may be overridden to be more public, not more private.

Q.70. What are different types of inner classes?

Ans. **Nested top-level classes.** Member classes, Local classes, Anonymous classes.

Nested top-level classes: If you declare a class within a class and specify the static modifier, the compiler treats the class just like any other top-level class.

Any class outside the declaring class accesses the nested class with the declaring class name acting similarly to a package. e.g., outer.inner. Top-level inner classes implicitly have access only to static variables. There can also be inner interfaces. All of these are of the nested top-level variety.

Member classes: Member inner classes are just like other member methods and member variables and access to the member class is restricted, just like methods and variables. This means a public member class acts similarly to a nested top-level class. The primary difference between member classes and nested top-level classes is that member classes have access to the specific instance of the enclosing class.

Local classes: Local classes are like local variables, specific to a block of code. Their visibility is only within the block of their declaration. In order for the class to be useful beyond the declaration block, it would need to implement a more publicly available interface. Because local classes are not members, the modifiers public, protected, private, and static are not usable.

Anonymous classes: Anonymous inner classes extend local inner classes one level further. As anonymous classes have no name, you cannot provide a construction.

Q.71. Are the imports checked for validity at compile time? e.g. will the code containing an import such as java.lang.ABCD compile?

Ans. Yes the imports are checked for the semantic validity at compile time. The code containing above line of import will not compile. It will throw an error saying, can not resolve symbol

symbol Olas ABCD

location: package io

import java.io.ABCD;

Q.72. What is the difference between declaring a variable and defining a variable?

Ans. In declaration we just mention the type of the variable and it's name. We do not initialize it. But defining means declaration + initialization.

E.g., String s; is just a declaration while String s new String ("abed"); Or String s = "abed"; are both definitions.

Q.73. Can a top level class be private or protected?

Ans. No. A top level class can not be private or protected. It can have either "public" or no modifier. If it does not have a modifier it is supposed to have a default access. If a top level class is declared as private the compiler will complain that the "modifier private is not allowed here". This means that a top level class can not be private. Same is the case with protected.

Q.74. What is Externalizable interface?

Ans. Externalizable is an interface which contains two methods readExternal and writeExternal. These methods give you a control over the serialization mechanism. Thus, if your class implements this interface, you can customize the serialization process by implementing these methods.

Q.75. When you serialize an object, what happens to the object references included in the object?

Ans. The serialization mechanism generates an object graph for serialization. Thus it determines whether the included object references are serializable or not. This is a recursive process. Thus, when an object is serialized, all the included objects are also serialized alongwith the original object.

Q.76. What happens to the static fields of a class during serialization?

Ans. There are three exceptions in which serialization does not necessarily read and write to the stream. These are

1. Serialization ignores static fields, because they are not part of any particular state.
2. Base class fields are only handled, if the base class itself is serializable.
3. Transient fields.

Q.77. Give a simplest way to find out the time a method takes for execution without using any profiling tool?

Ans. Read the system time just before the method is invoked and immediately after method returns. Take the time difference, which will give you the time taken by a method for execution.

To put it in code

```
long start System.currentTimeMillis();
method ();
long end System.currentTimeMillis ();
System.out.println ("Time taken for execution is" + (end - start));
```

Remember that if the time taken for execution is too small, it might show that it is taking zero milliseconds for execution. Try it on a method which is big enough, in the sense the one which is doing considerable amount of processing.

Q.78. What are wrapper classes?

Ans. Java provides specialized classes corresponding to each of the primitive data types. These are called wrapper classes. They are e.g., Integer, Character, Double etc.

Q.79. Why do we need wrapper classes?

Ans. It is sometimes easier to deal with primitives as objects. Moreover most of the collection classes store objects and not primitive data types. And also the wrapper classes provide many utility methods also. Because of these reasons we need wrapper classes. And since we create instances of these classes we can store them in any of the collection classes and pass them around as a collection. Also we can pass them around as method parameters where a method expects an object.

Q.80. What is the difference between error and an exception?

Ans. An error is an irrecoverable condition occurring at runtime. Such as OutOfMemory error. These JVM errors and you can not repair them at runtime. While exceptions are conditions that occur because of bad input etc. e.g. FileNotFoundException will be thrown if the specified file does not exist. Or a NullPointerException will take place if you try using a null reference. In most of the cases it is possible to recover from an exception (probably by giving user a feedback for entering proper values etc.).

Q.81. What are runtime exceptions?

Ans. Runtime exceptions are those exceptions that are thrown at runtime because of either wrong input data or because of wrong business logic etc. These are not checked by the compiler at compile time.

Q.82. How does an exception permeate through the code?

Ans. An unhandled exception moves up the method stack in search of a matching. When an exception is thrown from a code which is wrapped in a try block followed by one or more catch blocks, a search is made for matching catch block. If a matching type is found then that block will be invoked. If a matching type is not found then the exception moves up the method stack and reaches the caller method. Same procedure is repeated if the caller method is included in a try catch block. This process continues until a catch block handling the appropriate type of exception is found. If it does not find such a block then finally the program terminates.

Q.83. What are the different ways to handle exceptions?

Ans. There are two ways to handle exceptions,

1. By wrapping the desired code in a try block followed by a catch block to catch the exceptions, and
2. List the desired exceptions in the throws clause of the method and let the caller of the method handle those exceptions.

Q.84. Does garbage collection guarantee that a program will not run out of memory?

Ans. Garbage collection does not guarantee that a program will not run out of memory. It is possible for programs to use up memory resources faster than they are garbage collected. It is also possible for programs to create objects that are not subject to garbage collection.

Q.85. What is the difference between preemptive scheduling and time slicing?

Ans. Under preemptive scheduling, the highest priority task executes until it enters the waiting or dead states or a higher priority task comes into existence. Under time slicing, a task executes for a predefined slice of time and then reenters the pool of ready tasks. The scheduler then determines which task should execute next, based on priority and other factors.

Q.86. Can applets communicate with each other?

Ans. At this point of time applets may communicate with other applets running in the same virtual machine. If the applets are of the same class, they can communicate via shared static variables. If the applets are of different classes, then each will need a reference to the same class with static variables. In any case the basic idea is to pass the information back and forth through a static variable.

An applet can also get references to all other applets on the same page using the getApplets() method ofjava.applet.AppletContext. Once you get the reference to an applet, you can communicate with it by using its public members.

It is conceivable to have applets in different virtual machines that talk to a server somewhere on the Internet and store any data that needs to be serialized there. Then, when another applet needs this data, it could connect to this same server. Implementing this is non-trivial.

Q.87. What are the different scopes for Java variables?

Ans. The scope of a Java variable is determined by the context in which the variable is declared. Thus a java variable can have one of the three scopes at any given point in time.

1. **Instance:** These are typical object level variables, they are initialized to default values at the time of creation of object, and remain accessible as long as the object accessible.
2. **Local:** These are the variables that are defined within a method. They remain accessbile only during the course of method excecution. When the method finishes execution, these variables fall out of scope.
3. **Static:** These are the class level variables. They are initialized when the class is loaded in JVM for the first time and remain there as long as the class remains loaded. They are not tied to any particular object instance.

Q.88. Why can't my applet read or write to files?

Ans. Applets execute under the control of a web browser. Netscape and Internet Explorer impose a security restriction, that prohibits access to the local filesystem by applets. While this may cause frustration for developers, this is an important security feature for the end-user. Without it, applets would be free to modify the contents of a user's hard-drive, or to read its contents and send this information back over a network.

Digitally signed applets can request permission to access the local filesystem, but the easiest way around the problem is to read and write to remote files located on a network drive. For example, in conjunction with a CGI script or serviet, you could send HTTP requests to store and retrieve data.

Q.89. How can I create my own GUI components?

Ans. Custom graphical components can be created by producing a class that inherits from java.awt.Canvas. Your component should override the paint method, just like an applet does, to provide the graphical features of the component.

Q.90. How do I create a scrollable container?

Ans. The good is there is already a scrollable container as part of the java.awt package it's called

ScrollPane, and without this, you'd need to create one from scratch, using scrollbars.

Its easy to create an instance of ScrollPane, and to then add it to your applet or application. Simply create a new instance of ScrollPane, and then add it to your applet's canvas. Whatever size your applet is, the scroll pane will adjust to. Now as you add components, scroll bars will appear as needed. You can also change the size of the scrollbar via the setSize() method. Here's a quick example

```
// Create a scroll pane object
ScrollPane mycontalner = new ScrollPane();
//Add scroll pane to my current canvas (if I am an appet)
add(myContainer):
// Now I can add components to my container….
```

Q.91. How do I playback multimedia files? I'd like to display .avi, .mpg, and other movie form ats.

Ans. It'd be a tough task to write routines to playback a wide range of multimedia formats. Then you'd have to keep an eye out for new formats, write new code, and make it all so efficient that it can do real-time playback under a Java Virtual Machine. Fortunately, you don't have to do any of this!

Sun has been working on the Java Media Framework API, which offers an easy API to playback multimedia files. The API has been available for some time now, and implementations are now available from Sun, Intel, and others.

Q.92. My application/applet loads images, but they aren't drawn to the screen. What's going on?

Ans. I've encountered this problem a few times in my own applications. When you load an image (using java.awt.Toolkit.getImage), the function returns immediately, and the image is loaded asynchronously. An image isn't ready to be drawn, because it hasn't yet loaded. Depending on when the image is loaded, and when it is drawn, the problem can be intermittent and hard to track down.

If your application or applet MUST display the image, you can have it wait until the image is fully loaded. An animation applet, for example, may not have any useful work to do until the image(s) are loaded. To wait for images, you need to use the java.awt.MediaTracker class.

MediaTracker allows you to register an image with the tracker, and have your application or applet wait until the image is ready. Note that this isn't limited just to applets loading images ove- a network - from my own experience an application it can happen loading a small (<10ⱺ bytes) image from a local filesystem.

To register an image, you assign it an image number, and call the addlniage method. Then you can call the waitFor(int) or waitForAll( ) methods.

```
//Pass media tracker any component (such as a canvas or an applet)
MediaTracker tracker = new MediaTracker(this);
//Add images
```

```
tracker.add Image (mylmagel, 0);
tracker.add Image (mylmagel, 1);
// Wait for images
try{
tracker.waitForAll();
} catch (lnterruptedException ie) {}
```

Once you start the wait, your application will block until the image has loaded. Then, you can call java.awt.Graphics.drawlmage to display the image to your applet or application.

Q.93. How can I append an existing file in Java?

Ans. Appending to a file is fairly common as there is no support for file appending in JDK1 .02, and developers supporting that platform are forced to rewrite the entire file to a temporary file, and then overwrite the original. As most users support either JDK 1.1 or the Java 2 platform, you'll probably be able to use the following FileOutputStream constructor to append data:

public **FileOutputStream**(String name, boolean append) throws FileNotFoundException

Parameters:

name - the system-dependent file name

append - if true, then bytes will be written to the end of the file rather than the beginning

For example, to append the file 'autoexec.bat' to add a new path statement on a Wintel machine, you could do the following:

FileOutputStream appendedFile = new FileOutputStream

("c:\\autoexec.bat", true);

Q.94. How do I connect a Reader to an InputStream?

Ans. This is a very common question - after all, there aren't any SocketReaders, or PipedReaders. You need something to bridge the gap between a Reader, and an InputStream. That's where InputStreamReader comes into play.

InputStreamReader is a reader that can be connected to any InputStream - even filtered input streams such as DatalnputStream, or BufferedlnputStream. Here's an example that shows InputStreamReader in action.

// Connect a BufferedReader, to an lnputStreamReader which is connected to

// an InputStream in'.

BufferedReader reader = new BufferedReader (new InputStreamReader (in));

You can do the same with an OutputStream to a Writer (see OutputStreamWriter for more information).

Q.95. When should I use an InputStream, and when should I use a Reader?

Ans. This can be confusing, particularly if you're already familiar with InputStream, and keep getting deprecated APT warning messages. Let me simplify it for you.

- If you're reading data, such as bytes of information, you are best off to use InputStreams and DatalnputStream in particular.

- If you're reading in text, and want to be able to call a readLine() method, its best to use Readers, and BufferedReader in particular.

So what's the difference? Well, DataInputStream's readLine() method is deprecated, because of problems with this method. Readers offer an alternative - though placing a readLine() method in a BufferedReader still seems a little odd to me. Whether its buffered or not has little to do with the fact it can read lines of text - but its easy enough to live with.

Q. 96. How do I compare two strings?

Ans. A common error that we all make from time to time is incorrect string comparison. Even once you learn how to compare strings correctly, it's extremely easy to make a mistake and use the == operator.

When we compare primitive data types, such as two ints, two chars, two doubles, etc. we can use the == operator. We can also use the == operator to compare two objects. However, when used with an object, the == operator will only check to see if they are the same objects, not if they hold the same contents.

This means that code like the following will not correctly compare to strings

```
if ( string I == string2 )
{
System.out.println ("Match found");
}
```

This code will only evaluate to true if string1 and string2 are the same object, not if they hold the same contents. This is an important distinction to make. Checking, for example, to see if a String == "somevalue", will not evaluate to true even if a String holds the same contents.

To correctly compare two strings, we must use the .equals method ( ). This method is inherited from java.lang.Object, and can be used to compare any two strings. Here's an example of how to correctly check a String's contents:

```
if ( string.equals("abcdef") )
{
System.out.println ("Match found");
}
```

This is a simple, and easy to remember tip that will safe you considerable time debugging applications. Remember - never use the operator if you only want to compare the string's contents.

Q.97. How can I throw an exception without declaring it in a 'throws' clause?

Ans. Sometimes it is useful to throw exceptions, without explicitly declaring them in the throws clause of a method's signature. Any exceptions that extends java.lang.RuntimeException don't need to be declared. This means that it is safe to throw subclasses (like NullPointException), or to create your own.

Q.98. I'm confused about variables and their scope. What's the difference between a member variable and a local variable?

Ans. Simple! A member variable is a variable that belongs to an object, whereas a local variable belongs to the current scope. Hmm... Still confused?

When we define a class, we can give that class member variables. These variables are members of that class. Take, for example, the following class declaration.

```
public class MyClass {
int a;
int b;
}
MyClass has two member variables, a & b. When we define an object
instance of MyClass it will still have two member variables, a & b,
We can reference these members using the '. character.
// Create an instance of MyClass
MyClass obj new MyClass();
//Assign new values to a & b
obj.a 1;
obj.b = 65536;
```

These variables belong to MyClass, and are known as member variables. On the other hand, if we declare variables inside of a function, we call these local variables. These variables are local to a particular function, and not publicly accessible. For example, in the following function, we have no way of accessing the obj variable outside of the main(String[]) function.

```
public static void main (String args[])
{
MyClass obj new MyClass();
System.out.println ("A" + obj.a);
}
```

Q.99. What is an abstract class, and when should it be used?

Ans. Abstract classes are classes that contain one or more abstract methods. An abstract method is a method that is declared, but contains no implementation. Abstract classes may not be instantiated, and require subclasses to provide implementations for the abstract methods. Let's look at an example of an abstract class, and an abstract method.

Suppose we were modeling the behaviour of animals, by creating a class hierachy that started with a base class called Animal. Animals are capable of doing different things like flying, digging and walking, but there are some common operations as well like eating and sleeping. Some common operations are performed by all animals, but in a different way as well. When an operation is performed in a different way, it is a good candidate for an abstract method (forcing subclasses to provide a custom implementation). Let's look at a very primitive Animal base class, which defines an abstract method for making a sound (such as a dog barking, a cow mooing, or a pig oinking).

```
public abstract Animal
{
public void eat(Food food)
{
```

```
// do something with food....
}
public void sleep(int hours)
{
    try
{
// 1000 milliseconds * 60 seconds * 60 minutes * hours
Thread.sleep (1000 * 60 * 60 * hours);
}
catch (InterruptedException ie) { /* ignore *1)
}
}
public abstract void makeNoise( );
}
```

Note that the abstract keyword is used to denote both an abstract method, and an abstract class. Now, any animal that wants to be instantiated (like a dog or cow) must implement the make Noise method - otherwise it is impossible to create an instance of that class. Let's look at a Dog and Cow subclass that extends the Animal class.

```
public Dog extends Animal
{
public void makeNoiseO'{ System .out.println ("Bark! Bark!"); }
}
public Cow extends Animal
{
public void makeNoise() { System.out.println ("Moo! Moo!"); }
}
```

Now you may be wondering why not declare an abstract class as an interface, and have the Dog and Cow implement the interface. Sure you could - but you'd also need to implement the eat and sleep methods. By using abstract classes, you can inherit the implementation of other (non-abstract) methods. You can't do that with interfaces - an interface cannot provide any method implementations.

Q.100. What is Pure Java? I've heard that its 100%, so if I only use Java code and no external applications, is my code 'pure'?

Ans. 100% Pure Java code is code that conforms to the Java ideal of universal portability. Writing an application that doesn't exploit operating system/platform specific features is a great start, but you also have to write the code in a platform neutral way. This includes things such as not hardwiring the '1' symbol as a file separator on Unix systems, as this will fail on a Wintel system that use '\'. If you don't rely on the core Java API's, and instead use native methods, this can also disqualify' an application from being 100%.

Developers who wish to use the 100% Pure Java logo must have their application independently verified, using the Java Purity Checker software. Full details are available from Sun, but developers who wish to write portable code can read the 'cookbook' for writing pure applications for free.

Q.101. How do I kill a thread? The stop() method is deprecated in JDK1.2, so how do I shut it down?

Ans. The API documentation for JDK1.2 discusses an alternate mechanism for stopping threads, by having them continually poll a boolean flag to see if they should terminate of their own accord. This is an option, but if you have threads that become deadlocked or stall waiting for 110, sometimes you'll have to kill them the hard way.

Why shouldn't you normally use the Thread;stop() method? Well, it is deprecated as of JDKI.2 because it can potentially leave the system in an unsafe state. If a thread had a lock on an object (within a synchronized block), it might not release the object lock, causing problems at a later time. Note that this problem can affect older JVM implementations as well, JDK1.02 and JDK1 .1 are not immune.

So while you shouldn't use Thread.stopQ unless absolutely necessary, it is an acceptable way to kill a thread if it becomes stalled and you really need to shut it down fast.

Q.102. What is the difference between public, private, and protected keywords? Do I even need to use them?

Ans. We use these keywords to specify access levels for member variables, or for member functions (methods).

- Public variables, are variables that are visible to all classes.
- Private variables, are variables that are visible only to the class to which they belong.
- Protected variables, are variables that are visible only to the class to which they belong, and any subclasses.

Deciding when to use private, protected, or public variables is sometimes tricky. You need to think whether or not an external object (or program), actually needs direct access to the information. If you do want other objects to access internal data, but wish to control it, you would make it either private or protected, but provide functions which can manipulate the data in a controlled way.

Q.103. What does the 'extends' keyword mean?

Ans. Java, like other object-orientated languages, supports class inheritance. Inheritance allows one class to "inherit" the properties of another class. For example, all Java objects are inherited from the java.lang.Object class. This means that we can call the to String( ) method inherited from java.lang.Object, and get a string representation of any java object, such as an Integer, a Float, a Double, etc.

Take a look at the following example, which demonstrates the use of the 'extends' keyword.

```
public class A extends java.lang.Object {
public int number;
public String toString( ); {
  return new String("Value :" + number);
}
```

In this example, we implicitly state that we extend java.lang.Object, and override the functionality of the toString() method by providing our own function. Note that all classes, whether they state so or not, will be inherit from java.lang.Object.

Our next example shows a more common use of the keyword 'extends'. In this example, we inherit from class A, which means that B will also contain a field called number, and a function called toString( ).

```
public class B extends A {
public void increment() {
number++;
}
}
public class ABDemo {
}
public static void main (String args[]) {
// Create an instance of B B counter = new B();
//Increment B
counterincrement();
// Call toString() method System.out.println (counter.toString() );
    }
}
```

Even though we never defined a toString() method, or added a number field to the B class, it has inherited this information from A. This is a powerful feature of object-orientated programming, and can save significant time when developing classes.

Q.104. What's the difference between = & ==?

Ans. One of the most common programming mistakes that one can make is to confuse the equal sign () with a double equal signs (==). While experienced programmers can still make the same mistake, knowing the difference between the two is a good way to avoid it.

When we wish to assign a value to a variable or member, we use the equals sign. As an example, the following would assign the value of three to the variable a.

a = 1 + 2;// assignment operation

When we wish to make a comparison, such as in an if statement, we use the double equals sign (==). A simple example would be the following

if (a == b) then System.out.println ("Match found!");

Now consider what would have happened if we used an assignment operator instead. A would be assigned the value of B - destroying the current contents of A and giving us an incorrect comparison. Finding this type of error can be difficult, because the two operators look so similar. So why does Java use such confusing operators? Java draws its roots from C, which shares the same problem. Unfortunately, its something that all Java programmers must learn to live with.

Q.105. What does the ++ or – – signs after a variable mean?

Ans. These operators date back to the days of C programming. These operators increment or decrement a variable by one. They're quite handy for using in expressions, because they will increment or decrement the variable after the expression has been tested.

A common example of their use is in for loops. Consider the following loop, which counts from one to ten.

```
for (int i=1; i<=1 0; i++) {
System.out.println (i);
}
```

In this case, the variable is incremented by one each time, until the terminating condition of greater than ten has been reached. It could just have easily been a while loop, or other expression.

Q.106. How can I find out who is connected to my server?

Ans. If you write applications that supply TCP services via the StreamSocket class, its extremely easy to determine the IP address and port of the remote connection. The accept method returns a Socket (which is used to communicate with the remote client). The Socket class has a getInetAddress(), and a getPort() method - all instances of socket can provide you with a unique identifier at a given point in time.

As far as finding out exactly who (as opposed to what machine) is connected to your server, you might want to have some form of authentication phase so that as a client connects, you can uniquely identify the user. If you create a lookup table, at a later stage you can lookup the P address and port to determine the user.

Q.107. What exactly are servlets?

Ans. Most programmers will be familiar with the concept of server-side programming. Content can be created at the client end, through JavaScript, Dynamic HTML, or applets - but it can also be created at the server end through CGI scripts, server side applications, and now servlets.

Servlets are pieces of Java code that work at the server end. Servlets have all the access to resources on the serve- that a CGI script do, and aren't normally limited by the restrictions on file and network access that iava applets have traditionally been held back by. Servlets also offer substantial performance advantages for developers and webmasters, because unlike CGI scripts, do not fork off additional processes each time a request is made from a browser.

Servlets may take a little while to approach the same amount of usage as CGI scripts, but they are growing in popularity. Aside from the obvious advantage of portability, the performance advantages are significant, and its likely that in the future the use of Java serviets will become widespread. Developers keen to adopt skills should certainly focus on this new trend in server side programming, as the number of developers with servlet experience is (currently), small.

Q.108. How do I get parameters from a HTML form when using servlets?

Ans. When extending javax.servlet.http.HttpServlet, you should override either of the following two methods:

public void doGet(HttpServletRequest req, HttpServletResponse res)

public void doPost(HttpServletlrequest req, HttpServletResponse res)

Both of these methods accept as a parameter a HttpServletRequest instance. This allows the servlet to obtain information about the browser request, including the parameters passed to the servlet. By using the String getParameter(String) method, you can request any parameter you need. If the parameter is not present, a null value will be returned.

Q.109. How do I send cookies from a servlet?

Ans. HTTP is a stateless protocol, which makes tracking user actions difficult. One solution is to use a cookie, which is a small piece of data sent by a web browser every time it requests a page from a particular site. Servlets, and CGI scripts, can send cookies when a HTTP request is made - though as always, there is no guarantee the browser will accept it.

Cookies are represented by the javax.servlet.http.Cookie class. Cookie has a single constructor, which takes two strings (a key and a value).

```
// Create a new cookie
Cookie cookie = new Cookie ("counter", "1");
```

Adding a cookie to a browser is easy. Cookies are sent as part of a HTTPServletResponse, using the addCookie(Cookie) method. You can call this method multiple times, but remember that most browsers impose a limit of ten cookies, and 4096 bytes of data per hostname.

Public void doGet (HttpServletRequest request, HttpServletResponse response)

throws IOException

```
{
response.addCookie(new Cookie("cookie_name", "cookie value"));
}
```

Q.110. How can I use a quote" character within a string?

Ans. When we use literal strings in Java, we use the quote (") character to indicate the beginning and ending of a string. For example, to declare a string called myString, we could this :-

```
String myString = "this is a string";
```

But what if we wanted to include a quote (") character WITHIN the string. We can use the \ character to indicate that we want to include a special character, and that the next character should be treated differently. \" indicates a quote character, not the termination of a string.

```
public static void main (String argsfl)
{
System.out.println (If you need to 'quote' in Java");
System .out.println ("you can use single V or double \" quote");
}
```

This allows us to include quote characters within a string. Its not something you'll need to do often, but when you need it, this tip will come in handy!

Q.111. What exactly are Java Beans?

Ans. Java Beans are components that can be used to assemble a larger Java application. Beans are classes that have properties, and can trigger events.

To define a property, a bean author provides accessor methods, that can get and set the value of a property. A bean tool should inspect the class for methods matching the get/set pattern, and allow you to modify the object's properties.

```
public class My First Bean
{
private String name;
public MyFirstBean()
{
name = new String("MyFirstBean");
}
public String getName()
{
return name;
}
public void setName( String newName
{
Name = newName;
    }
}
```

This is a very simple bean, within minimal functionality. It triggers no events, and has a single property, but does introduce you to the basics of beans. For more information on beans, check out the following resources:

- JavaBeans - a new component architecture
- Java.sun.com - Beans

Q.112. How can I generate random numbers?

Ans. Generating random numbers is simple. Provided as part of the java.util package, the Random class makes it easy to generate numbers. Start by creating an instance of the Random class

```
// Create an instance of the random class
Random r = new RandomO;
```

Now, you must request a number from the generator. Supposing we wanted an integer number, we'd call the nextlnt() method.

```
// Get an integer
int number r.nextInt();
```

Often you'll want numbers to fall in a specific range (for example, from one to ten). We can use the modulus operator to limit the range of the numbers. This will give us the remainder of the number when divided by ten (giving us a range –9 to +9). To eliminate negative numbers, if the number is less than one we'll add ten to it. This gives us random numbers between one and ten!

```
// Accept only up to ten
int random number = number % 10;
```

```
if (random_number < 1) random_number = random_number + 10;
```

Creating random numbers in an application or applet really isn't that difficult, Just remember to limit the range of your numbers, and to import the java.util.Random class.

Q.113. What causes out of memory exceptions?

Ans. The dreaded OutOfMemoryException is something that no Java programmer ever wishes to see. Yet it can happen, particularly if your application involves a large amount of data processing, or is long lived - such as a server that responds to requests and is expected to run indefinitely.

There are several reasons that out of memory exceptions can be thrown. Either the virtual machine your Java program is running on may have a limit to the amount of memory it will give access to, the system on which your program is running may have run out of physical and virtual memory, or your application may just be consuming too much memory. In the first case, you may be able to modify the maximum heap size of the virtual machine, in the second or third you'll need to redesign your application.

Designing applications for minimal memory consumption isn't an easy task, and isn't specific only to Java programming. There are many techniques available, such as buffering data to disk that isn't needed at the moment, to using more efficient algorithms or subdividing tasks into smaller pieces. This is more of a design problem that a Java one - however there are some steps you can take to avoid your program crashing when it runs out of memory.

For a start, in your main method (or those you identify as likely to cause problems), catch OutOfMemoryExceptions. This way your application can terminate gracefully. Also, be sure to clear any data that you know you'll no longer require. The automatic garbage collector looks for objects that contain no references, so be sure to set your objects to null when you're finished. Finally, you can always examine the amount of free memory by calling the freeMemory() method of the system Runtime object. Here's how:

```
Runtime runtime Runtime .getRuntime
System.out.println ("Free memory : "- + runtime.freeMemory( ));
```

If you realize that you're going to be performing large amounts of data processing (and consuming large amounts of memory), it might be a good idea to check before beginning. Here's to no more OutOfMemoryExceptions!

Q.114. How do I create a .JAR file?

Ans. Java Archive (JAR) files allow developers to package many classes into a single file. JAR files also use compression, so this can make applets and applications smaller.

Creating a .JAR file is easy. Simple go to the directory your classes are stored in and type:

```
jar -cf myfile.jar * class
```

If your application or applet uses packages, then you'll need to do things a little differently. Suppose your classes were in the package mycode.games.CoolGame - you'd change to the directory above mycode and type the following :- (Remember to use /on UNlXsystems)

```
jar -cf myfile.jar .\mycode\gamesCooIGame\*.class
```

Now, if you have an existing JAR file, and want to extract it, you'd type the following

```
jar -xf myfile.jar
```

Working with JAR files isn't that difficult, especially if you've used the Unix 'tar' command before. If you're planning on packaging an applet for Internet Explorer, or an application for Microsoft's review, you might also want to consider .CAB files.

Q.115. How can I convert my Java classes to an executable .EXE file for Windows?

Ans. This is a very common question asked in the comp.lang.java newsgroup. Its often useful to have an executable application when deploying your applications to a specific platform, but remember to make your .class files available for users running Unix/Macintosh/other platforms.

Microsoft used to provide a free system development kit (SDK), for Java, which includes the jexegen tool. This will convert class files into a .EXE form. The only disadvantage is that users need a Microsoft Java Virtual Machine (JVM) installed. Microsoft no longer supports this however, and you should transition to a new Win 32 Java system. See http://java.sun.com/ for the latest version of a Java interpreter for Winodws.

Though I've not used these tools personally, others have recommended Visual Age for Java, and Duckware's Java to Windows EXE (Java2Exe) application available from http://www.duckware.cori/j ava2exe/index.html.

JAVA PRACTICAL LAB

(SET – I)

Q.1. Create a switch statement that prints a message for each case, and put the switch inside a for loop that tries each case. Put a break after each case and test it, then remove the breaks and see what happens.

Ans.
```
class  Switchjava  {
public static void main( String args[])
{
int value=IntegerparseInt(args[0]);
for(int i=value;i<5;i++)
{
switch(i)
{
case 1 :System .out.println("Ajay");
case 2:System .out.printIn('Kumar");
break;
case 3:System.out.printIn("JAVA");
break;
default:System .out.prinIn('PROGRAMMER");
break:
}
}
}
}
```

Q.2. Create a class called Tank that can be filled and emptied, and has a termination condition that it must be empty when the object is cleaned up. Write a finalize() that verifies this termination condition. In main(), test the possible scenarios that can occur when your Tank is used.

Ans.
```
class  Tank
{
double tcap=100;
double temp=0;
protected void finalize(int x)
{
if(tcap<x)
{
System.out.printIn("Tank is Overflow");
}
else if(tcap==x)
{
```

```
System.out.println("Tank is Full");
double tfill=tcap-x;
System.out.println("Tank is now empty");
}
Else
}
System .out.println("Tank is empty by"+" "+-( 10-x));
{
}
}
}
class TankExa
{
public static void main(String arg[])
{
Tank tl=new Tank();
int i=Integer.parselnt(arg[O]);tl.finalize(i);
}
}
```

Q.3. Prove that the base-class constructors are always called and called before derived-class constructors.

Ans.

```
class ConBase
{
int i;
int j;
ConBase( )
{
i=10;
j=20;
System.out.println("i=".i);
System .out.println("j="+j);
}
}
class ConDer extends ConBase
int n;
int m;
ConDeri( )
{
n=10;
m=219;
System .out. println("n="+n);
System.out.pnintln("m="+m)
```

```
}
}
class ConsExa
{
public static void main(String args[])
{
ConDeri nl=new ConDen();
}
}
```

Q.4. Create a class with two constructors. Using this, call the second constructor inside the first one.

Ans.
```
class Cim
{
int i;
int j;
Cim( )
{
this.i= 10;
this .j=20;
System .out.println("i="+i);
System .out.println("j"+j);
}
cim(int x, int y)
{
i=x;
j=y;
system.out.printIn("i="+i);
system.out.printIn("j="+j);
this.cim();
}
}
class Consjava {
public static void main( String args[])
{
Cim nl=new Cim(20,10);
//Cim n2=new Cim();
}
}
```

Q.5. Create a program to copy of one file into other file.

Ans.
```
import javaio.*;
class Fileja1 {
```

```
public static void main(String arg[]) throws IOException
{
FileOutputStream fout;
FileInputStream f;
try
{
f=new FilenputStream ("rahul.java");
catch(FileNotFoundException e)
{
System.outprintln("File not found");
return;
}
try
{
fout=new FileoutputStream'("Jatin.java");
}
catch(FileNotFoundException e)
{
System.out.println("File open not found");
return;
}
int data;
try
{
do
{
data=f.read();
if(data!=-1)
fout.write(data);
System .out.println((char)data);
}while(data!=-1);
}
catch(IOException e)
{
} System.out.printIn ("File Error")
f.close();
fout.close();
}
```

Q.6. Create a class with a final method. Inherit from that class and attempt to override that method.

Ans. `class Anim`

```
{
final void meth()
{
System.out.println("ThiS is final method");
}
}
class Bnim extends Anim
{
void meth()
{
System .out.printIn ("Illegal");
}
class Finalexa
public static void main(String arg[])
{
Anim a=new Anim();
 Bnim b=new Bnim( );
 a.meth( );
b.meth();
}
}
```

Q.7. Create a base class with an abstract print() method that is overridden in a derived class. The overridden version of the method prints the value of an int variable defined in the derived class. At the point of definitions of this variable, give it a nonzero value. In the base-class constructor, call this method. In main() create an object of the derive type, and then call its print( ) method. Explain the results.

Ans.

```
abstract class SuperNim
{
abstract void print( );
SuperNim( )
{
print( );
}
}
class SubNim extends SuperNim
{
int n=5;
void print( )
{
System.out.println("n"="+n);
}
}
```

```
class InheNim
{
public static void main(String arg[])
{
SubNim s=new SubNim( );
s .print( );
}
}
```

Q.8. Write a program that generates 25 random int values. For each value, use an if-else statement to classify it as greater than, less than, or equal to a second randomly-generated value.

Ans.

```
class RandInt {
public static void main( String argsfl )
{
int value;
int a[]=new int [25];
for ( int counter = 1; counter <= 20; counter++)
{
value = (int) ( Math.random() * 6 );
a[counter]=value;
if ( a[counter]==a[counter-1] )
{
System.out.println("value is equal to previous");
}
else if( a[counter]>a[counter- 1])
{
System.out.println("value is greater than previous ");
}
else
System.out.println("value is less than previous ");
System .out.println(value);
}
}
}
```

Q.9. Write a program to find out number of space and number of word in string enter by keyboard.

Ans.

```
import java.io.*;
{
public static void main(String arg[])
throws IOException
```

```
{
char c;
inf s=0;
inf d=o;
InputStreamReader m=new InputStreamReader(System.in);
BufferedReader br =new BufferedReader(m);
System .out.println("Enter character 'q' to quit");
do
{
c=(char)br.read();
System .out.println(c);
}while(c!'q');
while(c!'q')
{
if(c! = "")
{
   d=d++;
            }
else
{
s=s++;
}
}
System.out.printIn("Total no of the sapace:" + s);
System.out.printIn ("Total no of the words :" +d);
}
}
```

SET-II

Q.1. Write a program to print message hello world.

Ans.
```
Class Intro
{
    Public static void main (String arg[])
    {
        System.out.println("Hello World");
    }
}
```

Q.2. Write a program to print command line arguments supplied by the programmer

Ans.
```
Class Command
    {
      public static void main (String arg [])
    {
      for (int i=0; i< arg.length; i++)
      {
         System.Out.println  (a[i]);
    }
  }
    }
```

Q.3. Write a program to concatenate two command line arguments supplied by the programmer.

Ans.
```
PROGRAM
Class Command1
    {
        public static void main (String arg[])
        {
            System.out.println(arg[0]+arg[1]) ;
        }
    }
```

Q.4. Write a program to calculate the sum of commandline arguments.

Ans.
```
Program
Class Sum
    {
        public static void main (string arg[])
        {
            int sum = 0;
            for (int i =0; i < arg.length; i++)
            {
```

```
                int num = Integer.parseInt(arg[i]);
                sum+ = num;
          }
          System.out.println("Sum is\t"+sum);
          }
     }
```

Q.5. Write a Program to find factorial of given command line number.

Ans. Program

```
Class Factorial
     {
  public static void main (String arg[])
     {
        int num = Integer.parseInt (arg[0]);
        int  fact = 1 ;
        for (int i = 1 ; i <=num; i++)
        {
        fact = fact * i;
        }
          System.out.println("Factorial of "+num+"is"+fact);
     }
   }
```

Q.6. Write a program to find the largest of 3 numbers

Ans. class largest

```
{
   public static void main (String arg[])
   {
      int large =0;
      int a = Integer.parseInt(arg[0]);
      int  b = Integer.parseInt (arg[1]);
      int c = Integer.parseInt(arg[2]);
      if (a>=b)
      {
         if (a>c)
         large=a;
         else
         large=c;
      }
         if (b>a)
      {
         if (b>c)
         large =b;
         else
```

```
        large=c;
      }
    System.out.println("The largest no is:"+large);
  }
    }
```

Q.7. Write a program to print real solutions of quadralic equation $ax^2 + bx + c = 0$,we take a, b & c as command prompt & use the formula.

Ans.
```
Calss quadratic
{
    public static void main (string arg[])
    {
            int a = Integer.parseInt (arg[0]);
            int b = Integer.parseInt (arg[1]);
            int c = Integer .parseInt (arg[2]);
             System.out.println ("quadratic equation is "+a+"X =
2+"+b+""x+"C+=0")
            int d = ((b*b)-(4×a×c×a×c));
            if (d<0)
        System.out.println("Real roots does not exist");
             if (d==0)
        System.out.println("equal real roots");
            if (d>=0)
        {
            double f = Math.sqrt (d);
            double x1 = ((-b)+f)/(2×a);
            double   x2 = ((-b)-f)/(2×a);
            System.out.println("Roots are "+χ1+""and"+χ2");
        }
    }
}
```

Q.8. Write a programe to print Fibonacci series till n^{th} value entered by user.

Ans.
```
Class Fibonacci
    {
        public static void main (string arg[])
        {
            int a = 0; b= 1; c=0;
            int n = Integer.parseInt (arg[0]);
            for (int i = 0; i< =n ;i++)
            {
                System.out.println(a);
                {
```

```
            c = a+b
            a = b;
            b = c:
        }
    }
  }
}
```

Q.9. Write a programe to find prime number till the nth, where 'n' is command prompt arguments by the user.

Ans.
```
class prime
  {
     public static void main(string arg[])
     int  n = Integer.parseInt (a[0]);
     int c =3 ;
     for (int i = 2; i<n; i++)
     {
        for (int  j = 2; j<c-1 ; j++)
        {
           if (c% j == 0)
           break;
        }
           if (j==c)
           {
                    System.out.println (c);
           }
           c++;
           }
        }
  }
```

Q.10. Write a program to check. Whether a string is palindrome or not using command prompt string.

Ans.
```
class Palindrom
  {
     public static void main (string arg[])
     {
        String S = arg  [0];
        int chk = 0, i = -I , k = s.length()-1, last = s.length()1;
        While (++i < K /2)
        {
           if (S.chratt(i)! = S.charAt (last--),
           Chk++;
```

```
            }
            if (chk==0)
            System.out.println("given command sequenceis palindromic");

        else
            System.out.println("given sequence is not palindromic");
    }
}
```

Q.11. Write a program that defines factorial class.describe its constructor.Overload constructor and instantiate its object.

Ans.

```
import java util.;
class factorial
{
    int n;
    factorial ()
    { n=1;}
    factorial (int n)
{    this n = n;
int calculate ()
    {
        int f = 1:
        for (int i = 1;i<n;i++)
    {    f = f *i:
    }
    returns (f);
}
voint show
}
    System. out. println ("number is "+n);
}
}
class fact
}
public static void main (string args[])
    {
Scanner sc = new Scanner (System.in);
        factorial obj1 = new factorial ();
        factorial obj2 = new factorial (5);
        obj1.show();
        System.out.println ("factorial is"+obj1.calculate());
        System.out.println("enter a number");
```

```
        obj1.n = sc.nextInt();
        System.out.println("factorial is "+obj1.calculate());
    }
}
```

Q.12. Write a program to define a complex class and perform arithmetic operation on 2 complex objects.

Ans.

```
class complex
    {
        float a,b;
        complex ()
        {  a = 0 ;
           b = 0;
        }
        complex (int a)
        }  b = a
           this. a = a ;
           this.b  =  b;
        }
        void show ()
        {  System. out .println (a+"i"+b); }
        complex add (complex C1 , complex c2),
        {
           complex c = new complex ();
           c.a = c1.a + c2.a ;
           c.b = c1.b + c2.b;
           return c ;
        }
    complex sub(complex c1, complex c2)
        {
           complex c = new complex ();
           c.a = c1.a - c2.a ;
           c.b = c1.b - c2.b;
           return c ;
        }
    complex mul(complex c1, complex c2)
        {
           complex c = new complex ();
           c.a = (c1.a * c2.a) - (c1.b * c2.b);
           c.b = (c1.a * c2.b) + (c1.b * c2.a);
           return c;
        }
```

```
    class Comp
  {
    public static voidmain (String args[]);
        {   complex ob = new complex () ;
      complex ob1 = new complex (5);
      complex ob2 = new complex (6,7);
      ob.show(); ob1.show(); ob2 show();
      ob = ob.add(ob1 , ob2);
      System.out.println("Sum is") ; ob.show();
      System.out.println("subtraction is");
      ob = ob.sub(ob1,ob2); ob.show();
      System.out.println("multiplication is");
      ob = ob.mul(ob1,ob2);ob.show();
    }
  }
```

Q.13. Write a programe that define matrix clam perform multiplication of 2 matrices.

Ans.

```
import  java.util  *;
class Matrix
{  int m [][] = new int [2][2];
   Matrix () {}
   void init ()
   {  scanner sc = new scanner (System.in);
      System.out.println ("enter values in matrix");
      for (int i = 0; i<2;  , i++)
      {  for(int j = 0; j<2; j++)
         { m [i][j] = sc.nextInt();} }
   {
   void show ()
   { System.out.println("matrix is");
        for (int i = 0 ; i<2 ; i++)
        { for (int j = 0; j<2; j++)
      {System.out.println(m[i][j]);        }                }
 }
Matrix mul (Matrix x, Matrix y )
   { Matrix Z = new Matrix();
      for (int i = 0; i<2; i++)
      for (int j = 0; j<2; j++)
      for (int k =0; k<2; k++)
         z.m [i][j]+ = x.m[i][k]*y.m [k][j];
      return z ;
   }
 }
```

```
    class Matrix_Demo
{
        public static void main (String args [])
    {
        Matrix a = new Matrix ();
        System.out.println("the o/p is");
        Matrix b = new Matrix ();
        a.init();
        b.init();
        a.show()
        b.show();
        Matrix c = new Matrix ();
        c = c.mul (a,b);
        c.show();
    }
}
```

Q.14. WAP that creater date class. Describe its constructor for instantiating instance variable one method named day Since jan 1 () that compute and return the no. of days since jan 1 of same year.

Ans.
```
import  java.util.scanner;
class date
{  int date, month year;
   date (int d, int m, int yr)
   {  day = d ;
      month=m;
      year = yr ;
   }
   int daysSincejanone()
   {  int cal = 0;
      year++;month++;day++;
      while (--year>2013)
           cal+=365;
      while (--month>1)
      { if (months-1==3¦¦month-1==5¦¦month-1==7¦¦month-1==8¦¦month-
1==10¦¦month-1==12)
         cal+=31;
         else if (month-1==2)
         cal+=28;
         else
            cal+=30;
      }
```

```
        while  (--day>0)
                cal++;
        return cal ;
    }
    public static void main (String args ())
    Scanner sc = new scanner (System.in);
    System.out.printIn ("enter day");
    int  j = sc.nextint();
    System.out.println("enter month");
    int j = sc . nextInt ()
    System.out.println("enter years");
    int k = sc .nextInt ();
    Date d = new Date (i,j,k);
    d.daysSinceJanOne();
    System.out.println("total number of days are:
  "+d.daysSincejanOne()");
    }
    }
```

Q.15. WAP to define on employee class perform constructor overloading.

Ans.
```
class  employee
{
    int id;
    int sal:
    employee()
    {
        System out.println ("Default Coustructor");
        id =0; sal = 0;
    }
    employee (int id, int sal)
    {
        System. out.println ("Parametrized coustructor");
        this.id = id;
        this.sal = sal;
    }
    employee (employee e)
    {
        id = e.id;
        sal = e.sal;
    }
    void show ()
    {
        System.out.println("employee id is "+id");
```

```
        System.out.println("employee salary is "+sal");
    }
}
class emp
    {
        public static void main(String arg [])
        {
            employee el = new employee ();
            el.show();
            employee e2 = new employee (21,2000);
            e2.show;
            employee e3 = neew employee (e2);
            e3.show ();
        }
}
```

Q.16. WAP that write line of integer and display each integer & sum of each integer.

Ans.

```
import java.util.*;
class ReadInteger
    {
        public static void main (String args[])
        {   Scanner sc = new scanner (System.in);
            intz [] = new int [5]
            int sum = 0 ;
            System.out.println ("enter the line of integer ");
            int n = sc. nextInt ();
            for (int i = 0; i<5; i++)
            {   z[i] = n%10;
                sum = sum+z[i];
                n=n/10;
            }
            for (int i =4; i>=0; i--)
            {
System.out.println("the line of integer is "+2(i));
            }
        System.out.println("the sum is"+sum);
    }
}
```

Q.17. Wap to demonstrate the use of Nested class.

Ans.

```
import java.utill.*;
class outer {int a, b;
{   class Inner
```

```
    { int c;
      void in ()
      {
         Scanner sc = new Scanner (System.in);
         System.out.println("enter a");
         a = sc.nextInt ();
         System.out.println("enter b");
         b = sc.nextInt ();
      }
      int sum ()
      { c = a+b ;
      return c;
      }
    }
void show()
    {
      Inner inner = new Inner (); //inner variable are not accesible
      inner.in();
      System.out.println("daight enter is "+a);
      System.out.println ("digit enter is"+b);
      System.out.println("sum is"+inner.sum());
    }
}
    class Demo
    {
      public static void main (String args [])
      {
         System.out.println("I'm main");
         Outer ox = new outer ()
         ox.show();
    }
}
```

Q.18. Wap to demonstrate the use of static keyword.

Ans.

```
input java .util.*;
class static
    { int a = 9;
      static int b = 4 ;
      static
         { int c = 29 ;//variable declared in static block is static
            System.out.println ("I'm static Block"+b+"+c);
         }
      static void show ()//static method can acces static function
```

```
        { Scanner sc = new Scanner (System.in);
          System.out.println(b+"");
          b = Sc.nextInt();
//value of static vanable can be charged
          System.out.println("b entered is"b);
        }
    public static void main (String args[])
    {
       System.out.println("Inside main");
       static.obj= new static ();
       obj.show();
       }
    }
```

Q.19. WAP to display of the characters, words and lines.

Ans.
```
import java.util. *;
class CalculateString
String S;
Void enter ()
{  Scanner sc = new Scanner (System.in);
   S = sc.next line ();                                          }
void calculate ()
{  chase arr [] = new char [200];
   arr = s.tocharArray ();
   System.out.println("the total no.of char are"+ arr.length);
   int line = 1, words = 0;
   for (int i = 0; i<arr.length;i++)
   {  if (arr[i]=='.')
         line++;
      else if (arr[i]=='')
         words++; }
         words ++;
      System.out.println ("total lines are ;"+line");
      System.out.println ("total no.of words:"+words);
   }
public static void main (String args[])
   {
   CalculateString ob = new CalculateString();
   ob.enter();
   ob.calculate ();
   System.out.println("\n\texecuted BY Jasmeet Kaur");
   }
}
```

Q.20. Create a class 2D shape with constructors and accessor methods for instance members height, width, name. Also create sub class circle.

Ans.
```
class  shape2D
{  double height , width;
   string name;
      shape 2D() {}
      shape 2D (double h, double w, string s)
      {  height = h;
         width=w;
         name = s;    }
      void setheight (double height)
         { this.height = height;                                    }
      void getweight (double width)
         { this.width = width ;                                     }
      double getheight ()
         { returnheight;                                            }
      double getwidth ;                                             }
         { return width;                                            }
      String getname ()
         { return name ;}
}
class Circle extends shape2D
{
   double r;
   Circle (){}
Circle ( double h , double w, String S, double r)
{  super (h,w,s);
   this.r = r; }
double getarea ()
{  System.out.println ("the area is"+(3-14*r*r);
   return 0;
}
}
Class ShapeDemo
{
   public static Void main (String args[])
   {
      Shape2D obj = new Shape2D (3.1,2"ABC");
      Circle ob = new Circle (12.5,33,"triangle",5);
      System.out.println("Name is"+ob.getname();
      System.out.println("with is"+ob.getwidth());
      System.out.println ("height is "+ob.getheight ());
```

```
        ob.getarea();
      }
    }
```

Q.21. To demonstrate the use of final key word.

Ans.
```
final class Great
{  int a,b,c ;
   Greate () {}
   Greate (int x, int y, int z)
   {  a = x;
      b = y ;
      c = z ;  }
   final double largest ()
      {
   if (a > =b)
      {  if (a>c)
         return a ;
         else return c ; }
      if (b>a)
         {  if (b>c)
            return b ;
            else return c;                                    }
      else return 0;
}

class Great1 // extends Great, final Class can't be inherited
{
   final double pi = 3.14 ;
   int r ;
   Great (int r )
   {  this . r =r ;
   }
      double largest ()
      {  return (pi *r *r); }
}
class GreatDemo
{
   public static void main (String args [])
   {
      Great ob = new Great (1,100-0);
      System.out.println("the largest no. from"+ob.a+"+ob.b+"and
+ob.C=")
```

```
        Great1 ob1 = new Great1 (2);
        radius "+ob1.r+"is"ob1.largest ();
        System.out.println ("executed by Jasmeen")
    }
}
```

Q.22. To demonstrate the use of abstract class.

Ans.
```
abstract class employee
{
    double salary;
    abstract double income (double s);
    void show ()
    {  System. out println ("inside Abstract class":); }
}
class Manager extends employee
{  double income (double sal)
    {  salary = sal ;
       return salary ; }
       void disp ()
       { System .out.println ("its an implemented subclass");
       }
}
class employeeDemo
{
    public static void main (String args [])
    {
        Manager obj = new Manager ();
        obj.show ();
        System.out.println("the salary of a manager is "+obj.income
(12,500));
        obj. disp();
        System.out.println ("execnted by Jasmeen");
    }
}
```

Q.23. Create abstract class 2D shape with method area. Define its constructors, accesor methods and abstract methods. Also creat sub class of 2D shape class as triangle, rectangle and circle using DYNAMIC DISPATCH.

Ans.
```
abstract class Shape2D
{  double height,width;
   String name ;
   Shape2D () {}
   Shape2D (double h, double w, string s)
```

```
    {  height = h ; width = w ; name = s ; }
       void setheight (double h)
          {  height = h ; }
       double getheight ()
          {  return height ;
       void setwidth (double w);
          {  width = w ; }
       double getwidth ()
          {  return width ; }
          string getname ()
             {  return name ; }
          abstract double area ();
}
class Rectangle extends Shape2D
{  Rectangle ()   {}
   Rectangle (double h , double w, String s)
   { super (h,w,s); }
   double area ()
      {  return (height * width); }
}
class circle extends shape2D
{  int r ; final double pi = 3.14 ;
   circle (int r)
   {  this.r = r ;   }
   double area ()
   {  return (pi*r*r);
}
class Triangle extends shape2D
{  Triangle (double h , double w, String S)
   {     super (h,w,s);
   double area ()
   {  return (0.5*width*height); }
}
class Shape 2Demo
{  public static void main (String args[])
      shape 2Dref ;
      Rectangle r = new Rectangle (10,20, "rect");
      Circle   c = new Circle (2);
      Triangle t = new Triangle (4,6,"right triangle");
      ref = r ;
      System.out.println("the area is ""+ref.area());
```

```
        ref = t;
        System.out.println("the area is "+ref.area());
        ref = t ;
        System.out.println("the arrea is "+ref.area());
    }
}
```

Q.24. To implement producer consumer problem using concept of Inter thread communication.

Ans.
```
Class Q
    {  int n ;
       boolean valueSet = false ;
       Synchronized int get ()
       {  if (! Value set)
          try { wait ();}                                    }
          catch (Exception e)
          {  System.out.println("Interpted exception");       }
             System.out.println ("got"+n);
             valueSet = false ;
             notify ;
             return n ;
          }
          synchronized void put (int n)
          {
             if (valueSet )
                  try { wait ();}
             catch (interuptedException ie)
             {
          this.n = n;
          valueSet = true;
          System.out.println ("put"+n);
          notify ();  }
 }
 class Producer implements Runnable
 {  Qq;
    Producer (Q q)
    {  this.q = q ;
       new Thread  (this,"producer".start ()};}
    public void run ()
    {  int i = 0
       while (true)
       {  q.put (i++);}}
```

```
}
class Consumer implements Runnable
{  Q q ;
   Consumer (Qq)
   { this.q =q;
      new Thread (this,"consumer".start ()};}
   public void run ()
   {  int i = 0 ;
      while (true)
      {  q.get ();}  }
}
Class PCFixed
{  public static void main (string ary {})
   {
   Qq = new Q ();
   new Producer (q);
   new Consumer (q);
   sysyem.out.printIn ("Press class-c to stop");
      {  q.get(); }
   }
}
```

Q.25. To create three threads by extending thread class. First thread display "Good Morning" enemy 1 sec then "Hello" display every 2 Sec and "Welcome" at 3 secs.

Ans.

```
Class HelloThread extends Thread
{  string name ;
   long time ; thread t ;
   HelloThread (String n , long trn)
   {  name = n ; time = trn;
      t = new Thread (this, name);
      System.out.println("new Thread"+t);
      +.start ();
   }
   public void run ()
   {
      try {
         for (int i = 5; i>0; i--)
            {  System.out.println(""+name);
            }  +.Sleep (time);
         catch (Interputed_Exception ie)
            {
               System.out.println(name+"Interupted"+e);
```

```
            }
        }
    }
Class HelloDemo Thread
    {
        public static void main (String arg[]) {
        new HelloThread ("good morning",1000);
        new HelloThread ("hello",2000);
        new helloThread ("welcome",3000);
        try {
            Thread.sleep (15000);
        }
        catch (InteruptedException e)
        {
            System.out.println("main Thread Interupted");
        }
        System.out.println ("Exiting main Thread");
    }
}
```

Q.26. Implement previous program by Implementing Runnable.

Ans.

```
Class HelloThread implement Runnable
{
    String str;
    Thread t ;
    HelloThread()
    { t = newThread (this, name);
        t.start();
    }
    public void run ()
        try {
            for (int i = 0 ; i < 5; i ++)
            {
            str = Thread.currentThread ().get Name();
            if (str.equals ("Good Morning"))
            { System.out.println (str);
            Thread.sleep(1000);
            }
            if(str.equal("hello"))
            { System.out.println (str);
             Thread.Sleep (2000);
            }
            if (str.equal("welcome"))
```

```
            {
                System.out.println(str);
                Thread.sleep (3000);
            }
        }
    }
}
    catch (InterruptedException e)
    {
        System.out.println ("interrupted exception");
} }
class HelloDemoThread
{
    public static void main (String args[])
    {
        HelloThread H1 = New HelloThread ();
        HelloThread H2 = new HelloThread ();
        HelloThread H3 = new HelloThread ();

        Thread t1 = new Thread (H1);
        Thread t2 = new Thread (H2);
Thread t3 = new Thread (H3);

t1. setName ("Good Morning");
t2. setName ("Hello");
t3. setName ("Welcome");
}
    }
```

Q.27. To create two threads : One for odd number of others for even number.

Ans.

```
Class MyThread extends Thread
    { public void run ()
        { int o = 1, e = 2;
            String str ;
            for (int i =0; i<5,i++)
            { str.Thread.currentThread ().getName();
                if (str.equals ("odd"))
                {System.out.println(str+"/n"+0); 0+=2; }
                if (str.equals("even"))
                { System.out.println(str"/n"+e);e+=2; }
            }
        }
    }
```

```
Class oddEven
{
    public static main (String arg[])
    {
        MyThread t1 = new MyThread ();
        MyThread t2 = new Mythread ();
        t1.setName("odd")
t2.set Name("even");
t1.start (); t2.start();
System,out.println("\n\t= executed by Jasmeet Kaur");
        }
    }
```

Q.28. To write Applet that displays a simple message.

Ans.

```
        import java.awt.*;
        import java.applet.*;
        /*<applet code="Message" height =200 width = 300>
<1 applet> */
public class Message extends Applet
{ string S;
        public void init ();
        {  s = "Inside init()";
        setBackground (color.CYAN);
        }
        public void start ()
        {
        s= s+"inside start ()";
        public void paint (Graphics g)
        {
            s= s+"inside paint ()Welcome!!";
            g.drawString (5,10,30);
            showstatus ("simple Message");
        }
    }
```

Q.29. To print a moving banner using Applet

Ans.

```
import java.awt.*;
import java.applet.*
/*<applet code ="BannerA" width = 300 height = 100></applet>*/
public class BannerA extands Applet implement Runnable
{  String s = "A moving Banner";
   Thread t = null;
   boolean stopflag;
```

```
    public void start ()
    {
        t = new Thread (this);
        stopflag = false;
        t.start();
    }
  public void run ()
    {
        char ch ;
        for (;;)
        { try {
                repaint ();
                Thread.sleep(200);
                ch = s.CharAt(0);
                s = s.substring (i,S,length());
                s = s+ch;
                if (stopflag) break;
            }
            catch (InterruptedException e)
                {  {
        }
    }
    public void stop ()
        { stopflag = true ;
        t = null;
    }
    public void paint (Graphics g)
    {
        g.drawstring (s,10,20);
        showstatus ("my status");
    }
}
```

Q.30. To create a parameterized banner by using applet.

Ans.

```
import java.awt.*;
import java.applet.*;
/*<applet code = "Banner Param "width = 300 height = 200>
<Param name = "Message" value = "think Before You speak">
</applet>*/
public class Banner Param extends Applet implements Runnable
{ String msg; Thread t=null; boolean stopflag;
   public void start ()
```

```
    {  msg = getParameter ("Message");
       if (msg == null)
             msg = "not found";
             msg = '''+msg;
       t = new Thread (this); t.start();
       stopflag = false;
 }
    public void run ()
 {  char ch ;
    for(; ;)
       { try { repaint ();
             Thread.sleep(200);
             ch = msg.charAt(0);
              msg = msg.substring(1,msg.length())
                    msg += ch; if (stopflag) break ;}
       catch (exception e){}
    }
 }
 public void paint (Graphics g)
 {
    g.drawstring (msg 10,20);
 }
    }
```

Q.31. WAP to read a file and display the file on screen with line number before each file.

Ans.

```
import java.io.*;
class file
{
   public static void main (String args[])
      {
         FileReader fr = new FileReader (arg[0]);
         BufferredReader br = new Buffered Reader (fr);
         String s;
         int i = 0;
         while ((s = br.readline())!= null)
         {
            i ++
            System.out.println(+i+""+s);
         }
         fr.close ();
         }
      }
```

Q.32. WAP that read a file name from user and display information about file existence, readable or writable.

Ans.
```
import java.io. * ;
class file10
   {
      static void println (String s)
      {
         System.out.println(s);
      }
      public static void main (string args[])
      {
         File f1 = new file(args [0]);
         printit("File Name;"+f1.getName()");
         printit(f1.exists()?;"exists":"does not exists");
         printit(f1.canWrite ()?"is writable":"is not write");
         printit (f1.canRead()?"is variable":"is not ");
         printit (f1.isFile ()?"is normal file":"may be");
         printit ("File Size"+f1.length()+"Bytes");
      }
   }
```

Q.33. WAP to output question "who is PM of India ?" and accept answer and print "correct" or "incorrect". Allow 3 attempts and then finally display the answer.

Ans.
```
import java.util.*;
class inquiz
{
   static int trial = 1 ;
   static string ans = "Narender Modi";
   public static void main (String arg[])
   {
      String s ;
      Scanner sc = new Scanner (System .in);
      System.out.println ("q.who is the Prime  Minister of India");
      while (trial<4)
      {
         s=sc.nextLine();
         if (s.equalsIgnorecase(ans))
            {
               System.out.println("Correct Answer");
               break;
            }
            else
```

```
                    System.out.println("Correct Answer");
                    break;
                }
                else
                    System.out.println("wrong Answer");
                    trial++;
                }
                is (trial== 4)
                {  System.out.println("Correct Answer"tans);
                }
        }
    }
```

Q.34. WAP to draw lines rectangles and ovals.

Ans.

```
        import java.applet.*;
        import java.awt.*;
    /*<applet code = "Rect"height = 200 width = 400>
    <applet>*/
    public class Rect extends Applet
    {
        public void init ()
        { setBackground (color.CYAN);}
        public void paint (Graphics g)
            {
                g.drawString ("Figures",10,20);
                g.drawRect (20,20,60,50);
                g.fillRect  (100,20,60,50);
                g.drawRound Rect (70,90,140,100,30,40);
                g.drawoval(400,300,20,30);
                g.filloval (200,200,50,60);
                g.drawline(10,10,200,200);
                g.drawline(30,30,150,350);
            }
    }
```

Q.35. Write an applet that computer payment of loan based on the amount of loan, rate and time.

Ans.

```
        import java.applet.*;
        import java.awt.*;
        import java.awt.event.*;
    /*<applet code = "Loan" width = 150 height = 300><applet>*/
        public class Loan extends Applet implements Actionlistner
        {  Text Field Prim, rate, time;
            Label h,r,t ans;
```

```
        Button.b1;string msg ;
        public void init ()
        {  b1 = new Button ("Click");
           p  = new Label ("enter Principle in Rs");
           r  = new Label (enter rate (heronaun));
           t  = new Label ("enter time in years");
           prim = new Textfield (10);
           rate = new Textfield(10);
           ans = new Label ("Ans");
           add (p);add (prim); add(r),add(rate);
           add (t),add (time);
           add (b1);
           add (ans);
     b1.addActionListener (this);
  }
  public void actionPerformed (ActionEvent ae)
     if (ae.getsource == b1)
        {  double s1,s2,s3,S;
  s1=Double.parseDouble(prim.getText());

        s2 = Double.parseDouble (rate.getText());
        s3 = Double.parseDouble (time.getText());
        s = s1+(s1*s2*s3*)/100);
           msg = "the amount is"+5;
        }
        else msg = "invalid output";
        ans.setText (msg);
     }
     public void paint (Graphics g)
        {
           g.drawString ("Loan",10,10);
        }
  }
```

Q.36. To develop a program to display table using swings.

Ans.

```
import java.awt.*;
import javax.swing.*;
/*<applet code = "JTableDemo"width = 400 height = 200>
</apet>*/
public class TableDemo extends JAplet
{
      public void.init()
      {  container content Pane = getContentPane ();
```

```
        Content Pane.setLayout (new Border Layout ());
        final string [] colHeads = ("rolNo","Name","Stream";)
        final object [] [] data = {
           { "10", "Simran","Cse","82"};
           { "32", "Priya", "ece" ,"76"};
        };
     JTable table = new JTable (data, colHeads);
  contentPane.add(jsp,BorderLayout;
     }
}
```

Q.37. To write on application for calculate using grid bag layout.

Ans.

```
import javax.swing.*;
import java.awt.*;
import java.awt.event.*;
public class Calculator extends Jframe implements ActionListener
{  JTextfield t = new JTextField();
   JButton []b = new Button [16];
   String [] buttonString = ("7","8","9","+";"4","5","6","-
","1";"2";"3";"x";"/")
   Calculator()
   {  setTitle ("Calculator");
      JPanel p = new JPanel (new GridBagLayout());
      GridBagContraints c = new GridBag Layoutconstraints();
      add (p) , p.setBackground (Color.CYAN);
      p.add(t,c);
      c.fill = GridBagConstraints.HORIZONTAL;
      for (int i = 0; i<16;i++)
      {  c.ipadx = 20; c.ipady = 15;
         c.insets = new insets (5,5,5,5);
         if ((i)%4 == 0) { c.gridy +=1;}
         b[i] = new JButton();
         b[i].setText (buttonString[i]);
         b[i].addActionLister (this);
         p.add (b[i],c);
      }
      setVisible(true);
   }
public void actionPerformed (ActionEvent ae)
{  String BtnCmd = ae .getAction Command ();
   System.out.println (btn.Cmd);
   processCmd (btnCmd);
}
```

```
public void processCmd (String)
    { Switch (S)
      { case"0": ; case"1":  ; case"2":  ; case "3": ;
        case "4": ; case "5":  ; case "6":  ; case "8":  ;
      if (opLock)
        { t.setText (" ");
          op.Lock = false ;}
          String tf = t .getText();
             tf = tf+s;
             t.setText (tf);
             break;
          Case "C": +.setText("")break;
          Case "+": operatorCmd ("+");break;
          Case"-" : operatorCmd ("-");break;
          Case "*": operatorcmd ("*");break;
          Case "/": operatorcmd ("/"); break;
          case "=" : operatorEval ();
        }
      public void operatorCmd (String S)
        {int n1 = Integer.parseInt (t.getText());
             currentoperator=s;currentoperand=n1;
             opLock = true : ?
      public static void main(String args[])
        {  new Calculator();
        }
    }
```

Q.38. Write a programe to demonstrate the use of URL Connection.

Ans.

```
import java net .*;
public class
  {
     public static void main (String []args)
     throws malformedURLException
     {
        URL hp = new URL ("http ://www.facebook.com/login.php");
        System.out.println ("Protocol:"=hp.getProtocol());
        System.out.println ("port:"+hp.getPort());
        System.our.println("Host:"+hp.getHost());
        System.out.println("file:"+hp.getField());
        System.out.println("ext:"+hp.getField());
        System.out.println("Ext:"+hp.toExtenalform());
     }
  }
```

Q.39. To develop a program to demonstrate the use of tabbed panes in swing.

Ans.

```
import.javax.swing.*;
import.java.awt.*;
import java.out.event.*;
public class MyPanes extends JFrame
   {  JTextField t1,t2;
      JTabbedPane t1;
      {
         setTitle ("Tabbed Panes Demo");
         tp = new JTabbedPane (JTabbedPane.Top);
         tp.add Tab3 ("Tabl", new JLabel ("This is the First
                                                   label"));
         tp.addTab ("Tab2"new JLabel ("This is Second Label"));
         tp.addTab("Tab3",New JLabel("This is Third Label"));
         add (tp);
         tp.setBounds (10,10,450,250);
         setLayout (Null);
         SetSize (490,310);
         SetDefault CloseOperation (JFrame.Exit_on_Cross)
         setVisible (true);
      }
   public static void main (string args [])
      {
         new MyPanes ();
      }
   }
```

Q.40. To develop a program demostrating the use of generic servlet class.

Ans.

```
import java.i0.*;
import javax.servelet.*;
public class first extends generic
   {
   public void Service (ServeletRequest req ServeletResponse res)
   throws JoException,ServeletException
   {  res.setContentType ("Text/html");
      printlnWriter out = res.getWriter ();
      out.print("<html><body>");
      out.print("<b> hello.generic servlet <\b>");
      out.println ("</body></html>");
   }
}
```

Q.41. To Develop a programe demonstrating the use of HTTPServlet Class.

Ans.

```
import javax.servlet.*;
import javax.servlet.http.*;
import java.io.*;
import java.util.Enumeratrom ;

public class QueryStringServlet extends Http Servlet
  { public  void doGet (Http ServletRequest req, HttpServletResponse
res) throw Exception
    { res.set ContentType ("text/html");
      printwriter out = res.getWriter();
      String s[] = req.getParameterValues ("neyo");
      if (S! = null)
        { int C=s.length;
          for (int i =0;i<l;i++)
          out.println (s[i]+"<br>");
          }
        String r = req.getPathInfo ();
        String r1 = req.getPathTranslated ();
        String r2 = req.getPathQueryString ();
        String r3 = req.getRequestURI();
        String r4 = req.getServletPath();
        out.println ("getPathInfo:"+r+<br>getPath Translated:
"+r1+"<br>get Query String: "r2+"<br>getRequestURI:"+r3+<br>get
ServletPath : "r4);
          }
    }
```

Q.42. To develop a program to set the given string in a desired font and color (font: Arial, Bold, 20)

Ans.

```
import javax.swing.*;
import java.awt.*;
import java.awt.event.*;
public class fontChanger implements ActionListener
{  JButton b1, b2;
   JTextField f;
   JLabel l ;
   fontChanger ()
   { JFrame f = new JFrame ("FontChanger");
     JButton b = new JButton ("Change Font");
     l = new JLabel();
     b.addActionListener(this);
```

```
        l.SetBounds (50,50,300,50);
        f.add (l); f.add (b);f.setSize(500,400);
        f.setVisible (true);
    public void actionPerformed (ActionEvent ae)
    {  Font f = new font ("Arial"; Font Bold;20);
        l.setFont (f);
        l.setForeground (Color.Green);
        l.setHorizontalAssignment(SwingConstants(ENTER))
    }
    public static void main (string args[])
    {
        new fontChanger (); }
    }
```

Q.43. To develop a program to design form having 2 textfulders and a button having swing components.

Ans.

```
import javax .swing.*;
import java .awt.*
import java.awt.event.*;
public class MyPro extends Jframe
{  JTextField t1, t2 ;
   MyPro ()
   {  t1 = new JtextField();
      JButton b = new Jbutton ("Click");
      b.setBounds(90,100,100,30);
      add(b);
      b. addAction Listener (new ActionListener);
      {  JOptionPane. showMessageDialog (rootPane,"Hello"
+t1.getText()+""+t2.getText ());
      }
      }
    t1.SetBounds (20,40,100,30);
    t2.SetBounds (140, 40, 100, 30)
    add(t1);add (t2);
    SetLayout (Null);
    SetSize (300,200);
    SetDefault Close Operation (Jframe.Exit_On-Gross)
    SetVisible (true);
    }
    public static void main (String arg [])
    {
       new MyPro ();}
}
```

Question Papers

Object Oriented Programming Using Java

Minor I

MCA - I Year (DELHI UNIVERSITY)

Time: 1 Hour Max. Marks: 25

1. Consider the following code segment. Find the error(s) if any and produce the output. Also explain your answer. (2 × 7)

(i)
```
byte b==110;
b=b* 2;
System.out.println("b"+b);
```

(ii)
```
int x=5;
System . out. println(x++)
int y=x; System.out.println("y"+y);
```

(iii)
```
int b=-156;
byte x =b;
System.out.println("x'+x);
System.out.println("b"+b);
```

(iv)
```
int i=3,j=6,k;
k=++i + j++ +3
System.out.println ("k"+k);
```

(v)
```
int i=5;
char c=15;
char d=i;
System.out.println("c"+c);
System.out.println("d"+d);
```

(vi)
```
double d= 23.34;
int i =d;
System.out.println("i"+i);
```

(vii)
```
int i=10;
char c=30;
double d=34.60
System.out.println((i+c+d));
```

2. Consider the following code segment and give the output. (3)

```
public static void main()
  {
     int j=45:
  {
     int i=10;
     System.out.println("i="+i);
  {
     int i = 23;
     System.out.println("i="+i);
     System.out.println("j="+j);
  }
```

3. Why is java called Platform Independent? Explain. (3)

MCA - Ist Sem.

Object Oriented Programming

Time: 1 Hour　　　　　　　　　　　　　　　　　　　　　　　　Max. Marks: 20

1. Write the output of the following code segments: (2 × 4)

(i)
```
int a=10,b=1;
a>>b+3
```

(ii)
```
int a=5,b=2, c=7;
a¦4+c>>b&7;
```

(iii)
```
int i=10,b=5;
if (i=j)
System.out.println("Condition satisfied"):
else
System.out.println("Condition not satisfied");
```

(iv)
```
int i=1;
s witch(i)
  case 0:
     System. out.println("Value of i is zero.");
  case 1:
     System.out.println("Value of i is one.");
  case 2:
     System.out.println("Value of i is two.");
  case 3:
     System.out.println("Value of i is three.");
  default:
     System.out.println("Vaiue of i is greater than three");
}
```

2. (a) Differentiate between overloading and overriding with the help of suitable example. (3 + 3)

(b) Design a class person having attributes name, age and address. Design various constructors to initialize the data of the class. Also write a member function Display () to display class data. (3)

GGSIPU, Delhi

End-Term Exams.

5th Sem., (B.Tech–CSE/IT), Dec. 2012

JAVA PROGRAMMING

Time: 3 Hours Max. Marks: 75

1.(a) What is use of System.gc( )?

(b) When a variable and class is called a 'final'? And what is its use?

(c) What are wrapper classes?

(d) Give some four methods of string buffer class.

(e) Why string objects are considered to be immutable?

(f) How does subclass call its base class constructors? Give example.

(g) Why multiple inheritances of classes is not there in java?

(h) What is the use of throw and throws clause?

(i) Why should the sleep ( ) method of thread class be enclosed in a try catch block?

(j) What is URL and give its format? (1.5 × 10 = 15)

UNIT-I

2.(a) Explain Abstract classes with an example program. Also, describe the properties of abstract classes? How is it different from interfaces? (7.5)

(b) What is a Package? Explain the Packages with an example and how to import packages. Explain the compiliation of a newly designed package. (7.5)

3.(a) Explain constructor overloading with an example. Also, describe the usage of super keyword. (7.5)

(b) Is there multiple inheritances in Java? If not, whether there is an alternative to implement multiple inheritances? (7.5)

UNIT-II

4.(a) Explain Inter Threads Communication and suspending, resuming and stopping threads. (7.5)

(b) Explain the concept of streams and about stream classes and classification. (7.5)

5. Design and implement a multithreaded client/server application in java, in which multiple clients send an integer to server, server find the cube of number, and return it to individual clients. (15)

UNIT-III

6.(a) What is Event Handling? Explain the various layout manager and menus. (7.5)

(b) Give the concept of adapter and inner classes. (7.5)

7.(a) What is a Servlet and what are the types of Servlets? (7.5)

(b) What is the need to go for Java Beans? (7.5)

UNIT-IV

8.(a) What is DTD? Explain its use. (7.5)

(b) Explain object models and collections using DHTML in detail. (7.5)

9.(a) Explain event model of dynamic HTML in detail. (7.5)

(b) How we can handle the multimedia data in HTML? (7.5)

GGSIPU, Delhi

End-Term Exams

5th Sem., (B.Tech–CSE/IT), Dec. 2013

JAVA PROGRAMING

Paper Code: ET1T303 Subject: Java Programming & Website Design

Time: 3 Hours Max. Marks: 75

Note: Q. No. 1 is compulsory. Attempt any four questions of remaining. (5 × 3 = 15)

Q.1. (i) Explain compare to () & char At() is reference to string.

(ii) List any two stream classes & their subclasses in Java.

(iii) What problems occur with global variables. Enlist & explain.

(iv) Explain wait () methods related to thread.

(v) Write a program to compare two strings.

Q.2. Describe use of final & super keywords with respect to inheritance. (15)

Q.3. (a) Write an applet 'program that accepts two input strings using <param> tag & concatenates them & display it in the status window. (10)

(b) Give the attribute of applet tag. (5)

Q.4. (a) Write a program to implement Fibonacci series using for loop control structure. (8)

(b) Explain with an example how to create a package. (7)

Q.5. (a) Explain left & right shift operators with examples. (7)

(b) What is a thread. Explain complete life cycle of thread. (8)

Q.6. (a) What is a container. Explain how components are added to a container. (7)

(b) What is multithreaded programming. Show how threads can be created in Java. (8)

Q.7. (a) Write a Java program to create a menu for a typical banking system. (12)

(b) How does Java achieve portability? (3)

Q.8. (a) Write a Java program to suitable the operation of a numerical calculator with the functions +, –, / & * (12)

(b) What are Java Beans? (3)

Q.9. (a) Why Java is considered as best language for internet applications. (4)

(b) Describe an utility that enables to configure a set of Beans, connect them together & produce a functional application. (8)

(c) How JDBC used with Java is advantageous. (3)

Q.10. (a) Write a program to check whether a given number is a palindrome. (7)

(b) Write a program that accepts number from user & converts it into binary using wrapper class methods. (8)

Appendix

A JAVA PROJECTS

Project: Editor in Java

SECTION 1

TABLE OF CONTENTS

1.1 INTRODUCTION OF THE PROJECT

The TEXT EDITOR makes provision for editing and applying different operation on textual materials i.e. cut, copy, paste, opening and saving the document, changing different forms of text. In this project we have worked a lot and devoted much time in understanding about how the internal process goes on in a notepad & what are the basic requirements for a TEXT EDITOR.

This project uses **JAVA** as a Front End. In introduction phase we can say that we'll understood lots of project facilities that should be provided in a best system and also how to manage the developing system. Working on this project was an interesting experience.

Key feature of the System:

The Software:

- Edit the textual material in a simple and sober way without any manual headache. The software include basic functionalities such as- new, open, saving, exiting the document.
- Notepad is a basic text editor you can use for simple documents or for creating Web pages. To create or edit files that require formatting, use WordPad. To open notepad, click Start, point to run command, write cmd, and then press enter, cmd prompt will open.
- To run the notepad, compile and run the java file using java commands from the location.

1.2 OBJECTIVES OF THE PROJECT

The main objective of this project is editing and formatting of the text.

- basic text editor you can use for simple documents or for creating Web pages. To create or edit files that require formatting, use WordPad.
- It can be a useful tool for anyone and everyone.

The project uses **JAVA** as Front End.

SCOPE & PURPOSE

Purpose

The purpose of doing this project is to create a framework that eases the editing and formatting of texts. It will help the concerned in following ways You should pick your program based on how complicated your document is. What kind of formatting do you need? Does the document include graphics or tables? Will people using other operating systems need to open or modify it? How large is the document? Are you creating a Web page?

Windows includes two word processing programs: notepadand WordPad. Each provides basic text editing capability, but you may have tasks that are better suited for one editor than the other.

Decide whether your document needs any of the following before you choose an editor.

Text formatting

Notepad provides only the most basic text formatting. You can specify a font and insert tabs. The font applies to the whole document, not an individual paragraph or word, and it is not saved with the file. If someone else looks at the file on another computer, that person will see whatever font is available.

WordPad allows you to create more complex documents, giving you most of the capability of a word processor. You can change the font for the entire document or just a word within it. With the click of a button, you can insert bullets into text in WordPad or align a paragraph to the right or left. All of this formatting is saved with your document, so no matter who opens it, it will appear as you created it.

Word processors provide even more text formatting options, such as automatically numbering lines of text, creating columns, or inserting frames.

Tables

If you plan to use tables in your file, you should probably create the document using a word processor. You can create a table in a Notepad or WordPad document, but you must count characters or insert tabs to align the columns. Most word processors will separate the columns and rows and automatically wrap text within columns.

Graphics

Notepad does not support graphics. You can insert graphics into a WordPad document and modify them by linking or embedding them in your document. Almost all word processors provide graphics support.

Page setup

Basic page setup is available with both Notepad and WordPad. You can set margins, add headers and footers, and orient your documents to print either vertically or horizontally. Your word processor may offer more options.

Large documents

The more elaborate the document, the longer it will take to open and modify. Notepad and WordPad are both compact programs that start and open files quickly, and work best when used with smaller files.

Word processors are intended for larger, more elaborate documents. A word processor gives you more control over your documents than Notepad or WordPad. Often you can add footnotes, annotations, and even generate a table of contents for your documents. Many word processors offer macros and templates to help you automate repetitive tasks, such as typing your name or formatting headings. Usually word processors will automatically check the spelling and grammar in your document.

Cross-operating system support

Notepad is a basic text editor that is most commonly used to view or edit .txt files, such as the Readme.txt files provided with your Windows software. Text-only files are critical if you share documents with someone using another operating system such as Macintosh or UNIX. WordPad also allows you to save your files as a Word document, so you can modify files created in Word even if you don't have the program yourself.

Multiple languages

WordPad and Notepad allow you to save your files in different formats, such as Unicode, providing you greater flexibility when working with documents that use different character sets or documents created by other programs.

Most word processors also allow you to save your files in a variety of formats. Some provide support for multiple languages, even including several dictionaries for checking spelling. In WordPad, documents that use multiple languages should be saved in rich text format (.rtf).

HTML and Web pages

Many people who use HTML to create Web pages or other documents find Notepad a useful tool for writing in HTML. Because Notepad supports only very basic formatting, you cannot accidentally save special formatting in documents that need to remain pure text. This is especially useful when creating HTML documents for a Web page because special characters or other formatting may not appear in your published Web page or may even cause errors.

Many word processors provide additional tools or converters to help you create HTML documents. But, if you are creating simple pages or if you want to make a few quick changes, Notepad opens files quickly. Also, Notepad shows all of the HTML tags so you can troubleshoot your page. Not all word processors or converters make the HTML code available.

If you only need to create simple documents, Notepad is your best choice. You need to use WordPad or another word processor for anything more complicated.

SECTION 2

SYSTEM ANALYSIS

TABLE OF CONTENTS

2.1 IDENTIFICATION OF THE NEED

This step is initiation of System Analysis. An overview of the client's requirement has been done. The basic need of the client to opt for such kind of project is analyzed.

As per current scenario text editors are needed by the people to format and edit their text, and timely generation of reports is the basic features of this project.

2.2 PRELIMINARY INVESTIGATION

They have to do the basic functionalities of a text editor and additional customized functionalities for individuals.

Modules in Computerized System

Module: Single Module

In this module, user can enter any sort of text , the software provides the tools to use the software. The user is allowed to enter the text but the user cannot open graphic files as it is a limitation for the text editor for that many word processors are available.

2.3 FEASIBILITY STUDY

Depending on the results of the initial investigation, the survey is expanded to a more detailed feasibility study. Feasibility study is a test of system proposal according to its workability, impact on the organization, ability to meet user needs, and effective use of resources.

The objective of the feasibility study is not to solve the problem but to acquire a sense of its scope . During the study, the problem definition is crystallized and aspects of the problem to be included in the system are determined.

Consequently, costs and benefits are described with greater accuracy at this stage.

It consists of the following:

1. **Statement of the problem:** A carefully worded statement of the problem that led to analysis.
2. **Summary of finding and recommendations:** A list of the major findings and recommendations of the study. It is ideal for the user who requires quick access to the results of the analysis of the system under study. Conclusion are stated, followed by a list of the recommendation and a justification for them.
3. **Details of findings:** An outline of the methods and procedures under-taken by the existing system, followed by coverage of the objectives and procedures of the candidate system. Included are also discussions of output reports, file structures, and costs and benefits of the candidate system.
4. **Recommendations and conclusions:** Specific recommendations regarding the candidate system, including personnel assignments, costs, project schedules, and target dates.

2.3.1 Technical Feasibility

This involves financial considerations to accommodate technical enhancements. If the budget is a serious constraint, then the project is judged not feasible. In our Mailing system only the cost of developing and maintaining the application will be taken into consideration by the company. There is no need for any special hardware.

2.3.2 Economical Feasibility

With the help of Mailing application it will lead to decrease in cost of communication which will be more than the cost of developing and maintaining the application. The time and security factor will also lead to economic profitability.

2.3.3 Operational Feasibility

This Application is very easy to operate as it is made user friendly. Main consideration is user's easy access to all the functionality of the Application.

SECTION 3

The basic objective of software engineering is to: develop methods and procedures for software development that can scale up for large systems and that can be used to consistently produce high quality software at low cost and with a small cycle time. That is, the key objectives are consistency, low cost, high quality, small cycle time, and scalability.

The basic approach that software engineering takes is to separate the development process from the software. The premise is that the development process controls the quality, scalability, consistency, and productivity. Hence to satisfy the objectives, one must focus on the development process. Design of proper development process and their control is the primary goal of the software engineering. It is this focus on the process that distinguishes it from most other computing disciplines. Most other computing disciplines focus on some type of the product-algorithms, operating systems, databases etc. while software engineering focuses on the process for producing products.

To better manage the development process and to achieve consistency, it is essential that the software development be done in phases.

Different Phases of the Development Process

(1) Requirement Analysis

Requirement analysis is done in order to understand the problem the software system is to solve. The problem could be automating an existing manual process, developing a new automated system, or a combination of the two. The emphasis in requirements analysis is on identifying what is needed from the system, not how the system will achieve its goals. There are at least two parties involved in the software development—a client and a developer. The developer has to develop the system to satisfy the client's needs. The developer does not understand the client's problem domain, and the client does not understand the issues involved in the software systems. This causes a communication gap, which has to be adequately bridged during requirements analysis.

(2) Software Design

The purpose of the design phase is to plan a solution of the problem specified by the requirements documents. This phase is the first step in moving from the problem domain to the solution domain. Starting with what is needed; design takes us toward how to satisfy the needs. The design of a system is perhaps the most critical factor affecting the quality of the software. It has a major impact on the later phases, particularly testing and maintenance.

The design activity is divided into two phases: System Design and Detailed Design. In system design the focus is on identifying the modules, whereas during detailed design the focus is on designing the logic for each of the modules.

(3) Coding

The goal of the coding phase is to translate the design of the system into code in a given programming language. Hence during coding, the focus should be on developing programs that are easy to read and understand, and not simply on developing programs that are easy to write.

(4) Testing

Testing is the major quality control measure used during software development. Its basic function is to detect errors in the software. Testing not only uncover errors introduced during coding, but also errors introduced during the previous phases. Thus, the goal of the testing is to uncover requirement, design and coding errors in the programs. Therefore, different levels of testing are used. Testing is an extremely critical and time consuming activity. It requires proper planning of the overall testing process. The output of the testing phase is the test report and the error report. Test report contains the set of test cases and the result of executing the code with these test cases. The error report describes the errors encountered and the action taken to remove the errors.

SECTION 4

SOFTWARE REQUIREMENT SPECIFICATION

PROJECT PLANNING

I was assigned the duty for developing a computerized system known as **"TEXT EDITOR"**. Working in team reinstates the team for some common guidelines and standard to be followed by all the team members across all team. For the optimum use of practical time it is necessary that every session is planned. Planning of this project will include the following things:

- Topic Understanding.
- Modular Break–Up of the System.
- Processor Logic for Each Module.
- Database Requirements.

Topic Understanding

It is vital that the field of application as introduced in the project may be totally a new field. So as soon as the project was allocated to me, I carefully went through the project to identify the requirements of the project.

Modular Break –Up of the System

- Identify the Various Modules in the System.
- List them in the Right Hierarchy.
- Identify their Priority of Development.

Description of the Modules

Modules

Module : Single Module

In this module, user enters a password and the software checks its validity. If the password is valid then he is allowed to enter, otherwise "Invalid User/Password" message is displayed. Different data access rights are assigned to different users. A new member can also be registered in this module.

Database Requirements

- Identify the Various Tables Required.
- Fields for these Tables.
- The Various Key Fields (for example Primary key and foreign key).
- Identify the Various Constraints like Not Null, Unique etc.

Software/Compilers Required To Develop This System

Software means a collection of program where the objective is to enhance the capabilities of the hardware machine.

The following paragraph defines the software of the proposed system development.

Operating System	: Win XP
Front end Tool	: Core Java, swings, applets, awt.
Back end	: Database provided in source code

Hardware Environment

Hardware is the term given to machinery itself and to various individual pieces of equipment. It refers to the physical devices of a computer system. Thus the input, storage, processing control and output devices are hardware.

Processor	:	Pentium-IV
RAM	:	128 MB
HDD	:	40 GB
FDD	:	1.44 MB
CD-ROM	:	52 X
Monitor	:	14 inches Color Monitor
Keyboard	:	104 Keys Keyboards
Printer	:	HP DeskJet 670 C

Tools/Environment Used

Tools

In a strict sense, tools are those things which are necessary to create some result.

"A Carpenter would use a hammer and saw to create furniture; a programmer would use a compiler and a program editor to create software".

Definition (Tool)

A tool is any device that, when used properly, improves the performance of a task, such as the development of computer information systems.

The tools used in the online user for wider ground.

The most basic, and most important, tool you can put at your disposal is a connection to the Internet and software to use that connection.

A good World Wide Web browser, electronic mail client, file transfer software, and the underlying networking software necessary to make it all run are requirements to get at the information available online.

With these tools, you/we will be able to locate information about practically any other Internet tools and techniques, including HTML tagging and translation software, secure transaction software, consulting services, World Wide Web server and browse tools and packages.

When developing an application, the web logic server can be viewed as a library of Java classes. Because of this you can use any development tool.

Client-Server Tools

For developing a web site the most frequently used architecture is client-server based. The client requests services and the server provides them.

Server

In a client-server structure, the computer that resides above another computer is called the server.

Client

The computers that reside at the lower level (below server level) are called clients.
In general, tools are grouped into the categories as under:

List of tools used in the development of system

Name of S/W Packages

Java

HTML

Window XP

Applets

Awt

SECTION 5

DESIGN

Definition of Analysis and Design

Analysis and design refers to the process of examining a business situation with the intent of improving it through better procedures and methods.

Overview of Analysis and Design

System development can generally be thought of as having two major components—analysis and design.

Introduction of User

The term user is widely used in the system analysis and design. The term end-user is widely used by the analysts to refer to people who are not professional information systems specialists but who can use computers to perform their Jobs. We can group end-user into four categories.

Hands-on Users actually interact with the system. They feed in data or receive output, perhaps using a terminal.

Indirect Users benefit from the results or reports produced by these systems but do not directly interact with the hardware or software.

These users may be managers of business functions using the system.

End-Users are not alike. Some are intermittent users. The end-user can also be a competitor, not an employee of the firm.

User managers have management responsibilities for application systems.

Senior Manager users are fourth type of users and are taking increased responsibility for the development of information systems.

Definition of System

In the broad sense, a system is simply a set of components that interact to accomplish some purpose. Systems are all around us. As computers are used more and more by persons who are not computer professionals, the face of systems development is taking on an additional dimension. Users themselves are undertaking development of some of the systems they use, as the executive in the vignette emphasized.

These different situations are represented by three distinct approaches to the development of computer information systems:

- Systems Development Life Cycle.
- Structured Analysis Development Method.
- Systems Prototype Method.

Systems Development Life Cycle

Systems development, a process consisting of two major steps of systems analysis and design, starts when management or sometimes systems development personnel realize that a particular business system needs improvement.

SDLC is classically thought of as the set of activities that analysts, designers and users carry out to develop and implement an information system.

Different parts of the project can be in various phases at the same time, with some components undergoing analysis while others advanced stages.

SDLC consists of following activities

- Preliminary investigation.
- Determination of system requirements.

- Design of system.
- Development of software.
- System testing.
- Implementation and evaluation.

Two main steps of development are:

- Analysis
- Design

ANALYSIS

Objectives

System analysis is conducted with the following objectives in mind:

- Identify the user's need.
- Evaluate the system concept for feasibility.
- Perform economic and technical analysis.
- Allocate functions to hardware, software, people, database, and other system elements.
- Establish cost and schedule constraints.

Create a system definition that forms the foundation for all subsequent engineering work. Both hardware and software expertise are required to successfully attain the objectives listed above.

DFD'S

0-Level DFD

DATABASE DESIGN

Introduction to Data Dictionary

Data dictionaries are an integral component of structured analysis, since data flow diagrams by themselves do not fully describe the subject of the investigation. The data flow diagrams provide the additional details about the project/system.

Data Dictionary (Definition)

A data dictionary is a catalog—a repository—of the elements in a system. These elements center on the data and the way they are structured to meet user requirements and organization needs. A data dictionary consists of a list of all the elements composing the data flowing through a system. The major elements are data flows, data stores, and processes. The data dictionary stores details and descriptions of these elements.

Describing Data Elements

Each entry in the data dictionary consists of a set of details describing the data used or produced in the system. Each item is identified by a data name, description, alias, and length and has specific values that are permissible for it in the system being studied.

SECTION 6

TESTING

Testing

It should be clear in mind that the philosophy behind testing is to find errors. Test cases are devised with this purpose in mind. A test case is a set of data that the system will process as normal input. However, the data are created with the express intent of determining whether the system will process them correctly. For example, test cases for inventory handling should include situations in which the quantities to be withdrawn from inventory exceed, equal and are less than the actual quantities on hand. Each test case is designed with the intent of finding errors in the way the system will process it. There are two general strategies for testing software: Code testing and Specification tests. In code testing, the analyst develops those cases to execute every instructions and path in a program. Under specification testing, the analyst examines the program specifications and then writes test data to determine how the program operates under specific conditions. Regardless of which strategy the analyst follows, there are preferred practices to ensure that the testing is useful. The levels of tests and types of test data, combined with testing libraries, are important aspects of the actual test process.

Levels of Testing

Systems are not designed as entire systems nor are they tested as single systems. The analyst must perform both unit and system testing.

Unit Testing

In unit testing the analyst tests the programs making up a system. For this reason, unit testing is sometimes called program testing. Unit testing gives stress on the modules independently of one another, to find errors. This helps the tester in detecting errors in coding and logic that are contained within that module alone. The errors resulting from the interaction between modules are initially avoided. For example, a hotel information system consists of modules to handle reservations; guest check in and checkout; restaurant, room service and miscellaneous charges; convention activities; and accounts receivable billing. For each, it provides the ability to enter, modify or retrieve data and respond to different types of inquiries or print reports. The test cases needed for unit testing should exercise each condition and option.

Unit testing can be performed from the bottom up, starting with smallest and lowest-level modules and proceeding one at a time. For each module in bottom-up testing a short program is used to execute the module and provides the needed data, so that the module is asked to perform the way it will when embedded within the larger system.

System Testing

The important and essential part of the system development phase, after designing and developing the software is system testing. We cannot say that every program or system design is perfect and because of lack of communication between the user and the designer, some error is there in the software development. The number and nature of errors in a newly designed system depend on some usual factors like communication between the user and the designer; the programmer's ability to generate a code that reflects exactly the systems specifications and the time frame for the design.

Theoretically, a newly designed system should have all the parts or sub-systems are in working order, but in reality, each sub-system works independently. This is the time to gather all the subsystem into one pool and test the whole system to determine whether it meets the user requirements. This is the last change to detect and correct errors before the system is installed for user acceptance testing. The purpose of system testing is to consider all the likely variations to which it will be subjected and then push the system to its limits.

Testing is an important function to the success of the system. System testing makes a logical assumption that if all the parts of the system are correct, the goal will be successfully activated. Another reason for system testing is its utility as a user-oriented vehicle before implementation.

System testing consists of the following five steps:

1. Program testing
2. String testing
3. System testing
4. System documentation
5. User acceptance testing

Program Testing

A program represents the logical elements of a system. For a program to run satisfactorily, it must compile and test data correctly and tie in properly with other programs. It is the responsibility of a programmer to have an error free program. At the time of testing the system, there exist two types of errors that should be checked. These errors are syntax and logic. A syntax error is a program statement that violates one or more rules of the language in which it is written. An improperly defined field dimension or omitted key words are common syntax errors. These errors are shown through error messages generated by the computer. A logic error, on the other hand, deals with incorrect data fields out of range items, and invalid combinations. Since the logical errors are not detected by compiler, the programmer must examine the output carefully to detect them.

When a program is tested, the actual output is compared with the expected output. When there is a discrepancy, the sequence of the instructions, must be traced to determine the probiem. The process is facilitated by breaking the program down into self-contained portions, each of which can be checked at certain key points.

String Testing

Programs are invariably related to one another and interact in a total system. Each program is tested to see whether it conforms to related programs in the system. Each part of the system is tested against the entire module with both test and live data before the whole system is ready to be tested.

System Testing

System testing is designed to uncover weaknesses that were not found in earlier tests. This includes forced system failure and validation of total system as it will be implemented by its user in the operational environment. Under this testing, generally we take low volumes of transactions based on live data. This volume is increased until the maximum level for each transaction type is reached. The total system is also tested for recovery and fallback after various major failures to ensure that no data are lost during the emergency. All this is done with the old system still in operation. When we see that the proposed system is successful in the test, the old system is discontinued.

System Documentation

All design and test documentation should be well prepared and kept in the library for future reference. The library is the central location for maintenance of the new system.

User Acceptance Testing

An acceptance test has the objective of selling the user on the validity and reliability of the system. It verifies that the system's procedures operate to system specifications and that the integrity of important data is maintained. Performance of an acceptance test is actually the user's show. User motivation is very important for the successful performance of the system. After that a comprehensive test report is prepared. This report shows the system's tolerance, performance range, error rate and accuracy.

Special Systems Tests

There are other six tests which fall under special category. They are described below:

Peak Load Test: It determines whether the system will handle the volume of activities that occur when the system is at the peak of its processing demand. For example, test the system by activating all terminals at the same time.

Storage Testing: It determines the capacity of the system to store transaction data on a disk or in other files. For example, verify documentation statements that the system will store 10,000 records of 400 bytes length on a single flexible disk.

Performance Time Testing: It determines the length of time system used by the system to process transaction data. This test is conducted prior to implementation to determine how long it takes to get a response to an inquiry, make a backup copy of a file, or send a transmission and get a response.

Recovery Testing: This testing determines the ability of user to recover data or re-start system after failure. For example, load backup copy of data and resume processing without data or integrity loss.

Procedure Testing: It determines the clarity of documentation on operation and use of system by having users do exactly what manuals request. For example, powering down system at the end of week or responding to paper-out light on printer.

Human Factors Testing: It determines how users will use the system when processing data or preparing reports.

SECTION 7

IMPLEMENTATION

Implementation

7.1 Hardware Requirement

7.2 Software Requirement

After completing the packaging process and produced distribution media for the application, it can run on a machine that has IIS4 and Windows 2000 Server operating systems.

7.1 HARDWARE REQUIREMENT

Hardware is the term given to machinery itself and to various individual pieces of equipment.

It refers to the physical devices of a computer system. Thus the input, storage, processing control and output devices are hardware.

Minimum Hardware Requirement of Client Side:

Processor: Any Pentium or Equivalent Machine

RAM: 128 MB

HDD: 4.1 GB or higher

14 inch Color Monitor

7.2 SOFTWARE REQUIREMENT

Software means a collection of program where the objective is to enhance the capabilities of the hardware machine.

Minimum Software Requirement of Client Side:

Operating System: Windows 98/2000/XP

SECTION 8

MAINTENANCE

Once the software is delivered and developed, it enters the maintenance phase. After implementation systems need maintenance. Beyond monkey testing during Software development some errors may not appear. During its usage by the end-user with actual data certain errors may disclose.

Therefore some residual errors or bugs remain in the system that must be removed as they are discovered. Many of these surfaces only after the system have been in operation sometimes for a long time. These errors once discovered need to be removed on an urgent basis for the smooth running of the system, leading to the software getting changed.

Though Maintenance is not a part of software development, it is an extremely important activity in the life of a software product.

Maintenance involves understanding the existing software (code and related documents), understanding the effects of change, making the changes-to both the code and documents-testing the new parts and retesting the old part.

For successful and smooth running of the system, maintenance is the prominent part of the project.

Any error, which hinders the functioning of any part of the project, may lead to bad impression of the developer.

There are major two types of errors: Compilation error and Runtime errors.

Compilation errors are errors during coding and are to be taken care of by the developer during development process.

Runtime errors are those which occur during running of the program. Whenever there is an occurrence of error an 'Error Window' opens in the middle of the screen displaying the type of error, Error Number and the Nearest Possible reason as to why the error has occurred. With the occurrence of this Error Window the operator (End-user) should note the type of error, the error number and the description of the error and should immediately report to the concerned Developer or Administrator. For example an error window which has appeared during the runtime process.

SECTION 9

COST ESTIMATION OF THE PROJECT

Cost in a project is due to the requirements for software, hardware, and human resources. Hardware resources are computer time, terminal time and memory required for the project. Software resources include the tools and compilers needed during development. The bulk of cost of software development is due to human resources needed. Cost estimates are determined in terms of person-months (PM).

SECTION 10

GANTT CHART

Gantt chart is a project scheduling technique. Progress can be represented easily in a Gantt chart, by coloring each milestone when completed. The project will start in the month of January and end after 4 months at the end of April.

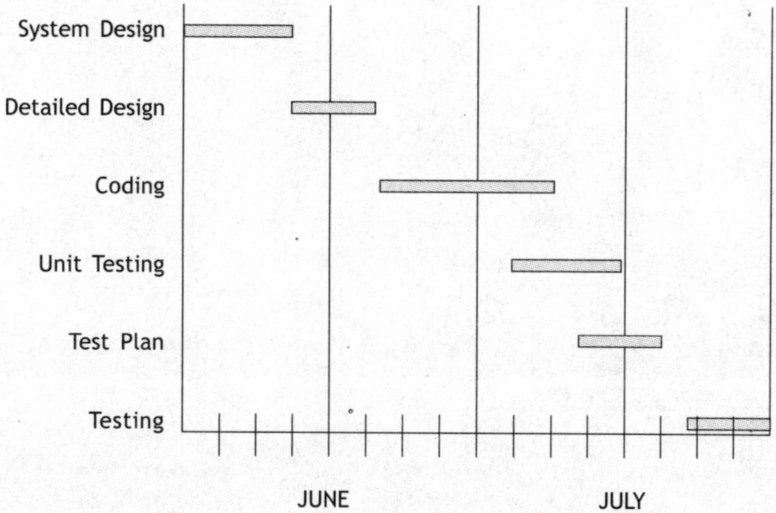

SECTION 11

FUTURE APPLICATION OF THE PROJECT

The Project can be upgraded to a fully Functionality notepad after adding some advanced features:-

In future we can have advanced text editors, we can increase the Option providing multiple functionalities that can provide the result on the basis of customization by different customers.

CONCLUSION

This project is designed to meet the requirements of **text editor**. It has been developed in **Java**.

For designing the system we have used simple data flow diagrams, structure charts. Overall the project teaches us the essential skills like:

(A) using system analysis and design techniques like data flow diagram, e/r diagram and structure chart in designing the system.

(B) understanding programming logic and language along with utilities like reports, screens etc. in Java.

Part-A

SCREEN SHOTS

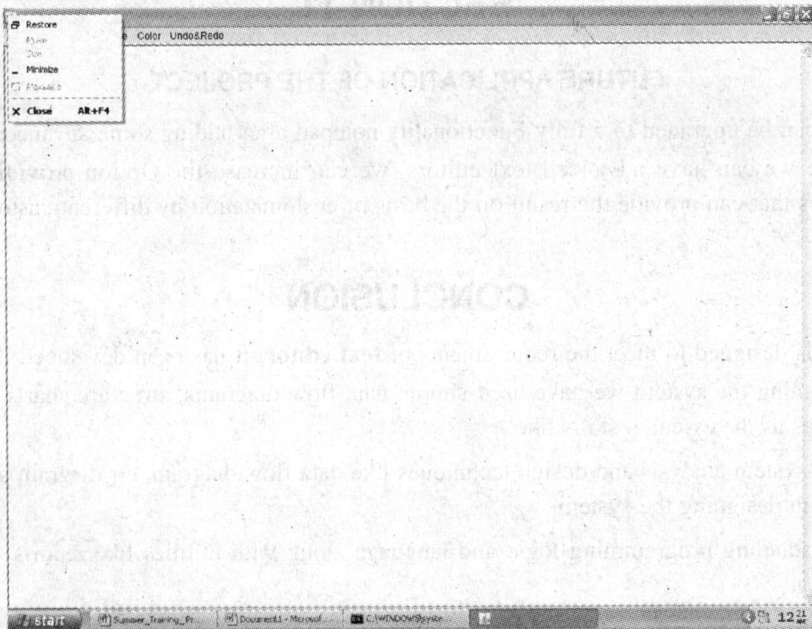

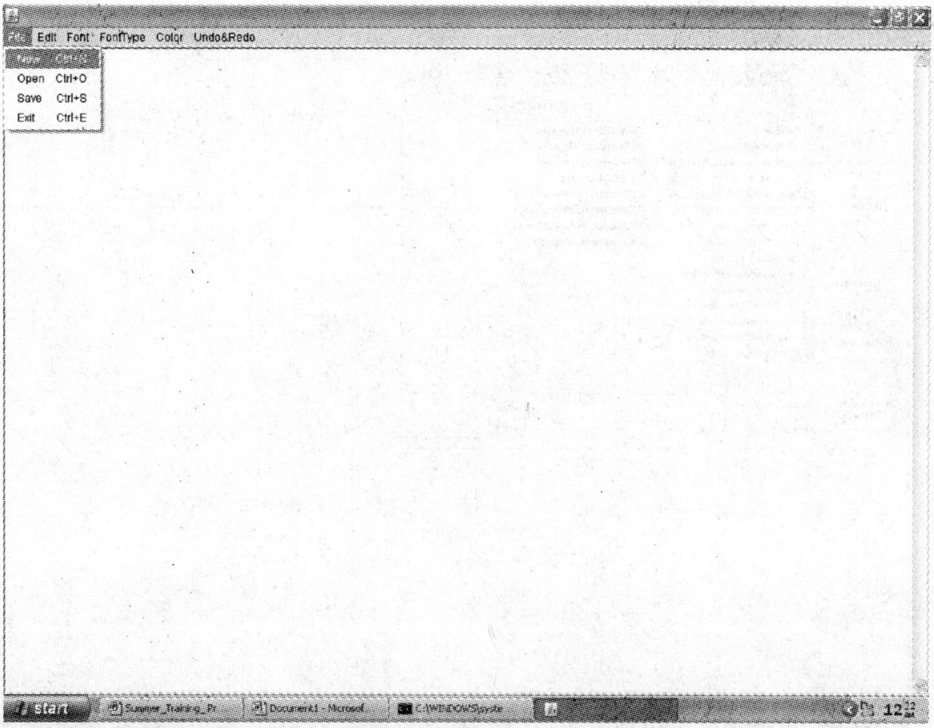
File Edit Font FontType Color Undo&Redo
New Ctrl+N
Open Ctrl+O
Save Ctrl+S
Exit Ctrl+E
start

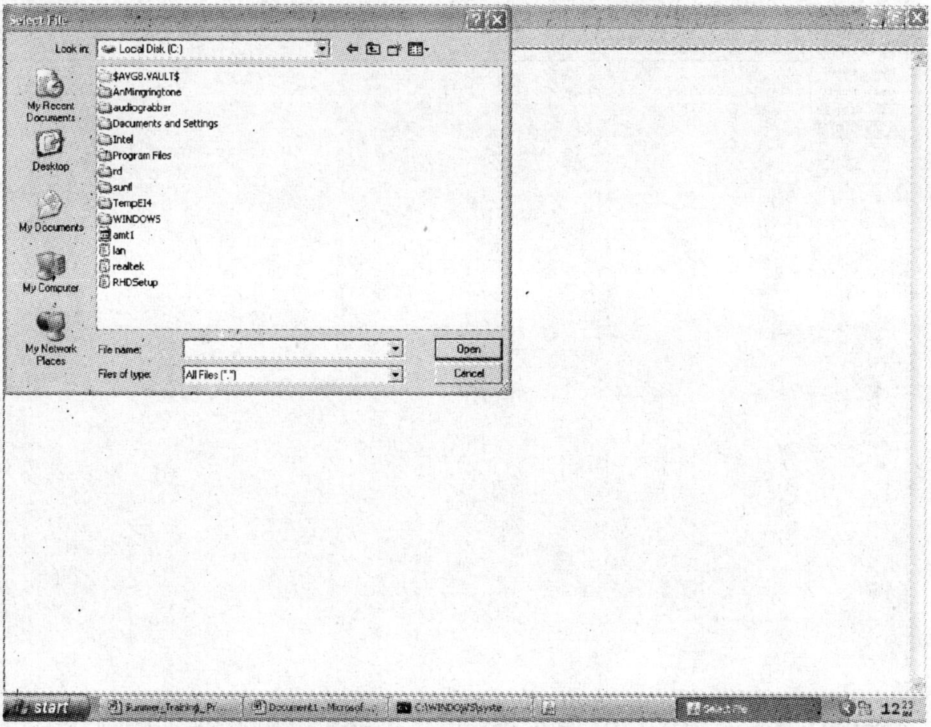
Select File
Look in: Local Disk (C:)
My Recent Documents
Desktop
My Documents
My Computer
My Network Places
$AVG8.VAULT$
AnMingringtone
audiograbber
Documents and Settings
Intel
Program Files
rd
sunf
TempEI4
WINDOWS
amt1
lan
realtek
RHDSetup
File name:
Files of type:
All Files (*.*)
Open
Cancel
start

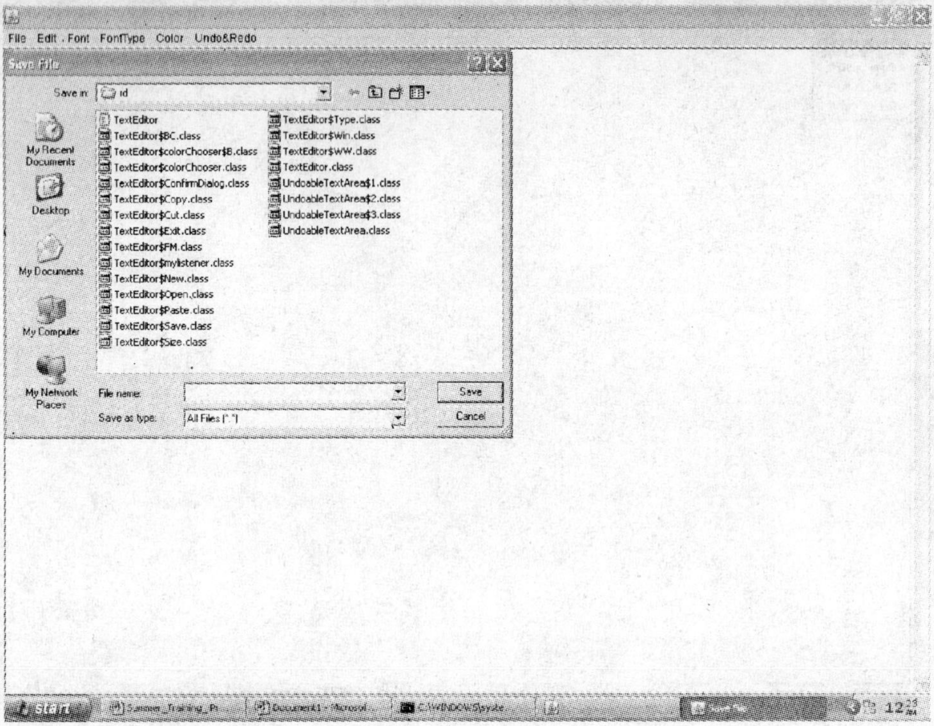
File Edit Font FontType Color Undo&Redo
Save File
Save in: rd
My Recent Documents
Desktop
My Documents
My Computer
My Network Places
TextEditor
TextEditor$BC.class
TextEditor$colorChooser$B.class
TextEditor$colorChooser.class
TextEditor$ConfirmDialog.class
TextEditor$Copy.class
TextEditor$Cut.class
TextEditor$Exit.class
TextEditor$FM.class
TextEditor$mylistener.class
TextEditor$New.class
TextEditor$Open.class
TextEditor$Paste.class
TextEditor$Save.class
TextEditor$Size.class
TextEditor$Type.class
TextEditor$Win.class
TextEditor$WW.class
TextEditor.class
UndoableTextArea$1.class
UndoableTextArea$2.class
UndoableTextArea$3.class
UndoableTextArea.class
File name:
Save as type: All Files (*.*)
Save
Cancel
start

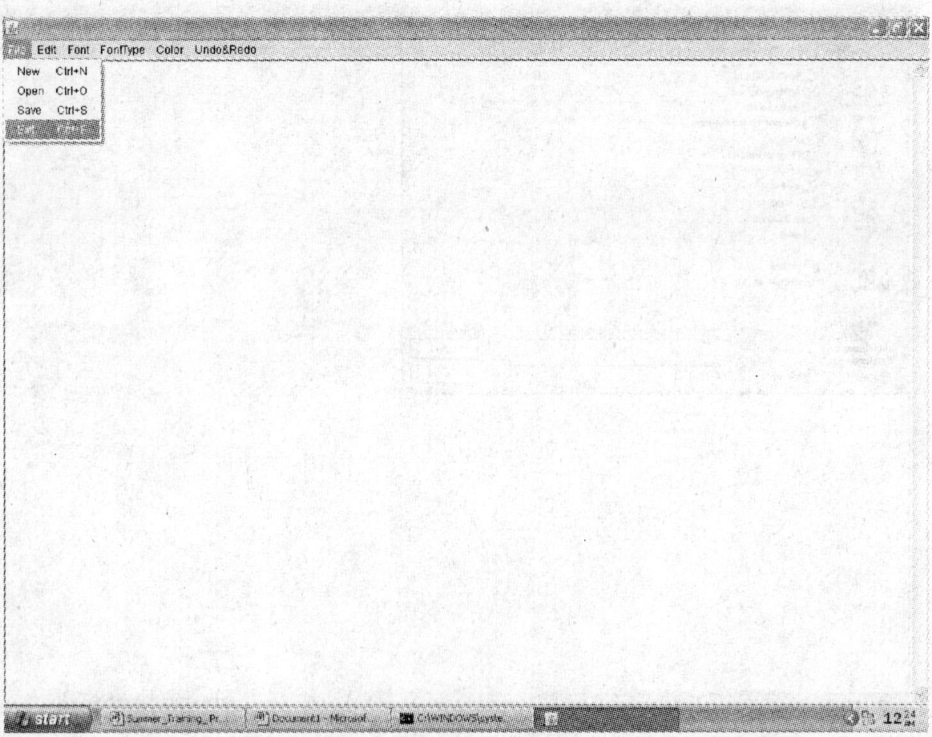
Edit Font FontType Color Undo&Redo
New Ctrl+N
Open Ctrl+O
Save Ctrl+S
start

File
Edit
Font
FontType
Color
Undo&Redo
Copy Ctrl+C
Paste Ctrl+V
start

File
Edit
Font
FontType
Color
Undo&Redo
Cut Ctrl+X
Copy Ctrl+C
Paste Ctrl+V
start

File Edit Font FontType Color Undo&Redo
Plain
Italic
Size

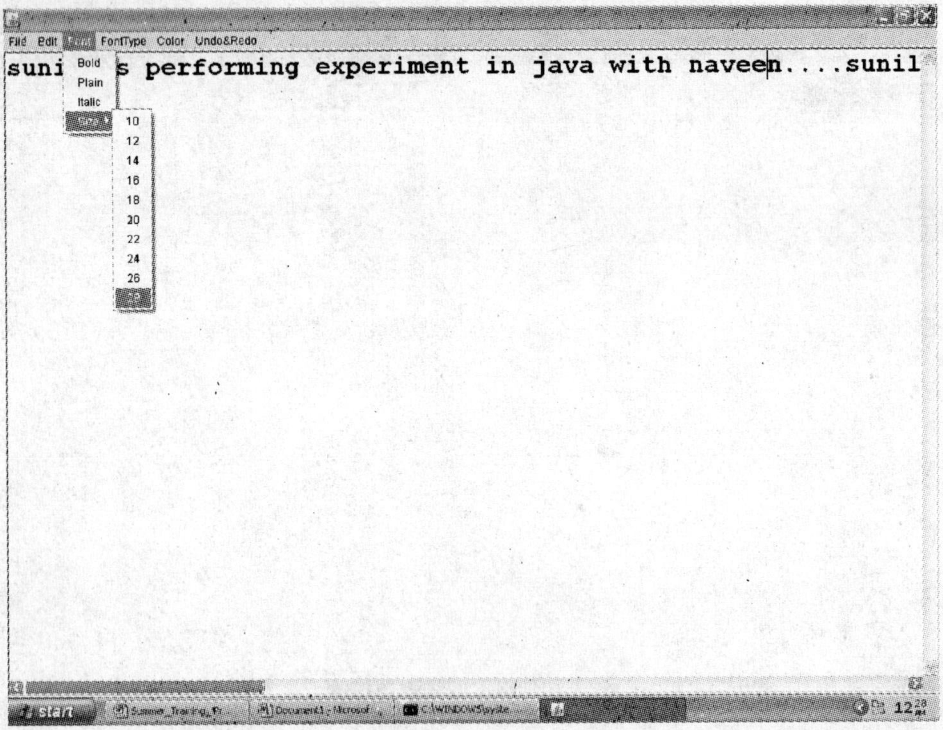
File Edit Font FontType Color Undo&Redo
suni s performing experiment in java with naveen....sunil
Bold
Plain
Italic
10
12
14
16
18
20
22
24
26

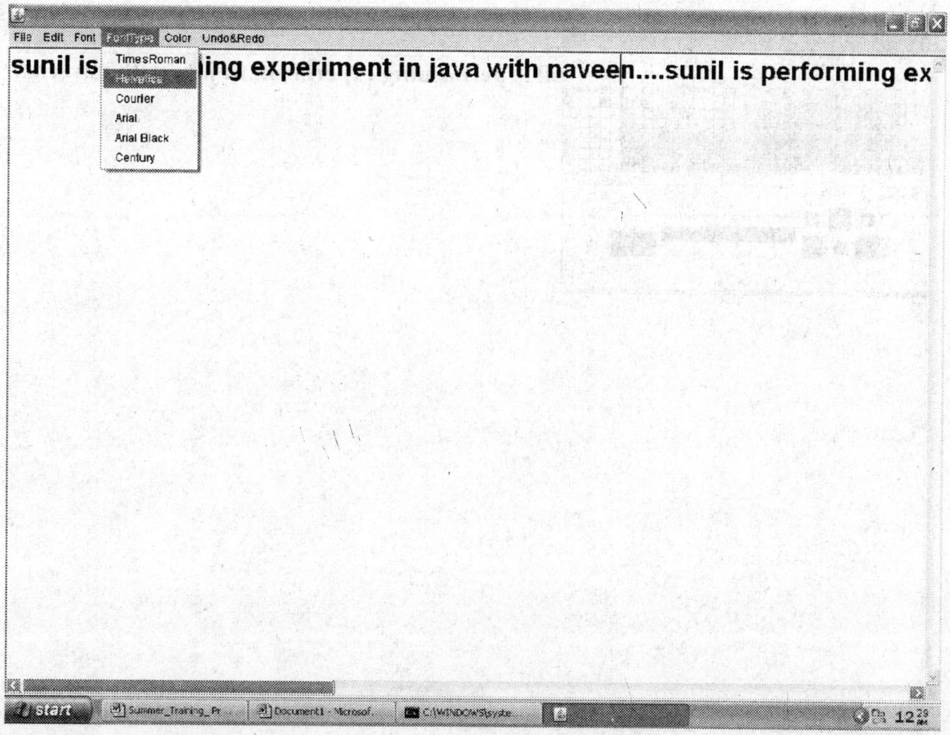
File Edit Font FontType Color Undo&Redo
TimesRoman
Helvetica
Courier
Arial
Arial Black
Century
sunil is ing experiment in java with naveen....sunil is performing ex
start
Summer_Training_Pr
Document1 - Microsof.
C:\WINDOWS\syste

File Edit Font FontType Color Undo&Redo
Background
Foreground
sunil is perfor periment in java with naveen....sunil is performing experiment
start
Summer_Training_Pr
Document1 - Microsof.
C:\WINDOWS\syste

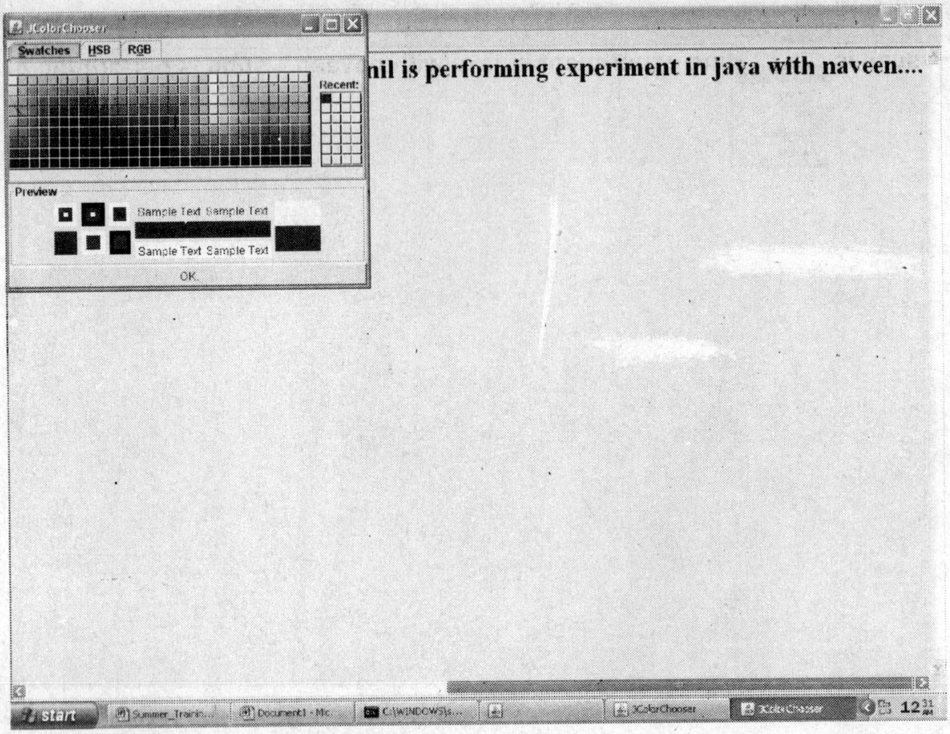
JColorChooser
Swatches
HSB
RGB
Recent:
Preview
Sample Text Sample Text
Sample Text Sample Text
OK
nil is performing experiment in java with naveen....
start
JColorChooser

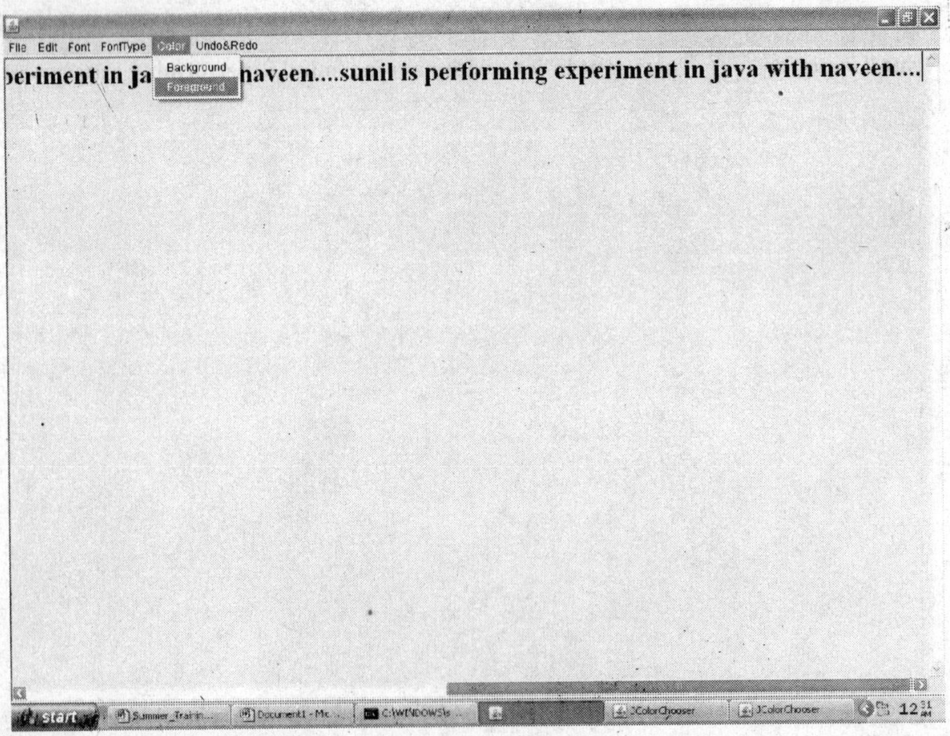
File Edit Font FontType Color Undo&Redo
Background
Foreground
periment in ja naveen....sunil is performing experiment in java with naveen....
start
JColorChooser

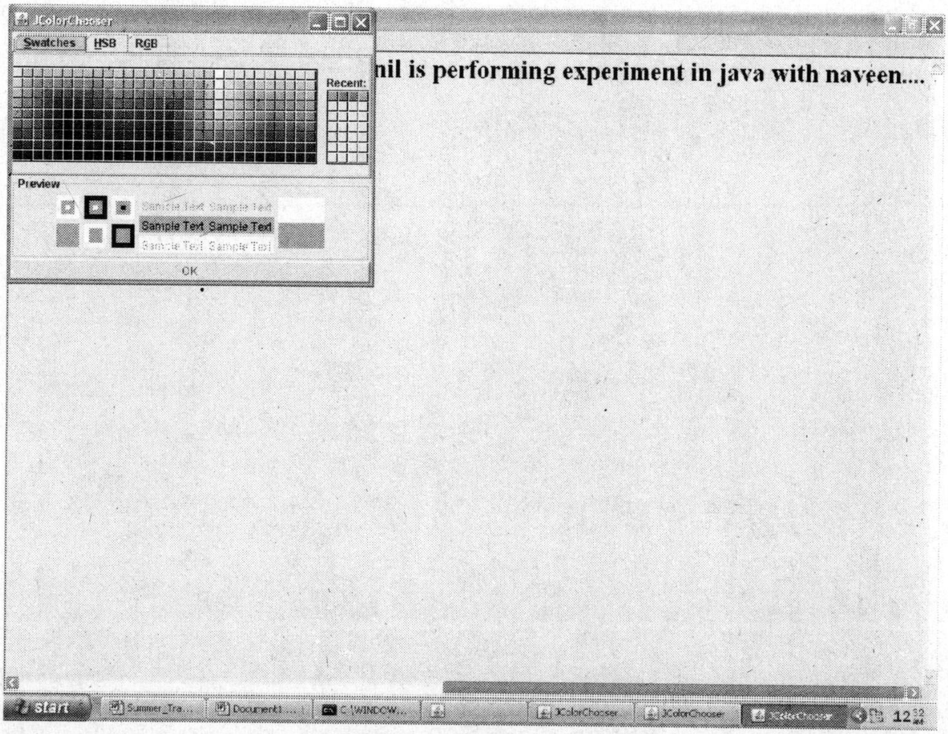
JColorChooser
Swatches
HSB
RGB
Recent:
Preview
Sample Text Sample Text
Sample Text Sample Text
Sample Text Sample Text
OK
nil is performing experiment in java with naveen....
start
Summer_Tra...
Document1 ...
C:\WINDOW...
JColorChooser
JColorChooser
JColorChooser

File Edit Font FontType Color Undo&Redo
sunil is performing experiment in java with naveen....sunil is performing experiment
start
2 Microsoft Off...
C:\WINDOWS\s...
JColorChooser
JColorChooser
JColorChooser

File Edit Font FontType Color Undo&Redo
Undo
Redo
sunil is performi[...]periment in java with naveen....sunil is performing experiment
start
JColorChooser
JColorChooser
JColorChooser

File Edit Font FontType Color Undo&Redo
Undo
Redo
sunil is performi[...]periment in java with naveen....sunil is performing experiment
start
JColorChooser
JColorChooser
JColorChooser

Part-B

SOURCE CODE

```
import java.awt.*;
import java.awt.event.*;
import java.awt.datatransfer.*;
import java.applet.*;
import java.io.*;
import javax.swing.*;
import javax.swing.undo.*;
import java.util.Hashtable;
class UndoableTextArea extends TextArea implements StateEditable
 {
 private final static String KEY_STATE="UndoableTextAreaKey";
 private boolean textChanged=false;
 private UndoManager undoManager;
 private StateEdit currentEdit;

 public UndoableTextArea()
 {
 super();
 initUndoable();
 }
 public UndoableTextArea(String string)
 {
 super(string);
 initUndoable();
 }
 public UndoableTextArea(int rows,int columns)
 {
 super(rows,columns);
 initUndoable();
 }
 public UndoableTextArea(String string,int rows,int columns)
 {
 super(string,rows,columns);
 initUndoable();
 }
 public UndoableTextArea(String string,int rows,int columns,int scrollbars)
 {
```

```
super(string,rows,columns,scrollbars);
initUndoable();
}

public boolean undo()
     {
          try
          {
               undoManager.undo();
               return true;
}
          catch(CannotUndoException e)
{
               System.out.println("cannot undo");
               return false;
}
}
public boolean redo()
{
          try
          {
               undoManager.redo();
               return true;
          }
          catch(CannotRedoException e)
{
System.out.println("cannot redo");
return false;
}
}


public void storeState(Hashtable state)
{
state.put(KEY_STATE,getText());
}

public void restoreState(Hashtable state)
{
Object data=state.get(KEY_STATE);
if(data!=null){
setText((String)data);
}
```

```
}

private void takeSnapshot()
{
if(textChanged)
{
currentEdit.end();
undoManager.addEdit(currentEdit);
textChanged=false;
currentEdit=new StateEdit(this);
}
}

private void initUndoable()
{
undoManager =new UndoManager();
currentEdit=new StateEdit(this);
addKeyListener(new KeyAdapter(){
public void keyPressed(KeyEvent event){
if(event.isActionKey()){
takeSnapshot();
}
}
});

addFocusListener(new FocusAdapter(){
public void focusLost(FocusEvent fe){
takeSnapshot();
}
});

addTextListener(new TextListener(){
public void textValueChanged(TextEvent e){
textChanged=true;
takeSnapshot();
}
});

}
}


public class TextEditor extends Frame
```

```
{
boolean b=true;
Frame fm;
FileDialog fd;
Font f;
int style=Font.PLAIN;
int fsize=12;
UndoableTextArea txt;
String filename,st,fn="untitled",dn;
Clipboard clip=getToolkit().getSystemClipboard();
TextEditor()
{
f=new Font("Courier",style,fsize);
setLayout(new GridLayout(1,1));
txt=new UndoableTextArea(80,25);

txt.setFont(f);
add(txt);
MenuBar mb=new MenuBar();
Menu fonttype=new Menu("FontType");
MenuItem one,two,three,four,five,six;
one=new MenuItem("TimesRoman");
two=new MenuItem("Helvetica");
three=new MenuItem("Courier");
four=new MenuItem("Arial");
five=new MenuItem("Arial Black");
six=new MenuItem("Century");

fonttype.add(one);
fonttype.add(two);
fonttype.add(three);
fonttype.add(four);
fonttype.add(five);
fonttype.add(six);
one.addActionListener(new Type());
two.addActionListener(new Type());
three.addActionListener(new Type());
four.addActionListener(new Type());
five.addActionListener(new Type());
six.addActionListener(new Type());

Menu fontmenu=new Menu("Font");
MenuItem boldmenu=new MenuItem("Bold");
```

```
MenuItem plainmenu=new MenuItem("Plain");
MenuItem italicmenu=new MenuItem("Italic");
fontmenu.add(boldmenu);
fontmenu.add(plainmenu);
fontmenu.add(italicmenu);
boldmenu.addActionListener(new FM());
plainmenu.addActionListener(new FM());
italicmenu.addActionListener(new FM());
Menu size=new Menu("Size");
MenuItem s1,s2,s3,s4,s5,s6,s7,s8,s9,s10;
s1=new MenuItem("10");
s2=new MenuItem("12");
s3=new MenuItem("14");
s4=new MenuItem("16");
s5=new MenuItem("18");
s6=new MenuItem("20");
s7=new MenuItem("22");
s8=new MenuItem("24");
s9=new MenuItem("26");
s10=new MenuItem("28");
size.add(s1);
size.add(s2);
size.add(s3);
size.add(s4);
size.add(s5);
size.add(s6);
size.add(s7);
size.add(s8);
size.add(s9);
size.add(s10);

s1.addActionListener(new Size());
s2.addActionListener(new Size());
s3.addActionListener(new Size());
s4.addActionListener(new Size());
s5.addActionListener(new Size());
s6.addActionListener(new Size());
s7.addActionListener(new Size());
s8.addActionListener(new Size());
s9.addActionListener(new Size());
s10.addActionListener(new Size());
size.addActionListener(new FM());
fontmenu.add(size);
```

```
Menu file=new Menu("File");
MenuItem n=new MenuItem("New",new MenuShortcut(KeyEvent.VK_N));
MenuItem o=new MenuItem("Open",new MenuShortcut(KeyEvent.VK_O));
MenuItem s=new MenuItem("Save",new MenuShortcut(KeyEvent.VK_S));
MenuItem e=new MenuItem("Exit",new MenuShortcut(KeyEvent.VK_E));
n.addActionListener(new New());
file.add(n);
o.addActionListener(new Open());
file.add(o);
s.addActionListener(new Save());
file.add(s);
e.addActionListener(new Exit());
file.add(e);
mb.add(file);
addWindowListener(new Win());
Menu edit=new Menu("Edit");
MenuItem cut=new MenuItem("Cut",new MenuShortcut(KeyEvent.VK_X));
MenuItem copy=new MenuItem("Copy",new MenuShortcut(KeyEvent.VK_C));
MenuItem paste=new MenuItem("Paste",new MenuShortcut(KeyEvent.VK_V));
cut.addActionListener(new Cut());
edit.add(cut);
copy.addActionListener(new Copy());
edit.add(copy);
paste.addActionListener(new Paste());
edit.add(paste);
Menu color =new Menu("Color");
MenuItem Bg=new MenuItem("Background");
MenuItem Fg=new MenuItem("Foreground");
Bg.addActionListener(new BC());
Fg.addActionListener(new BC());
Menu undo=new Menu("Undo&Redo");
MenuItem un=new MenuItem("Undo");
MenuItem re=new MenuItem("Redo");
re.addActionListener(new WW());
un.addActionListener(new WW());
undo.add(un);
undo.add(re);
color.add(Bg);
color.add(Fg);
mb.add(edit);
mb.add(fontmenu);
mb.add(fonttype);
mb.add(color);
```

```
mb.add(undo);
setMenuBar(mb);

mylistener mylist=new mylistener();
addWindowListener(mylist);
}

class WW implements ActionListener
{
public void actionPerformed(ActionEvent e)
{
String se=e.getActionCommand();
if(se.equals("Undo"))
txt.undo();
if(se.equals("Redo"))
txt.redo();

}
}
class mylistener extends WindowAdapter
{
public void windowClosing(WindowEvent we)
{
if(!b)
System.exit(0);
}
}
class New implements ActionListener
{
public void actionPerformed(ActionEvent ae)
{
txt.setText(" ");
setTitle(filename);
fn="Untitled";
}
}
class Open implements ActionListener
{
public void actionPerformed(ActionEvent ae)
{
FileDialog fd=new FileDialog(TextEditor.this,"Select
File",FileDialog.LOAD);
fd.show();
```

```
if((fn=fd.getFile())!=null)
{
filename=fd.getDirectory()+fd.getFile();
dn=fd.getDirectory();
setTitle(filename);
readFile();
}
txt.requestFocus();
}
}


class Save implements ActionListener
{
public void actionPerformed(ActionEvent ae)
{
FileDialog fd=new FileDialog(TextEditor.this,"Save
File",FileDialog.SAVE);
fd.setFile(fn);
fd.setDirectory(dn);
fd.show();

if(fd.getFile()!=null)
{
filename=fd.getDirectory()+fd.getFile();
setTitle(filename);
writeFile();
txt.requestFocus();
}
}
}

class Exit implements ActionListener
{
public void actionPerformed(ActionEvent ae)
{
System.exit(0);
}
}
void readFile()
{
BufferedReader d;
StringBuffer sb=new StringBuffer();
```

```
try{
d=new BufferedReader(new FileReader(filename));
String line;
while((line=d.readLine())!=null)
sb.append(line+" ");
txt.setText(sb.toString());
d.close();
}catch(FileNotFoundException e){
System.out.println("File not found");
}catch(IOException e){ }
}

public void writeFile()
{
try{
DataOutputStream d=new DataOutputStream(new FileOutputStream(filename));
String line=txt.getText();
BufferedReader br=new BufferedReader(new StringReader(line));
while((line=br.readLine())!=null)
{
d.writeBytes(line+" ");
}d.close();
}catch(Exception e){
System.out.println("File not found");
}
}
class Cut implements ActionListener
{
public void actionPerformed(ActionEvent ae)
{
String sel=txt.getSelectedText();
StringSelection ss=new StringSelection(sel);
clip.setContents(ss,ss);
txt.replaceRange(" ",txt.getSelectionStart(),txt.getSelectionEnd());
}
}
class Copy implements ActionListener
{
public void actionPerformed(ActionEvent ae)
{
String sel=txt.getSelectedText();
StringSelection clipstring=new StringSelection(sel);
clip.setContents(clipstring,clipstring);
```

```
}
}
class Paste implements ActionListener
{
public void actionPerformed(ActionEvent ae)
{
Transferable cliptran=clip.getContents(TextEditor.this);
try{
String sel=(String)cliptran.getTransferData(DataFlavor.stringFlavor);
txt.replaceRange(sel,txt.getSelectionStart(),txt.getSelectionEnd());
}catch(Exception e){
System.out.println("not starting flavor");
}
}
}
class Win extends WindowAdapter
{
public void windowClosing(WindowEvent we)
{

ConfirmDialog cd=new ConfirmDialog();
if(!b)
{
System.exit(0);
}
}
}



class ConfirmDialog extends JPanel
{
public ConfirmDialog()
{
int result;
result=JOptionPane.showConfirmDialog(this,fn+" not saved do you want to
save"/*,"Message Box",JOptionPane.QUESTION_MESSAGE*/);
switch(result)
{
case JOptionPane.YES_OPTION:
FileDialog fd=new FileDialog(TextEditor.this,"Save
File",FileDialog.SAVE);
```

```
fd.setFile(fn);
fd.setDirectory(dn);
fd.show();
if(fd.getFile()!=null)
{
filename=fd.getDirectory()+fd.getFile();
setTitle(filename);
writeFile();
txt.requestFocus();
}
System.out.println("Yes button pressed");
break;
case JOptionPane.NO_OPTION:
dispose();
System.exit(0);
System.out.println("NO button pressed");
break;
case JOptionPane.CANCEL_OPTION:
setVisible(true);
//b=false;
repaint();
System.out.println("Cancel button pressed");
break;
case JOptionPane.CLOSED_OPTION:
System.out.println("Closed button pressed");
break;
}
}
}

class Size implements ActionListener
{
public void actionPerformed(ActionEvent e)
{
int style=f.getStyle();
String w=e.getActionCommand();
if(w=="10")
{
f= new Font("Courier",style,10);
txt.setFont(f);
fsize=f.getSize();
repaint();
}
```

```
if(w=="12")
{
f= new Font("Courier",style,12);
fsize=f.getSize();
txt.setFont(f);
repaint();
}
if(w=="14")
{
f= new Font("Courier",style,14);
fsize=f.getSize();
txt.setFont(f);
repaint();
}
if(w=="16")
{
f= new Font("Courier",style,16);
txt. setFont(f);
fsize=f.getSize();
repaint();
}
if(w=="18")
{
f= new Font("Courier",style,18);
txt.setFont(f);
fsize=f.getSize();
repaint();
}
if(w=="20")
{
f= new Font("Courier",style,20);
txt.setFont(f);
fsize=f.getSize();
repaint();
}
if(w=="22")
{
f= new Font("Courier",style,22);
txt.setFont(f);
fsize=f.getSize();
repaint();
}
if(w=="24")
```

```
{
f= new Font("Courier",style,24);
txt.setFont(f);
fsize=f.getSize();
repaint();
}
if(w=="26")
{
f= new Font("Courier",style,26);
txt.setFont(f);
fsize=f.getSize();
repaint();
}

if(w=="28")
{
f= new Font("Courier",style,28);
txt.setFont(f);
fsize=f.getSize();
repaint();
}


}
}
class FM extends Applet implements ActionListener
{
public void actionPerformed(ActionEvent e)
{
String b=e.getActionCommand();
if(b=="Bold")
{
f= new Font("Courier",Font.BOLD,fsize);
style=f.getStyle();
txt.setFont(f);
}
if(b=="Plain")
{
f= new Font("Courier",Font.PLAIN,fsize);
style=f.getStyle();
txt.setFont(f);
}
```

```
if(b=="Italic")
{
f= new Font("Courier",Font.ITALIC,fsize);
txt.setFont(f);
}
repaint();
}
}

class Type implements ActionListener
{
public void actionPerformed(ActionEvent e)
{
String lbl=e.getActionCommand();
if(lbl=="TimesRoman")
{
f=new Font("TimesRoman",style,fsize);
txt.setFont(f);
}
if(lbl=="Courier")
{
f=new Font("Courier",style,fsize);
txt.setFont(f);
}
if(lbl=="Helvetica")
{
f=new Font("Helvetica",style,fsize);
txt.setFont(f);
}
if(lbl=="Arial")
{
f=new Font("Arial",style,fsize);
txt.setFont(f);
}
if(lbl=="Arial Black")
{
f=new Font("ArialBlack",style,fsize);
txt.setFont(f);
}
if(lbl=="Century")
{
f=new Font("Century",style,fsize);
txt.setFont(f);
```

```
}

repaint();
}
}


class BC implements ActionListener
{
public void actionPerformed(ActionEvent e)
{
st=e.getActionCommand();
JFrame jf=new JFrame("JColorChooser");
colorChooser c=new colorChooser();
c.setSize(400,300);
c.setVisible(true);
}
}


class colorChooser extends JFrame
{
Button ok;
JColorChooser jcc;
public colorChooser(){
setTitle("JColorChooser");
jcc=new JColorChooser();
JPanel content=(JPanel)getContentPane();
content.setLayout(new BorderLayout());
content.add(jcc,"Center");
ok=new Button("OK");
content.add(ok,"South");
ok.addActionListener(new B());
}

class B implements ActionListener
{
public void actionPerformed(ActionEvent e)
{
System.out.println("Color Is:"+jcc.getColor().toString());
if(st.equals("Background"))
txt.setBackground(jcc.getColor());
```

```
if(st.equals("Foreground"))
txt.setForeground(jcc.getColor());
setVisible(false);
}
}
}

public static void main(String args[])
{
Frame fm=new TextEditor();
fm.setSize(800,600);
fm.setVisible(true);
fm.show();
}
}
```

References

[1] Herbert Schildt, "Java Programming", TMH, 2014.

[2] N. B. Venkateshwarlu, E.V. Prasad, "Learn Object Oriented Programming Using Java: An UML based", S. Chand and Company Ltd., First Edition, 2010.

[3] Tonny Gaddis, "Starting out with JAVA Programming", Wiley India, Reprint 2000.

[4] Deitel and Deitel, "JAVA—How to Program", 3/ed, Pearson Asia, 1999.

[5] Cay S. Hortsmann and Gary Cornell, "E-book Core Java Programming", Vol II, Sun Microsystems Press.

[6] http://ibm.com/DeveloperWorks

[7] http://www.drjava.org/

[8] http://javaboutique.internet.com/demoIDEs/

[9] Hason, Java Notes for Programming Languages and Advanced Programming, http://www.cs.biu.ac.il/~hasonz

[10] Rajiv Chopra, "Object-Oriented Software Engineering", 3rd Edition, Katsons, 2013.

[11] E. Balagurusamy, "Programming with JAVA—A Primer", 5th Edition, TMH, 2015.

[12] Rajiv Chopra, "Modern Software Engineering", 1st Edition, I.K. International Publishers, 2014.

NEW AGE

JAVA Programming

A Supplement

- JVM
- Sandbox Models
- Socket Programming
- RMI

Dr. RAJIV CHOPRA

NEW AGE INTERNATIONAL PUBLISHERS

GGSIPU, Delhi

End Term Exams

5th Sem., (B.Tech–CSE/IT), Dec. 2016

JAVA PROGRAMING

Paper Code: ETCS-307 Subject: Java Programming

Time: 3 Hours Max. Marks: 75

Note: Attempt any five questions including Q. No. 1 which is compulsory. **(5 × 5 = 25)**

1.(a) Define constructor. Write various types of constructors.

(b) What is meant by Byte Code in Java?

(c) Explain about creation of classes and creation of objects in java with example.

(d) Write a program to create two threads, one thread will print odd numbers and second thread will print even numbers between 1 to 20 numbers.

(e) Write a short note on Buffered Streams.

2.(a) Write a program to create a vector with seven elements, first 2 are integers, next 2 are strings and remaining are float. Remove element at 3rd position and insert new element at 5th location. Display the updated vector. **(8)**

(b) Explain the following methods related to thread (i) wait ( ) (ii) sleep( ). **(4.5)**

3.(a) Describe the levels of access protection available for packages. **(6)**

(b) What do you mean by exception handling? Explain the use of various Keywords used for exception handling with suitable example. **(6.5)**

4.(a) Explain different methods for changing priorities for threads. **(4.5)**

(b) Write Code for creating a closable window using AWT classes, to receive following inputs.

User Name, Sex, Qualification, Address, Submit and Reset button. **(8)**

5.(a) What is 'this' pointer? How does 'this' pointer can be used in java program? Explain with example. **(4.5)**

(b) Write the syntax of iteration statement of Java. **(4)**

(c) Explain about Overloading of methods in Java. **(4)**

6.(a) Define Inheritance. Give various forms of Inheritance and write a Java program on single inheritance. **(6)**

(b) Define an Applet? What is the use of an Applet? Describe the life cycle of an Applet. **(6.5)**

7.(a) Define Container Class. Give a suitable example. **(4.5)**

(b) Write short note on **any two** of the following: **(2 × 4 = 8)**

(i) Security promises of JVM

(ii) Wrapper classes

(iii) AWT Components

(iv) Remote Method Invocation

JAVA VIRTUAL MACHINE (JVM)

Java platform consists of a JAVA VIRTUAL MACHINE and a package of ready made software components. It is shown in Fig. 1. This package is known as Java Application Programming Interface (API).

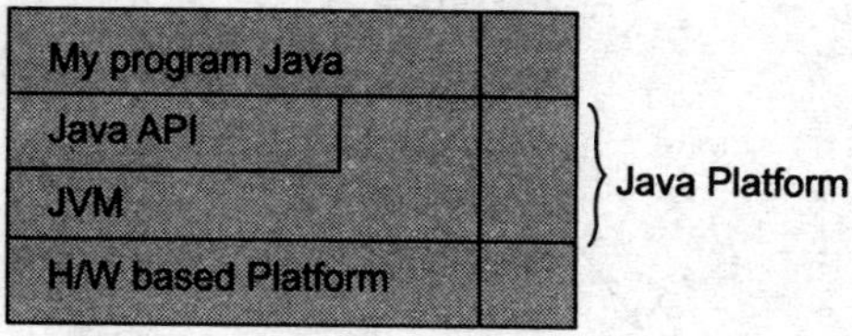

Fig. 1. JVM

As we know that all programming languages use compilers to convert source code into machine code for a specific computer. But Java is somewhat different because Java produces a bytecode of a source code and this bytecode is run by this JAVA VIRTUAL MACHINE (JVM). *Also understand that JVM is actually software* and *not a hardware unit*. Its job is to convert bytecode into machine code for a specific computer. Thus, we can say that JVM is an interpreter for a bytecode. Java bytecodes were made machine-independent so that they could be run on a variety of machines. That is why, you need only JVM for each platform. Also **note that these bytecodes are not machine specific**.

From Fig. 1, it is crystal clear that Java platform has two main components:

(*a*) JVM—JAVA VIRTUAL MACHINE.

(*b*) JAVA API—JAVA APPLICATION PROGRAMMING INTERFACE.

JVM is the base for the Java platform and is ported onto various hardware-based platforms. While Java API is a large collection of ready-made software components that provides many useful capabilities like GUI (Graphical User Interface). The Java API is grouped into libraries of related classes and interfaces and these libraries are known as **packages** (to be discussed later). Figure 2 shows a program running on the Java platform.

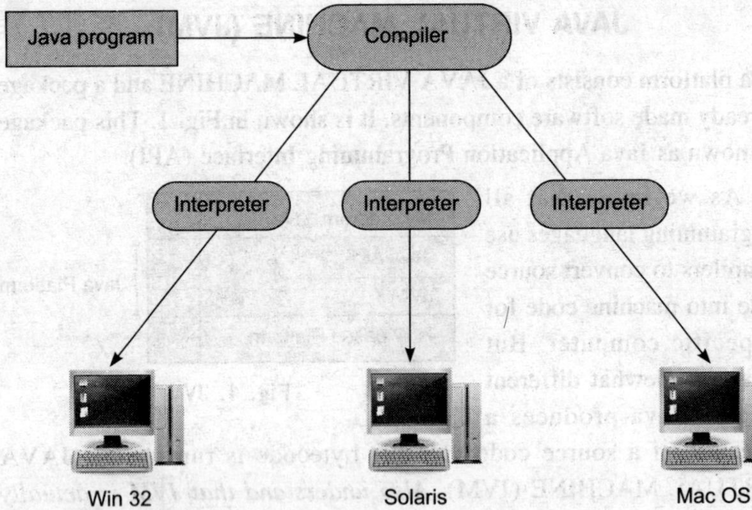

Fig. 2. Snapshot of Java running program

From Fig. 2, it is crystal clear that the JAVA API and the virtual machine insulate the program from the hardware. Native code is the code that after you compile it, the compiled code runs on a specific hardware platform. But as a platform-independent environment, the Java platform can be a bit slower than the native code. But smart compilers, smart interpreters and just-in-time bytecode compilers can bring performance closer to that of native code without threatening portability.

Java Programs normally undergo five phases:

I. **Edit (E):** Programmer writes program and stores program on disk.

II. **Compile (C):** Compiler creates bytecodes from program.

III. **Load (L):** Class loader stores bytecodes in memory.

IV. **Verify (V):** Verifier ensures bytecodes do not violate security requirements.

V. **Execute (E):** Interpreter translates bytecodes into machine language.

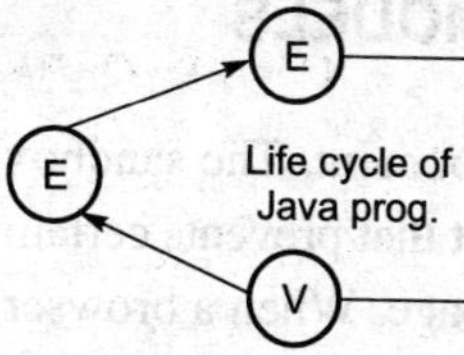

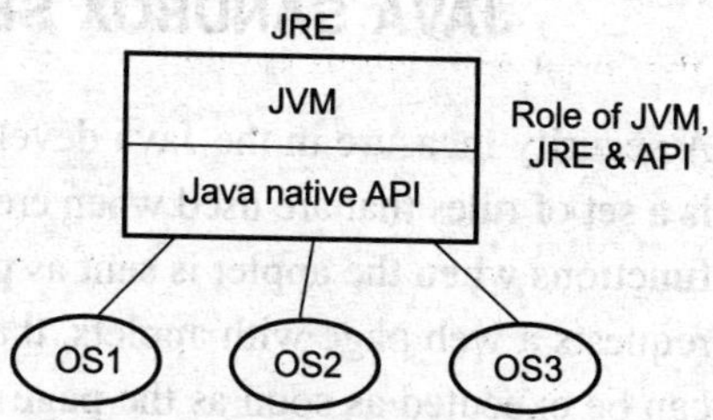

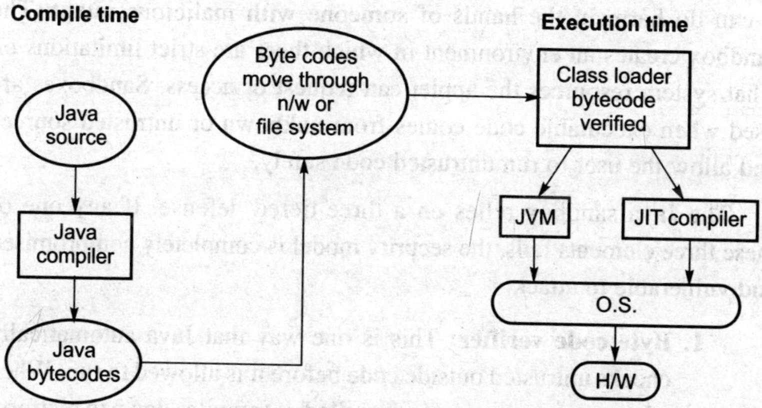

Fig. 3. Bytecode verification process in Java

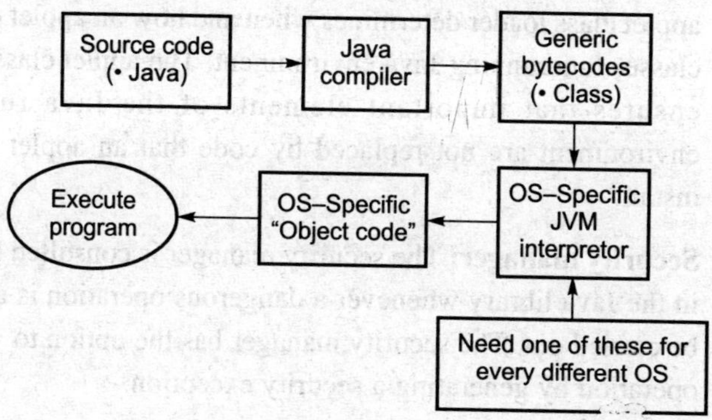

Fig. 4: Compilation process in Java

JAVA SANDBOX SECURITY MODELS

A security measure in the Java development environment. The sandbox is a set of rules that are used when creating an applet that prevents certain functions when the applet is sent as part of a web page. When a browser requests a web page with applets, the applets are sent automatically and can be executed as soon as the page arrives in the browser. If the applet is allowed unlimited access to memory and operating system resource it can do harm in the hands of someone with malicious intent. The sandbox creates an environment in which there are strict limitations on what system resources the applet can request or access. Sandboxes are used when executable code comes from unknown or untrusted sources and allow the user to run untrusted code safely.

The Java sandbox relies on a three-tiered defense. If any one of these three elements fails, the security model is completely compromised and vulnerable to attack.

1. **Byte code verifier:** This is one way that Java automatically checks untrusted outside code before it is allowed to run. When a Java source program is compiled, it compiles down to platform independent Java byte code, which is verified before it can run.
2. **Applet class loader:** All Java objects belong to classes, and the applet class loader determines when and how an applet can add classes to a running Java environment. The applet class loader ensures that important elements of the Java run-time environment are not replaced by code that an applet tries to install.
3. **Security manager:** The security manager is consulted by code in the Java library whenever a dangerous operation is about to be carried out. The security manager has the option to veto the operation by generating a security exception.

Platform Security Model

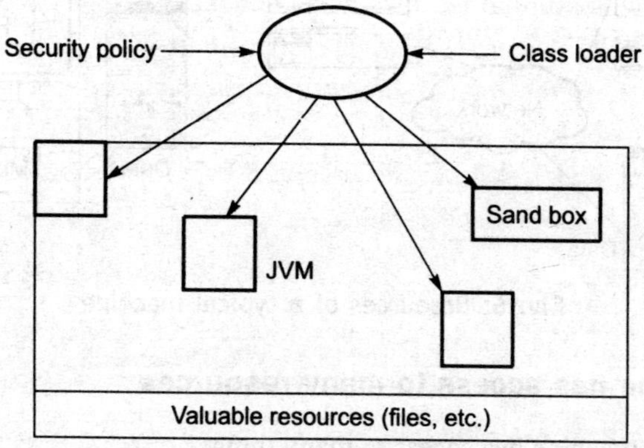

Fig. 5. Platform security model

In computer security, a sandbox is a **security mechanism** for separating running programs. It is often used to execute untested code, or untrusted programs from unverified third parties, supplies, untrusted users and untrusted websites. A sandbox typically provides a tightly controlled set of resources for guest programs to run in, such as scratch space on disk and memory. Network access, the ability to inspect the host system or read from input devices are usually disallowed or heavily restricted.

The idea behind this model is that when we allow a program to be hosted on our computer, we want to provide an environment where the program can run, but we want to confine the program's run area within certain bounds. We may decide to give the program certain toys to play with i.e. we may decide to let it has access to certain system resources, but in general, we want to make sure that the program is confined to its sandbox.

The Java sandbox is responsible for protecting a number of resources, and it does so at a number of levels. Consider the resources of a typical machine as shown in Fig. 6.

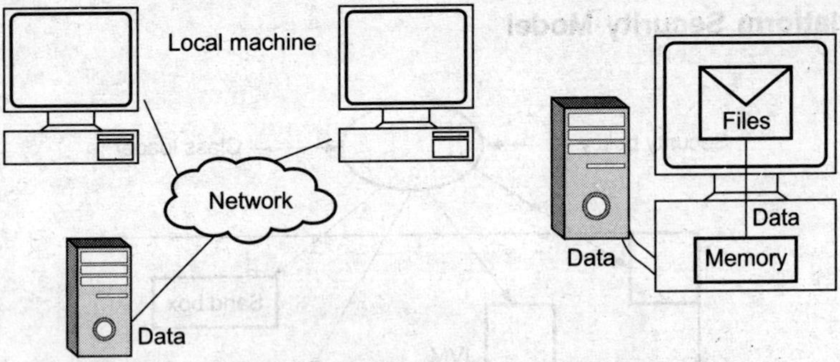

Fig. 6: Rosources of a typical machine

A Machine has access to many resources

The user's machine has access to many things:

1. Internally, it has access to its local memory (the computer's RAM)
2. Externally, it has access to its filesystem and to other machines on the local network.
3. For running applets, it also has access to a web server, which may be on its local (private net), or may be on the internet.
4. Data flows through this entire model, from the user's machine through the network and (possibly) to disk.

→ Each of these resources needs to be protected, and those protection from the basis of Java's security model.

→ We can imagine a number of different sized sandboxes in which a Java program might run:

1. A sandbox in which the program has access to the CPU, the screen, keyboard, and mouse and to its own memory. This is the minimal sandbox - it contains just enough resources for a program to run.
2. A sandbox in which the program has access to the CPU and its own memory as well as access to the web server from which it was loaded. This is often thought of as the default state for the sandbox.

3. A sandbox in which the program has access to the CPU, its memory, its web server and to a set of program specific resources (local files, local machines, etc.) Ex: A word processing system might have access to the docs directory on the local filesystem, but not to anyother files.

4. An open sandbox, in which the program has access to whatever resources the host machine normally has the access.

   The sandbox, thus, is not a one-size-fits-all model. Expanding the boundaries of the sandbox is always based on the notion of trust. Since the inception of Java technology, there has been strong and growing interest around the security of the Java platform as well as new security issue raised by the deployment of Java technology.

   From a technology provider's point of view, Java security includes two aspects:

→ Provide the Java platform as a secure, ready-built platform on which to run Java-enabled applications in a secure fashion.

→ Provide security tools and services implemented in the Java programming language that enable a wide range of security-sensitive applications, for example in the enterprise world.

The Original Sandbox Model

The original security model provided by the Java platform is known as the **sandbox model,** which existed in order to provide a very restricted environment in which to run untrusted code obtained from the open network. **The essence of the sandbox model** is that local code is trusted to have full access to vital system resources (such as the file system) while downloaded remote code (an applet) is not trusted and can access only the limited resources provided inside the sandbox.

This model is illustrated in the Fig. 7.

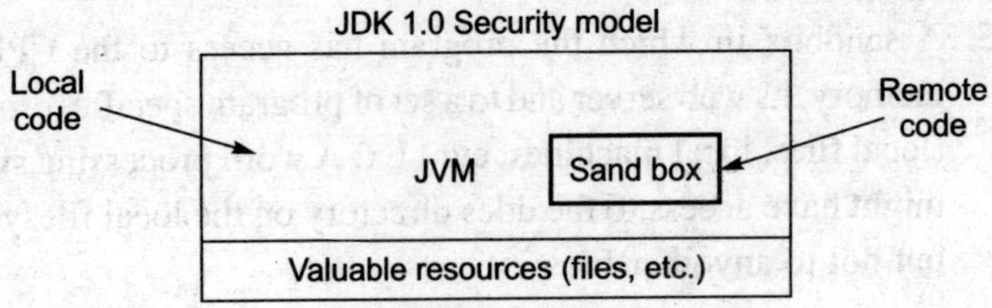

Fig. 7: Original sandbox model

→ The sandbox model was developed through the Java Development Kit (JDK), and was generally adopted by application built with JDK 1.0, including Java enabled we browsers.

→ Overall security is enforced through a number of mechanisms.

→ First of all, the language is designed to be typesafe and easy to use. The hope is that the burden on the programmer is such that the likelihood of making subtle mistakes is lessened compared with using other programming languages such as C or C++.

→ Second, compilers and a bytecode verifier ensure that only legitimate Java bytecode are executed.

→ Moreover, a classloader defines a local name space which can be used to ensure that an untrusted applet cannot interfere with the running of other program.

→ Finally, access to crucial system resource is checked in advance by Security Manager class that restricts the actions of a piece of untrusted code to the bare minimum.

JDK 1.1 introduced the concept of a "signed applet" as illustrated by the Fig. 8. In that release a correctly digitally signed, applet is treated as if it is trusted by the end system that receives the applet. Signed applets, together with their signatures are delivered in the JAR (Java Archive) format. In JDK 1.1, unsigned applets still run in the sandbox.

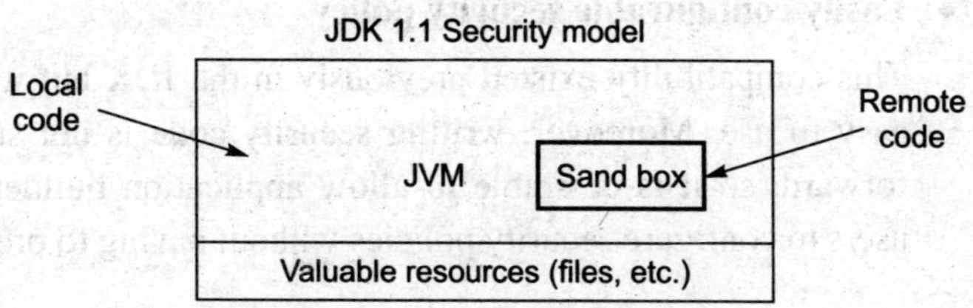

Fig. 8. Signed applet

Evolving the Sandbox Model

The new Java SE Platform Security Architecture, illustrated in the Fig. 9, is introduced primarily for the following purposes.

Java 2 Platform Security Model

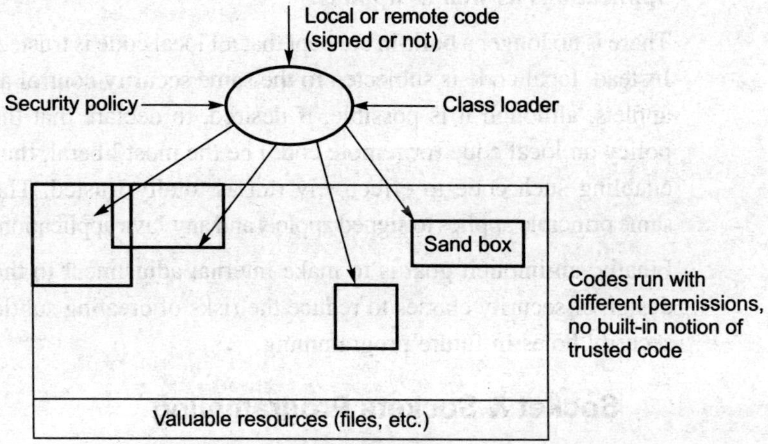

Fig. 9. New Java 2 platform security model

- **Fine grained access control**

  This capability existed in the JDK from the beginning but to use it, the application writer had to do substantial programming. The Hot Java Browser 1.00 is such an example.

  However, such programming is

  → extremely security sensitive

  → requires sophisticated skills

  → depth knowledge of Computer Security.

- **Easily configurable security policy**

  This compatibility existed previously in the JDK but was not easy to use. Moreover, writing security code is not straight forward, so it is desirable to allow application builders and users to configure security policies without having to program.

- **Easily extensible access control structure**

  Upto JDK 1.1 in order to create a new access permission you had to add a new check method to the security Manager class. The new architecture allows typed permission and automatic handling of all permission of the correct type. So new method in the Security Manager class needs to be created in most cases.

- **Extension of security checks to all Java programs, including applications as well as applets.**

  There is no longer a built-in concept that all local code is trusted. Instead, local code is subjected to the same security control as applets, although it is possible, if desired, to declare that the policy on local code (or remote code) be the most liberal, thus enabling such code to effectively run as totally trusted. The same principle applies to signed applets and any Java application.

  Finally, an implicit goal is to make internal adjustment to the design of security classes to reduce the risks of creating subtle security holes in future programming.

Socket & Sockets Programming

A **Socket object** is the Java representation of a TCP connection. *When a socket is created, a connection is opened to the specified destination.* Stream objects can be obtained to send and receive data to the other end.

I. The Constructors for Socket Class

Constructors for socket class takes two arguments:

1. The name (or IP address) of the host to connect to,
2. And the port number on that host to connect to.

The host name may be given as either a string or as an InetAddress object.

In either case, the port number is specified as an integer.

The Methods of Socket Class

Two methods are very important methods and they are:

- **Get Input Stream( )**
- **Get Output Stream( )**

} **return stream objects that can be used to communicate through the socket.**

A close ( ) method is provided to tell the underlying O.S. to terminate the connection.

Also some methods are provided to retrieve information about the connection such as the local and remote port numbers and an InetAddress representing the remote host.

II. The Server Socket class

It represents a listening TCP connection. Once an incoming connection is requested, the serversocket object will return a socket object representing the connection. In normal use, another thread would be spawned off to handle the connection. Then serversocket is free to listen for the next connection request.

The Constructors for Server Socket class

Both constructors take as an argument the *local port number* to listen for connection requests. A constructor is provided that also takes the maximum time to wait for a connection as a 2nd argument.

Methods of Server Socket class

Two methods are used —

- **accept( ):** This method will block the calling thread until a connection is received. A socket object is returned representing this new connection.
- **close( ):** This method tells the O.S. to stop listening for requests on the socket.

NOTE: Methods are also provided to retrieve the host name the socket is listening on (in InetAddress form) and the port number being listened to.

III. The DatagramSocket class

The *DatagramSocket* represents a connectionless datagram socket. This class works with the Datagram, packet class to provide for communication using the UDP protocol.

the constructors for DatagramSocket

As we know that UDP is a connectionless protocol, you do not need to specify a host name when creating a DatagramSocket. But only the port number on the local host is specified.

Another constructor is there that takes no arguments. When this constructor is used, the port number will be assigned arbitrarily by the O.S.

The Methods

Two most improtant methods are:

- **Send ( )**
- **Receive ( )**

IV. The DatagramPacket class

DatagramPacket objects represent one packet of data that is sent using the USP protocol.

The Constructors

It provides two constructors:

- for outgoing packets.
- for incoming packets.

The **incoming version** takes as arguments a **byte array** to hold the received data and an **int** specifying the **size of the array**.

The **outgoing version** also takes the **remote host name** and the **port number** on that host to send the packet to.

The Methods

There are four methods in this class:

- **getData ( )**
- **getLength ( )**
- **getAddress ( )**
- **getPost ( )**

These methods allow the data, datagram length and addressing (InetAddress and port number) information for the packet to be extracted.

V. The Inet Address class

This class represents a host name and its IP numbers. The class itself also provides the functionality to obtain the IP number for a given host name (just as C's gethostbyname ( ) function on UNIX)

The Constructors

There are no explicit constructors for Inet Address objects you can use –

(*a*) A static class method, getByName ( ), which returns a reference to an Inet Address.

(*b*) Because some hosts might be known by more than one IP address, there also is a method, getAllByName ( ), which returns an array of InetAddress objects.

The Methods

Methods do exist that will return a string representation of the host name that the InetAddress represents–getHostName ( ). And an array of the raw bytes of the address—getAddress ( ).

Also, equals ( ) method is used for the comparison of address objects.

The class also supports a to string ( ) method for printing out the host name and IP address.

Programming Sockekts in Java

The main issue here is—*How to open a socket?* Two cases arise:

Case-1: If you are *programming a client*, then you would **open a socket** as follows:

Socket My client;

My client = new socket ("Machine name", Port number);

Where "*Machine name*" is the machine you are trying to open a connection to, and "*Port Number*" is the port (a number) on which the server you are trying to connect to is running.

But please note that when you select a port number, keep in mind that port numbers between 0 and 1,023 are reserved for privileged users (*i.e.*, super user or root). These port numbers are reserved for standard services like e-mail, FTP and HTTP. When selecting a port number for your server, select one that is greater than 1,023.

Also note that to handle exception in this case, we may write–

```
Socket MyClient;
  try{
        MyClient = newSocket("Machine name",
PortNumber);
  }
  catch (IOException e){
        System.out.println(e);
  }
```

Case-2: If you are *programming a server*, then you would open a socket as follows:

```
ServerSocket MyService;
   try{
      MyService = new ServerSocket(PortNumber);
      }
catch (IOException e){
      System.out.println(e);
}
```

Please note that when implementing a server you also need to create a socket object from the server socket in order to listen for and accept connections from clients. That is,

```
Socket clientsocket = null;
  try{
     ServiceSocket = MyService.accept();
     }
catch (IOException e)
     {
     System.out.println(e);
}
```

How to create an Input stream?

Case-1: *On the client–side*, you can use the DataInputstream class to create an input stream to receive response from the server:

```
DataInputstream input;
  try{
 input = new DataInputstream
 (MyClient.getInputStream());
     }
 catch (IoException e){
 System.out.println(e);
 }
```

The class *Data Input Stream* allows you to read lines of text and Java primitive data types in a portable way. It has methods like read, readchar, readInt, readDouble and readline.

Case-2: *On the server–side,* you can use DataInputStream to receive input from the client:

```
DataInputStream input;
  try{
 input = new DataInputstream
 (ServiceSocket.getInputStream ( ));
     }
 catch (IoException e)
     {
 System.out.println(e);
 }
```

How to create an output stream?

Case-1: *On the client side,* you can create an output stream to send information to the server socket using the class *PrintStream* or *DataOutputStream* of Java.io:

```
Printstream output;
  try{
output = new PrintStream
(MyClient.getOutputStream());
    }
catch (IOException e){
System.out.println(e);
}
```

The class *PrintStream* has methods for displaying textual representation of Java primitive data types. It has write and println methods. If you want to use DataOutpputStream then you may write:

```
Dataoutputstream output;
  try{
output = new DataOutputStream
(MyClient.getOutputStream());
    }
catch (IOException e)
    }
    System.out.println(e);
}
```

The class *DataOutputStream* allows you to write Java primitive data types. The method WriteBytes ( ) is used here.

Case-2: *On the server side,* you can use the class *PrintStream* to send information to the client.

```
PrintStream output;
  try{
output = new PrintStream (ServiceSocket.
getOutputStream());
    }
Catch (IOException e)
    {
    System.out.println(e);
}
```

How to close sockets?

It is a good programming practice to close the input and output streams before you close the socket.

Case-1: *On the client–side,*

```
try{
    Output.close();
    Input.close();
    MyClient.close();
    }
catch (IOException e){
    System.out.printin(e);
}
```

Case-2: *On the server side,*

```
try{
    Output.close();
    Input.close();
    ServiceSocket.close();
    MyService.close();
    }
Catch (IOException e)
    {
System.out.println(e);
}
```

NOTE:

	Object	Class
Client	MyClient	Socket
Server	MyService	ServiceSocket

Just remember the following points regarding sockets:

1. Socket interface was *defined by Berkeley* UNIX.
2. It represents an *interface* to the TCP/IP networking subsystem.

3. It is widely used in *Internet software* but not required by the protocols.

4. They are *adopted by SUN* too and thus are available on all SUN-UNIX machine and in Java.

5. It's *functionality* was copied by Winsock.

6. It is an *abstraction* of underlying data communication layers.

7. `import java.net.* ;` provides access to network classes in Java.

8. *Default socket* uses a *TCP/IP connection.*

9. Sockets provide *full-duplex communications*. So, they include a *Dataoutput stream* and a *DataInput stream.*

10. To *create a socket*, *connect* it to a *host* and a *port* and *open* the socket as follows–

```
Socket s = null;
  try{
s = new Socket ("cecasun.utc.edu", 80);
DataOutputStream out = new DataOutputStream
(s.getOutputStream());
DataInputStream in = new DataInputStream
(s.getInputStream());
//now read bytes from "in" and
//Write bytes to "out"
    ....
    ....
    out.close();
    in.close();
    s.close();
  }
Catch (IOException e)
{...}
```

11. Also note that you must close the input/output streams before closing the socket.
12. Do not close just one of the streams as a socket is always full duplex.
13. Sockets in Java are easier to program than in C or C++.
14. Socket class provides methods like–
    - **close** ( )—throws IOException.
    - **getInetAddress** ( )—returns an InetAddress object.
    - **getPort** ( )—returns an int.
    - **getInputStream** ( )—throws IOException returns Inputstream object.
    - **getOutputStream** ( )—throws IOException returns Outputstream object.

Socket Programming With TCP

As explained earlier, the processes running on different machines communicate with each other by sending messages into *sockets*. We can also say that each *process* is analogous to a *house* and the *process's socket* is analogous to a *door*. The *socket is the door* between the *application process and TCP*. The application *developer* has the control of everything on the *application-layer side* of the socket. But it has a little control of the *transport-layer side*. He has the ability to fix a few TCP parameters like maximum buffer and maximum segment sizes.

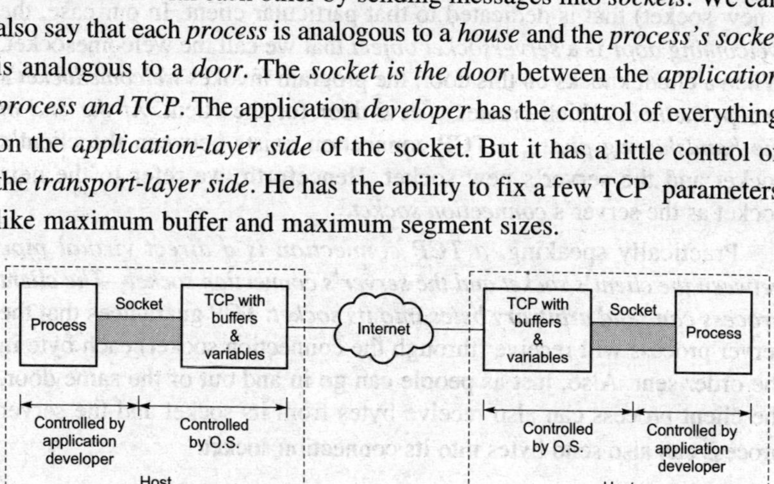

Fig. 10. Processes Communicating through TCP Sockets

Working: The *client* has the job of initiating contact with the server. For server to be able to react to the client's initial contact, the server has to be ready. This implies two things:

1. The server program cannot be dormant *i.e.*, it must be running as a process before the client attempts to initiate contact.
2. The server program must have some sort of door (*i.e.*, socket) that welcomes some initial contact from a client (running on an arbitrary machine).

NOTE: Using our house/door analogy for a process/socket, we will sometimes refer to the client's initial contact as "knocking on the door".

Please note that with the server process running, the client process can initiate a TCP connection to the server. This is done in the client program by creating a socket object. When the client creates its socket object, it specifies the address of the server process, namely, the IP address of the server and the port number of the process.

After creation of the socket object, TCP in the client initiates a *three-way handshake* and establishes a TCP connection with the server. This is *transparent* to the client and server programs. During the 3-way handshake, the *client process knocks* on the welcoming *door of the server process*. When the server, *hears the knocking*, it creates a new door (*i.e.*, a new socket) that is dedicated to that particular client. In our case, the *welcoming door* is a *serversocket object* that we call the welcomesocket. When a client knocks on this door, the program invokes *welcomeSocket's accept method*, which creates a new door for the client. *At the end of the handshaking phase*, a TCP connection exists between the client's socket and the server's new socket. Henceforth, we refer to the new socket as the server's *connection socket*.

Practically speaking, *a TCP connection is a direct virtual pipe between the client's socket and the server's connection socket—The client process can send arbitrary bytes into its socket*. TCP guarantees that the server process will receive (through the connection socket) each byte in the order sent. Also, just as people can go in and out of the same door, the client process can also receive bytes from its socket and the server process can also send bytes into its connection socket.

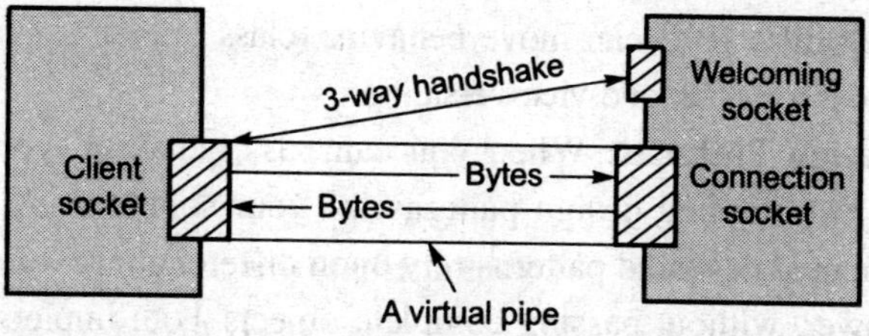

Fig. 11. Client socket, welcoming socket and connection socket.

Also note here that as sockets play a central role in client-server applications, so client-server application development is also known as **Socket programming.**

RMI–Remote Method Invocation

Java RMI allows you to write distributed objects using JAVA. RMI provides a simple and direct model for distributed computation with Java objects. These objects can be new Java objects or can be simple Java Wrappers around an existing API. A *golden rule*:–

"Java embraces the "Write Once, Run Any where" model while RMI extends the Java model to be run everywhere".

Please understand that as RMI is centered around Java, it brings the power of Java safety and portability to distributed computing. You can move behavior, such as agents and business logic, to the part of your network where it makes the most sense.

RMI connects to existing and legacy systems using the standard Java native method interface, JNI. RMI can also connect to existing relational database using standard JDBC package. Also remember that these RMI/JNI and RMI/JDBC connections let you use RMI to communicate today with existing servers in non-Java languages, and to expand your use of Java to those servers.

Advantages of RMI over traditional RPC systems

1. **Object-orientation:** RMI can pass full objects as arguments and return values, not just predefined data types. This means that you can pass complex types like a standard Java hashtable object, as a single argument. In existing RPC systems you would have to have the client *decompose* such an *object* into *primitive data types*, ship those data types and to recreate a hashtable on the server.

2. **Mobility:** RMI can move behavior (class implementation) from client to server and vice-versa.
3. **Design Patterns:** When you can pass behavior, you can use object-oriented design patterns in your solutions. All object-oriented designed patterns rely upon different behaviors for their power, without passing complete objects–both implementations and type. The benefits provided by the design patterns movement are lost.
4. **Safe and secure:** RMI uses in-built Java security mechanisms that allow your system to be safe when users download implementations. RMI uses security manager defined to protect systems from hostile applets.
5. **Easy to Write /Easy to Use:** RMI makes it simple to write remote–Java servers and Java clients that access those servers. *A remote interface is an actual Java interface*. A server has approx. 3 lines of code (LOC) to declare itself a server and otherwise is like any other Java object. This simplicity makes it easy to write servers for full-scale distributed object systems quickly and to repidly bring up prototypes and early versions of software for testing and evaluation. RMI program's maintenance is also easy.
6. **Connects to existing/legacy (old) systems:** RMI interacts with existing systems through Java's nature method interface, JNI. Using RMI and JNI you can write your client in Java.

   When you use RMI/JNI to connect to existing servers, you can rewrite any parts of your server in Java when you choose to and get the full benefits of Java in the new code.

   Based on similar lines, RMI interacts with existing relational databases using JDBC without modifying existing non-Java source that uses the databases.
7. Any RMI based system is *100% portable* to any JVM (Java Virtual Machine) as is an RMI/JDBC system.
8. **Parallel computing:** RMI is multi-threaded. It allows your servers to exploit Java threads for better concurrent processing of client requests.